AF605839

CHAEKGEORI

THE POWER AND PLEASURE OF POSSESSIONS IN KOREAN PAINTED SCREENS

A volume in the SUNY series in Korean Studies

Hongkyung Kim, Editor

CHAEKGEORI

THE POWER AND PLEASURE OF POSSESSIONS IN KOREAN PAINTED SCREENS

Edited by Byungmo Chung and Sunglim Kim

With essays by Sunglim Kim and Joy Kenseth,
Kris Imants Ercums, Ja Won Lee, Sooa McCormick,
Byungmo Chung, and Jinyoung Jin

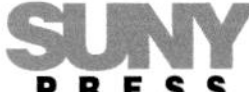
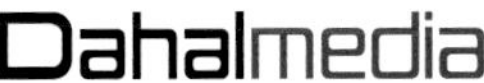

Cover image: Anonymous, Chaekgado, Plate number 2

Printed in Republic of Korea
Published by Dahal Media
Book design by Seoul Selection & Dahal Media
Distributed in North America by State University of New York Press, Albany

For information, contact State University of New York Press, Albany, NY (www.sunypress.edu),
Dahal Media, Seoul, Korea (www.dahal.co.kr)

Produced to accompany The Power and Pleasure of Possessions in Korean Painted Screens,
an exhibition on view at
Charles B. Wang Center, Stony Brook University, 29 September – 23 December 2016
Spencer Museum of Art, University of Kansas, 15 April – 11 June 2017
The Cleveland Museum of Art, 5 August – 5 November 2017

Sponsors: KOREA KF FOUNDATION GALLERY HYUNDAI

Contributors:
Byungmo Chung, professor of Korean art, Gyeongju University, Korea
Ja Won Lee, Jane and Morgan Whitney fellow, The Metropolitan Museum of Art, New York
Jinyoung Jin, Director of Charles B. Wang Center, Stony Brook University
Joy Kenseth, professor of Renaissance and Baroque art, Dartmouth College
Jungsil Jenny Lee, visiting assistant professor of Korean art, University of Kansas
Kris Imants Ercums, curator of Asian art, Spencer Museum of Art, University of Kansas
Sooa McCormick, Assistant curator of Asian art, The Cleveland Museum of Art
Sunglim Kim, assistant professor of Korean art, Dartmouth College

Chaekgeori / edited by Byungmo Chung and Sunglim Kim
ISBN: 978-1-4384-6811-2 (hardcover : alk. paper)

Library of Congress Control Number: 2017935503

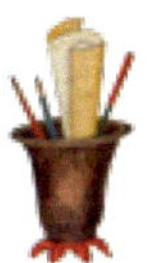

Table of Contents

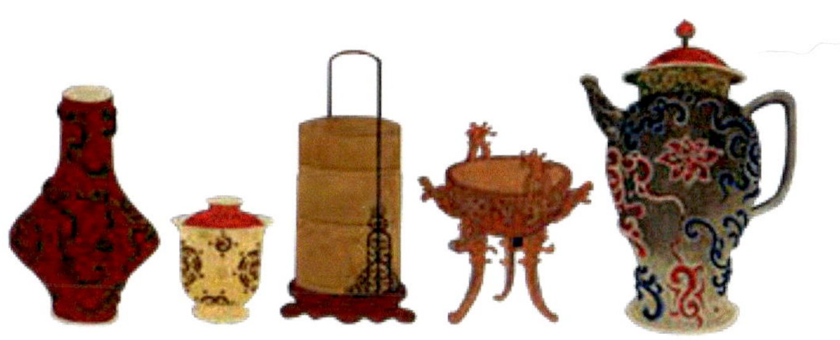

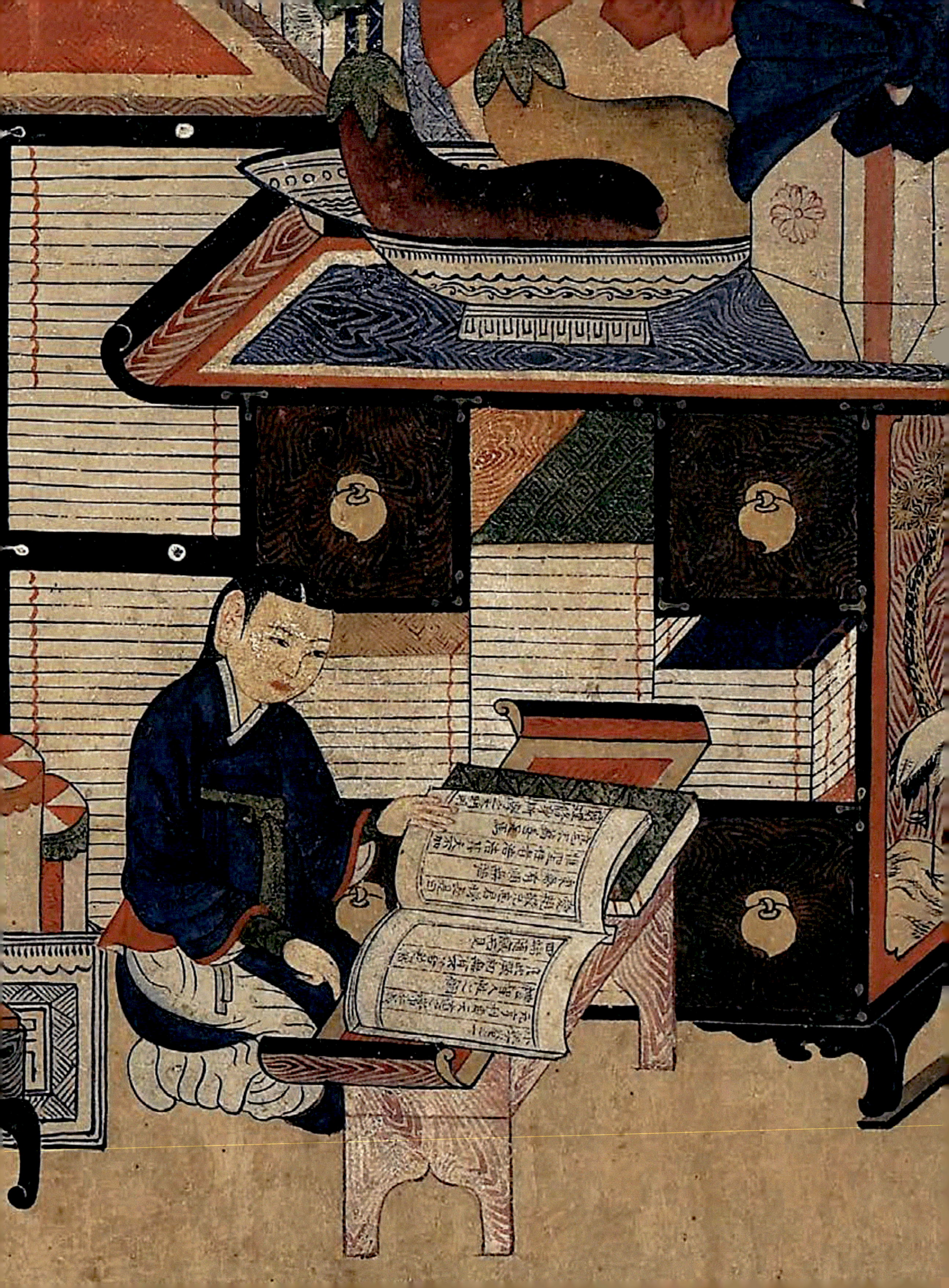

Foreword

Since its founding in 2002, the Charles B. Wang Center has been bringing an ever-deepening understanding and appreciation of Asian arts and cultures to diverse local, national, and international audiences. I am proud to announce that Stony Brook University is furthering the Wang Center's mission of showcasing programs of the highest caliber by being the first host of a U.S. tour of a special exhibition on Korean screen painting.

The Power and Pleasure of Possessions in Korean Painted Screens offers an opportunity to learn about *chaekgeori* screens from the Joseon dynasty of eighteenth- and nineteenth-century Korea. This exhibition features a genre of painting that emphasizes books as a symbolic embodiment of knowledge, power, and social reform—a theme we are eager to share with our students and the surrounding community. Books, and education in general, have the power to transport us to worlds far beyond our imagination, acting as agents to create change in our lives. *The Power and Pleasure of Possessions in Korean Painted Screens* reveals a timeless and universal curiosity in cultural exchange, humanistic values, and the pursuit of knowledge, which can also be a bridge for intercultural understanding and dialogue.

As the largest single-site employer on Long Island, with more than 25,000 students, more than 2,500 faculty, and more than 14,000 employees, Stony Brook offers a range of exhibitions and cultural programs to the University community that extends beyond campus into the communities of Nassau and Suffolk counties. This exhibition on chaekgeori screens is sure to reach broad and new audiences.

Much behind-the-scenes work goes into hosting an exhibition, so I wish to express my heartfelt gratitude to the Korea Foundation for generously offering this exquisite collection to the Charles B. Wang Center. I also want to thank Dr. Byungmo Chung of Gyeongju University and Dr. Sunglim Kim at Dartmouth College for their meticulous preparation, and the Cleveland Museum of Art and the Spencer Museum of Art of the University of Kansas for their cooperation in organizing the U.S. tour of *The Power and Pleasure of Possessions in Korean Painted Screens*. I hope you enjoy this significant exhibition.

Samuel L. Stanley Jr.
President
Stony Brook University

Foreword

The Spencer Museum of Art is dedicated to cultivating the study and interpretation of objects of cultural significance for students, faculty, and the public. In order to learn and contribute to teaching and research, we purposely reach toward cultural understanding through material things that stir imaginative powers and intellectual curiosities. *The Power and Pleasure of Possessions in Korean Painted Screens* is especially relevant during the first year of implementing our mission in newly renovated galleries. The screens will serve as potent symbols within a light-filled gallery space that aspires to encourage and contribute to an atmosphere of educational achievement.

For the Spencer Museum of Art, a university art museum, the exhibition also provides an opportunity to bring the concepts of *chaekgeori* to a broad audience, questioning notions of refinement and elite company in the context of a large public university. We are honored to welcome these visual compositions replete with beauty, history, and meaning to instruct audiences in the visual representations of knowledge. We are also eager to look attentively in order to think about what the screens express to our changing world—theoretically and practically—as objects. What can we find that will inspire us to reflect on and conceptualize our own places in the world?

Will we ask, as King Jeongjo did, "Do you see them?"

Can we answer, as his officials did in the eighteenth century: "Yes, we see them?"[1]

The exhibition builds on a strong history of East Asian art at the University of Kansas, both in the Kress Department of Art History and within the Spencer Museum. Curators and faculty enthusiastically join to support the exhibition and have developed a rich set of programs including an academic conference. *Guo Ziyi's Banquet* will make its first debut after conservation as part of the Spencer Museum's collection during the exhibition, representing the most significant example of late Joseon painting traditions in the collection.

I wish to express my gratitude to the Korea Foundation and to the many colleagues and scholars within distinguished institutions who have produced this ambitious project: the Hood Museum of Art at Dartmouth College, the Charles B. Wang Center at Stony Brook University, and the Cleveland Museum of Art. Finally, my thanks to Dr. Kris Ercums, who brings this exhibition of chaekgeori to the University of Kansas.

Saralyn Reece Hardy
The Marilyn Stokstad Director
Spencer Museum of Art, University of Kansas

1. Kim 2014, 7.

Foreword

In 1916 the Cleveland Museum of Art officially opened its doors to the public. As old as the museum itself, the history of our Korean art collection demonstrates that a philanthropic vision and international collaborations between institutions and individuals can inspire artistic creativity and promote intellectual advancement.

Among the museum's earliest Korean acquisitions were Goryeo-period celadon pieces donated by Cleveland industrialist John Long Severance (1863–1936), the son of Standard Oil treasurer Louis H. Severance (1838–1913). About two hundred such works are believed to have been given to the elder Severance by Koreans to express their profound gratitude for his donation toward establishing the first modern hospital in Seoul, later named the Severance Hospital. These elegant pieces stand as visual testimony to the bond forged between Cleveland and Korea at the turn of the nineteenth century.

In 2013, a generous grant from the Korea Foundation helped establish a gallery solely dedicated to Korean art, the first such gallery in the museum's history. In addition, a grant from the National Museum of Korea funded the purchase of new display cases in 2015, the same year we welcomed Dr. Sooa Im McCormick, the museum's first curator devoted to Korean art. We thank the Korea Foundation and Gallery Hyundai for their financial support and their strong commitment to the promotion of Korean art and culture. We are also thrilled to announce that through collaborative research between Dr. McCormick and Dr. Byungmo Chung, along with support from the Overseas Korean Cultural Heritage Foundation, the museum's *chaekgeori* screen was found to be the work of the famous court painter Yi Taekgyun (b. 1808). This recent discovery proves again how collaborations between institutions and scholars are indispensable for the advancement of knowledge.

William M. Griswold
Sarah S. and Alexander M. Cutler Director
The Cleveland Museum of Art

Foreword

The Korea Foundation is most pleased to co-host *The Power and Pleasure of Possessions in Korean Painted Screens*, an exhibition to be on view at three prominent venues in the United States: the Charles B. Wang Center at Stony Brook University, the Spencer Museum of Art at the University of Kansas, and the Cleveland Museum of Art.

This exhibition is the first event of its kind to introduce the still-life paintings on screen panels known as *chaekgeori* that date from the eighteenth to nineteenth centuries of Korea's late Joseon dynasty. The works on display have been carefully selected from the collections of Korean museums and private collectors. In addition, a variety of contemporary artworks inspired by the traditional chaekgeori will also be featured.

As an institution that strives to enhance international good will and friendship, and to promote the interests of Korea among the world's peoples through various exchange programs, the Korea Foundation is hopeful that visitors to this exhibition will have a chance to appreciate the elegant beauty of Korea's chaekgeori paintings and to familiarize themselves with the culture and people of Korea. In addition, it is impressive to see how the influences of traditional Korean arts have been a source of inspiration for the contemporary artworks of today's artists.

This touring exhibition has been made possible thanks to the cooperative efforts of many organizations and professionals. Above all, I would like to express my sincere gratitude to three venues and their staffs: the Charles B. Wang Center at Stony Brook University, the Spencer Museum of Art at the University Kansas, and the Cleveland Museum of Art. These prestigious institutions are also valued partners of the Korea Foundation which have helped to advance our mutual interests through a variety of previous cultural exchange endeavors.

Also, I would like to extend my personal appreciation to Dr. Byungmo Chung of Gyeongju University and Dr. Sunglim Kim of Dartmouth College for their dedicated efforts, which have been instrumental in the organization of this touring exhibition.

Lastly, I wish to express my heartfelt thanks to the Gallery Hyundai and its staffs for arranging all the artworks for the exhibition. Also, I need to acknowledge the other contributors, who have so generously made available their treasured screen paintings so as to enhance the exhibition's overall splendor.

Sihyung Lee
President
The Korea Foundation

Foreword

As someone who has dealt with modern and contemporary Korean artworks for a long time, I consider Korean folk painting, which has continued from the eighteenth to the early twentieth century as being the most representative of what it means to be "Korean." While contemporary Korean art thrives in various forms, it is my belief that Korean folk painting of the late Joseon period has been the foundation of all others.

Since the opening of Gallery Hyundai in Insa-dong in 1970, I have encountered various Korean folk paintings, ranging from elegant and alluring court paintings to skillfully executed folk paintings. My coming into contact with them has increased my admiration for the exceptional artistic skills of our ancestors. Although *chaekgeori* screens are not widely known internationally, the genre is one of the most charming genres in Korean art, and for the longest time, I have dreamed of organizing an exhibition that would gather dispersed folk paintings and publicize them internationally.

Discussions about such an exhibition began three years ago during preparations for *Chaesaekhwa: Polychrome Painting of Korea*, organized by Professor Byungmo Chung at Gyeongju University. Acting as a bridge between the professor and collectors, I helped locate certain paintings. Then Professor Chung brought Dong Guk Lee, director of the Seoul Arts Center, into the conversation; after discussions with few Korean folk painting experts, plans for a joint exhibition with the Seoul Arts Center and Seoul Calligraphy Art Museum were made. In June 2016, the exhibition opened—the first show in the renovated Seoul Calligraphy Art Museum. Now, with support from the Korea Foundation, the exhibition is traveling to the United States. The tour for *The Power and Pleasure of Possessions in Korean Painted Screens* includes the Charles B. Wang Center at Stony Brook University, the Spencer Museum of Art at University of Kansas, and the Cleveland Museum of Art.

We are indebted to the Leeum, Samsung Museum of Art, Seoul Museum, Korean Folk Village, Sungok Memorial Hall, Chosun Minhwa Museum, Gana Art, and many private collectors for parting with their works of art for the duration of the show. Furthermore, I want to express my gratitude to the Korea Foundation and to Professor Chung and Professor Sunglim Kim at Dartmouth College, who organized the traveling exhibition; and to Joy Kenseth, professor at Dartmouth College; Jinyoung Jin, director of Charles B. Wang Center; Kris Imants Ercums, curator at the Spencer Museum of Art; Jungsil Jenny Lee, visiting assistant professor at the University of Kansas; Sooa Im McCormick, assistant curator at the Cleveland Museum of Art; and Ja Won Lee, Jane and Morgan Whitney Fellow at the Metropolitan Museum of Art, for their contributions to this catalogue.

Myung Ja Park
President
Gallery Hyundai

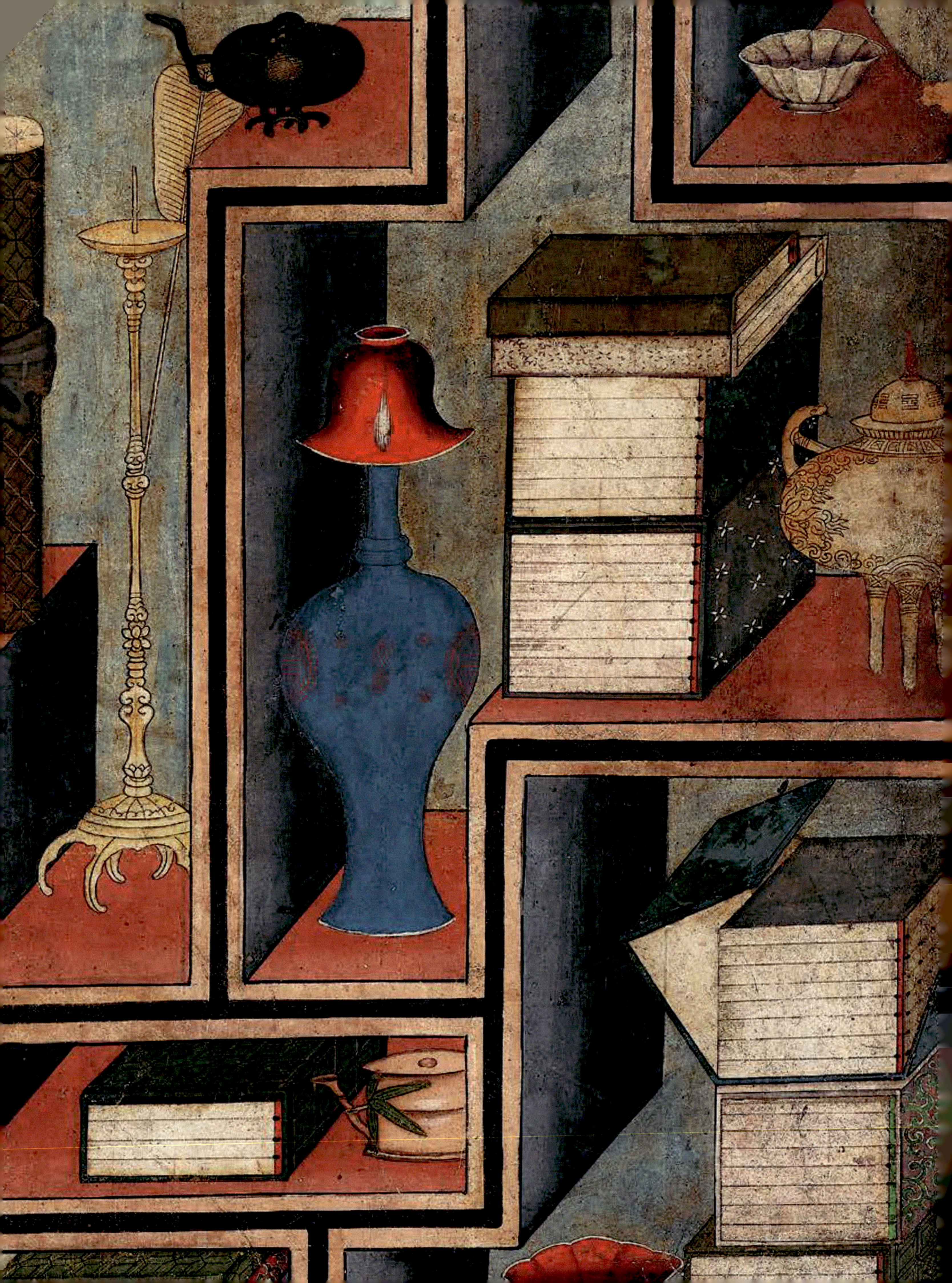

Introduction

Chaekgeori Screens in Material Culture

Byungmo Chung and Sunglim Kim

The Power and Pleasure of Possessions in Korean Painted Screens introduces a genre of Korean still-life painting called *chaekgeori* to a U.S. audience. Colorfully painted chaekgeori screens first appeared in the late eighteenth century, became very popular and widespread in the nineteenth century, and have lately been reinterpreted within contemporary Korean art. The *Power and Pleasure of Possessions in Korean Painted Screens* is the first major exhibition of this genre to include screens from private collections and various Korean institutions. Most of the screens are on view abroad for the first time, and the Korean public is also getting its first look at some of them.

The general term for Korean still life is *munbangdo*, which means scholar's accoutrements. The munbangdo category includes several kinds of subject matter. The most popular subject among the literati is *munbang sau* (the "Four Friends of the Scholar's Studio")—that is, paper, brush, ink, and inkstone—but books, painting and calligraphy, writing tables, musical instruments, collectible rocks, auspicious plants, a board game called *baduk*, and wine jars also appear. The other subjects are *bakgodo* (painting of ancient bronze, porcelains, and jade vessels), *gimyeong jeoljido* (painting of vessels and cut-flowers), and chaekgeori (books and things, books and scholar's utensils, or scholar's accoutrements).

Three types of chaekgeori screen exist. The first to appear was *chaekgado* (bookshelf-style chaekgeori, also known as trompe l'oeil chaekgeori). These screens depict books, ceramics, bronze vessels, flowers and plants, and other precious and foreign objects and curios in a multishelved frame structure (plates 1, 2). This style was preferred by the court and elite classes known as the *yangban*. The second type is tabletop or folk-style chaekgeori which was popular among commoners. Folk-style chaekgeori render subjects playfully, with lots of color, in more relaxed compositions. Stacks of books are placed on tabletops with other objects like symbolic fruits and flowers, furniture, and sometimes mythical animals (plates 14, 15). The third type is "isolated" or "floating" chaekgeori. In floating chaekgeori books and scholarly utensils and other objects are depicted independently (not stacked together) and float on a blank background without any structure or sense of gravity (plates 19, 20). They are often vividly painted in mineral colors and later chemical polychrome inks on silk or paper in multipanel folding screens.

Late-eighteenth-century Korea was a peaceful and prosperous time under the cultivated and scholarly King Jeongjo. With a population of about 200,000, Hanyang (modern day Seoul), the capital of the Joseon dynasty, was the country's commercial and cultural center. The country had recovered from the foreign invasions of the late sixteenth and early seventeenth centuries—the Japanese invasions of Korea (1592–98) and the Manchu invasions of 1627 and 1636—and had re-established its diplomatic relationships with neighboring China and Japan. Both the Qing dynasty of China under the Qianlong Emperor and the Edo period of Japan under the Tokugawa shogunate enjoyed social stability, economic and population growth, and flourishing cultures. Among them, Korea followed the most austere and strict form of Neo-Confucianism, which frowned upon any kind of frivolous consumption of material objects. It was when this conservative aesthetic began to weaken that chaekgeori made its appearance.

Under the strong leadership of two monarchs, King Yeongjo (r. 1724–76) and King Jeongjo (r. 1776–1800), Korean scholars developed a school of thought called *Silhak* (Practical Learning), which gained much popularity among Joseon intellectuals. Silhak argued for reforming Korea's rigid Neo-Confucian social structure, including land reform, encouraged commerce and the study of science and technology, and advocated for empirical and experimental approaches to solving social problems. One branch of Practical Learning was the *Bukhak* (Northern Learning), movement. Visiting Beijing and witnessing the advancement of Chinese material life, the scholars of the Northern Learning movement promoted "Improvement of Life through Practical Utilization." They established a close social network, introduced their Chinese friends and acquaintances to other Koreans in their network, and worked closely together. Embracing foreign models, especially the scientific teachings of the West, they encouraged manufacturing, trade, commerce, and even material consumption, although the Joseon monarchy did not support the last.

These forward-looking men traveled back and forth to China on regular tributary missions. One exemplar is Hong Daeyong, who visited China in 1765, where he encountered Chinese scholars, Jesuit missionaries, and a plethora of new material culture. Hong saw a Italian-style trompe l'oeil painting at the South Catholic Church in Beijing and recorded his wonder at first seeing realistic illusory painting in his *Yeongi* (Beijing Memoir). His awe at Chinese progress, questioning of Korea's rigid Neo-Confucianism, and impressive artistic experience continued through his protégé Bak Jiwon, who traveled to China in 1780 and wrote the most influential travelogue of his period, *Yeolha ilgi* (The Jehol Diary). Bak Jiwon's close friend and another Northern Learning scholar, Bak Jega, also wrote about Chinese advances in his *Bukhakui* (*Discussion of Northern Learning*), stating the importance of commerce and noting the progress of China in areas such as transportation, castles, roads, and bridges. His book may be one of the critical intellectual backgrounds of chaekgeori screens, which derive their visual content from the embrace of material culture advocated by the Practical Learning and Northern Learning movements.

The six essays in this exhibition catalogue stand to deepen our understanding of chaekgeori screens and their cultural significance.

The first essay, "From Europe to Korea: The Marvelous Journey of Collectibles," was written by Sunglim Kim and Joy Kenseth. This essay traces the possible European origins of the bookshelf chaekgeori screen style by exploring the history of the Renaissance collecting culture of the West and its transmission to Beijing through Jesuit missionaries. Korean envoys then encountered Western painting, artistic techniques, and foreign collectible objects in Beijing and took the ideas back to Korea, where they were given visual form by Korean artists. The chaekgeori screens, once they were approved and enjoyed by the royal court, changed stylistically as they became popular and were appreciated by a broader audience of viewers.

In the second essay, "Books as Things in Korean Chaekgeori Screen Paintings," Kris Imants Ercums transposes the conventional English translation of chaekgeori from "books and things" to "books as things" in order to highlight the deeper social significance of books as visual embodiments of reading and literary achievement in chaekgeori paintings. The essay first examines the social space in which books existed by considering paintings of "elegant gatherings," in which learned individuals were depicted collectively engaging with antiques and literary objects; in the process the author briefly traces the emergence of the chaekgeori painting tradition. Ercums then examines how contact between Qing China and Joseon Korea stimulated transnational textual and literary exchanges, especially as attested in travel literature written by educated Korean elites, who procured books during their annual tributary missions to the Chinese capital. The essay concludes by considering the implication of books as seen in the mesmerizing installation *End of the End* by contemporary Korean artist Kibong Rhee (b. 1957), in which books assume metaphysical form and appear to fly or float, as seen in isolated or floating-style chaekgeori.

Third, Ja Won Lee's "Pursuing Antiquity: Chinese Bronzes in Chaekgeori Screens" examines the trend in art collecting and its impact on visual culture in the late Joseon dynasty in order to highlight the intellectual and artistic motivations of collectors and artists. It is significant to note that chaekgeori screens rendering Chinese bronze vessels parallels the growing trend of appreciation for Chinese bronze vessels. This allows Joseon court painters to incorporate certain aspects of Chinese bronze vessels in their works using various sources. The essay demonstrates that Joseon collectors expressed their passion for Chinese antiques to elucidate how the collecting practice contributed to the emergence of chaekgeori screens.

The fourth essay, Sooa McCormick's "Taste of Distinction: Paintings of Scholars' Accoutrements," explores the objects depicted on a chaekgeori screen in the collection of the Cleveland Museum of Art. The essay examines the impact of late Ming Chinese aesthetic sensibilities on the late Joseon ruling elites' collecting habits and, more significantly, on the iconographic program of chaekgado, bookshelf-style chaekgeori. By exploring chaekgado as an emblem of highly refined taste, McCormick convincingly shows how the material world depicted in chaekgado acts as both urban stage and agent to fashion a late-eighteenth- and nineteenth-century Korean literatus's ideal self: a classic, yet trendy, scholar. An exciting part of the story is the author's discovery of the identity of the artist of the screen in the collection of the Cleveland Museum of Art in the collection of the Cleveland Museum of Art. Acquired as anonymous work in 2011, the ten-panel chaekgeori screen now has been identified as the work of Yi Taekgyun, one of the most influential chaekgeori painters active in the later half of the nineteenth century. McCormick discovered the artist with the help of Byungmo Chung and Heon-gang Seo.

Fifth, Byungmo Chung's essay, "The Allure of the Chaekgeori, the Scholar's Accoutrements," investigates the artistic developments from bookshelf-style chaekgeori to folk-style chaekgeori. By comparing and contrasting the two styles in terms of function, composition, and artistic expression, Chung argues that folk-style chaekgeori, though sharing certain subject matter and artistic styles with bookshelf-style chaekgeori, had a completely different orientation and aspirations. This essays shows how folk-style chaekgeori expresses the commoner's hopes for happiness, shows aspirations for social advancement, and creates spaces for fundamental human desires. In terms of style, folk-style chaekgeori becomes. unfettered, spontaneous, and natuarally "irrational," where Japanese folklorist Yanagi Muneyoshi, along with other modern and contemporary viewers, perceive its mysterious allure.

While the previous five essays focus on chaekgeori screens in the premodern period, "The Evolution of Chaekgeori: Its Inception and Development from the Joseon Period to Today" by Jinyoung Jin concentrates on how the genre is used by artists of today. No other genre or medium in Korean art, in both literati and folk painting, has so engaged and documented the images of books and collectible commodities. As a medium for chronicling and exploring material culture, and issues of image and identity as symbolized through objects, chaekgeori has been revived by Korean artists of the late twentieth and early twenty-first century, reflecting Korea's increasing economic power and participation in the global culture. The essay draws comparisons between eras and traces the elements of chaekgeori from the past to the present by examining the work of contemporary Korean and Korean-American artists Airan Kang, Stephanie S. Lee, and Kyoungtack Hong, who have adapted the visual vocabularies of chaekgeori to fit our own time.

These seven scholars have approached and interpreted chaekgoeri screens in rich and diverse manners. Some explore the aesthetic and cultural tastes of the ruling elites of the late Joseon dynasty from visual evidence contained in chaekgeori screens, along with literary sources. Others attempt to decode the symbolic meanings of varied objects depicted in chaekgeori to access the hopes, imagination, and aspirations of the Joseon people. Others explore stylistic developments and examine pictorial traditions, and apply insights useful for examining contemporary art works. By considering the ways in which chaekgeori screens played their roles in material culture, we hope to illuminate the complex relationships between this art form, the commissioners and buyers who possessed and enjoyed it, the artists who used their artistic creativity and imagination to develop it, and the society for which it was made. Though little known outside of Korea, chaekgeori painting provides an exciting window into the entangled relationships between objects and people, and between Korea and a wider world.

ESSAYS

Sunglim Kim and Joy Kenseth

From Europe to Korea: The Marvelous Journey of Collectibles in Painting

Kris Imants Ercums

Books as Things in Korean Chaekgeori Screen Paintings

Ja Won Lee

Pursuing Antiquity: Chinese Bronzes in Chaekgeori Screens

Sooa McCormick

Taste of Distinction: Paintings of Scholars' Accoutrements

Byungmo Chung

The Mystical Allure of the Chaekgeori, Books and Things

Jinyoung Jin

The Evolution of Chaekgeori: Its Inception and Development from the Joseon Period to Today

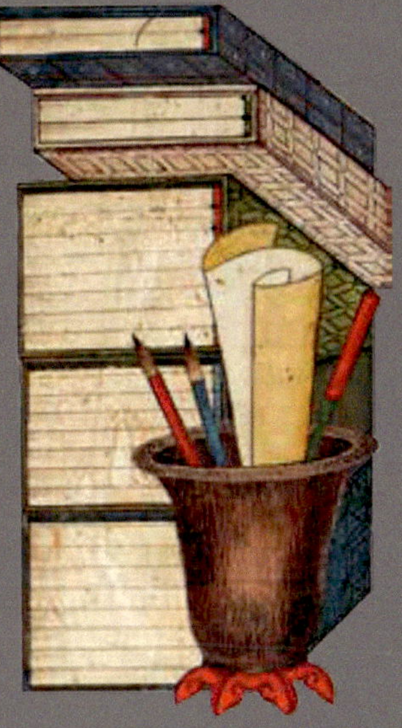

From Europe to Korea: The Marvelous Journey of Collectibles in Painting

Sunglim Kim and Joy Kenseth

Chaekgeori (scholar's accoutrements), a unique Korean form of still-life painting, first appeared in the late eighteenth century and flourished in the nineteenth century. Chaekgeori paintings, usually large multipanel folding screens that come in varying styles, represent an uncharacteristic break from traditional forms of Korean painting. Without available documentation, the origins of chaekgeori painting have not been completely understood, but art historians have speculated about possible sources.[1] It is possible to trace similar Renaissance painting and the transmission of its techniques to Korea through Jesuit missionaries, who had ongoing artistic activities in Beijing. Regardless of source, Korean artists and patrons developed chaekgeori painting in a creative and distinctive manner, using it to express their identities, hopes, and aspirations. This story is especially interesting because representing objects in painting was contrary to Neo-Confucian teachings of austerity and simple living, which profoundly engraved in the life of Korean ruling classes.

Two characteristic features of chaekgeori painting provide convincing evidence that we need to look westward for its origins. Both are primary features of *chaekgado* (bookshelf-style chaekgeori) screens. First is the prevelant feature of side-by-side shelves in more than one vertical column and complex shelves that do not conform to continuous horizontal and vertical divisions (plate 2). Korean shelves, both before and after the appearance of chaekgeori, were single-column only and had simple horizontal divisions (fig. 1). The closest example to the shelving depicted in chaekgeori paintings is the *duobaoge* (Chinese display shelf of collectible treasures), which appeared during the Qing dynasty (fig. 2). The second foreign feature in chaekgeori painting is Western artistic techniques such as linear perspective, chiaroscruo (the use of light and shadow to achieve a sense of volume), and trompe l'oeil (literally, "fool-the-eye"). While never completely accurate, linear perspective convincingly enough suggests shallow depth in the depiction of the shelves (plate 9). Spatial recession is also rendered through shadowed walls in the shelves. Even though Korean painters did not depict shadows cast by objects, they adopted chiaroscuro in lightly modeling the three-dimensional objects that

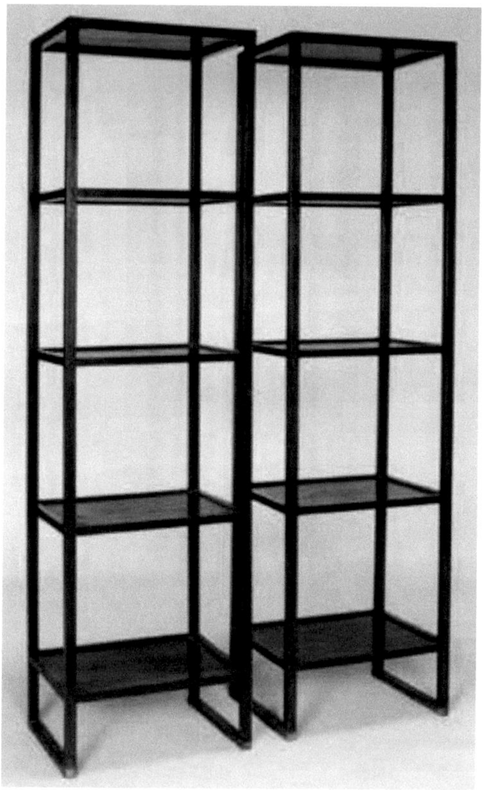

Figure 1. Korean. *Display cabinet*, Joseon dynasty.

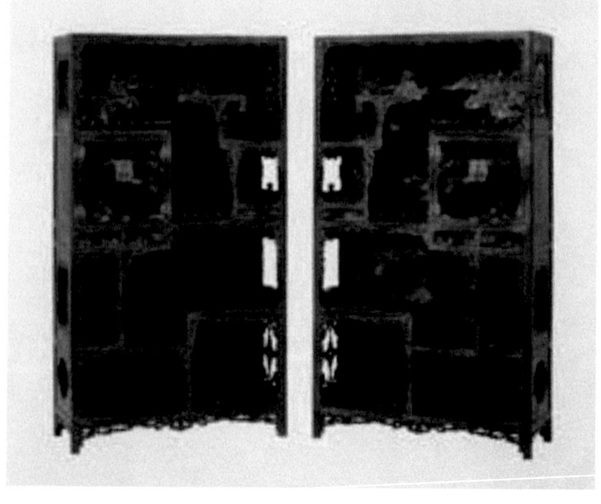

Figure 2. Chinese. *Duobaoge (Display Cabinet of Treasures)*, Qing dynasty.

appear in chaekgeori painting. None of these features was traditional in the limited depiction of objects previously found in Korean art.

Art historian Kay E. Black was the first to introduce the trompe l'oeil painting of Chinese duobaoge attributed to the seventeenth-century Italian Jesuit missionary Father Giuseppe Castiglione as a prototype for Korean chaekgeori painting.[2] Even though this clue is central to the origins of these screens, we do not find any other similar examples of freestanding Chinese painting of duobaoge. Instead, a key difference between Qing China and Joseon Korea is that Qing Chinese collectors displayed their actual collectibles in duobaoge, while Joseon Korean collectors had their collectibles or "objects of desire" depicted in paintings, that is, chaekgeori screens, and enjoyed possessing and displaying the screens as much as the objects. Both three-dimensional and two-dimensional formats, however, provide similar opportunities, through the selection of objects and the way they are displayed, to make statements about the ideals, status, and personalities of the owners. Keeping this in mind, let us unfold the story of the eastward journey of collectibles in painting, beginning in Europe.

Europe: The Age of the Marvelous

During the Renaissance, Europeans' curiosity about new and exotic things blossomed with the discovery and exploration of new continents. After Christopher Columbus sailed to America in 1492, Europeans explored North and South America, Asia, and Africa. From 1519 to 1522, Ferdinand Magellan's crew circumnavigated the Earth, proving that it is round. The work of Nicolaus Copernicus in the early sixteenth century and Galileo Galilei in the early seventeenth century challenged the Eurocentric outlook and made people interested in the worlds beyond. This period has been described as "the age of the marvelous."[3] Shiploads of novel and fabulous things arrived from Asia, the Americas, and Africa. Curiosities from the New World aroused people's desire for encyclopedic knowledge, and in the sixteenth and seventeenth centuries everyone who had the means, from monarchs and princes to amateur collectors, became interested in collecting and displaying the new curiosities in one place.

In 1654, a visitor to the museum of the Danish naturalist Ole Worm reported that in this place "is found and can be examined with wonder, odd and curious rarities and things among which a large part have not been seen before, and many royal persons and envoys visiting Copenhagen ask to see the museum on account of its great fame and what it relates from foreign lands, and they wonder and marvel at what they see."[4] Worm's guests had every reason to be astonished, for the museum's contents were a bewildering mixture of remarkable *naturalia* (natural) and *artificialia* (man-made) objects. An illustration of the museum's interior (fig. 3) shows huge tortoise shells, an armadillo, the spiral tusk of a narwhal, a sawfish saw, oddly shaped antlers and horns, the skin of a polar bear, and a host of other exotic animal fragments that the professor had acquired over a period of thirty or so years. Displayed together with Worm's natural specimens was his vast collection of ethnographic artifacts—man-made objects that came from the Americas, China, Turkey, and other distant lands. A kayak was suspended from the ceiling of his museum, while spears, bows and arrows, articles of clothing, and musical instruments were arranged on the walls and shelves. On one shelf containing bone fragments and the preserved remains of various sea creatures, two statuettes were displayed—one of a male nude and the other a replica in miniature of the sixteenth-century sculptor Giovanni da Bologna's *Rape of the Sabine Woman*.

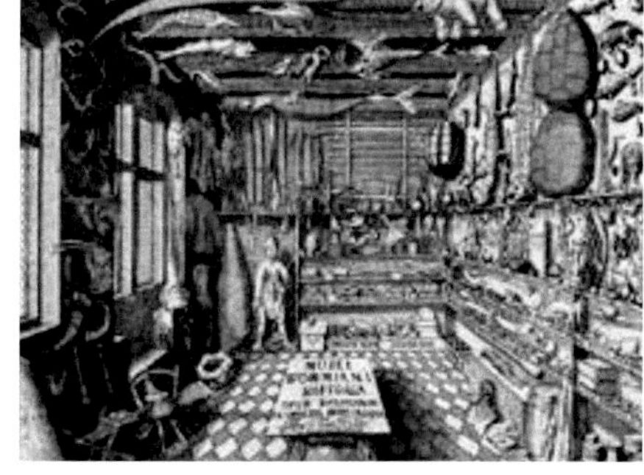
Figure 3. Interior of Ole Worm's museum. Frontispiece to Ole Worm, *Museum Wormianum seu historia rerum rariorum* (Leiden, 1655).

Worm's collection seems an extraordinarily odd and illogical assemblage: natural and man-made objects were freely intermixed, but in the sixteenth and seventeenth centuries collections of this general type were common. Not all of them had the character of Worm's, as many were comprised chiefly of paintings, sculptures, or antiquities, while others displayed works of nature and of art in about equal proportions. The rarities that Worm installed in his museum contrasted noticeably, for instance, with those found in the gallery of the Medici grand dukes in Florence. Its rooms "were heaped up [with] rare exquisite things," according to one visitor.[5] Antique busts and statues lined the corridors; gold and silver plates, scientific instruments, and wonderfully turned items in ivory were installed in adjoining rooms. The most splendid room of the gallery, the Tribuna, was loaded with treasures, including precious gems and medals, finely made bronze statuettes, and masterpieces by Raphael, Michelangelo, Titian, and Dürer. The display of wealth and the prominence of works of art clearly set the gallery apart from Worm's museum. But the two collections nonetheless had some commonalities. In both, the oddities of nature vied for attention with rarities fashioned by human hands, and the beholder was confronted with a truly stunning assortment of objects.

Diversity, abundance, and a love for the singular, the odd, and the uncommon were the traits of the majority of sixteenth- and seventeenth-century museums, or, as many of them were also called, cabinets of curiosities or *Kunst- und Wunderkammern* (rooms of art and marvels).[6] Collections of rarities and other heterogeneous items were not entirely new, however, as they had been assembled in earlier periods, most notably in fifteenth-century private studies (*studioli*). Here, their owners, either alone or in the company of friends, could study and admire antiquities, rare manuscripts, and natural curiosities as well as fine hand-crafted objects. For example, from the fifteenth century, the collection of Piero di Cosimo de' Medici at his family palace in Florence contained natural curiosities, but it was celebrated for its extraordinary manuscripts, antiquities, and gems. In his account of the grand duke's *studiolo*, the Florentine architect and sculptor Antonio Filarete tells how Piero, suffering from gout, had himself carried into his study where he would while away the hours admiring his rare books, statuettes, vases of gold and silver, and engraved jewels and precious stones.[7]

In the next century the sites for collections changed, moving from studioli designated for contemplation and private study to more public galleries or museum spaces. The contents of the collections also changed, reflecting the impact of the voyages of discovery and increased trade with distant lands. Exotic objects, both natural and man-made, were avidly collected and, together with European rarities and antiquities, were installed on shelves, in cupboards, and in the nooks and crannies of ever more museums, galleries, and curiosity cabinets. By the second half of the sixteenth century collections of this type had become widespread.[8] Established not just by monarchs and princes but also by natural scientists and members of such professions as medicine, law, and education, they were found all over Europe and by some estimates numbered in the thousands.[9]

The proliferation of such museums, indeed the tremendous expansion of collecting in general, was a distinctly Renaissance phenomenon, a manifestation of the period's inquisitiveness, its preoccupation with understanding all aspects of the physical world, and its emphasis on individual human achievement. The new idea that lay behind the creation of the early museums was the aspiration for comprehensive knowledge, a belief that in the course of a lifetime a man could know everything. Indeed, as humanist ideas spread across Europe, there was a corresponding increase in all-embracing, encyclopedic collections. In his famous *Oration on the Dignity of Man*, first published in 1496, the humanist Giovanni Pico della Mirandola gave eloquent expression to the belief in man's privileged status in the world and his capacity to acquire comprehensive knowledge. God placed man at the center of the world, he declared, because from that vantage point he could more easily survey all that the world contains. But, according to Pico, man's comprehension and appreciation of God's work is not obtained automatically. Rather, by the exercise of his God-given free will and his intellectual powers he should search out the causes of things, the ways of nature, the plan of the universe, and the mysteries of the heavens and the Earth.[10]

Following the first-century AD example of Pliny the Elder, whose *Natural History* increasingly became an important source of inspiration, sixteenth-century naturalists such as Konrad Gesner and Ulisse Aldrovandi produced vast compendia in which they attempted to inventory and describe all forms of life known to them.

The desire for universality also was evident in gardens, with their great diversity of botanical specimens, menageries, statues, and waterworks, and in the subject matter of paintings, especially pictures showing ideal assemblages of animals in a Garden of Eden atmosphere or those representing collections themselves consisting of widely diverse, unusual, and exotic objects. But it was in the cabinets of curiosities and Kunst- und Wunderkammern of the time where the desire for comprehensiveness or encyclopedism was most prominent and most vigorously pursued.

In his 1565 publication *Inscriptiones vel tituli theatri amplissimi*, the Flemish doctor and artistic advisor Samuel Quiccheberg offers detailed guidelines for properly organizing collections. According to Quiccheberg, the exhibits of the ideal museum would allow one to gain knowledge of the universe and God: they would reveal the creative ingenuity of man and his maker and, furthermore, would reflect the personality of the one who had brought the museum into being. Although Quiccheberg's elaborate scheme was never realized in any museum, his manual often determined the kinds of objects collectors purchased and, more significantly, served as a model for museum catalogues. His view of a comprehensive museum, one in which the naturalia and artificialia together would give insight into God's universe, was shared by many at the time and continued to be a guiding principle for numerous collectors in the seventeenth century.

The most spectacular collection in Northern Europe during the late sixteenth century was that assembled by the Habsburg emperor Rudolph II. Located at the Hradschin Palace in Prague, its thousands of items included paintings, sculptures, exquisitely wrought decorative arts, ethnographic objects, instruments of astrology, alchemy, and magic—every conceivable type of natural curiosity.[11] A museum shaped by the emperor himself and reflecting his varied interests and tastes, it was, according to Thomas DaCosta Kaufmann, "a form of *representatio*," whereby "Rudolph's possession of the world in microcosm . . . [was] . . . an expression of his symbolic mastery of the greater world."[12] Other princely collections carried a similar cosmological meaning. The Tribuna of the Medici grand dukes, for example, was designed in such a way that the power of the ruler was seen as an integral part of God's universal order.[13] The universality of such collections and their lavish displays of wealth served to glorify the owner, asserting his preeminence in the world of men as well as his favored position within the larger cosmological scheme. Although, after the publications of Copernicus and Galileo, man no longer stood at the center of the universe, the princely collector was able to place himself in the middle of a world of his own making.

The collections formed by those in less powerful positions were not overlaid with elaborate political or cosmological symbolism, but they often served as status symbols and sometimes were a means to climb the social ladder. When a private citizen created a cabinet or museum of wide-ranging items, it gave evidence of his catholic tastes and the breadth of his learning. In short, it identified him as a scholar and a gentleman and provided the locus for his intellectual pursuits. Indeed, the rise of collections coincided with the elevation of the status of the scholar who was not a passive observer of the world but an active and engaged participant, investigating, questioning, and describing its myriad parts.[14] Worm's museum, described earlier, while it delighted and astounded princes and other dignitaries, was meant as a place for study. Worm had assembled his collection chiefly for his students at the University of Copenhagen, to enlighten young minds about the discipline of natural history.[15] A collection's usefulness as a site for study was sometimes underscored by the inclusion of reference books, as shown, for example, in the 1599 catalogue of the collection of the Neapolitan pharmacist Ferrante Imperato (fig. 4), which includes an impressive collection of books, carefully stacked on shelves for handy

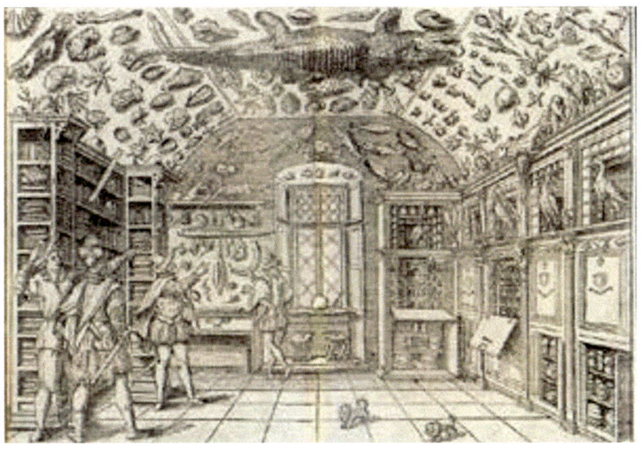

Figure 4. Interior of Ferrante Imperato's museum. Frontispiece to Ferrante Imperato, *Dell'Historia natural*, book 28 (Naples, 1599).

reference or consultation.[16]

The fame of curiosity cabinets and Kunst- und Wunderkammern spread rapidly in the seventeenth century, especially when catalogues were produced to accompany the collections. As Paula Findlen has observed, catalogues are "the most important object produced from a collection." They do not merely list but interpret the objects in a collection, serving as "repositories of multiple intersecting stories that textualized and contextualized each object."[17] By means of the published catalogue, collectors could display their erudition, advertise their trades, and introduce the collection to audiences far and wide. Catalogues that contained images of the collection also gave readers a glimpse of its appearance and the manner in which its objects were displayed. Following the publication of Imperato's *Dell'Historia Naturale* in 1599, catalogues usually included a frontispiece giving a view into the collection (figs. 3, 4). Although many of these illustrations presented idealized rather than realistic depictions of the curiosity cabinets, museums, or Kunst- und Wunderkammern, they nonetheless provided viewers with some sense of the diversity and quantity of the objects in the collector's possession.

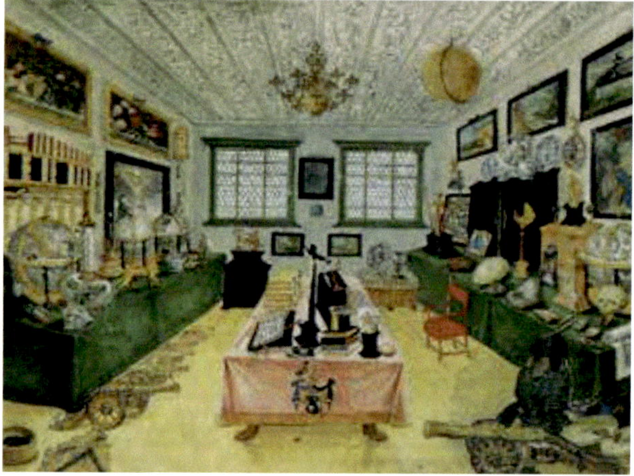

Figure 5. Joseph Arnold (Austrian, 1782–1819). *Kunstkammer of the Dimpfel Family of Regensburg*, 1668. Ulm Museum, Germany.

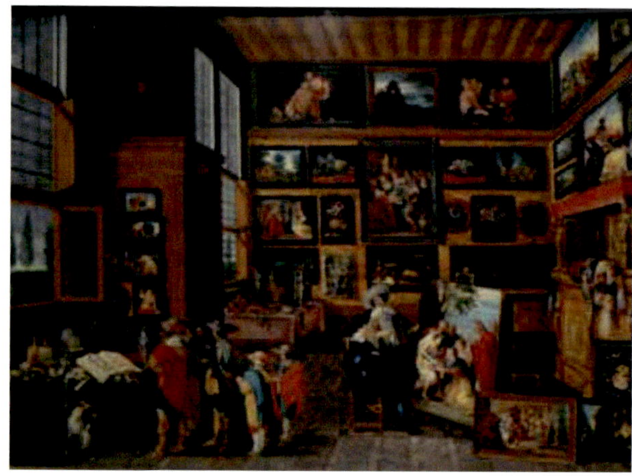

Figure 6. Hans Jordaens III (Flemish, ca. 1595–1643) and Cornelis de Baellieur (Flemish, 1607–1671). *Kunstkammer*, ca. 1630(?). Oak, 186 x 120 cm. Kunsthistorisches Museum, Vienna, Gemäldegalerie, 716.

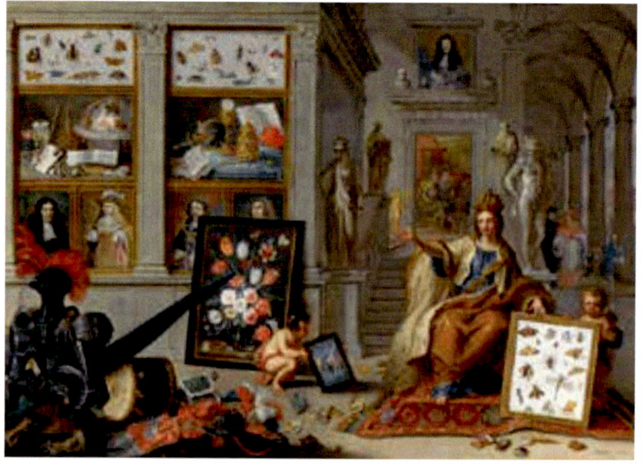

Figure 7. Jan van Kessel the Elder (Flemish, 1626–1679) and Erasmus Quellinus II (Flemish, 1607–1678). *Allegory of Europe*, 1670. Worcester Art Museum, Worcester.

In the course of the sixteenth and seventeenth centuries and well into the eighteenth, a large number of paintings also offered views of the cabinets and collections of Europeans. Some, like Joseph Arnold's *Kunstkammer of the Dimpfel Family of Regensburg* (fig. 5) have the effect of straightforward visual documentation, while others tended to be idealized views of collections (fig. 6).[18] Idealized or not, such images gave testimony to the abundance and variety of objects that collectors amassed and proudly put on display. In yet other instances, paintings were produced as evocations rather than documents or idealized views of curiosity cabinets. For example, *Allegory of Europe* (1670) by the Flemish artists Jan van Kessel the Elder and Erasmus Quellinus II (fig. 7) is an imaginary view that presents a wide array of naturalia and artificialia.[30] Similar mixtures of nature and art appear in imagined partial views of collections (fig. 8) and in trompe-l'oeil pictures of collectors' shelves and portable cabinets (figs. 9, 10, 11). Many trompe-l'oeil pictures were themselves collected in Kunst- und Wunderkammern and cabinets of curiosities on account of their capacity to fool the viewer's eye through artistic cunning or sleight-of-hand.[19] These demonstrations of an artist's illusionistic skills made the objects that were found in a cabinet vividly

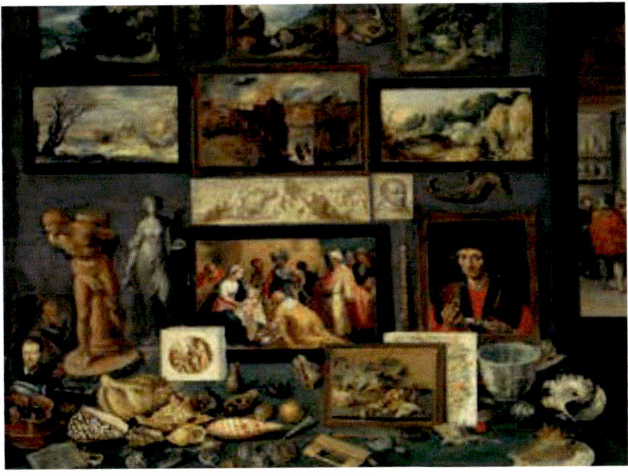

Figure 8. Frans Francken the Younger (Flemish, 1581–1642). *Kunst- und Rariätenkammer*, ca. 1620/25. Oak, 74 x 78 cm. Kunsthistorisches Museum, Vienna, Gemäldegalerie, 1048.

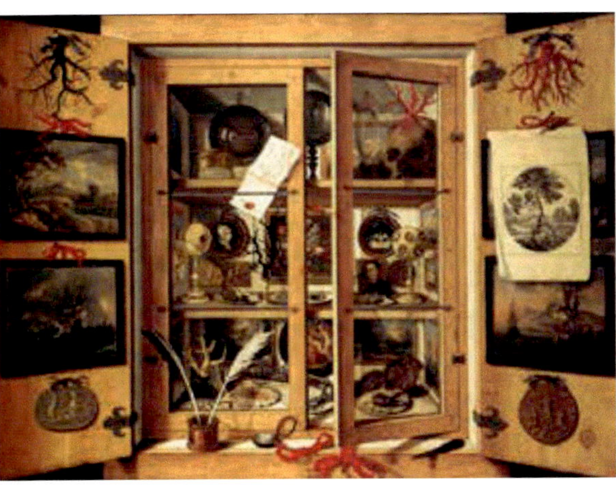

Figure 9. Domenico Remps (act. Italy, 1650–1700). *Cabinet of Curiosities*, 1690s. Opifcio delle Pietre Dure, Florence.

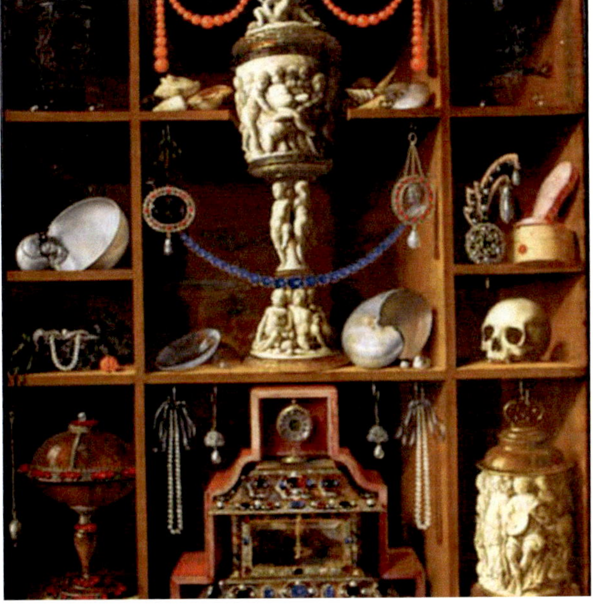

Figure 10. Georg Hainz (German, 1630–1700). *Cabinet of Curiosities*, 1666. Kunsthalle, Hamburg.

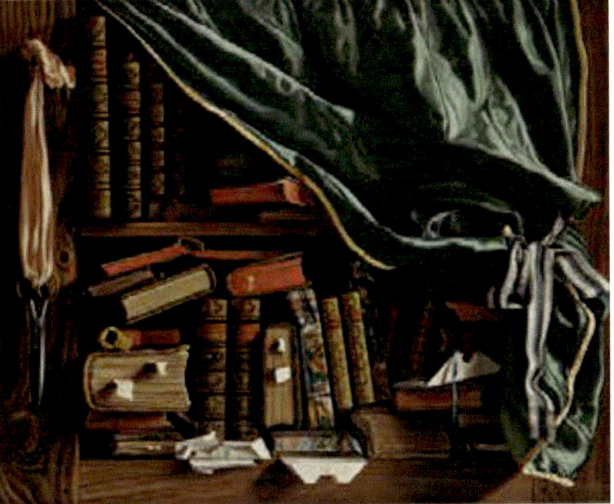

Figure 11. François Foisse (Brabant) (French, 1708–1763). *Still Life with Books*, ca. 1741. Oil on canvas, 61.6 x 77.2 cm. Wadsworth Atheneum Museum of Art, Hartford, The Ella Gallup Sumner and Mary Catlin Sumner Collection Fund, with additional contributions in memory of Frank B. Gay, former Director of the Wadsworth Atheneum (1911–1927), 1939.244.

present to the viewer. Indeed, long after the actual curiosity cabinets, the theaters of nature and art, and the Kunst- und Wunderkammern disappeared, these pictures and the museum catalogues remain as eloquent reminders of the collections and collecting habits of Europeans in the sixteenth, seventeenth, and eighteenth centuries.

China: Where West Meets East

China has a longer history and culture of collecting, displaying, and cataloguing objects than does Europe. However, until the late seventeenth century, the Chinese generally collected art objects, rather than natural objects or foreign curiosities.[20] As in Europe, Chinese emperors were a driving force in the foundation of collections of arts and antiquites, and they were major patrons of artists and artistic projects as a way to preserve or promote their cultural and political power.[21]

In the eighteenth century the early Qing emperors were especially passionate and aggressive in building the imperial collection and sponsoring art and architectural projects.[22] A large part of their artistic enthusiasm arose from their non-native Han Chinese background. By the late seventeenth century, the early Manchu rulers had pacified the native Han Chinese militarily, but in order to rule, these foreign rulers had to earn the respect of their Chinese subjects, who viewed these barbaric outsiders with cultural condescension. The Manchu rulers had to demonstrate their interest in not only maintaining but also excelling at Chinese traditions. They had to hone their public image as learned scholar-gentlemen with profound knowledge of the Confucian classics and a deep appreciation of art and antiquities. But at the same time, compared to the preceding conservative Ming emperors, the Manchu were more open-minded and very much interested in the new Western science, mathematics, art, and architecture. Therefore, it was an opportune time for Italian and French Jesuit missionaries to encounter and befriend the Chinese rulers.

Jesuit missionaries were the main conduits by which European ideas came to the Chinese court.[23] Italian missionaries first became active in China in the late sixteenth century, bringing with them all manner of ideas, technologies, and art forms. The first and most prominent European to enter the Forbidden City was the Italian Jesuit priest Matteo Ricci.[24] After twenty years of working in the provinces, Ricci was finally allowed to enter Beijing and founded a small mission in the capital in 1601. Even though he never met the Ming Emperor Wanli, he was invited to court and there he taught the eunuchs and befriended the Chinese scholar-officials.[25] Ricci's Jesuit missionary work was continued by the German Jesuits Adam Schall vol Bell and John Schreck, who arrived in Beijing in 1622. They brought the first telescope ever seen in China. Schall met the Korean Crown Prince Sohyeon while the latter was kept as a hostage in Beijing during the 1636 Manchu Invasion, and the two became friends.[26] When Sohyeon returned to Korea in 1644, he brought home Western books on astronomy, mathematics, and Catholicism, an image of Jesus, and a globe.[27]

The knowledgeable, skilled, and adaptable Jesuit priests charmed the Manchu emperors and Chinese intellectuals with a treasure trove of scientific instruments and other Western tools that they brought from Europe, as well as with their scientific and artistic knowledge. This material influx carried along with it European conventions of artistic representation, and by the mid-eighteenth century, the court academy of the Qing rulers included European painters and architectural designers, sculptors, cartographers, printmakers, glassmakers, and clockmakers. Their specialized knowledge and technical expertise were highly appreciated by the seventeenth- and eighteenth-century Kangxi, Yongzheng, and Qianlong emperors.

In fact, it was the Jesuit missionaries who transmitted the idea of gathering one's collection in one place or on display shelves and openly exhibiting it. In China, collecting natural objects and oddities was not traditional (with a few exceptions such as unique rocks and plants), but collecting art and antiques had a long history among the elites. Instead of openly displaying their collections, however, Chinese collectors usually stored them and only occasionally pulled them out for view by themselves or with like-minded colleagues. Therefore, the public display of collections appears to be a Renaissance European concept brought to China

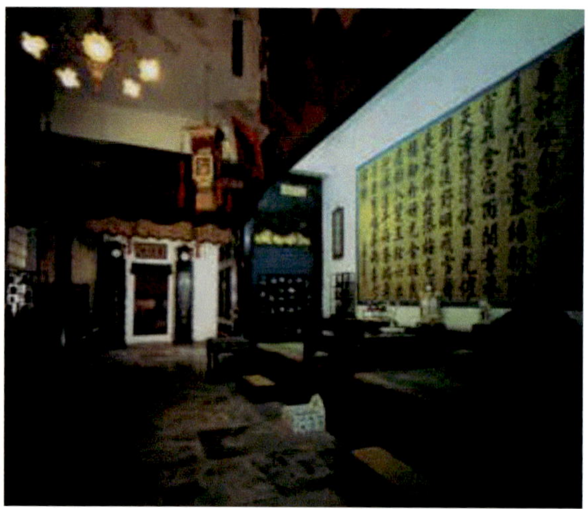

Figure 12. Several duobaoge in the Hall for Mental Cultivation (*Yang Xin Dian*). Forbidden City, Beijing.

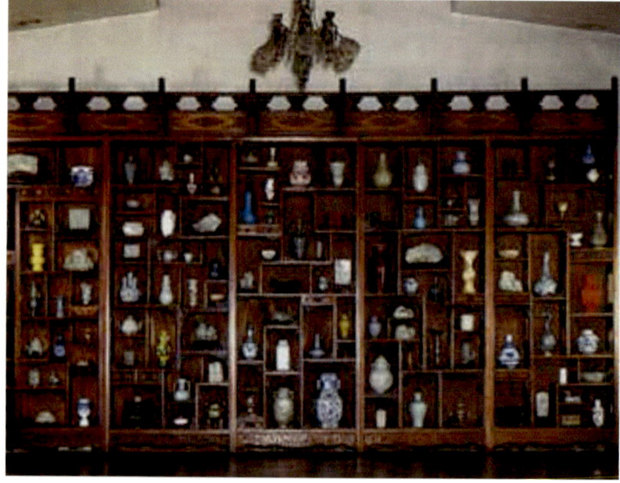

Figure 13. Duobaoge in the Hall for the Enjoyment of Beauty (*Shu Fang Zai*). Forbidden City, Beijing.

by the Jesuits. But the concept of the microcosm, or the gathering of an encyclopedic collection in one small site, which implies that the owner's purview is all-inclusive, very much appealed to the Qing rulers. Perhaps for this reason, by the eighteenth century open display shelves decorated the halls of the Qing court (fig. 12). These multishelved cabinets were called *duobaoge*. The most representative duobaoge is the one in Shufangzai, the library of Emperor Qianlong, where a cabinet filled with various ceramics from different periods occupies an entire wall (fig. 13).

An example of duobaoge featured in Chinese painting is shown in one panel of a twelve-panel screen called *Yongzheng's Screen of Twelve Beauties* (1732) (fig. 14). Here, a seated court lady in Han Chinese attire is surrounded by a diverse and tasteful collection of antiques displayed in a multishelf duobaoge. Even though the screen is a group of "fantasy" pictures depicting idealized views of women engaged in various pastimes, rather than portraits of actual consorts, the objects in the duobaoge are all representations of identifiable antiques in the imperial collection.[28] However, the Chinese never painted duobaoge as a freestanding subject, so Chinese painting prototypes cannot account for the sudden appearance of Korean chaekgeori painting.

The Jesuits were also valued for their artistic and technical skills, and the Qing emperor Kangxi asked the Jesuits to send a trained European painter to Beijing. Upon this request, several European painters came to Beijing to paint for the emperor and to teach Western techniques to the court artists. Very often, the Jesuit painters who served at the Chinese painting academy were under close control and had to tolerate the restrictions and confiment of court life. Therefore, it is not surprising to hear Father Denis Attiret complain: "To be on a chain from one sun to the next; barely to have Sundays and feast days on which to pray to God; to paint almost nothing in keeping with one's own taste and genius; to have to put up with a thousand other harassments . . . all this would quickly make me return to Europe if I did not believe my brush useful for the good of religion and a means of making the Emperor favorable towards the Missionaries."[29]

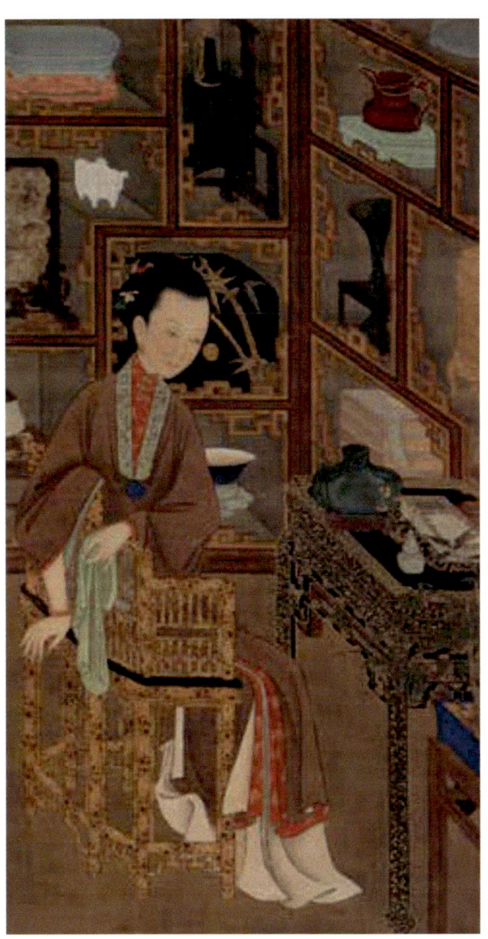

Figure 14. Anonymous, Chinese. *Twelve Beauties at Leisure Painted for Prince Yinzhen, the Future Yongzheng Emperor*, 1732 (detail). Twelve-panel screen. Ink and color on silk, 194 x 98 cm (each panel). Palace Museum, Beijing.

The Italian Jesuit Giuseppe Castiglione, who arrived in Beijing in 1715, truly satisfied both the demanding emperor Yongzheng and his successor Qianlong, who cherished Castiglione very much.[30] Born and trained in Milan, where the European "illusionistic cupboards" were invented, Castiglione trained as a professional painter and remained a lay brother throughout his Jesuit career. He developed his painting from the Bolognese tradition of illusionistic perspectival painting and was an expert at linear perspective. He participated in translating into Chinese an Italian book about the subject, *Perspective Pictorum et Architeorum* (1693) by the Milanese painter Andrea Pozzo.[31] He and other Jesuits, including Ferdinand Verbiest, Giovanni Gheradini, and Matteo Ripa, trained Chinese artists in linear perspective. For example, Verbiest, a Flemish mathematician-astronomer who worked at the Chinese imperial observatory, taught perspective techniques to his Chinese disciple Jiao Bingzhen, who later became a prominent court artist.

The masterful perspective painting of Giuseppe Castiglione attracted Qianlong's interest. The emperor commissioned "scenic illusion painting" (*tongjinghwa* in Chinese), which is illusionitic trompe l'oeil painting, to decorate his palatial halls.[32] Likewise, the walls in the South Catholic Church and the observatory in Beijing were decorated in illusionistic trompe l'oeil technique. One Chinese observer left us with a written description of a painting by Castiglione on the walls of the South Catholic Church in Beijing:

> In the [South Church], there are two paintings in perspective executed by Lang Shining [Giuseppe Castiglione]. They cover the whole of the two walls, vertically and horizontally, to the east and west of the parlor. If you are standing at the foot of the west wall, close one eye and look at the completely raised bead curtains. The window to the southwest is ajar. Rays of sunlight are playing on the ceiling. Scroll books closed with ivory needles and jade pins fill the library. There is a magnificant cabinet containing "curios" that sparkle from top to bottom. To the north stands a table. And on the table [is] a vase containing a bouquet of pheasant's feathers. A brilliant feather fan appears in the setting sun. In the rays of the sun [are] the shadow of the fan, the shadow of the vase, the shadow of the table—all perfectly rendered. . . . You are tempted to enter. . . . You stretch out your hand and suddenly realize that you are facing a wall.[33]

This is a valuable record of the existence of trompe l'oeil paintings by Castiglione, even though the actual artworks in the church were destroyed by a fire in 1775 and other such paintings by Castiglione have not been found. However, the painting of duobaoge in trompe l'oeil manner attributed to Castiglione, which was introduced by Kay E. Black, shows a striking similarity with Korean chaekgeori in subject matter, complex shelving, chiaroscuro, and linear perspective. Even though the painting holds an inscription, "I am privileged to address the Emperor thusly, painted with respect by Lang Shi-ning," many art historians think the painting was probably done by his Chinese disciples at the Painting Academy or by a copyist in later years.[34]

In Beijing, Korean visitors were as entranced by the new Western influences as the Chinese. From the mid-seventeenth century, members of the Korean elite visted the Chinese capital regularly through Korean tributary missions. Every year Korea sent about three, each consisting of two to three hundered individuals, including the envoys and their interpreters, physicians, and government and military officials, as well as the required staff and laborers. Among them were many forward-looking Korean scholars of the Northern Learning school, as described in the Introduction to this catalogue. In Beijing one of the must-see sights for the envoys, especially the Northern Learning scholars, was the South Catholic Church and its environs, where the envoys interacted with Western missionaries, experienced advanced Western technology, and acquired books, prints, and paintings, while others had their portraits painted in the Western manner.[35]

There are numerous records of Korean visitors who were amazed by the realistic, Baroque-style depictions of scenes, objects, and people on the church walls.[36] In 1720 a young scholar, Yi Giji, accompanied the tributary mission of his father, Prime Minister Yi Imyeong, and saw the mural at the South Catholic Church. He recorded his astonishment at the painting with this commentary:

> At first, upon entering the hall and looking at the wall, it appeared as if there was a big niche on the wall that was filled with clouds and people, and I felt dizzy by illusions of ghosts and spirits that turned into phantoms. But upon closer examination, I realized that it was a painting on the wall. It is hard to say that human techniques have reached up to such a high level. Also, the wooden members of the painted architecture cross one another, creating shadows, corners, sharp edges, and space so that one can turn around the corner and hide in the space behind.[37]

One of the Northern Learning scholars, Bak Jiwon, who visited the South Catholic Church in 1780 wrote:

> The figures and clouds on the walls and ceiling of the church seem hard to describe with usual written or spoken languages, also hard to figure out with ordinary mentality. There was some unknown force stemming from the eyes of the figure that tried to pull out my eyes when I was about to look at it. I abhorred the way the figures pry into my thoughts. When I was about to

> say something, suddenly they broke their silence and roared aloud like a thunder. Upon closer examination, rather rough strokes of ink were applied sparsely, and only the areas of their ears, eyes, noses, and mouths, and the body hairs, mustache, skin, and sinews were marked with thin brush lines. The features were represented with hair-splitting exactitude, and they look as if [they are] moving and breathing; their light and dark sides were well represented with the proper application of light and shade. In the painting there was a woman holding a child of about five or six years old; the child squints at the woman with his sick face, and the woman turns away her head as if to avoid the child's eyes. . . . . When I looked up the high ceiling, numerous babies [putti] were playing amid the clouds of five colors as if suspended in midair. Their wrists and shins looked plump, their skin, warm if touched. Suddenly the viewers were struck with the sight of the falling babies, and stretched out their arms and pulled their heads back to receive them.[38]

This descripton shows that Korean envoys observed the dimensional realism and modeling of Western painting with amazement. They also realized that the "secret" behind this trompe l'oeil painting was closely related to Western math. After seeing the illusionary painting at the observatory in 1765, the scholar-official Hong Daeyong described his impressions of a wall painting there, and then remarked: "They say that the principles behind Western painting are not only outstanding thoughts but also the laws of planning and dividing, which all come from mathematics."[39]

Scholars of the Northern Learning school were keely interested in Western math and geometry and its relationship to perspective painting and the painting of objects based on actual observation. They brought Western books translated into Chinese back to Korea and also Western paintings, as well as Western gadgets. Thus, artistic techniques and Western objects such as clocks, eyeglasses, and zithers seen on Korean chaekgeori paintings are closely related to the intellectual thoughts and scholarship of the Northern Learning scholars and reflect the latest trends in painting in contemporary China.

Korea: Object and Identity [40]

Every year during the late-seventeenth, eighteenth, and nineteenth centuries, Korean evoys returned from China laden with ideas, as well as books, paintings, and all manner of novel and foreign objects to disseminate back in Korea. With an inflow of Chinese and foreign objects, late Joseon Korea experienced an unprecedented introduction to consumer culture. While the scale of the new materialism in Korea did not match the flourishing consumer culture of late Ming and Qing China and Edo Japan, nonetheless, and perhaps inevitably, Korea's traditional, asustere Confucian culture began to dissolve under the onslaught of alluring material imports.

As more and more luxury items began to flood in from China, Korea was caught up in the rise of collecting and consumer culture, as described in the essays by Ja Won Lee and Sooa McCormick in this catalogue. This was a noteworthy shift because early Joseon society was dominated by deeply embedded, centuries-old Confucian values of austerity and humility. The humble and modest life was considered the ideal life, as reflected in the phrase *wanmul sangji* (meaning "dallying too much with objects kills one's will").[41] For centuries, Confucian condemnation of material pleasure had effectively prevented Korean Confucian literati from enjoying, possessing, and collecting pleasurable objects. In the eighteenth and nineteenth centuries, however, scholars and government officials began to both distance themsleves from the ethic of austerity and steadily increase their "dalliances with objects," as we see in portraits of government officials and other elites and numerous chaekgeori paintings.

Chinese books and antiques began to appear in Korean portraits from this period. Unlike Chinese examples, in which material objects or servants are often included to imply the sitter's social and economic status, the poses and props in traditional Korean portraits were relatively austere. Portrait sitters were dressed in either official or scholar's garments and sat in a three-quarter view on simple chairs, hiding their hands, and without any extra accoutrements. However, from the eighteenth century on, sitters began to commission private portraits in much more relaxed poses, sometimes displaying their hands, along with selected accoutrements and symbolic objects (fig. 15). In the 1863 portrait of Regent Yi Haeung by the court painter Yi Hancheol (fig. 16), Yi Haeung, wearing his crane robe and dragon cap, proudly displays many imported luxuries, including a Chinese sword, encased book, Western clock, jade-carved seal, blue-and-white porcelain ink-paste case, brush and dragon-decorated inkstone, Buddhist rosary, eyeglasses, jade cup, and bronze incense burner. The fact that this regent, who was a conservative and staunch proponet of Korean isolationism, presented himself with such imports reveals major changes in Joseon values and material culture.

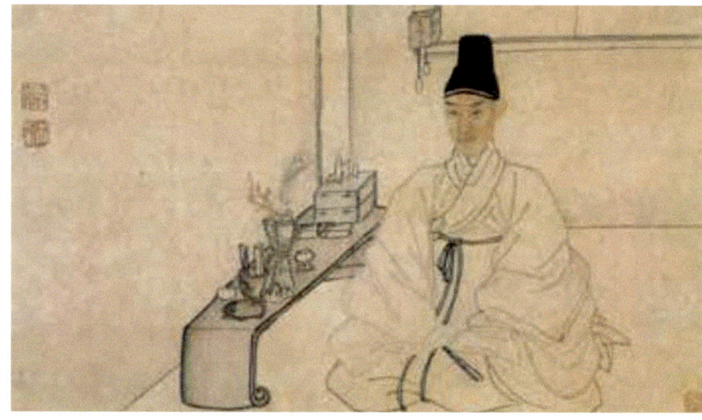

Figure 15. Kim Hongdo (1745–1806/14). *Portrait of a Literatus*, 18th century. Ink and light color on paper, 27.5 x 43 cm. Chosun Art Museum, Pyongyang.

However, while portraiture underwent significant transformations, in chaekgeori still-life painting we see an entirely new genre arise from foreign roots to give visual form to an increasingly materialistic culture. It is interesting to note that even though in China duobaoge appeared as a backdrop in court paintings, it never developed as an independent painting subject. Conversely, the real-life duobaoge or European-style curio cabinet was never popular in Korea; instead Koreans limited themselves to translating its three-dimensional form into two-dimensional painting. This is likely because the deeply embedded Confucian values of modesty, austerity, and simplicity, as well as economic and political limitations, would have prevented Joseon Koreans from featuring curio cabinets with treasured objects in their homes. In fact, early chaekgeori paintings were far from displays of consumption; they were displays of proper scholarship.

The most characteristic feature of Korean chaekgeori is the presence of large numbers of books (plate 3), which reflects the elevated position of books in Joseon society and Koreans' passion for them. However, as much as books were prized by the Korean literati, they were not always freely available. Because books were a principal means of acquiring knowledge and transmitting ideas and information, they could undermine royal power and cultural institutions, and so Korean monarchs regulated their production and circulation. With accessibility to books in Korea limited, the regular tributary missions to Beijing were some of the best opportunities for the literati to purchase books. In Beijing, Korean diplomatic envoys, armed with long lists of books for themsleves and their friends back home, roamed around the bookstores and spent much time searching for, reading, and copying books. As Kris Ercums shows in his "Books as Things" in this catalogue, the Korean passion for books was very well known in China.

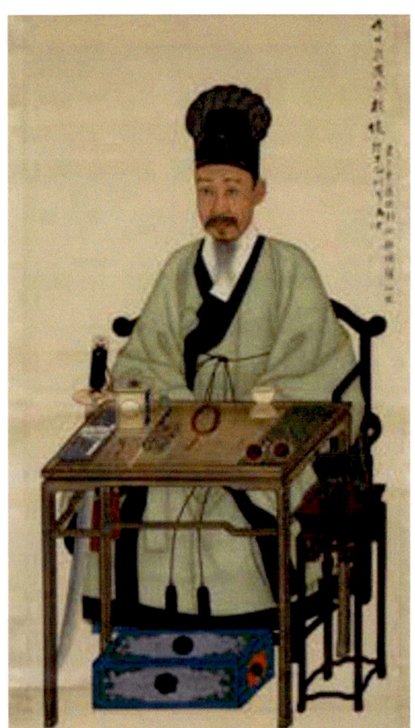

Figure 16. Yi Hancheol (1812–after 1890) and Yu Suk (1827–1873), *Portrait of Yi Haeung*, 1869. Hanging scroll. Ink and color on silk, 133.7 x 67.7 cm. Seoul Museum of History.

The early nurturing and spread of chaekgeori in Joseon Korea is most attributable to one critical figure, the late-eighteenth-century King Jeongjo. Known for his deep admiration for books, Jeongjo founded Gyujanggak, the famous palace library. Jeongjo was also an able painter and a great patron of painting. In 1783 he established a system of "court painters-in-waiting," consisting of ten extraordinary court painters who worked diretly under the guidance of the king himself. In 1784, chaekgeori became one of the major subjects in the formal examinations for court painters-in-waiting, and it continued to be an examination subject for almost a century, until 1879.[42] The kind of chaekgeori painting promoted by Jeongjo was appropriately austere in the Confucian painting tradition, but chock full of books.

King Jeongjo had both personal and political reasons for promoting chaekgeori. In 1791, he wrote:

> Looking back at the bookshelf behind the throne, His Highness asked his officials, "Do you see them?" "Yes, we see them," answered the officials. Then, His Highness smiled and said: "These are not real books but paintings. [Cheng Yi] once said that if one occassionally entered one's study and touched one's books, it would please one, even though one was unable to read books regularly. I came to realize the meaning of the saying through this painting. For the titles of the books [in the painting], I wrote the Confucian Classics and those of Zhuangzi."[43]

From this statement, we see that Jeongjo viewed chaekgeori painting as a vicarious substitute for reading and studying, as he did not have as much time to spend with his books as he wanted. Behind his throne he placed a chaekgeori screen, instead of the typical royal theme of *irworobongdo* (Sun, Moon, and Five Peaks screen). We see that as an artist himself, he had an aesthetic interest in chaekgeori, especially in its illusionistic aspect, and enjoyed tricking his officials with its trompe l'oeil technique. Chaekgeori was the new thing, so it enabled the king to present a public image of a monarch who was an up-to-date and accomplished literatus.

However, for Jeongjo, chaekgeori was more than a personal preference. As indicated, books were a means of maintaining power and authority and a device by which monarchs could promulgate and instill their governing ideologies. Therefore, in order to recommend proper readings, Jeongjo selected appropriate book titles of the Chinese classics for the books to be represented in court chaekgeori. Jeongjo was also fully aware of, and equally disturbed by, the increasing importation of Chinese luxury objects. He expressed his concern about the scholar-official's increasing culture of collecting sumptuous imported luxuries:

> Lately the habits of the high officials have become very queer, and they try to disrupt the Chosŏn order and instead want to learn Chinese ways. Not ony through [vulgar] books, but also to show off their highbrow culture. Inksticks, screens, brusholders, chairs, antiques—they lay out all these imported items, drink tea, smoke scents. . . . I cannot mention them all one by one. Even I, who stay deep in the palace, know this by hearsay, and there must be deep and widespread harmful effects scattered all over.[44]

Unfortunately, no chaekgeori painting produced under the direct guidance of Jeongjo has survived. However, a twelve-panel folding screen from the National Palace Museum provides us with an idea of what kind of chaekgeori King Jeongjo probably enjoyed and promoted (plate 10). Each panel of this screen is divided into three or four simple horizontal shelves, most of which hold piles of books and no imported luxury objects. There is the mixture of Korean and Chinese books, which can be distinguisehd by size, casings, and stitches. Imported Chinese books were smaller and had four stitches for bindings. The book covers were thin, so multiple volumes were encased in a silk-covered box. Often indigo in color, Chinese book boxes were splendidly patterned and had ivory latches. Korean bookcase covers were larger and had five stitches. These covers were thick papers stamped in abstract patterns with no latches. Unlike Jeongjo's apparent practice of including the titles of books, however, no book titles appear in this painting. This chaekgeori painting, with no luxurious objects but filled with books, clearly reflects not only Jeongjo's ascetic scholarly taste, but also his political agenda.

As indicated by King Jeongjo's concern, the immense flow of Chinese luxuries, antiques, and books from Beijing, especially late Ming essays and manuals on how properly to enjoy material culture, spurred an interest in material objects and the desire to acquire and appreciate antiquities, paintings, and calligraphy in late Joseon society. Chaekgeori paintings began to depict increasing numbers of luxurious objects, and in content and style became increasingly unbound by Confucian ideas of order and austerity. By the nineteenth century, chaekgeori paintings were popular as household decorations among the ruling elite and prosperous commoners. Conflicting but coexisting values and outlooks, ranging from austere and scholarly Confucianism to flamboyant and sensual materialism, are reflected in equally diverse range of chaekgeori styles.

Yet, we cannot understand the rise and role of chaekgeori painting as a function of increasing materialism alone. The late Joseon was also a period of immense social realignment, as the traditional aristocratic class, the *yangban,* was challenged by an emerging professional and technical class, the *jungin.* The jungin included foreign language interpreters, medical officials, legal officials, and geomancers, and other wealthy merchants, and all acquired financial stability through their professions and other privileges. This group was as intellectually cultivated as the yangban literati and emulated the lofty and scholarly yangban taste, but at the same time wanted to display their affluence, diverse interests, and distinctive identities. As a group, and as individuals, they were eager to create and broadcast their identities as prosperous yet refined intelligentsia and men of letters.[45] This nouveau rich group emerged as a primary market for chaekgeori painting.

In this socially mobile time, chaekgeori appeared as a perfect agent to deliver messages and craft self-identities for patrons. All chaekgeori paintings follow the established tradition of painting reading (*dokhwa*) in East Asian literati culture, in which paintings deliver messages through extensive visual symbolism. Carefully selected and presented symbolic and auspicious items were coded for communicating statements of desire and identity. A chaekgeori screen painting by the court painter Yi Eungnok [Yi Hyeongnok] now in the Asian Art Museum in San Francisco (hereafter, the AAM chaekgeori) is typical of chaekgeori symbolism (plate 4).[46] A bronze vessel on the bottom shelf on the far left panel holds two peacock feathers and a coral branch, which is a common symbolic combination in both Chinese and Korean painting. According to the *Book of Changes,* the peacock is a cultured bird of nine virtues and represents one of the three top ranks of civil service positions. Likewise, coral is a precious object, and in China civil officers of the first rank wore coral buttons on their hats. Thus, the coral branch and peacock feathers are usually interpreted as an aspiration to achieve the highest official rank. The two Buddha's hand (fingered citrons) and pomegranates in a bowl in the center of the screen are also symbolic. With its shape of fingers grasping or holding something, probably money, a Buddha's hand fruit is interpreted as symbol of wealth. The pomegranate with its numerous seeds symbolizes fertility or abundance. Thus, the Buddha's hand citrons, in combination with the pomegranate, can be read as the hope for wealth, many blessings, and many sons. When we decipher all the coded messages of the objects in the AAM chaekgeori painting, and in all chaekgeori paintings, we find messages of Confucian values and auspicious aspirations.

As noted in the introduction to this catalogue, there are several types of chaekgeori paintings. The wealthy jungin and yangban, who were the commissioners and consumers of chaekgeori paintings, used the bookshelf style that caught the attention and favor of King Jeongjo and later became widespread among the elite. The jungin especially did not stop at imbuing their screens with these coded messages, they also used them to announce their identities and express their personalities. Chaekgeori paintings are multipanel folding screens. Large and typically positioned behind the owner's seat as a backdrop, they provided context for the host and, even when the master of the room was absent, remained for visitors to contemplate. Therefore, chaekgeori screens were used to create an image of the sitter. With this in mind, we can examine and compare the implied personalities and possible identities expressed by two very different chaekgeori screens.

The traditional sedate, formal style is exemplified by the AAM chaekgeori screen just described, in which the objects are neatly organized on the shelves and have their own spaces. However, another eight-panel folding screen, *Chaekgeori behind a Leopard-Skin Curtain* in the Leeum Museum in Seoul (plate 16), delivers a very different message. Eight long leopard skins are hung as a curtain, with two skins raised to reveal the scene behind. The space behind the curtains contains a plethora of objects. If the owner of the orderly and relatively austere AAM chaekgeori screen exhibited his refinement, tranquility, scholary focus, and complete control of the objects, the commisioner/owner of this chaekgeori painting wants us to know that he is immensely wealthy, but also casual, spontaneous, exuberant, and involved in numerous activities. With the many hints provided, viewers can visualize him: a middle-aged man (from the eyeglasses) with scholarly manners (he was reading a book right before he left the room) and elegant taste (with his antiques and and accountrements), yet he is a sociable fellow who enjoys his leisure time, as we see in the elegant tea service and *golpae* (Korean domino game) tiles. He must be a well-off gentleman who can enjoy luxurious imports such as coral and other Chinese objects. Symbolizing bravery and warding off demon spirits, the leopard is an auspicious animal, and by the nineteenth century leopard skins were extremely rare and expensive. Therefore, the leopard-skin curtain brags of incredible affluence. Finally, the *Leopard Skin* screen is unique among bookshelf chaekgeori in its use of a drawn curtain to reveal an apparently unarranged slice of life. Thus, in its form as well as its content, this screen sends the message that its owner was not afraid to be different and experimental.

As we see in these two paintings, chaekgeori screens were not merely decorative displays of luxurious objects with generic symbolism, they were customized to signal the kind of person the owner was, believed himself to be, or wanted others to believe he was. Art historians today cannot be sure to what extent the objects depicted were accurate representations of someone's actual possessions or were objects of imagination and desire. But we can assume that what we see in these screens reflects the Joseon people's desires and ideals for themselves and their surroundings.

As time went by, chaekgeori became popular with and accessible to less affluent people and took on a different form. They were mass-produced rather than personalized for particular patrons, and, designed to appeal to that new audience, they are highly colorful and playful. Departing from the bookshelf format, these minhwa chaekgeori (folk-style or tabletop) were more like European still lifes, with books and objects piled on and around small tables (plate 23). The paintings were grouped in screens, and were smaller in scale to fit modest homes. While scholarly objects such as books, inkstones, inksticks, brushes, and papers remained prominent, testament to the scholarly ambitions of all levels of Korean culture, small pieces of furniture and indigenous objects for leisure time also appear, along with numerous symbolic fruits and vegetables such as grapes, cucumbers, eggplants, and watermelons, whose many seeds augur feritility and prosperity. Minwa chaekgeori sometimes also contain images of auspicious animals, including carp, goldfish, buttlerflies, and tigers to represent longevity, success, and marital harmony. These paintings symbolize in visual form the spiritual and emotional well-being of the home and its residents, as well as their idealized material comforts. Yet if the owners could not afford the expensive objects depicted, the paintings themselves could be primary objects of aesthetic pleasure in the home. Long ignored by art historians as mere folk art, tabletop chaekgeori have recently attracted scholarly interest and are examined further in Byungmo Chung's essay in this catalogue.

While patrons and buyers exploited how chaekgeori screens could be used to deliver personal and cultural messages, the painters explored the artistic potential of the new genre. In fact, one of the most exciting aspects of chaekgeori painting is how it became a vehicle for stylistic experimentation. Not only did chaekgeori painters experiment with European painting techniques, including Western perspective, modeling, and illusionism appropriated from European models via China, they also delved into a kind of optical abstraction not seen in Western painting until the twentieth century.

While it is outside the scope of this essay to go into detail about the wide-ranging stylistic experimentation present in both bookshelf and tabletop chaekgeori, it appears that Korean chaekgeori painters, having fashioned a new genre based on European and Chinese models, with new content based on dazzling new imports, felt unconstrained by traditional Korean painting styles. But equally, as powerful and astonishing as Renaissance realism was to its Korean observers, chaekgeori painters did not mimic European aesthetics. Instead, Korean artists adopted some aspects of Renaissance illusionism, such as linear perspective, modeling, and chiaroscuro, but in most cases, two-dimensional design seemed as important or more important to them than three-dimensional realism. In tabletop chaekgeori, the objects and the backgrounds intertwine in delightful shapes, confusing the eye and shifting the focus from volumetric objects to surface interplays of texture, pattern, and design (plate 34). In bookshelf chaekgeori, the geometric structure provided by the "shelves" and books tends to dominate the objects. In both bookshelf and tabletop chaekgeori screens, the bookcase-cover patterns consistently become design opportunities that flatten the space (fig. 17). What appears so "modern" to our eyes is the way in which these artists used chaekgeori as a platform through which to create a dialogue between abstraction and reality.

A Rich Cultural Artifact

Korean chaekgeori screens, partly because of their cross-cultural character (in the case of the bookshelf style) and their symbolic and abstract features (in the case of the tabletop style), appeal to contemporary viewers in both East and West and have recently become a coveted art object for Korean galleries in art museums in the West. This collaborative essay by a Renaissance and Baroque art historian and a Korean art historian has traced the possible origins of chaekgeori painting. Putting art objects and other collectibles on public display in decorative shelves was a widespread activity in Renaissance Europe by the sixteenth century, where such collections reflected the Renaissance ideal—the acquisition of comprehensive knowledge—and broadcast the power and erudition of the owners. This collecting culture arose alongside the development of linear perspective and phenomenal realism in painting.

In the seventeenth and eighteenth centuries, these European ideas and techniques were transmitted to China through Jesuit missionaries, who assured their continuing welcome in Beijing by captivating the Chinese monarchs with Western science, technology, and trompe l'oeil painting. The Chinese court adopted the use of display shelves containing fabulous objects to impress visitors and symbolize the reach of their power. In Beijing, Korean government officials and intellectuals, who visited the capital regularly as part of official tributary missions, interacted with the Jesuits and Chinese, exchanging books, objects, and ideas. Forward-looking Koreans were eager to partake in the progressive ideas and activities they saw taking place in China. The Korean visitors were awestruck by Renaissance realism and clearly saw the relationship between advances in technology and possibilities for artistic ingenuity.

Over two centuries, huge numbers of books, painting manuals, paintings, art objects, Chinese antiques, and other luxury items poured into Korea from China. These cultural curiosities and interactions were visually manifested in Korea in chaekgeori painting. The Korean elite used bookshelf chaekgeori screens depicting their collections—or idealized collections—much as the Renaissance princes and Chinese court did: as public statements of wealth, power, and erudition. Korean commoners enjoyed tabletop chaekgeori as sensual visual luxury items and symbols of scholarly aspirations, prosperity, and family harmony. Compared to the more traditional Korean painting genres, chaekgeori painting has relatively short history, yet it is a rich cultural artifact that opens up myriad research opportunities and still has much to reveal about early modern Korean aesthetics, sensibilities, hopes, and aspirations.

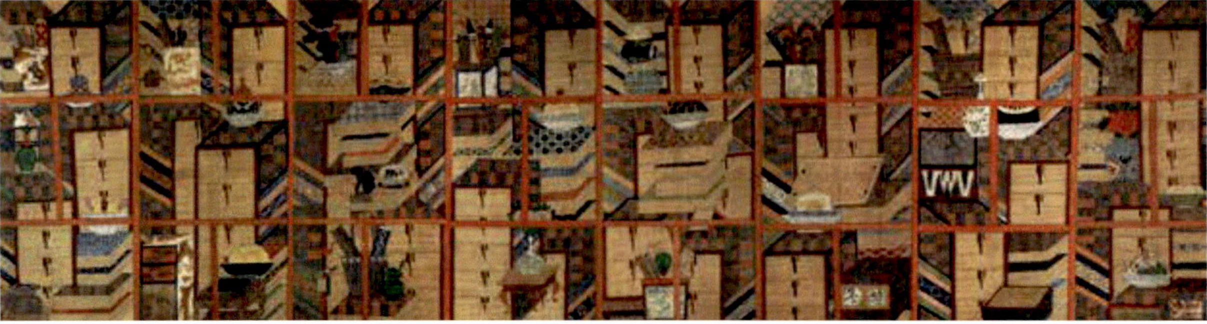

Figure 17. Anonymous. *Chaekgeori*, late 19th to early 20th century. Eight-panel screen (now framed). Ink and color on paper, 83 x 305.5 cm. Leeum, Samsung Art Museum, Seoul.

This essay is a collaborative work of two art historians, Joy Kenseth and Sunglim Kim. Joy Kenseth is a professor at Dartmouth College specializing in Renaissance and Baroque art. She curated the exhibition *The Age of the Marvelous* at the Hood Museum in 1992. Sunglim Kim is an assistant professor at Dartmouth College specializing in Korean art.

1 Korean art historians have pointed out some similarities between Korean chaekgeori paintings and Chinese duobage and/or duobaogejing. Kay E. Black introduced a Chinese trompe l'oeil painting attributed to Italian Jesuit priest Giuseppe Castiglione that may be a prototype for Korean chaekgeori painting; see Black and Wagner 1998, 23–35. Chinese art historian Jerome Silbergeld extends the chaekgeori's connection further to the Italian Renaissance; see Silbergeld 2014, 1-2. For chaekgeori's Western connection, see Yi, S. 2014; Jungmann 2013, 67–87.

2 Black and Wagner1998, 24–26.

3 Kenseth, 1991.

4 This source, not identified, is cited in Dam-Mikkelsen and Lundack 1980, xix–xx. Parts of this essay are drawn from an earlier discussion of cabinets of curiosity, Kenseth 1991.

5 This is the observation of Richard Lassels, who visited the gallery in 1650. From his unpublished journal, cited in Jane S. Whitehead, " 'The Noblest Collection of Curiositiys': British Visitors to the Uffizi, 1650–1789," in Barocchi and Ragionieri 1983, 290. Lassels described the contents of the gallery in detail in Lassels 1670, part I, 160–75.

6 The terms used to describe the early collections were numerous and varied from region to region. The variations on the most familiar terms were considerable. Balsiger 1970, 740–66, provides a helpful glossary of these terms and other words related to the history of collecting. Excellent discussions of the terms used to describe collections in the early modern period and of the transformation of the *studiolo* to *galleria* can be found in Findlen 1989, 59–78, and Findlen 1994, 97–150.

7 Filarete 1890, 666–69. An English translation of Filarete's treatise is also available, Filarete 1965.

8 The literature on museums of the early modern period is vast. Schlosser 1908 was the first modern study of the phenomenon of European cabinets of curiosities. More recent scholarship in this area includes the previously cited studies by Balsiger and Findlen; Lugli 1983; Impey and MacGregor 1985; Pomian 1987; Hooper-Greenhill 1992. Another interesting essay on this subject is Giuseppe Olmi, "Dal 'Teatro del Mondo' ai mondi inventariati. Aspetti e forme del collezionismo nell'età moderna," in Barocchi and Ragionieri 1983, 243–44. Many other discussions of early modern museums and collecting practices can be found in Preziosi and Farago 2004.

9 Pomian 2987, 64.

10 Mirandola 1956. The relevant passages from this essay appear on pages 5–8, 34, 43–44.

11 Discussions on Duke Albrecht's collections can be found in Thoma and Brunner 1970; Scherer 1931; and Lorenz Seelig, "The Munich Kunstkammer, 1565–1807," in Impey and MacGregor, 76–89. As to Rudolf II's collections, see Eliška Fučíkova, "The collection of Rudolf II at Prague: Cabinet of Curiosities or Scientific Museum?" in Impey and MacGregor 1985, 47–53. See as well the essays regarding Rudolf's collection in Fu íkova 1997.

12 Kaufmann 1978, 27.

13 For a discussion of the Tribuna and its iconographic program, see Heikamp 1964, 11–30.

14 See Schulz 1990, 205, and Findlen 1989, 64 and *passim*.

15 For information regarding Worm's collection, see, in addition to Dam-Mikkelsen and Lundaek 1980, the essay by H. D. Schepelern, "Natural Philosophers and Princely Collections: Worm, Paludanus and the Gottorp and Copenhagen Collections," in Impey and MacGregor 1985, 121–27.

16 See the following for discussions of Imperato's collection: Accordi 1981, 43–56; Neviani 1936, 57–74, 124–45, 191–210, 243–67.

17 Findlen 1994, 36.

18 Paintings that offer idealized views of collections are discussed Filipczak 1987.

19 In the seventeenth century trompe-l'oeil paintings were found in such collections as those of the Danish monarchs, Rudolf II at Prague, the Medici, and the Archduke of the Southern Netherlands. See Gundestrup 1991 and Eliška Fučík 1997.

20 To learn about Chinese collecting culture, see Li and Watt 1987.

21 Xu and Li 2016.

22 Zhang 2003; Ho 2004; Kleutghen 2015. See also the film *The Emperor's Eye: Art and Power in Imperial China*

by Lisa Hsia, which sheds light on the priceless treasures of China's imperial art collection, relating them to the political climate of their time. The film makes an argument that the tale of a passionate collector, Emperor Qianlong, whose pursuit to create the greatest art collection in the world, was actually his hope for his own immortality.

23 Bailey 1999; Saravia 2012.

24 See Hsia 2010; Fontana 2011; Laven 2011.

25 Ibid.

26 Yi, S. 2014, 14 and 17.

27 Ibid.

28 For detailed stuides of the objects appearing in this screen, see Peng 80–95.

29 Paludan 1998, 197.

30 To learn about Giuseppe Castiglione's artistic activities and court life in China, see Beaurdeley and Beaurdeley 1971; Musillo 2016.

31 Ibid.

32 See Kleutghen 2015.

33 Beaurdeley and Beaurdeley 197, 93–94. The original Chinese quotation is from Mikinosuke Ishida, "A Biographical Study of Giuseppe Castiglione," *The Memoirs of the Research Department of the Toyo Bunko*, no. 19 (1960).

34 Black and Wagner 1998, 24–25.

35 In Beijing, there were three Jesuit Churches. The South Church was built in 1601 followed by the East Church in 1650 and finally the North Church in 1693. For the records of meetings and interactions between Korean envoys and Western Jesuits, see Sin 2013.

36 The Korean visitors' impressions of trompe l'oeil paintings are found in their travelogues. See Yi, S. 2014, 17–31.

37 The translation is by Yi, S. 2014, 21. The original text is from Yi Giji's "Seoyanghwa gi [Record of Western painting]" in his writing collection *Iramjip*, vol. 2.

38 The translation is by Yi Kawon in *Hanguk myeongjeo daejeonjip*, vol. 22, 339–40. The original text is from Bak Jiwon's "Yanghwa [Western painting]" in his *Yeolha ilgi*, book 3.

39 Yi, S. 2014, 23.

40 This part of essay is a shortened and revised version of Kim 2014, 3–32.

41 The context is the Lord of Shao's petition to King Wu of Zhou (r. 1122–15 BC), requesting that the latter should refuse certain extravagant tributes from a tribe to the west of China. The argument is based on a distinction between *yiwu* (extraordinary things) and *yongwu* (useful things), and the warning against the baleful consequences of enjoying the former. The *Documents* is a collection of documents written between the time of the legendary Emperor Yao and the early Zhou dynasty.

42 The term "cheakga" first appeared in 1784, when King Jeongjo selected this as the third and final topic in the painting examination, and the term "chaekgeori" first appeared in 1788 in the *Daily Journal of Gyujanggak*. See Kang, G. 2001, 79–95.

43 Recorded by O. Jaesun in *Hongje jeonseo* [Collected works of King Jeongjo], 162, *Ildeuknok* [Records of diaologues with King Jeongjo and his subjects], *Munhak* [Literature].

44 Recorded by Kim Josun in ibid., *Huneo* [Admonition].

45 For the rise of the *jungin,* see Kim 2009.

46 See Kim, S. 2014, 14.

Books as Things in Korean Chaekgeori Screen Paintings

Kris Imants Ercums

A lifetime of books has meant delights without end.
Yi Hwang (Toegye, 1501–1570)

The abundance and variety of objects in chaekgeori decorative screens evince a delight in material things that captivated Korean elite and wealthy artistic audiences of the late Joseon period (plate 9). Although the objets d'art depicted in chaekgeori, commonly translated simply as "books and things," fluctuated over time, the inclusion of books remained a defining characteristic of this genre of decorative color screens.[1] The enduring, essential characteristic of books is further underscored in other variant terms for this painting genre: *chaekgado* (pictures of bookshelves), *seogado* (picture of bookshelves), and *chaekga munbangdo* (picture of a study [with] bookshelves). The appearance of either *chaek* or *seo*, two words that can generally be understood as "book," in all of these terms reveals the central importance of books in chaekgeori screen painting.

However, rather than approaching these decorative screens as "books and things," a subtle interpretative shift is possible, demonstrating "books as things" in conjunction with the wealth of other precious commodities depicted in chaekgeori. As Karl Marx poignantly remarked, "a commodity appears at first sight an extremely obvious, trivial thing. But its analysis brings out that it is a very strange thing, abounding in metaphysical subtleties and theological niceties."[2] By approaching books as things in chaekgeori, the manifold relationships between the world and materiality come into focus. Books emerge as more than mere objects, but rather as spatial embodiments of reading and literary achievement.

The focus on the human-object interaction of books situates books not as mere objects but rather provides a fuller understanding of the transformative, expanded meaning of books in chaekgeori. Such an approach to books in chaekgeori builds on Martin Heidegger's definition of "the thing" as more than a mere object-in-itself and posits books in chaekgeori as superseding their original, intended function as textual objects.[3] As Bill Brown observes in his seminal article on "thing theory" in literature, "we look through objects because there are codes by which our interpretive attention makes them meaningful, because there is a discourse of objectivity that allows us to use them as facts."[4] Brown goes on to note that the way in which objects assert themselves as things further reveals a subject-object relationship.[5] Considering books as things expands them not only beyond the mere object-in-itself—unfolding and transforming into something beyond the book as a receptacle for ideas—but also as a stage for enacting thought. The book in chaekgeori operates as a material *habitus*, that is, an unfixed context in which social practice and significance endures. The interpretive transitions away from the typical understanding of chaekgeori as books and things to books as things attempts to penetrate the object and within it locate the subject and, in doing so, sketch the contours of the complex roles that objects play in our lives.

The Space of Books

Paintings of "elegant gatherings" (Korean: *ajip*; Chinese: *yaji*) portray the way in which educated peer groups collectively engaged with antiquities and literary objects, and perhaps provide a good starting point for discussing the sociocultural significance of books in chaekgeori. While paintings of elegant gatherings range from works that document events historically attested to imagined and idealized compositions, they all share a common intention that "commemorated the association of allied men and celebrated the political and social order that defined and supported their alliance."[6] An example from late imperial China that documents a historical elegant gathering is *The Elegant Gathering in the Apricot Garden* (*Xingyuan yaji tu*) after the thirteenth-century artist Xie Huan, which memorializes a meeting of nine men on 6 April 1437 that was organized by Grand Secretary Yang Rong (fig. 1). The composition is carefully staged to highlight the social prestige and sophistication of the attending officials, all of whom are attired in formal robes of office and framed by literary and antique things that grant the meeting its atmosphere of elegance, refinement, and literary accomplishment. In contrast, rather than depicting a historical assembly, the eighteenth-century Korean painting *Elegant Gathering of Eminent Scholars*, a work attributed to Kim Hongdo (fig. 2), demonstrates how imagined representations of such assemblages used a cultural framework that was well understood among the educated aristocracy of Joseon Korea. It is within the social space constructed in elegant gatherings that things like books and antiquities operated as spatial embodiments of education and refinement, much like chaekgeori.

While the exact origins of chaekgeori may never be definitively established, as Sunglim Kim explains, "the early nurturing and spread of chaekgeori in Joseon Korea is most attributable to one critical figure, King Jeongjo."[7] An ardent bibliophile, Jeongjo not only established the royal library, Gyujanggak, but also commissioned chaekgeori to adorn his formal office at the Changdeokgung Palace.[8] He also designated chaekgeori an official genre in the qualifying examinations for the Royal Bureau of Painting in 1784.[9] Furthermore, his fondness for chaekgeori even propelled him on one occasion to substitute for the iconic Sun, Moon, and Five Peaks screen (*irworobongdo*)—a symbol of the monarch that served as the requisite backdrop in the throne room of Joseon kings—a chaekgeori screen.[10] Yet, even more significant than King Jeongjo's promotion of these decorative screens was the way in which he deployed them as a deliberate strategy for his intellectual authority. "*Chaekgeori* paintings," Kim observes, "provided a deliberate and ingenious way for the king [Jeongjo] to admonish high officials against reading inappropriate—or even, as the king saw it, threatening or dangerous—books."[11]

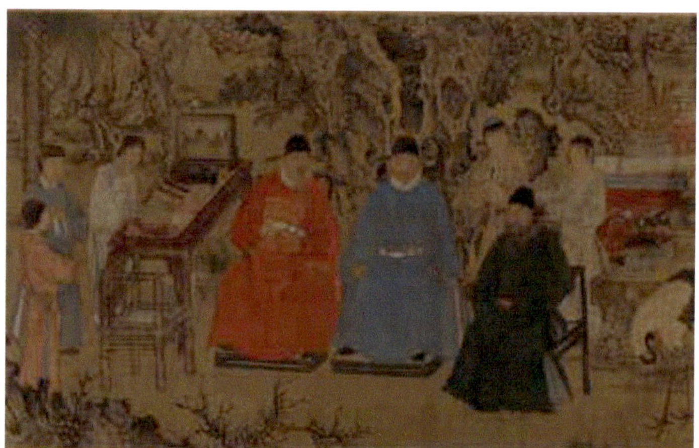

Figure 1. After Xie Huan (1377–1452). *Elegant Gathering in the Apricot Garden* (*Xingyuan yaji tu*) (detail), ca. 1437. Handscroll. Ink and color on silk, 37.1 x 243.2 cm (image). The Metropolitan Museum of Art, New York, Purchase, The Dillon Fund Gift, 1989.141.3.

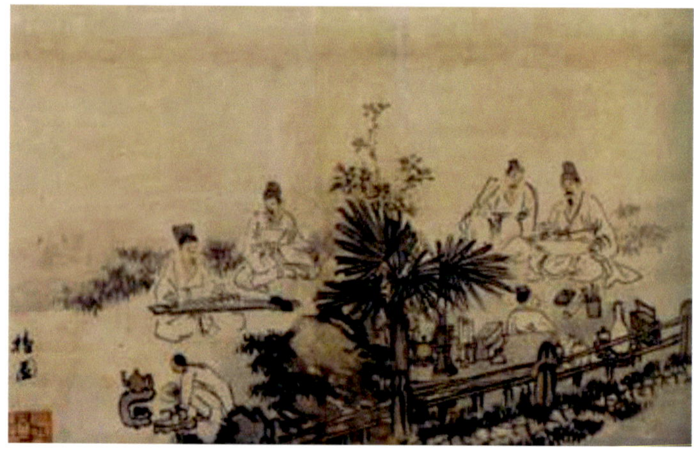

Figure 2. Attributed to Kim Hongdo (1745–1806/14). *Elegant Gathering of Eminent Scholars*, ca. late 18th century. Ink on paper. Private collection.

As chaekgeori gained popularity at the royal court, the aristocratic *yangban* class of educated scholar-officials soon began to commission similar decorative screens for use in their private residences. As seen in the painting *Leisurely Reading* by

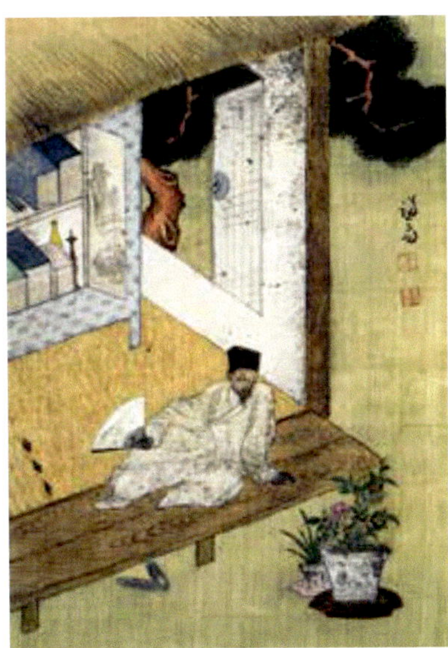

Figure 3. Jeong Seon (1676–1759). *Leisurely Reading*, ca. mid-18th century. Ink and color on silk. Gansong Art Museum, Seoul. Image credit: creativecommons.org

sixteenth-century artist Jeong Seon (fig. 3), which portrays a scholar pensively gazing into his garden from the edge of a study replete with a bookshelf of neatly stacked volumes, the chaekgeori with its symbolic content of books and refined antiquities was emblematic of the Confucian values of the yangban, who were, by and large, devoted to intellectual and literary pursuits.[12] Within yangban residences, chaekgeori were most likely located in the *sarangchae* (men's quarters), a multifunctional room for dinning, sleeping, reading, and receiving guests, in which books were typically displayed.[13] According to the *Gourd Song* (*Heungbuga*), a *pansori* (narrative song) composed in the nineteenth century by Shin Jaehyo, the sarangchae typically featured a six- or eight-panel folding screen, and thus, one can speculate that chaekgeori could have been displayed in this room of a yangban private residence.[14] This assertion is further corroborated by Yi Gyusang, who in *Manuscript of One Dream* (*Ilmonggo*, circa mid-18th century) claimed that chaekgeori were a ubiquitous feature in yangban houses of the eighteenth century.[15] Furthermore, as the genre grew in popularity, chaekgeori could also be found in the households of wealthy *jungin* (technocrats within the Joseon government) and middle-class merchants.[16] The nineteenth-century Scholar Yu Jaegeon recounts that he owned an illusionistic chaekgeori by Yi Yunmin that delighted visitors.[17]

Procuring Books

Transnational contact between China and Korea from the late seventeenth to early nineteenth centuries greatly stimulated the development of textual and literary culture in Joseon Korea. For the educated yangban class, annual tributary missions to Yanjing (present-day Beijing) were the principal means for procuring Chinese books and other desired commodities.[18] Although the prestigious post of chief ambassador was typically awarded to distinguished officials at court, there were hundreds of minor positions open to younger, junior officials, who often availed themselves of the opportunity to travel to China.[19]

An early Qing-period Chinese bibliophile and collector, Jiang Shaoshu, describes how visiting Joseon envoys set out to buy books in the Chinese capital:

> The people of Joseon like books most. Once the [Joseon] envoys, which are limited to fifty or sixty people, arrive to pay tribute [in China], [they begin to look for] old literature, new books, and popular novels that are not available in Korea. In the morning, they would set out for the market with a list of books they had compiled, asking people about them, and not hesitating to spend large sums of money to bring them back to [Joseon]. This is why so many unusual books are to be found in the collections of Joseon.[20]

Not only does Jiang relate to the bibliomania of the visiting Joseon envoys, he praises them for their erudition and skill in book publishing:

> I once saw [a copy of] *Huanghua Ji*,[21] which had been carved [by Koreans]. The carved blocks of this book were fine and the mulberry paper was as crystal clear as jade.[22] The light-yellow book casing from Joseon[23] was truly astonishing. The way that the people of Joseon cherish books is truly astonishing.[24]

The procurement of books in China by Joseon envoys was also occasionally undertaken by kingly request. In his travel journal *Return to Yantai* (*Yeondaejaeyu-rok; Yantai zai youlu*), Yu Deukgong records that prior to the Joseon tributary mission to China of 1776, King Jeongjo had instructed the head emissary Seo Hosu (to obtain a complete copy of the monumental *Gujin tushu jicheng (Complete collection of ancient and modern illustrations and writings)*, which amounted to a staggering 5,020 volumes packed in 502 cases.[25]

The way in which envoys from Joseon procured books on tributary missions to Yanjing further underscores the relationship between books and other commodities. Take for instance the account of Hong Daeyong recorded in his travelogue *Damheon yeongi* (Damheon's memoirs of Yanjing) from 1795, which chronicles his forays to a commercial market area in southern Yanjing known as Liulichang.[26]

> This market has all kinds of books, stone inscriptions, ancient vessels, antiques, and curios. Many of the merchants here are *hsiu-ts'ai* [*xiucai*][27] from the southern cities who have come to the capital to take the examination or seek offices, and that is why, while walking around the market, you will occasionally see a famous scholar. . . .
>
> There are seven areas devoted to bookshops. On three walls are mounted bookcases having as many as ten shelves. The books are all neatly arranged in regular folding cases, each with its ivory clasps and paper labels. The total number of books in any given area cannot be less that several myriads. However, long you can keep looking up, you cannot read all of the labels without getting dizzy.[28]

As noted in Hong's account, Liulichang was not only full of bookshops but abounded with antiquities such as fine ceramics and bronzes as well as literary objects including brushes, ink, paper, and inkstones that comprised the so-called Four Treasures of the Study (*munbangsau / wenfang sibao*), all of which are essential parts of chaekgeori.[29]

For Hong, "life abroad was undeniably exciting and liberating; like many travelers, he must have enjoyed a certain indulgence, a suspension of the rules and restraints that inevitably inform life in one's own country."[30] Hong reveled in the intellectual life he found in Yanjing, where he became fascinated with mathematics and astronomy; and was mesmerized by the illusionistic perspective in the tromp l'oeil wall murals adorning the Catholic South Church.[31] Whereas most visiting Korean envoys avoided speaking colloquial Chinese, preferring to engage in written communication known as *pildam* (brush talk) Hong was exceptional, as he not only had several close Chinese friends, but also conversed freely in vernacular, spoken Chinese.[32]

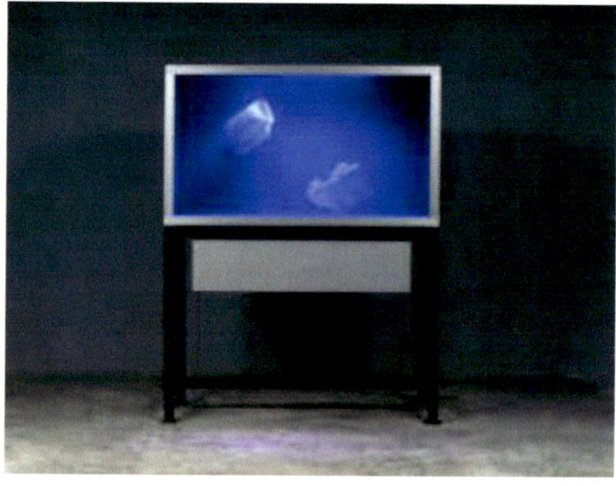

Figure 4. Kibong Rhee [Yi Gibong] (b. 1957). *End of the End*, 2008. Aluminum, steel, water pump, blue lamp, acrylic box, water, and handmade book. 52.5 x 65.2 x 200 cm. Courtesy of the artist and Kukje Gallery, Seoul, Korea.

Implications of Books

In the mesmerizing installation by contemporary Korean artist Kibong Rhee (fig. 4), two books glide through a glowing blue tank like a pair of manta rays.[33] The books are copies of *Tractus Logico-Philosophicus*, a 1921 philosophical treatise by Ludwig Wittgenstein that broadly aims to define the relationship between language and reality. Described by art critic Jinsang Yoo as "seeds of reason drifting in the sea at the beginning of the world," Rhee's work demonstrates the metaphorical transformation of a book from a mere object-in-itself to a thing encoded with interpretative attention that makes it meaningful (fig. 5).[34] As the two books caress one another in their

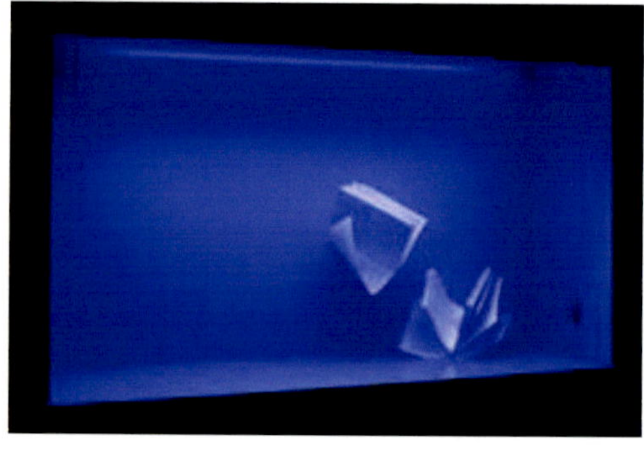

Figure 5. Kibong Rhee. *End of the End*, 2008 (detail).

languid drift, Rhee's *End of the End* visualizes the Buddhist concept of *anātman* (nonself), resounding with "metaphysical echoes."[35]

Similarly, the books in chaekgeori are depicted not as mere objects of textual and literary value but, because of the human-object interaction, as things with metaphysical significance. This expansive, transformed reading of books is particularly noticeable in later manifestations of chaekgeori referred to as the "isolated type" (plate 15).[36] In this version, the illusionistic bookshelf presentation vanishes and books with other things seem to float in space as if levitating, just as in Rhee's installation. It is in how we use books, not only in the reading of them but in their reassuring presence in our homes, studies, and libraries, that we discover their fullest meaning. King Jeongjo reflected further on this feature of books in his observations on the central value of chaekgeori, remarking that "great scholars of the past said that if one occasionally entered one's study and touched one's desk, it satisfied the mind, even though one was unable to read books regularly."[37]

Epigraph: Toegye, quoted in McCune 1983, 55.

I am grateful to Weitian Yan for his assistance with Chinese translations; however any mistakes are my own.

1 Black and Wagner 1993, 63.
2 Marx 1990, 168.
3 Heidegger 1971, 161–84.
4 Brown 2001, 4.
5 Ibid.
6 Burkus-Chasson 2002, 315.
7 Kim, S. 2014, 7.
8 Ibid.
9 Jungmann 2014, 280.
10 Kim 2014, 7.
11 Ibid., 8.
12 Han 1970, 247–48.
13 Choi 2007, 87.
14 Ibid., 91.
15 Kim, S. 2014, 44n. See *18 segi Joseon Inmulji* [Biographies of Joseon people from the eighteenth century] (Seoul: Changjak gwa bipyeongsa, 1997), 150–51.
16 The *jungin* were technocrats within the Joseon government that became increasingly wealthy by the nineteenth century, see also Kim, S. 2009, 25–32.
17 Jungmann 2014, 279.
18 A prominent literary figure and politician of the time, Heo Gyun, is said to have purchased more than 4,000 volumes during his tributary missions to China in 1614 and 1615. For examples of extensive Joseon book collections, see Kim, S. 2009, 41.
19 Ledyard 1974, 3.
20 The original Chinese text is as follows: 朝鮮國人最好書, 凡使臣入貢限五六十人或舊典, 或新書, 或稗官小說, 在彼 所缺者, 日出市中, 各寫書目, 逢人遍問不惜重值購回。故彼國反有異書藏本也. Jiang 1921; *Chaoxian* 2016. Several studies cite Chen Jiru's *Taiping Qinghua* 太平清话as the source for this observation.

21 Korean: *Hwanghwajip*. This a collection of response poems composed by Ming envoys to the Joseon court, see Wang, K. 2011, 144–49.

22 Chinese:蠶紙 *canzhi* paper on which the silkworm moth has deposited its eggs.

23 Chinese:海邦 *haibang* (country by the sea).

24 The original Chinese text is as follows: 余會見朝鮮所刻皇華集乃中朝敕封使臣與彼國文臣唱和之什鏤板精整且蠶紙瑩潔如玉海邦緗帙洵足稱奇. Jiang 1921; see note 22 above.

25 See also Jin 2010, 245. Yu Deukgong was a Silhak scholar best known for his important work on Korean history, *Balhae-go* 渤海考, 1784.

26 Damheon is the style name (號 *ho*/*hao*) of Hong Daeyong. For an extensive survey of the travel literature of Korean envoys in Liulichang, see Huang and Yu 2004, 10–13.

27 *Xiucai* 秀才 (flowering talent) is roughly equivalent to a bachelor's degree in the Chinese imperial examination system.

28 Ledyard 1982, 25.

29 For a history of Liulichang, see Wang, Y. 1963.

30 Ledyard 1982, 65–66.

31 Yi, S. 2014, 23. See also Jungmann 2014, 280.

32 Ledyard 1982, 65–66.

33 I am reminded of Hans Waanders' intervention of a field guide from the 1950s that resulted in the following passage: "Books can fly where they want to when they want to. So it seems to us, who are earthbound. They symbolise a degree of freedom that we would nearly give our souls to have," in Finlay 2001, 14.

34 Yoo, S. 2008, 7.

35 Ibid., 8.

36 Black and Wagner 1973, 63.

37 Black and Wagner 1998, 23.

Pursuing Antiquity: Chinese Bronzes in Chaekgeori Screens

Ja Won Lee

Joseon court painters began to produce chaekgeori screens in the late eighteenth-century, when a considerable number of collectors expressed their interest in Chinese antiques. Not only does this genre manifest certain European painting techniques, such as linear perspective and chiaroscuro, it also reflects a growing trend of appreciation for Chinese bronze vessels among Joseon collectors. An examination of this particular trend in art collecting and its impact on visual culture gives evidence of the cultural significance of collecting Chinese antiques and highlights the intellectual and artistic motivations of collectors and artists during the late Joseon dynasty.

Scholarly research in both Korea and the West has been devoted to chaekgeori screens in terms of their origins, symbolism, function, the identification of artists, and the inspiration of European painting styles.[1] In spite of the historical and cultural value of Chinese antiques, however, Chinese bronze vessels in chaekgeori screens have gained little attention in previous studies. Examining the depiction of Chinese bronze vessels offers a way to understand how chaekgeori screens visualized Joseon collectors' aesthetic preferences.

Collecting Chinese Antiques

As is well-known, after the fall of the Ming dynasty in China most Joseon intellectuals regarded the new Manchu rulers, who established the Qing dynasty, with disdain.[2] However, scholar officials who visited China from the reign of King Jeongjo onward sought a more intensive contact with Qing scholars and became increasingly interested in Qing culture. Scholars of the *Silhak* (Practical Learning) and *Bukhak* (Northern Learning) movements, which emerged in the late seventeenth century and attempted to reinvigorate Joseon intellectual life and culture, particularly sought innovative knowledge and technologies, and developed a penchant for accumulating Chinese art and cultural objects.[3] Joseon envoys, who provided information on Chinese antiques in their travel records called *Yeonhaengnok* (Records of the journey to Beijing), played a critical role in encouraging the practice of collecting Chinese bronzes. The Practical Learning scholar Bak Jiwon, for instance, described and recorded the names, forms, and value of Chinese bronzes after he had examined such vessels at antique stores in Beijing.[4] He also emphasized that one should be equipped with knowledge and a discerning eye in order to truly appreciate artworks and antiques. Furthermore, he underscored the significance of Chinese illustrated books, such as the catalogue of the imperial bronze collection *Xiqing gujian* (Catalogue of Xiqing antiquities) of 1749, as essential references for collecting Chinese antiques and gave advice on the purchase of archaistic bronze vessels produced during the Ming and Qing dynasties:

> Zhou [ritual vessels] Shiwang *dui* [tureens], Si *dui*, Yi *dui*, the Shang Mother Yi *li* [cauldrons with three hollow legs], the Zhou Mian Ao *li*, the Shang tiger-head sacrificial vessel, [and] the Zhou Xin sacrificial vessel, are all found in *Bogutu* [Illustrated catalog of antiques, 1120s]. However, the recent publication, *Xiqing gujian* has far better illustrations. Therefore, one should

first look for this publication. Look at the names [of vessels], then examine the illustrations carefully. First choose refined vessels, [then] go to the workshop [directly] or to Yingfusi and Baoguosi [districts in Beijing where well-established antique shops were located] on market day, you will definitely find them.[5]

Joseon envoys also roamed the bookstores of the Chinese capital and brought large numbers of books home, ranging from literature to catalogues. It is therefore highly likely that illustrated catalogues such as *Bogutu* or *Xiqing gujian* were circulated among the Joseon collectors. Apart from Bak Jiwon, another leading scholar, Yi Deokmu, who visited China in 1778, also emphasized the importance of the *Xiqing gujian* for collecting Chinese antiques in his book *Cheongjanggwan jeonseo* (Collected writings of Cheongjanggwan).[6] As both scholars state, *Xiqing gujian*, which had been commissioned by Emperor Qianlong, who amassed the largest collections of all times, not only includes the inscriptions on ancient bronzes but reproduces their shapes and surface decoration.[7] The various bronze vessels were depicted with great accuracy in these publications, providing Joseon painters with the most valuable material for portraying Chinese antiques.

While Bak Jiwon's above-mentioned text was apparently meant as information and advice, other members of the Joseon elite also began to show a growing interest in Chinese bronze vessels. The collection of Chief State Councilor Nam Gongcheol is an early example. Not only did Nam acquire a number of Chinese books, paintings, and antiques throughout his life, he also built a pavilion, Godong seohwagak (Pavilion for Appreciating Antiques, Paintings, and Calligraphy), for storing his collection, which also included paintings and calligraphy.[8] In his *Geumneungjip* (Collected works of Geumneung) of 1815, Nam specifically mentions his collection of ritual bronzes of *ding* (tripod vessel) and *yi* (ale container) types.[9] He wanted to distinguish himself from other collectors of lesser social standing (the nouveau riche) as a literatus, who understood true taste and elegance in reclusion, evoking the notion of "pure appreciation" (*cheongsang*).[10] Economic growth and urbanization occurred during the late Joseon dynasty, and, as with the earlier Ming trend, collecting Chinese objects soon became popular in Korea among the yangban elites and *jungin*, a secondary status group that grew in wealth and influence in the late Joseon dynasty.[11] Nam's statement reflects the phenomenon that, among yangban elites, collecting functioned as a distinct marker for cultural identity. Based on Nam's writing, it is difficult to distinguish what types of Chinese bronze vessels he actually possessed. Yet, his and other collectors' comments give evidence to the rising interest in Chinese bronze vessels in late-eighteenth- and early nineteenth-century Korea.

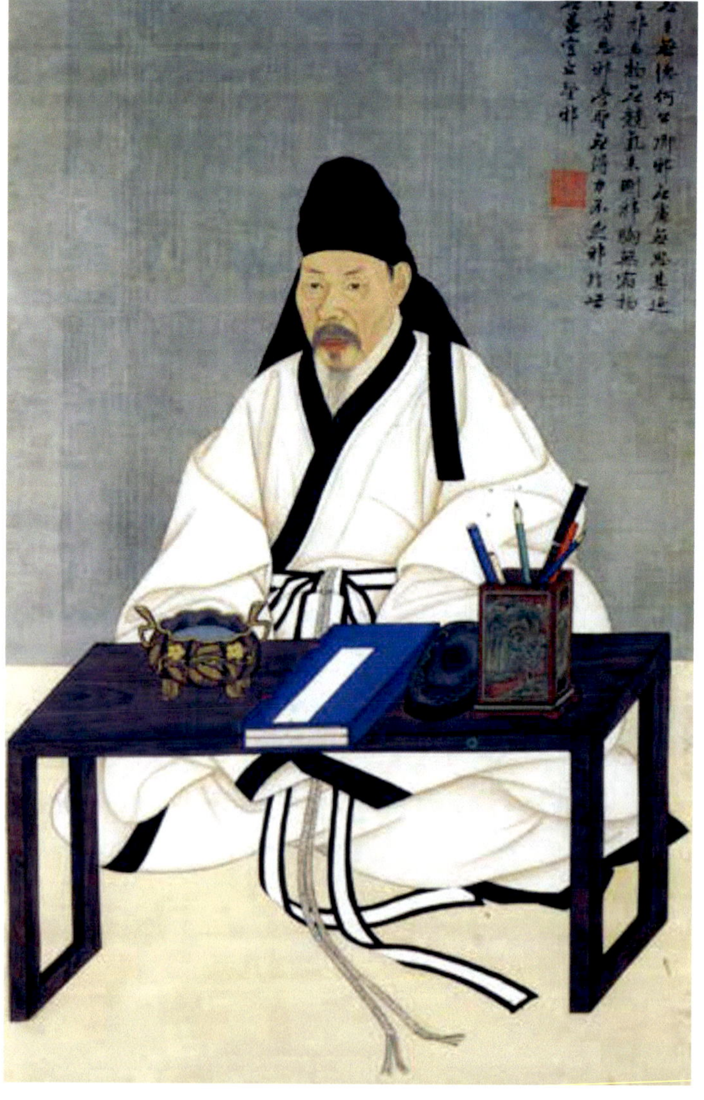

Figure 1. Anonymous. *Portrait of Yun Dongseom*, late 18th century. Color on silk, 97.1 x 57.4 cm. Leeum, Samsung Museum of Art, Seoul.

The portrait of Yun Dongseom (fig. 1), who acquired a number of Chinese antiques, provides a further glimpse at the importance of collecting Chinese bronzes.[12] Portrayed in a three-quarter view, he wears a plain white robe (*yabok*) and a

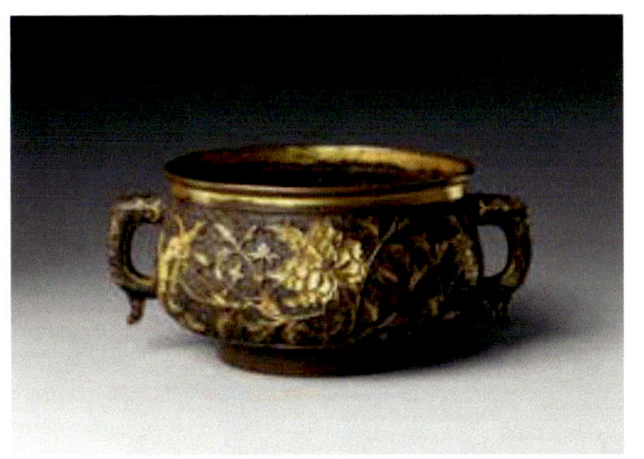
Figure 2. Attributed to Hu Wenming (Chinese, act. late 16th–early 17th century). *Incense Burner*. Bronze with gilding, H. 15.9 cm, W 7.3 cm. The Metropolitan Museum of Art, New York.

black hat. Given that Yun purchased Chinese antiques in Beijing on his tributary mission in 1771, the gold-inlaid incense burner on his desk was likely selected based on his collection.[13] These gold lines may have been inspired by the design scheme of archaic bronze vessels, particularly of the late Ming dynasty. The flowery ornament and rounded shape of the incense burner in this portrait is similar to that of the incense burner attributed to Hu Wenming in the Metropolitan Museum of Art (fig. 2).[14] However, it is important to note the differences between the two bronzes, particularly the scallop-shaped body, handles, and shape of the legs, which resemble the shape of a ding, one of the bronzes Joseon collectors prized. In addition to the records by Bak Jiwon, Yi Deokmu, and Nam Gongcheol, *Portrait of Yun Dongseom* offers the cultural background for the depictions of Chinese bronzes in chaekgeori screens and allows us to trace the visual sources that guided Joseon artists.

Representation of Chinese Bronzes in Chaekgeori Screens

Although Korean chaekgeori were to a certain degree inspired by Chinese and European painting, they developed into an independent and highly popular genre of screen painting during the Joseon dynasty.[15] The eight-fold screen *Books and Scholarly Utensils behind a Curtain* by the court painter Jang Hanjong (plate. 1) is an early extant example of rendering a bronze vessel with stacks of books, scholarly utensils, porcelain cups, and vases behind a tied-back curtain decorated with a pattern of double happiness characters (囍). On the sixth panel, the cylinder-shaped bronze with three flanges supported by three legs has two loop handles on the circular mouth rim and a lid with a red knob (fig. 3). Positioned on a small circular stand, it echoes the characteristics of the archaistic bronze vessels produced during the late Ming and early Qing periods, such as *Censer with Cover and Stand* in the Saint Louis Art Museum (fig. 4).[16] The comparison with a *fangding* (rectangular cauldron) depicted on *Pictures of Ancient Playthings* of 1728, a handscroll now in the British Museum, also offers evidence that the lids and stands reached their popularity in this period.[17]

Books and Scholarly Utensils behind a Curtain in the National Palace Museum of Korea, produced in the late nineteenth century by an anonymous artist (fig. 5), shares with Jang Hanjong's painting the display of precious objects, a bronze incense burner with a lid and stand, and the Baroque-style curtain that frames it. Here, however, the illustrated collectables float in an undefined space. One of the most intriguing items is the bronze incense burner at the bottom of the second panel (fig. 6). Not only does the artist exaggerate the shape of the body and legs, but he also maintains the traits of archaistic bronze vessels. In other words, the narrow neck, elongated legs, upright handle, and lid suggest it might have been modeled on a censer similar to a second censer by Hu Wenming, *Archaistic*

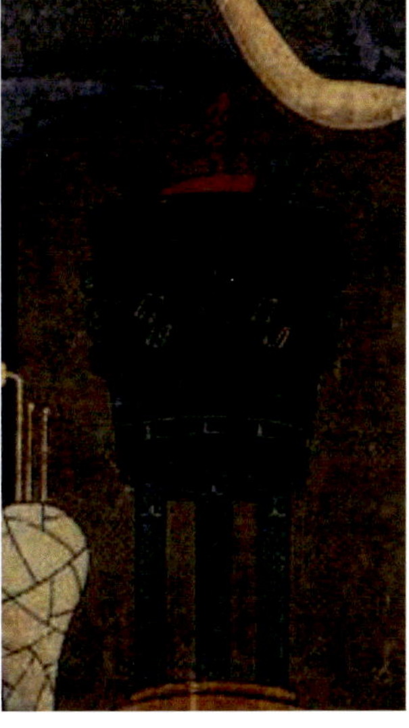
Figure 3. Jang Hanjong. *Books and Scholarly Utensils behind a Curtain* (detail of plate1)

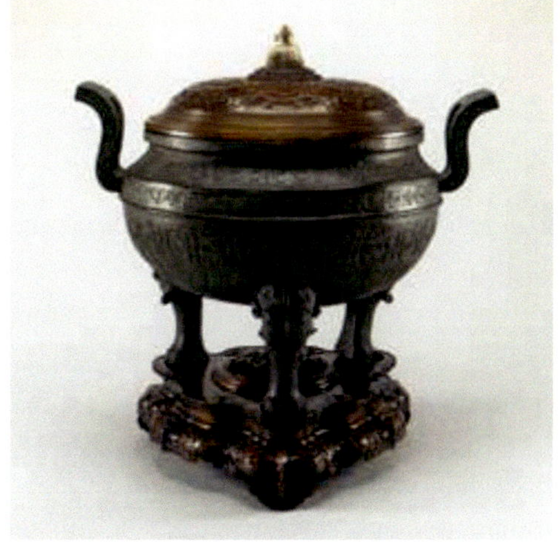
Figure 4. Chinese, Ming (1368–1644) or Qing dynasty (1644–1911). *Censer with Cover and Stand*, 17th–early 18th century. Bronze with pigment, wood, and jade, 66.7 x 65.2 cm. Saint Louis Art Museum, Partial and promised gift of Robert E. Kresko, 6:2005a-c.

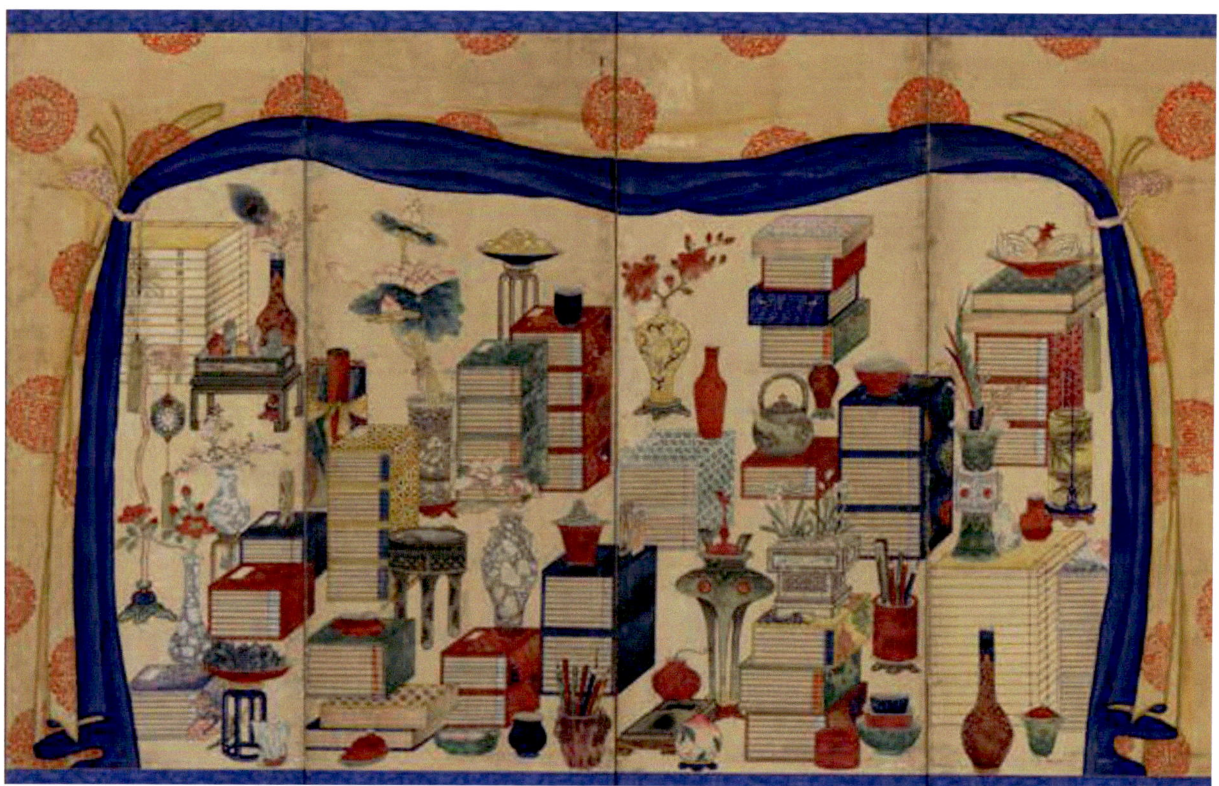

Figure 5. Anonymous. *Books and Scholarly Utensils behind a Curtain*, late 19th century. Four-panels. Color on paper, 142.8 x 57 cm (each panel). National Palace Museum of Korea, Seoul.

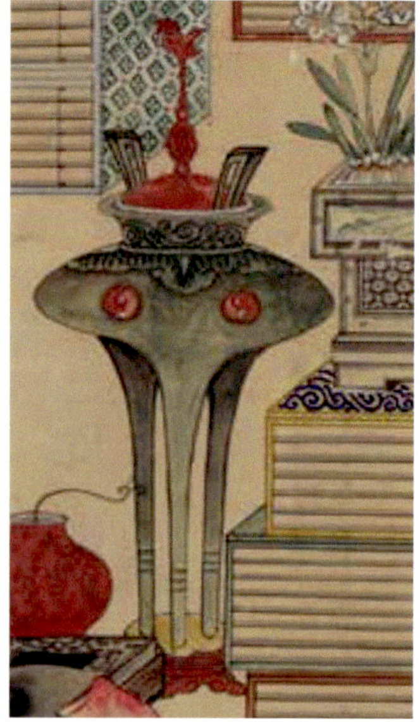

Figure 6. Anonymous. *Chaekgeori behind a Curtain* (detail of figure 5)

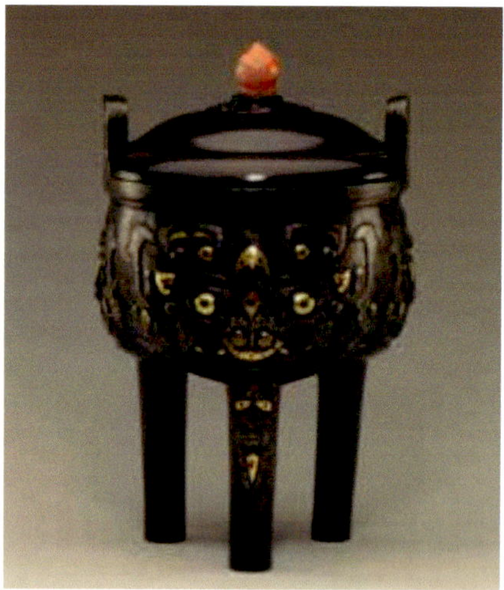

Figure 7. Hu Wenming (Chinese, act. ca. 1572–1620). *Archaistic Tripod Censer with Cover*, early 17th century. Bronze with gold and silver inlay, wood, and agate, H. 21 cm (overall). Saint Louis Art Museum, Partial and promised gift of Robert E. Kresko, 7:2005a,b.

Tripod Censer with Cover, also in Saint Louis (fig. 7). The most distinguishing features of this vessel are its lid with a red knob and the "yellow eyes" (黃目) decoration, which originates from the *taotie* (motif of zoomorphic mask from Shang and Zhou dynasty) of ancient bronzes and has been transformed into big circular red eyes on the screen.[18] The difference between the painting and the bronze vessel strongly suggests that the artist did not use a real object as a reference. As Burglind Jungmann has pointed out in her study of European inspiration in chaekgeori screens, instead of looking at real objects Joseon court painters used sketchbooks handed down through workshops over generations.[19] The original source of inspiration, however, were most likely the bronze vessels produced during the Ming and Qing dynasties that were imported to Joseon Korea and found their way into the households of royalty or wealthy collectors. That their stands had been crafted especially for them underscores their value as collectibles and gives them visual prominence.

Another important court painter of the nineteenth-century, Yi Hyeongnok [Yi Eungnok], carefully depicted

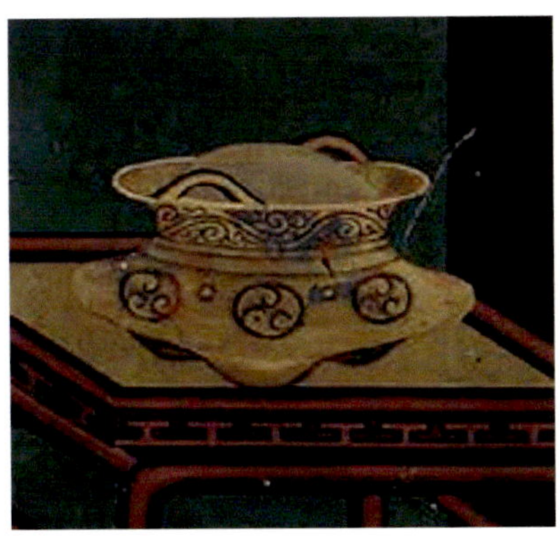

Figure 8. Yi Hyeongnok. *Books and Scholarly Utensils* (detail of plate 5)

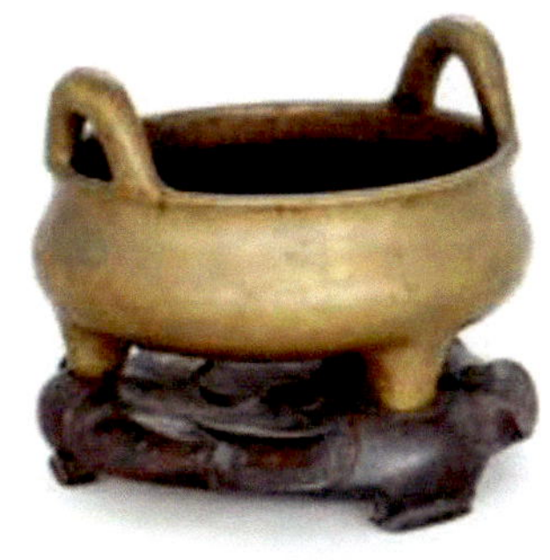

Figure 9. *Xuande Incense Burner*. Bronze, H: 14.5 cm; D: 21 cm. Grassi Museum of Ethnography Leipzig.

stacks of books with precious objects such as Chinese bronze vessels, flowers in vases, jade ornaments, and a clock, using linear perspective and the illusion of three dimensions to deliver precise visual effects (plate 5).[20] Together with various shapes of Chinese porcelains, Yi Hyeongnok illustrates four Chinese bronzes: a *xuande*-type (宣德) censer on the first, a fangding on the second, and ding on each of the sixth and eighth panels. What inspired Yi Hyeongnok in depicting Chinese bronze vessels? The incense burner on the first panel (fig. 8) resembles the *Bronze Censer* bearing the royal mark "Xuande" housed in the Grassi Museum of Ethnography in Leipzig (fig. 9); see, for instance, its two loop handles, inwardly curved neck, and flattened round shape supported by three stubby feet.[21] According to *Qing bi cang* (Collecting the pure and rare) by Zhang Yingwen, xuande-type censers were desirable items for collectors in China.[22] The fact that this Bronze Censer demonstrates one of the examples of Chinese bronzes collected in the late Joseon dynasty suggests that Yi Hyeongnok's screen represents Joseon collectors' aspiration to the xuande-type censers.

The two tripod vessels on the sixth and eighth panels of Yi's screen are characterized as archaic bronze vessels because each has a lid and stand. Specifically, the one on the eighth panel (fig. 10) has an inwardly curved neck, elongated legs, upright handle, red lid, and circular stand. Similarly, another *Books and Scholarly Utensils* by Yi Hyeongnok, in the Leeum, Samsung Museum of Art (fig. 11), presents a ding with a lid standing on a circular pedestal at the bottom of the sixth panel (fig. 12). The vessel's inwardly curved neck below the mouth rim is decorated with a flat band of repeated angular pattern, and whirl patterns ornament the belly. While the two vessels have slightly different shapes and decoration, Yi Hyeongnok maintained the characteristics of archaic bronze vessels by depicting elongated legs, lid, and stand in both bronzes. Interestingly, the ding on the sixth panel, (fig. 13) an incense burner with a lid standing on top of a pedestal, is very similar to the one in the previously discussed painting by Jang Hanjong. The cylinder-shaped body with three flanges supported by three legs and the lid and stand are evidence that both artists used the same archaic bronze vessels as references. The slightly more harmonious design of Jang Hanjong's incense burner suggests that he may have seen a real object.

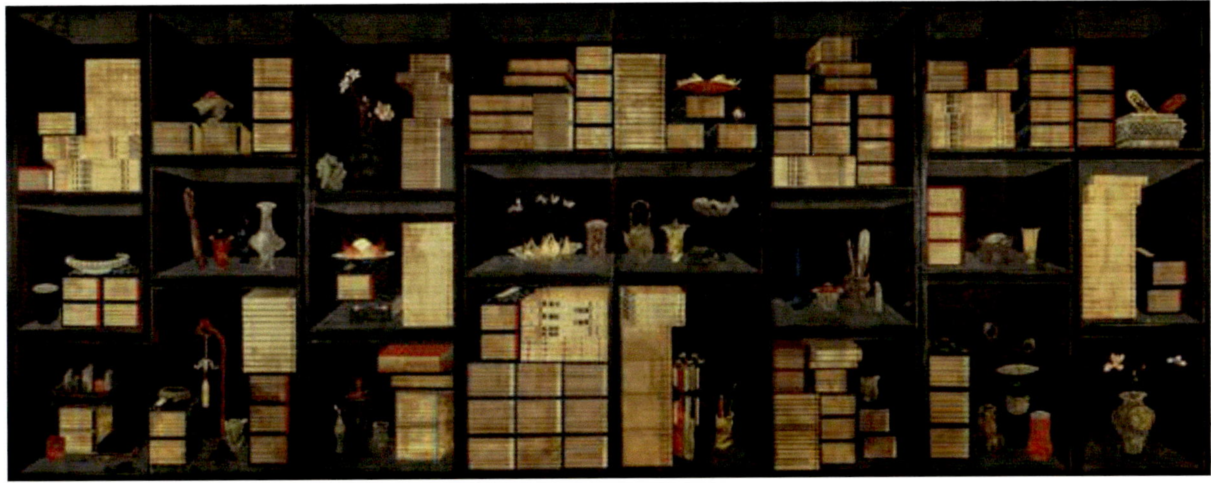

Figure 11. Yi Hyeongnok. *Books and Scholarly Utensils*, 19th century. Eight panels. Color on paper, 202 x 438.2 cm. Leeum, Samsung Museum of Art, Seoul.

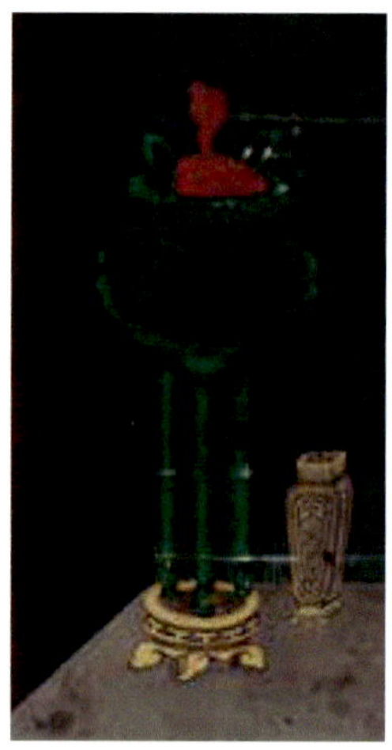

Figure 10. Yi Hyeongnok. *Books and Scholarly Utensils* (detail of plate 5)

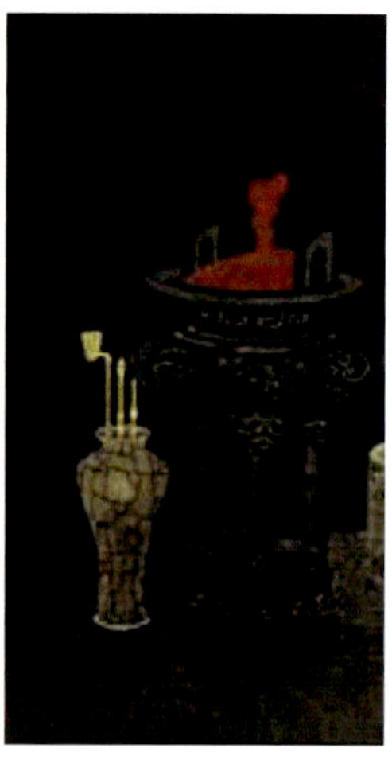

Figure 12. Yi Hyeongnok. *Books and Scholarly Utensils* (detail of plate 11)

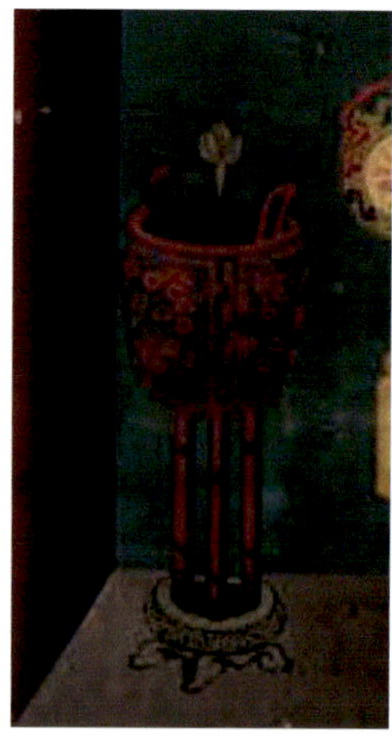

Figure 13. Yi Hyeongnok. *Books and Scholarly Utensils* (detail of plate 5)

In contrast, the unbalanced structure between the body and legs in Yi Hyeongnok's screen indicates that he worked from sketches or paintings by the previous generation of court painters.[23]

While the two tripod vessels in Jang Hanjong's screen are reminiscent of archaistic bronzes, the fangding offers some insight into another possible source. It appears that Yi Hyeongnok relied on the illustrated catalogue of the imperial bronze collections of the Qing dynasty (*Xiqing gujian*) as a reference. For instance, the rectangular cauldron appearing on the second panel has a rectangular-shaped mouth and a rounded belly supported by four flat legs (fig. 14). The shape of the body, the form of the legs, and the location of flanges are identical to those of the *Zhou Lu Ding Er* (fig. 15), a square cauldron of the ancient Zhou dynasty from the *Xiqing gujian*. Yet, this similarity does not mean that Yi Hyeongnok copied the bronze vessels exactly from the *Xiqing gujian*. There are certain discrepancies in the decoration, for instance, in the side-view beaked dragon designs on the upper body and the four dragon-shaped legs. Yi Hyeongnok gave the beaked dragon motif a rounder shape and added three small circles at the belly. While he sought to convey an illusionistic effect by applying chiaroscuro to achieve verisimilitude, he took some liberties in rendering the details of this motif.

The *Xiqing gujian* was an important pictorial resource for depicting Chinese bronze vessels for Joseon court painters when they worked in a different genre, on screens that exclusively show ancient Chinese bronzes. *Screen of Ritual Vessels* in the National Palace Museum of Korea (fig. 16) displays a variety of vessels accompanied by a title on the top and inscriptions in seal script and regular script on both sides. A bronze vessel at the top of the third panel, *Zhou Wen Wang Ding* (*Ding for King Wen of Zhou*), has upright handles on the wide mouth rim, a squared belly with four flat yet decorative legs, and a rectangular design on the body (fig. 17). The lower part of its belly is decorated with a taotie and its legs are adorned with animal design patterns. This bronze vessel, in fact, is identical with the *Ding for King Wen of Zhou* found in the *Xiqing gujian* with regard to its title, inscription, shape, and surface decoration. The comparison shows that court painters reused models they had employed for another genre in their chaekgeori screens. In other words, their sketchbooks contained a repertoire of models for collectibles deriving from various sources.

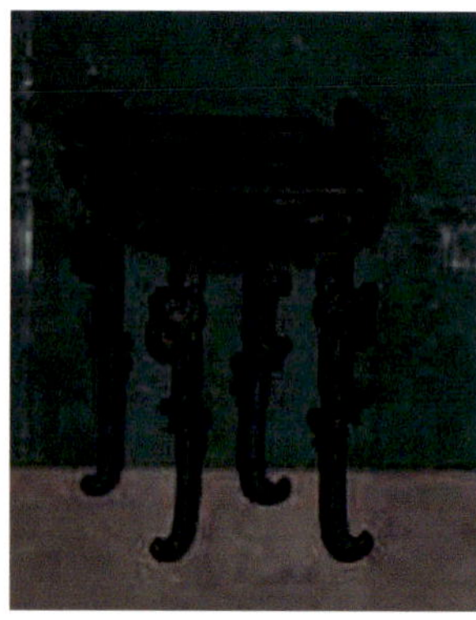

Figure 14. Yi Hyeongnok. *Books and Scholarly Utensils* (detail of plate 5)

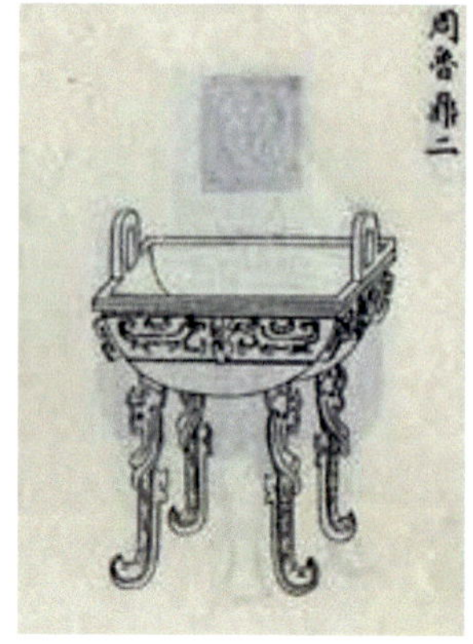

Figure 15. *Zhou Lu Ding Er*, as reprodced in *Xiqing gujian*

The motifs of Chinese bronze vessels found in Yi Hyeongnok's paintings appear repeatedly in another chaekgeori, for instance, in the National Palace Museum of Korea (fig. 18). Similarities in the design of the depicted bronze vessels imply that other Joseon artists copied their motifs from Yi Hyeongnok's paintings or from sketchbooks that were made on the basis of his designs. Insofar as the artists had an opportunity to select the object that they were willing to or commissioned

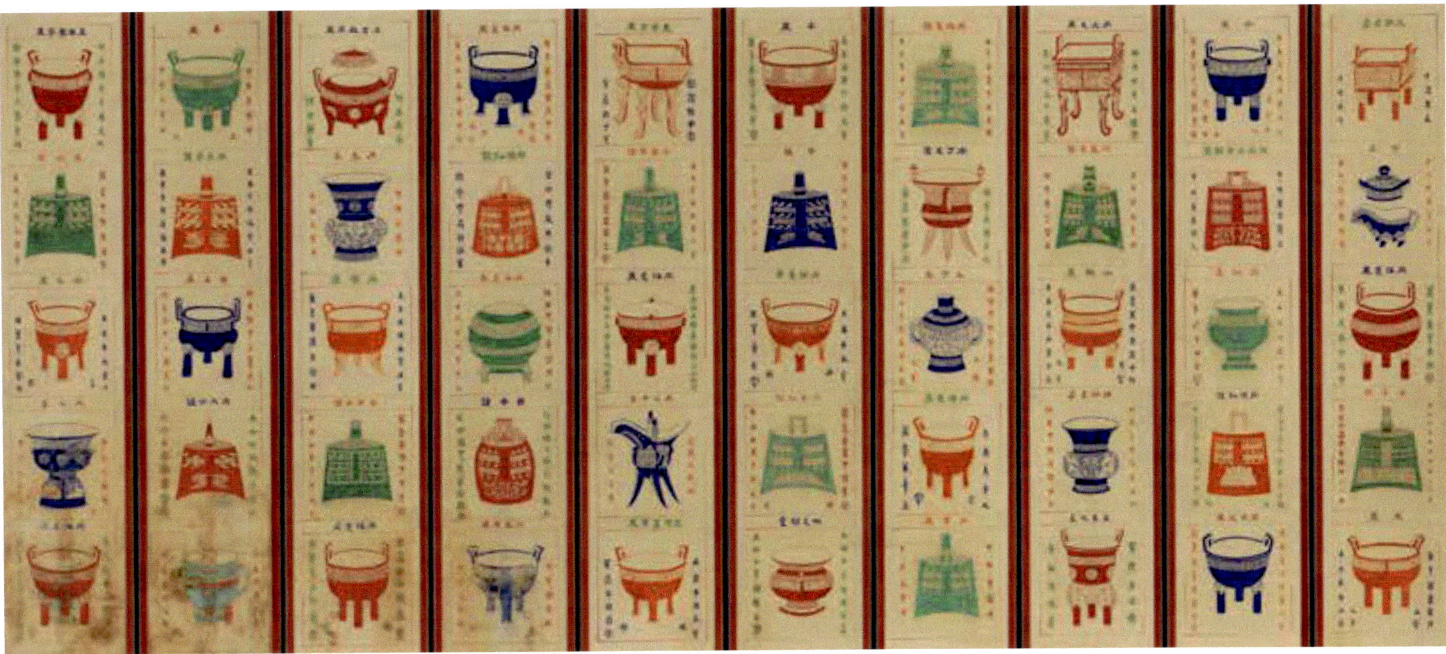

Figure 16. Anonymous. *Screen of Ritual Vessels*, late 19th–early 20th century. Ten panels. Color on silk, 242.5 x 345 cm. National Palace Museum of Korea, Seoul.

to depict, the bronze vessels in Yi Hyeongnok's paintings reflect a favored design scheme of bronzes among Joseon collectors.

Although the *Xiqing gujian* contains different types of antiques, Yi Hyeongnok repeatedly depicts the same shapes of bronze vessels in his paintings. *Zhangwuzhi* (Treatise on superfluous things), written by the late Ming connoisseur Wen Zhenheng, offers evidence as to what types of Chinese bronze vessels were recommended for the knowledgeable and cultivated collector. In his book, Wen evaluated ancient bronzes and ranked them on the basis of the desirability of owning bronzes.[24] The Joseon elite had great respect for Ming material culture and referred to guidebooks such as *Zhangwuzhi* for their colleting activities. It is thus reasonable to infer that chaekgeori screens reflect the preferences of Joseon collectors. Their special interest in tripod vessels likely resonated with a wider audience of commoners, who tried to imitate the elite. That chaekgeori depicting these vessels became part of popular Korean culture signifies both an appreciation of ancient Chinese culture and their owners' quest for social prestige.

Joseon collectors' passion for antiques thus contributed to the emergence of a new type of pictorial object: chaekgeori screens. Court painters appropriated the motifs of Chinese bronzes produced during the Ming and Qing dynasties in their chaekgeori screens. Significantly, the appearance of chaekgeori screens rendering Chinese bronze vessels parallels the growing appreciation of Chinese bronze vessels in the late Joseon dynasty. Given the rising interest in Chinese antiques among Joseon collectors, chaekgeori screens may have substituted for the actual Chinese objects that Joseon collectors were eager to acquire as a way of

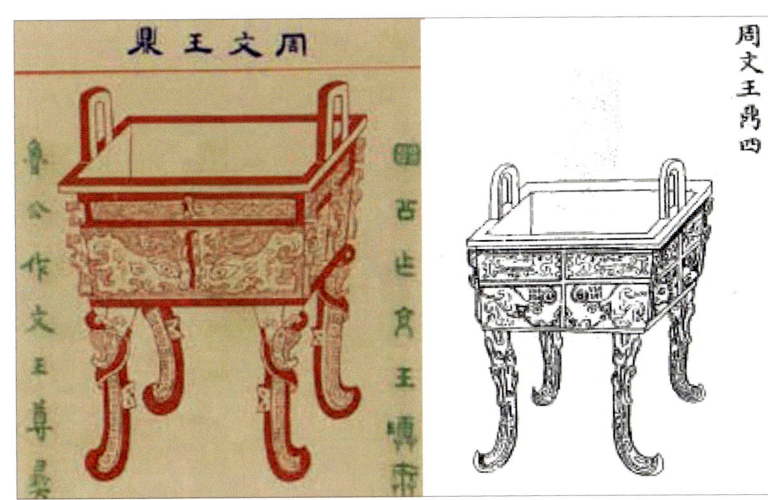

Figure 17. Anonymous. *Screen of Ritual Vessels* (detail of figure 15) (left). *Zhou Wen Wang Ding*, as reproduced in *Xiqing gujian* (right).

displaying their quest for a higher social status through their elite tastes.

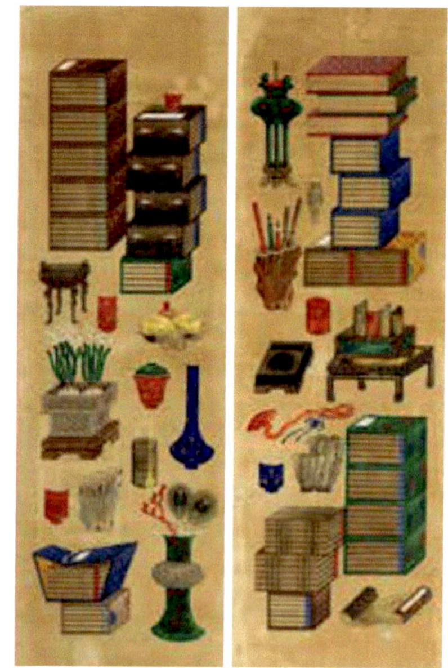

Figure 18. Anonymous. *Books and Scholarly Utensils.* 19th century. Two panels. Color on paper, 145.2 x 47 cm (each panel). National Place Museum of Korea, Seoul.

Symbols of Culture

Examining written sources in terms of social context and intellectual climate provides evidence of how Joseon collectors perceived Chinese bronzes as a symbol of culture in the course of their cultural exchanges. Over centuries of interaction between China and Korea, many important cultural materials, including books, paintings, and other valuable artifacts, were brought to Korea. In particular, Joseon envoys viewed and imported Chinese antiques and illustrated catalogues that served as references for Joseon court painters in their chaekgeori screens. In addition to real objects, the *Xiqing gujian* provided models for the court artists in depicting objects, thereby compensating for their inability to access actual ancient Chinese bronzes. Remarkably talented, Joseon artists combined shapes and motifs from diverse sources to create new decorative shapes and ornaments that echoed the approach of collectors in appreciating Chinese antiques.

I would like to express my sincere gratitude to Dr. Burglind Jungmann for critical comments and insightful guidance. I am deeply grateful to Dr. Sunglim Kim for invaluable suggestions.

1 For research in Korean, see Kang, K. 2001; Sin, M. 2010; *Chaekgeori* 2012; and Jeong, B. 2015. Among the illustrated objects, Chinese porcelains have been singled out for study. Bang Byeongseon and Kim Eunkyeong discussed chaekgeori in relation to the origin and types of Chinese porcelains; Bang 2007 and Kim, E. 2012. For research in English, see Black and Wagner 1993; Black and Wagner 1998, 22–35; Jungmann 2013; Pak 2013; Kim, S. 2014; and Jungmann 2014.

2 It took Joseon elites more than a century after the fall of the Ming dynasty to overcome their aversion to the Manchu rulers who had established the Qing dynasty in 1644 and whom they regarded as "barbarian." Joseon scholars paid more attention to Chinese objects and new technologies in order to advance the society. Jeong, JH 2010.

3 By emphasizing practical ways to reform society in terms of economic, social, and political aspects, Silhak scholars made a great contribution to Korea's intellectual history between the late seventeenth and early nineteenth centuries. For instance, a leading scholar Jeong Yagyong turned his attention to geography, economics, and medicine. Bukhak is considered a part of the Silhak movement. Scholars such as Bak Jiwon, Hong Daeyong, and Bak Jega further focused on economic development and argued for the necessity of advanced techniques through active acceptance of Qing culture and technology. Yi, U. 1982, 106-15; and Jeong, M. 2007.

4 Bak, J. 2007, 3:113–17 (Pilseseol).

5 Bak, J. 1968, 555. The original text reads as follows: 周師望敦，兕敦，翼敦，商母乙鬲，周蔑敖鬲，商虎首彝，周辛彝己上 俱載博古圖中，近日新刻 西淸古監 製式尤精 先於書肆 索見 西淸古監，按名審圖，先講其式樣 精雅入賞者，次於廠中 或隆福報國寺市日，索之俱有不爽. Modified English translation from Pak 2013, 201.

6 Yi, D. 1986, 134.

7 Feng 2002.

8 A large number of Chinese paintings and calligraphies derived from the collecting activities of his grandfather Nam Yongik and his father, Nam Yuyong, but Nam himself also accumulated works of art and antiques through his own acquisitions in China. Nam Gongcheol wrote 116 inscriptions, mostly regarding Chinese paintings and calligraphy, referring to famous Chinese literature. For an analysis of Nam Gongcheol's collecting practice and attitude toward Chinese art, see Mun 1996; Mun 1997; Sin, Y. 2011.

9 置亭龍山廣陵之間。多植梅菊松竹。時以幅巾野服。出往逍遙。客至。焚香淸坐。討論經史。傍列古今法書名畫銅玉彝鼎。評品賞玩。泊然無榮利之慕。Nam 2001, 555.

10 Chang Chin-Sung points out the notion of pure appreciation in the tradition of the famous Northern Song scholar and artist Su Shi. He also notes the conflicts between conflict between yangban and nouveau riche; Chang 2013. For the similar phenomenon in China, see Zeitlin 1991.

11 Hong, S. 1999, 231–54; Kang 1999, 277-316.

12 Hwang Jungyon notes that the idea of pursuing reclusive lifestyle through art collecting started by Heo Gyun in the seventeenth century and expanded by Yun Dongseom in the eighteenth century; Hwang 2012, 105.

13 *Inmul ro* 1999, 236–37; Kim, S. 2014, 10–11.

14 Chang Chin-Sung notes the similarity between the incense burner in *Portrait of Yun Dongseom* and one attributed to Hu Wenming; Chang 2011, 174–76. For more information on an incense burner in the Metropolitan Museum of Art, see Leidy et al. 1997.

15 Kay Black and Edward W. Wagner have proven that Joseon chaekgeori screens were inspired by Chinese paintings such as *Books and Scholar's Utensils* (*Duobaoge tu*) attributed to Giuseppe Castiglione [Lang Shining]; Black and Wagner 1998, 24–25.

16 For the characteristic of later Chinese bronzes, see Hu et al. 2008.

17 Stuart 2011, 695, fig 2

18 One of the most popular motifs taotie was originally found on Chinese bronzes during the Anyang period (ca. thirteenth century–ca.1027 BC) of the Shang dynasty (ca. 1600–1045 BC). The taotie motif also was described on the archaic bronzes produced in the later period. For the meaning and characteristics of taotie motifs, see Bagley et al. 1990; and Whitfield 1993.

19 Jungmann 2013, 84, and Jungmann 2014, 281–82, 292.

20 Since court painters formed style of "dynasties" and passed their knowledge and techniques on to their descendants, it is obvious that Yi Hyeongnok learned how to depict chaekgeori screens from his father, Yi Yunmin, a court painter who is known to have excelled in the genre. Kay Black suggests that Yi Hyeongnok's style followed that of his grandfather Yi Jonghyeon based on the relationship between Yi Jonghyeon and Kim Hongdo, who was the earliest painter known to have painted chaekgeori screens; Black and Wagner 1993, 64.

21 This incense burner presents one of the examples of Chinese bronze vessels collected in Korea. The museum acquired this incense burner from a German collector, H. Sänger, who purchased it in Korea. For Sänger's collection, see *Korean Art Collection* 2013. I greatly appreciate Dietmar Grunmann, a curator of the Grassi Museum of Ethnography Leipzig in Germany, for an opportunity to view this incense burner.

22 Zhang, Y. 1968.

23 Yi Hyeongnok illustrates the same whirl pattern for different shapes of bronze vessels: the bronze censer in xuande type (fig. 8) and ding vessel with a lid and stand (fig. 12). This also suggests that he used the design and shape of bronzes from workshop or iconographic sketches.

24 Wen 2011, Clunas 1991.

Taste of Distinction: Paintings of Scholar's Accoutrements

Sooa McCormick

Taste classifies, and it classifies the classifier.
Pierre Bourdieu, *Distinction: A Social Critique of the Judgement of Taste*

First produced around the second half of the eighteenth century, *chaekgado* (literally, "pictures of bookshelves") flourished throughout the nineteenth century.[1] This still-life genre was a product of an epoch when Korean men of letters began collecting and surrounding themselves with tasteful antiquities and utilitarian objects as a way to display their status. By that time, status was no longer the result of birth but of sophisticated consumption. [2]

A typical iconographic repertoire of a chaekgado can be seen in a ten-panel folding screen that the Cleveland Museum of Art (hereafter CMA screen) acquired in 2011 (plate 6). The CMA screen consists of thirty-five compartments. Multiple volumes of books occupy twenty-seven of the sections, and a variety of objects ranging from scholarly utensils to antiquities—all of which would have adorned the scholar's desk and bookshelves—are displayed on the shelves of the remaining compartments, either with or without books.[3]

Although many chaekgado screens were painted by different hands, their iconographies are more or less the same.[4] Such aspects of conventionality suggest us that a typical chaekgado was a not pictorial representation of a specific collector's bookshelf, but rather a standardized assortment of collectibles that the painters very likely devised in order to reflect their patrons' collective taste. Considering the fact that the chaekgado was first developed and used as a royal emblem during the reign of King Jeongjo and soon became popular as a furnishing item for aristocrats' guest room and study, there is little doubt that the iconographic program was generated by some of the leading court painters serving in the late eighteenth-century Korean royal court.[5]

The iconographic repertoire of chaekgado consisted of complex elements involving ruling classes' tastes, their collecting habits, and ideological sources. Such complexity, however, has been overlooked, assuming that all painted objects in chaekgado are simply auspicious symbols: books as knowledge, pomegranates as fertility, fingered citrons as either fertility or good fortune, narcissus flowers as longevity, peonies as wealth, crackle-pattern vases as longevity, and so forth.[6] This interpretative method derives from the conventional approach of earlier scholars in treating polychrome paintings such as chaekgado as art for common folk. In the course of archival research on royal records, contemporary Korean scholars such as Kang Kwanshik have revealed that various types of polychrome paintings, including chaekgado, were initially created primarily for members of the ruling classes: the royal house, court officials, and aristocrats.[7]

Nevertheless, in the current scholarship the powerful ethos of the literati and the tastes that governed the ruling classes' aesthetics and that, more importantly, contributed significantly to the iconographic programs of chaekgado have still remained largely unexplored. This essay explores the way in which the material world presented in chaekgado conveyed deliberate aesthetic choices and functioned both as stage and agent for the projection of identity.

Books

Books, the primary motif of chaekgado screens, were traditionally associated with power and social distinction. This was particularly true for Joseon society in which civil service examinations functioned to select men of literary talent for government posts. Until the late eighteenth century, however, books had not received much attention in Korean visual culture.[8] In contrast to China and Japan, Korean central and local government offices were the two main agencies that oversaw book publication and circulation until the second half of the nineteenth century, when bookshops began to appear.[9] In the absence of wide market availability, books were very difficult to acquire and their variety was extremely limited, even if personal finances were not an obstacle.

Yet, by the late eighteenth century, a large number of books on diverse topics flooded in from China and found homes on the bookshelves of scholars in Korea. Also, shopping for books on Beijing's famous Liulichang Street, which was crowded with book and antique shops, became a fashionable activity of Korean book collectors. King Jeongjo, one of the most famous Korean bibliophiles, amassed a large collection of Chinese books, most of which were purchased in Liulichang shops.[10] Such royal examples spurred great interest among court officials, aristocrats, and even the nouveau riche in collecting books and building special edifices in which to store their burgeoning collections. For example, Yi Uihyeon, a Korean court official who visited Beijing in 1720 and 1732, purchased 1,416 volumes during his first trip.[11]

While some high-ranking court officials were able to shop for books during diplomatic missions to Beijing, many had to pursue their hobby with the help of a new group of professionals: book brokers, who managed the marketing and circulation of books. By the end of the century, hundreds of brokers were actively working in Hanyang, the capital of the Joseon dynasty.[12] The degree to which Korean readers at that time broadened their access to books can be seen in part on a six-panel folding screen from the collection of the Brooklyn Museum of Art (plate 11). The screen depicts volumes ranging from Confucian classics to writings by Korean scholars to Chinese vernacular novels.[13]

Strangely, the Brooklyn screen is the unique case. The majority of chaekgado, in fact, do not provide the titles of the books they depict.[14] The specific reason for the anonymity of multiple volumes of books requires further investigations, yet one can speculate that chaekgado painters did not treat books as actual objects, but rather as symbols that announced their patrons' status and the wealth that allowed them to amass a large collection of books.

The Multilevel Bookshelf

A variety of uniquely shaped display shelves started to furnish scholars' studios in Korea around the late eighteenth century. The *sabang takja* (four-direction shelf), a display case with three or four tiers and all four sides open, was one of the most common pieces of furniture in the scholar's study.[15] In the typical scholar's room, one sabang takja unit usually stood alone. Multiple units were never assembled in one place, as chaekgado imagery would suggest. Rather than depicting sabang takja in their chaekgado, artists depicted a particular type of Chinese curio cabinet known as a duobaoge, a display case for myriad books and collectibles.[16] For many Korean visitors who traveled to Beijing for diplomatic or tourism purposes, duobaoge displayed in the Liulichang antique stores must have been marvels to behold. Yi Uihyeon, for example, wrote about his experience seeing a duobaoge, recalling: "At the corner of the room, there was a display shelf. Precious dishes and jade trays, and numerous rare objects were arranged in that shelf.[17]

While it is difficult to determine whether duobaoge were imported into late Joseon Korea, as many scholars have suggested, chaekgado painters had opportunities to see examples of these chiness curio cabinets in intricately carved or painted wooden wall panels.[18] It is not clear why chaekgado painters chose to depict the exotic Chinese duobaoge rather than the indigenous Korean sabang takja. Such a tendency for appreciating for exotic foreign luxuries over indigenous ones, in fact, was one of the most notable features of chaekgado.

In the late eighteenth and nineteenth centuries, Goryeo-period celadons were acquired and circulated among many Korean collectors,[19] but they were never painted in chaekgado. The painted objects are conspicuously foreign antiquarian objects. As highlighted in an essay co-authored by Sunglim Kim and Joy Kenseth in this publication, chaekgado certainly served as a cabinet of curiosities among Korean collectors with a global taste that stored and displayed all types of exotic materials from porous limestone from Lake Tai, Jiangsu Province in China, to rhinoceros horn possibly from India or Indonesia.

Three Friends of Incense

One of the most frequently painted motifs in chaekgado is the "three friends of incense" a grouping that includes an incense burner in the shape of an ancient ritual tripod, a covered lacquer box for powdered incense, and a slender vase containing incense tools (a pair of metal chopsticks and a spade) (figs. 1, 2). Although not as conspicuous as other items, incense accoutrements were regarded as essential accessories of a scholar's life in late Ming books on connoisseurship. In his *Zunsheng bajian* (Eight Treatises on the Nurturing of Life), a late Ming-period Chinese text well known among early modern Korean collectors,[20] Gao Lian recommended the following types of incense burners for the scholar's study:

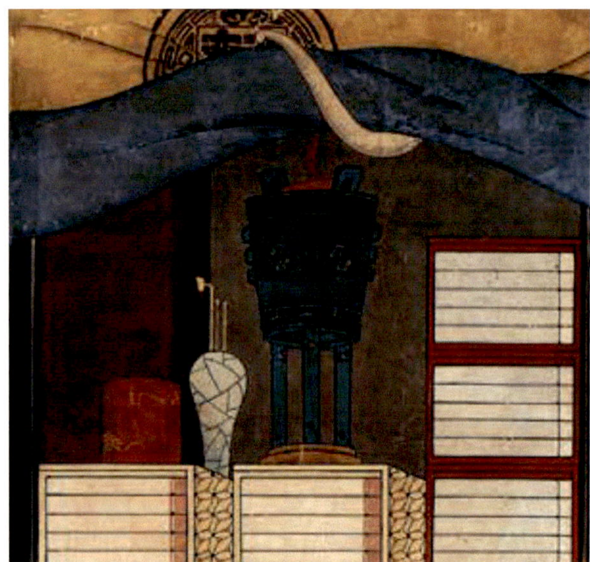

Figure 1. Three friends of incense (detail of plate 1)

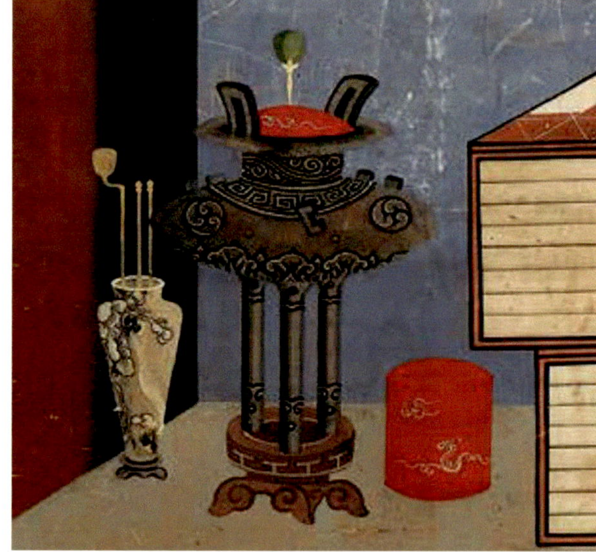

Figure 2. Three friends of incense (detail of plate 7)

> Next to the stone pot, you can place an incense burner, a flower vase, a vase containing a pair of incense chopsticks and an incense spade, and a container for powdered incense. The qualities of these four objects can vary and only erudite Confucian scholars have an ability to make a discerning choice. For the incense burner, the following three kinds are desirable: Ru type burner, Ding type burner, incense burner with spear-shaped handles. The width of the burner cannot be greater than three inches.[21]

Another late Ming text of *Kao pan yu shi* (Desultory Notes on Furnishing on the Abode of the Retired Scholar) praises incense as the most beneficial of useful things. The author contends that it has the capacity to raise the spirit, foster concentration, promote sleep, and even put lovers in the mood for romance.[22] Considering how widely the three friends of incense were accepted as scholarly objects appropriate for decorating the scholar's studio since the late Ming, it is not surprising to see them in a number of late Ming and Qing informal portraits (fig. 3) and erotic paintings that depict a romantic encounter between a scholar

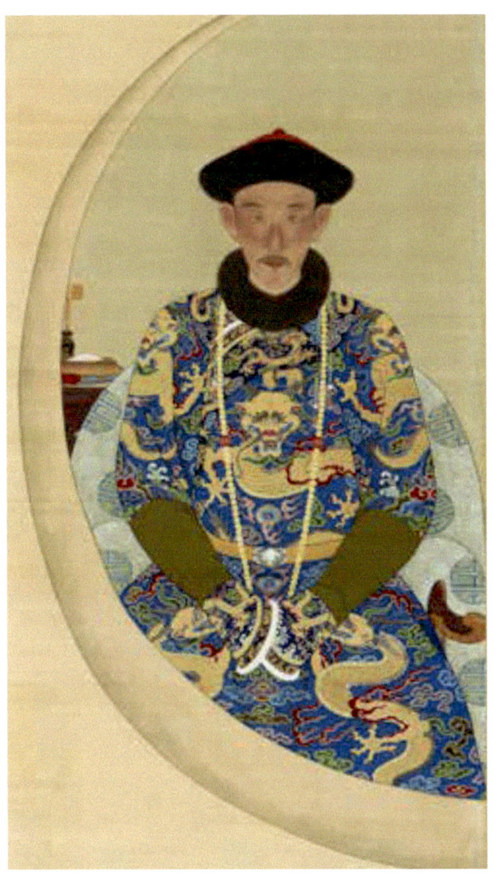

Figure 3. Anonymous. *Portrait of Yinxiang, Prince Yi Looking through a Window*, 1720s. Hanging scroll. Ink and color on silk, 143.5 x 72.5 cm. Arthur M. Sackler Gallery, Smithsonian Institution, Washington, DC. Photo credit: Purchase — Smithsonian Collections Acquisition Program and partial gift of Richard G. Pritzlaff (Image courtesy of Freer Gallery of Art, Smithsonian Institution)

and a beauty. It is highly possibly that for the same reason as late Ming and Qing scholars, Joseon Korean literati collectors pursued the three friends of incense as items to permeate their elegant taste, in addition to their practical function to foster concentration.

Bronze Vessels

Chinese bronze vessels were some of the most desirable objects for late eighteenth- and nineteenth-century Korean collectors.[23] In the essay compiled after his visit to Beijing, Hong Daeyong reported that he had paid about three ounces of silver for the two pieces of the rectangular bronze vessel often called *King Wen's Rectangular Vessel* at a Liulichang antique shop.[24] King Jeongjo, in his *Taehoseok gi* (Record of Taihu), announced that he had finally acquired two types of bronze vessels from antiquity: a compressed, low globular container with three conical feet and a pair of upright loop handles, called a *xuande* incense burner, and a rectangular bronze vessel with four legs in the shape of stylized dragon called *Wenwang ding* or King Wen's Rectangular Vessel. He displayed his new acquisitions along with a miniature taihu rock on the ledge of the window in his study.[25]

Ja Won Lee in her essay in this publication identifies a xuande-type incense burner and wenwang ding in chaekgado, for example, the third panel of the CMA screen (fig. 4) and the first panel of a ten-panel screen from the National Museum of Korea (fig. 5).[26] Besides these two types of bronze vessels, a zun-type vessel was often portrayed holding a branch of corals and peacock feathers (fig. 6). The ensemble of the slender zun-type bronze vase with a branch of flowers originated from an aesthetic trend that had been fashioned originally by late Ming scholar-collectors. Bak Jiwon, an esteemed Korean scholar-collector, recommended that his readers select the slender bronze vessels of the *gu*, *zun*, and *zhi* types to hold flowers because they would help to purify one's mind.[27]

Nevertheless, not all collectors could afford to acquire genuine bronze vessels. The nineteenth-century Korean scholar Yi Yuwon related that one of his friends carved wood in the shapes imitating ancient bronze vessels and painted them with blue and gold pigments to make them appear aged. According to Yi, those faux bronze vessels often looked remarkably similar to ancient vessels from the Han and Jin periods.[28] This anecdote reveals that there was a large market for fabricated antiquarian objects and explains why connoisseurship came to be recognized as essential for scholars. In fact, some scholar-collectors in late eighteenth- and nineteenth-century Korea, profited as connoisseur thanks to their keen eyes.

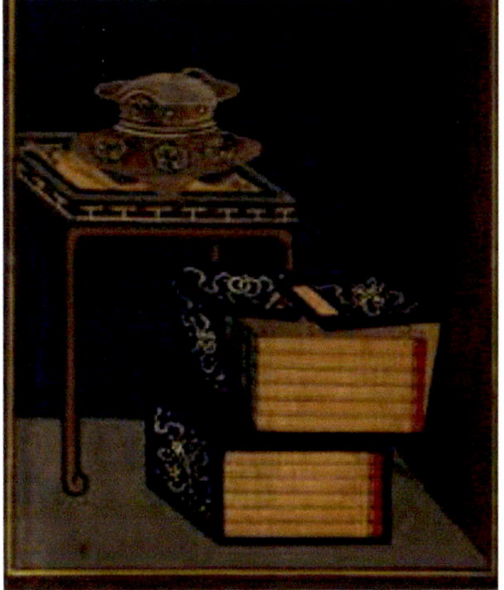

Figure 4. Globular incense burner (detail of plate 6)

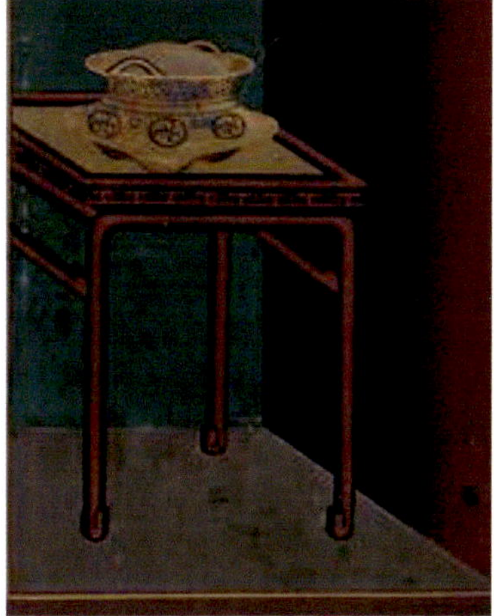

Figure 5. Globular incense burner (detail of plate 5)

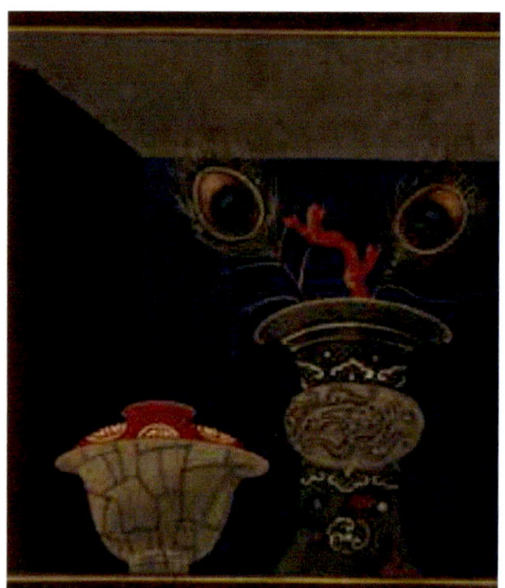

Figure 6. Zun-type bronze vase (detail of plate 1)

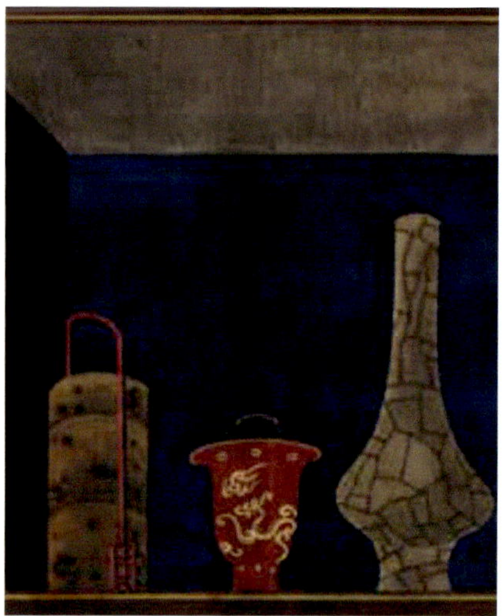

Figure 7. Guan/ge vase (detail of plate 6)

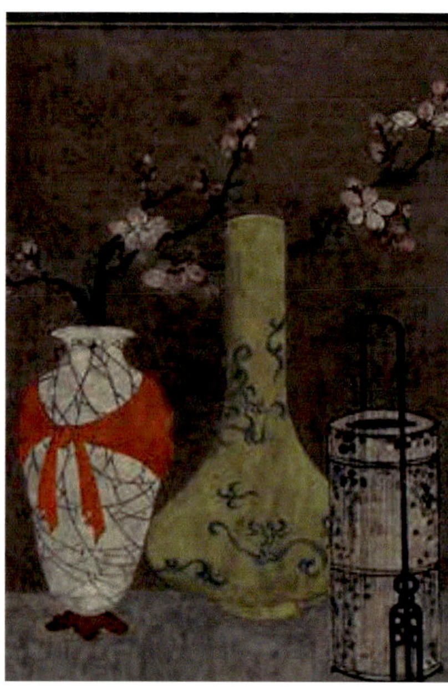

Figure 8. Guan/ge vase for holding cut flowers (detail of plate 8)

Crackle-Glaze Stoneware with a Branch of Flowers

Among the antiquarian objects depicted in chaekgado, stoneware covered with greenish-gray glazes with crackle patterns known as *guan* and *ge* wares were some of the most prized objects among late Joseon-period collectors (figs. 7, 8).[29] Bang Byeongseon discusses how the popularity of ge wares in late eighteenth- and nineteenth-century Korea led to the mass production of fake guan or ge wares.[30] In chaekgado, guan and ge wares stand out as vases for holding cut flowers. In his advice for decorating a scholar's studio, the famous eighteenth-century Korean scholar-collector Yi Deokmu, for instance, stated that "if cut flowers are placed in bronze vessels or *ge* wares, they will last for a long time.[31]

In the depiction of cut-flowers in chaekgado, one can find an aesthetic sensibility strongly advocated by late Ming Chinese literati-connoisseurs including Wen Zhenheng, the author of *Zhangwuzhi* (Treatise on Superfluous Things). Wen advised to his readers not to hold more than two varieties of flowers, since too many gives the appearance of wine shop.[32] The austere appearance of cut-flowers, indeed, is well-matched with the simple archaic guan and ge wares.

Testifying to the popularity of guan and ge ware, Bak Jiwon advised acquiring examples with large "cracked-ice"' patterns in the glaze, warning that glazes with smaller crackling should be avoided.[33] In fact, the use of cracked-ice as a name was a late Ming invention meant to evoke the seasonal change from late winter to early spring—the "early spring" theme much beloved by landscape painters. The glazed effect even reminded scholars of a line from the *Daodejing* (Book of the Way) that describes a sage as "shrinking, as ice when it melts."[34] Without doubts, late Joseon-period Korean collectors' predilections for stoneware with cracked-ice glazes were greatly indebted to the aesthetics of late Ming connoisseurs.[35]

Wen Zhenheng defined ge wares as the most desirable ceramics for the scholar's study because they were "objects of connoisseurship and not convenient for daily use."[36] In his *Ping shi* (History of the Flower Vase), another late Ming scholar, Yuan Hongdao, condemned the use of "pompous" blue-and-white Ming porcelains for the display of flowers. The book explains:

> If a vase is sturdy enough, then the same is true of pottery. This makes one aware of the fact that precious antique vases are not mere baubles. Impecunious and unimportant scholars, however, have not the wherewithal to possess such things, and even to get hold of a porcelain vase or two from such kilns as those of the Xuande and Chenghua reign years makes one feel like a beggar who has suddenly come into a fortune.[37]

While "pompous" blue-and-white or colorful enamel-glazed ceramics populated the surfaces of screens for the common folk, in most chaekgado the austere, cracked-ice antique stoneware remains prominent. This shows how widely early-modern Korean intellectuals, patrons of chaekgado embraced Ming-period Chinese scholars' aesthetic sensibilities as a mark of sophistication and erudition.

Wooden Stands

Bronze incense burners, stoneware with cracked-ice glazes, plates of flowers or fruit, scholars' rocks, and even fish tanks are often represented atop custom-made wooden stands. A six-panel folding screen from a private collection exemplifies the use of various shapes of wooden stands with different textures (plate 2).[38] For instance, a root-wood stand with a distinct rugged surface serves as a prop for a tray that holds a group of colorful enamel-painted tea cups (the second panel), and a shiny, polished wooden stand is used to support a plate of rocks and assorted orchids (the third panel). In many chaekgado, a stack of piled books often serves as a sort of platform for displaying various objects.

According to Jan Stuart, the practice of displaying selected objects—particularly ceramic vessels—on pedestals can be traced to the Neolithic Period, but the convention of exhibiting large numbers of objects in diverse media was new in the late Ming.[39] *Gudong shisan shuo* (Thirteen Commentaries on Antiquities) emphasized the reasons for displaying objects on pedestals:

> In the old days, there were many stands or supporting bases for antiques. All objects must be supported and something must prop them up. To set up an object without a stand causes trouble because it can be easily damaged but to support it is to manage it so it can play out its usefulness.[40]

The late Ming practice of equipping antique bronzes with custom-made wood supports and lids aimed to highlight their historical importance. According to Jonathan Hay, although the xuande-type incense burner was extremely stable, late Ming and Qing collectors often placed such censers on their own customized low stands. Hay argues that the use of the low stand for the burner was more about emphasizing the importance of the piece than about stabilizing it.[41] The special treatment of certain prized objects such as a xuande-type incense burner, as Hay observed in late Ming and Qing collectors' display practice, can be well observed in chaekgado, for example, a xuande-type incense burner and plates of precious flowers and exotic fruits are almost always depicted resting on a customized table or a pedestal, although using wooden stands as propping tools never became widely practiced in Korea.

Fruits and Flowers

In many chaekgado, books are often arranged alongside selected fruits and flowers, which past scholars have discussed with respect to their auspicious symbolism. [42] For example, the narcissus is traditionally interpreted as a symbol of longevity; pomegranate fruits are associated with fertility and prosperity; the fingered citron is emblematic of longevity and wealth (figs. 9, 10).[43] This conventional, interpretive approach is well suited to late folk-art variations of chaekgado, yet it may not be the most appropriate method for decoding the iconographic language of the earliest chaekgado, which, as noted above, originated as a royal emblem and evolved into the most popular item with which to furnish a scholar's studio.

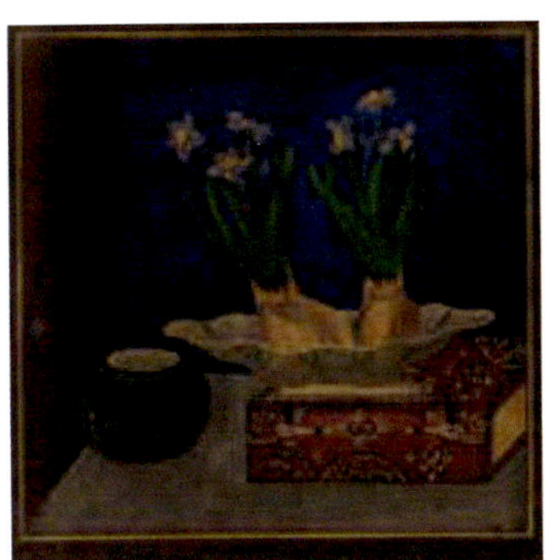

Figure 9. Narcissus flowers (detail of plate 6)

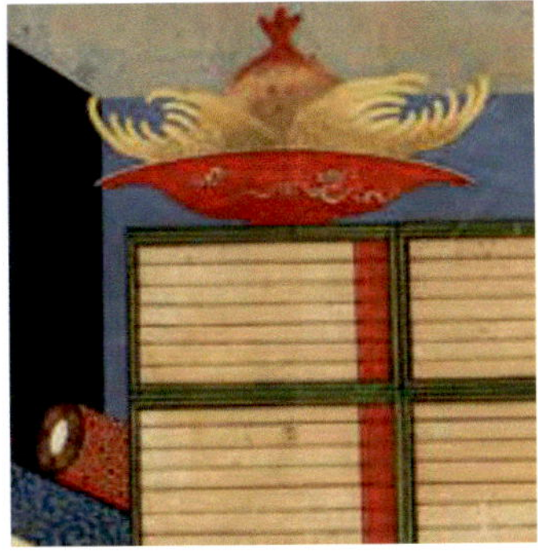

Figure 10. Pomegranates and fingered citrons (detail of plate 7)

A number of Ming texts on connoisseurship, widely read by late Joseon intellectuals, indicate that narcissus and fingered citrons were essential for enhancing the sensorially refined environment of the scholar's room. *Bencao gangmu* (Compendium of Materia Medica) by the late Ming scholar Li Shizhen, for example, dedicates a section to explaining the use of fingered citrons. Li encouraged his readers to place them on the top of writing desks, where they would encourage relaxation and concentration, and advised that they be placed together with minced garlic to enhance their sweet aroma.[44] This may explain why fingered citrons and narcissus also often appear in the informal Ming and Qing portrait type that depicts a scholar in his study (fig. 11) as well as in erotic paintings (fig. 12).

Probably, for the same reason, chaekgado painters might have included fragrant fruits and flowers, which were often planted in the scholar's garden. Narcissus was certainly one of the most popular flowers among scholars not only for its fragrance, but also its poetic implication. A nineteenth-century Korean scholar famous for his encyclopedic knowledge, Jeong Yagyong, describes narcissus as having a distinctive aroma, one that cannot be appreciated by the common people. Quoting the Northern Song scholar Huang Tingjian, Jeong compared the narcissus to an immortal who has left behind the dusty world.[45] Kim Jeonghui, another famous calligrapher and scholar who was influential in the late nineteenth-century Korean art scene, composed a number of poems and essays about the narcissus blossom, comparing it to an enlightened immortal and a scholar with a pure mind.[46]

The imagery of narcissus continued to be painted in later folk-style screens called gimyeong jeolji, yet the flower's association with the "pure mind of immortal sages" was lost in the folk-art versions. For the nouveau riche patrons of such later, folk-style screens, the narcissus was more meaningful as a symbol of longevity. The shift in meaning from the "pure mind of immortal sages" to the "longevity of Daoist immortals" in the case of the narcissus shows the importance of taking into account major changes in the social context and audience of an object.

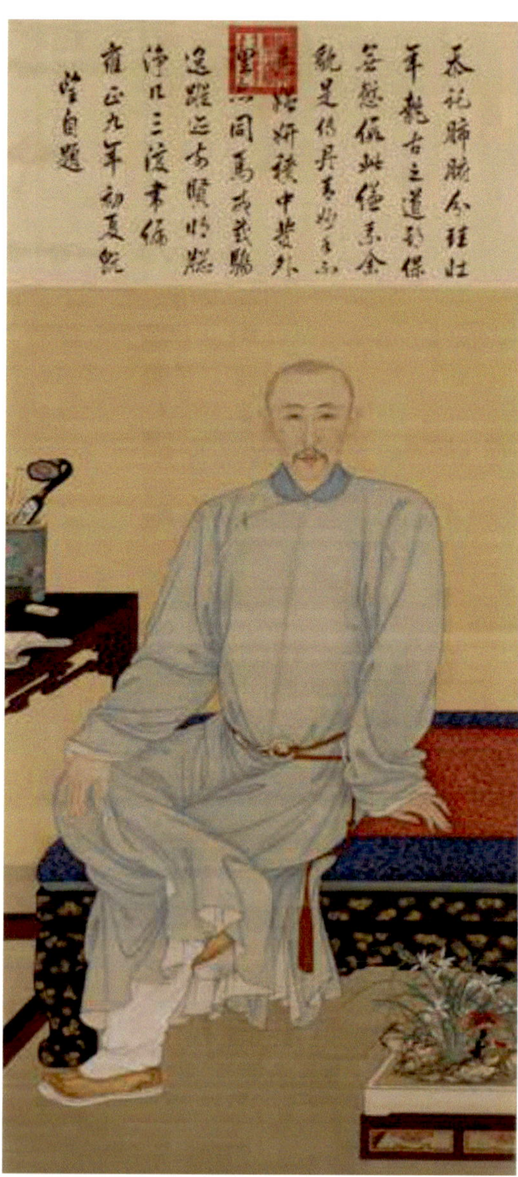

Figure 11. Anonymous. *Portrait of Yinli, Prince Guo*, 1713. Hanging scroll. Ink and color on silk, 158.8 x 88.9 cm. Arthur M. Sackler Gallery, Smithsonian Institution, Washington, DC. Photo credit: Purchase — Smithsonian Collections Acquisition Program and partial gift of Richard G. Pritzlaff. (Image courtesy of Freer Gallery of Art, Smithsonian Institution)

Scholars' Rocks

Since the Northern Song dynasty in China, small, eccentrically shaped rocks and precious stones such as malachite and lapis lazuli were displayed on tabletops and regarded as the epitome of scholarly taste.[47] The Northern Song period scholar, calligrapher, and connoisseur Mi Fu, for instance, had an unusually shaped *lingbi* stone on his desk, and the episode in which he bowed to the stone and called it "Elder Brother" was famous.[48]

By the late Ming dynasty in China, an elementary understanding of stone lore was considered basic knowledge for any educated person. In 1613, scholar-collector Lin Youlin compiled and published the *Suyan shipu* (Suyuan Stone Catalogue), which combined Song period books on rocks such as Du Wan's *Yunlin shipu* (Yunlin Stone Catalogue), with illustrations of hundreds of different types of stone. Taihu, lingbi, and ying are three representative types of rocks that appealed the most to scholar-collectors.[49] The craze for eccentrically shaped stones to decorate one's garden and study room continued throughout the Qing period in China. The painter Wang Yemei, for instance, wrote in his *Yemei shipu* (Yemei Stone Catalogue), "On my tables were placed grotesque stones and in my courtyard were

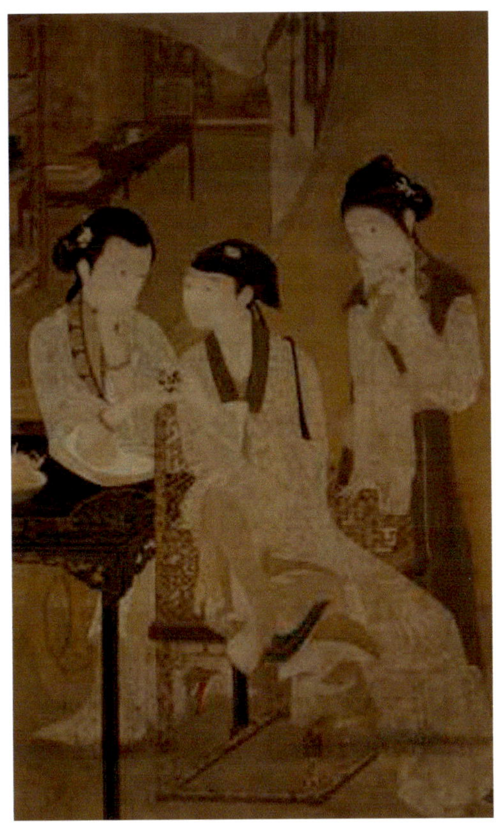

Figure 12. Anonymous. *Amorous Meeting in a Room Interior*, late 18th century. Hanging scroll. Ink and color on silk, 198.5 x 130.6 cm. Freer Gallery of Art, Smithsonian Institution, Washington, DC. Photo credit: Gift of Charles Lang Freer. (Image courtesy of Freer Gallery of Art, Smithsonian Institution)

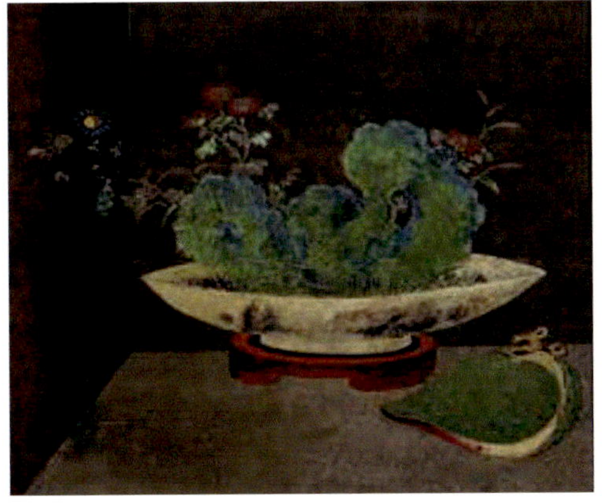

Figure 13. Plate of precious minerals (detail of plate 8)

installed supernatural stones so that I could enjoy and appreciate them during breaks in my study.[50]

In his *Taehoseok-gi*, King Jeongjo recounted how much he had sought a miniature taihu rock suitable for his study and in 1774, he finally acquired one.[51] In justifying his obsession with scholars' rocks, he referenced Confucian sayings that appeared in many late Ming scholars' books, asserting that benevolent and wise men could find enjoyment only in taihu rocks. Jeongjo lamented that even skillful painters were not good at representing the iridescent, bluish-black surfaces of the scholars' rocks.[52] This record strongly suggests that the inclusion of miniature scholars' rocks in chaekgado screens may have been initiated in the royal court.

According to a number of records from the *Nokchwijae*, the special examination given to court-painters-in-waiting, King Heonjong asked his court painters to produce images of scholars' rocks. A record dated to the seventh day of the fifth lunar year in 1849 indicates that the king asked examinees to paint miniature scholars' rocks and narcissus; another record dated to the twenty-eighth of the fifth lunar year in 1849 reveals that the examinees were required to render images of a stone with elegant and beautiful patterns resting on a desk.[53] Royal records such as these provide an explanation for why many chaekgado include images of miniature scholars' rocks as an important component of scholars' bookshelves (plate 3).

Interestingly, the scholars' rocks frequently painted in chaekgado are often either green or blue, suggesting that they are not taihu rocks, whose color typically ranges from gray to light brown (fig. 13). Possibly, they are precious minerals such as malachite and lapis lazuli, which were used as a substitute for rare taihu rocks yet were still considered to be the scholars' rocks. Yi Yuwon, was extremely proud of possessing three taihu rocks in his garden and even composed a song dedicated to them.[54] But, not everybody was lucky as he was in acquiring elegantly shaped taihu rocks. According to Yi, there was a large market for counterfeit taihu rocks. Bak Seonsu, a grandson of the famous scholar-connoisseur Bak Jiwon, was adept at producing faux taihu rocks from clay and painting them with bluish-purple pigments.[55]

Seals

From the late eighteenth-century screen by Jang Hanjong (plate 1) to the late nineteenth-century screen by Yi Taekgyun (plate 6), images of seals are often nestled atop the stacked books. Multiple blocks of seals in chaekgado reflect Korean collectors' growing interest in making their own seals, as well as collecting ancient seals of famous men of letters. For Joseon-period Korean intellectuals, seals were not mere objects to claim ownership of paintings or books. The seventeenth-century scholar Kim Sangheon was known for his large collection of seals. He wrote a book, *Gunok sogi* (Record of a Group of Jades) to share his passion for the art of carving seals. There, Kim defined seals as a medium to express the spirit of archaism, which allowed one to commune with the spirits of the sages of the past.[56] Such an attitude toward seals was widely shared to later Korean scholar-collectors.

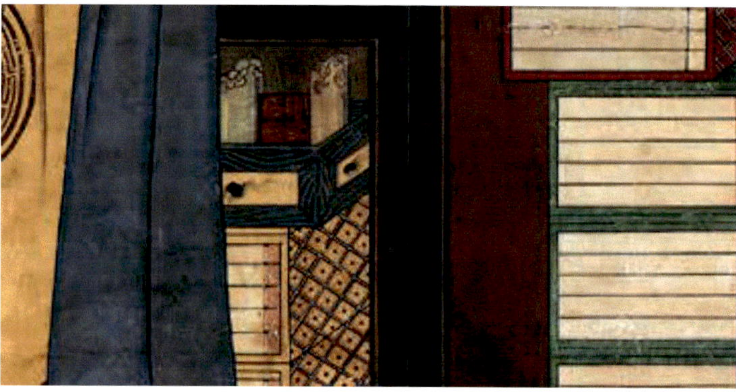

Figure 14. Jang Hanjong's seal (detail of plate 1)

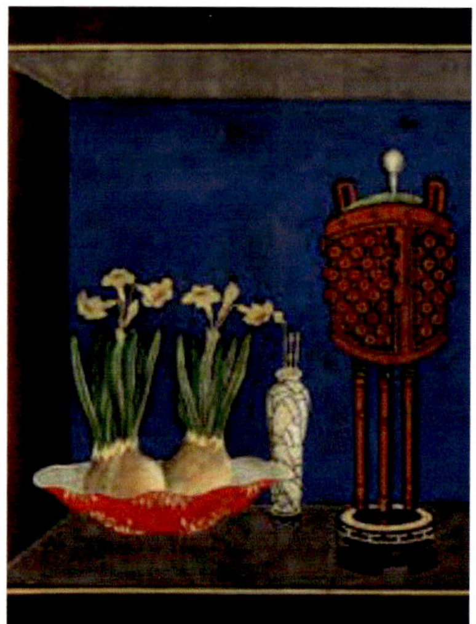

Figure 15. Red incense burner with a tripod decorated with raised studded bosses (Detail of Kang Dalsu chaekgado, Ten-panel folding screen, color on silk, 143 x 384 cm. Private collection.

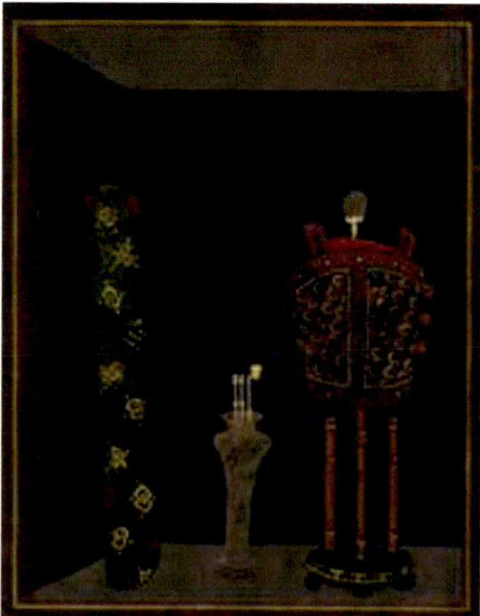

Figure 16. Red incense burner with a tripod decorated with raised studded bosses (Detail of plate 6)

In chaekgado, seals as painted objects can also reveal the painter's identity. There are about twelve chaekgado screens known to include the seals that identify their creators. The eight-panel folding screen at the Gyeonggi Provincial Museum, for example, features on its last panel a seal (fig. 14) that identifies the artist as Jang Hanjong, who was active in the late eighteenth century, serving as court painter. The painter's seal included as part of the overall iconographic program is often referred to as a "hidden seal" because of its discreet manner.

When the practice of adding the painter's seal to chaekgado began is not known, but one can conjecture that it was started around the late eighteenth century. Except for a limited number of works, court painters rarely left their seal on their products for the royal house.[57] Therefore, it is highly possible that existing chaekgado bearing the painter's seal were not for royal usage, but rather for other privileged groups: court officials, aristocrats, and even the nouveau riche. To such groups of patrons, the painter's seal must have been seen as a charming selling point to attract customers who wished to own a product by painters who used to serve or were still serving for the royal house. Chaekgado screens that bear the hidden seals are following: four screens—from the Leeum, Samsung Museum of Art, the National Folk Museum of Korea (plate 14), the Gansong Museum of Art, and the Pyongyang Korean Central History Museum—contain seals that identify the artist as Yi Hyeongnok. Three screens—from the National Museum of Art, the Gyeongsan City Museum, and the Asian Art Museum of San Francisco (plate 4)—feature seals that identify Yi Eungnok as their painter. Two screens—one from the Tongdo Monastery Museum and one from the Birmingham Museum of Art, Alabama —are known to include Yi Taekgyun seal. Finally, at least one screen bears the seal each of Kang Dalsu and Han Eungsuk, respectively.[58]

Three painters who shared the same family name, Yi—Yi Hyeongnok, Yi Eungnok, and Yi Taekgyun—are in fact the same person who served in the royal court as a painter during the second half of the nineteenth century. Yet, having changed his name twice, Yi did not alter either the iconographic program or his painting style.[59] Yi's "jaded" style, which makes his hand more recognizable and seems to have served as his brand, influenced his followers such as Kang Dalsu (active in the second half of the nineteenth century). Kang seems to have faithfully Yi's established iconographic vocabularies such as a bright green zun-type bronze vessel decorated with roundels or whorl circles, a red incense burner with a tripod decorated with raised studded bosses (figs. 15, 16) and so forth.[60]

The CMA screen, which I used as the focus of my exploration of the overall iconographic program of chaekgado, bears Yi's typical iconographic and stylistic features, but because the seal on the third panel is illegible to the naked eye, the screen remained anonymous. In March 2016, as part of the Overseas Korean Cultural Heritage research team, Heon-gang Seo came to survey the museum's Korean art collection. He photographed the seal at high resolution, hoping to make it more legible. Through the process of color separation, Seo was able to render the right half of the seal legible and thus detect the character "Taek and gyun" Dr. Byungmo Chung compared this seal to those of other chaekgado painters and verified that it indeed identifies Yi Taekgyun. This is the name Yi Hyeongnok took in 1871 at the age of sixty-four. Therefore, we finally conclude that Yi is the creator of the CMA screen (figs. 17, 18).

Taste of Distinction

Pierre Bourdieu's theory about "class habitus" explains that one's taste, informed by one's socioeconomic status, identifies and distinguishes one's identity.[61] The selection of certain types of artful utilitarian objects, antiquities, and exotic fruits and flowers and their careful arrangement in chaekgado were intricately woven into the ruling classes' strong desire to cultivate elegant taste in tune with the literati spirit. In this sense,

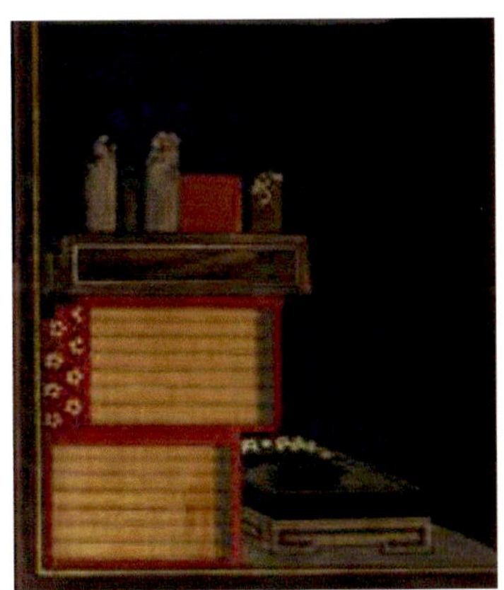

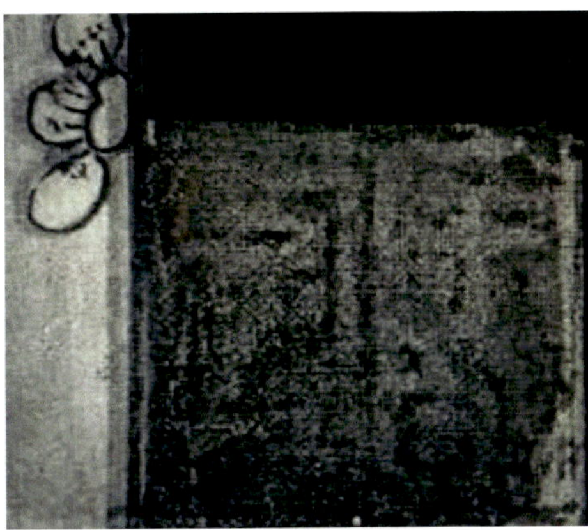

Figure 17. Yi Taekgyun's seal on the third panel of the CMA screen (detail of plate 6) (Image courtesy of the Overseas Korean Cultural Heritage Foundation; photograph: Seo Heunkang)

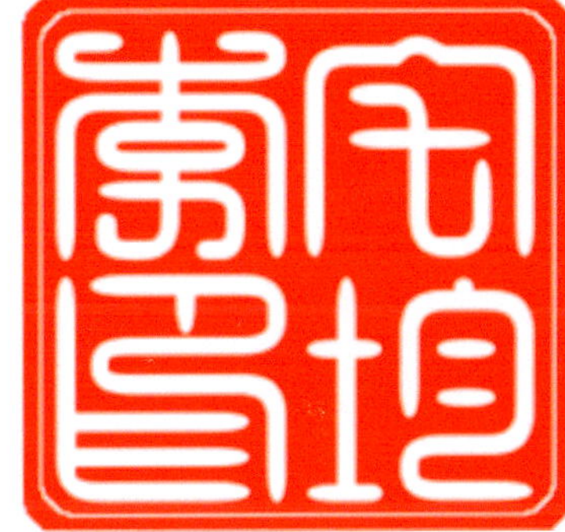

The image of the seal is painted to show the carved surface of the seal, so the characters in the painting are in reverse

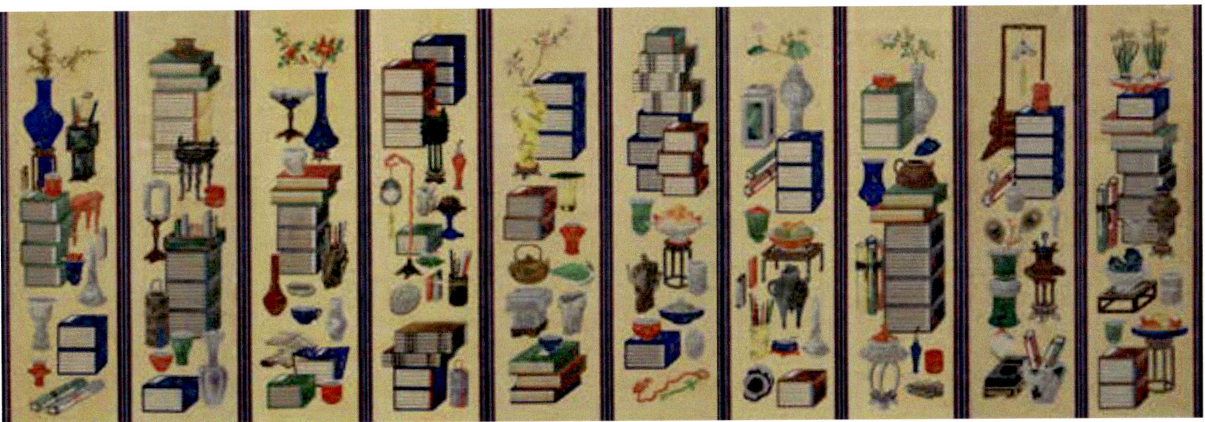

Figure 18. Yi Taekgyun, after 1871, Ten-panel folding screen, color on paper (Image Courtesy of Tongdo Monastery Museum)

the material world depicted in chaekgado is not a physical assemblage of things, but it was the product of cultural practices and exchanges of materials and knowledge. Also, it was a language to utter the early modern Korean ruling classes' passion for novelty and for refined consumption in tune with late Ming-period Chinese literatus' aesthetic sensibility.

I am very grateful to Prof. Chin-sung Chang, Dr. Susan Bergh, and Dr. Clarissa von Spee for their insightful suggestions and comments.

1 The chaekgado is the prototype of later developed paintings that depict books and other collectible objects. It is part of a larger category called chaekgeori, or paintings of books and things. Around the same time in China, the imagery that depicts luxuries and antiquities; *bogutu* [Illustration of antiquities], *bai gu* [One hundred antiquities] were the popular decorative motif for porcelain, furniture, textile and so forth. Instead of focusing on duobage tradition as the sole artistic inspiration for chaekgado, the connection between Qing decorative arts and Korean chaekgado is worth for further investigation.

2 Wen Zhenheng's *Zhangwuzhi* [Treatise on superfluous things] explicitly show how much the aesthetic skill of discriminating the elegant and the vulgar occupied the late Ming-period Chinese elites' life. For the translation and interpretation of Wen's text, See Clunas, 1991.

3 The complete list of the painted motifs in the CMA screen is as follows: A red container decorated in a gilded dragon pattern (first panel); a brush holder possibly made of bamboo, a red container with a lid for storing seal paste, and a brush washer with gilding on blue ground (second panel); a group of ink seals (one seal facing forward) resting on a pile of books, an ink stone resting on its own customized wood stand, and a globular incense burner placed on a sizable table (third panel); a brownish gray yixing tea pot paired with a green tea cup, a plate of pomegranates and fingered citrons propped by its customized wooden stand (fourth panel); a wood-root container possibly for storing scrolls of paper, a slender vase to hold an incense spade and chopsticks paired with a tall

incense burner with a red lacquer lid, and a gray container with black spotted pattern that holds two rolls of scrolls (fifth); a three-tier lunch container, a red cup with a lid, and a slender vase with crackle pattern, and a plate of narcissus flowers and a water container (sixth); a roll scroll, a slender vase to hold an incense spade and chopsticks paired with a red incense burner with a tripod decorated with raised studded bosses, and a peach-shaped charm hung on a red wooden stand (seventh); a bronze vase with a central swelling section that holds a branch of coral and a peacock feather, a lidded tea cup with crackle pattern, and a cup possibly carved of rhinoceros horn (eighth); a red plate decorated with gilding, a bright green bronze vase decorated with roundel or whorl circle patterns that holds a branch of cut-flowers, possibly peonies, and a red cup decorated with gilding (ninth); a wood-root brush holder paired with a water dropper in the shape of mountain (tenth).

4 Both a ten-panel screen in the National Museum of Korea and a ten-panel screen in a private collection in the United States are dated to the late nineteenth century and both feature images of colorful Qing enameled vases with wrapped-cloth designs, transparent glass vases, European clocks, and so on. In terms of iconographic languages, these two chaekgado are exceptionally different from the majority of chaekgado.

5 Sin, M. 2010, 179–80.

6 For the discussion of the symbolic meanings of the painted objects in chaekgado, see *Chaekgeori* 2012, 168–70.

7 Kang Kwanshik scrutinized *Naekgak ilryeok* records and discovered that many polychrome paintings were commissioned for royal usage; Kang, K. 2001B. For his identification of the longstanding misconception concerning polychrome paintings, see Kang K. 2001A.

8 Images of stacked books also appear in informal portraits of scholars in late eighteenth-century and nineteenth-century Korea and China. Notable Korean examples include *Leisurely Reading* by Jeong Seon (Kansong Museum of Art); *Portrait of Yi Haeung*, ca. 1869, by Yi Hancheol and Yu Suk (Seoul Museum of History); and *A Scholar Playing the Mandolin* by Kim Hongdo (Leeum, Samsung Museum of Art).

9 For further reading regarding government-sponsored publications, see Kang, M. 2001, 60–61; Jeong, JH. 2011.

10 For further information concerning King Jeongjo's book collection, see Jeong, H. 2012.

11 Yi Uihyeon, *Yeonhaeng japji* section from *Dogokjip*, quoted from Kang, M. 1999B. For further reading on Joseon envoys' book shopping at the Liulichang, see Kim, Y. 2006; Sin, I. 2009.

12 Among many books either purchased directly from Beijing or delivered by book brokers were late Ming scholars' books on connoisseurship, interior decoration, flower arrangements, and gardening, all of which aimed to help cultivate "elegant" taste. Yuan Hongdao's *Ping shi* [History of vase], Gao Lian's *Zunsheng bajian* [Eight treatises on the nurturing of life], and Wen Zhenheng's *Zhang wu zhi* [Treatise on superfluous things] were widely read by early modern Korean collectors. For further reading, see Hwang 2010; An 2012.

13 *Korean Art Collection Brooklyn* 2006, 263. There is a four-panel folding screen in the Museum of Fine Arts, Boston. Although further research is necessary, it may be another example in which the titles of books are provided and may even be related to the six-panel folding screen in the Brooklyn Museum.

14 Kho Youenhee in her 2014 lecture at the Hengso Museum of Keimyung University introduced the idea that folk-style chaekgeori screens contained various types of Confucian classics and Chinese novels.

15 According to Jonathan Hay, display cabinets came into use in the late seventeenth century; Hay 2010, 324.

16 Although the overall shape of the display case followed that of duobaoge, Jang Hanjong, for example, included a number of distinctive elements of Korean furniture such as black marbling patterns of persimmon wood and the use of sliding panels on the base of the bookshelf.

17 Yi Uihyeon, "Jap ji [Miscellaneous record] in *Gyeongja yeonhaeng japji* [Miscellaneous record of journey to Beijing in the year of Gyeongja]. Translation by the author.

18 Lee Wonbok points out similarities between Korean chaekgado and Chinese duobaoge; see Lee, W. 1992, 103–26. Furthermore, the discussion about the chaekgado and its similarity to a Chinese trompe l'oeil painting attributed to Giuseppe Castiglione, the Italian Jesuit painter, and suggested as a possible prototype for Korean chaekgado; see Black and Wagner 1993. Furthermore, Bak Simeun proposed that chaekgado might have been indirectly inspired by the European studiolo tradition, which flourished during the Renaissance period; Bak, S. 2002. Recently, Sunglim Kim developed Bak's initial speculation further; Kim, S. 2014.

19 Jeong Yagyong composed a poem about narcissus flowers contained in a Goryeo period celadon vessel. Jeong Yagyong, "Songpa sujak," in *Dasan simunjip* [Dasan's complete poems and essays].

20 For example, in his book *Imwon gyeongje ji* [Administration of our daily life in woods and fields], Seo Yugu quoted Gao Lian's *Eight Treatises on the Nurturing of Life*, as well as the famous Southern Song connoisseur text *Dong Tian Qing Lu Ji* [Record of the pure registers of the Cavern Heaven] by the thirteenth-century writer Zhao Xigu; see Chang 2009.

21 The original text reads: 幾外爐一,花瓶一,匙箸瓶一,香盒一.四者等差遠甚,惟博雅者擇之.然而爐制惟汝爐,鼎爐,戟耳彝爐三者為佳.大以腹橫三寸極矣.瓶用膽瓶,花觚為最,次用宋磁鵝頸瓶,余不堪供; Gao Lian, *Zunsheng bajian*. Translation by the author.

22 Hay 2010, 362.

23 Bang 2007; Sin, M. 2010, 178.

24 The original text reads: 以銀三兩二錢.買文王鼎二而歸; Hong, D. 2016. Translation by the author.

25 Jeongjo 2016. According to this record, Jeongjo acquired them in 1774, two years before his enthronement.

26 Ja won Lee, 44–52.

27 Bak, J. 2016.

28 Yi, Y. 2016B.

29 The word *guan*, which literally means "official" wares, was initially used during the Northern Song period in China, and *ge* means "elder brother" wares. The origin of both words relates to a legend of two brother potters from the Zhang family during the Southern Song period. By the late Ming period, guan and ge wares, both featuring crackle glaze, were considered to be of the same type.

30 Bang 2007, 232.

31 Scholars have pointed out the ubiquitous usage of crackle-glaze stoneware and ancient bronzes in chaekgado; however, they have not explained the reason why cut flowers are almost always displayed in such vessels. Yi, D. 2016.

32 Clunas 1991, 44.

33 Bak, J. 2016.

34 Hay 2010, 136.

35 For a discussion of the Ming period dichotomy, see Jang 2016.

36 For a discussion of the dichotomy between utility and pleasure, see Clunas 1991, 84–85.

37 Campbell 2003, 84.

38 Jonathan Hay observed that late Ming and Qing decorative artists paid considerable attention to various patterns and textures on the surface and called such an artistic feature "diversified surfacescape"; Hay 2010, 237–58.

39 Stuart 2011, 705.

40 The English translation is provided in ibid.

41 Hay 2010, 254–55.

42 Sin, M. 2010, 185; Kim, S. 2014, 14.

43 For Chinese symbolism, see Bartholomew 2006.

44 Meining Wang, a summer intern in the Asian department at the Cleveland Museum of Art, found this passage and translated it: 俗呼為佛手柑.有長一尺四,五寸者.皮如橙柚而厚,皺而光澤.其色如瓜,生綠熟黃.其核細.其味不甚佳而清香襲人.南人雕鏤花鳥,作蜜煎果食.置之幾案,可供玩.若安芋片於蒂而以濕紙圍護,經久不癟.或擣蒜罨其蒂上,則香更充溢; Li, S. 2003.

45 Jeong, Y. 2016.

46 Kim, J. 2016, vol. 10.

47 Hu 2011, 1.

48 Wang, J. 1992, 178.

49 Hu 2011, 3.

50 Ibid., 117–18.

51 Jeongjo 2016.

52 King Jeongjo referenced the Song period Chinese writer Du Wan's *Yunlin Shipu* (*Rock Catalogue of Cloudy Forests*, 1133). Du Wan's book was not printed until the late Ming period. Clunas 1996, 73.

53 Kang, K. 2001B, 501.

54 Yi, Y. 2016A.

55 Yi, Y. 2016B.

56 Bak, C. 2010.

57 Many polychrome paintings that depict bird and flowers, Daoist themes, and historical episodes were painted for the royal usage in the late Joseon period, but the painter's seal are rarely found in those works.

58 Kang Dalsu's ten-panel folding screen is in a private collection. Kang seems to have closely followed Yi Hyeongnok's [Yi Eungnok, Yi Taekgyun] style. Han Eungsuk's ten panel screen was first introduced in Black and Wagner 1993.

59 For the name change, see Black and Wagner 1993.

60 For this reason, Yi's screen, the CMA screen was previously mistaken to be Kang Dalsu's work.

61 Bourdieu 1996. For more information on material consumption as means of presenting the self, see Goffman 1959.

The Mystical Allure of Chaekgeori, Books and Things

Byungmo Chung

> The piece captivated me instantly. It bore an almost mystical beauty. But when I looked again with all the wisdom at my disposal, I understood that only a few works of art were so capable of rendering wisdom powerless. Perhaps this is because this picture was composed—from the perspectives of us modern people—entirely of irrationalities.[1]

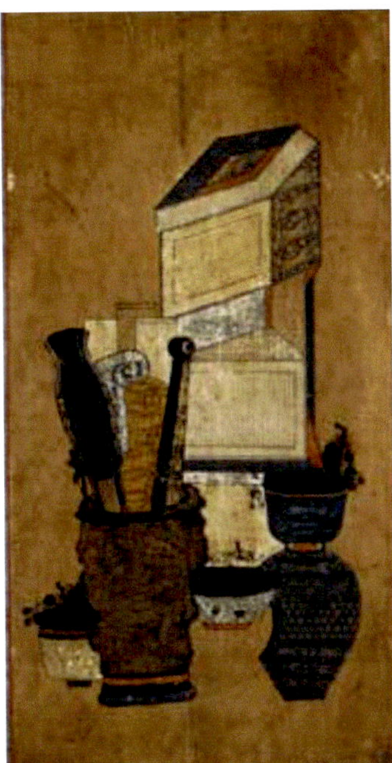
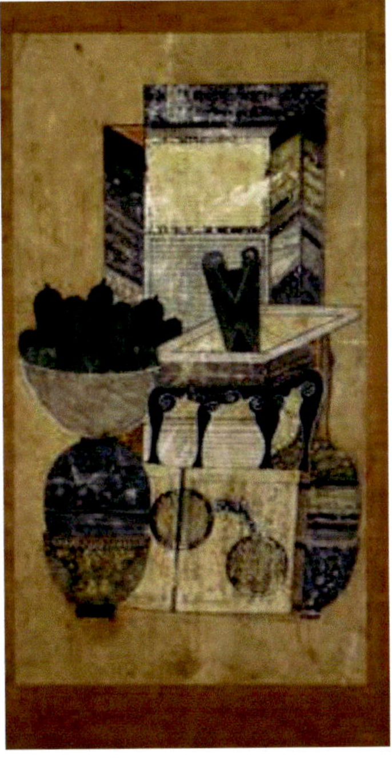

Figure 1. Anonymous. *Chaekgeori*, late 19th century. Colors on paper, 64 x 31.8 cm and 52.8 x 28 cm. The Japanese Folk Crafts Museum. Photo credit: Dahal Media

The above excerpt is from the 1959 essay "The Curious Folk Painting of Joseon" by Yanagi Muneyoshi regarding the two-panel screen *Chaekgeori* (fig. 1) he saw at the Japanese Folk Crafts Museum in Tokyo. The screen had been donated by Okamura Kichiemon and Miyosawa Motozu. Through this article the value and beauty of folk painting [minhwa] was introduced to the world. Muneyoshi's disciple and textile designer Serizawa Keisuke would go on to say: "I have seen many beautiful works of art, but Joseon still-life paintings struck me the most forcefully. For a few moments everything around me faded away as I was drawn into this irresistible painting. I found the scene surprisingly alluring and was overjoyed."[2]

The chaekgeori folk painting that captivated Yanagi and Serizawa more than a century ago has recently become a topic of interest in the West. In 2008, the Metropolitan Museum of Art held a chaekgeori exhibition entitled *Beauty and Learning*, which showcased the genre in the United States for the first time. Inspired by this exhibition, at my suggestion the Gyeonggi Provincial Museum hosted a chaekgeori exhibition, *From the Study of Joseon Scholar to the Study of Modern People*, in 2012. The exhibition showcased the historical continuity of chaekgeori paintings from the traditional to the modern, suggesting an artistic evolution from late eighteenth- to twenty-first–century folk painting that belies the idea that chaekgeori paintings are relics of the past and demonstrates instead that this genre of painting continues to develop in our culture today.

Paintings of books are also found in China and the West. But only in Korea did such art define the tastes of an era. Paintings of books and bookshelves gained popularity during the reign of Jeongjo and remained in vogue until the Korean War, a period of nearly two hundred years. Korea is the only country where the imagery of books became an independent genre. The Koreans' love for books was uniquely intense: during his reign, Jeongjo engaged in the world's first "academic politics" (literally, "book politics" which means a policy of capability, over caste) and founded a royal library for scholars, all of which gave rise to the first still-life book paintings known as chaekgeori.

Chaekgeori was a painting genre enjoyed not only in the court, but also among commoners. Chaekgeori originally produced in the court were adapted by the common folk and became known as folk-style chaekgeori. While chaekgeori of the court are strictly formal and focused on faithful depiction, folk-style chaekgeori unfold a colorful world brimming with imagination.

Until now, research has focused on royal paintings of chaekgeori, usually providing objective scholarship such as names of artists and their appearance in literature. By contrast, an objective approach to folk-style chaekgeori is more difficult, because it belongs to the world of mystery beyond our wisdom, as Yanagi Muneyoshi said, and little is written about it. In short, we can truly only explore these paintings by relying on intuition. Within this framework the most objective proof of these characteristics will be drawn, but realistically the most probable course will be to compare characteristics of folk-style chaekgeori to those of court-style chaekgeori.

Curiosity, Hapiness, And Eroticism

> These are not books; this is a painting of books.[3]

King Jeongjo said the above to his subjects in 1791 after installing a folding-screen painting known as chaekgado (bookshelf painting) behind his throne. This exchange signaled the start of the unprecedented popularity of bookshelf paintings. Some chaekgeori had been produced before, as early as 1783, but the king's declaration brought chaekgeori to the forefront. Jeongjo replaced, with chaekgado, the Sun and Moon with Five Peaks folding screen that had traditionally stood behind the throne as an important royal emblem. This act amounted to a defiance of palace customs and a political declaration to his subjects that he would put books at the forefront of his rule and reign with an emphasis on books and academics. Because of Jeongjo's "academic politics" chaekgeori began in earnest in Korea.

King Jeongjo announced that chaekgado served as a royal emblem symbolizing the correction of future benighted writings.[4] "Benighted writings" referred to popular contemporary writing styles comprising the latest literary trends from the Qing dynasty. As Joseon's dealings with the Qing dynasty increased, Joseon was flooded with Qing popular literature deemed problematic by Jeongjo. The king responded with a policy to stem the tide of Qing literature and revive Joseon classics. At first this policy was enacted to prevent literature from the Roman Catholic Church from entering Korea, but in order to avoid future contention between the Namin and Noron political factions, even the importation of contemporary Qing literature was forbidden. This decree was proclaimed in the year Sinhae (1791), which was one year before the Restoration Policy, which entailed literary-style reforms.[5] The chaekgado folding screen was used as visual propaganda to signal the beginning of the reforms.

Court officials formed factions, and the rivalries aroused by these divisions dogged the Joseon kings. Yeongjo (Jeongjo's grandfather) and Jeongjo developed *Tangpyeongchaek* (Policy of Impartiality) to diffuse the partisan strife among their subjects and to strengthen royal authority. Jeongjo, who advanced the Impartiality Office, sought to bolster his position as king by returning to classical Korean literature, a move symbolized by his chaekgado folding screen.

But it was simply not realistic to rein in the artistocratic factions with academics alone, as they tended to be composed of the most skilled politicians and learned scholars of their time. To rein them in would require greater political skill and academic understanding than they possessed. This was why the king would often stay up all night to read and deepen his knowledge. He was skilled enough to write a 100-book series in 180-volumes called *Hongjae jeonseo* (Complete works of Hongjae) and was confident enough to debate academics with literati.[6] This was why he defied custom and placed the chaekgado folding screen behind his throne. The act was a declaration of war against the divided officials; a declaration that Jeongjo would rule by books and academics.

Using academics as a way of ruling has historical precedent. The ancient Chinese philosopher Xunzi emphasized that a king must be both a politician and a teacher. The king ruled over the people, but he also had to be capable of imparting knowledge. Yeongjo put this philosophy into practice, and Jeongjo followed in his predecessor's footsteps by dedicating himself to study.[7]

So great was King Jeongjo's love for chaekgeori that the genre gained popularity among the noble class as well. The Jeongjo-era scholar Yi Gyusang wrote in his book *Ilmongo* (Manuscript of one dream): "The world calls these works 'chaekga.' The pictures are in full color, and there is not a wall in a nobleman's house without one. Kim Hongdo is particularly expert in this genre."[8] This excerpt attests to the spread of court-style chaekgeori aristocrats.

Court-style chaekgeori feature accoutrements such as porcelain pottery, bronzes, stationery, and flower vases. Like the miniature antique boxes and display shelves often used in China, these paintings increased a preference for material culture. The accoutrements featured in court-style chaekgeori are not Korean, but Chinese or Western. The porcelain, bronzes, and stationery were from China, and alarm clocks, clocks, and eyeglasses were from the West.[9] The chinoiserie trend that swept the royal courts of European countries in the late seventeenth century had also quietly made its way into the upper classes of Joseon society. But where Europe favored China's blue-and-white porcelain, Joseon favored single-color porcelain, mainly because blue-and-white wares were already being produced in Joseon and were not a subject of exotic curiosity.

That chaekgeori were filled not with Korean, but Chinese and Western articles reflects a preference for luxuries among the upper classes. For about 150 years Joseon had been an isolated country, until after the Japanese invasion in 1592 and the second Manchu invasion in 1636. During Jeongjo's reign in the late eighteenth century, trade with China began in earnest for the first time, and the trend toward foreign luxury goods increased.[10] Active trade with Qing was suggested to improve Joseon's depressed economy, and many cultural items were brought back to Korea through Joseon missions to imperial China.[11] Jeongjo was a critic of this phenomenon, outraged that nobles saw elegance and sophistication in using Chinese products for even the most mundane things, such as furniture and rice bowls.

Painted objects seen in chaekgeori were in actuality flowing into Korea. However, the nobles' love of foreign goods was not necessarily a negative trend. It can be interpreted as the attempts of the intellectual classes to finally get a glimpse of the outside world. Because there were limitations on Joseon citizens visiting China and the West, the nobles of Joseon used articles originating from such places to learn more about them.

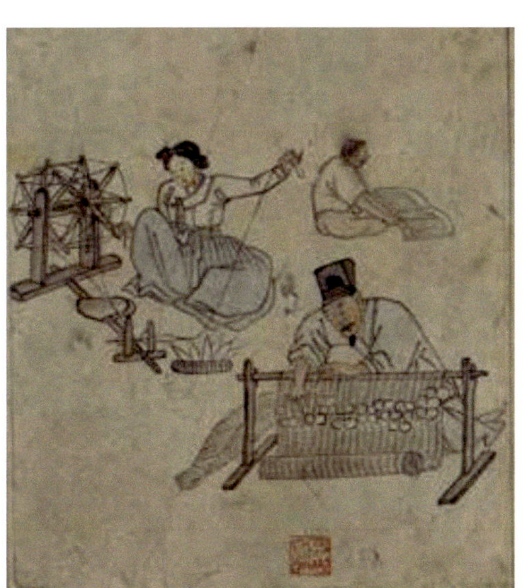

Figure 2. Kim Hongdo. *Mat-Weaving,* late 18th century. Colors on the paper, 26.9 x 22.6 cm. National Museum of Korea. Photo credit: National Museum of Korea

Commoners' views on books differed from those of King Jeongjo and the nobility. They had no reason to solidify the power of the monarchy, no interest in collecting curios, and little desire to get a glimpse of the outside world. To commoners, books were a symbol of realistic success and a means of achieving it. Kim Hongdo's *Mat-Weaving* (fig. 2) depicts the people's attitudes toward books. In the painting the father weaves mats, the mother spins thread, and the son reads a book larger than himself. This image poses the question: Why is the son exempt from his family's labor? Is it, as scholar Bak Jiwon once said, because even a housewife and a farmer hard at work would be happy to watch their children study?[12] The answer can be found in the *banggeon* (headpiece), worn by the father. The banggeon shows that the wearer is a yangban, a member of the noble class.

That the father is doing menial labor like a commoner in spite of his status makes it clear that he failed to obtain a government post. In other words, the son is exempt from household labor because he must study, pass the civil service exams, and restore himself—and the family—to its former glory.

The nineteenth-century scholar Jeong Yagyong once said, "The work of studying and reading with a great goal in mind, of collecting books on all manner of topics for storage, copying, or recording, and of treasuring and enjoying books must serve as the foundation for elevating one's family."[13] Reading as the basis for elevating the family is, as Jeong cites, a quote from the Song dynasty scholar Zhu Xi. Also, *Guwen zhenbao*, a collection of Chinese prose, states that with books the poor may gain riches and the rich gain nobility.[14]

Folk-style chaekgeori feature many auspicious animals and plants. Court-style chaekgeori feature books alongside curios imported from China, but folk-style chaekgeori showcase flowering plants, flowers and birds, and other plants and animals. Such motifs neither promoted royal power nor offered a glimpse into the outside world, but stood as auspicious symbols of hope for many sons, for social advancement, and for happiness. Chaekgeori paintings were transformed from political tools and reflections of the gentry's love of antiques into pictures of everyday life.

Chaekgeori from a private collection (plate 21) is a quintessential example of this transformation. The watermelon featured prominently at the center of the image—in spite of the work's genre as a painting of books—symbolizes the change. The books are relegated to the background, with fruits and flowers, including not only the watermelon but also lotus flowers and peaches, taking center stage. This piece shows how emphases reversed. The plants and fruits that have usurped the books' place in the spotlight are auspicious symbols for a happy life. The watermelon represents fertility, the kingfishers pecking at the lotus denote passing the civil service exams, and the peaches signify longevity. Along with the books symbolizing social advancement, the picture is replete with auspicious symbolism. As *Chaekgeori* shows, folk-style chaekgeori became, fundamentally, symbols of happiness.

Here a curious trend becomes apparent. Not only were the books robbed of the spotlight by fruits and plants, they were relegated to stands for bowls containing orchids and peaches. This may be seen as an insult to the books, which is odd considering the great respect afforded books by gentlemen scholars of Joseon. Bak Jiwon once declared that they were not to be used as pillows—that one should not yawn, stretch, or spit in the presence of a book, and that even a sneeze should be done while turned away.[15] This chaekgeori shows that, to commoners, happiness in life (symbolized by plants and flowers) was considered at least as important as social advancement (symbolized by books). It also indicates that the nobility began to break away from a focus on pretense and face-saving to engage more practical interests.

Having become symbols of happiness, folk-style chaekgeori were also a space for eroticism, serving a fundamental human desire. *Chaekgeori* (fig. 3) in the collection of the Musée National des Arts Asiatiques Guimet depicts symbols of femininity on the upper shelves, such as ginkgo fruits and sewing tools. The bottom right shows a man's shoes and accoutrements. Bedding and a pillow are laid out on the platform in the middle, and a man's and a woman's clothing are scattered haphazardly upon it as though cast away in a hurry. This implies that something is taking place between the owners of the

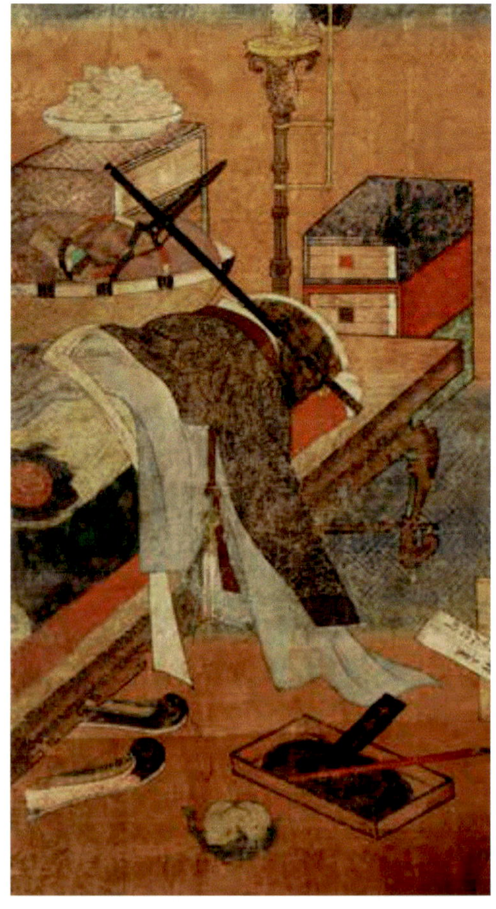

Figure 3. Anonymous. *Chaekgeori*, late 19th century. Colors on paper, 63.5 x 34.5 cm. Musée National des Arts Asiatiques Guimet. Photo credit: Dahal Media

clothes just off-frame on the left. This is an erotic work. The eroticism suggested by the objects, the bedding, and the clothes demonstrates the height of Korean metaphorical usage.[16] Professor Kang Woobang praised this work as "a masterpiece, a labor of love."[17] King Jeongjo, however, might have been outraged at the sight of such a work.

Joseon-era studies were the exclusive domain of men. There are rare examples (plate 19) of paintings of a woman's study, however. In one such chaekgeori the focus rests on books and a decorative safe used to store valuables and perhaps make-up. Above these items sit ceramics and articles tailored to female preference, beneath them rest a woman's silk slippers and perfume bottles. This chaekgeori does not function merely to make objects from a woman's private study public, however, but registers a quiet yet firm cry from its canvas. The watermelon roughly pierced by a decorative knife elicits a macabre feeling. Watermelons symbolize the bearing of many sons because of the fruit's many seeds. In most folk paintings this meaning is conveyed by the genteel slicing off of the top of the watermelon, thus revealing the seeds inside. But why in this instance would the central image of a beautiful painting be the subject of a ghoulish stabbing? Perhaps the commissioner of the painting wished to communicate a message that challenges male-centered culture by denying the watermelon its symbol of fertility.

The Secret of Irrational Composition

> In a word, we were more interested in structural composition than in the nature of beauty or the existence of the subject itself.[18]

The penetrating words above by modern artist Lee Ufan characterize minhwa in general and are particularly apt as descriptors of chaekgeori. The allure of chaekgeori hinges on the beauty of its composition, and many people love these paintings for that reason. Chaekgeori perhaps best reveal the innate skill of Koreans in the art of composition.

In 1788, Jeongjo ordered the royal painters-in-waiting Sin Hanpyeong and Yi Jonghyeon to paint chaekgeori as they pleased, but when their works turned out to be "strange to the eyes," the artists were exiled. On that very day, Jang Hanjong, Kim Jaero, and Heo Yong were newly appointed as royal painters-in-waiting.[19] Their role was to paint chaekgeori in line with Jeongjo's purposes. Jang Hanjong's *Chaekgado* at the Gyeonggi Provincial Museum (plate 1) was likely created around this time.

A single known chaekgado piece is framed, not by drapes but by a door (fig. 4). Like the works of Jang Hanjong, these screens were likely produced during Jeongjo's reign. These early chaekgado, where the subjects are framed by drapes or doors, seem to represent Jeongjo's reverence for books. For him, books were not simply media by which knowledge was passed on, but items upon which his rule depended. As is

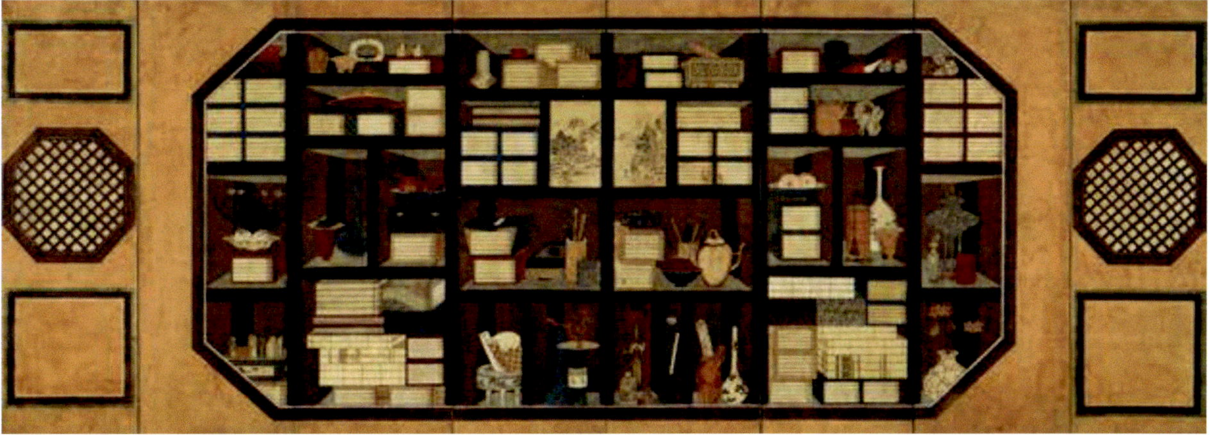

Figure 4. Anonymous. *Chaekado,* late 19th century. Colors on paper, 139.2 x 369.1 cm. Private collection. Photo credit: Dahal Media.

apparent in the mural of the deceased in Anak Tomb No. 3, in *Portrait of King Taejo (fig. 5)* at Gyeonggi Shrine in Jeonju, or in shamanic paintings, drapes were used as props that elevated the status of the subject.

In the nineteenth century Yi Hyeongnok became well known as a chaekgeori painter.[20] Although Yi's grandfather Yi Jonghyeon was banished because his works displeased Jeongjo, he was an excellent painter of studies. His father, Yi Yunmin, was popular among noble families for his paintings of studies. With this pedigree, Yi Hyeongnok painted so realistically that people approached his paintings to look very closely, after which they laughed because the bookshelves looked so real. The artist was famous for this sort of work.[21] Twice he changed his name, to Yi Eungnok in 1864, and to Yi Taekgyun in 1871. In his season as Yi Eungnok, he painted *Chaekgado* in the National Museum of Korea (plate 5) with a much more concise composition than preceding court-style examples and newly set green as the background color rather than the standard brown. Also, during the time he used the name Yi Taekgyun, he used blue for the background (plate 6). He appears to have constantly experimented in background colors.

As chaekgado beloved by kings and the upper classes spread to commoners, the genre took a step in a completely different direction. The most notable change is the unfettered freedom present in folk-style chaekgeori. The confining forms of chaekga with its stiff books and accoutrements are reinterpreted in the imaginations of minhwa artists, becoming free and lyrical. As Yanagi Muneyoshi said, the folk-style chaekgeori is an expression of freedom unburden from established artistic norms. This is why the composition of folk-style chaekgeori is irrational; yet this irrationality is expressed perfectly naturally. Yanagi Muneyoshi contended that the mysterious allure of folk-style chaekgeori began with its irrational nature. Having been educated in modern Western visual art, he believed that linear perspective and shading techniques were rational and scientific, but upon being exposed to this genre he realized that even unscientific, irrational expressions could make a deep impression. Yanagi's description of such art as "mysterious" was no exaggeration. Unconventional, random, and impulsive irrationality is in and of itself what makes folk-style chaekgeori so alluring.

The spaces depicted in folk-style chaekgeori do not abide by science or common-sense logic. Articles are placed in unnatural ways, books and accoutrements float in the air, and the colors and patterns used do not correspond to reality. Where royal painters looked at a bookshelf and painted it as seen, folk-style chaekgeori reflected the artist's taste. For example, without exception court-style chaekgeori invoked Western perspective techniques, while folk-style chaekgeori employed traditional Eastern inverse perspective or multiple view points. This is like ingesting a Western steak versus being reborn through the savory, luscious foods of Korea such as *doenjang* (fermented bean paste) and kimchi. Court-style chaekgeori imitated the newest, including Western, styles. They were realistic, and reproducing the three-dimensional effect was an important task. Folk paintings, however, sought a practical composition for their small canvases and made use of Korean styles to meet their tastes. Thus the free imagination imbued in folk painting gave rise to a chaekgeori painting style utterly different from that seen in the royal courts.

Folk-style chaekgeori folding screens are about one-quarter to one-third the height of those used in the court. Since the spaces commoners lived in were small, their folding screens by necessity were also small. Would the impressive impact of chaekgeori paintings be lessened in tandem with this reduction in size? Minhwa artists began carefully to assemble books and personal items within the smaller frame of the paintings, drawing them very close together, as if in a single mass. This contraction of the space between objects led to more of a two-dimensional effect, or sometimes a cross between 2D and 3D, thus creating an abstract image. Like stuffing many items into a small bundle or armoire, folk-style chaekgeori paintings presented a sense of life's wisdom compressed into a tiny space.

Similar to ancient tomb murals from Goguryeo, scale in minhwa was determined by the importance of the subjects featured in the work. Independent of actual size, objects deemed important were drawn larger than the others. *Chaekgeori* (fig. 5), from a private collection, is a combination of chaekgeori and portrait that seems reminiscent of *Gulliver's Travels*: a Lilliputian child, smaller than a book, sits

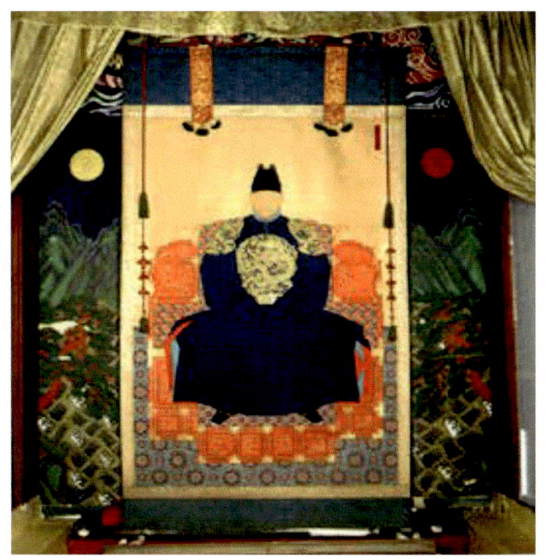

Figure 5. Anonymous. *Portrait of King Taejo*, 1872. Colors on silk, 220 x 105.9 cm. Gyeonggi Shrine in Jeonju. Photo credit: Cultural Heritage Administration

reading his own book in front of a table for Buddhist texts. Upon closer examination, it becomes clear that the boy is reading *Sohak*, an ethics textbook for Joseon-era children. By manipulating scale, a chaekgeori is formed within a chaekgeori. The fact that the boy in the painting is smaller than the books indicates that though he is a person, he is peripheral to the painting. While the screen is small, the composition places books at the center and manages to pack in a boy, accoutrements, and plants around the revered books.

The clustered composition of folk-style chaekgeori makes it difficult to see at first glance, but the composition of these paintings is unrealistic and irrational in several ways. Some objects, in fact, seem to be levitating. Folk-style chaekgeori do not cling to the absolute realism of the court style, but focus instead on the composition and the beauty of the image.

Another *Chaekgeori* (fig. 6) from a private collection bears a strikingly clear composition, but it is problematic from a purely realistic perspective. Furniture and covered books act as stands for other covered books, vases, and porcelain wares. But such objects are only narrowly balanced on the edges of their stands—were they to be placed in such ways in reality, they would fall immediately. The composition would not be possible outside a zero-gravity environment, yet it appears natural to the eye because of the idiomatic perspective found exclusively in folk painting. The addition of a pheasant, golden chicken, and phoenix, among other auspicious beasts, also plays a role in transforming the space into an unrealistic one.

Over time, folk-style chaekgeori paintings became flatter and more abstract.[22] *Chaekgeori Munjado* (plate 35) is almost reminiscent of the abstract works of French fauvist painter Henri Matisse in its two-dimensional composition. Upon close examination, the flat and geometric covered books become clearer. Books come together with more realistic flowers and animals, creating a delicate balance between the realistic and the abstract without veering too much in the latter direction. Surprisingly, this very modern painting comes from the historically rural folk painting tradition in Gangwon Province.

Painting flat spaces with abstract appearance is a tradition in Korean visual art. However, this two-dimensionality does not indicate deficient technique or skill. This style demonstrates a preference of traditional Korean artists, as can be seen in the murals of Goguryeo tombs and Buddhist art from the Goryeo Dynasty. *Portrait of King Taejo*, painted in 1396 at the dawn of the Joseon Dynasty, is a representative work of the traditions set after Korea's Three Kingdoms Period. The extant

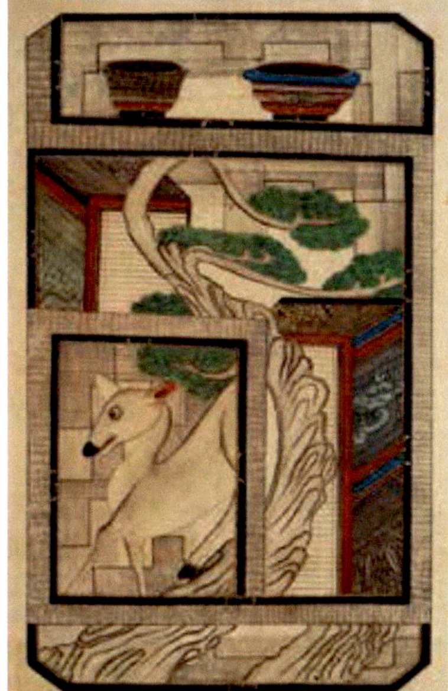

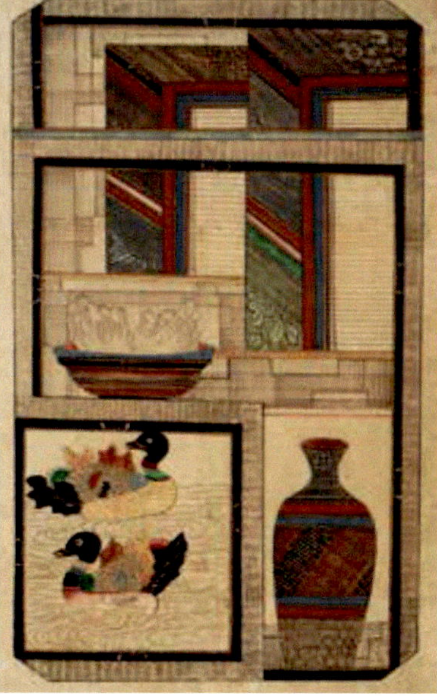

Figure 6. Anonymous. *Chaekgado,* late 19th century. Colors on paper, each 77 x 49 cm. Musée National des Arts Asiatiques Guimet. Photo credit: Dahal Media

version of the portrait, housed in the Gyeonggi Shrine in Jeonju, is a copy made in 1872, but it is a precise and faithful reproduction of the original.[23] This portrait was painted in a flat style, as seen in the planar depiction of the king's seat and footstool.

The affinity for traditional flat perspective passed directly from traditional art to folk painting. The flat perspectives of folk painting are not modern or revolutionary, but an extension of tradition. When paintings with a realistic sense of perspective and depth were brought into Joseon from China, such pictures were eventually adapted into a flatter style. Flat perspective is part of Korean artistic taste, which includes a preference for refreshing simplicity. Yeong-seop Byeon of Korea University posits that flat perspective stems from a deep-rooted aesthetic sense borne of the many layered mountain landscapes in Korea, along with a refreshing sense of space.[24]

Some folk-style chaekgado, however, incorporate bookshelves like those of the court style. Though shorter folding screens limit the space available, a small canvas is not a problem in the hands of an imaginative artist. The *Chaekgado* from the Musée National des Arts Asiatiques Guimet (fig. 6) is an example of a work where imagination runs free even in the limited frame of the bookshelves that so restricted the court. This work is relatively small at only 77 cm in height, but it nonetheless presents a successful composition of bookshelves. In spite of their size, the shelves are home to a vast and endless world of imagination. Some of the covered books are not shown in their entirety, implied instead through glimpses, and vases hover between shelves freely. The most surprising feature is the shelf filled with water, with two ducks playing in it. This painting is a testament to the artist's endless imagination.

Surprisingly, the revolutionary geometric world depicted in these folk-style chaekgeori is a faithful extension of tradition. Beauty in emptiness, free perspective, and flatness are defining characteristics of traditional Korean art. The folk artist's revolutionary imagination added to these traditions, affording chaekgeori a refreshing and modern look.

Harmonizing Life and Dreams

> Chaekgeori behind a Leopard Skin Curtain (plate 16) is a wholly unique masterpiece, a collaboration between two artists of different generations. The folding screen was originally a simple eight-panel work featuring leopard skins, but the center was later cut out and the skins pulled back. The eight-panel leopard skins act as a drape, eliciting in viewers' curiosity about the scene behind it. Perhaps that was why the owner of the screen had an artist expose the secret room by drawing open part of the drape. If the artist had painted a nude woman in the style of Francisco Jose de Goya y Lucientes instead of a scholar's study, the piece could pass for a modern work of art.[25]

The emergence of never-before-seen chaekgeori is always a pleasant surprise. The quote above describes *Chakgeori* behind a leopard skin curtain (plate 16), a work in which leopard skins act as a drape. The general term used to describe the skins is *hopi*, written with the characters for "tiger" and "skin," even though the skins in question come from leopards. The above quote by folklorist Zayong Zo, who once owned this work, highlights his imaginative interpretation. If his interpretation is correct, most folk-style chaekgeori did not use drapes as a feature. The leopard skins cover about one-third of this work, and through the gap created by the furtive lifting of the skins, a realistic scene of a bookstand stacked with books and a pair of glasses, along with the haphazardly placed surrounding accoutrements and ornaments, is visible. That there is a bookstand rather than bookshelves and the leopard skins do not seem as solid as those found in court paintings suggest that this work was done by a skilled folk-style artist.

The crossing of genres was not at all taboo in folk-style chaekgeori.[26] Folk style chaekgeori combined not only with its natural cousin, *munjado* (ideographs, Calligraphy of Character Pictures), but also with *hwahwehwa* (flowering plant pictures), *hwajohwa* (flower-and-bird paintings), landscape paintings, and portraits, thereby expanding the scope of stories it could tell and images it could portray. Different kinds of stories came together and created new ones; hwahwehwa were inserted into chaekgeori paintings, infusing soft lyricism into what could easily have become simply rigid paintings of books; imaginary beasts were painted into the pictures to lead the chaekgeori viewer into a fantastic, dreamlike world; people were added to make the images more approachable. Such combinations vastly diversified and enriched the strict and orderly world of chaekgeori.

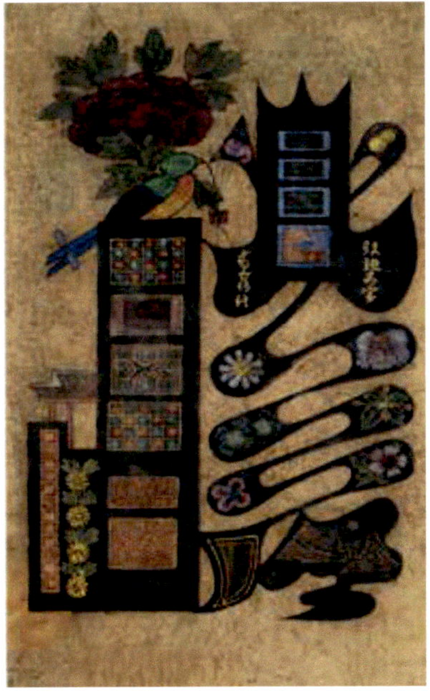

Figure 7. Anonymous. *Shin(信)jado,* late 19th century. Colors on paper, 25.2×12.6in. Private collection. Photo credit: Dahal Media

Though different genres, chaekgeori and munjado blend well together because they are both centered on academics. *Shinjado* (fig. 7), from a private collection , is an example in which chaekgeori is incorporated into munjado. Though the painting itself is an ideograph, the strokes that compose the characters are made up of books. In addition, the books are depicted only with flat patterns on them. The second and third strokes of the character 信 (shin) are composed of books standing upright and laid sideways, respectively. *Shinjado* shows how freely genres were mixed in folk painting.

Among works that display a blending of genres, however, only in folk painting is the imagination so fantastical as to mix bookshelves with auspicious creatures. Imagine how the simplicity of the scholar's study flies away when a phoenix makes its nest there, a giraffe walks about, a lion roars, and a tiger growls. The scene is reminiscent of Disney animation, yet this kind of scene is not uncommon in folk painting.

The Lee Ufan collection at the Musée National des Arts Asiatiques Guimet includes a work that is a cross between chaekgeori and *seosudo* (a painting of auspicious beasts) (fig. 8). The upper part of the folding screen is a chaekgeori, while the bottom part is a flower-and-bird painting, with both genres in one image. Between the two juts a fantastic, jagged mountain range. In the midst of everything, auspicious beasts float above the landscape like UFOs. It is an arbitrary combination possible only in folk painting. The chaekgeori part of the painting is also curious, with vases floating above the books, showing how even realistic and mundane objects and scenes can be used to express fantastical worlds.

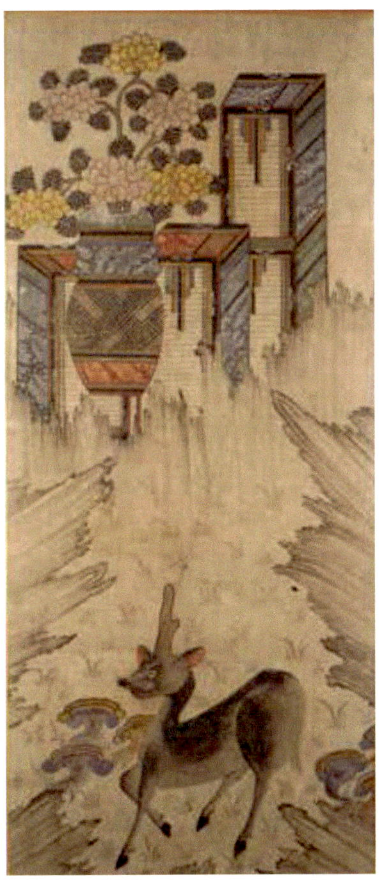

Figure 8. Anonymous. *Chaekgeori,* late 19th century. Colors on paper, 110 x 43 cm. Musée National des Arts Asiatiques Guimet. Photo credit: Dahal Media

The idea that chaekgeori paintings mixed well with auspicious creatures offers a glimpse of the contemporary perception of the kind of world this would create. The two-panel *Chaekgeori* with the turtles and birds at the Gahoe Museum (plate 30) is a work that alludes to the direction folk-style chaekgeori was heading in the crossing of genres.

"The pair of turtles emanates auspicious energy, and behind the covered books is a vase. Its scent stirs and gives life to a spring breeze, coaxing a song out of the pair of hundred-year birds."[27] This quote describes the function of the auspicious creatures and the vase in the painting. The turtles provide auspicious energy, and the vase creates an aromatic spring breeze, with these meanings conveyed by a pair of hundred-year birds (symbolizing longevity).

This chaekgeori exceeds the idea of the standard still-life painting: it overflows with a mystery and vitality that raise folk painting to a new, personified level of still life.

The most masterful cross between chaekgeori and auspicious beasts is found in *Chaekgeori* at the Chosun Minhwa Museum (plate 28). In this work, the dragon and the books are so intertwined that it is difficult to tell if it is centered on the dragon or the books. To be more specific, the dragon and a toad are wrapped around the books. The antennae of the dragon and the toad are connected, implying a relationship between the two. Dreams of dragons or toads have traditionally been omens of giving birth to a son, which means that this particular imagery is a symbol of fertility. These features show that this work is infused with the hopes of giving birth to many sons who will excel academically and succeed in life.

In folk painting, reality and fantasy that cannot be combined in life are brought together in harmony.

There is no border between the two worlds. These paintings suggest the belief that utopia is no longer a far distant place, but is right here by our side. In folk-style chaekgeori, reality is like a dream, and dreams are reality.

The Synergy between Tradition and Lively Imagination

Court-style and folk-style chaekgeori paintings share subject matter and form, but the worlds they aimed to depict differed dramatically. The paintings passed from political emblems to decorative furnishing for festivities, and became paintings reflecting desires of the heart. This change reflects the differences in life ambitions across classes, illustrated through the same subject matter. Court-style chaekgeori paintings played a role in easing economic difficulties by means of their inclusion in material cultural exchanges with China, while folk-style chaekgeori afforded visions of a blessed life by depicting an ideal world via a real-world medium. These changes in chaekgeori paintings illuminated the dream life of the nation's people between the late nineteenth and early twentieth centuries. To theme, such paintings offered a window into the world of a luxurious, faraway land. Bearing sons, finding success, and living happily were of the utmost urgency. These realistic desires, however, were not plainly revealed but were expressed indirectly and metaphorically; despite the very real problems people had, the presentation of desires through idealized and fantastical worlds offers a glimpse of the spirit and taste of Korean folk painting.

Chaekgeori decidedly show that the artistic capacity of Koreans is firmly rooted in compositional beauty. Court chaekgeori employed the Western techniques of perspective and shading to realize a solid, realistic image, while folk-style chaekgeori revived a Korean aesthetic sensibility, one that created a world of unique modern images by blending the subject matter with free imagination. Yanagi Muneyoshi and Serizawa Keisuke, on viewing a folk-style chaekgeori painting, admired the mysterious allure that was the effect of synergy between tradition and lively imagination.

The mixing of painting genres sprang spontaneously from folk-style chaekgeori paintings. Several painting genres, including ideograms, bird-and-flowers, landscapes, and portraits were combined with chaekgeori. Of note is the sudden appearance of auspicious, imaginary animals among the books. Although the desires represented in these images were very real, they were expressed in a metaphorical, lyrical, fantastical manner. A certain auspicious energy is found in these paintings, and like expressing a fragrant breeze, there is a spirit and taste that can only be found in folk painting. Thus, rather than accepting chaekgeori as a realistic world, people recognized it as fanciful space hovering between the real and the ideal.

Although chaekgeori is an unknown genre to many people, this aspect of Korean culture emanated from a deep-seated love for books. Korean scholars have not paid much attention to the genre, yet there has already been some international interest. In the future, setting forth this aspect of Korean cultural heritage more fully will be a worthy endeavor. In the end, King Jeongjo's words, "These are not books, this is a painting of books," was a declaration that instigated a trend in a unique genre of Korean still-lifes, chaekgeori.

Translated by Slin Jung and Diana Evans

1 Yanagi 1981, 504–8.

2 Ibid.

3 The original reads:「提學臣吳載純辛亥錄」, 顧視御座後書架。謂入侍大臣曰。卿能]見之乎。對曰。見之矣。笑而教曰。豈卿眞以爲書耶。非書而畫耳。昔程子以爲雖不得讀書。入書肆。摩帙。猶覺欣然。予有會於斯言。爲是畫。卷端題標。皆用予平日所喜玩經史子集。而諸子則惟莊子耳。仍喟然曰。今人之於文。趣尙一與予相反。其耽觀者。皆後世病文也。安得以矯之。予爲此畫。蓋亦有寓意於其間者矣. King Jeongjo, *Hongjae jeonseo* [King Jeongjo, vol. 1], 162, "Ildeungnok munhak [Quotes from King Jeongjo]," in Kang, K. 2016B, 591–92.

4 Ibid.

5 Regarding the relationship between the Restoration Policy and chaekgeori, see Chung, Byungmo, "Chaekgeori ui yeoksa, eoje wa oneul" [The history of *chaekgeori*: past and present]," in Joseon seonbi 2012, 173–77. Regarding the Restoration Policy, see Kim, T. 2012.

6 Jeong, O., 2001; Jeong, O. 2013.

7 Kim, M. 2000.

8 The original reads: 俗目之曰,冊架,畵必染丹靑,一時貴人壁,無不塗此畵,弘道善此技; see Yi, G. YEAR, "Hwajurok"; Hongjun Yoo, "Danwon Kim Hongdo yeongu noteu [Research notes on Danwon Kim Hongdo]," in Yoo, H. 1990; Yoo, H. 1992.

9 Bang, 2007; Kim, E. 2012; Kang, M. 2015.

10 Chung 2011, 74–79; Sin, S. 2011, 155–79.

11 Yeonhaeng 2012.

12 Bak, J. DATE. [Other notes from this website have a URL and date accessed; see biblio].

13 "Giyanga [A young man from Giyang]," in *Dasan simunjip* (Dasan poetry collection). [Other notes from the Korean Classics website have a URL and date accessed; see biblio].

14 貧者因書富富者因書貴, from "Wanghyeong gonggwon hagmun 王荊公勸學文 [ENGLISH]," in *Gomunjinbo* [Guwen Zhenbao] 古文眞寶.

15 "In the presence of a book, do not yawn; in the presence of a book, do not stretch; in the presence of a book, do not spit, and should you need to cough, turn away from the book before doing so. Do not lick your fingers to turn the pages, and do not use your nails to mark a book. [...] Do not use a book as a pillow, do not cover a bowl with a book, and do not put volumes of books out of order. Keep dust off the books and silverfish away, and dry out your books in sunlight whenever the chance presents itself. When borrowing a book, correct any errors and leave a note; if there are any tears, fix them, and if the binding is broken, re-bind the book before returning it to the owner." Bak, J. 2016.

16 Chung 2011, 97–101.

17 Kang, W. 2015.

18 Lee, U. 1977.

19 "Although I commanded that artists Sin Hanpyeong, Lee Jonghyeong, and others paint their pictures as they saw fit, they ought to have painted the "chaekgeori" properly. As they have chosen to create pictures that are very strange to my eyes, they will be exiled together, far away." For the original, see Kang, K. 2001B, 589–90.

20 For more on Yi Hyeongnok's *Chaekgeori*, see Wagner 2007 and Min, G. 2015.

21 Yu, JG. 1857.

22 Cambon 2015.

23 Lee, S. 2010.

24 Byun 2014.

25 Cho 1974, 188.

26 Chung 2013.

27 The original text reads: 有一雙龜瑞氣濃書匣而匣後置花盎香動春風其內養一雙百年鳥向人能言語. Ibid.; Joseon seonbi 2012, 134.

The Evolution of Chaekgeori: Its Inception and Development from the Joseon Period to Today

Jinyoung Jin

Promoted by King Jeongjo as a political tool to maintain societal conservatism against an influx of ideas and changes from abroad, the genre of painting known as chaekgeori became one of the most enduring and prolific art forms of the Joseon dynasty. Chaekgeori replaced traditional court paintings of symbolic natural features and elements with paintings of books. Intended initially as a way to prolong the disciplined lifestyle of Confucian Joseon and thereby maintain the social and political order of the kingdom under his rule, Jeongjo not only endorsed books that conformed to his ideals, but also, perhaps less intentionally, promoted images of books as symbolic elements that transcend the originals being embodied. In doing so, he objectified books as valuable physical entities and commodities to be desired. It is this inherent duality, hand in hand with increases in foreign influences, that fueled the proliferation of chaekgeori paintings as an outlet of expression.

Chaekgeori was a form that captured the changing Korean society and its values, which were becoming increasingly individualistic and materialistic as a new wealthy class emerged to take advantage of opportunities outside of the traditional economic structure and boundaries set by class prejudices.

A Vehicle of Knowledge and a Departure from Tradition

Known to be a devoted admirer of books, Jeongjo is credited with establishing the palace library and sponsoring numerous scholarly publications during his reign.[1] It is no surprise then that he would combine his enthusiasm for books and fondness of paintings with a political objective that was intended to preserve order against perceived threats of external forces. A presumption can be made that Jeongjo, acting as both a benefactor of foreign communication and a protector of traditional Confucian ideals, deliberately used a new painting style—chaekgeori—as a way to influence and selectively filter ideas and culture coming from abroad in the late Joseon dynasty. By encouraging court painters to adopt books as a main subject of royal screen paintings, even going so far as to replace the backdrop screen behind his throne in a dramatic break from past practices, Jeongjo embraced power of books and the ideas contained within them.[2] In this boldly defined capacity, books in chaekgeori paintings can inspire, teach, and in turn possess the power to shape a society.

King Jeongjo's approach was a fine and carefully calculated balancing act; he introduced new ideas by encouraging intellectualism, but he also observed Confucian ideals of learning and societal order. Yet the influence of his contemporary, the pragmatic scholar Bak Jiwon, can be seen as having an opposite effect, spurring a materialistic demand for books and knowledge. Bak commented on the influx of foreign goods and books as well as the collecting habits of the Chinese literati class in his travel journal *Yeolha ilgi* [Diary of a journey to Jehol], published in 1780. Bak had made an extensive tour to what was then the northern territory of the Chinese Qing Empire (including the cities of Shenyang and Beijing, as well as Rehe Province), and in his travels searching out, negotiating, and purchasing antiques and books, he noted a different attitude among the Chinese elites when compared to the Korean elites:

> While I was traveling, I noticed many people trading items in a temple. They often buy dishes, clothes. They were also in search of particular antiques, newly published books. I understood that it would be entertaining and convenient to do it by themselves instead of locating items through servants.[3]

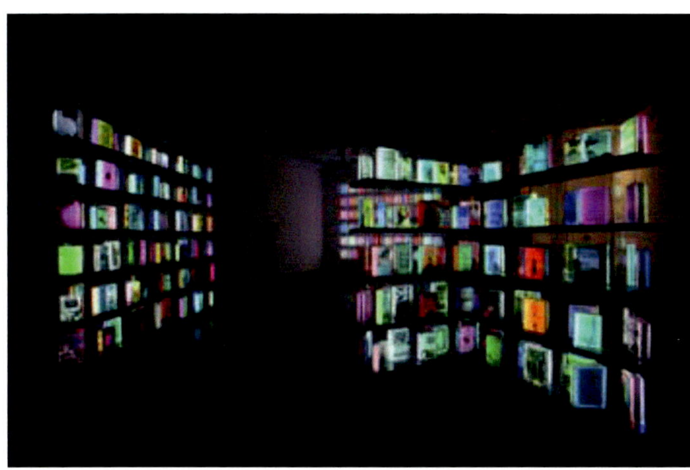

Fig. 1. Airan Kang (b. 1960). *Digital Book Project—The Luminous Poem*, 2011. Custom electronics, LEDs, and resin, dimensions variable., Gallery Simon, Seoul , Photo by Hong Soon Park.

Inspired by Bak's journal, collecting books from China became an obsessive preoccupation among the Joseon literati. Many scholars who had access to the practical and scientific knowledge of the West thought that such knowledge, provided through books, would eventually improve Joseon society. In this way, assembling pictorial books became a metaphor of social transit and a symbol of scholarly power. At the same time, books were hard to come by. Jeongjo's esteem for and love of books, combined with the scarcity of books in Joseon Korea due to royal censorship, spurred an increased fascination with books not just as simple vehicles of knowledge but also as valuable commodities. This desire for books set in motion a significant social and cultural shift toward materialism. In this sense, chaekgeori became a powerful and complex modern sociopolitical apparatus. And, of course, both Jeongjo and Bak believed in the idea of books as transformative agents and both helped propagate chaekgeori as a popular art form.

Through the aforementioned concepts and history of chaekgeori, books in the works of contemporary artist Airan Kang can be understood to embody knowledge, power, and transformation. The legacy of books as signifiers can be seen in her *Digital Book Project*, an installation where books on display appear to glow from within (fig. 1). For nearly a decade, Kang has presented various iterations of books in this ongoing project. As evident in many of the works in this series, by way of illumination, Kang dissolves materiality of physical books and fuses it with ephemeral depictions of data to make us visualize the evolution of books as a source of knowledge in the digital era. In her works, books glow, inspire, and attract viewers, yet they simultaneously invite and forbid access as they are the embodiment of ideals. This aspect of her work can be directly compared to representations of books in chaekgeori paintings, where books are a symbol of ideas, inaccessible objects that ultimately surpassed original meaning and being. Similarly, just as careful arrangements of forms were important in the initial acceptance and successive developments of chaekgeori paintings, the physical form of the books in Kang's work are still important in order to maintain recognizable identity.

In our increasingly paperless and digitized society, Kang's electronically luminescent books, although mere brightly lit shells, form vital connections to the physical world. She depicts books as still holding an inner luminescence, an artistic decision that seems to be an argument against the practice of appreciating books as material commodities. Yet, simultaneously, she also appears to be supporting Jeongjo's practice of appreciating books as tangible symbols of Confucian values. As the books in the chaekgeori paintings did in the past, the *Digital Book Project* attempts to organize a complex, communal world of multiple ideas to categorized personal experimentation and enjoyment. In addition, by choosing to illuminate the books from within, Kang symbolizes the curiosity and zeal that motivated Joseon literati in the eighteenth century to accelerate the development of their society into the modern era.

Consumption and the Proliferation of Materialism

Although no known chaekgeori paintings made under Jeongjo's direct supervision are believed to have survived, it is generally presumed that the first of the royal chaekgeori paintings consisted of books organized in a methodical manner so as to convey order, hierarchy, and discipline.[4] However, as the genre proliferated among the masses, the subject of chaekgeori expanded to include other personal items symbolic of wealth. While books symbolized the scholastic status of the paintings' owners, more exotic objects represented a high economic status and reflected shifting culture in what used to be a Confucian society that held that materialistic possessions were unworthy or even below its idealism.

This change in attitude, expressed in chaekgeori paintings over time, was the result of increasing exposure to outside cultures, particularly of China directly and even of Europe indirectly through China and Japan, where large number of emissaries were able to purchase and bring back objects and materials that further enticed the desire to possess the very latest and the exotic.[5] Additionally, as a side effect of growing trade functions, a new class called the jungin emerged as the facilitator of these cultural exchanges and began to unsettle socioeconomic order of Joseon.[6] Unhinged from the traditional social and economic settings, in addition to gaining their fortune outside of the family- and birth-based social structure, this newly formed class of wealth was less concerned with Confucian ideals and, perhaps as a way to make up for their lack of birthright status, expanded the range of chaekgeori painting subjects further by including materialistic elements to counter the status quo. Once started, the desire to consume, possess, and display wealth spread from the merchants to the traditional class of literati as well. The result, evident in many surviving chaekgeori paintings from the period, is a mixture of books and consumable objects, such as imported eyeglasses, clocks, compasses, telescopes, leathers, ceramics, and the like, that often compete for prominence and the attention of viewers.

This expansion of acceptable subjects for chaekgeori paintings from the Joseon era onward reflects a rising tide of materialism, an influence very much at work in the art of Stephanie S. Lee. Having used the foreshortening drawing technique of chaekgeori as the predominant visual structure of her works, Lee's paintings can be considered commentaries on a post–Korean War society that is heavily materialistic, a society where one's identity and socioeconomic status are perceived to be closely linked to one's material possessions. In her work, Lee playfully juxtaposes objects both old and new, along with their embodied meanings, to represent a significant transformation in Korean society's values visually. Thus, she uses a well-established understanding of chaekgeori's historical value as an artistic tool that captured a transitioning Joseon dynasty to illuminate contemporary material culture while also inviting viewers to contemplate the role of status and the meaning of self-identity within modern societies.

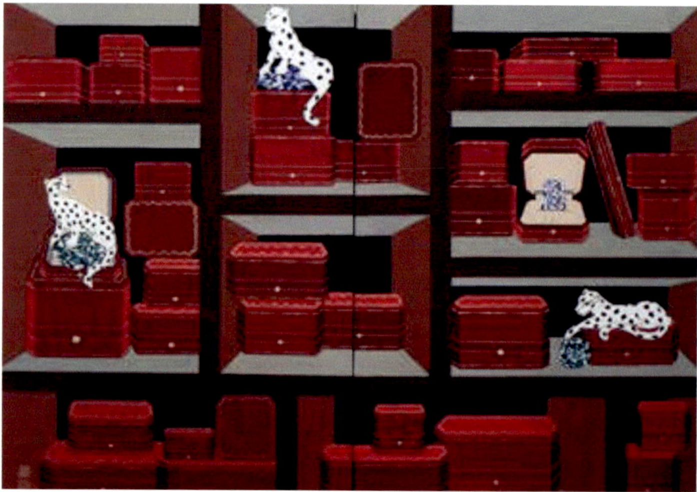

Fig. 2. Stephanie S. Lee (b. 1977). *Cabinet of Desire I*, 2016. Natural mineral pigment, colored and gold pigment, ink on Korean mulberry paper, 94 x 5.1 cm (each panel).

In Lee's 2016 diptych *Cabinet of Desire I* (fig. 2), books are completely absent. What at first appear to be formalistic chaekgeori paintings of books actually depict luxury gift boxes, particularly those of Western brands. In portraying these conspicuously foreign and exotic material goods, Lee seems to suggest complete transformation of a society where Confucian values, historically represented by books, are no longer present. This is a clear representation of modern society's complete shift from an enlightened set of Confucian ideals toward a superficial materialism.

In Lee's 2015 painting *Desire* (fig. 3), books, calligraphy brushes, tea, and fruit—all of which are symbolic of Jeongjo's ideal society—are illuminated by the sun. In contrast, the adjoining panel *Modern Desire* (fig. 4) depicts luxury gifts and alcohol lit by the moon, suggestive of a society where materialistic indulgences of night coexist and compete with what was once ideal without being able to merge and be reconciled. Lee symbolizes this historical movement further with her choice to set the two sides of the diptych in points of time, emphasizing a movement from Confucian day to materialistic night. The disparate set of objects in the paintings furthermore indicate a society where these two sets of values coexist and are reconcilable. This shift in values in chaekgeori is not a modern phenomenon; it was implicit even in Jeongjo's use and commission of paintings.

Lee's paintings display a diverse and affluent collection of luxuries typically out of the financial reach of the ordinary person. However, these extravagant objects are not used to reveal the negative aspects of materialism. Rather, we can interpret in them how the extravagantly materialistic yearnings of humanity can serve as a positive element of modern society. Using outlay and composition similar to traditional folding screens, Lee suggests that the ideal life that we all yearn for is not unattainable and can easily be found in one's own mundane, quotidian existence. Additionally, she takes the opportunity to investigate and reflect on the never ending aspirations and desires of human beings. She attempts to show the contrast of "the old" and "the new" by juxtaposing them, under the light of the sun and of the moon. While the objects of desire may have metamorphosed with the passage of time, the undying desires of human beings—wealth, health, beauty, knowledge, and fame—have not changed.

Lee has abstracted "consumption" as the theme for her contemporary chaekgeori by actively seeking personal gratification through images of books and commodities, as if the popular demand of chaekgeori was an envious imitation of elite conspicuous consumption.

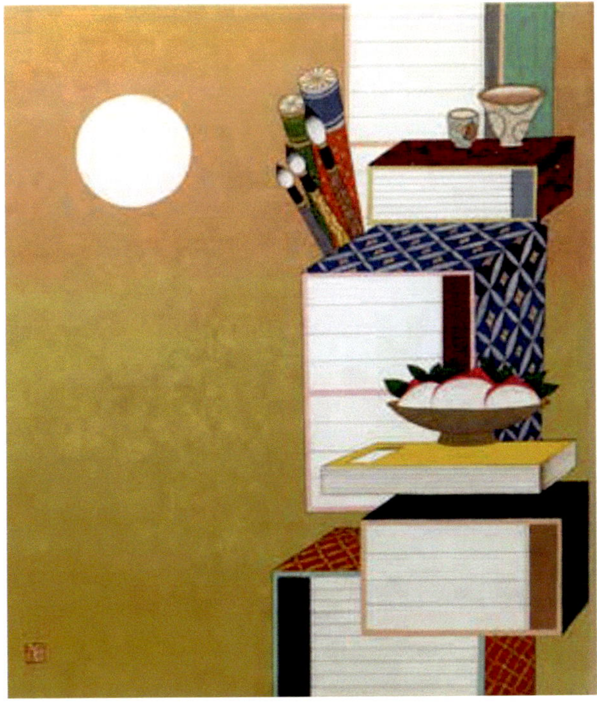

Fig. 3. Stephanie S. Lee (b. 1977). *Desire*, 2015. Colored and gold pigment, ink on Korean mulberry paper, 78.7 x 4.5 cm.

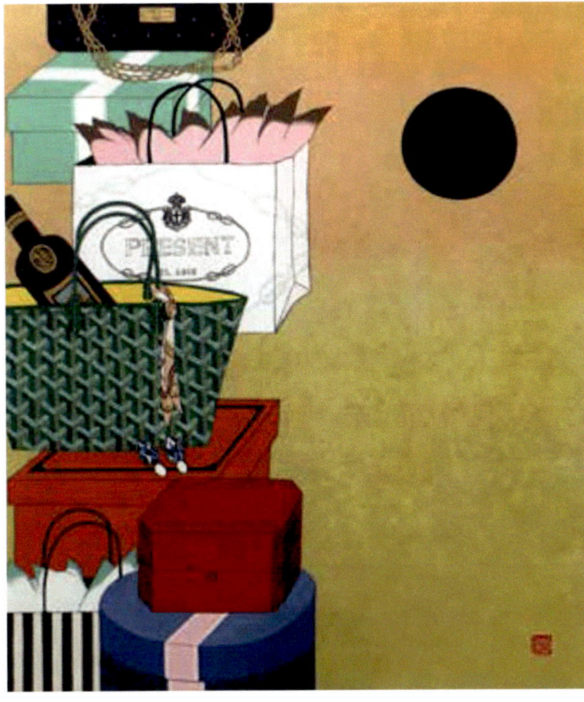

Fig. 4. Stephanie S. Lee (b. 1977). *Modern Desire*, 2015. Colored gold pigment, ink on Korean mulberry paper. 78.5 x 4.5 cm.

Chaekgeori beyond Politics and Consumption

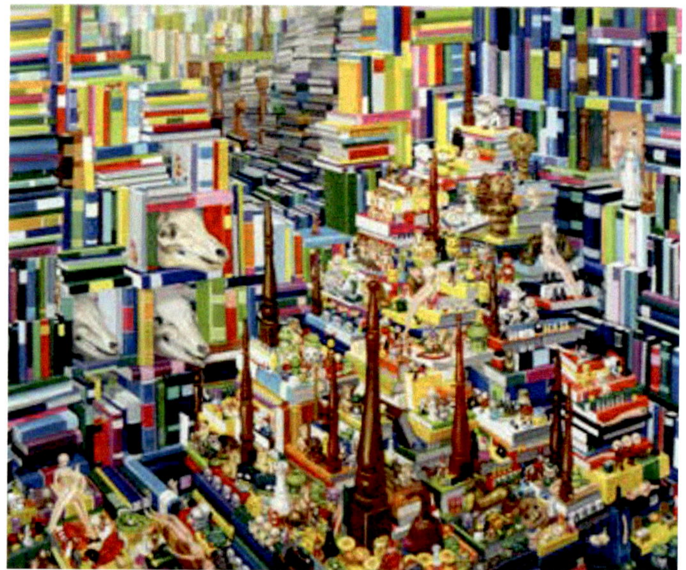

Fig. 5. Kyoungtack Hong (b. 1968). *Library 3*, 1995–2001. Oil on canvas, 181 x 226.1 cm.

One of the late nineteenth-century chaekgeori paintings owned by the National Palace Museum of Korea (plate 10) is commonly believed to approximate closely the initial form and content of chaekgeori paintings promoted by King Jeongjo. This is a bookshelf-style chaekgeori (chaekgado) consisting almost entirely of books and devoid of other materialistic objects. The bookshelf serves as the framework of this ten-panel screen painting, and it indicates the sensuous pleasure of owning and maintaining what is suggested to be an unlimited collection of books. However, when placed in the context of Joseon society, where the fabrication and distribution of books were highly regulated as a vehicle for sociopolitical and economic control, the embodied economic and scholastic status represented by the sheer quantity of the books in the painting is staggering. This abundance can therefore be understood as depicting an ecstatic frenzy of greed that went squarely against the austere and almost monastic modus operandi of the Joseon Confucianism that Jeongjo intended to promote. Although presumably to a lesser degree, Jeongjo himself admitted to such pleasure.[7] Thus, we can see how the pleasure of indulgence and the excess of materialism can be seen even in a painting expressly commissioned to promote only ascetic Confucian values.

Kyoungtack Hong's *Library* series exploits this duality. Although Hong paints still lifes with a proliferation of books, birds, and plants, the results often are surrealistic and have vanity-infused overtones. This effect, clearly intentional, is in many ways due to the banal and ubiquitous connotations of many of today's mass-produced objects and how said objects are inherent to the fabric of our daily lives. Whereas in traditional chaekgeori paintings objects take on a privileged aura, worthy of attention and rising to the level of beauty, in Hong's paintings the materials of old—Chinese ceramics, rolls of fabric, lacquered stationery boxes, flowers, and fruit—yield to plastics, mass-produced disposables, and impersonal objects. Skewed by sheer volume and quantity, these objects no longer hold the aura of affluence. Mass production negates not only art in the traditional sense, but also the notion of personal possession, originality, and personal taste that had made chaekgeori such a popular painting genre throughout Jongjo's Joseon and beyond.

However, Hong's innovation of the chaekgeori genre is not limited simply to the replacement of books with disposable commodities. He also experiments with depth and form. To overcome the disconnect induced by differing concepts of materiality, abundance, and other associated values, Hong offers alternatives. Where traditional chaekgeori paintings focus on objects, emphasized by their three-dimensional qualities set against flat fields, Hong pays particular attention to the space beyond the drawing planes and renders the objects contained within almost meaningless.

In Hong's *Library 3* (fig. 5), thousands of books become spatial defining objects, backgrounds, and pedestals for hundreds of mass-produced toys that, due to sheer quantity and a preconceived notion of their value, are of little importance. What makes *Library 3* so interesting are the figures that are not within but rather outside of the book walls. The cornucopia of mass-produced objects that appears to stretch infinitely is thus interrupted and its meaning rendered insignificant by seemingly small figures. On the left side of the painting, three skulls occupy the space. Symbolizing death, they serve as a stark contrast to the durable plasticity of the toys, as if to forecast impending doom. On the right side, through a small opening, a face, partially blocked by a statue of the Virgin Mary, stares back at the viewers. With the Virgin Mary serving as an ironic yet quintessential representation of Western religion, ethics, and humanity, Hong reminds viewers that there is more to life than ownership of uncountable objects that no longer have any value. These ideals and belief frameworks may be a way to escape materialistic immersion and reach higher ideas of ethics and redemption.

Books again become space-defining context in Hong's *Library—Mt. Everest* (fig. 6). In contrast to *Library 3*, there are no plastic toys and the overall composition is much simpler. In some ways, the restrained contents of the painting—a comprehensible amount of books, a chalice, an owl, a candelabra, a dog sculpture made of chrome—harkens back to an earlier style of chaekgeori where strategic employment of exotica promoted elevated values. Here, books and bookshelves form a frame that opens to an almost photorealistic image of Mt. Everest. The deliberately fake-looking books pale in comparison to the vastness of nature represented in the background, suggestive of the limited knowledge one can gain from books alone. The owl in the bottom-right corner of the painting represents the goddess of wisdom ready to lead the audience to the natural world. Again, Hong offers an alternative to the chaekgeori genre through an expanded representation of space and a near inversion of the traditional meanings of the objects embodied in such paintings, both in an artistic and also in a socioeconomic-political sense.

In our world of mass-produced objects, reinforced by a culture of disposability, books have lost the special panache of exoticism and luxury that used to reflect auspiciously on the personal proclivities of the owner. Once symbolizing the lofty aspirations of scholarship and material desires, in Hong's paintings those aspirations are clearly unfulfilled. Although material desires still remain, those desires are currently frustrated in contemporary society by the prevalence of uncountable objects possessing little inherent meaning.

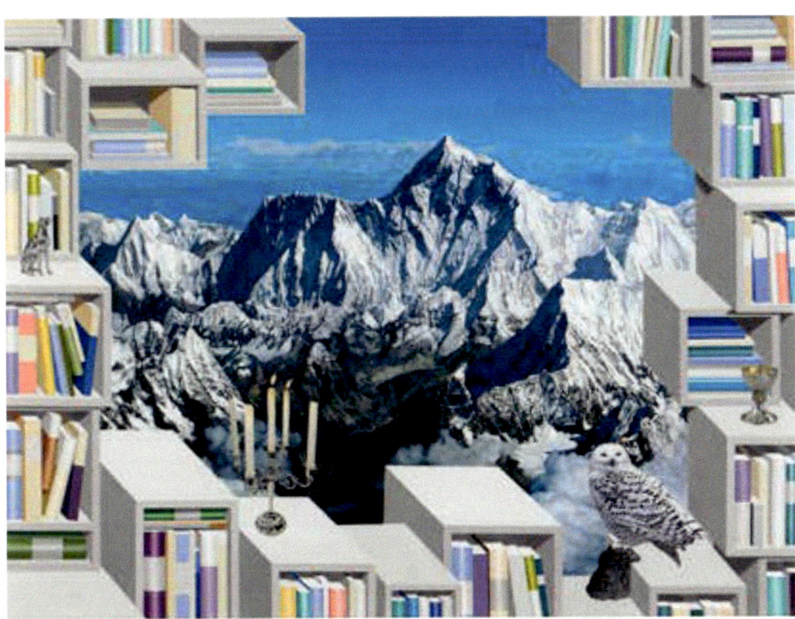

Fig. 6. Kyoungtack Hong (b. 1968). *Library—Mt. Everest*, 2014. Acrylic and oil on linen, 194 x 259 cm.

Continuing Tradition

The significance of any art consists largely in the work's ability to carry and communicate embodied meaning. For the past two centuries, no other genre or medium in the entire tradition of Korean art, in both literati and folk paintings, so engaged and documented the culture of consumption as chaekgeori did. Today, a diverse body of artists continues this tradition into the twenty-first century, coming together to examine contemporary Korean society and its social, cultural, and political attitudes and ideals.

In showcasing through light the inner essence of books, Airan Kang's *Digital Book Project* is truly an acknowledgement of Korea's history and the opposing yet complementary forces of Confucian intellectualism and materialistic indulgence. Kang dissolves the material of the book in her art, proving that the value of a book lies not in physical form or even actual content, in how it in itself signifies whether it is Confucian or materialistic or both.

Stephanie S. Lee's paintings, however, explicitly reflect the dual symbolic nature of books and a contemporary culture based on materialism. Chaekgeori has always been a highly symbolic mode of painting. The fact that the genre originated and was popular during a time when a Confucian society was transitioning into a more materialistic one makes it a fitting and valuable tool to innovate and experiment with in our own increasingly materialistic era.

Likewise, Kyoungtack Hong's paintings are similar to chaekgeori in basic format, namely how they depict and emphasize an abundance of objects to express mass production in a consumer society. However, Hong's works point its audience toward possibilities of ethics and redemption in the overwhelming plastic abundance of modernity.

Drawing the lineage and making comparisons to the traditional form and objectives of chaekgeori with modern examples suggests one way to facilitate a better understanding of the diverse Korean society that, from Confucian Joseon to the hyper-materialistic culture of today, is in constant flux.

The Charles B. Wang Center showcased chaekgeori screens alongside the works of a diverse body of contemporary artists who continue this genre into the twenty-first century. Seven contemporary artists featured in the exhibition were Seongmin Ahn, Kyoungtack Hong, Patrick Hughes, Airan Kang, Young-Shik Kim, Stephanie S. Lee, and Sungpa.

1 Kim, S. 2014, 7.

2 Jeong, J. 2011, 223.

3 Bak 2009, 170–91.

4 Chung 2011, 65–66.

5 Kang, M. 2015, 10–13. This book is devoted to early adaptations of eyeglasses, telescopes, and alarm clocks in eighteenth-century Joseon.

6 Sunglim Kim identified the emergence of the jungin as urban bourgeois who fostered the connoisseurship of chaekgeori painting. The jungin class refers to middle-class people whose status lay between the literati and merchant classes. They were skilled administrators, such as interpreters and traders who traveled with official amboys. Kim, S. 2014, 11–13.

7 Ibid., 7.

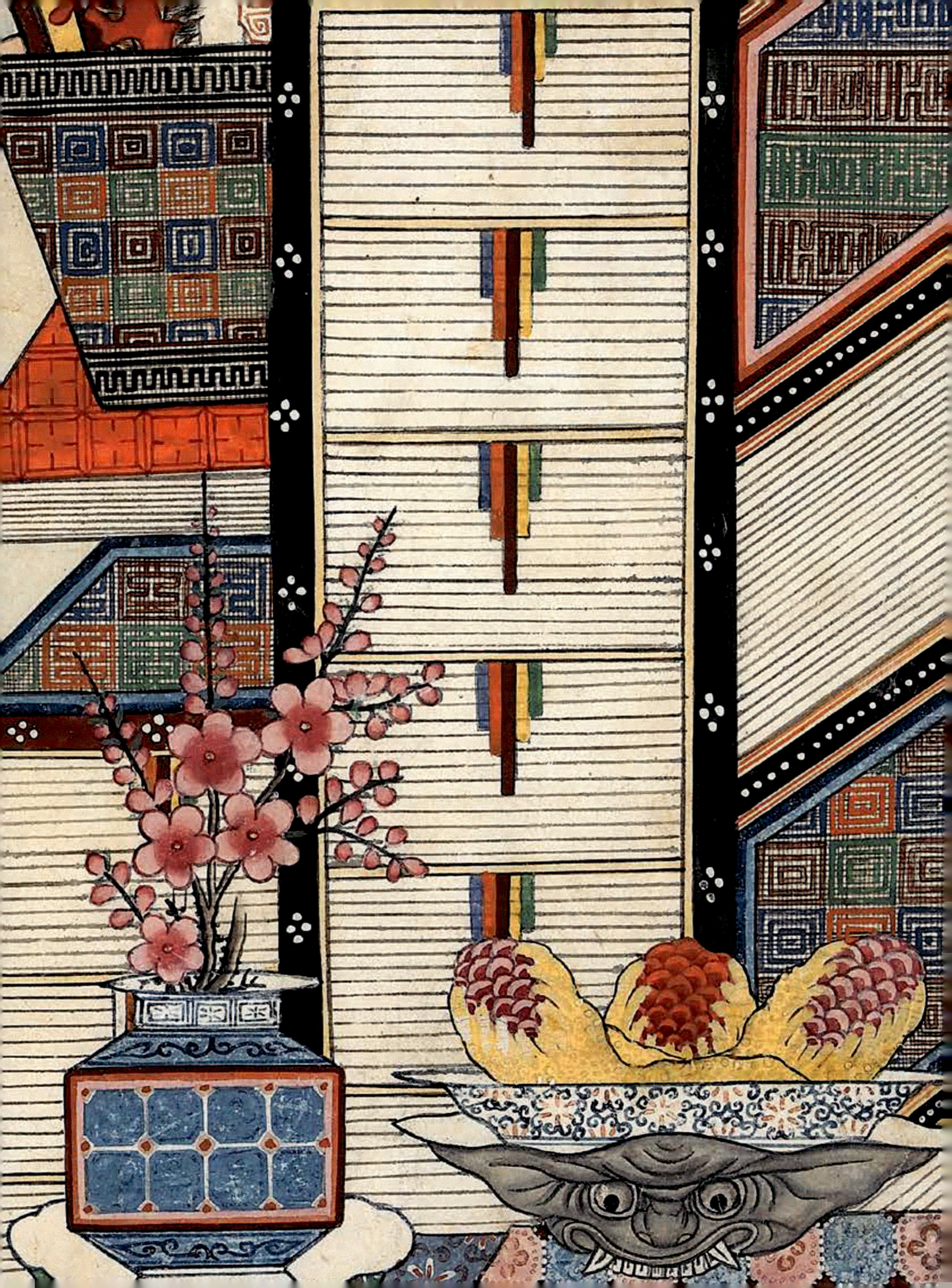

CHAEKGEORI

Books and Things

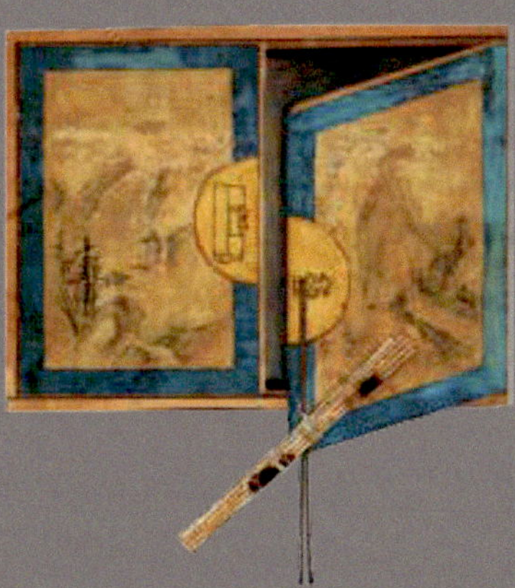

Catalogue entry authors

BC	Byungmo Chung
JJ	Jinyoung Jin
JJL	Jungsil Jenny Lee
JL	Ja Won Lee
SK	Sunglim Kim
SM	Sooa McCormick

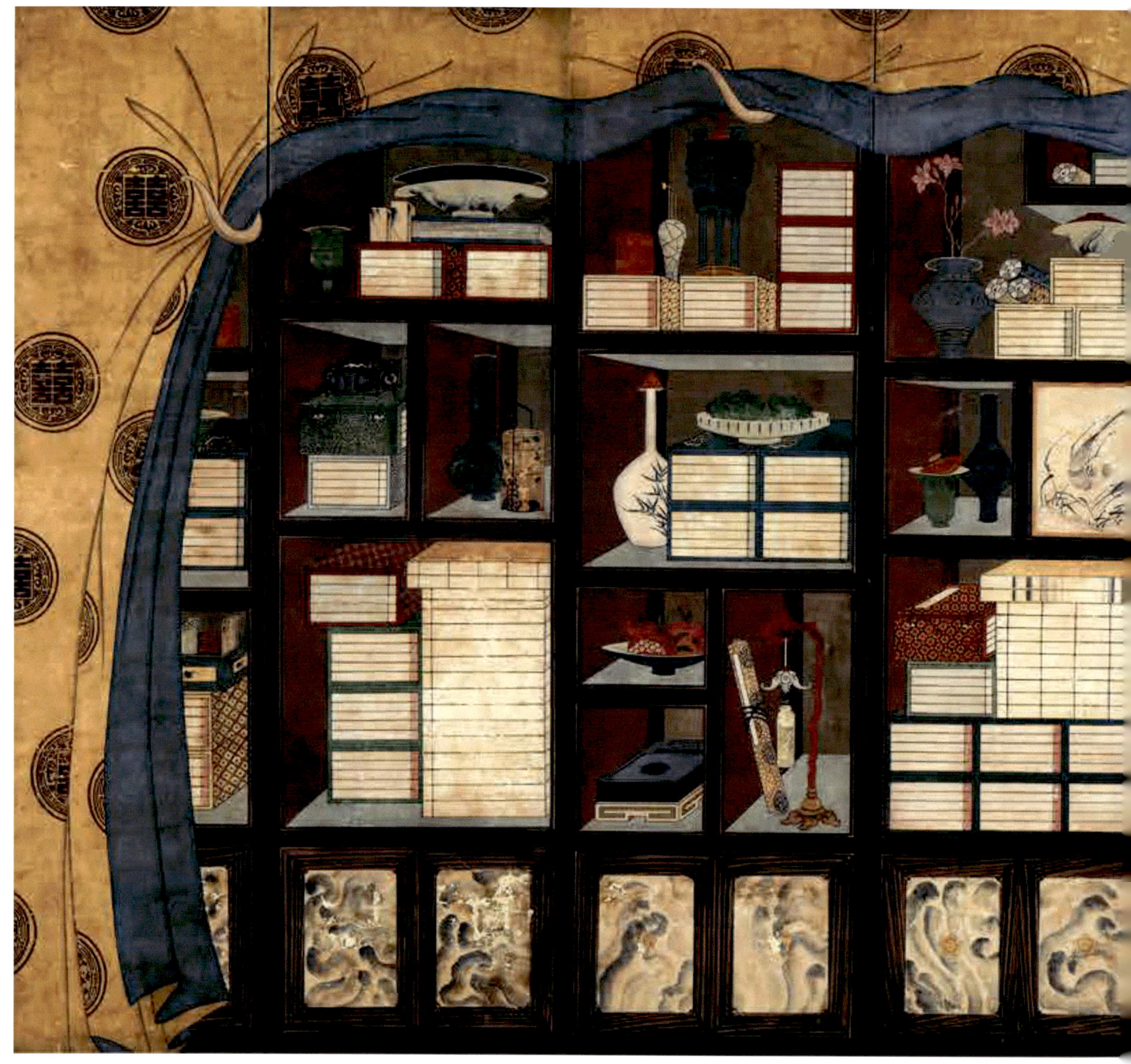

1 *Chaekgado*

Jang Hanjong (1768–1815), late 18th century
Eight-panel folding screen
Color on paper, 195 x 361 cm (overall)
Gyeonggi Provincial Museum, Yongin

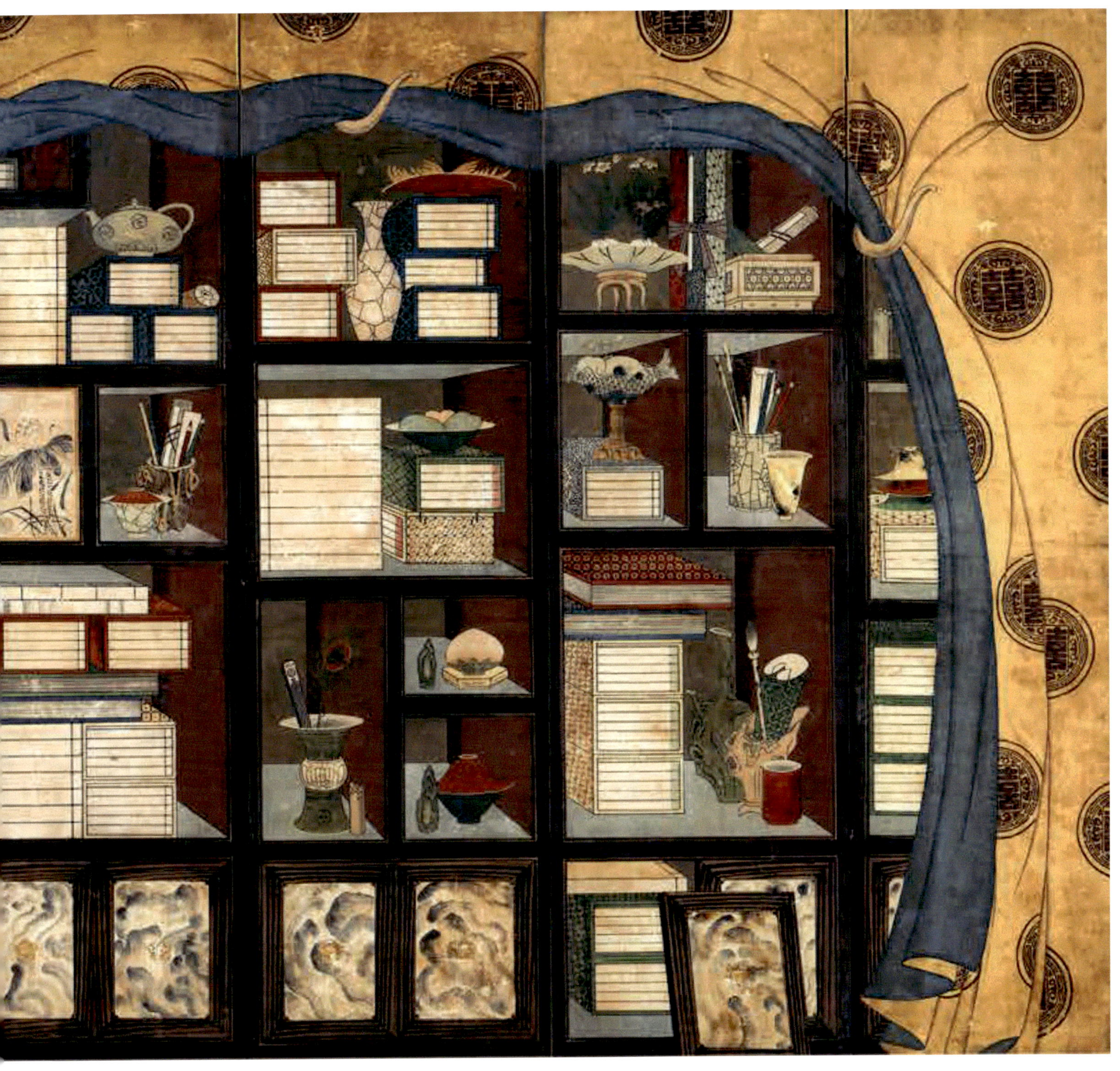

On the 18th day of the 9th month 1788, King Jeongjo exiled two leading court painters, Sin Hanpyeong and Yi Jonghyeon, because he was dissatisfied with the drafts they had submitted for chaekgeori screens. While that day must have been a humiliating one for the two senior painters, it provided an excellent opportunity for young Jang Hanjong and his fellow painters Kim Jaegong and Heo Yong to start their careers as painters-in-waiting. With that opportunity, chaekgeori seemed to have become one of Jang's specialties.

In this screen, the bookshelves make a dramatic appearance as if their owner had just lifted a drapery to reveal his collection to his guests. Jang carefully arranged a myriad of exported Chinese objects: ancient bronze vessels, a yixing clay teapot, colorful porcelains, and stoneware with crackle patterns. The artist also highlighted some of the characteristic features of Korean display shelves: paintings of bird and flowers, which were often pasted over the inside panels of cabinet doors, and black marbling of persimmon wood panels. BC, SM

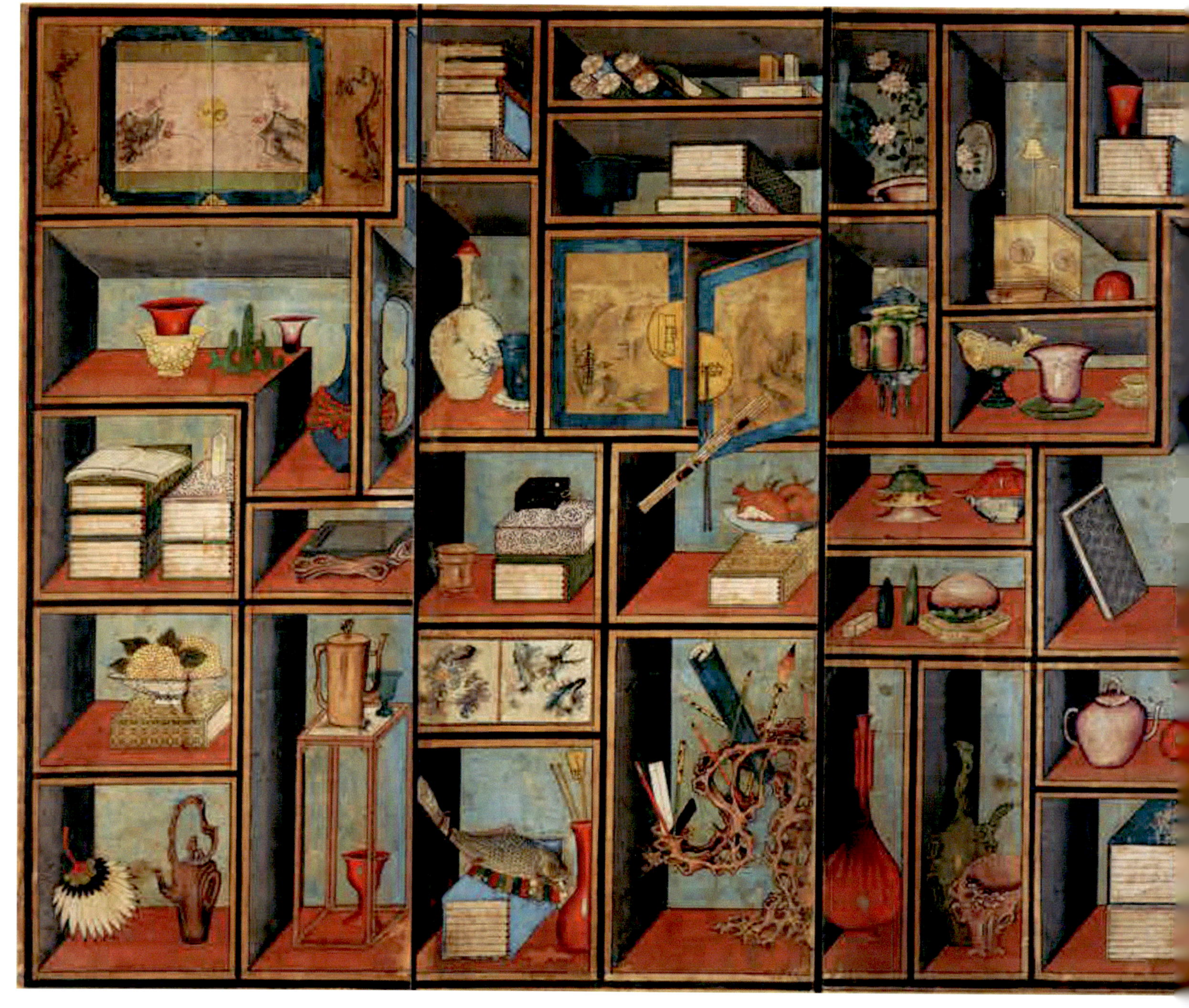

2 *Chaekgado*

Anonymous, late 18th–early 19th century
Six-panel screen
Ink and color on paper, 153 x 352 cm (overall)
Private collection

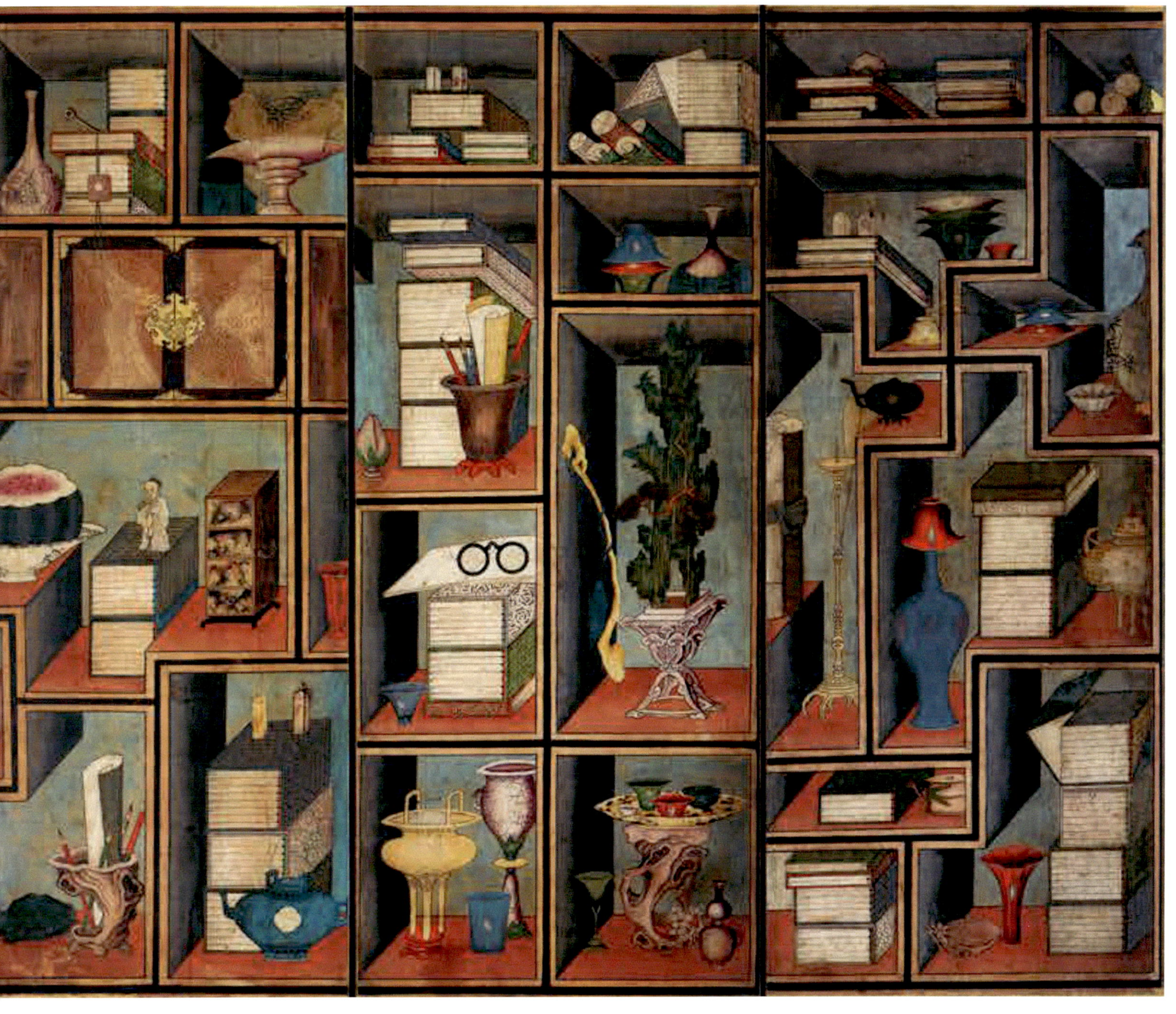

This screen is filled with curios imported from China. A mixture of books and commodities (such as imported Chinese ceramics, brushes, paper, eyeglasses, and the like) compete for pride of place and the attention of the viewer. The objects symbolize the inquisitiveness and zeal that motivated the Joseon literati of the eighteenth century to accelerate the development of their society. The Western techniques of trompe l'oeil, linear perspective, and shading are used here to give a sense of depth and presence to the furniture and accoutrements. BC, JJ

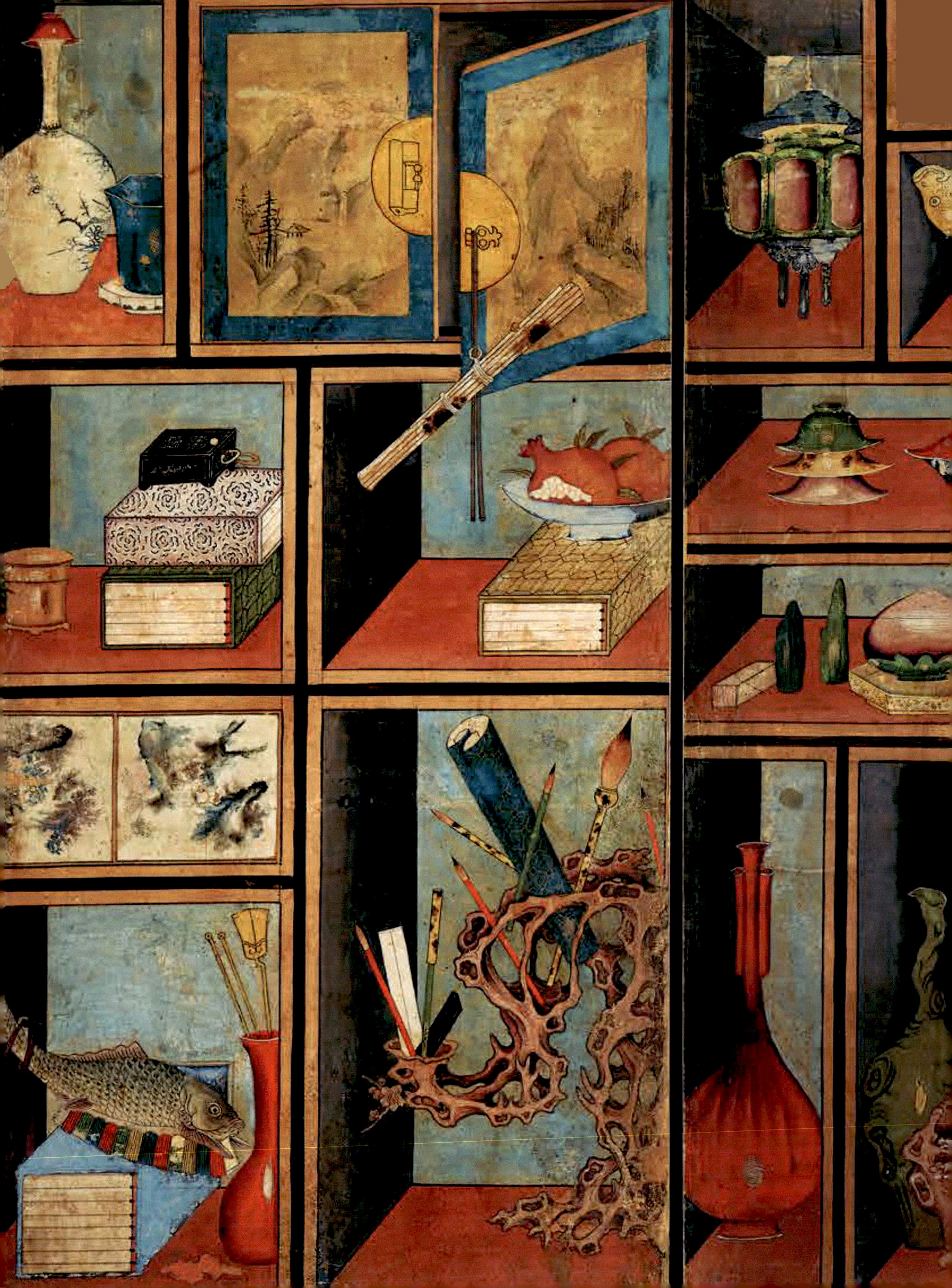

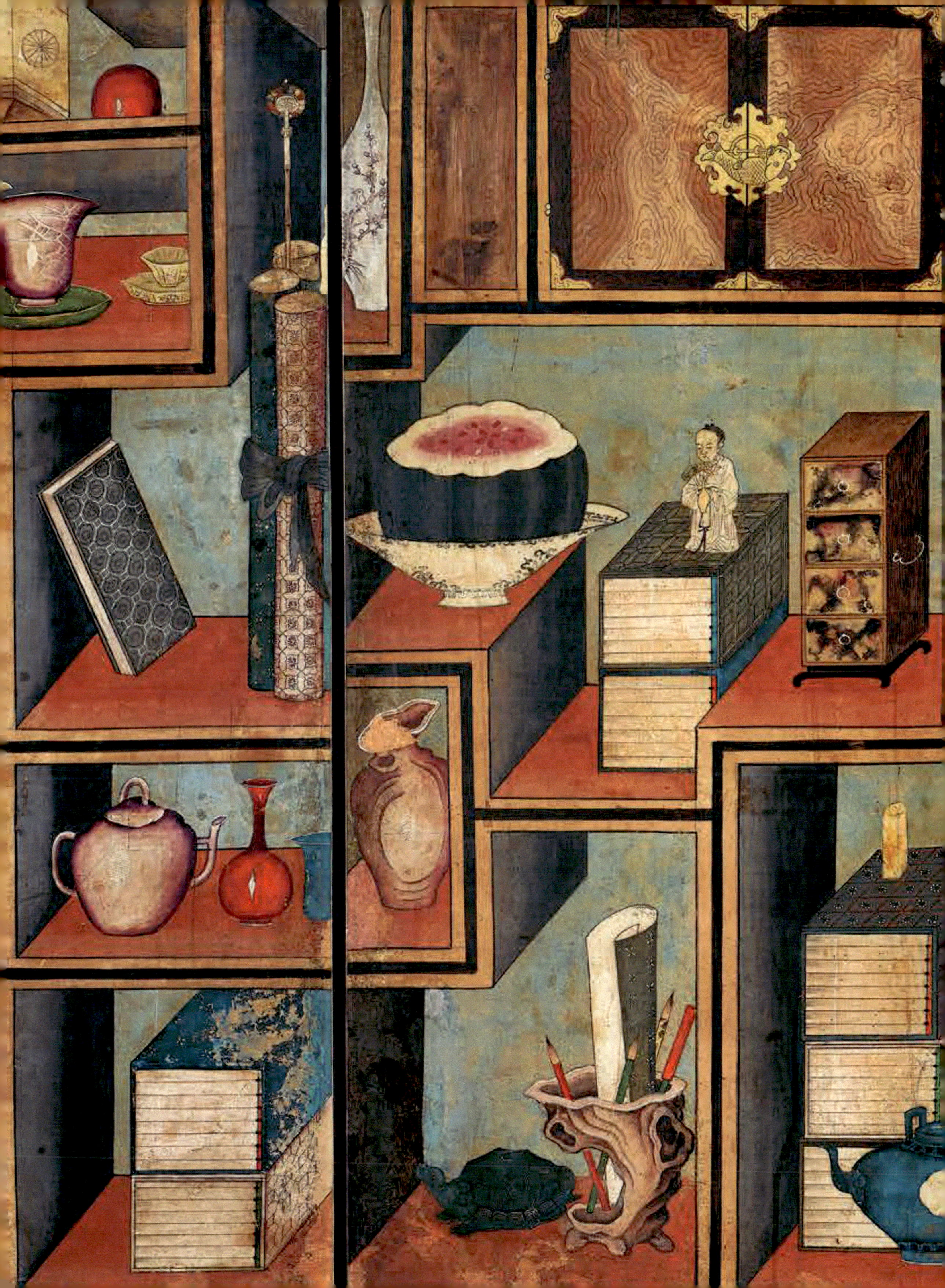

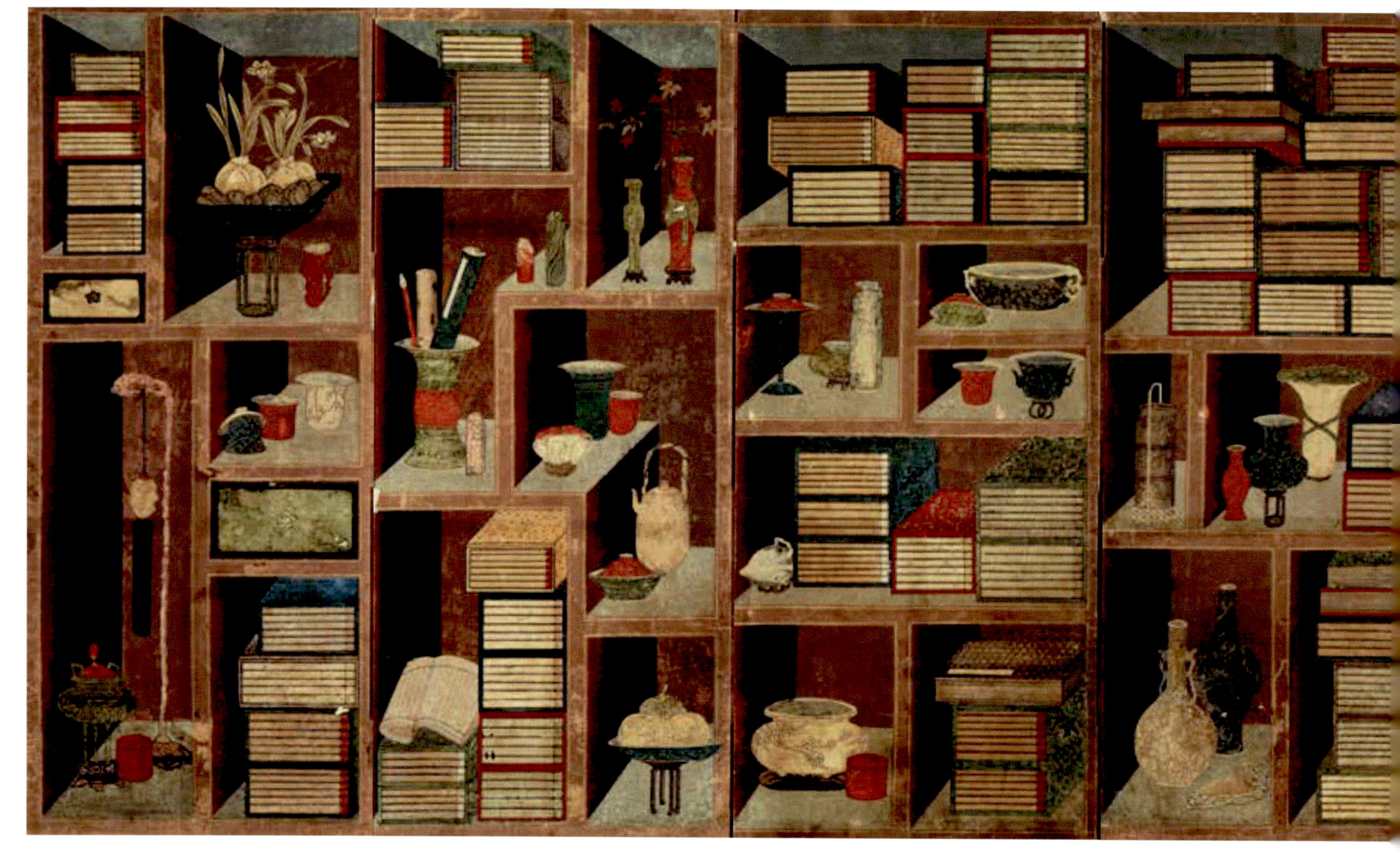

3 *Chaekgado*

Anonymous, late 18th or early 19th century
Eight-panel screen
Ink and color on paper, 112 x 381 cm (overall)
Private collection

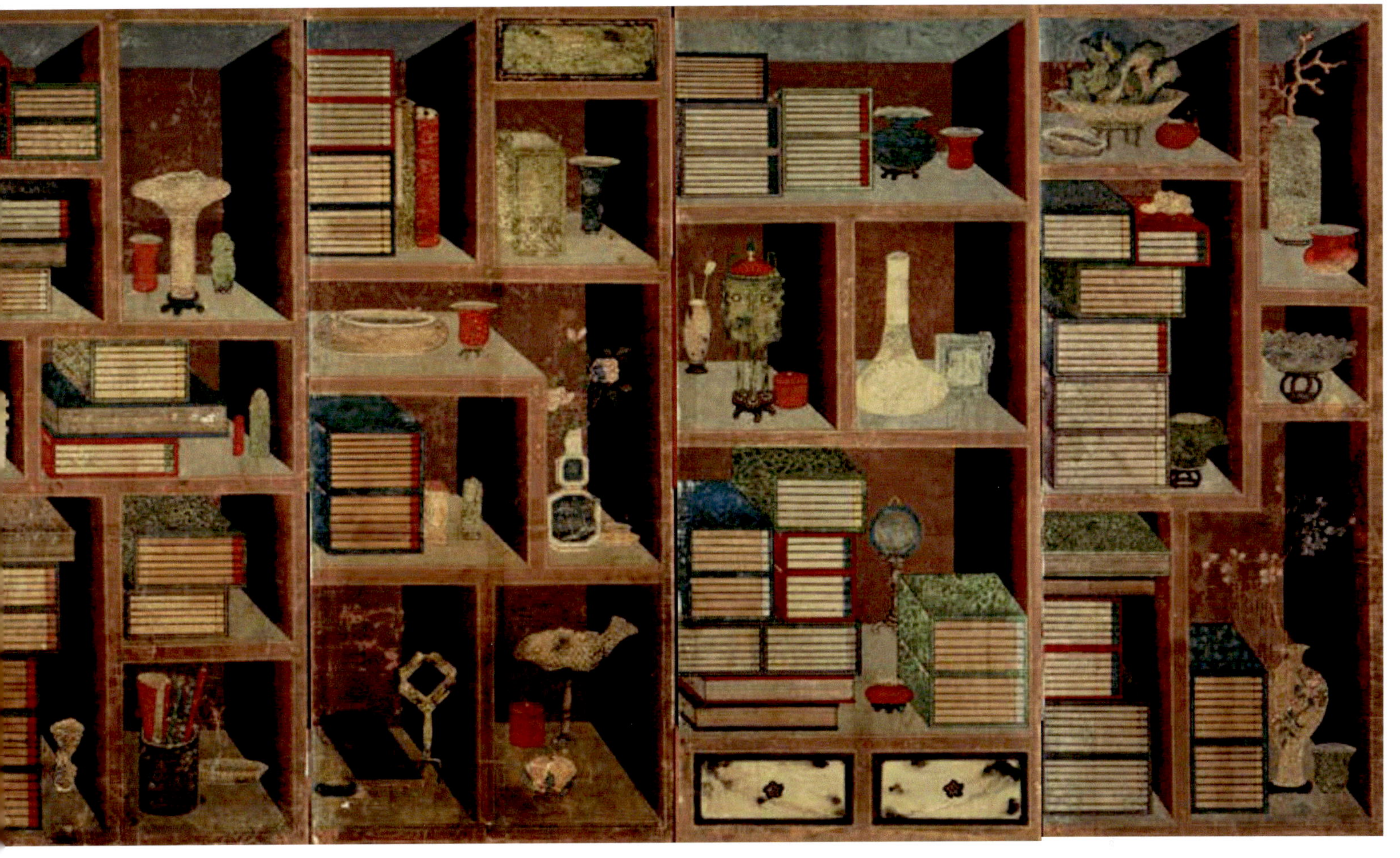

This complex composition of this chaekgado is striking. The fifty-three sections are arranged to perfection, and the drawers placed in between add touches of change to the painting. Though the image makes use of European-origined linear perspective, the vanishing point is not at the center, but slightly above. The work also features items not depicted in other chaekgado, and the accoutrements are adorned with intricate ornamental patterns in gold. The brown tone of the work and the presence of the drawers indicate a date of the late eighteenth or early nineteenth century, similar to Jang Hanjong's chaekgado (plate 1). The seal names the painter, "Giwon," but his identity is not known. This work is said to have been from the royal court. BC, JL

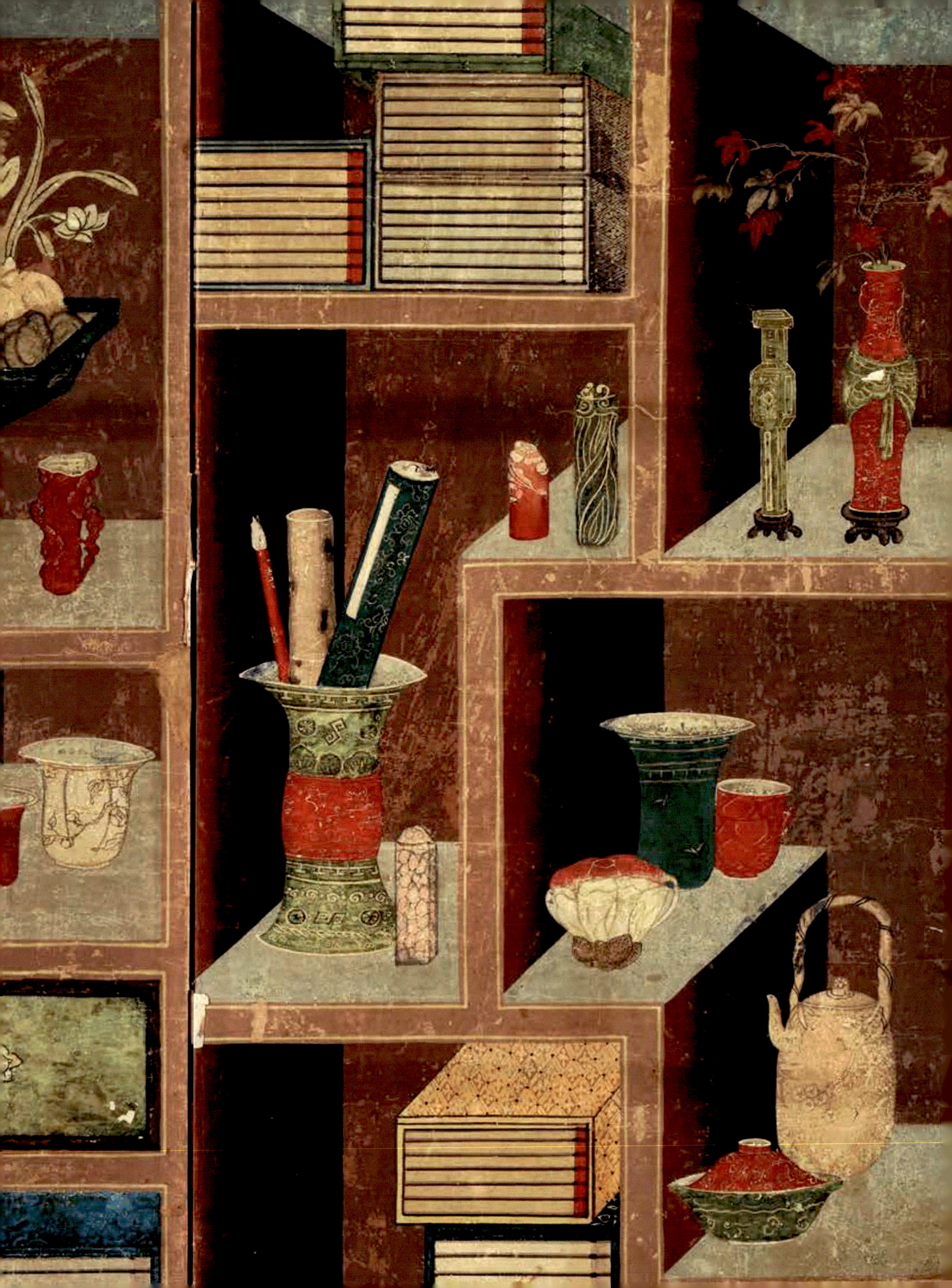

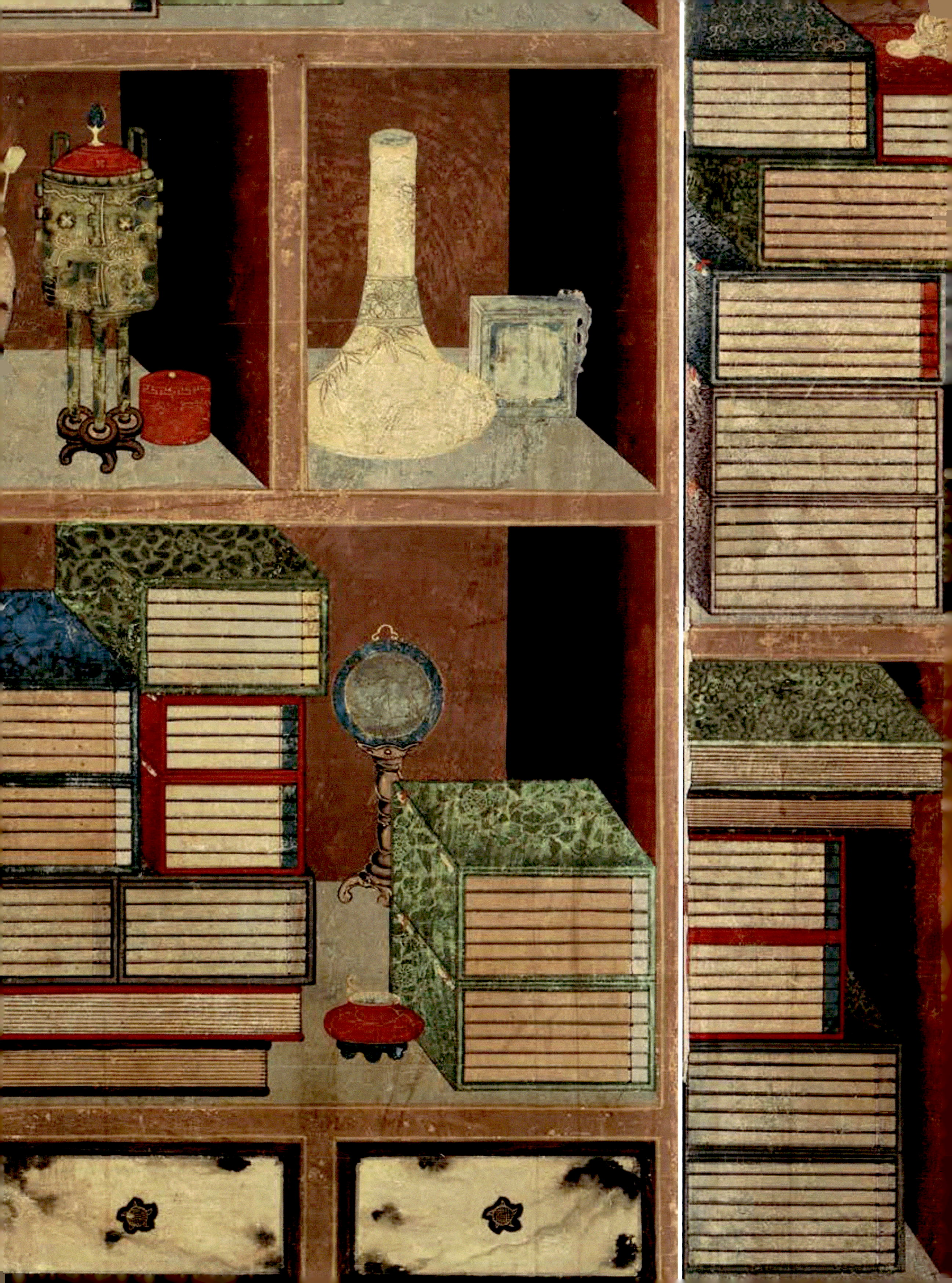

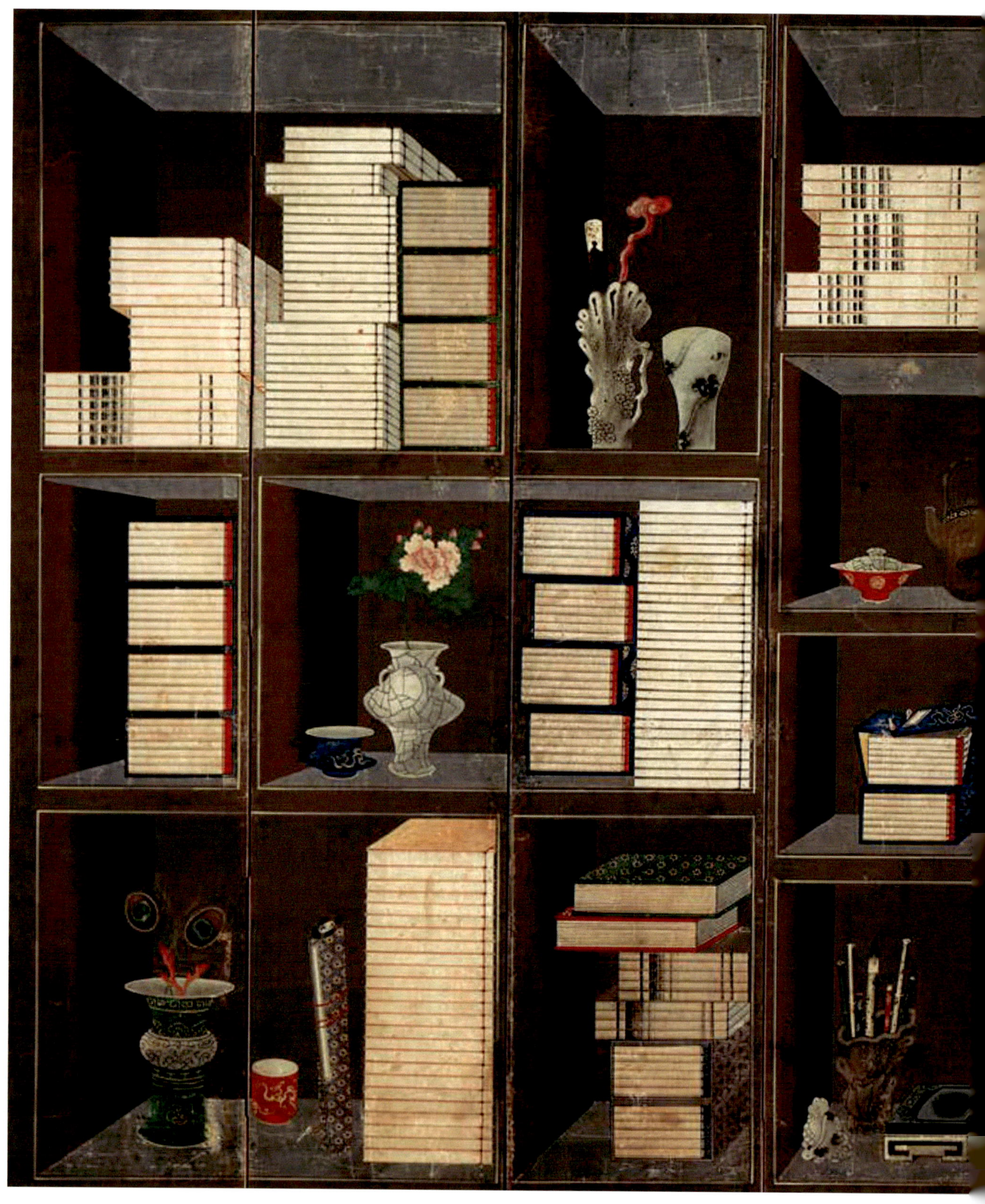

4 *Chaekgado*

Yi Eungnok [Yi Hyeongnok] [Yi Taekgyun] (1808–after 1871), 1860s
Eight-panel folding screen
Ink and color on paper, 203.8 x 289.6 cm (overall)
The Asian Art Museum–Chong-Moon Lee Center for Asian Art and Culture, San Francisco
Acquisition made possible by the Koret Foundation, the Connoisseurs' Council and Korean Art and Culture Committee.
Re-mounting funded by the Society for Asian Art, 1998.111

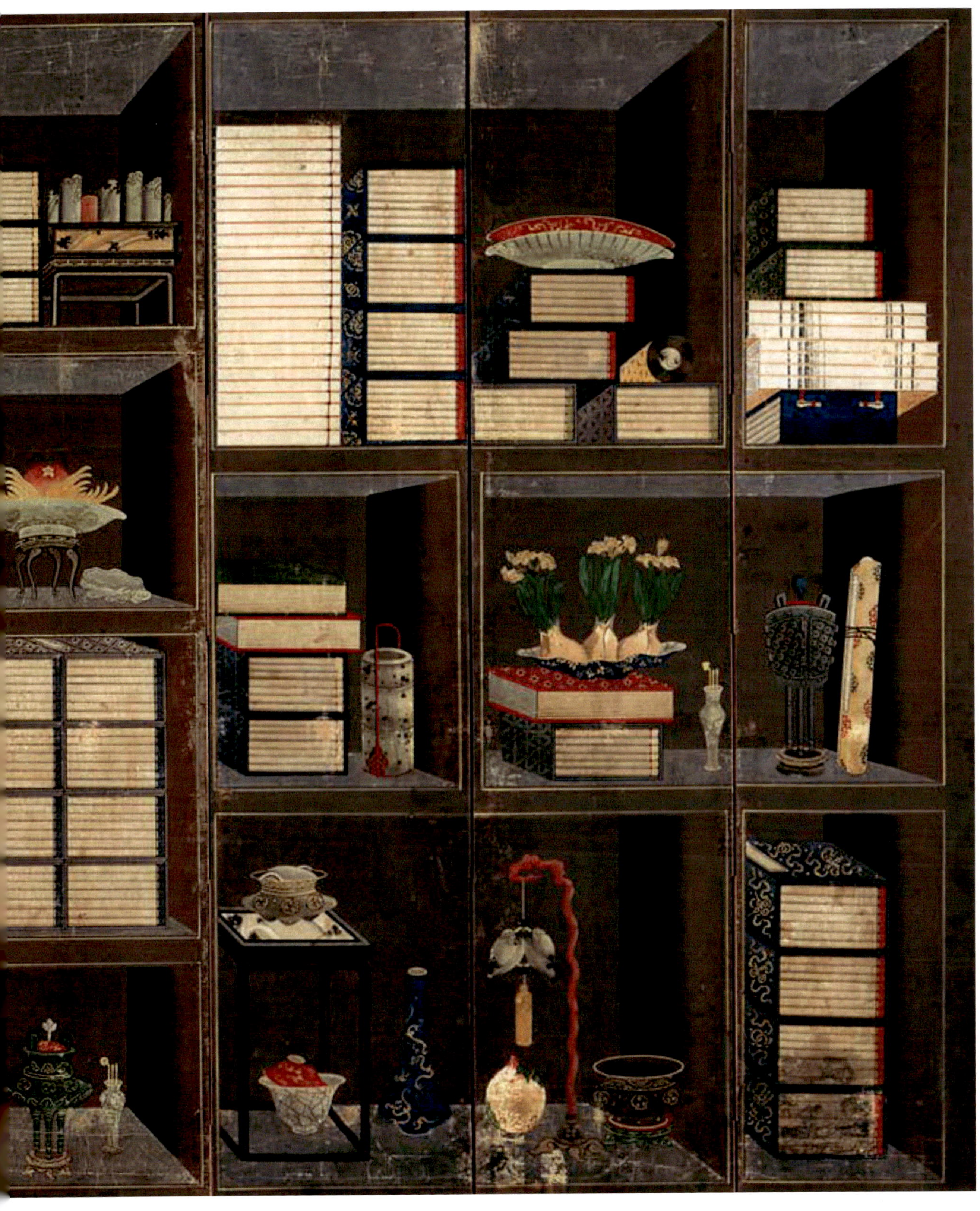

In this screen, the painter expresses his mastery of linear perspective and chiaroscuro, two major European pictorial languages that had been introduced to Korea around the late eighteenth century. The seal on the top shelf of the fourth panel from the right identifies Yi Eungnok, the most famous chaekgado painter in the late nineteenth century, as the painter of the screen. While he did not portray the shadow of each object as cast naturally, he endeavored to express a sense of depth by employing dark-brown shading.

It is generally believed that before Yi changed his name from Hyeongnok to Eungnok, he used brown, the most naturalistic color for a wood bookshelf, and began using dark green after he became Eungnok. However, in this screen, Yi Eungnok used brown for the back of his screen. Despite the name change, Yi here maintained the iconographic repertoire he had used while active under the name Yi Hyeongnok. BC, SM

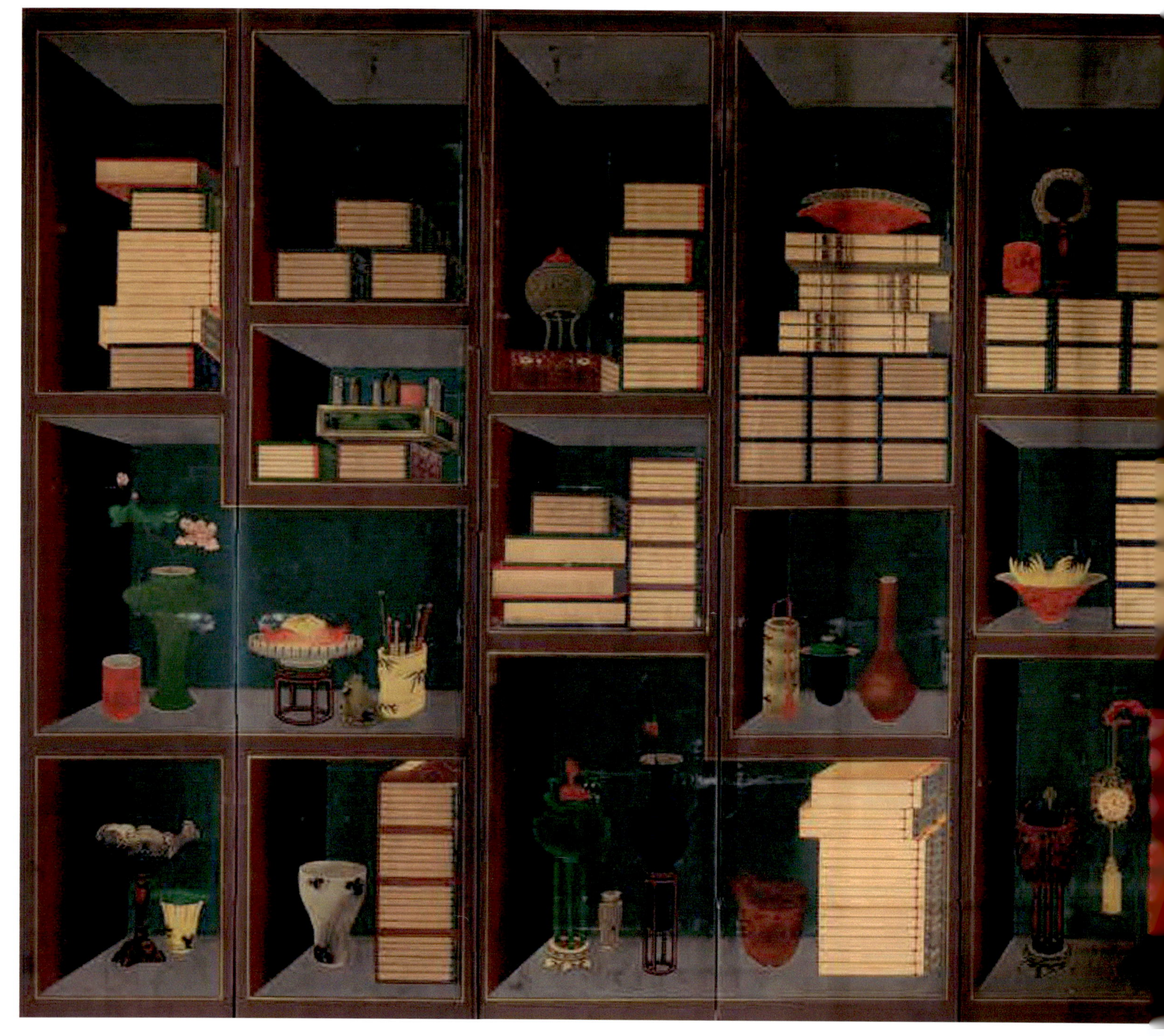

5 *Chaekgado*

Yi Eungnok [Yi Hyeongnok] [Yi Taekgyun] (1808–after 1871), before 1864
Ten-panel folding screen
Ink and color on paper, 153 x 352 cm (overall)
National Museum of Korea, Seoul

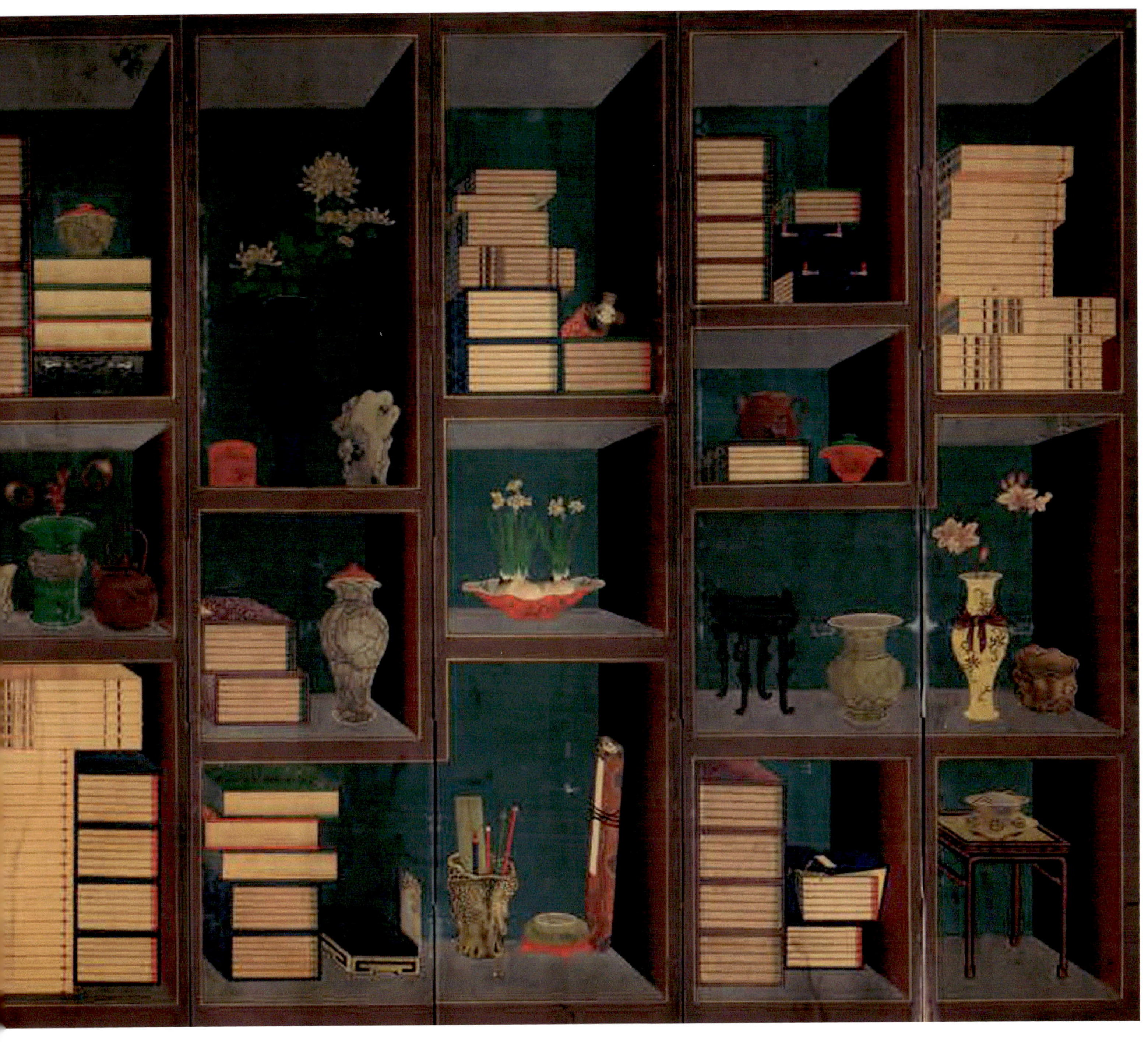

Consisting of thirty-two compartments, this screen displays multiple volumes of books and a variety of objects ranging from scholarly utensils to antiques, all of which would have adorned the scholar's desk and bookshelves. Many of the painted objects were not indigenous Korean luxuries, but rather imported from China. For example, ancient bronze vessels and incense burners, a yixing clay tea ewer, stoneware with crackle patterns, a fish-shaped water container, and a European clock. Korean collectors sought after such objects at Beijing's Liulichang antique street.
BC, SM

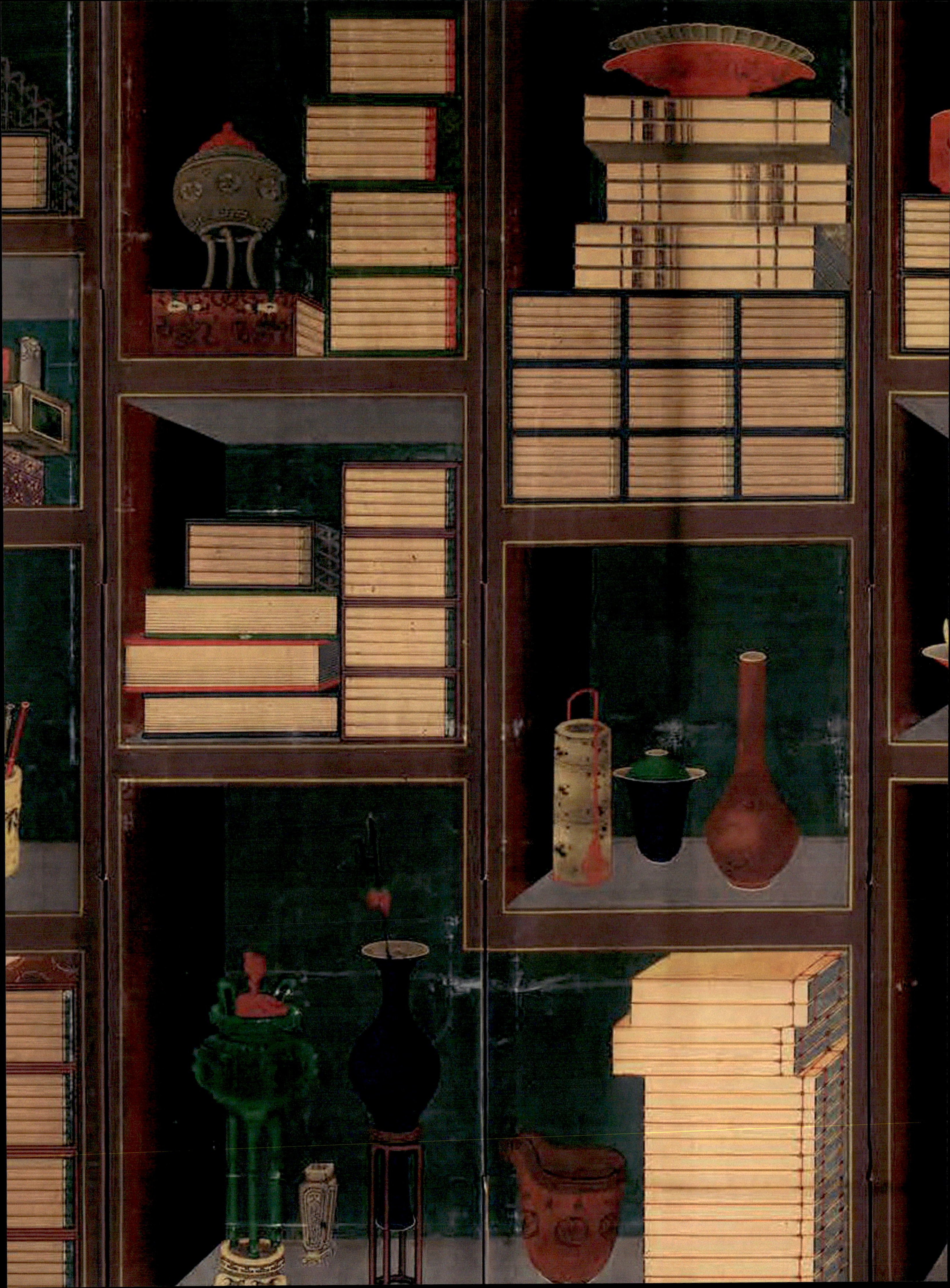

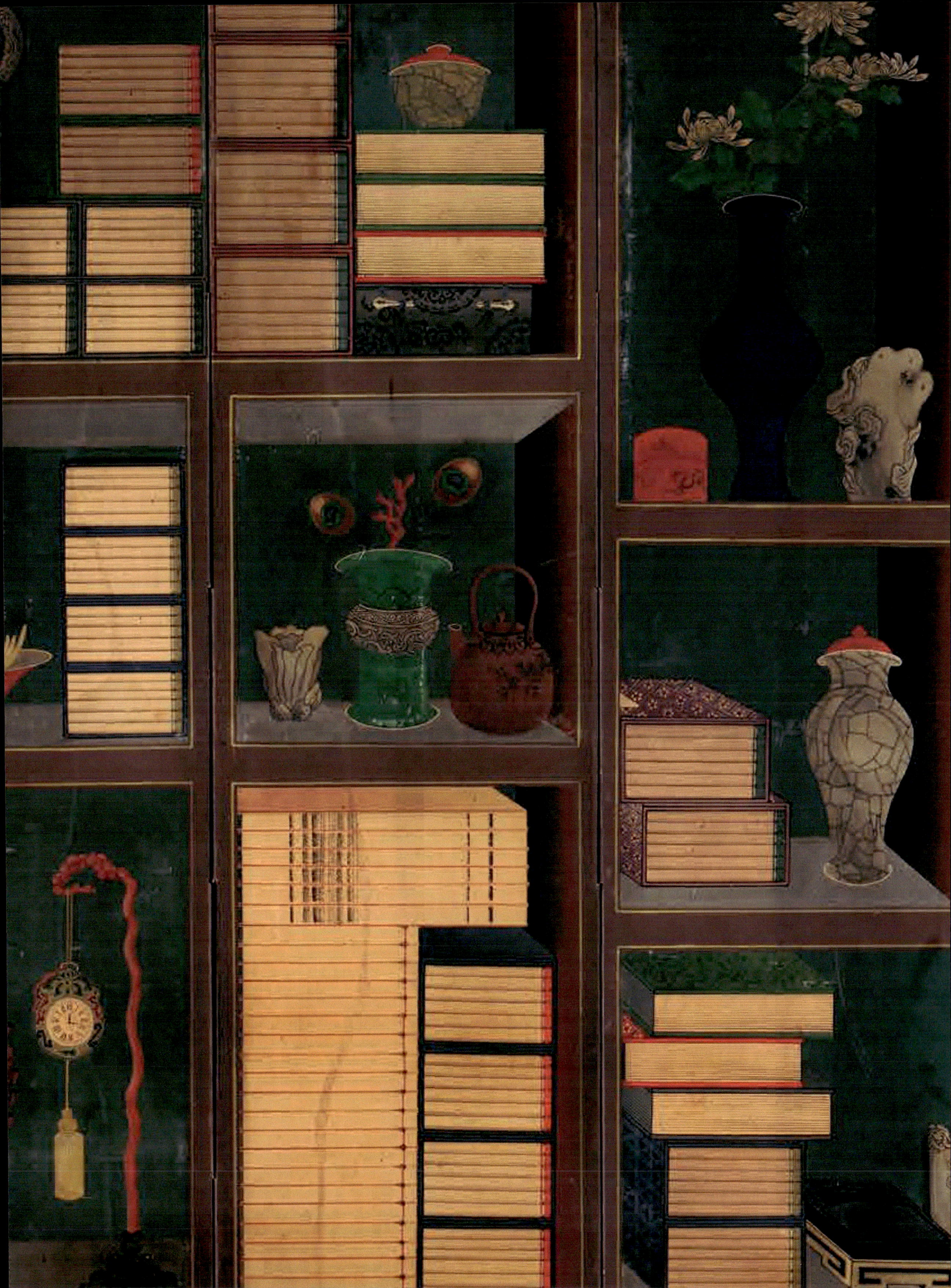

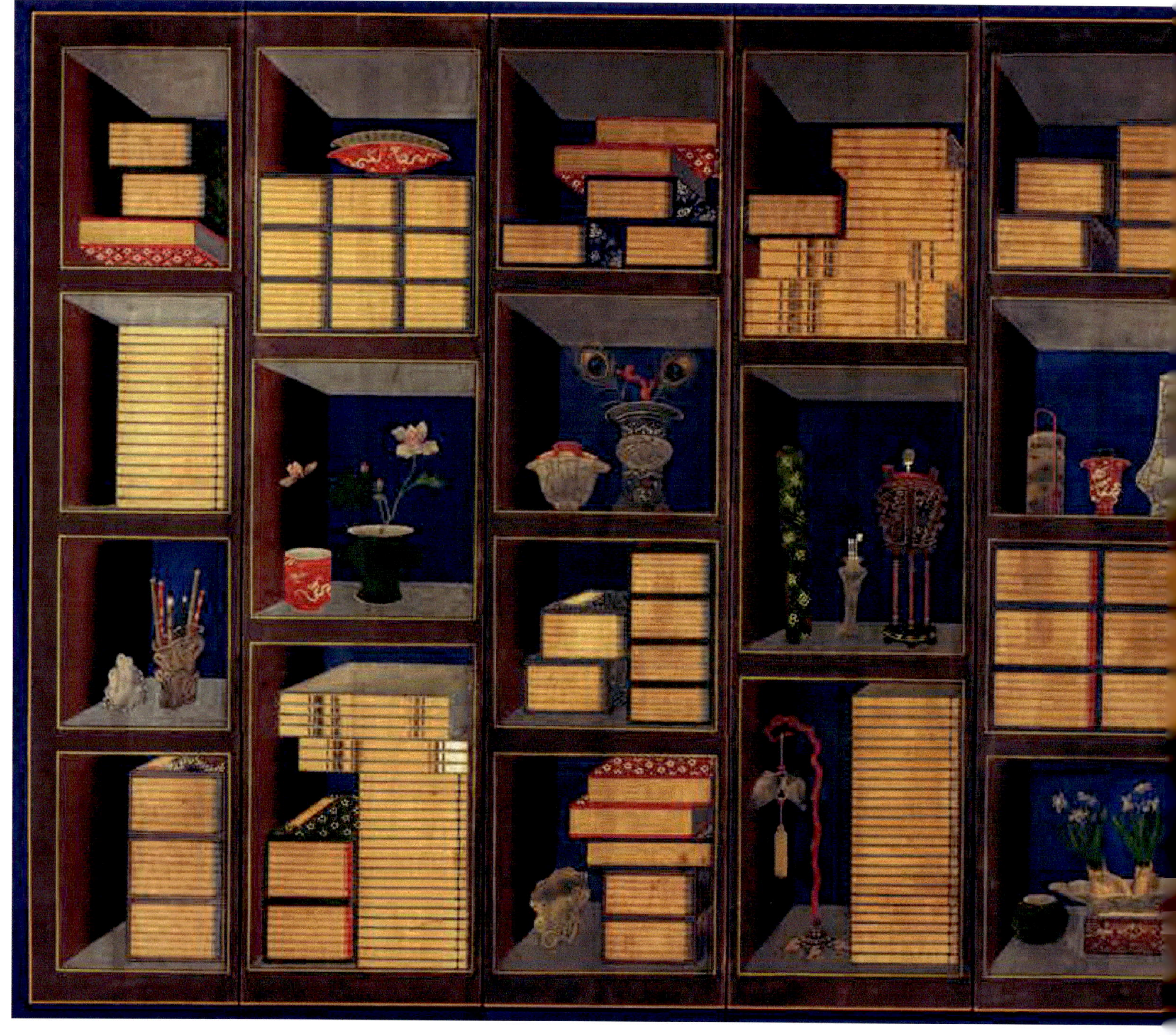

6 *Chaekgado*

Yi Taekgyun [Yi Hyeongnok] [Yi Eungnok] (1808–after 1871)
Ten-panel folding screen
Ink and color on silk, 197.5 x 395 cm (overall)
The Cleveland Museum of Art, Leonard C. Hanna Jr. Fund, 2011.37

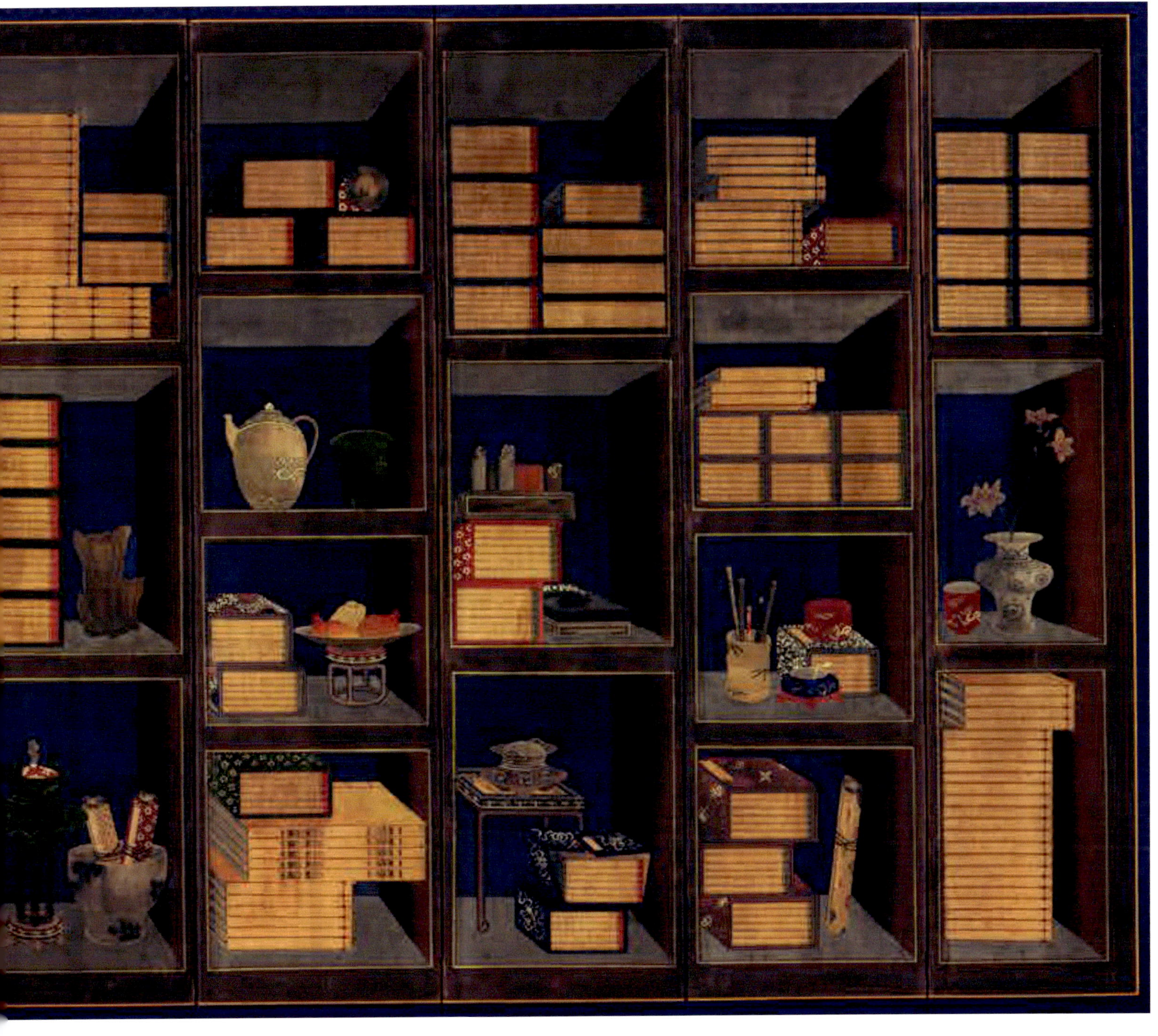

Artful yet utilitarian objects, carefully curated, were often paired or grouped to identify their functions in the scholar's life. For instance, a bamboo brush pot with a seal paste container; a tall, lidded bronze incense burner with a slender vase used to hold an incense spade and chopsticks; a clay yixing teapot with a tea cup and a wood-root container used to hold paper scrolls; a three-tier tortoise shell-patterned lunch container with a slender wine bottle; and a wood-root brush pot with a water dropper.

Because of its seal, this screen has recently been attributed to Yi Taekgyun, one of the most influential chaekgado painters of the late nineteenth century (see pp. 50-62). Two others by Yi Taekgyun are known to include the artist's seal: a ten-panel folding screen in the collection of Tongdo Monastery Museum in Korea, and a ten-panel folding screen in the collection of the Birmingham Museum of Art in Alabama. SM

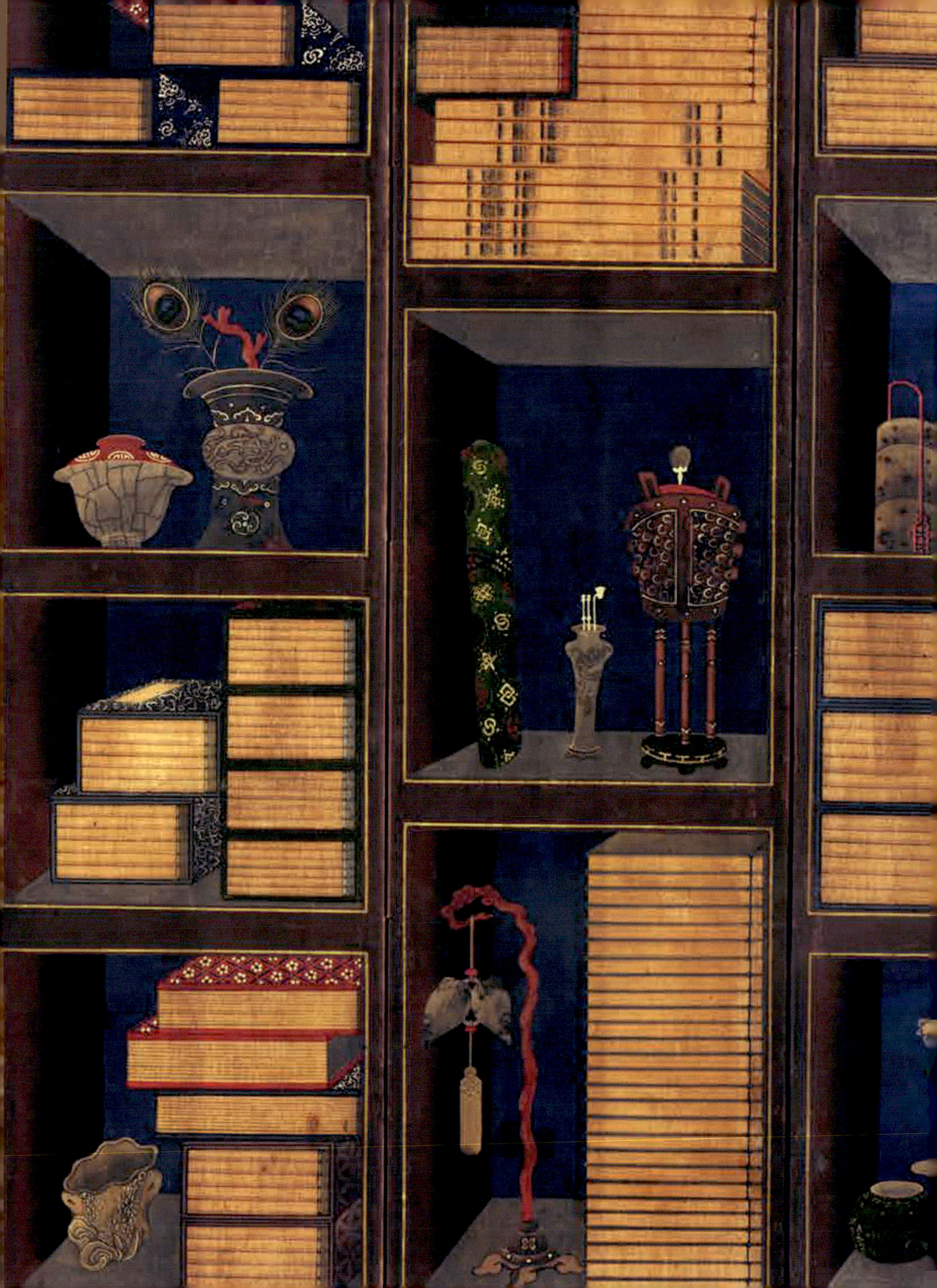

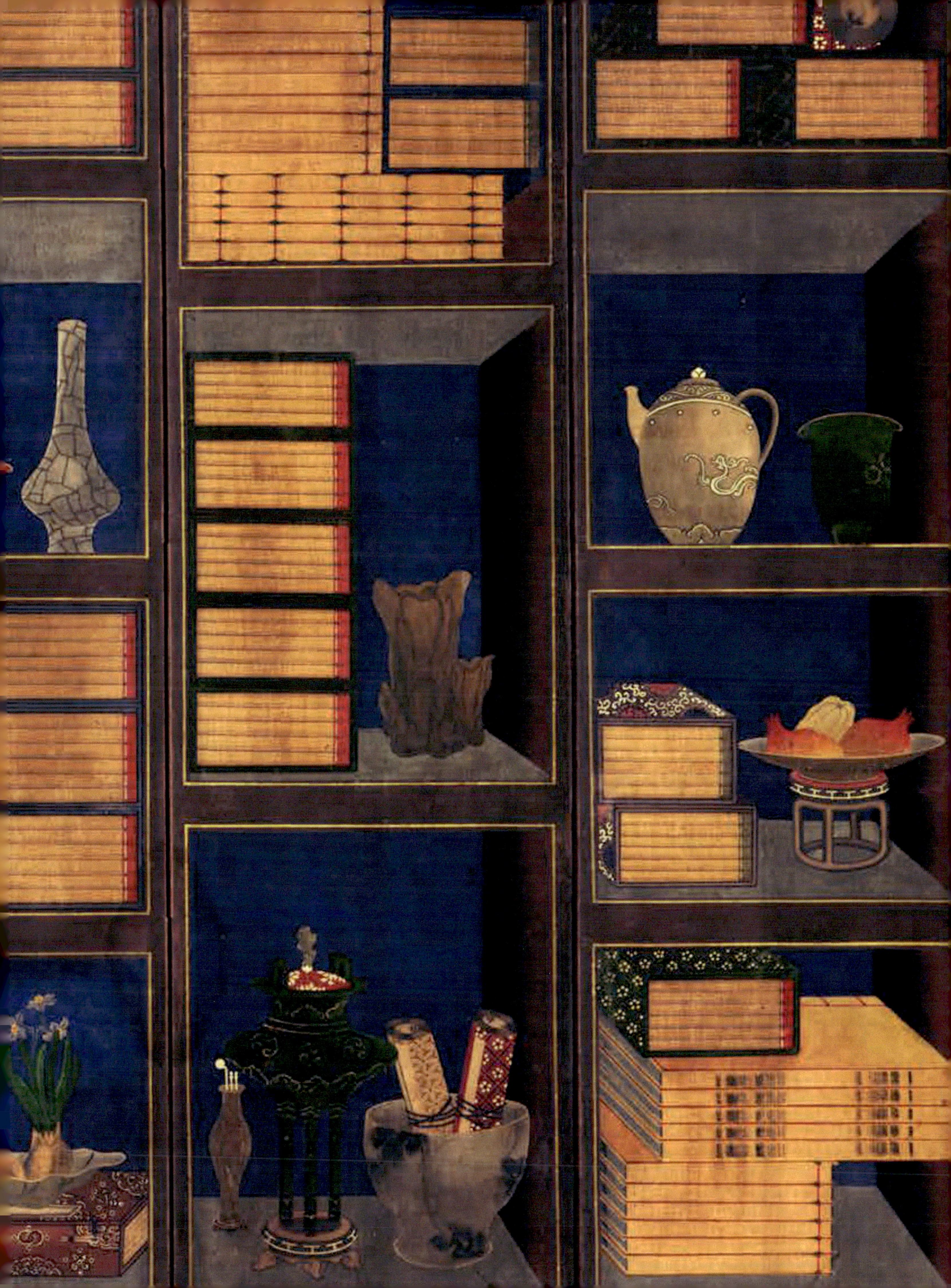

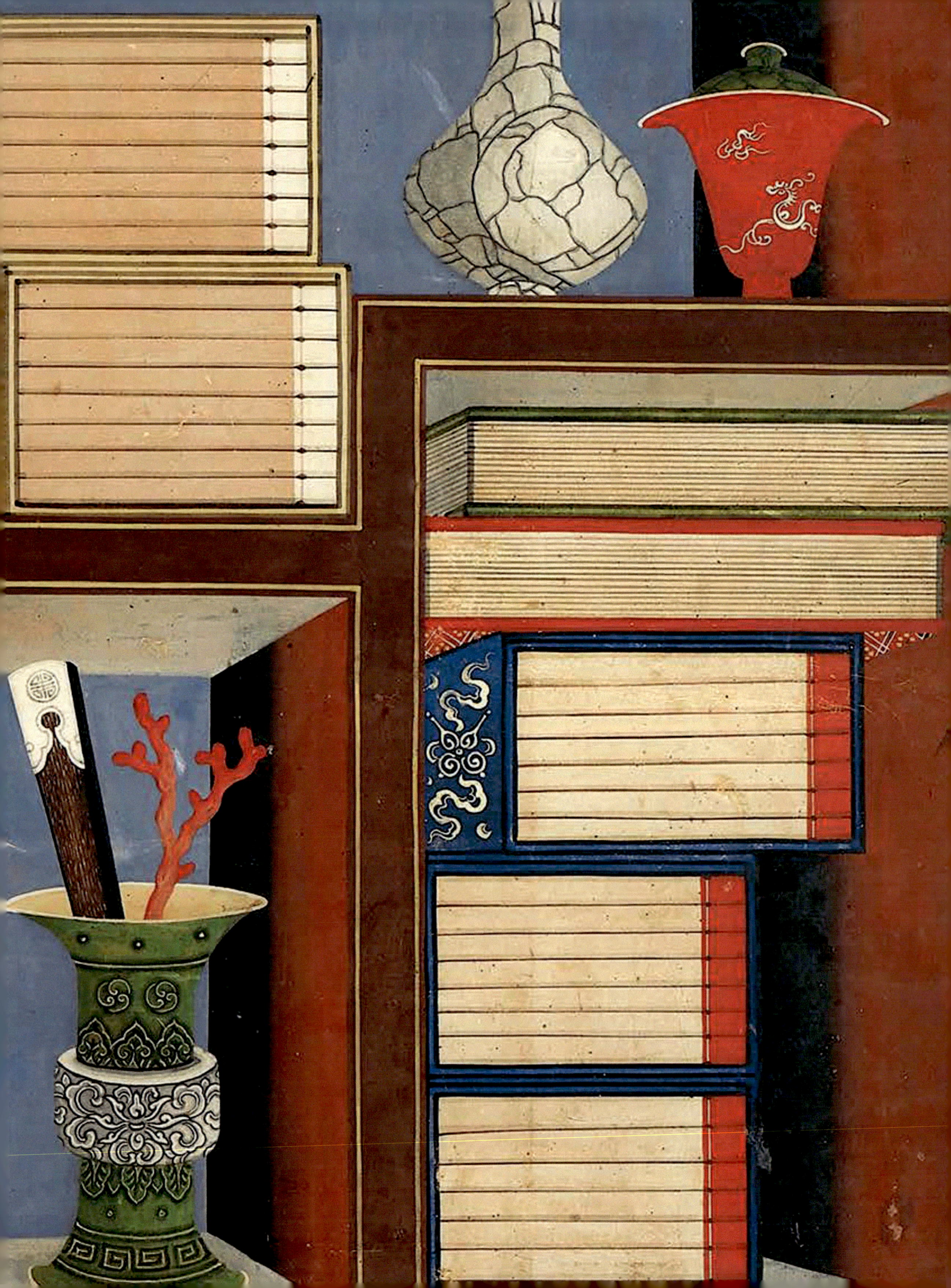

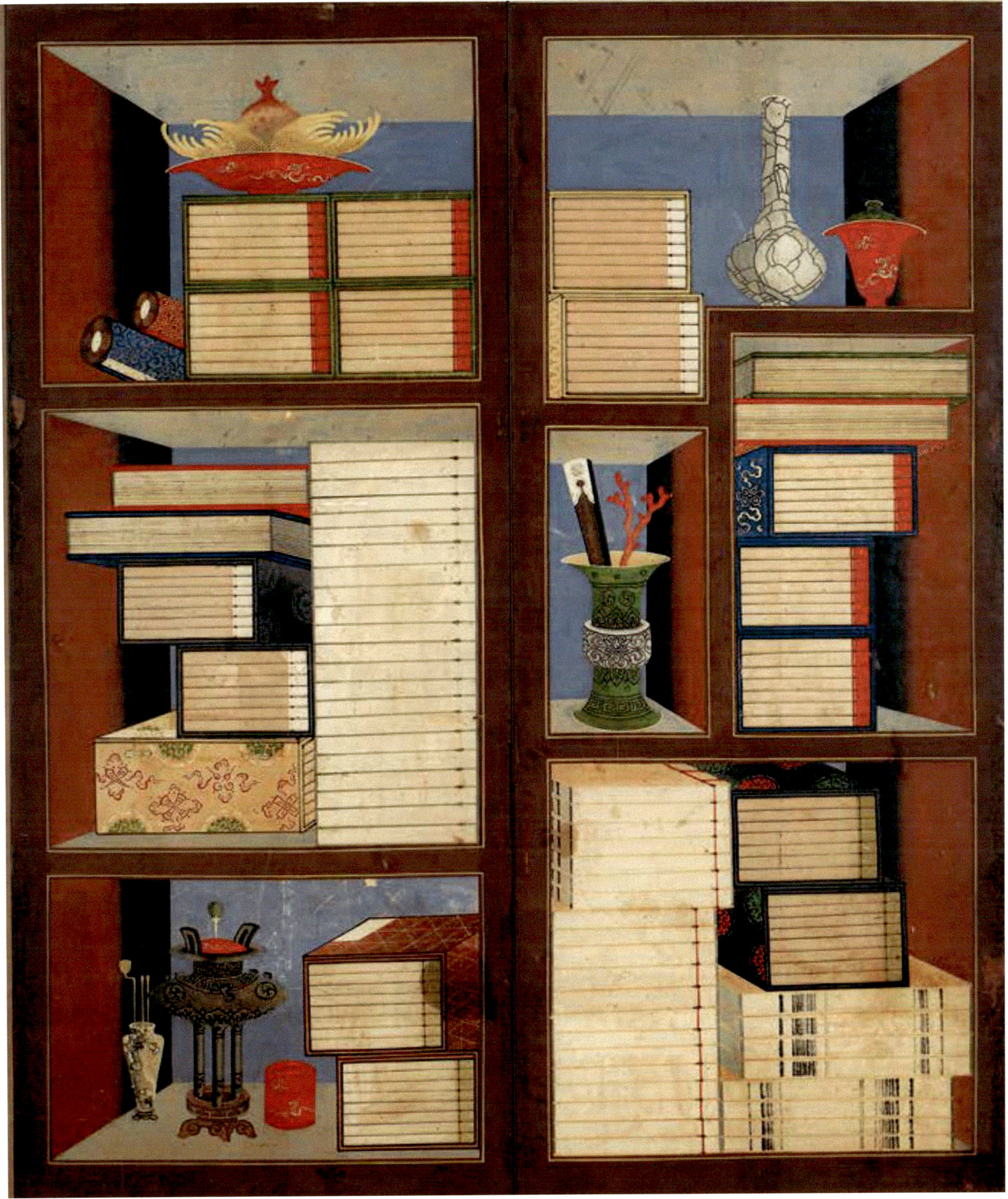

7 *Chaekgado*

Anonymous, late 19th century
Two-panel folding screen
Color on silk, 121.5 x 50 cm (each panel)
Seoul Museum of History

This two-panel folding screen was previously in the collection of the Unhyeon Royal Palace, the former residence of Yi Haeung, who acted as the regent from 1866 to 1873 for his son, King Gojong. Although composed of only two panels, this screen has all the charming features of late-nineteenth-century chaekgado. The artist quite confidently used two primary European pictorial techniques: linear perspective and chiaroscuro. Each section contains the typical assortment of books and scholarly items. The screen does not bear the artist's seal, nevertheless, its stylistic and iconographic language strongly echoes the style of Yi Hyeongnok, the leading chaekgeori painter during the second half of the nineteenth century. BC, SM

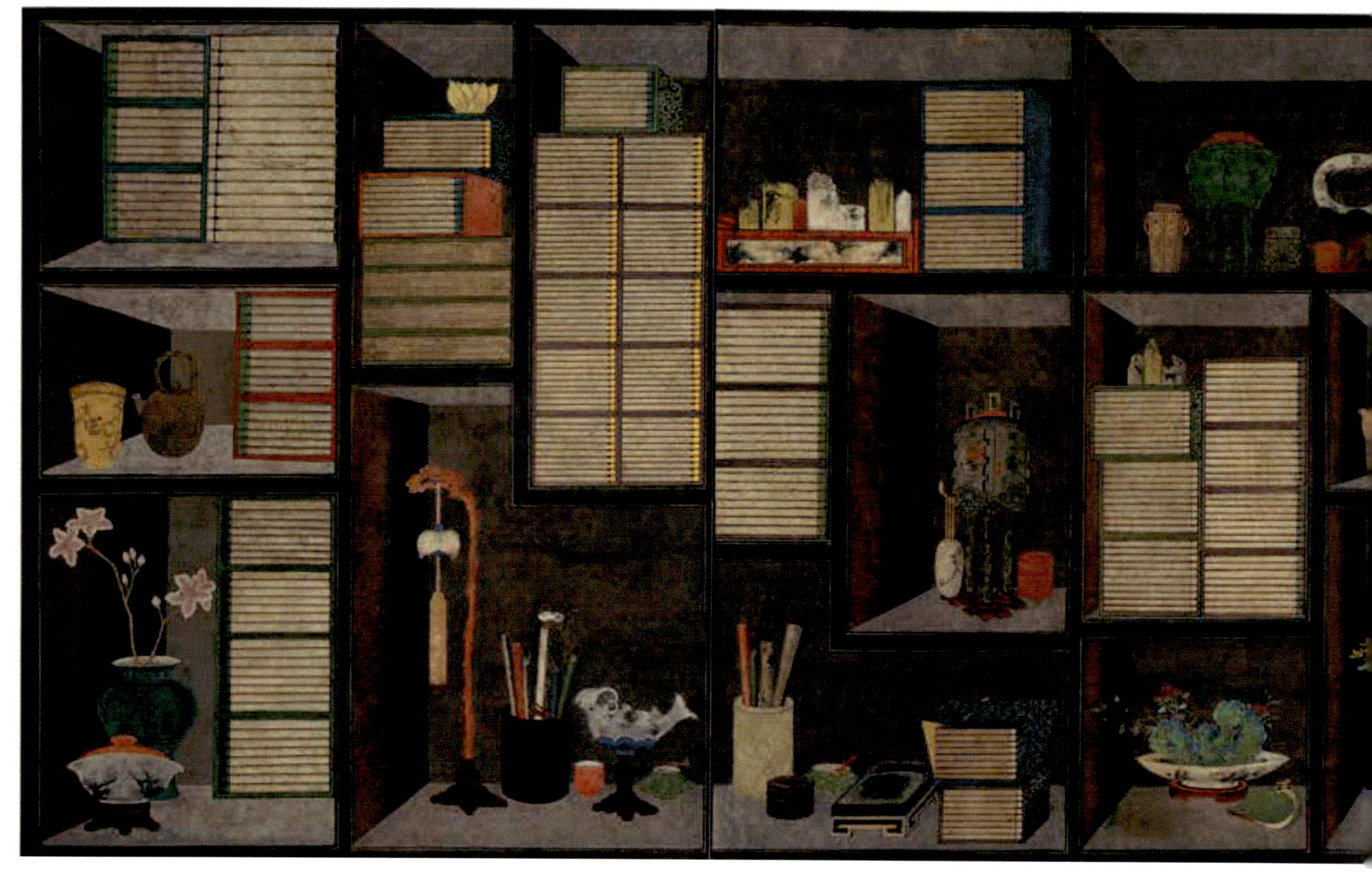

8 *Chaekgado*

Anonymous, late 19th century
Eight-panel screen
Ink and color on paper, 119 x 51 cm (each panel)
Korean Folk Village, Yongin

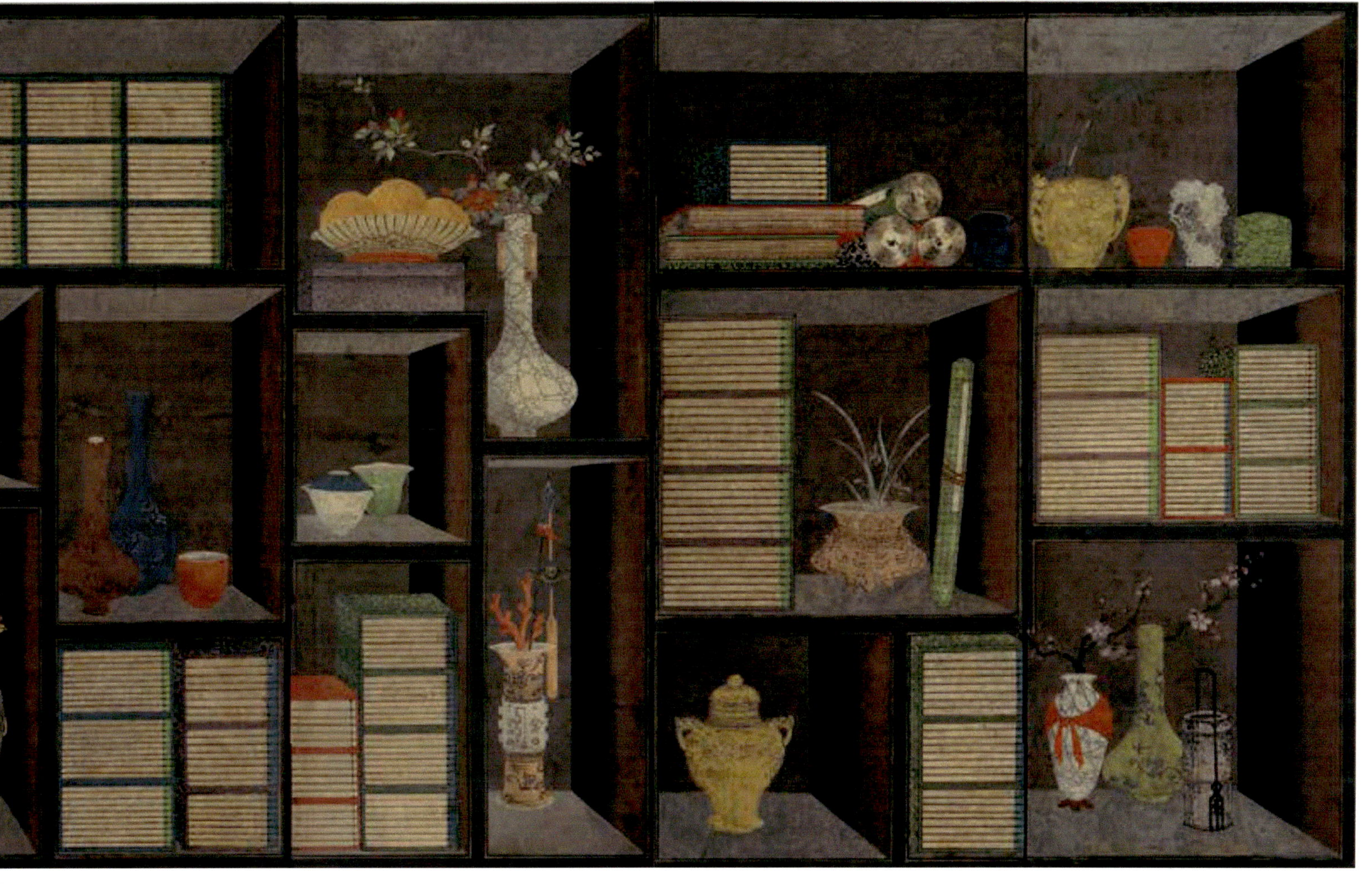

By encouraging court painters to adopt books as the main subject of royal screen paintings, King Jeongjo embraced the power of books and the ideas contained within them. He even went so far as to replace the screen behind his throne with this work—a truly dramatic break from tradition. In this bold capacity, the books in chaekgeori paintings inspire, teach, and possess the power to shape society. This work is a masterpiece in terms of its solid, simple composition and attention to detail. Bookshelves compose the frames of the piece, and on the shelves are books and accoutrements in varied, harmonious, and spacious arrangements. With Western shading techniques, these objects appear more real and three-dimensional within the deep spaces created by trompe l'oeil. This work is also notable in its use of traditional dark brown colors. BC, JJ

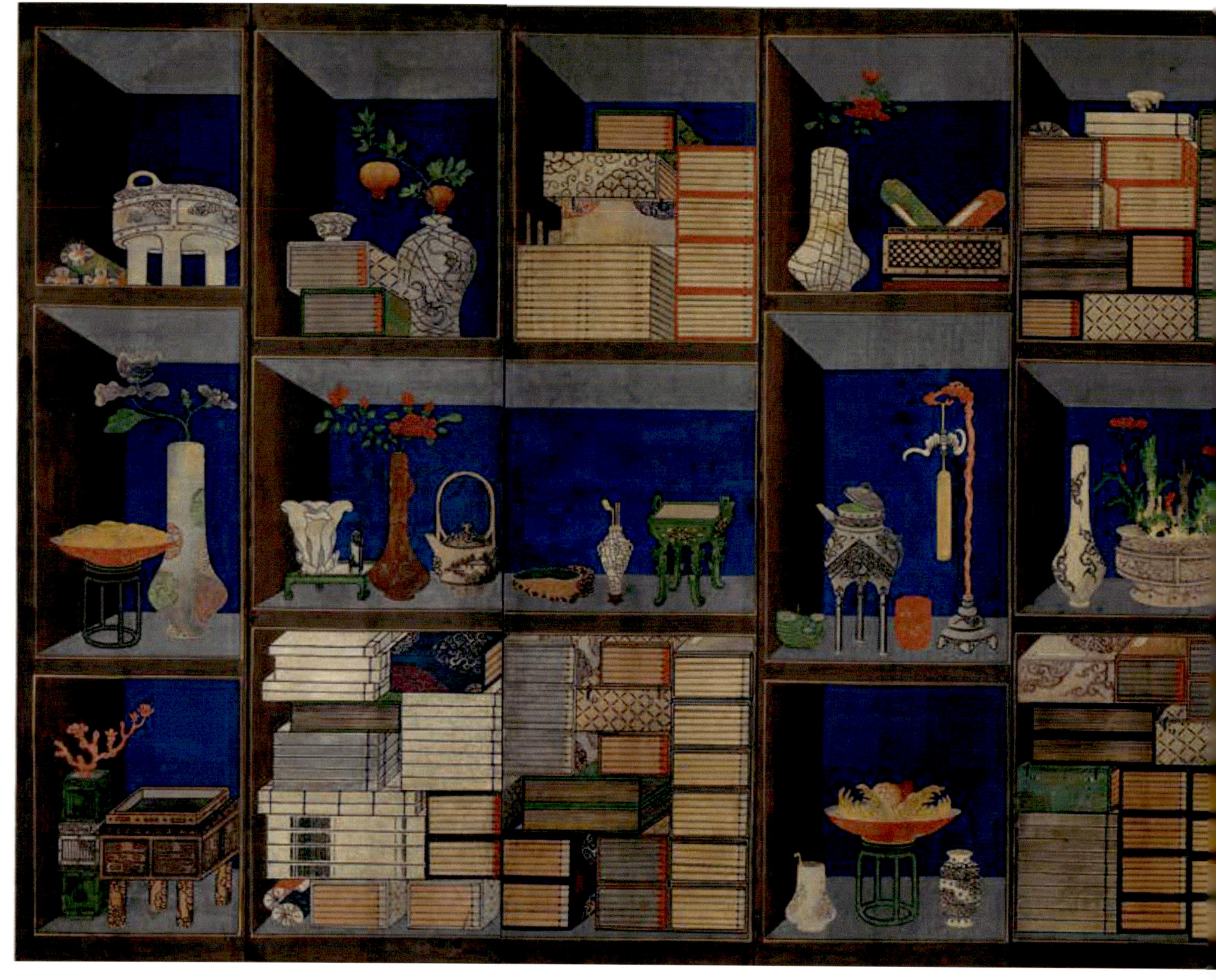

9 *Chaekgado*

Anonymous, late 19th century
Ten-panel screen
Ink and color on paper, 149 x 450 cm (overall)
Private collection.

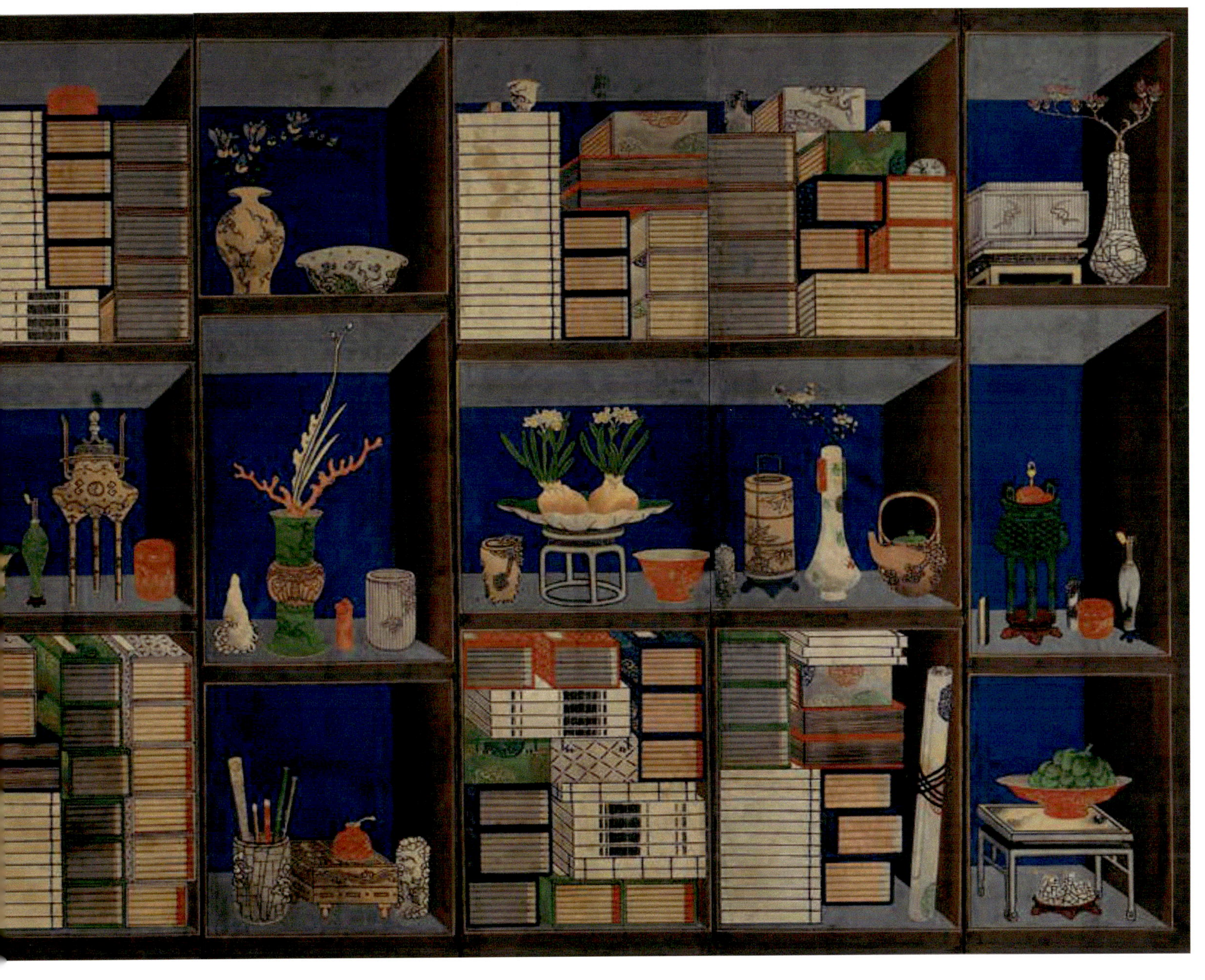

This ten-panel screen has a distinct rhythmical balance, with a full stack of books and luxurious objects boldly set off against a deep blue background. Chaekgado screens with blue backgrounds grew popular in the late nineteenth century, replacing the older, traditional brown background screens perhaps because the blue mineral pigments from Europe that reached Korea through China were more affordable at the time. The conspicuously presented objects fill more shelves than do the books, occupying twice as much space in the bookshelf. Arranging the objects horizontally in order maximizes the objects' visibility to viewers. Most of the vessels contain floral plants or precious fruits with symbolic meanings. BC, JJL

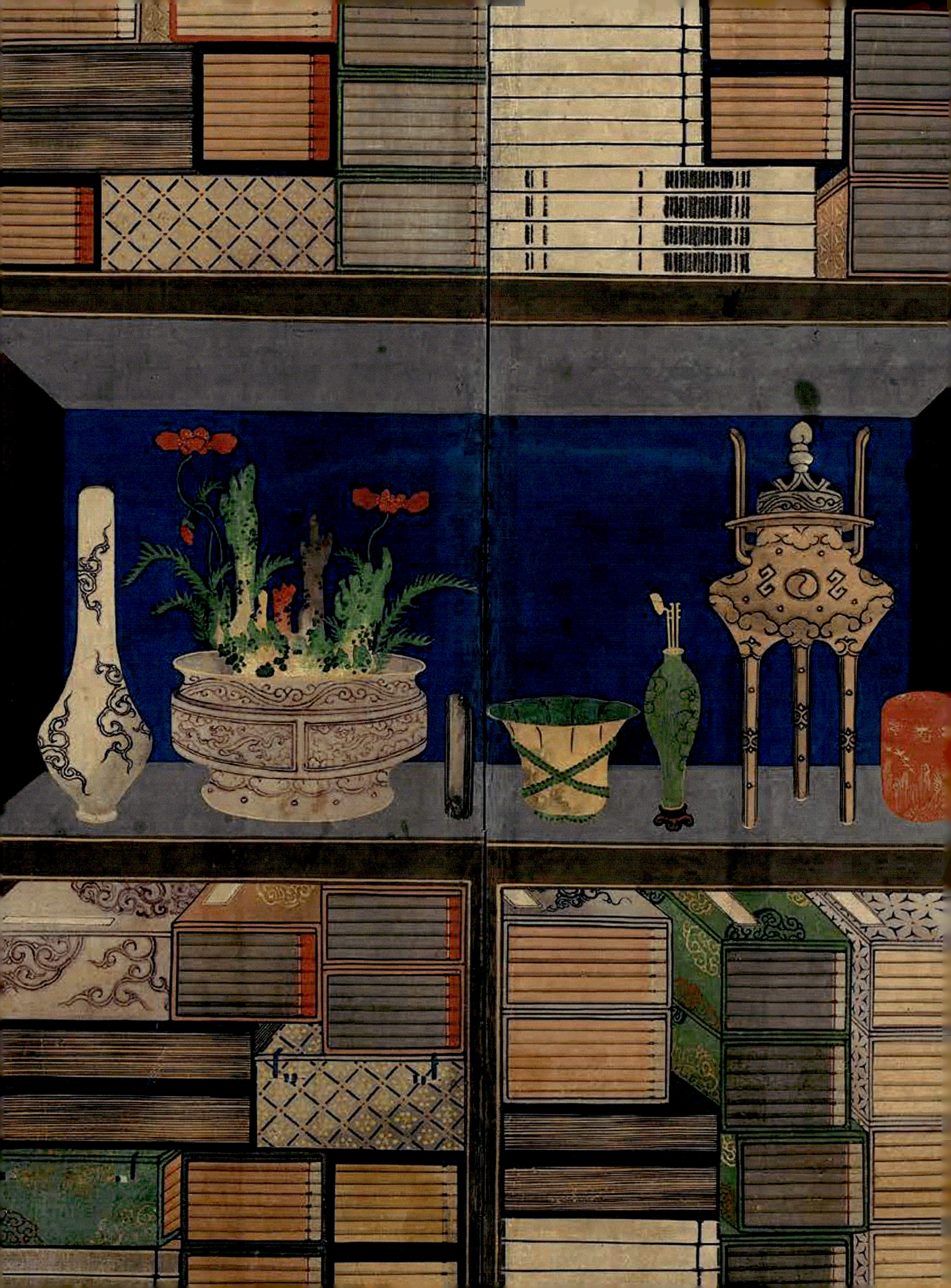

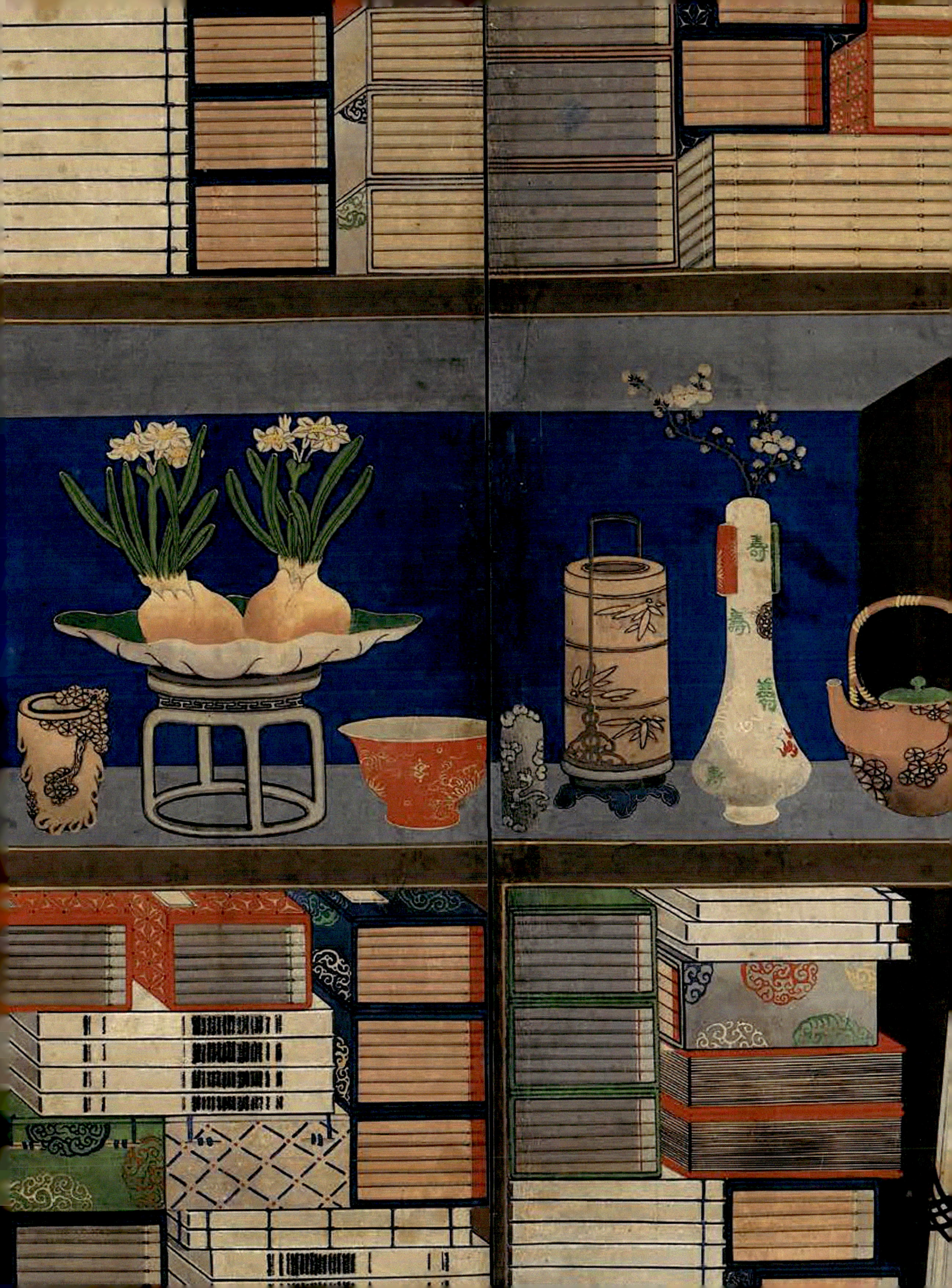
壽
壽
壽
壽

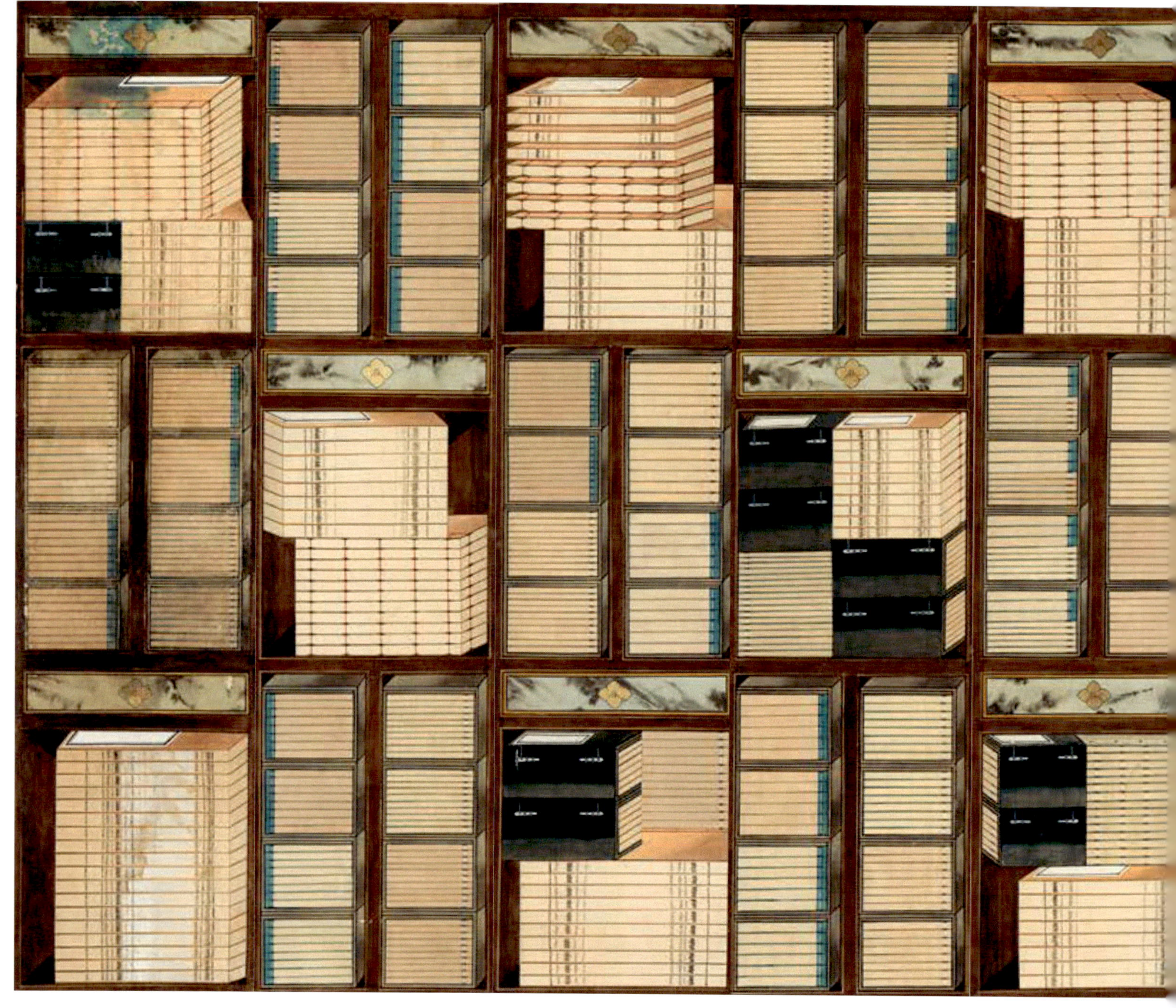

10 *Chaekgado*

Anonymous, late 19th century
Ten-panel folding screen
Ink and color on paper, 161.7 x 39.5 cm (each panel)
National Palace Museum, Seoul

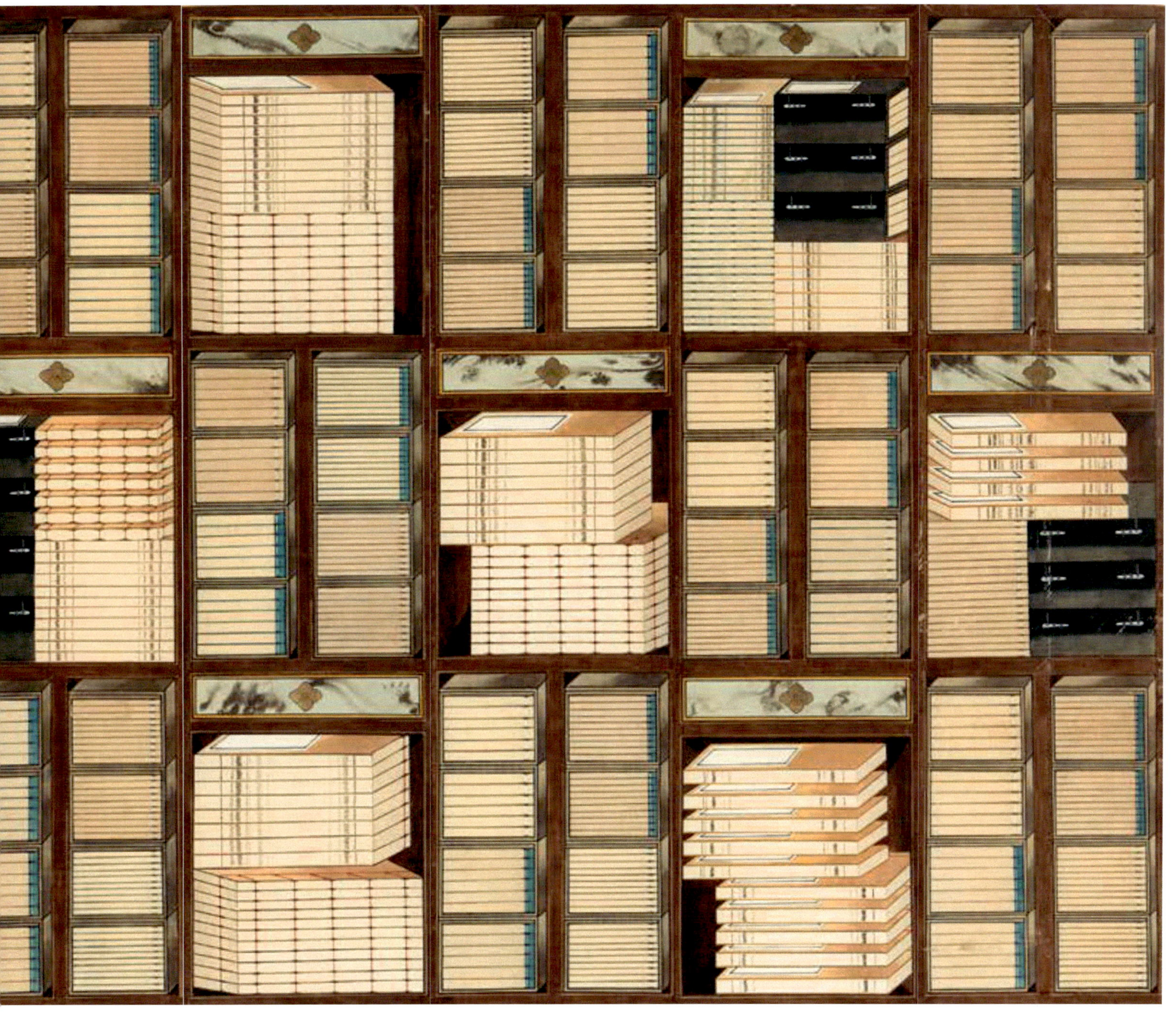

Most existing chaekgado represent books along with scholar's accoutrements and prized collectible items such as ancient bronze vessels, but this ten-panel screen exclusively depicts books, some housed in brocade cases and staged in a variety of positions. Scholars speculate that this screen may be close to a type that King Jeongjo favored and placed behind his throne as a royal emblem. Although this screen is not dated to Jeongjo's reign, the books depicted in it may still have been intended to echo the king's cultural policy to emphasize the importance of both Confucian classics in the foundation of the Joseon state and the morality of individual subjects. This screen is an excellent example of how art and politics intersected to express regal political messages without sacrificing creativity. BC, SM

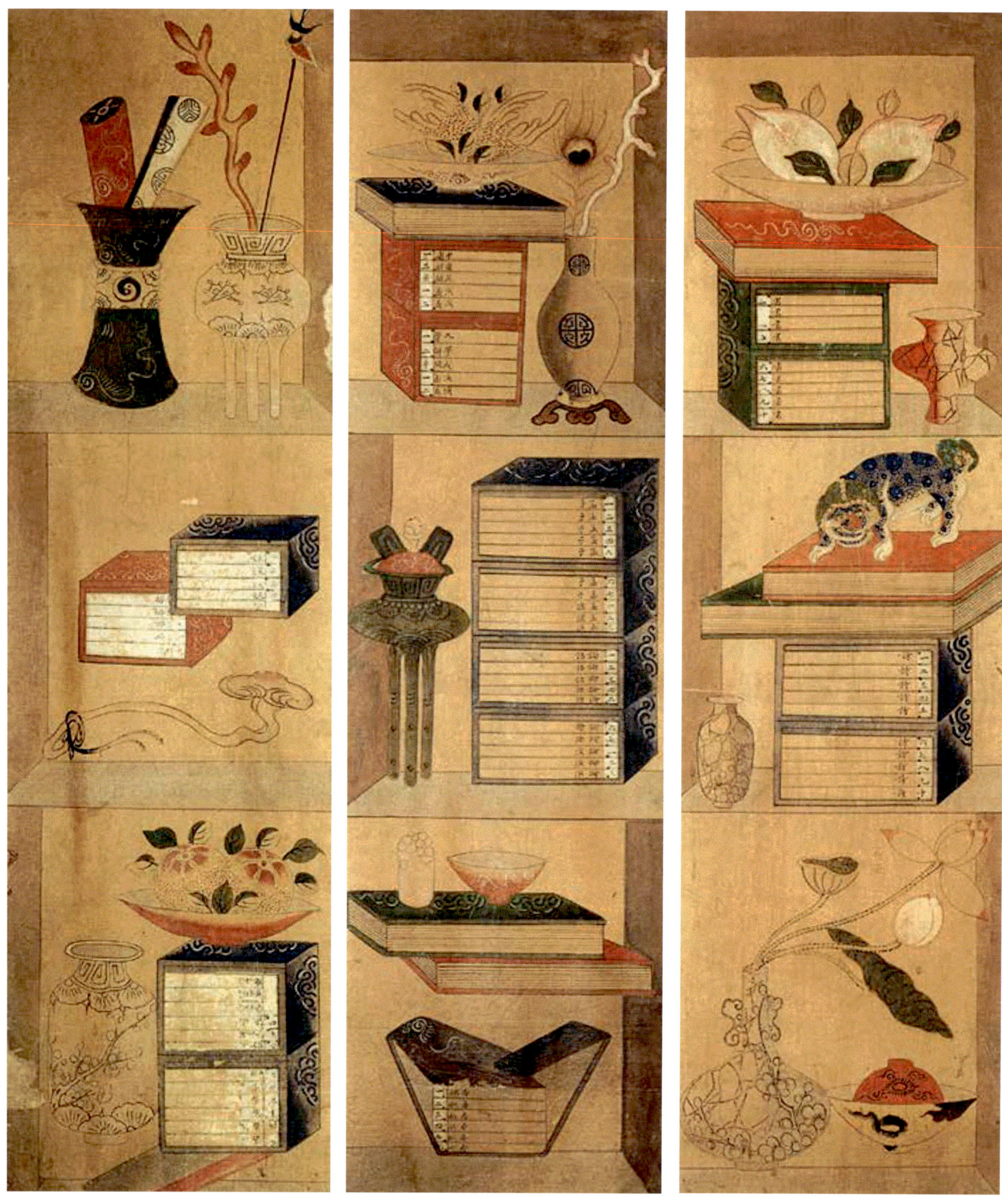

11 *Chaekgado*

Anonymous [Cheon Seok (act. mid-19th century)?], 1864
Six-panel folding screen
Ink and light color on paper, 153 x 39.4 cm (each panel)
Brooklyn Museum of Art, Gift of James Freeman, by exchange, 74.5

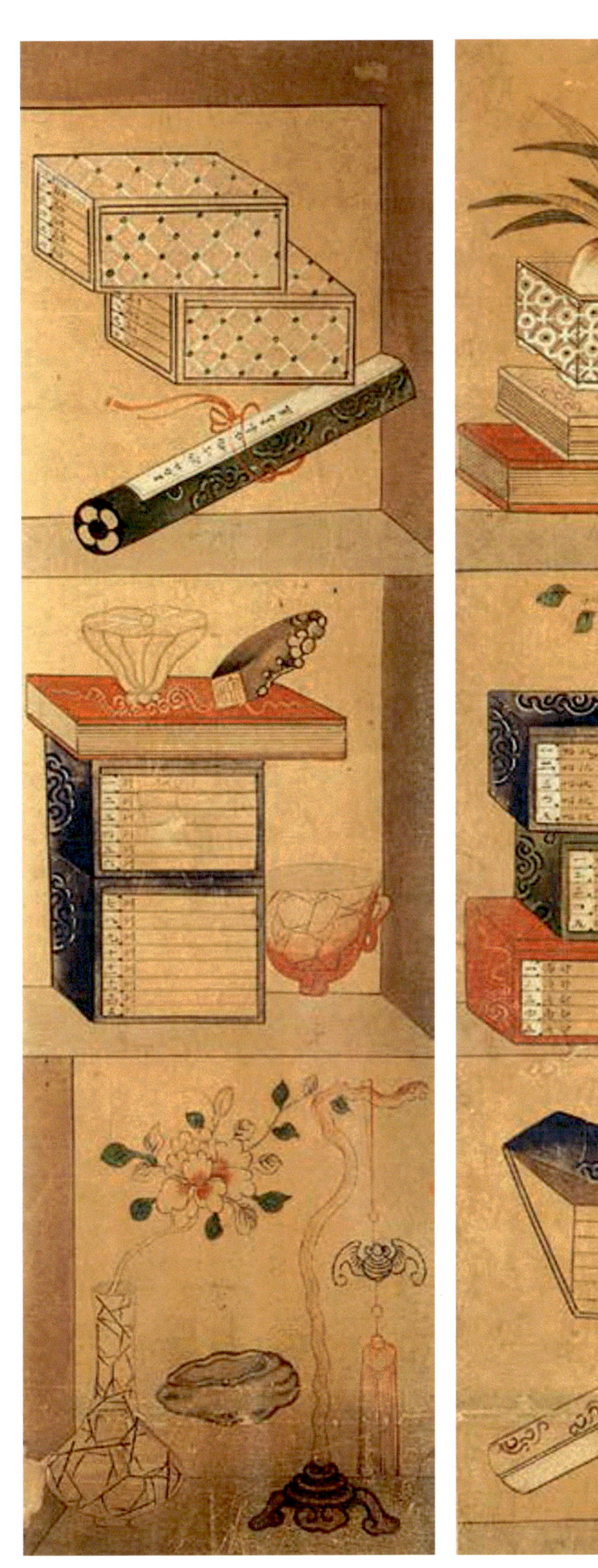

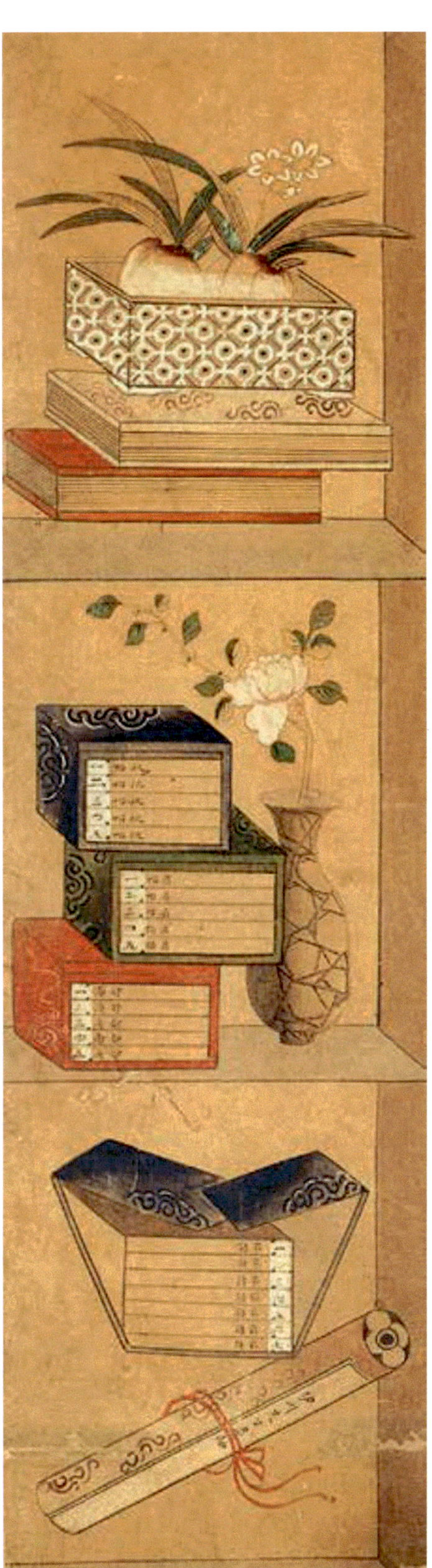

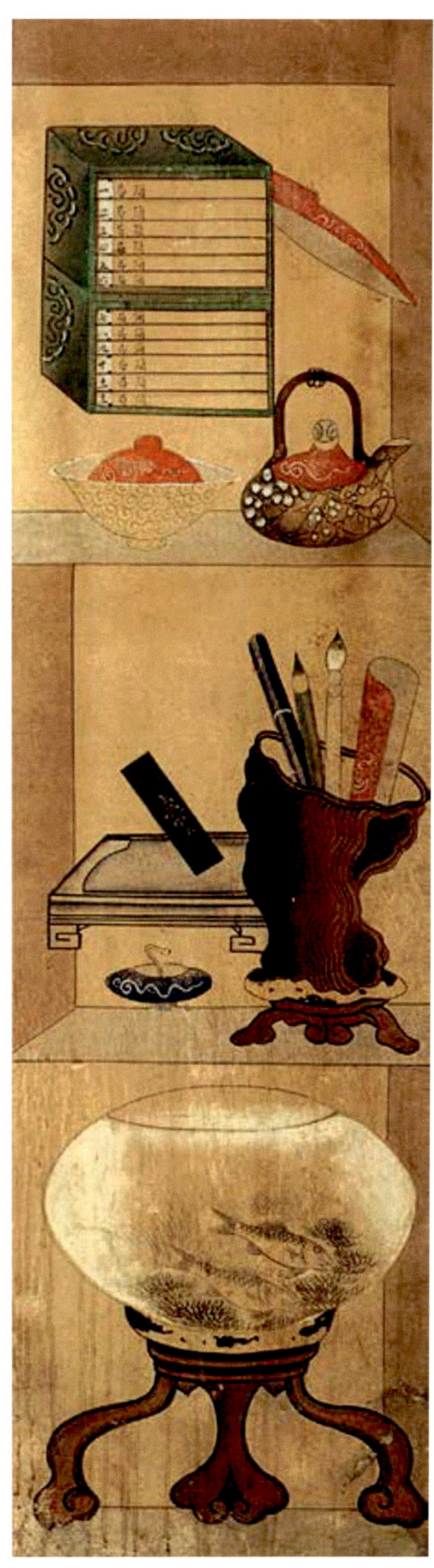

Unlike the majority of existing chaegado, this screen depicts volumes ranging from Confucian classics such as the *Analects, Mencius*, the *Book of Documents,* and the *Book of Poetry*; writings by Korean scholars such as *Ganyi jip* by Choe Rip (1539–1612), *Jeong'am jip* by Min Woosu (1694–1756), and *Chusa-cheop* (an album of calligraphy) by Kim Jeonghui (1786–1856); and Chinese vernacular novels such as *Story of the Western Wing* and *Chronicles of the Eastern Zhou Kingdoms*. The patron may have made a special request for the inclusion of such books, or the painter may simply have included those books popularly read among Korean intellectuals at that time. According to the inscription, the screen was created in the year of Gapja, which corresponds to 1864, and was made for the occasion of the First Full Moon Festival (Daeboreum). The third panel of the screen bears the painter's seal, which reads "Cheon Seok." SM

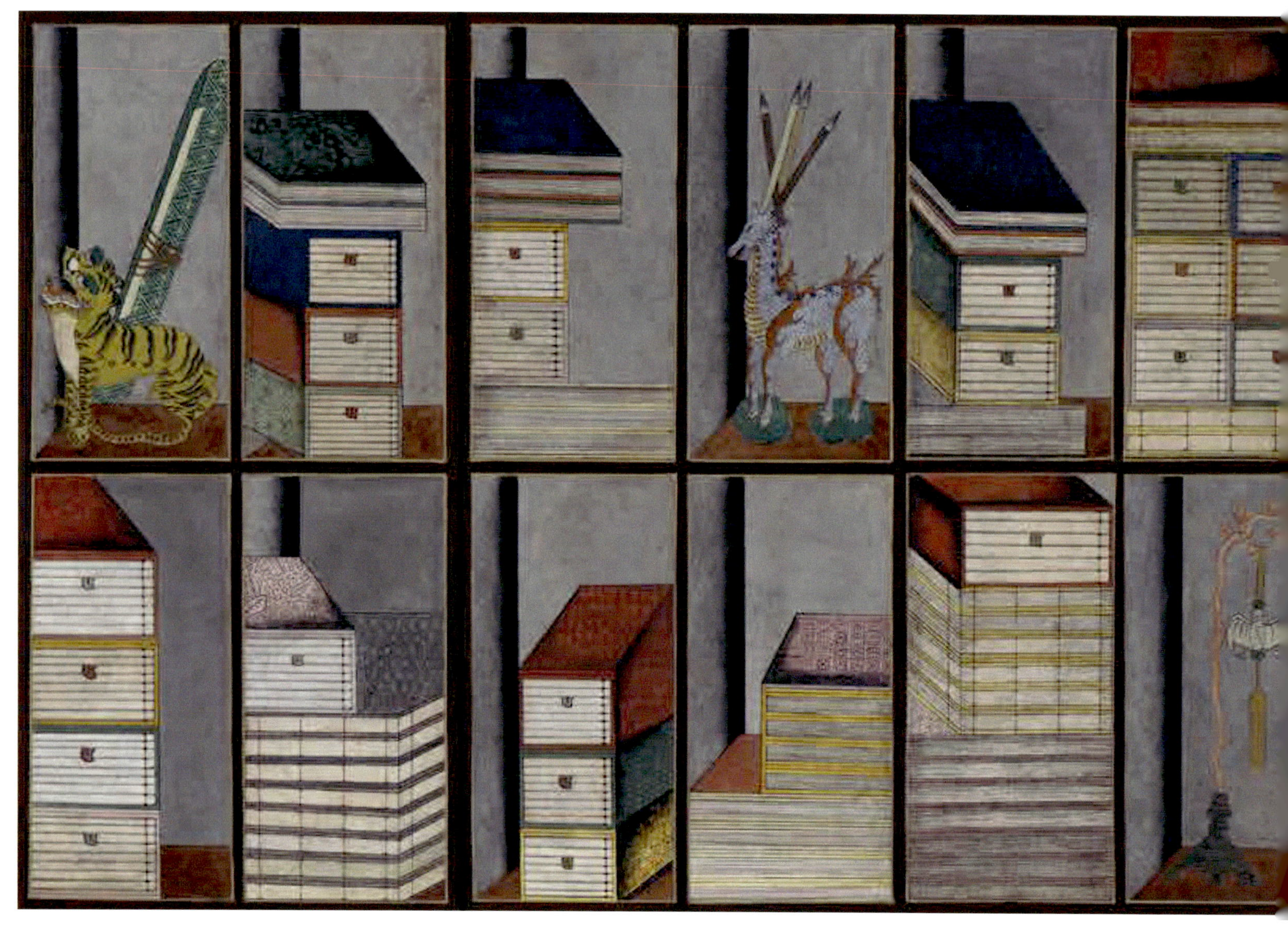

12 *Chaekgado*

Anonymous, early 20th century
Six-panel screen
Ink and color on paper, 83 x 41 cm (each panel)
Private collection

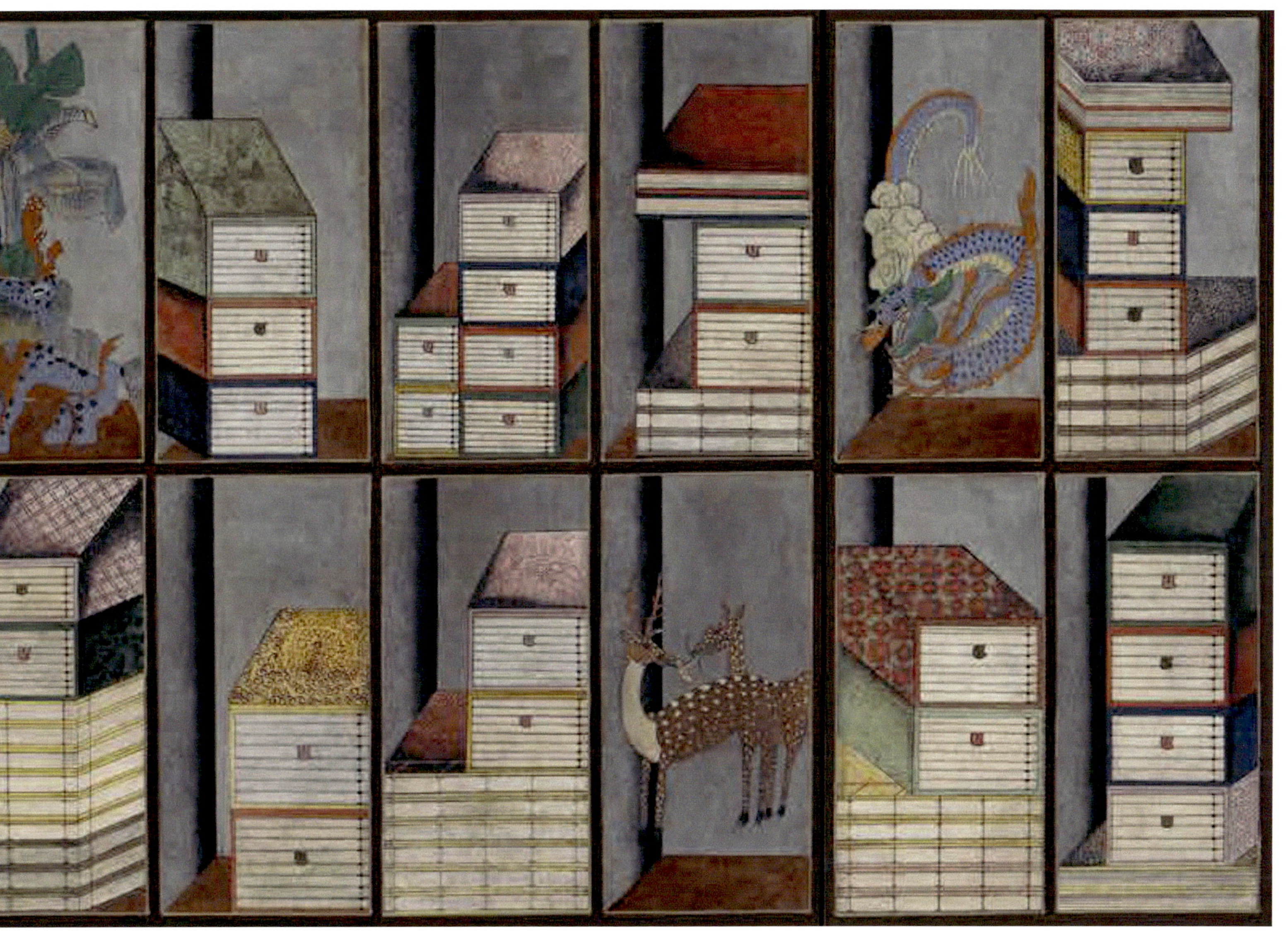

The traditional form of chaekgeori served as an impetus for creativity. Unlike other folk-style chaekgeori, which includes diverse objects, such as ceramics, fruits, and flowers, this chaekgeori screen contains only books and mythical and auspicious creatures—a dragon, a deer, a lion, a giraffe, and a tiger. The structure of the screen is formal and regular; each panel has four bookshelves. Even though the shelves show one side, the books are placed in various directions and some auspicious animals stand up in the middle of a shelf. Therefore, this screen shows a combination of bookshelf format and folk-style chaekgeori elements, and illustrates a dramatic break from conventional chaekgeori in its depiction of mythical and auspicious creatures in prominent locations on the bookshelves. Doing so expands the confined rigid space of academia into the imaginative world of myth. The artist depicted the stack of books in reverse perspective and used shading to indicate three dimensionality. BC, JJ

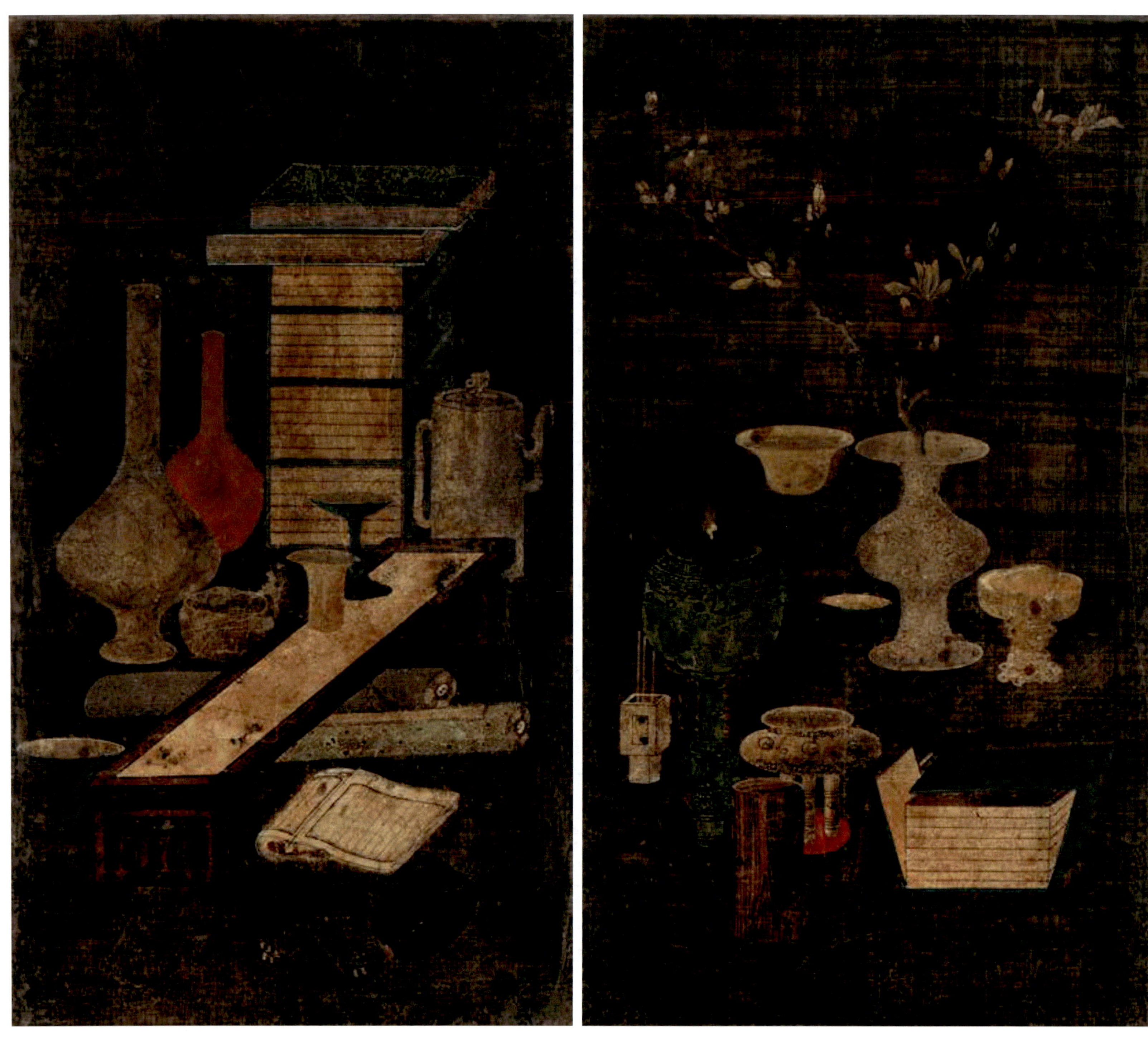

13 *Chaekgeori*

Anonymous, late 18th century
Eight-panel folding screen
Ink and color on paper, 144.8 x 391.2 cm (each panel)
Seoul Museum

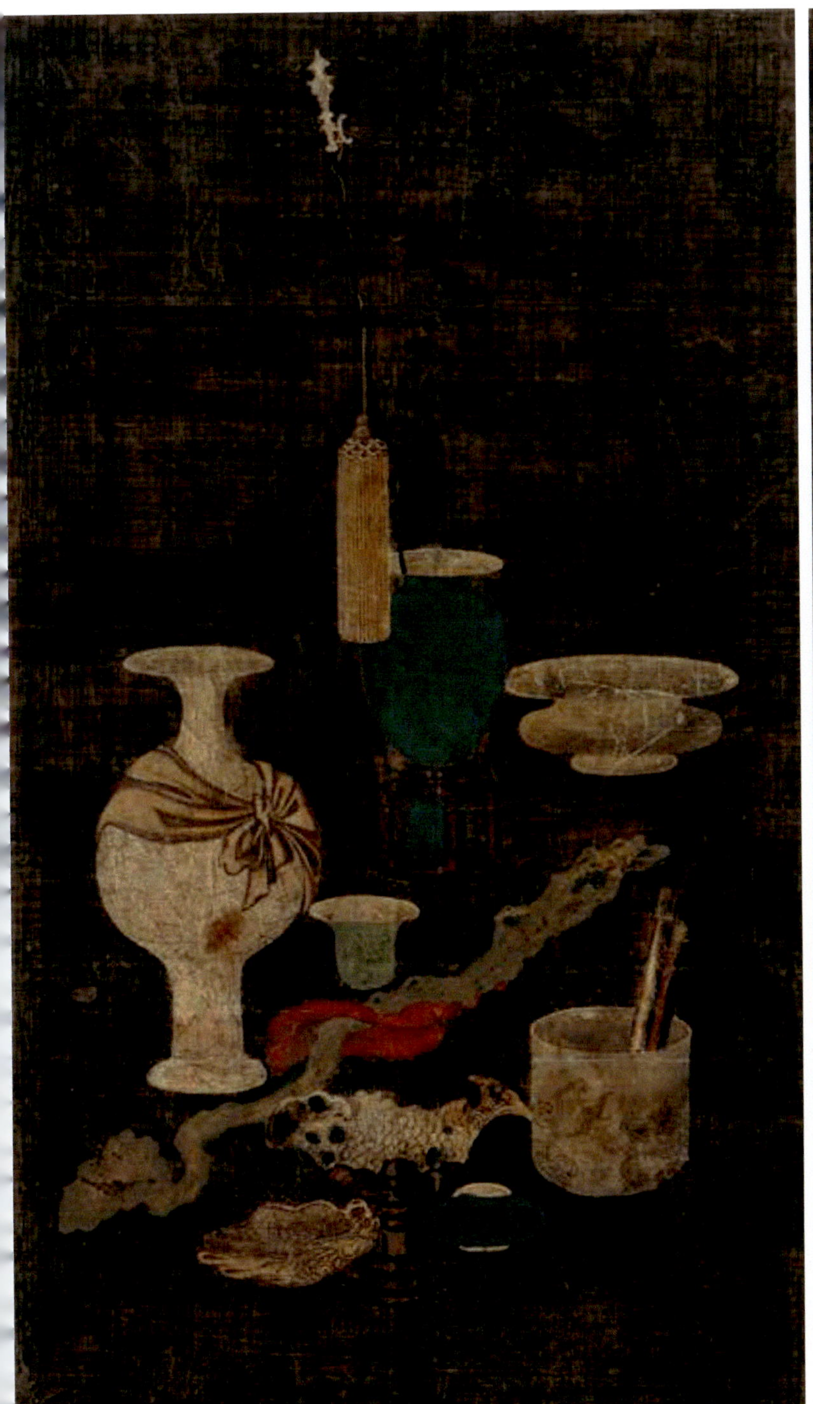

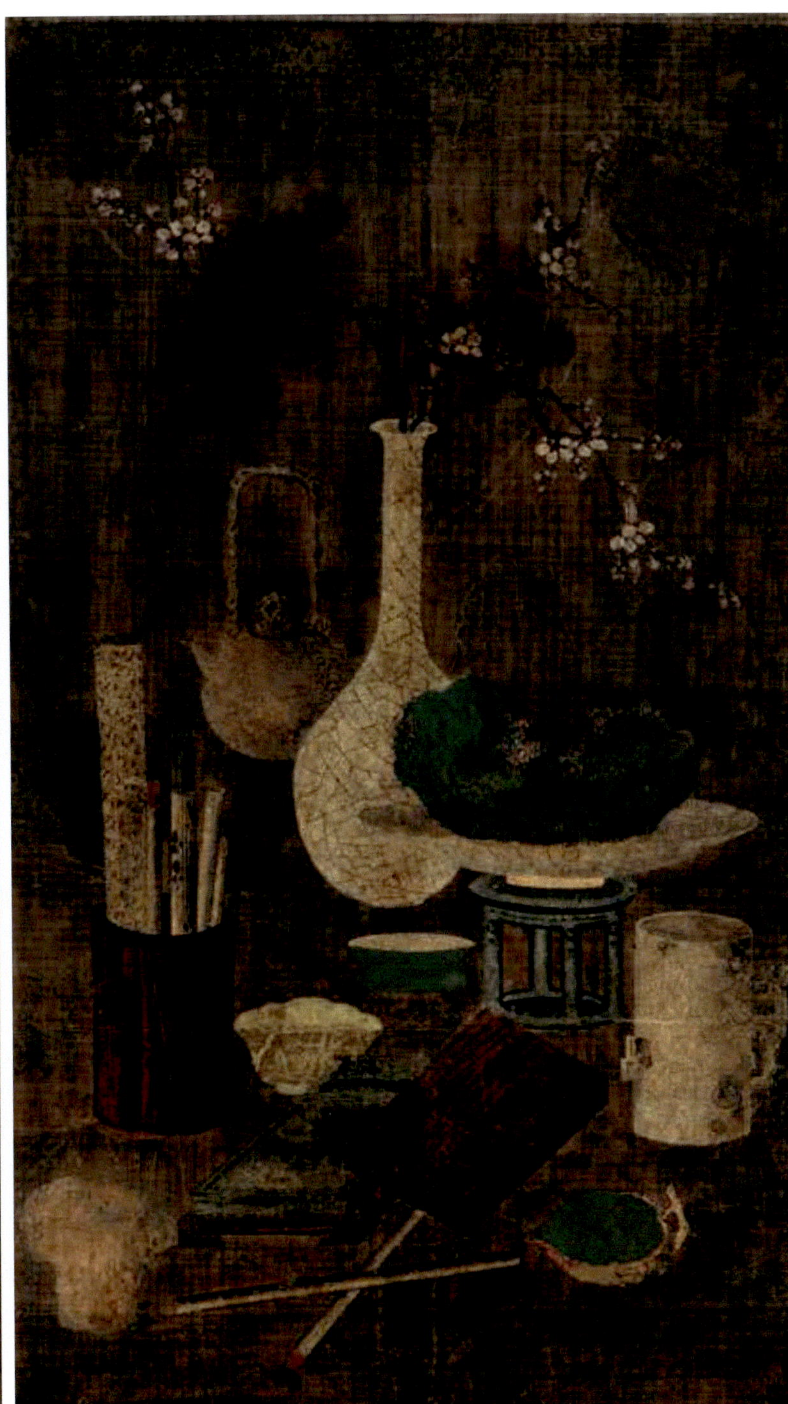

Dated to the late eighteenth century, this painting may be one of the earliest chaekgeori screens. While many screens developed out of late Qing cabinets of curiosities (*duobaoge*), this screen seems to have a more stylistic affinity with a group of paintings called Painting of Pure Offering, which were often used to celebrate the New Year during the Ming and Qing periods in China. This second source strongly implies that the pictorial vocabularies of Korean chaekgeori tradition are not limited to duobaoge.

Each panel depicts multiple stacks of books housed in a colorful brocade, elegantly displayed with accessories and other objects related to the scholar's sophisticated lifestyle. Flowers representing each season are portrayed: plum blossoms for winter, magnolia for spring, lotuses for summer, and chrysanthemums for autumn. Although the colorful pigments have now lost their brightness, originally they must have created a pleasant contrast with the shimmering black-lacquer background. BC, SM

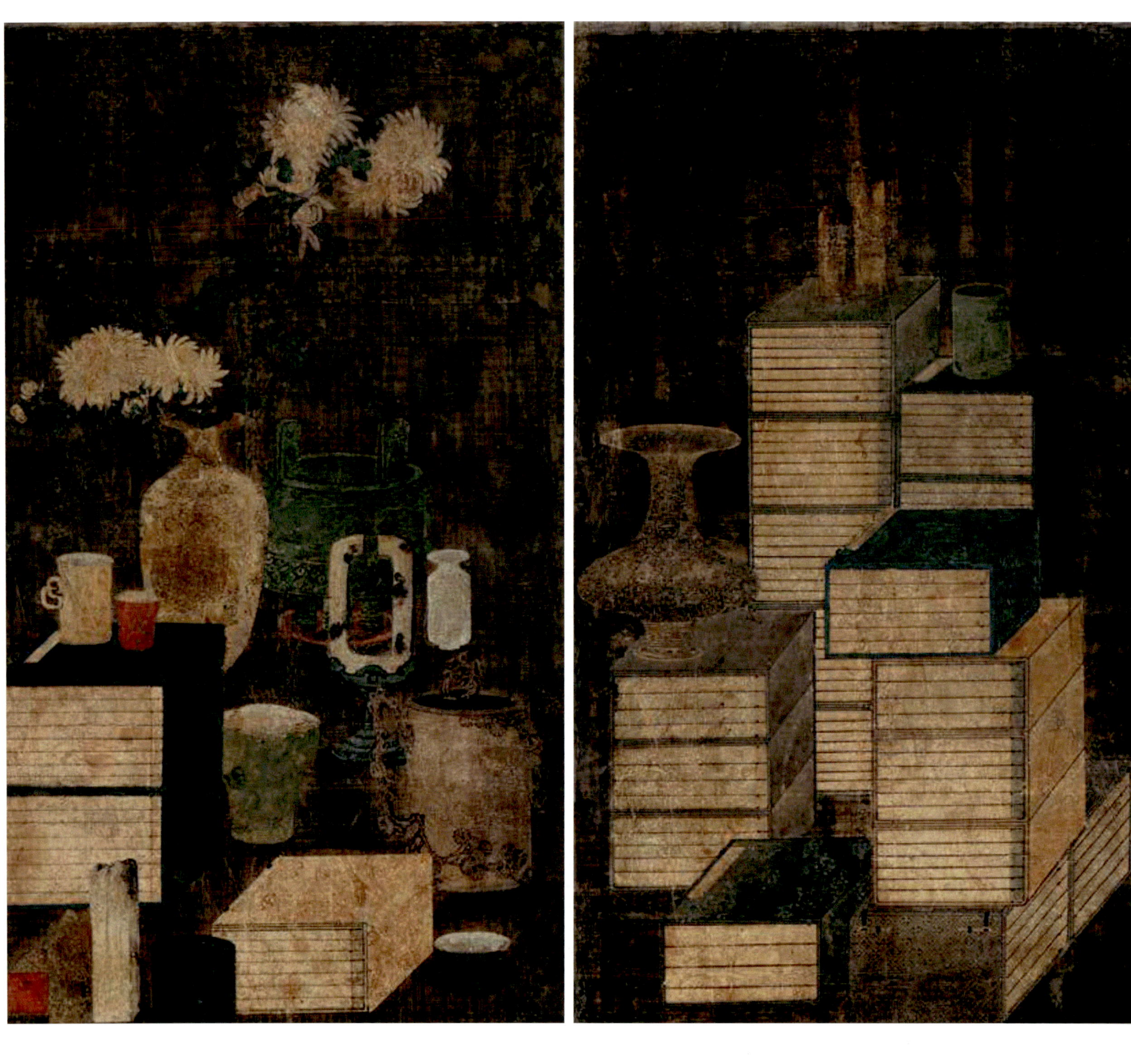

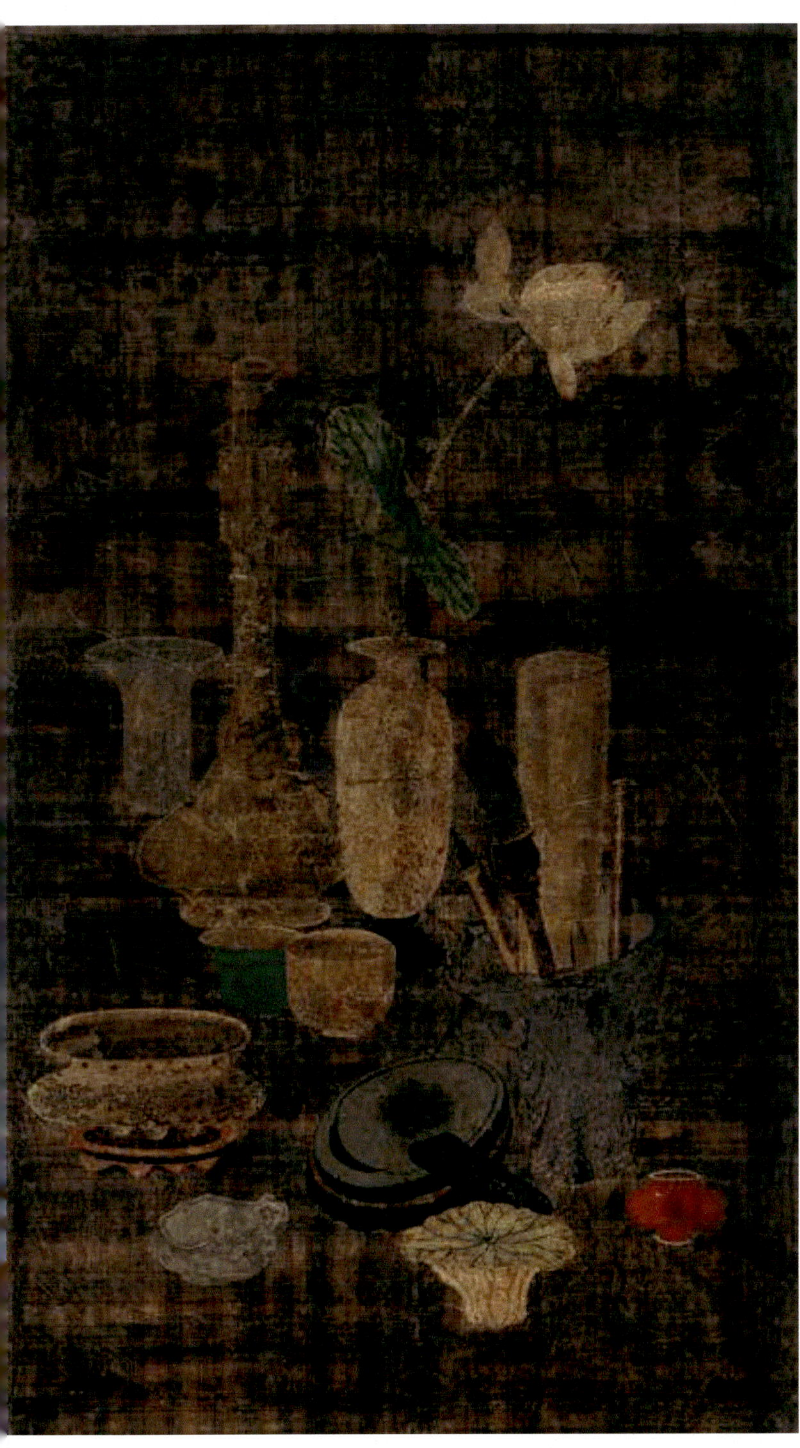

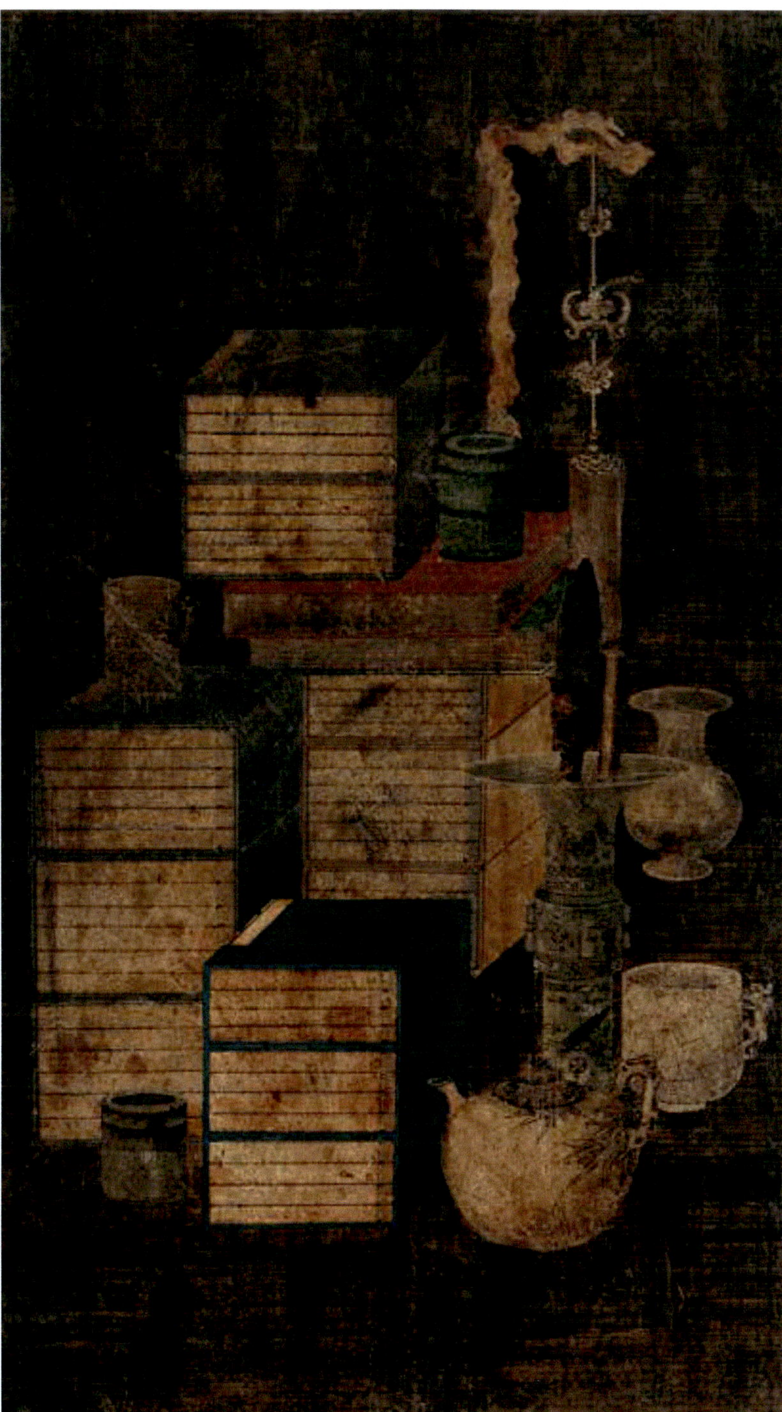

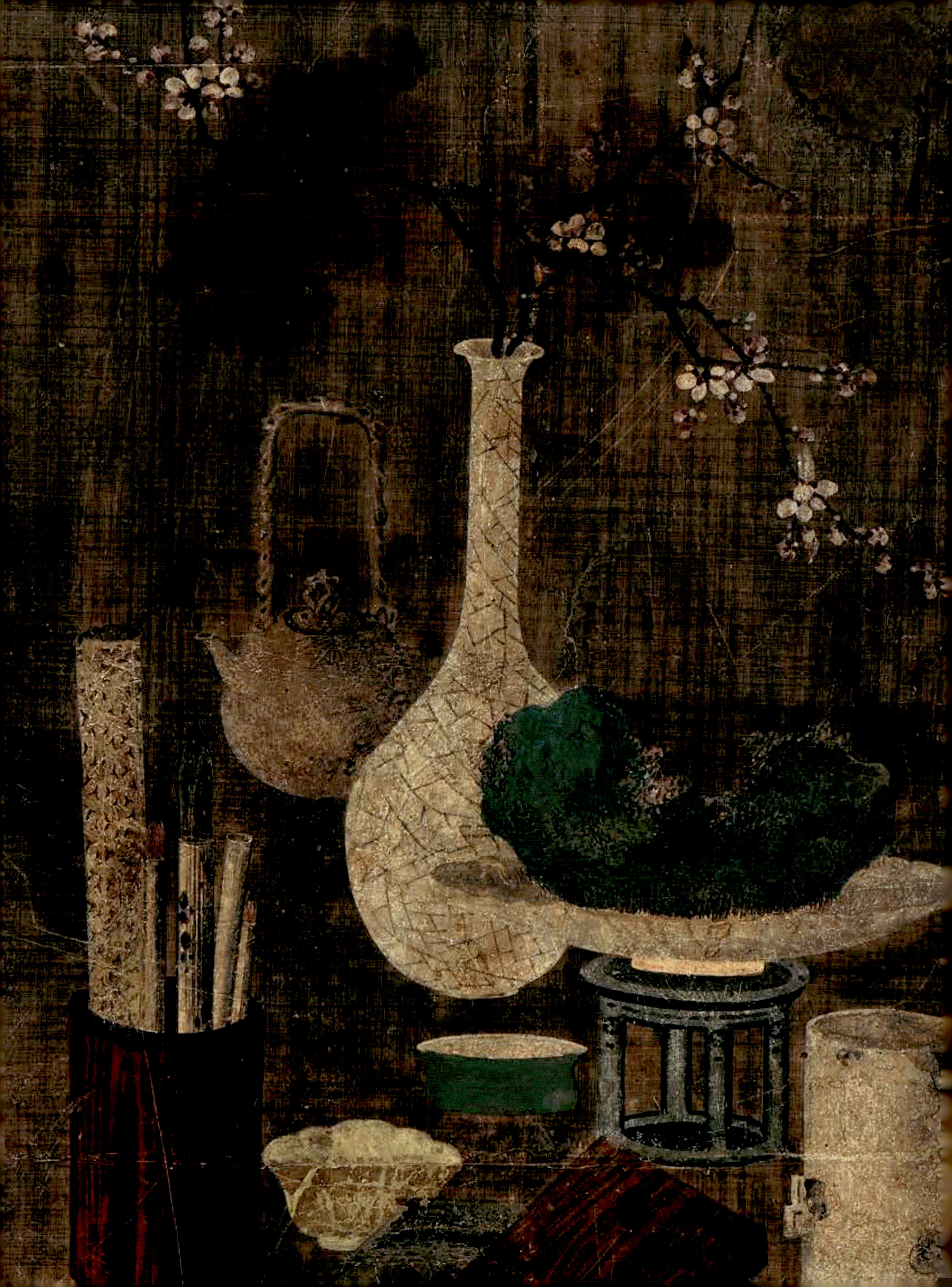

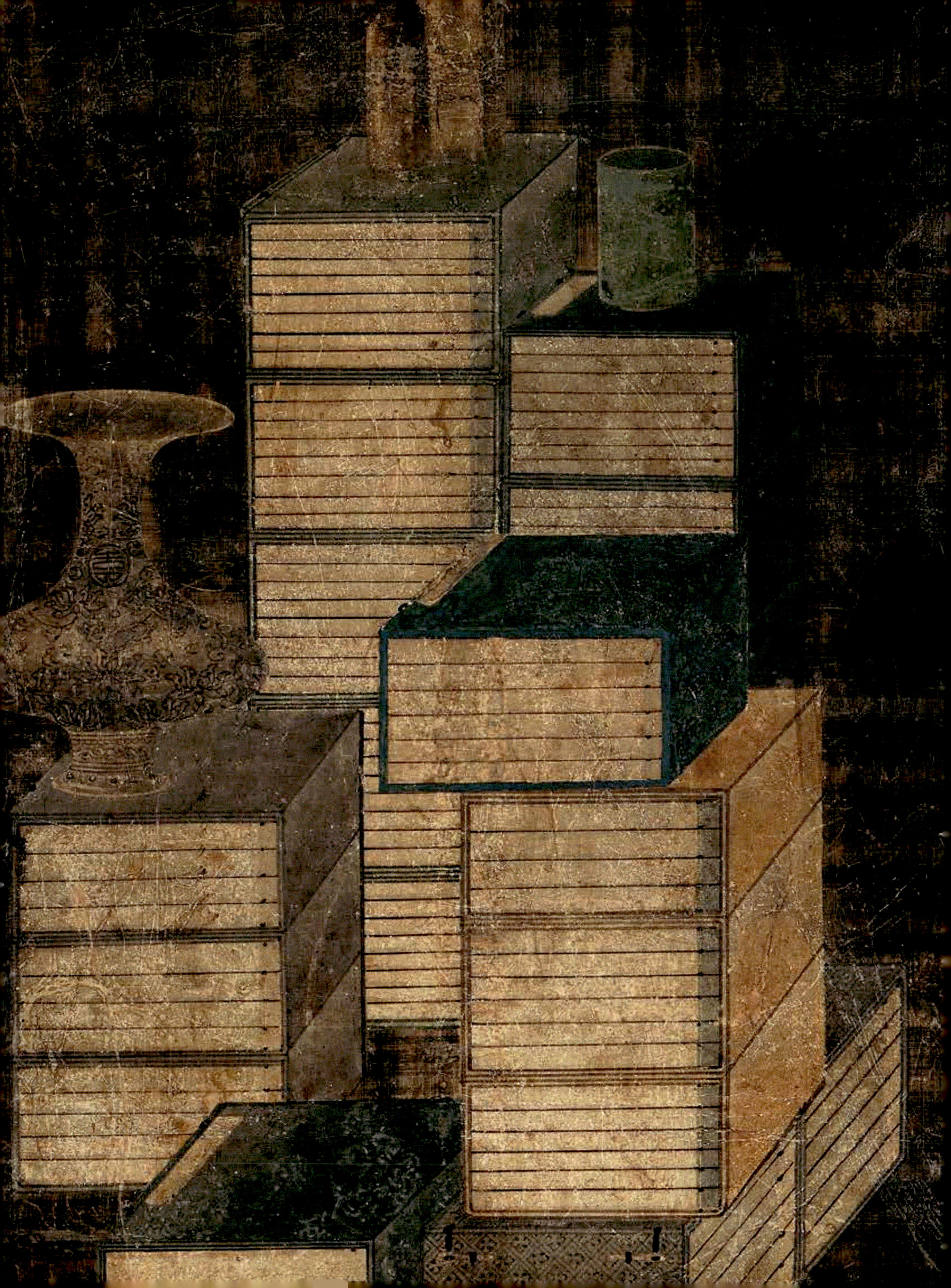

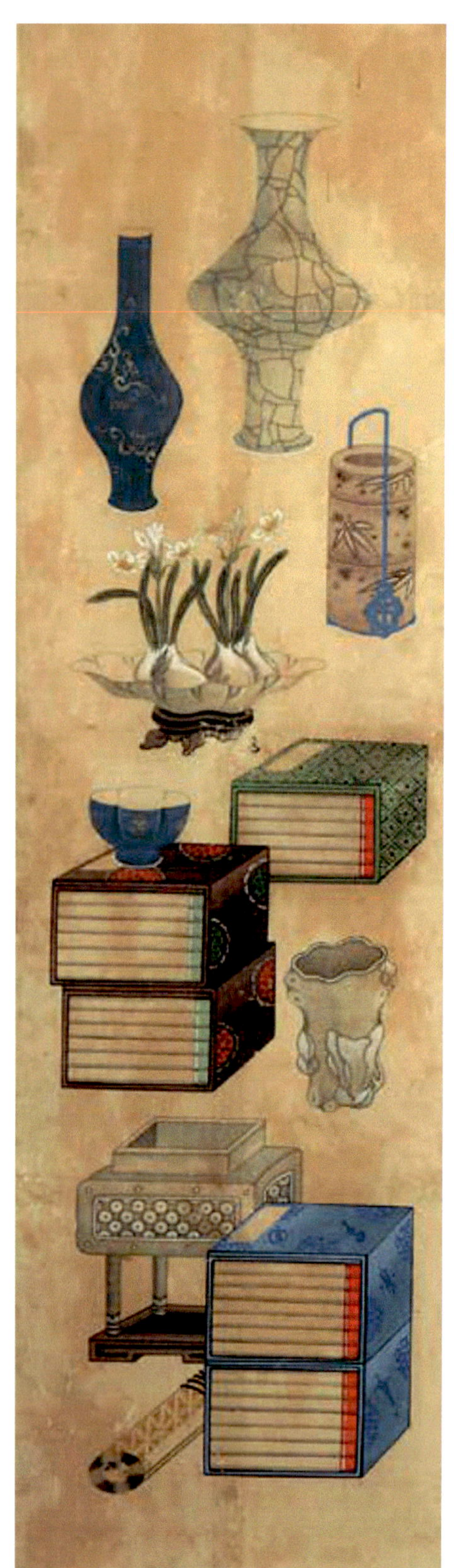
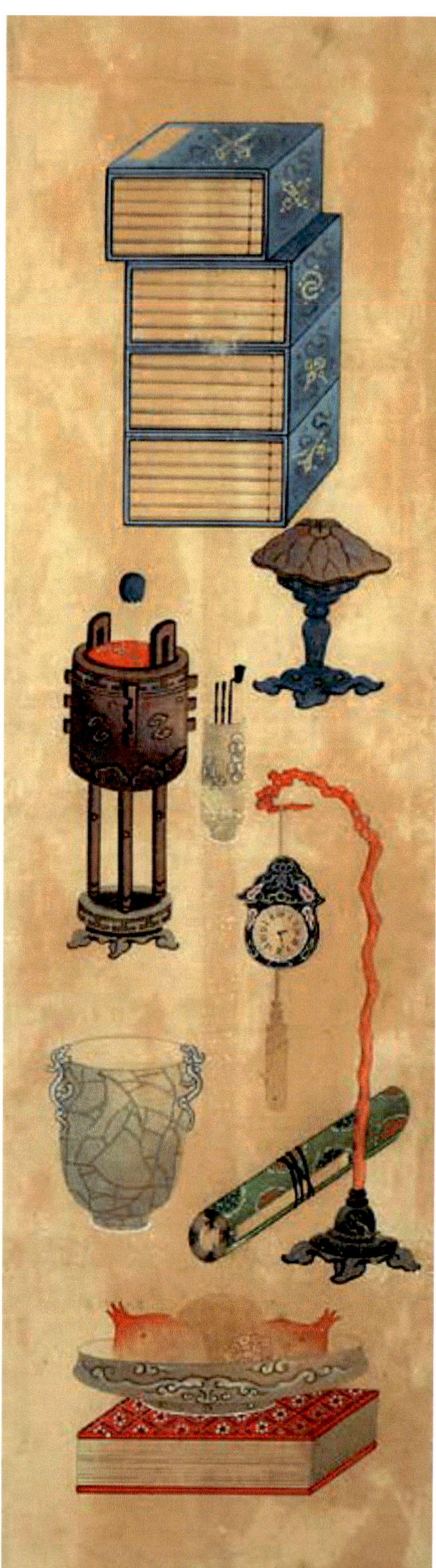
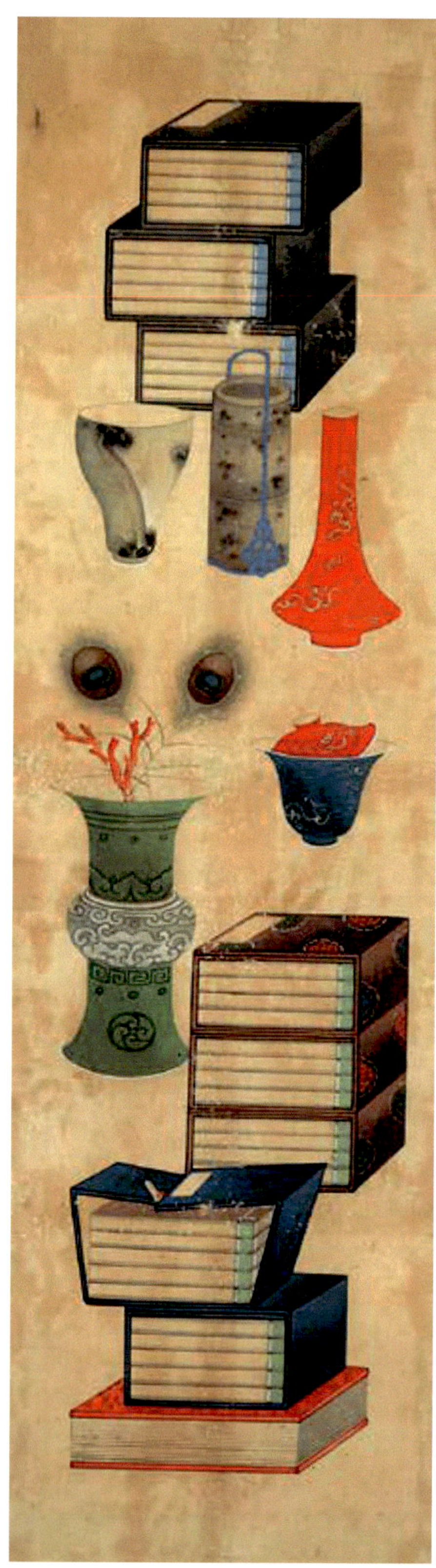

14 *Chaekgeori*

Yi Hyeongnok [Yi Eungnok] [Yi Taekgyun] (1808–after 1871), before 1864
Six-panel screen
Ink and color on paper, 154.5 x 38.5 cm (each panel)
National Folk Museum of Korea, Seoul

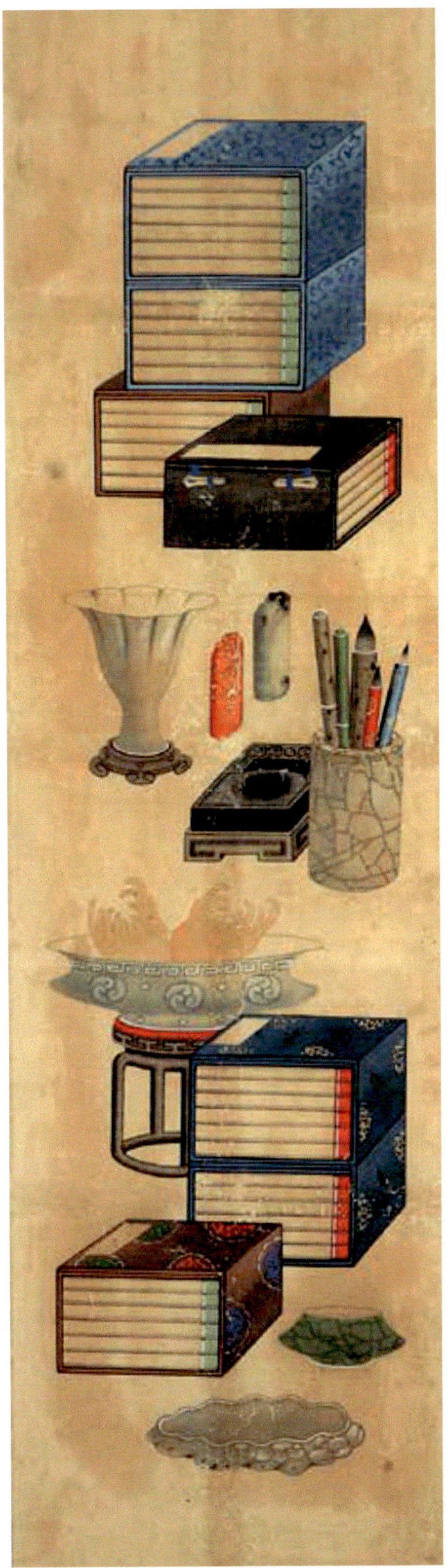

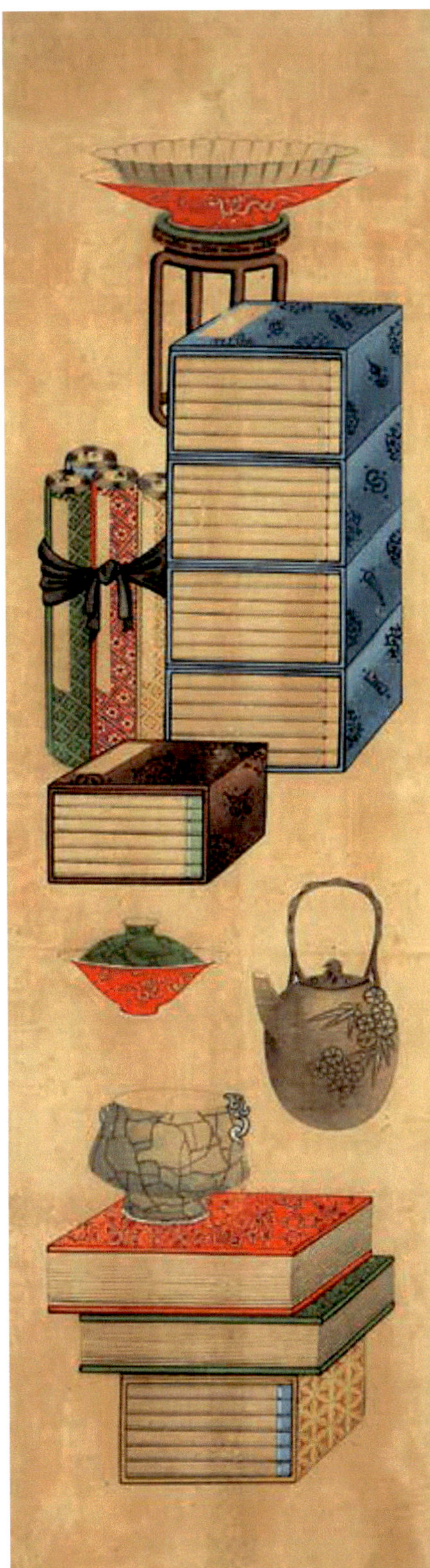

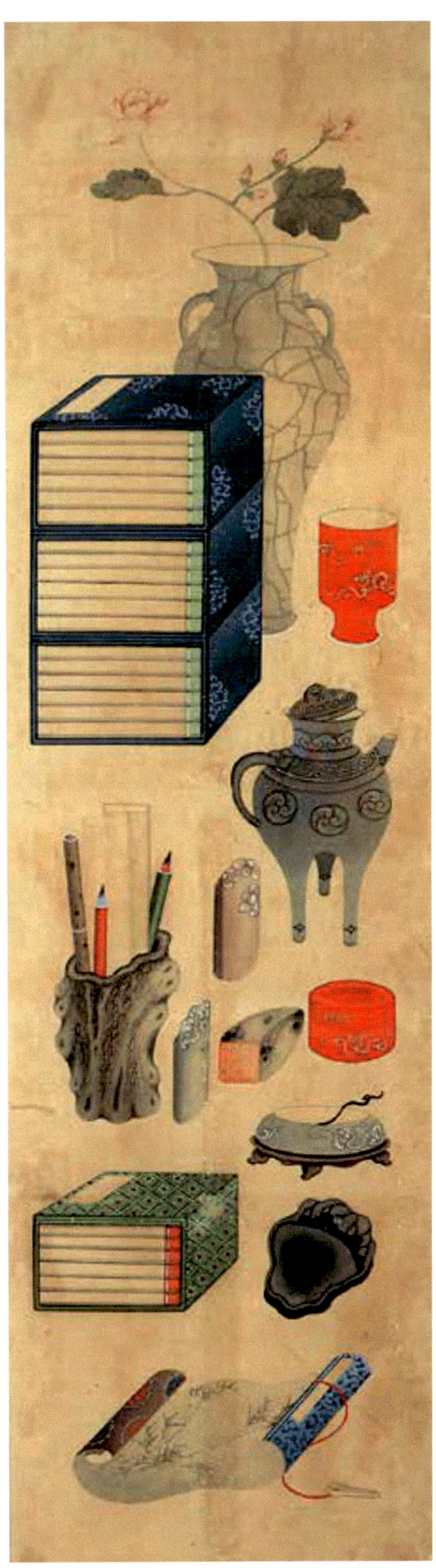

This "isolated" or "floating" chaekgeori was painted by Yi Hyeongnok. His family was skilled in the genre, beginning with his grandfather Yi Jonghyeon. While Yi Jonghyeon failed to please King Jeongjo with his paintings and was exiled, he was renowned for his munbangdo(painting of scholar's accouterments). His son Yi Yunmin was also famous among the nobles for his munbangdo. As talented as his forefathers, Yi Hyeongnok created such realistic and detailed depictions that people mistook his paintings for the real thing, only to draw closer and be amused at having been fooled. When the frames provided by chaekgado were eliminated, the structures of chaekgeori changed from horizontal to vertical. Such chaekgeori are of a different world than the early munbangdo. The books are piled up high, and the accoutrements stand up as though reaching into the air. Further, the narrow and tall frames of this folding screen give each panel a sense of individuality, making the images look even taller. Freed from frames, chaekgeori became a space for flaunting the beauty of vertical composition. Though each screen is packed with books and accoutrements, each is singular in a show of incredible variety. This elegant folding screen is one of Yi Hyeongnok's early works. BC

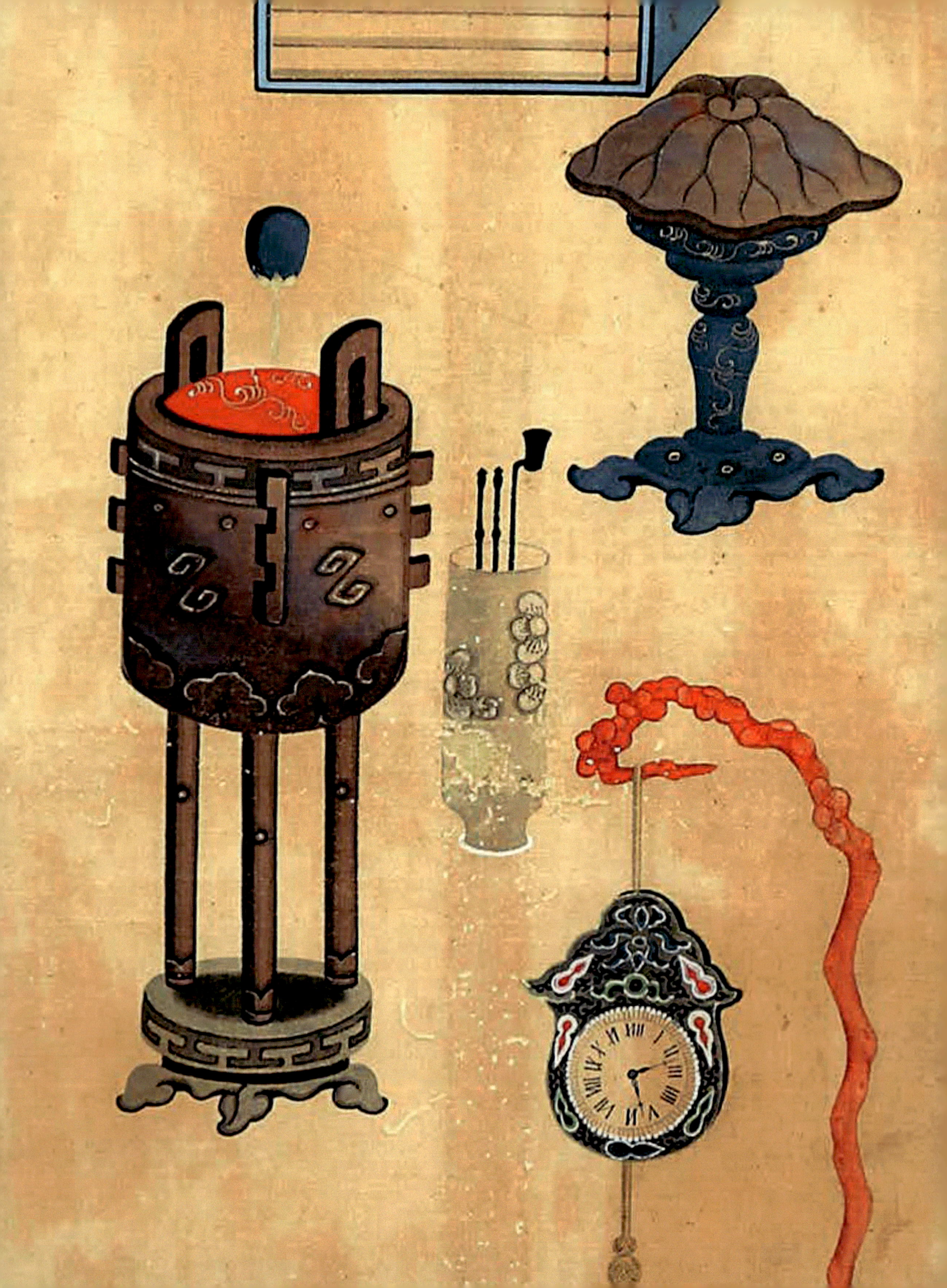

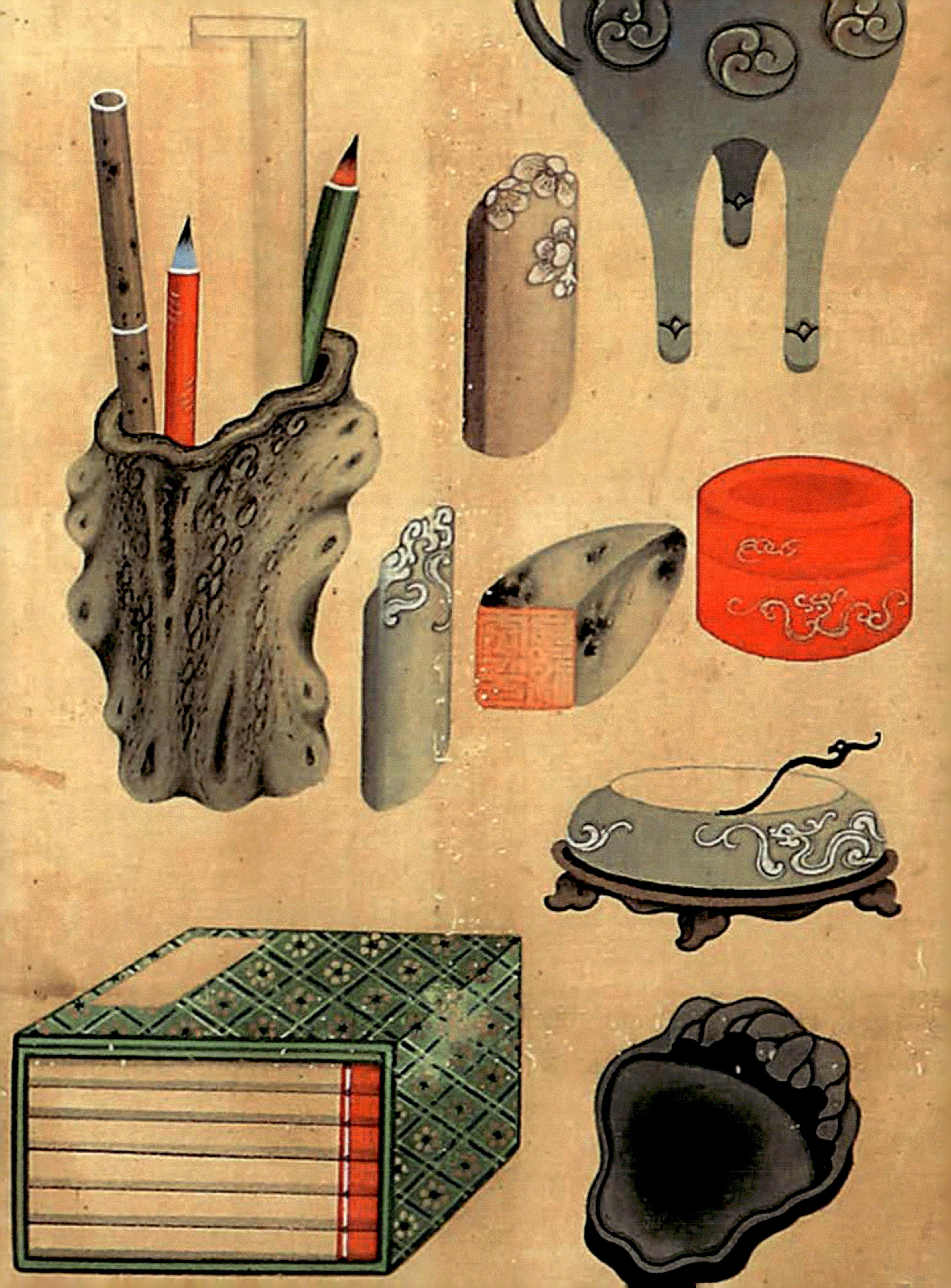

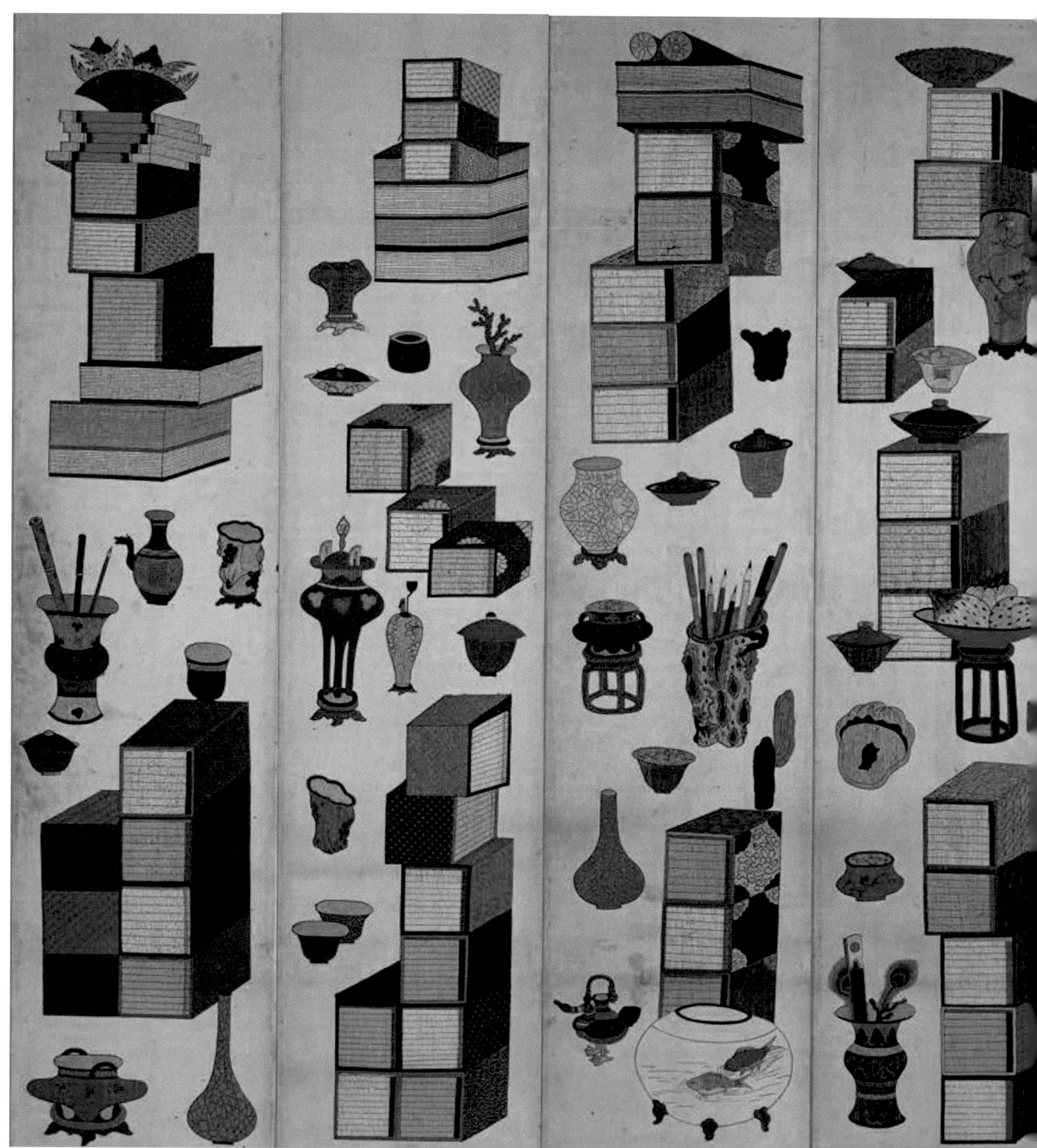

15 *Chaekgeori*

Anonymous, late 19th century
Eight-panel screen
Embroidery on silk, 166 x 38.5 cm (each panel)
Korean Folk Village, Yongin

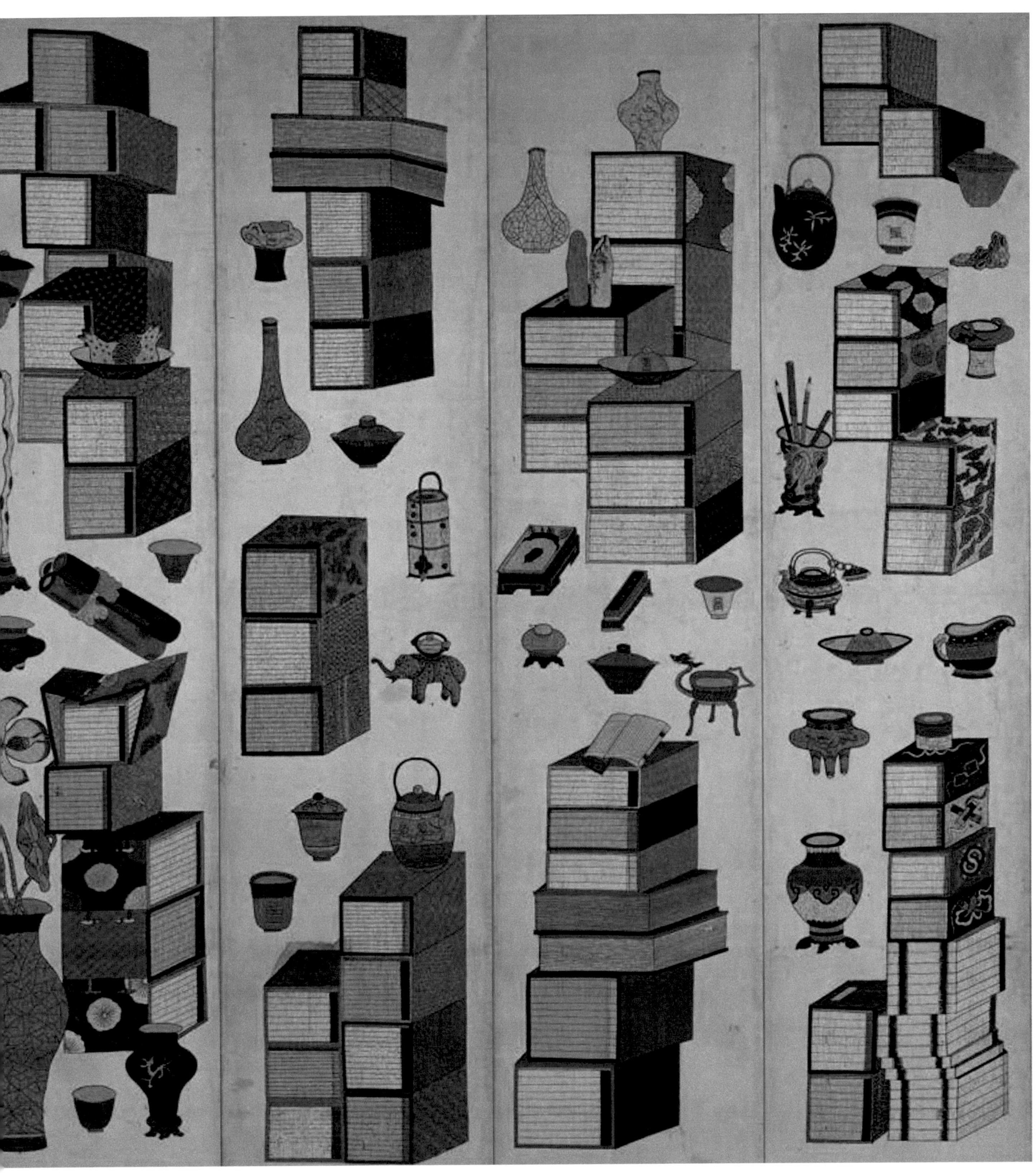

This large chaekgeori is a work of embroidery. Piles of books are placed at multiple levels without bookshelves, and the scholarly accoutrements are arranged between them. This work uses Western-style perspective, but the application of the technique is not entirely correct. Yet this imperfection makes the work even more unusual, and beautiful, in its unnaturalness. One factor that contributes to the piece's striking aura is its size. It is simply on a scale unheard of in the realm of painted chaekgeori.

The dyed indigo thread in the embroidery gives the screen an original, even modern look. The technique, at once soft and deep, belongs to the renowned Anju region style from North Pyongan Province in North Korea. The embossed surface of embroidered books and objects enhances the tangibility and weight of the objects hovering above the screen. Further, the embroidery implies the potential collaboration with female artisans on the initial drawing of the arrangement. This work is a masterpiece among embroidered chaekgeori. BC, JJL

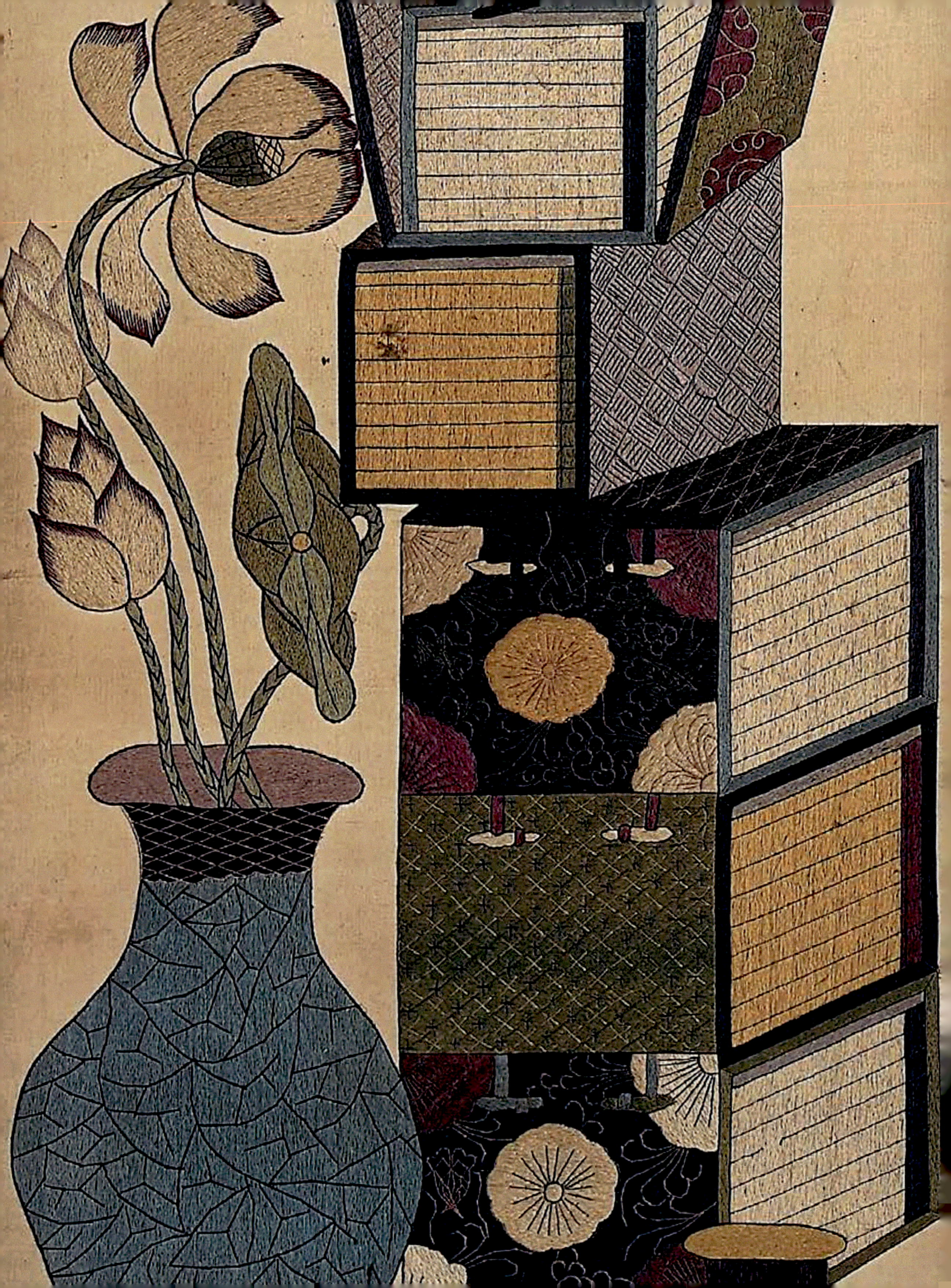

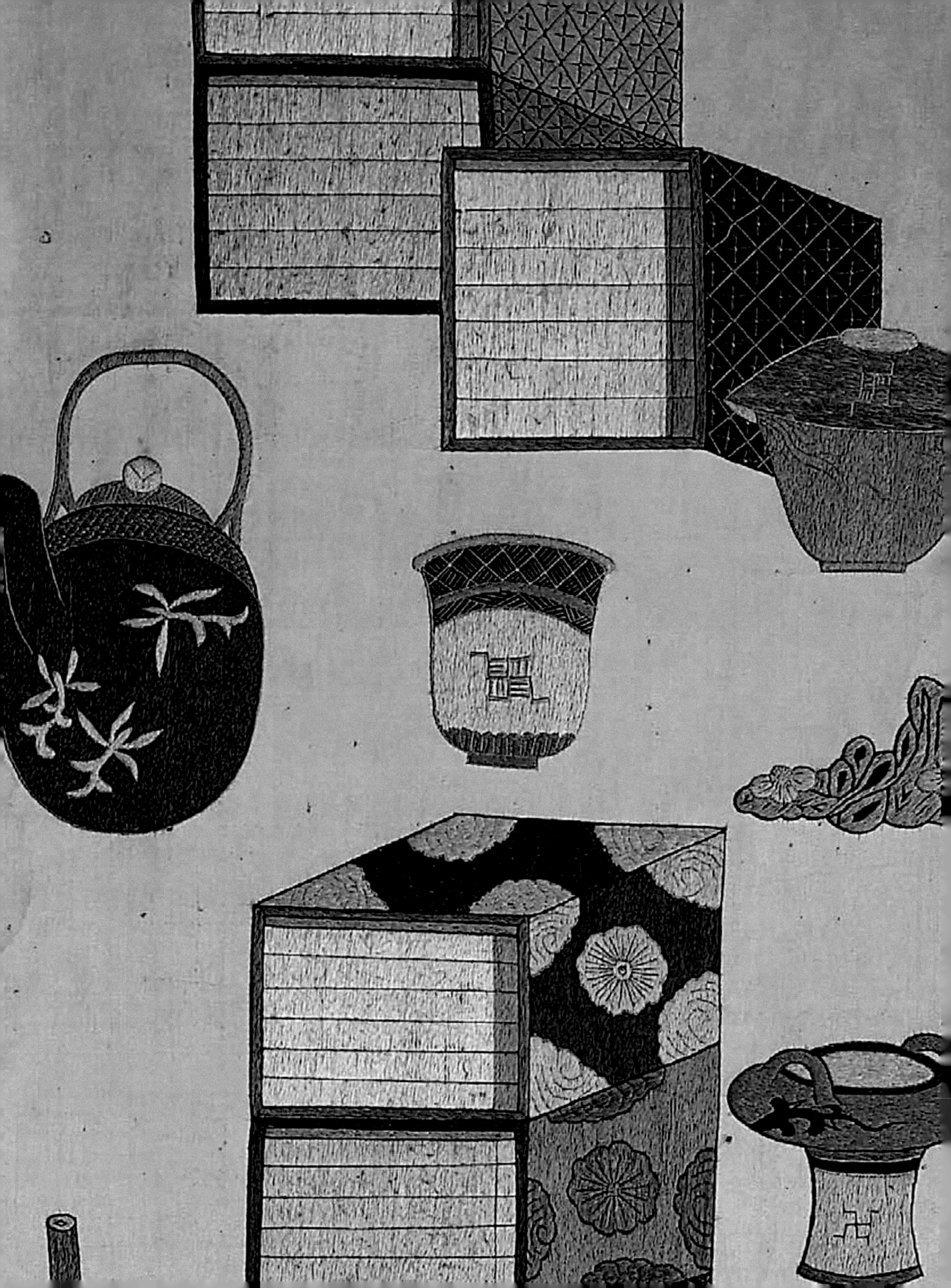

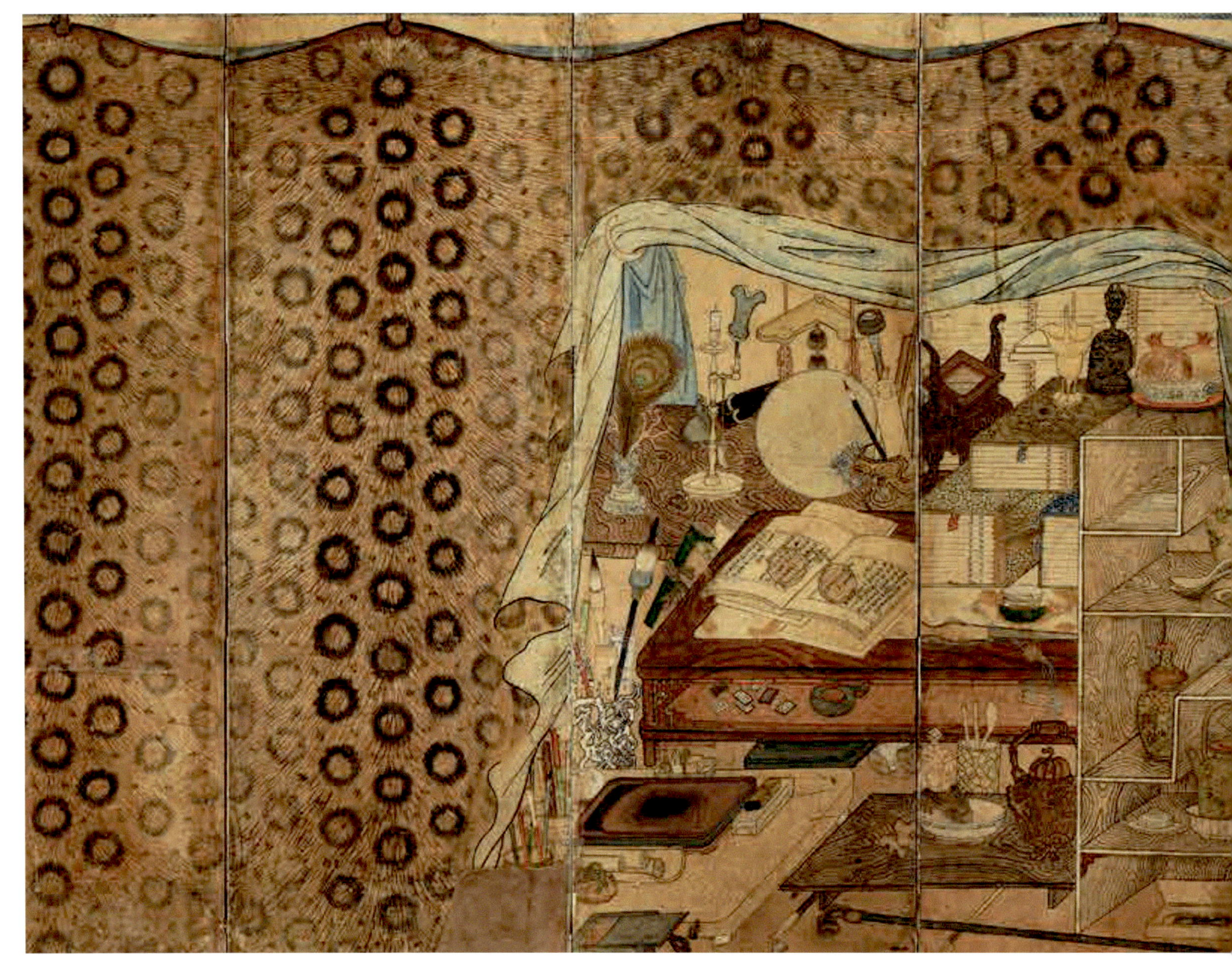

16 *Chaekgeori* behind a Leopard-Skin Curtain

Anonymous, late 19th century
Eight-panel folding screen
Ink and color on paper, 128 x 355 cm (overall)
Private collection

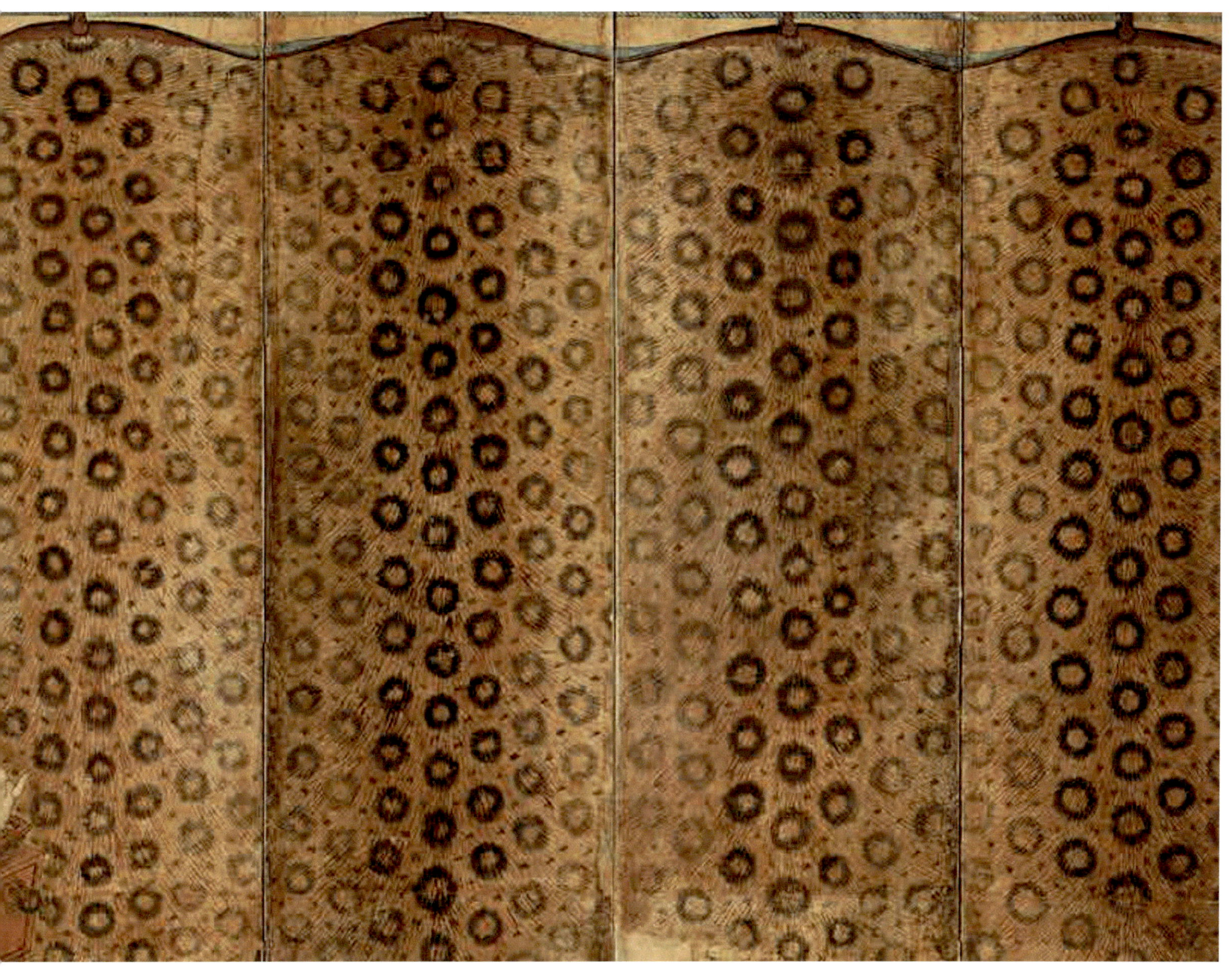

This eight-panel folding screen once depicted a leopard skin over its entire surface. At some point, its owner commissioned an artist to paint over sections of the two panels with images of books and scholarly accoutrements, perhaps due to the growing popularity of chaegkeori as a furnishing for scholars' studies. A similar type of screen combining the imagery of a leopard skin and chaekgeori is in the collection of Gyeonggi University Museum in Suwon.

The painted objects here, ranging from ancient bronze vessels, peacock feathers, a pair of reading glasses, a long pipe for smoking, musical instruments, and a set of *golpae* blocks, a traditional Korean domino game, give the scene an air of bravura. In a certain sense, this screen is not a simple still life of assorted objects, but perhaps an insightful portrayal of a man who could spend a day without worrying about the lofty matters of life.
BC, SM

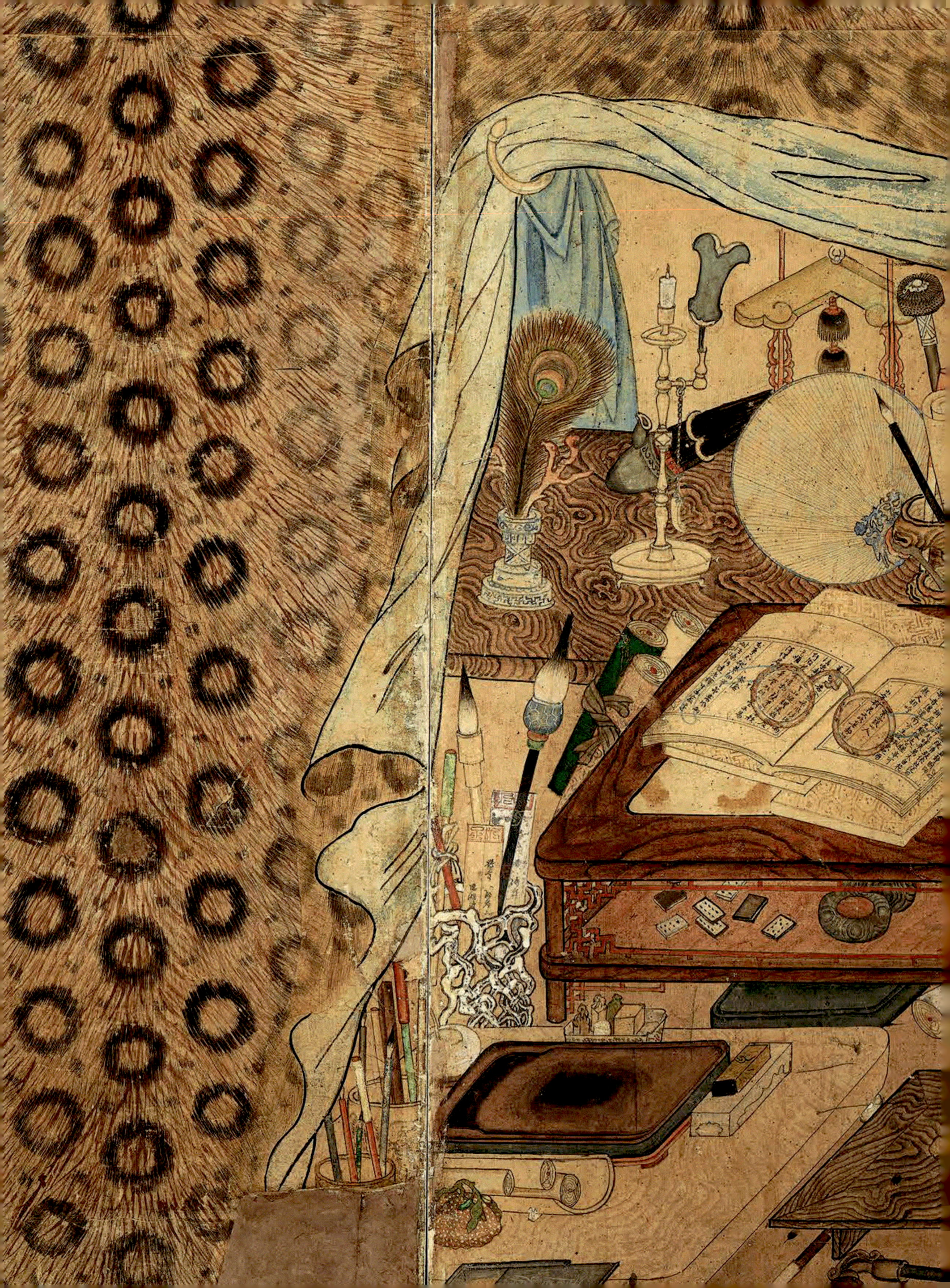

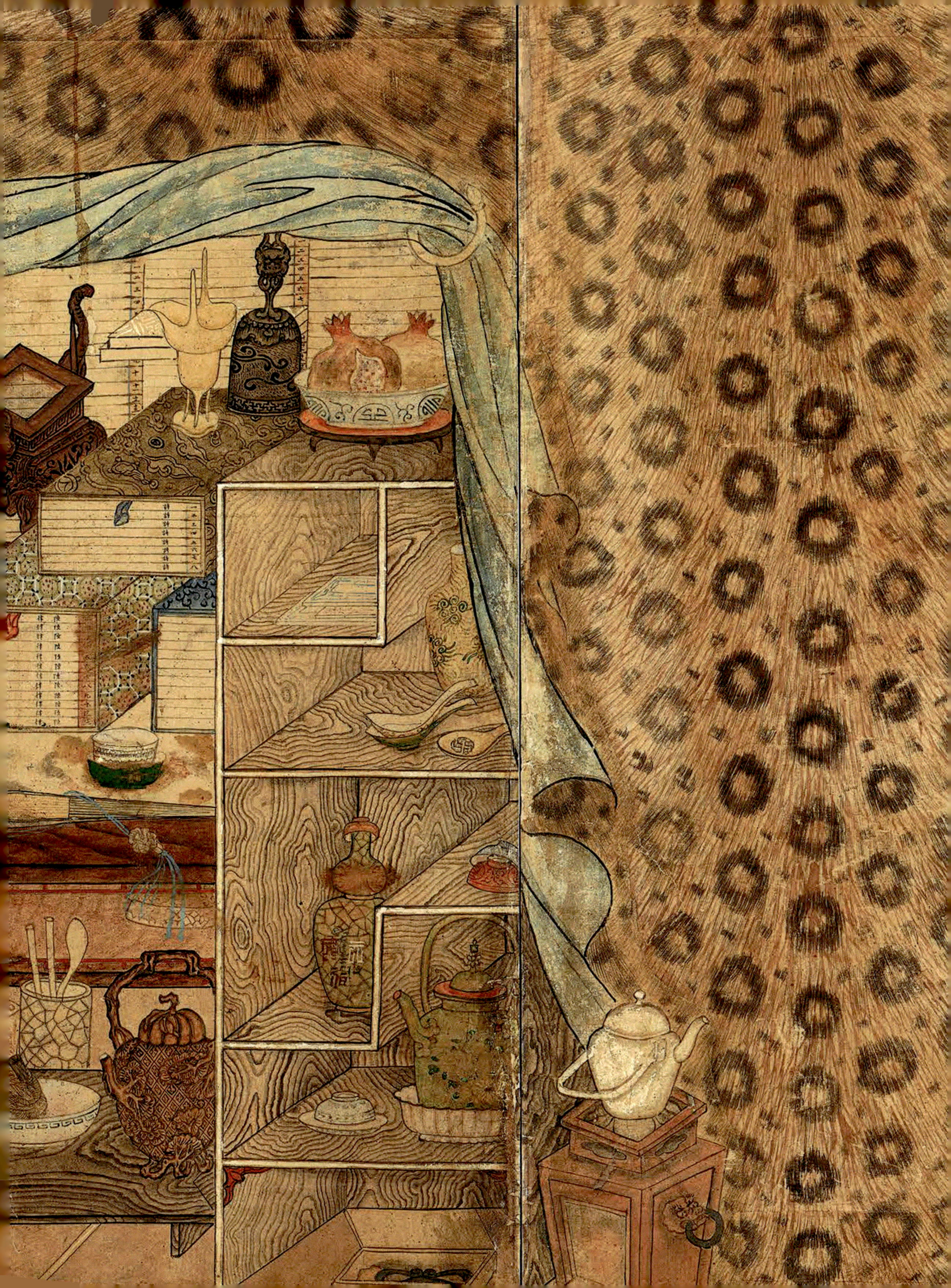

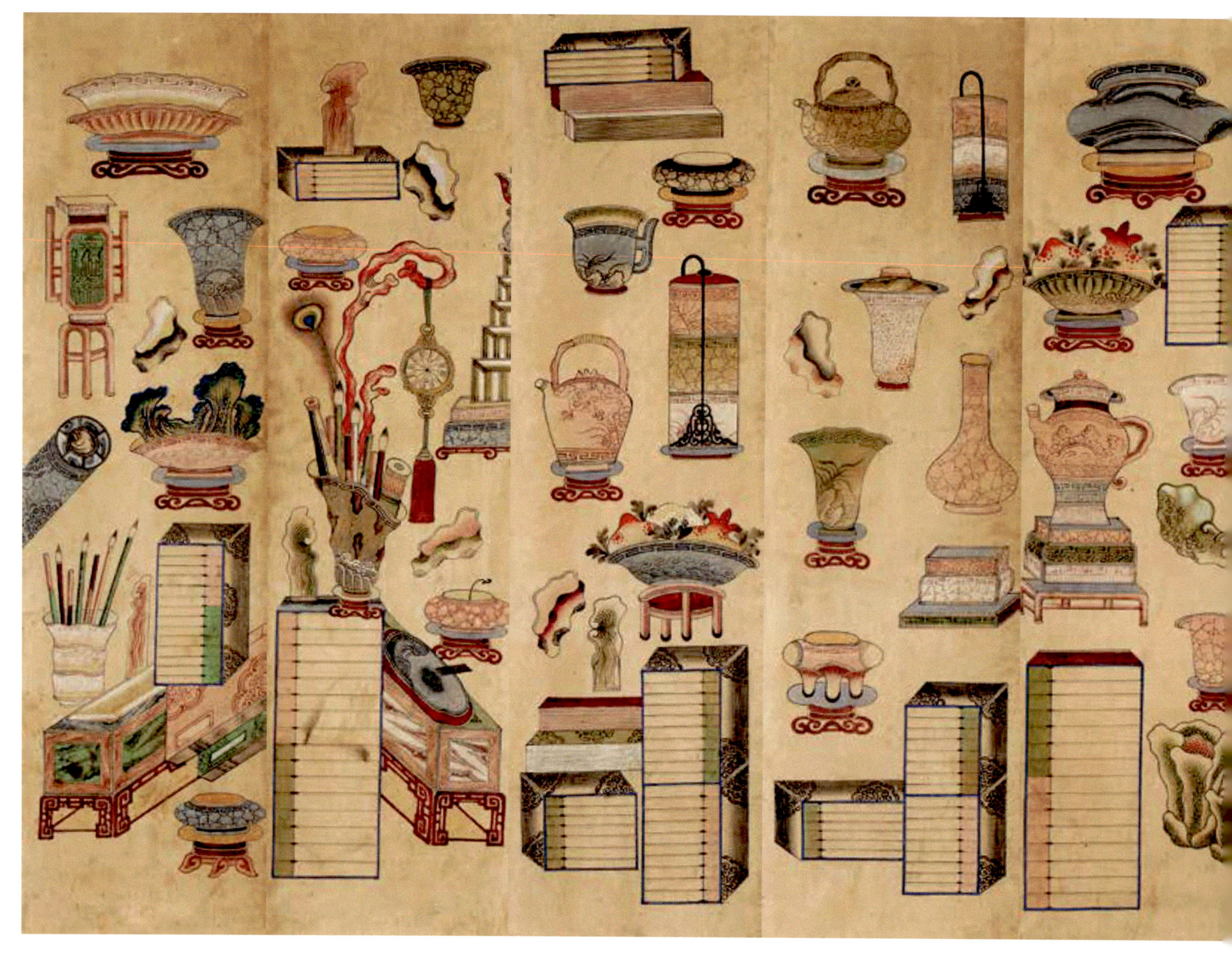

17 *Chaekgeori*

Anonymous, 19th century
Ten-panel folding screen
Ink and color on silk, 172.7 x 43.2 cm (each panel)
Philadelphia Museum of Art, Purchased with funds contributed by the Korea Heritage Group, the Hollis Family Foundation Fund, and the Henry B. Keep Fund, 2002-74-1

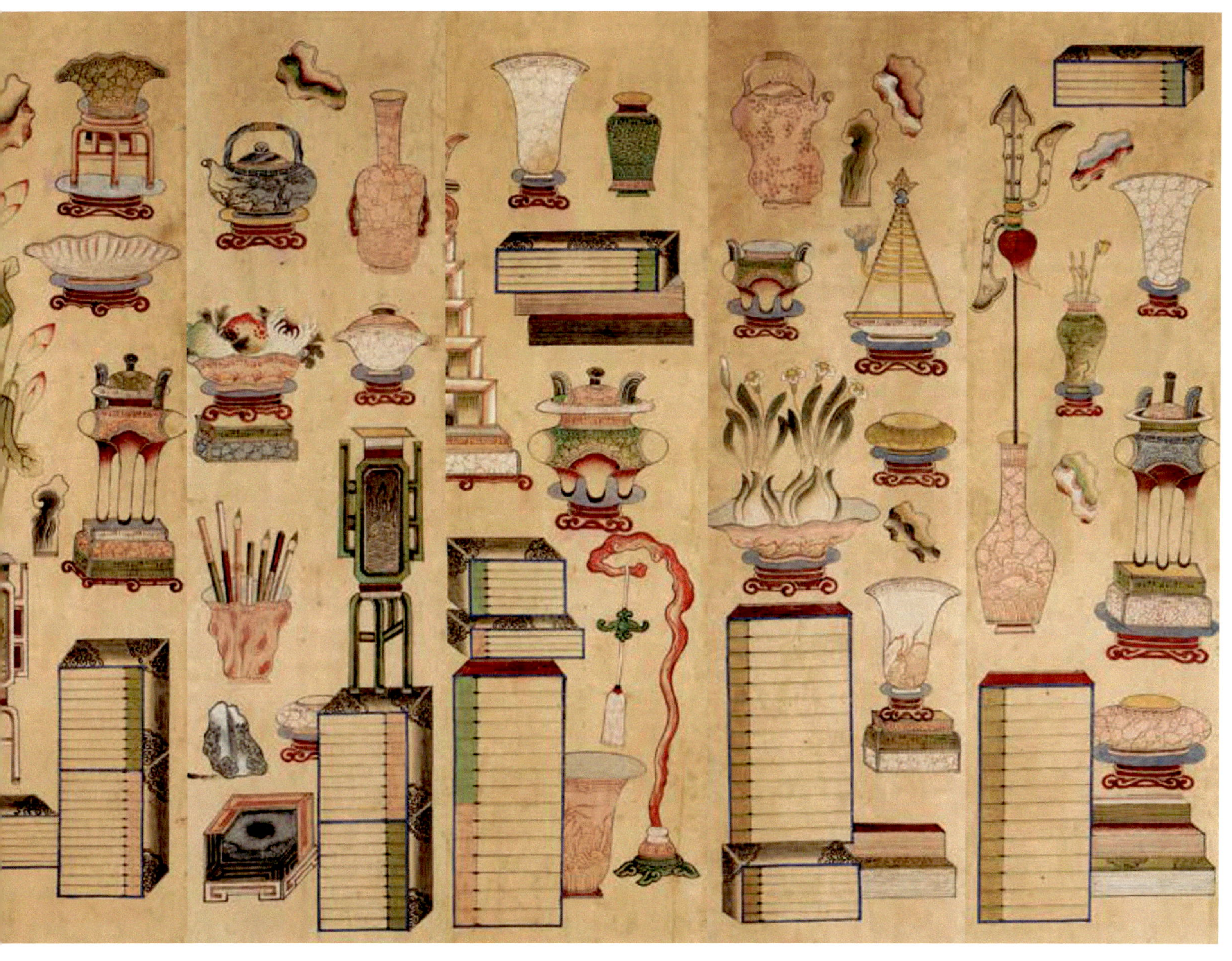

In this folding screen, objects are no longer shelved in bookcases, but rather spread all over the picture surface, as if floating on air. Many of the painted objects are scholarly items (books, brushes, ink stones, and seals) as well as antiquities to adorn the scholar's desk (a bowl of precious minerals, a bowl of fragrant fingered citrons, vases with crackle pattern, and a number of ancient bronze vessels). In addition to these objects, which often can be found in majority of chaekgeori screens, new items were added to symbolize the patron's aspiration for social and economic success. For instance, the three-pronged spear in a slender white vase with crackle pattern and wave design may symbolize success as a military officer. The European pocket watch hung on a branch of coral along with a peacock feather not only symbolizes bureaucratic promotion, but also implies that by the late nineteenth century well-to-do people could afford a timepiece made in a foreign land. SM

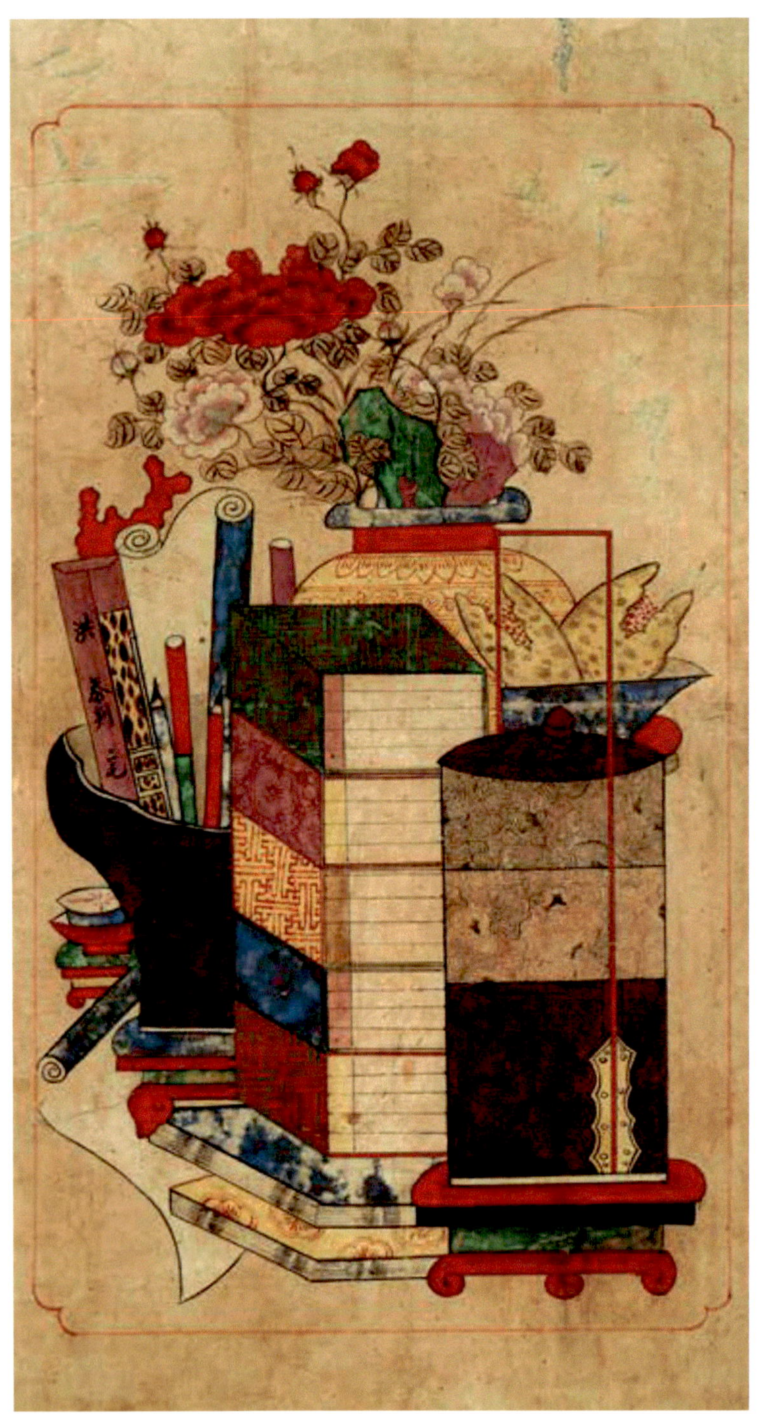

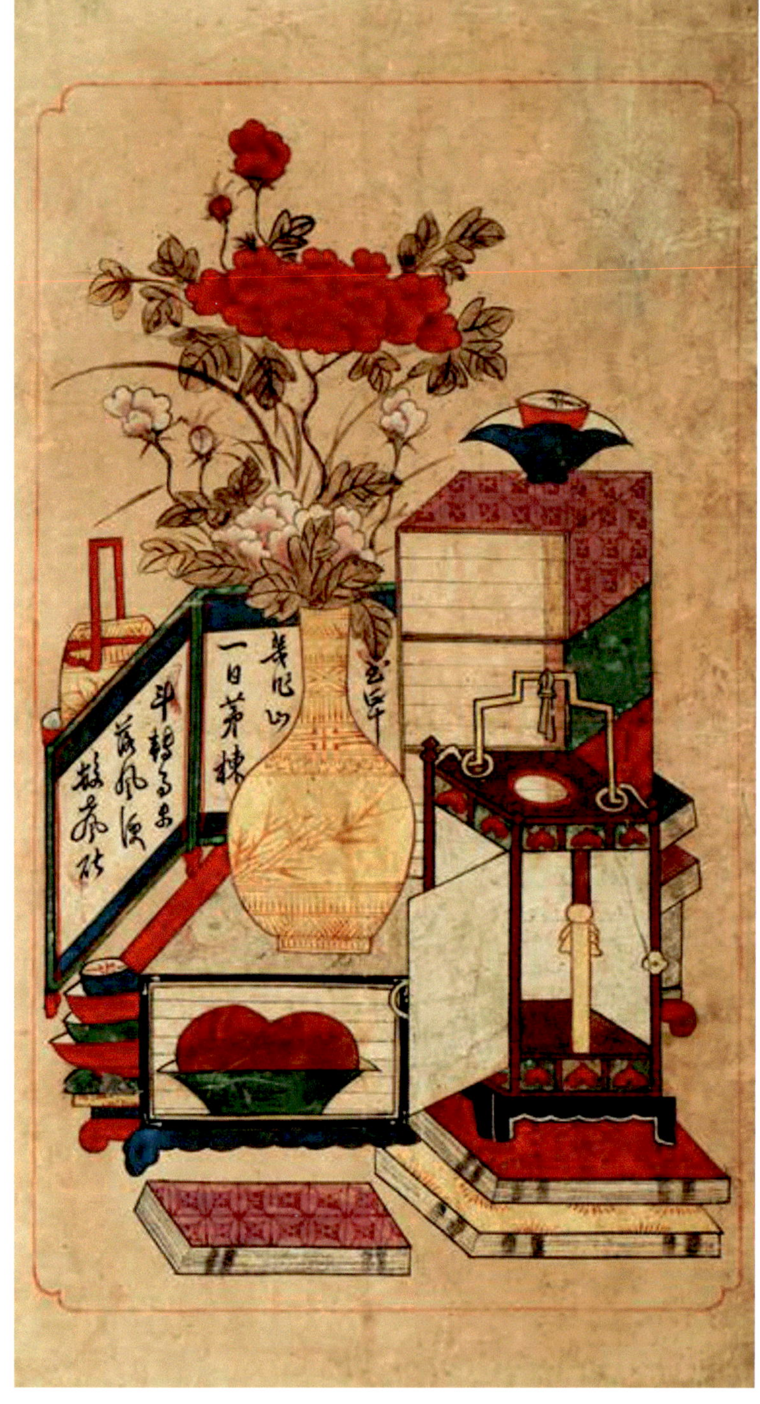

18 *Chaekgeori*

Anonymous, 19th century
Eight-panel screen
Ink and color on paper, 129.5 x 304.8 cm (overall)
Private collection

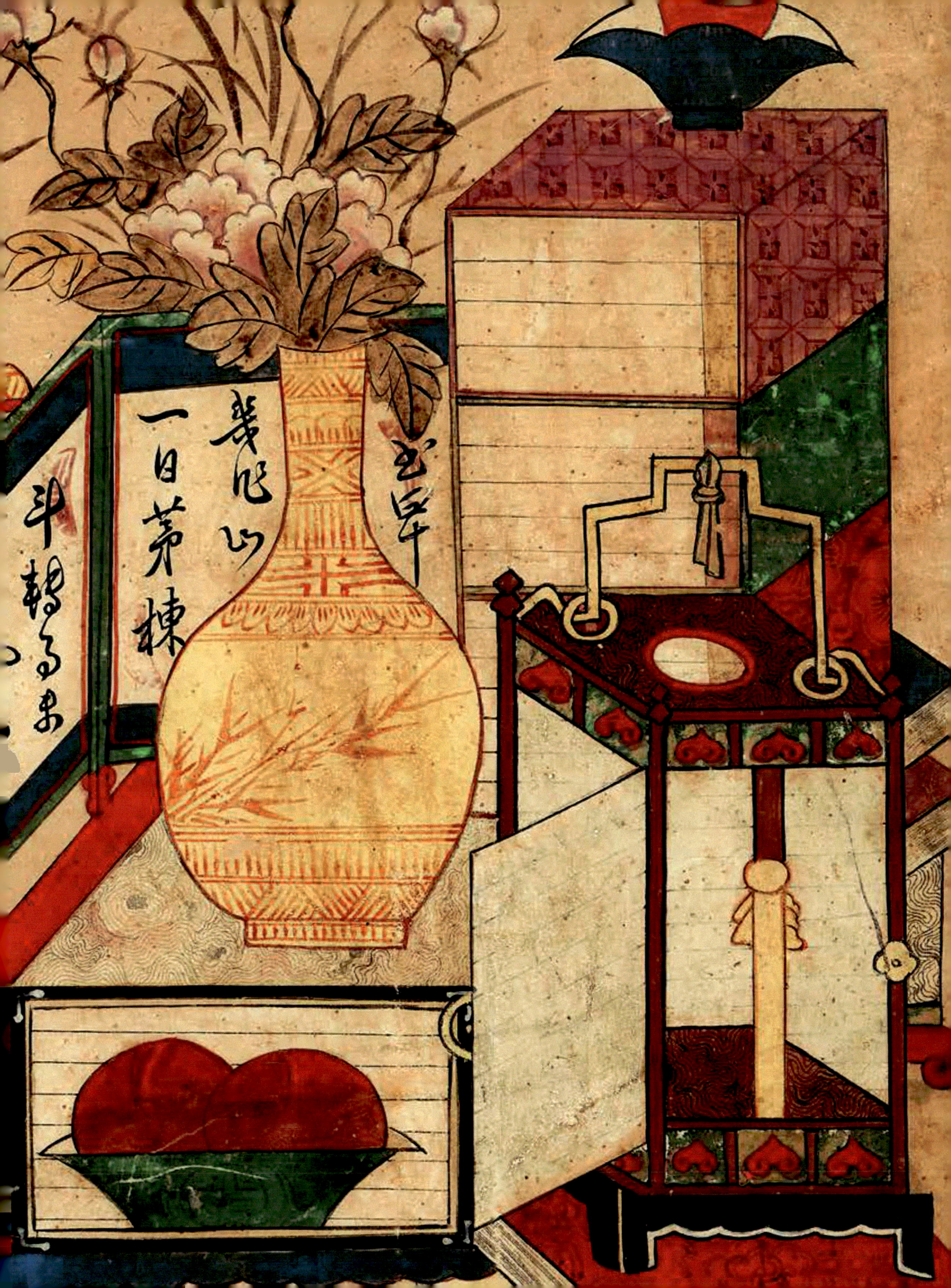

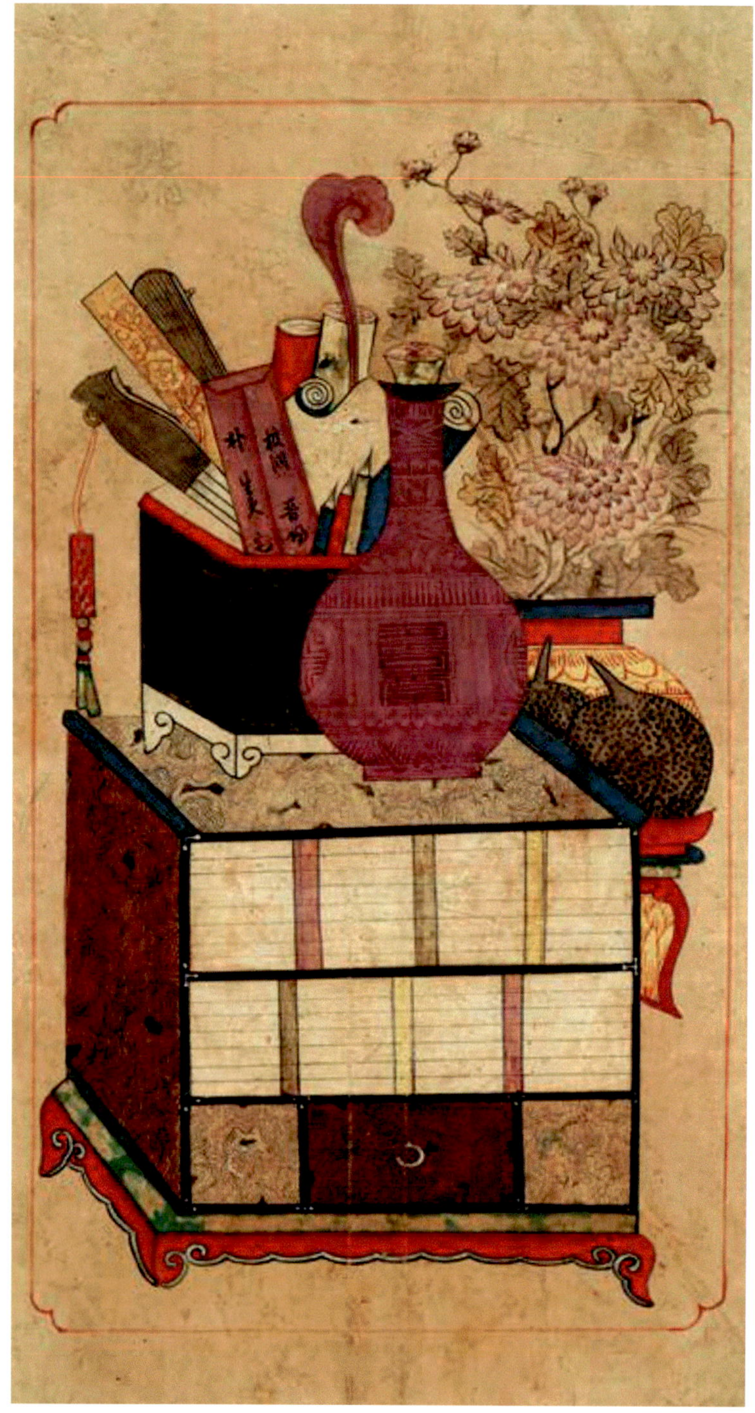

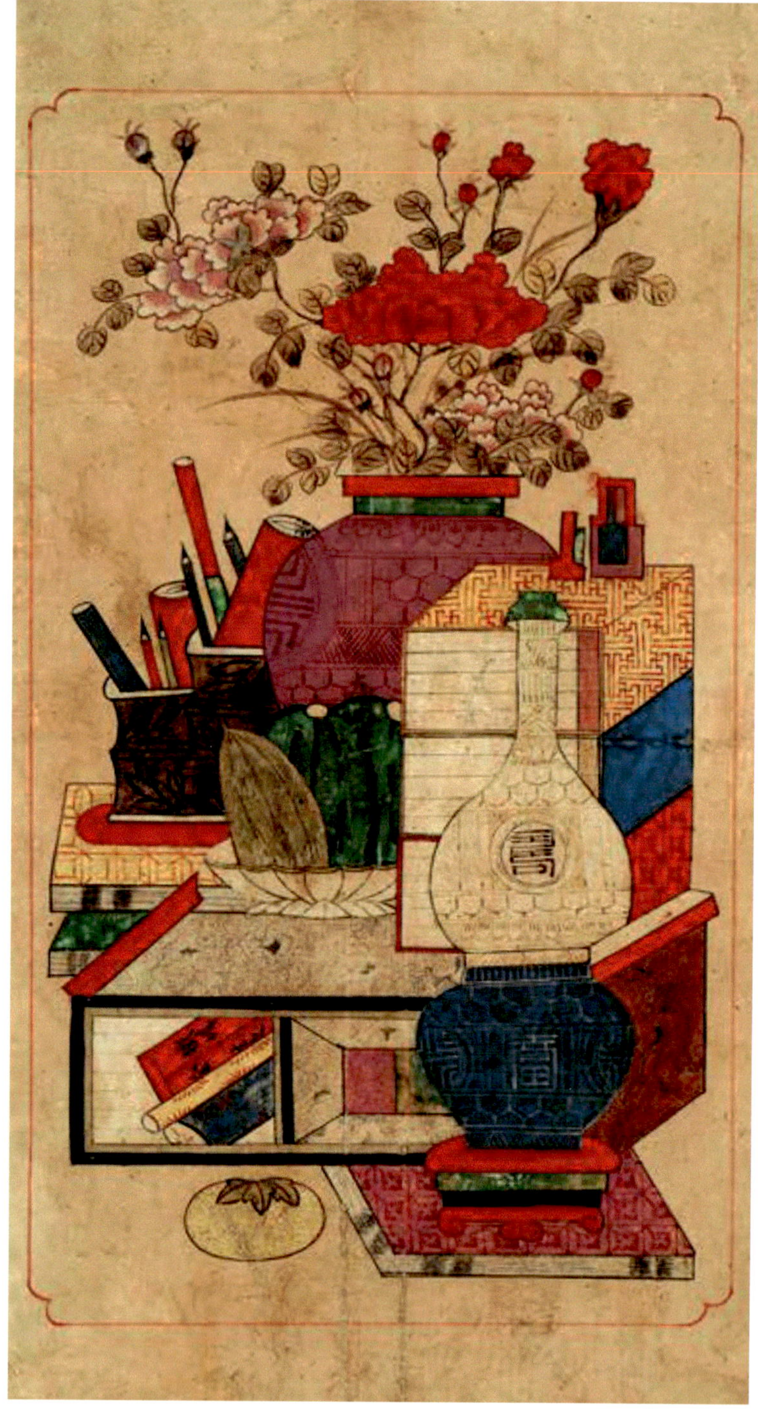

This chaekgeori is an example of exquisite detail in a balanced composition. Each of the eight panels is compactly filled with stationery, flowers, fruits, and collectible commodities, such as a porcelain vase, an incense burner, a teapot, and a pair of eye glasses. Also, the upper part of each panel contains flowers that represent the four seasons and add brilliance and brightness. Symbolic fruits, such as watermelon, grapes, Korean melon, pomegranates with lots of seeds, and eggplants in phallic shape, represent the patron's aspiration of fertility and lots of offspring. Books are pushed back or partially blocked by other everyday objects and small furniture, so that the main protagonist in this chaekgeori screen is not clear. The artist experimented with colorful and detailed patterns on book covers, surfaces of small tables, and fronts of small cabinets to enhance the screen's dazzling embellishment. BC, SK

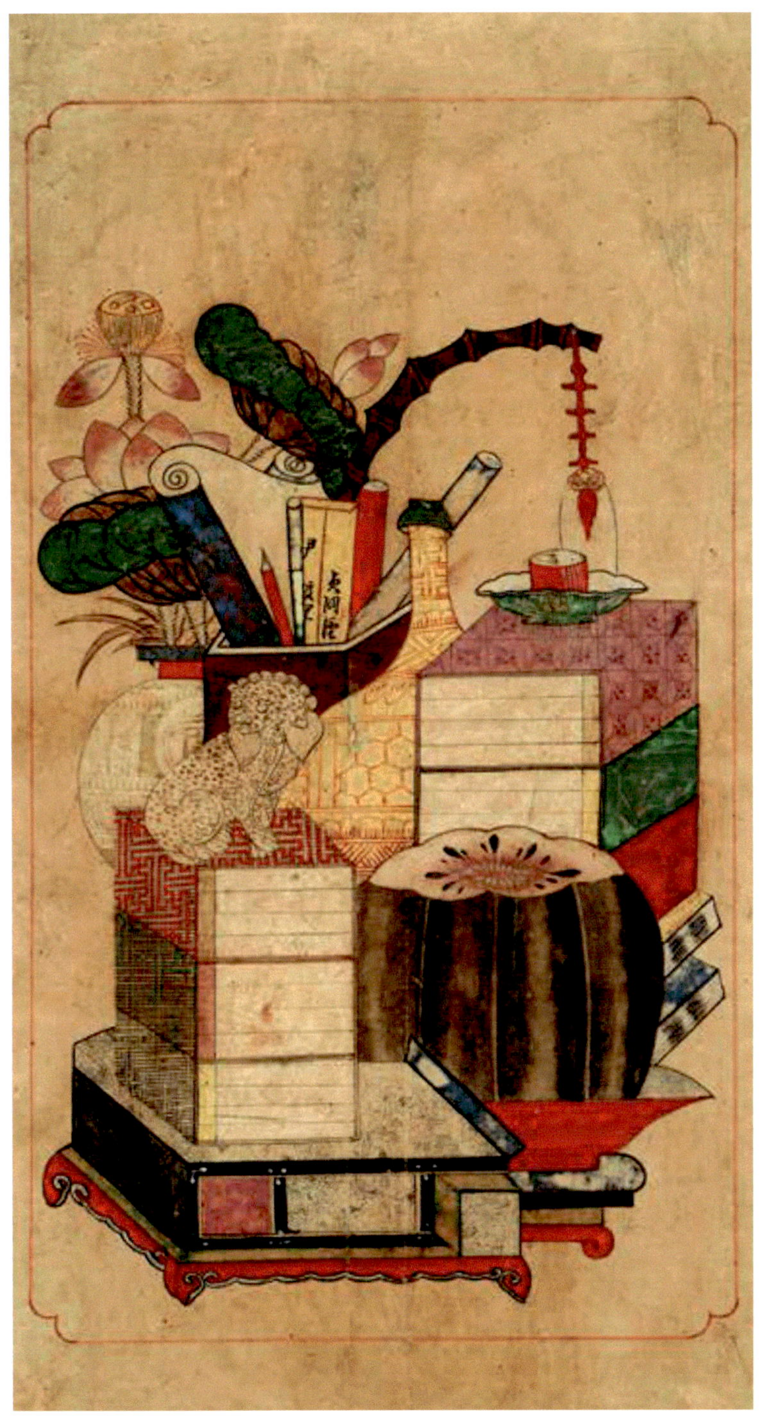

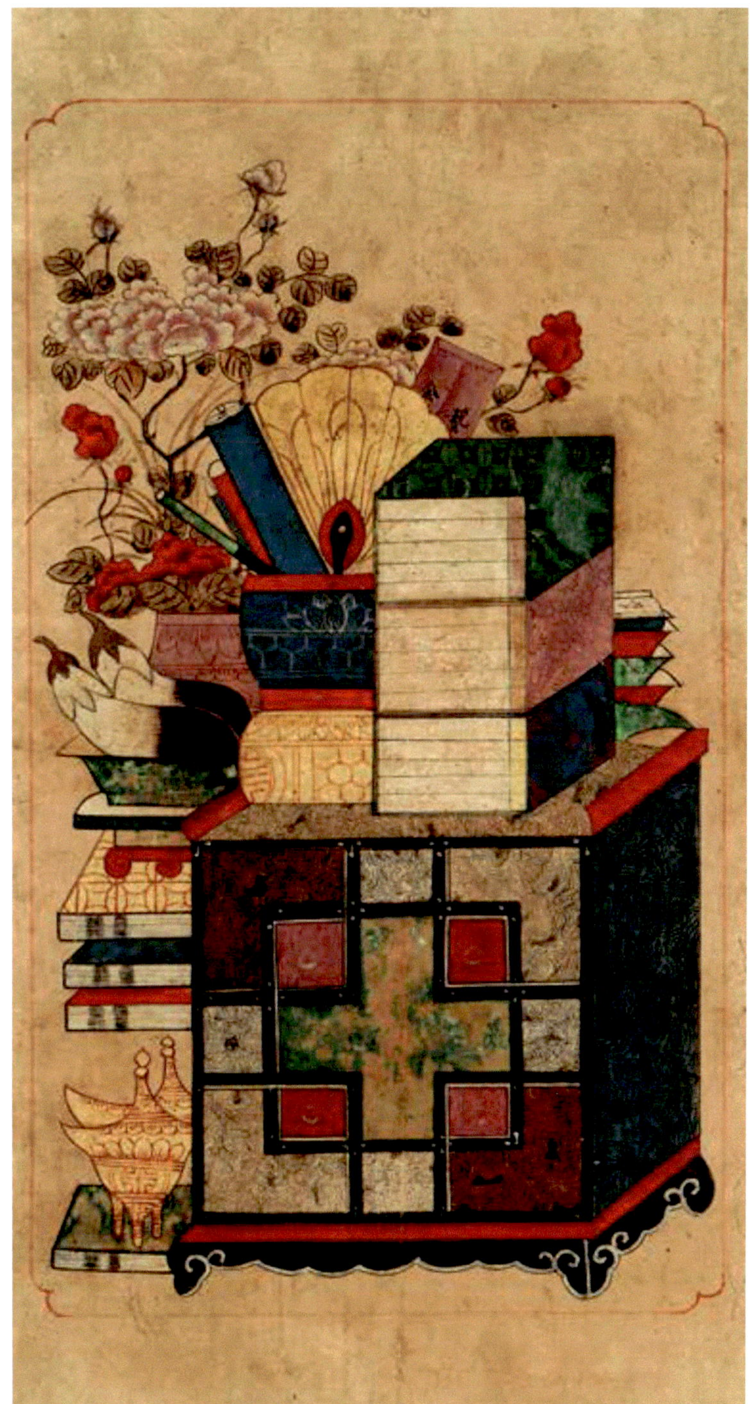

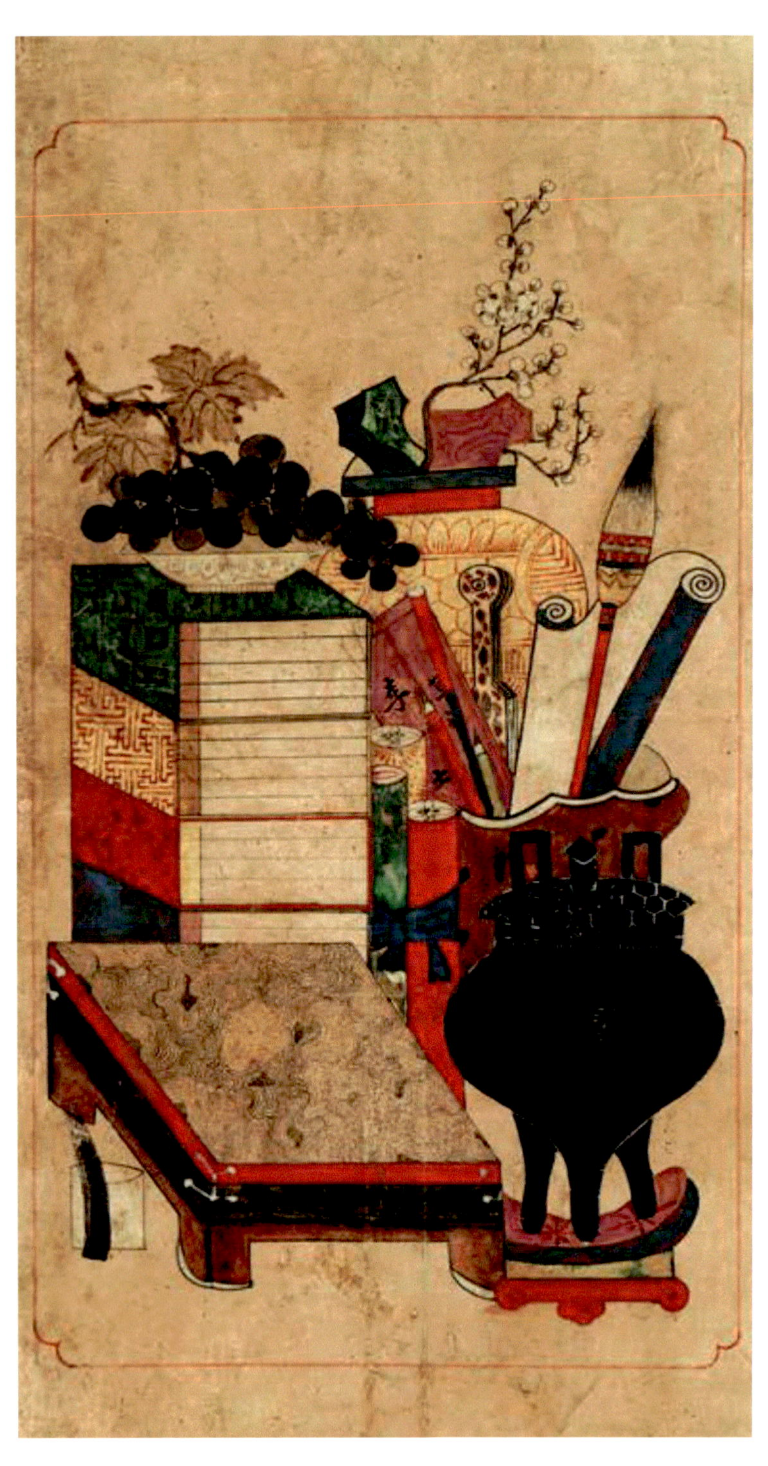

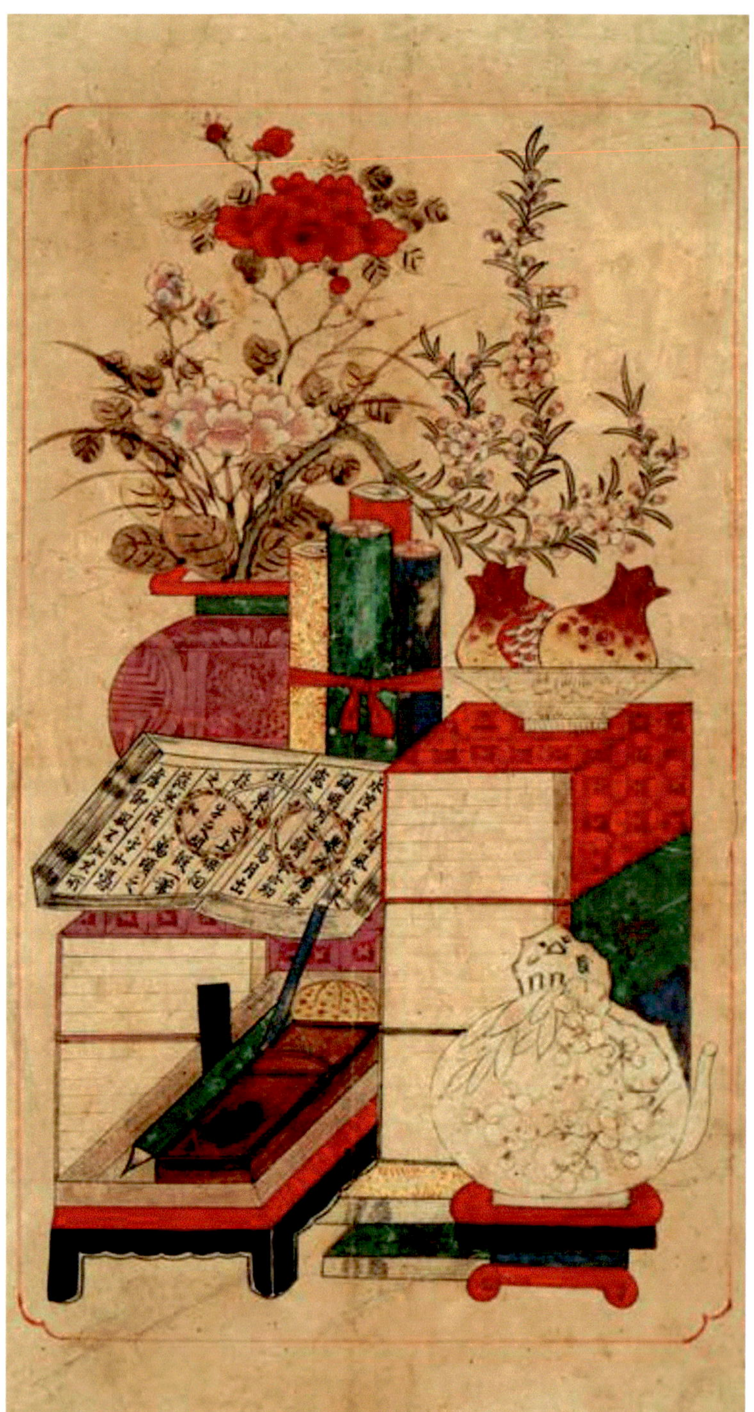

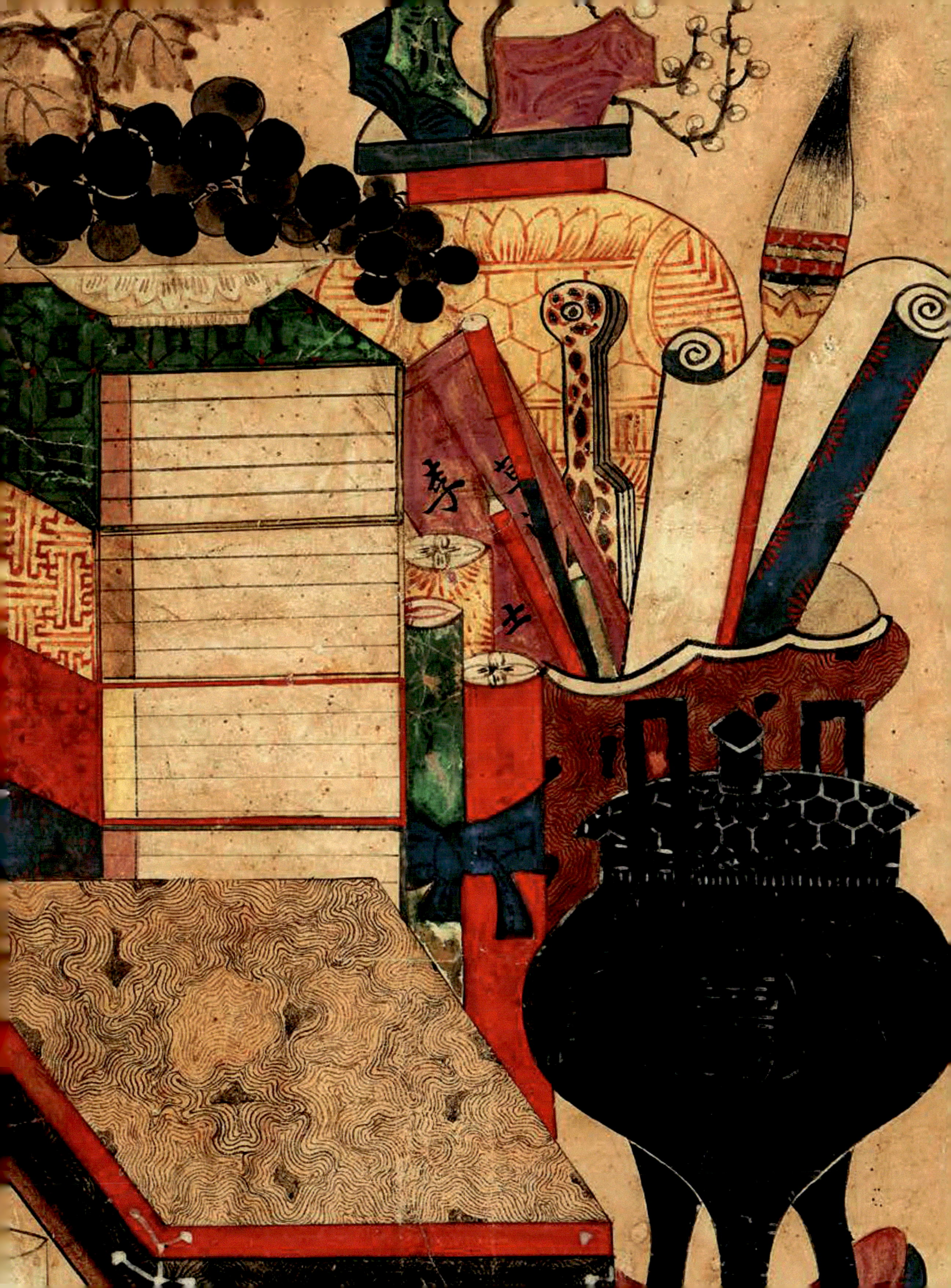

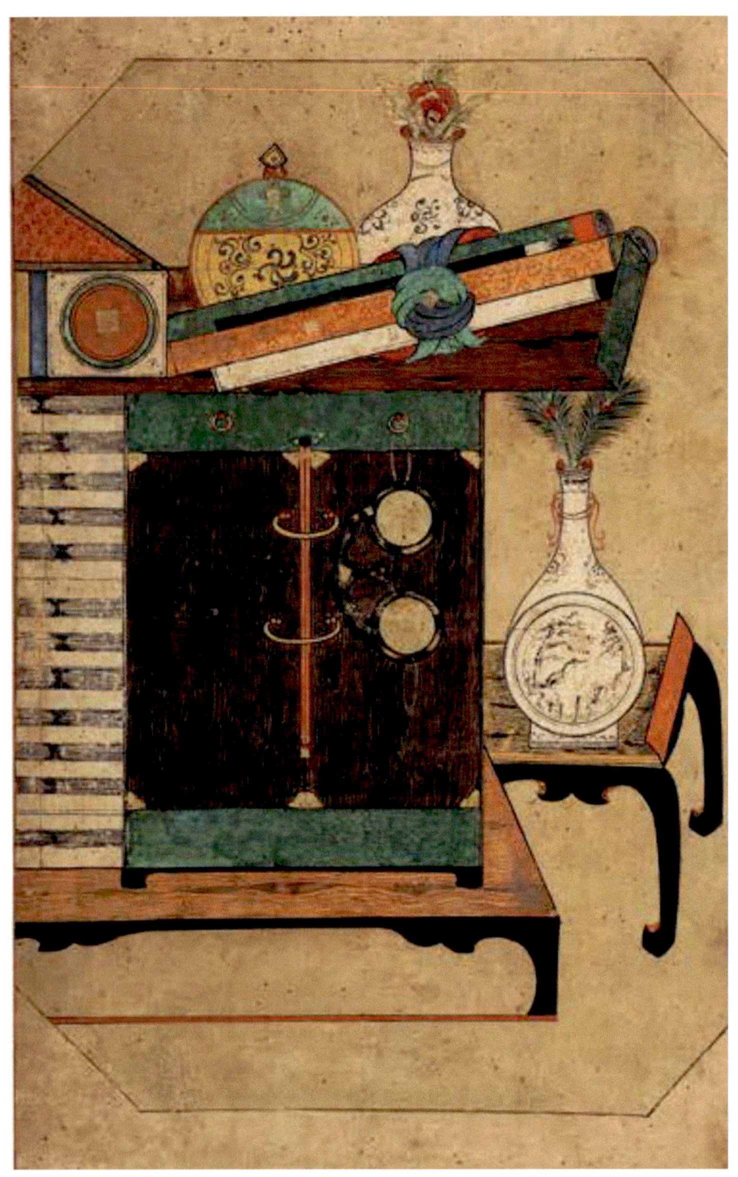
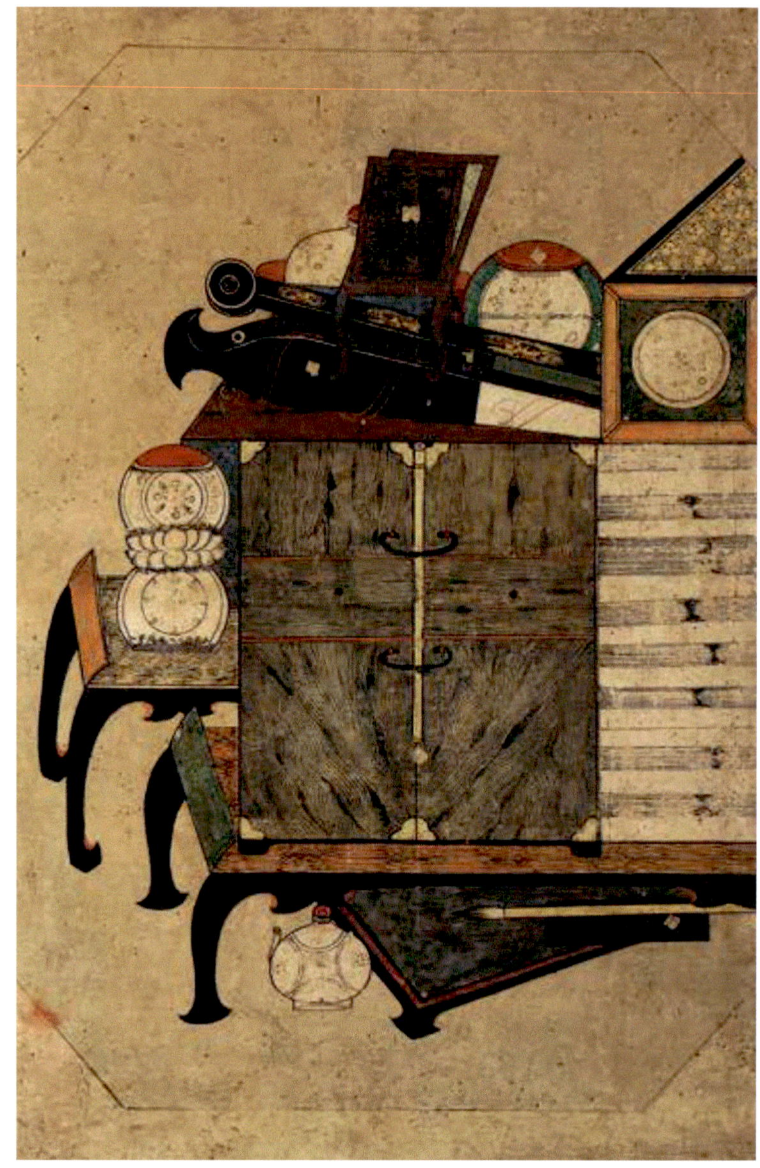

19 *Chaekgeori*

Anonymous, late 19th century
Eight-panel screen
Ink and color on paper, 47.3 x 30.5 cm (each panel)
Private collection

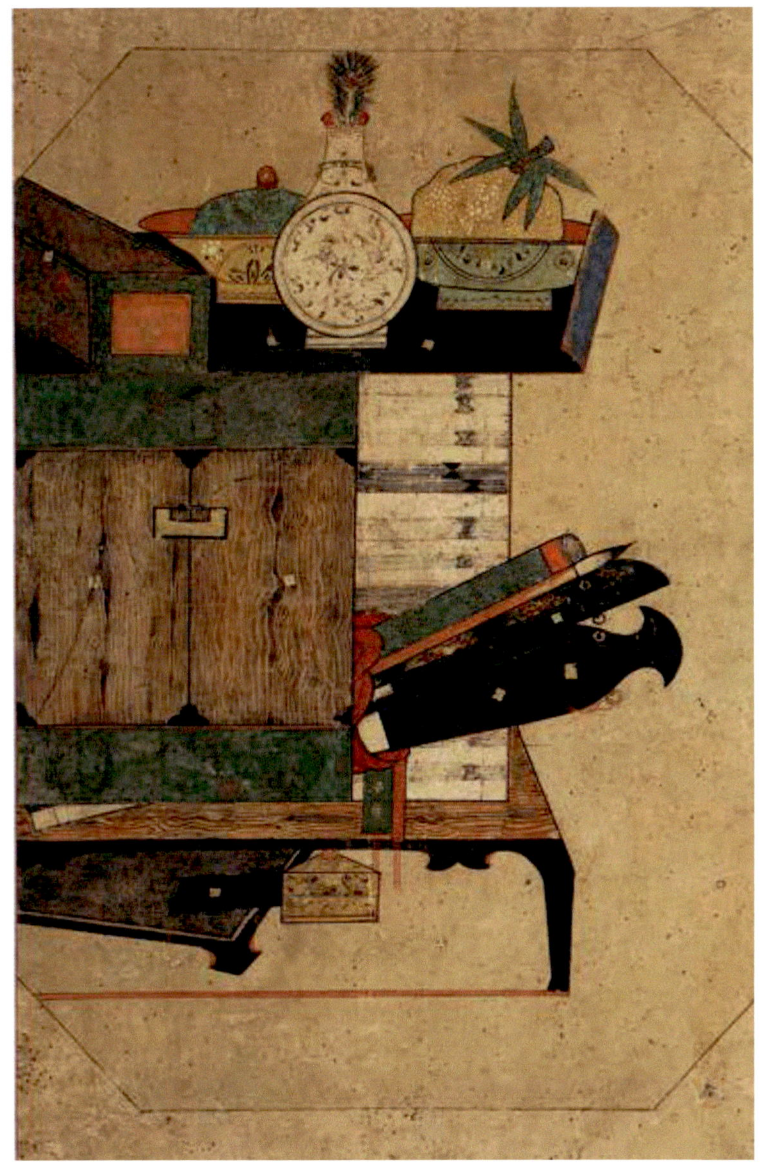

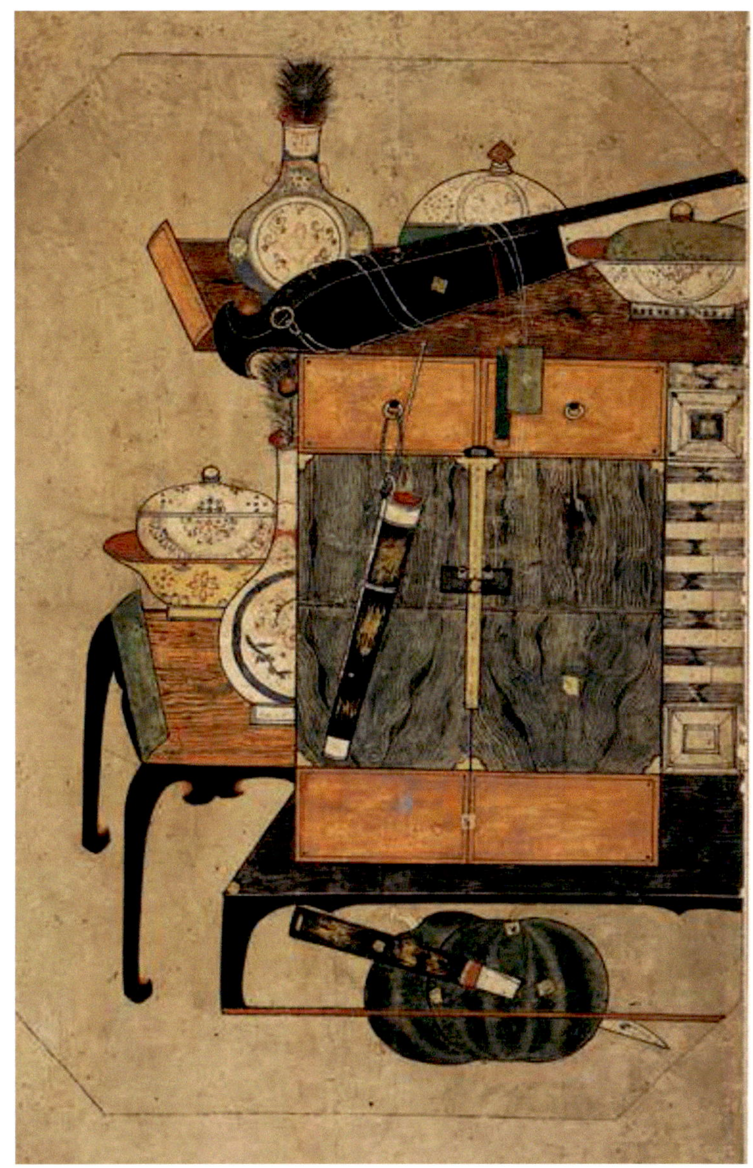

The screen is a striking departure from typical chaekgeori compositions. The most eye-catching feature is the off-center placement of the books and furniture. The landscape paintings of the Joseon dynasty often have asymmetrical compositions, but asymmetry is unusual in chaekgeori screens.

The objects—furniture, perfume bottle, women's shoes made of leather, luxurious pottery—signal that the screen was made for a female owner. The watermelon in the last panel symbolizes fecundity, but there is a subtle and surprising twist here. The knife stabbed right into the middle of the watermelon implies a passive yet powerful resistance to the limited social role of women during the Joseon dynasty. The extraordinary composition and intricate textures that characterize this work mark it as a masterpiece of folk-style chaekgeori. BC, JL

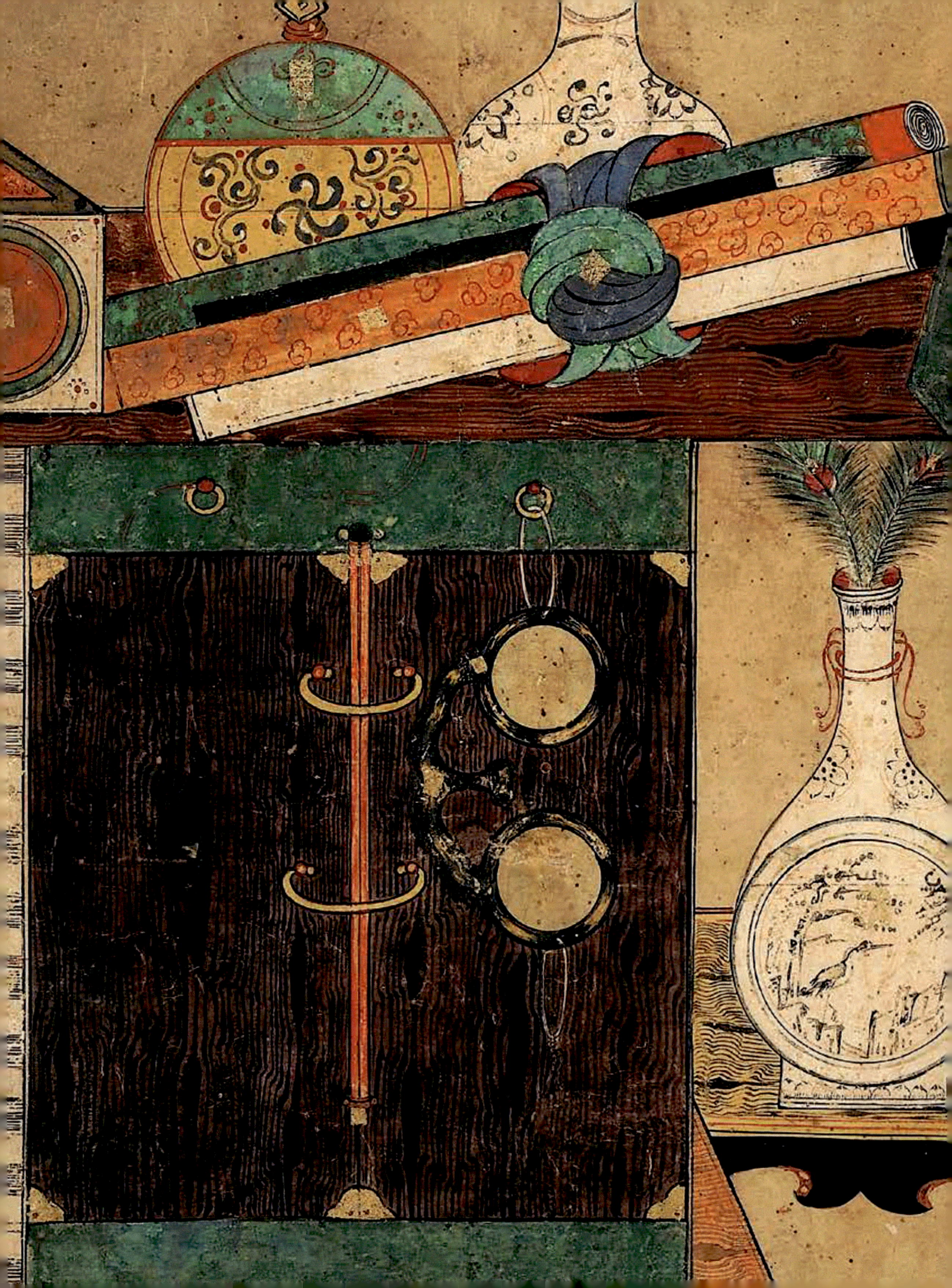

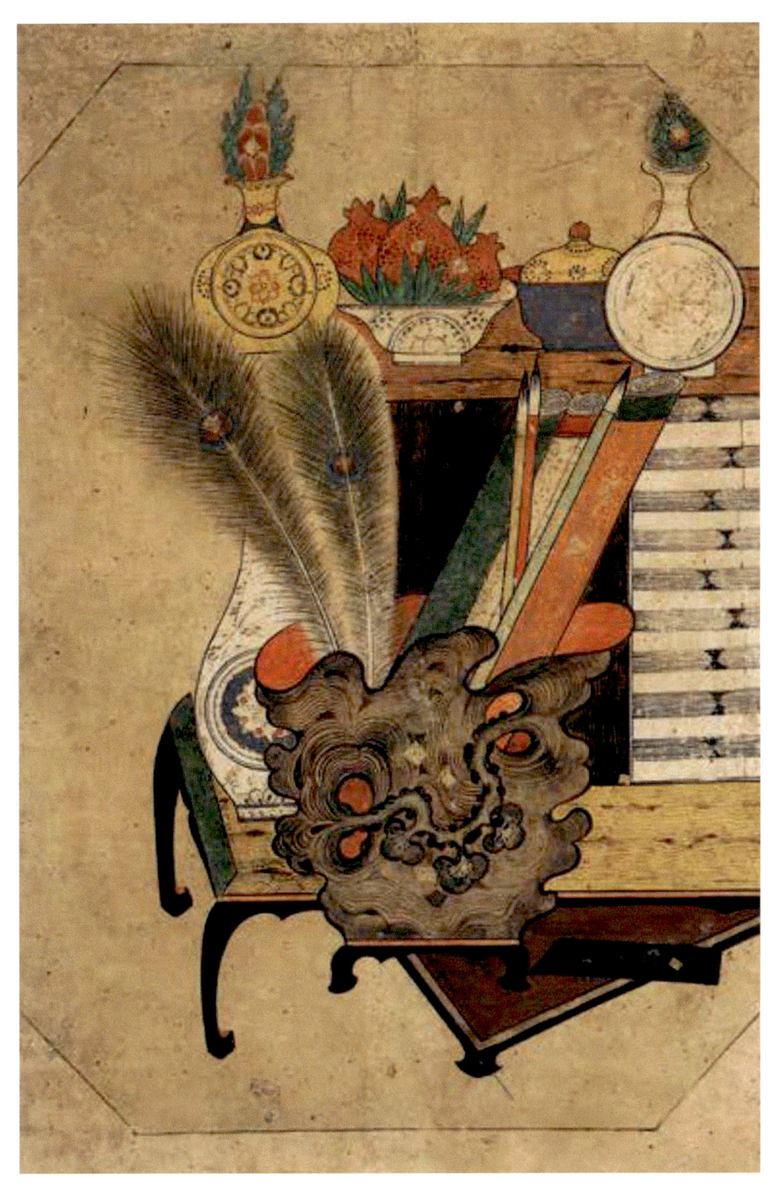

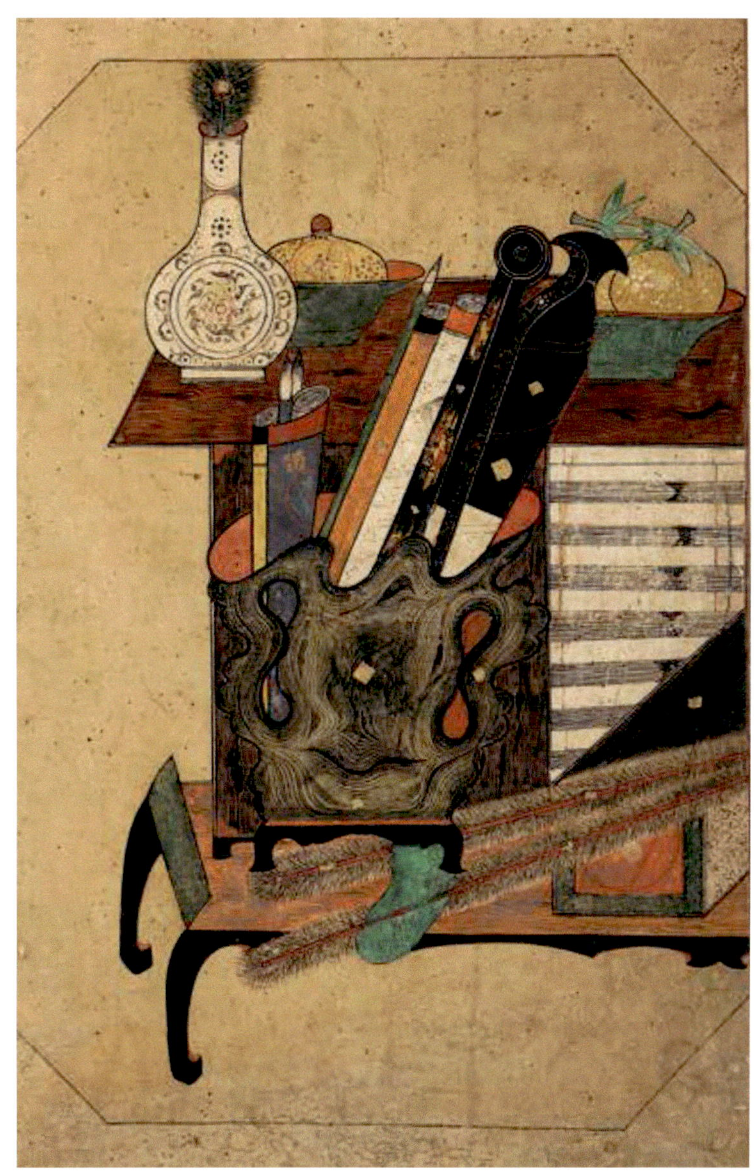

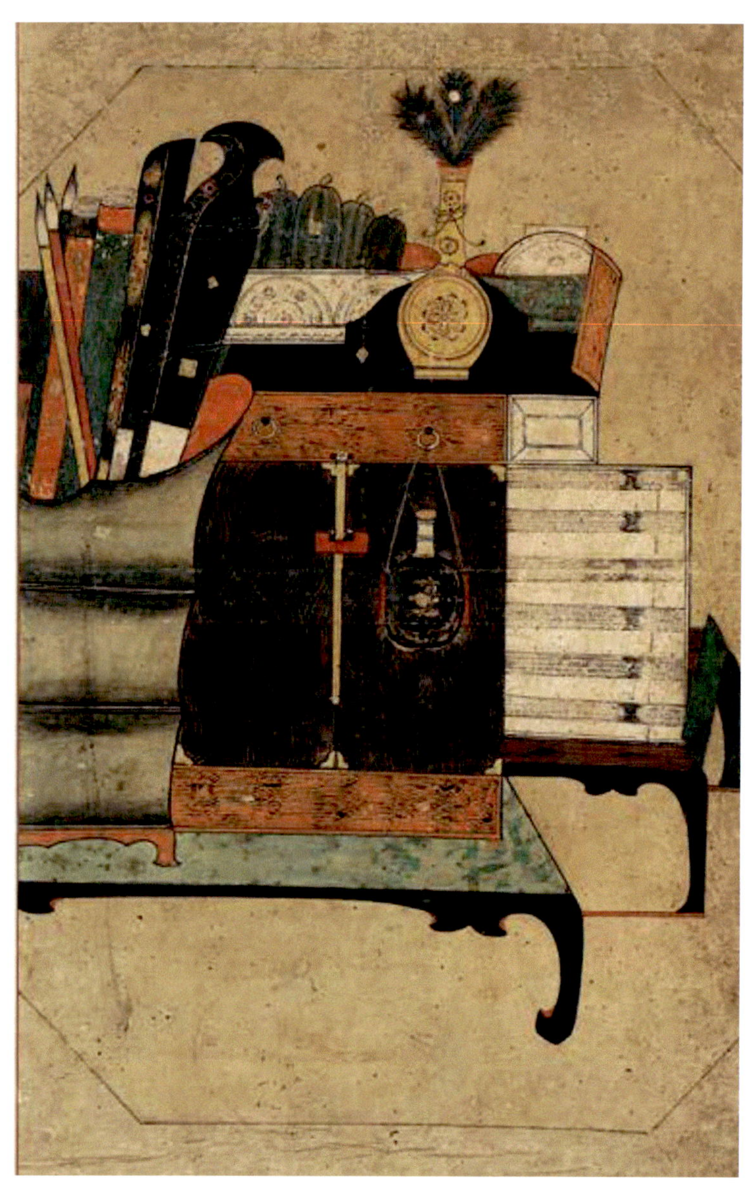

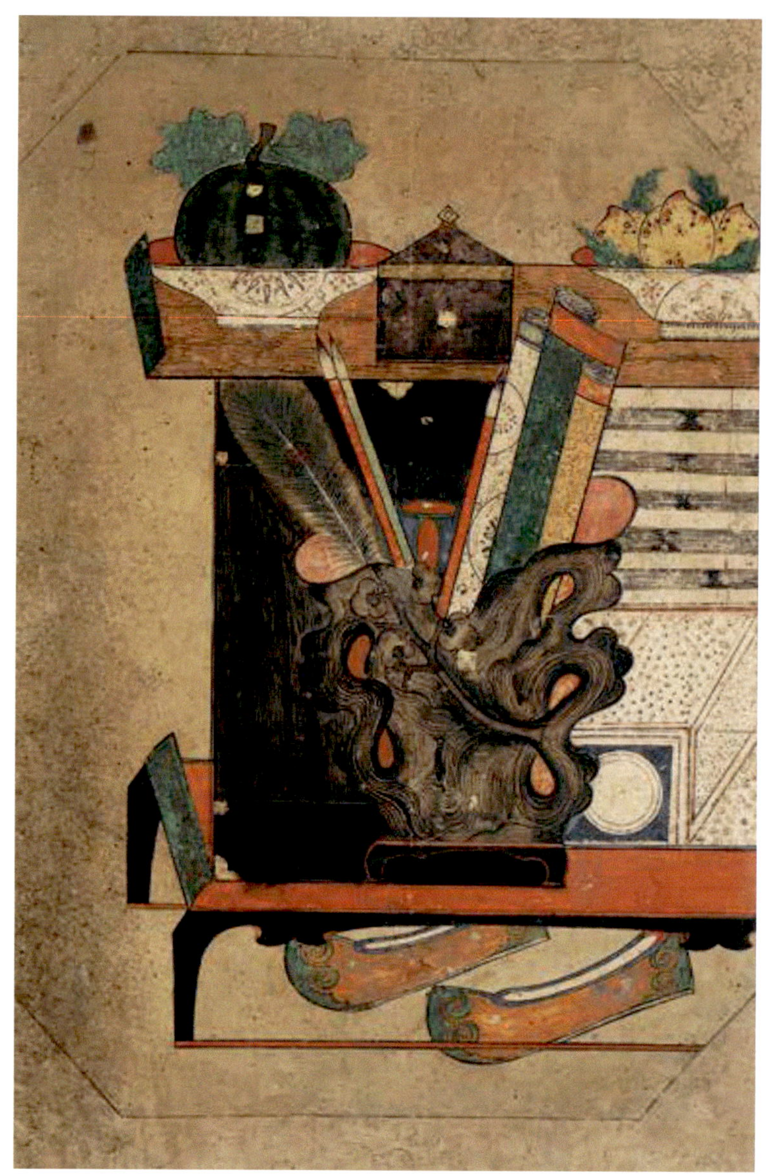

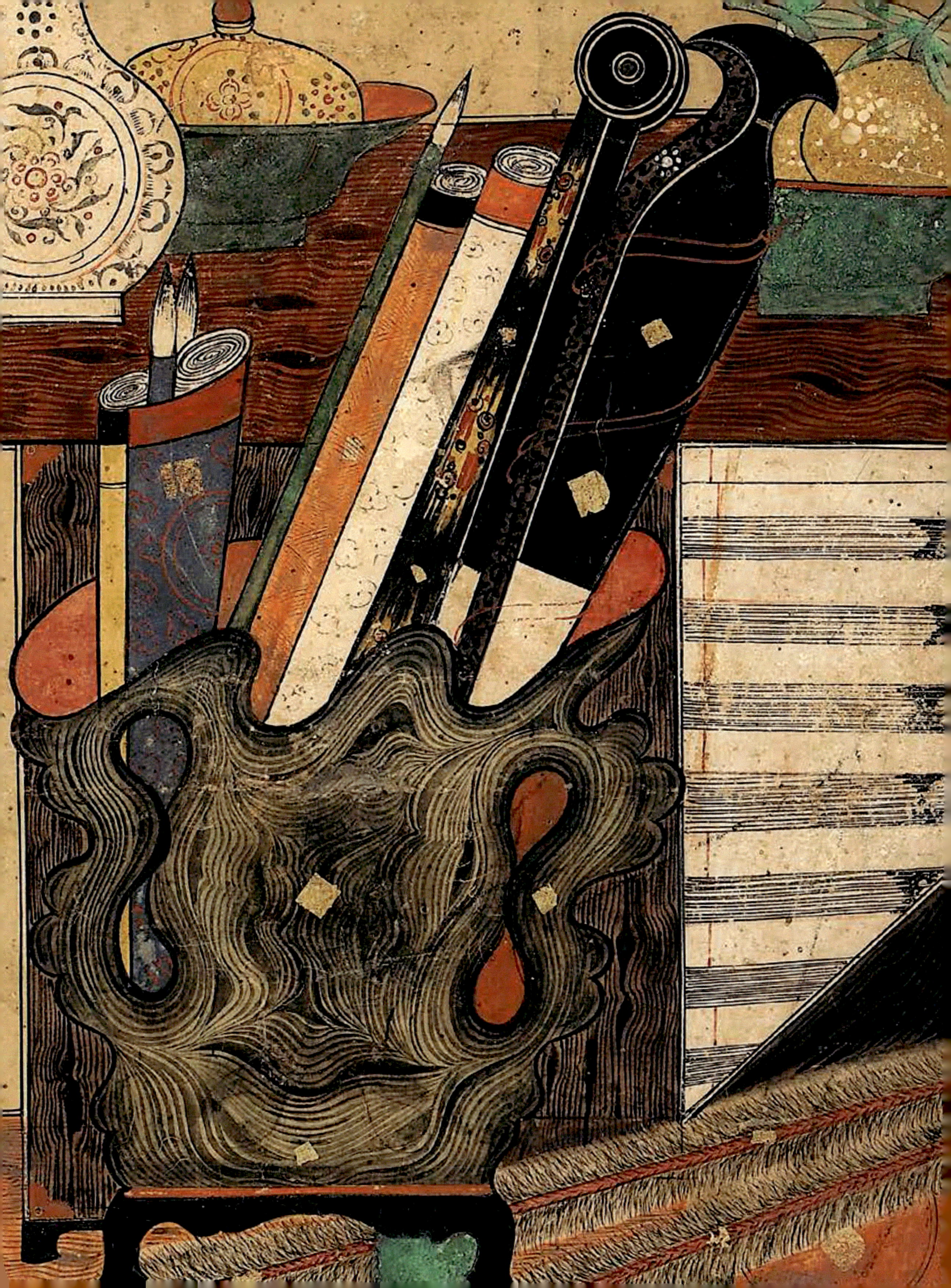

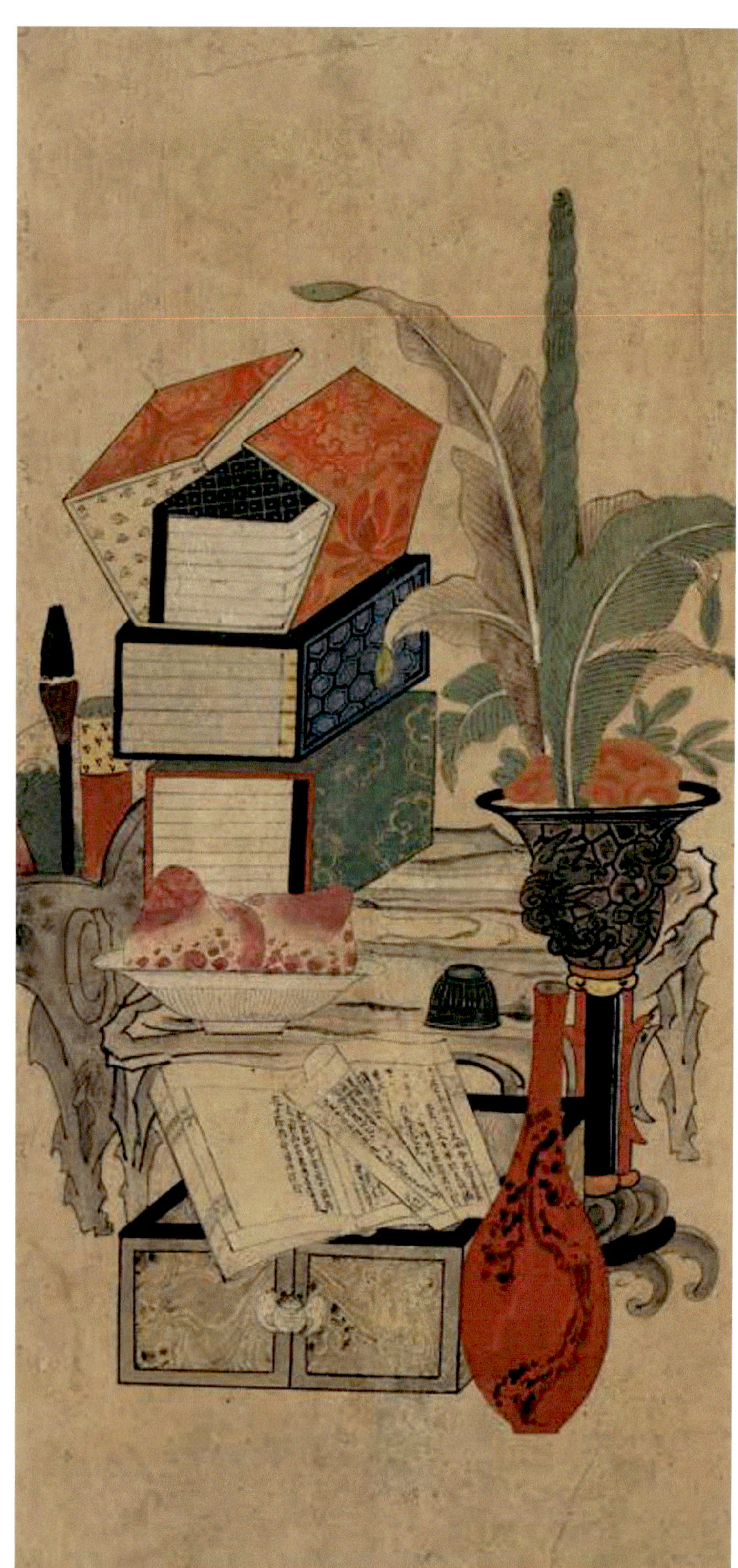

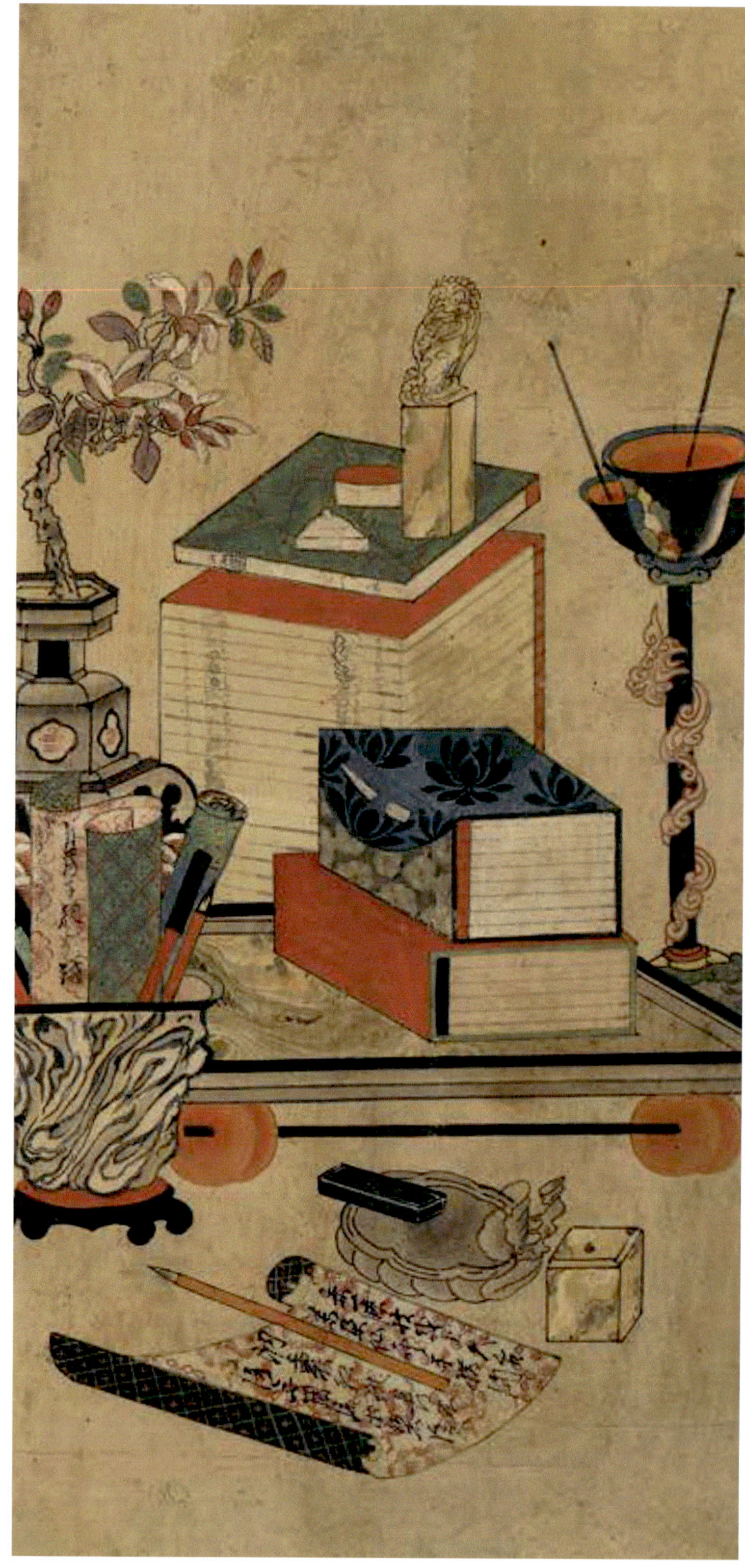

20 *Chaekgeori*

Anonymous, late 19th century
Eight-panel screen
Ink and color on paper, 68 x 35 cm (each panel)
Private collection

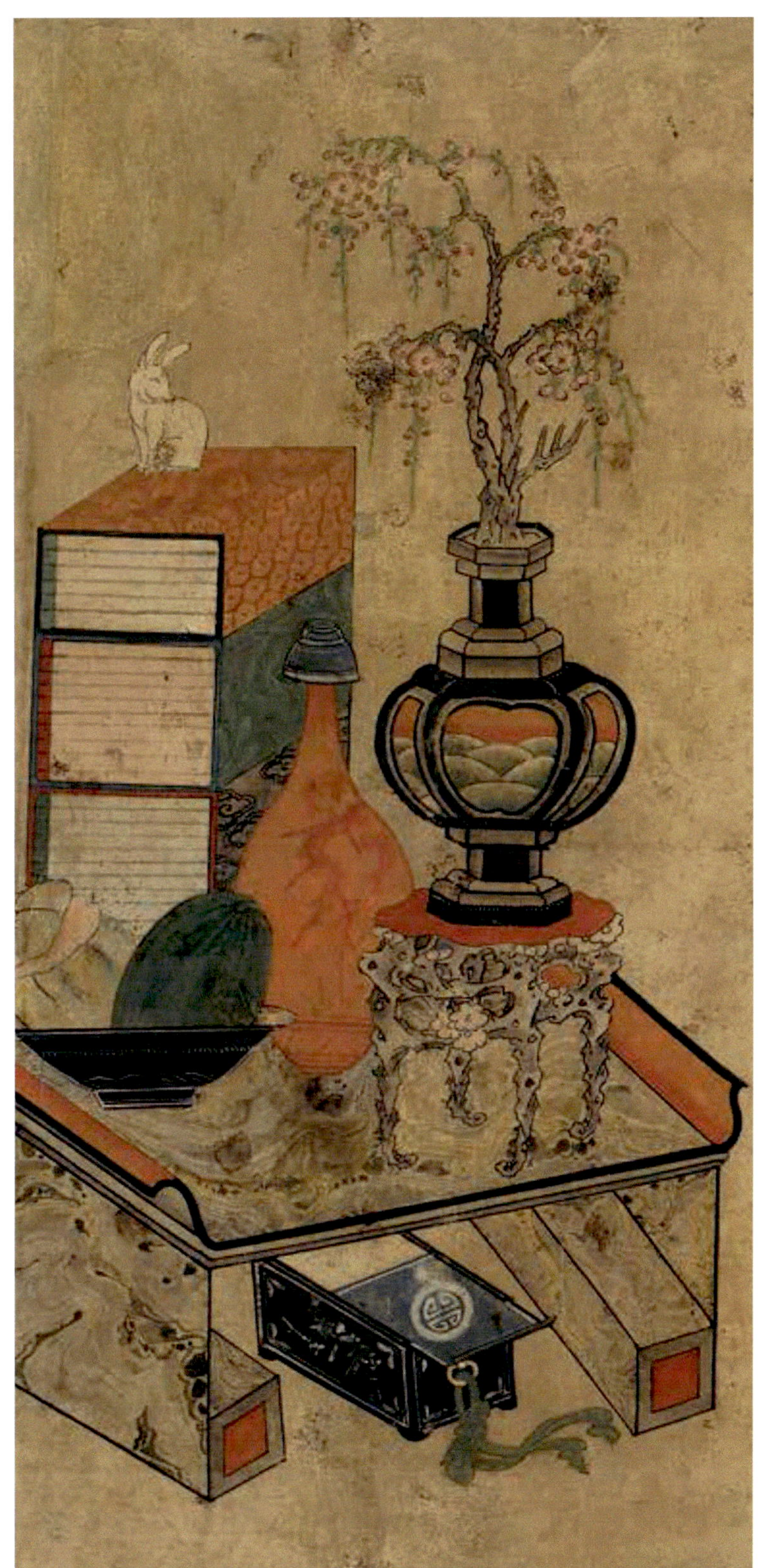

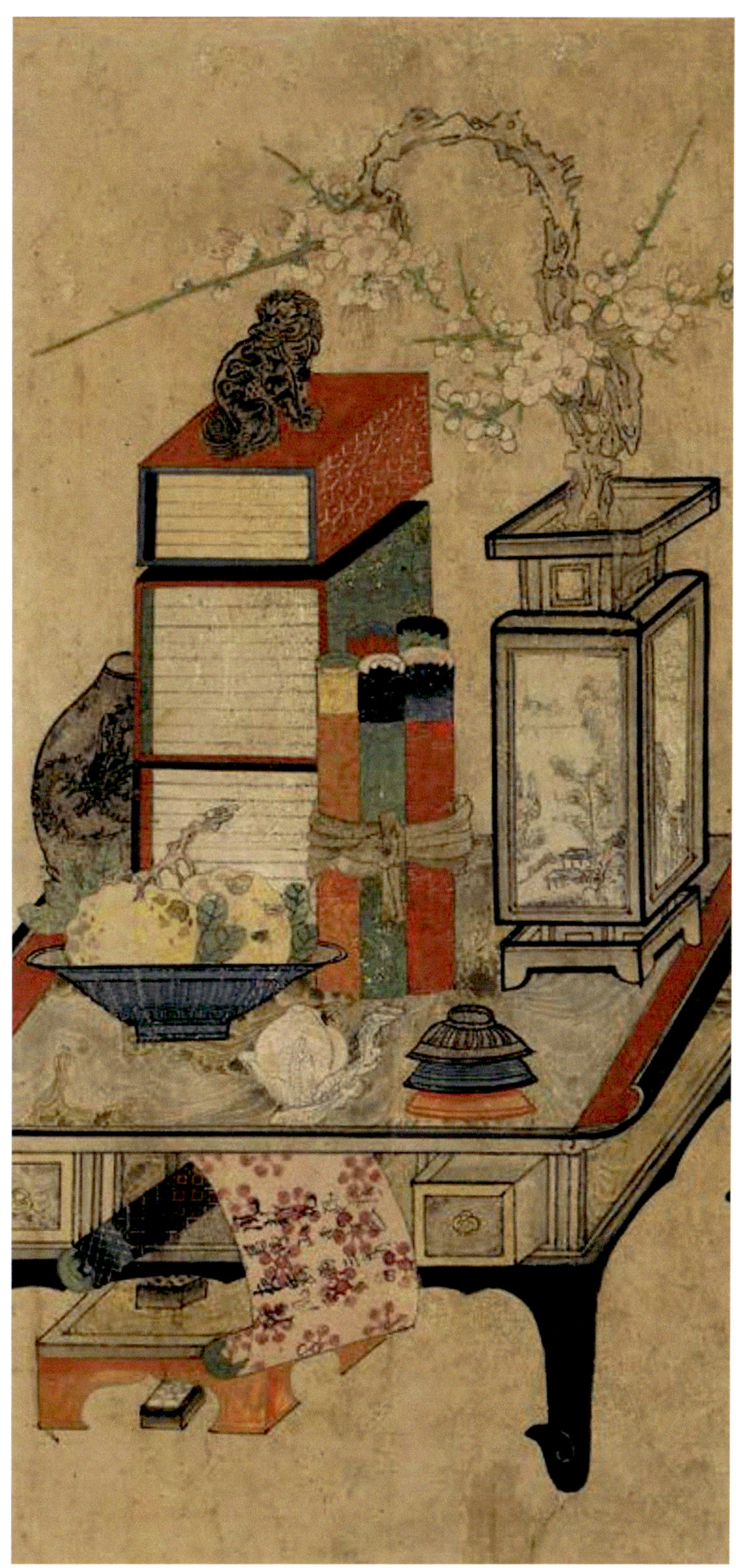

As the chaekgeori genre became popular art and increasingly desired among the common people, the subject expanded to include other personal items symbolic of wealth. While books denoted the scholarly status and the aims of the painting's owner, more exotic objects represented high economic status. Many items within the painting still have traditional symbolic meanings. The peacock feathers are a symbol for high rank government officials. The plum blossoms symbolize endurance, strength, and good news while the citron fruit symbolize wealth, prosperity, and the blessing of posterity. They do not overpower each other but rather are complementary to express the desires of commoners and a growing shift in Korean culture at the time: an ascetic, Confucian society was beginning to take more interest and put more value in materialistic possessions. BC, JJ

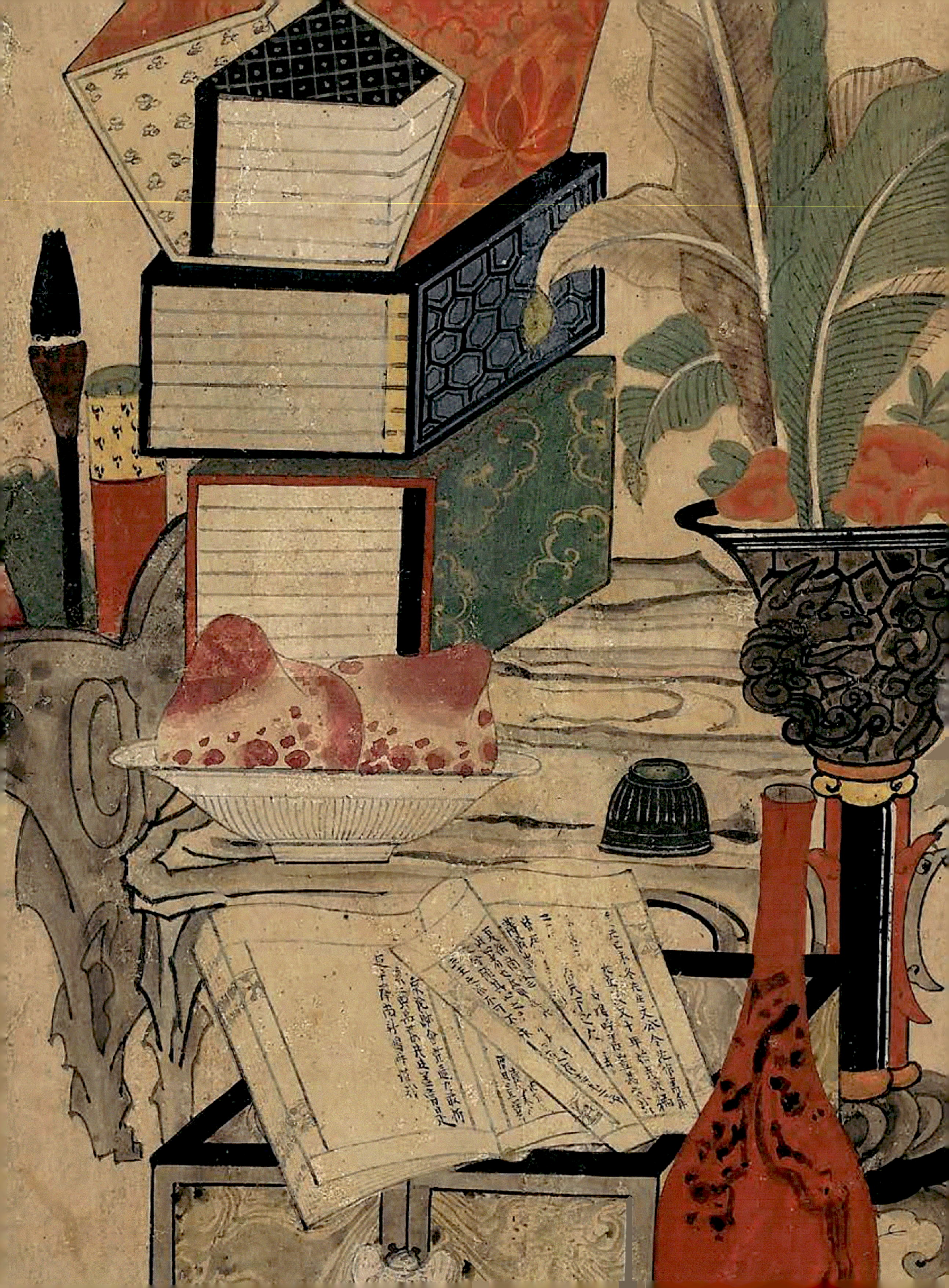

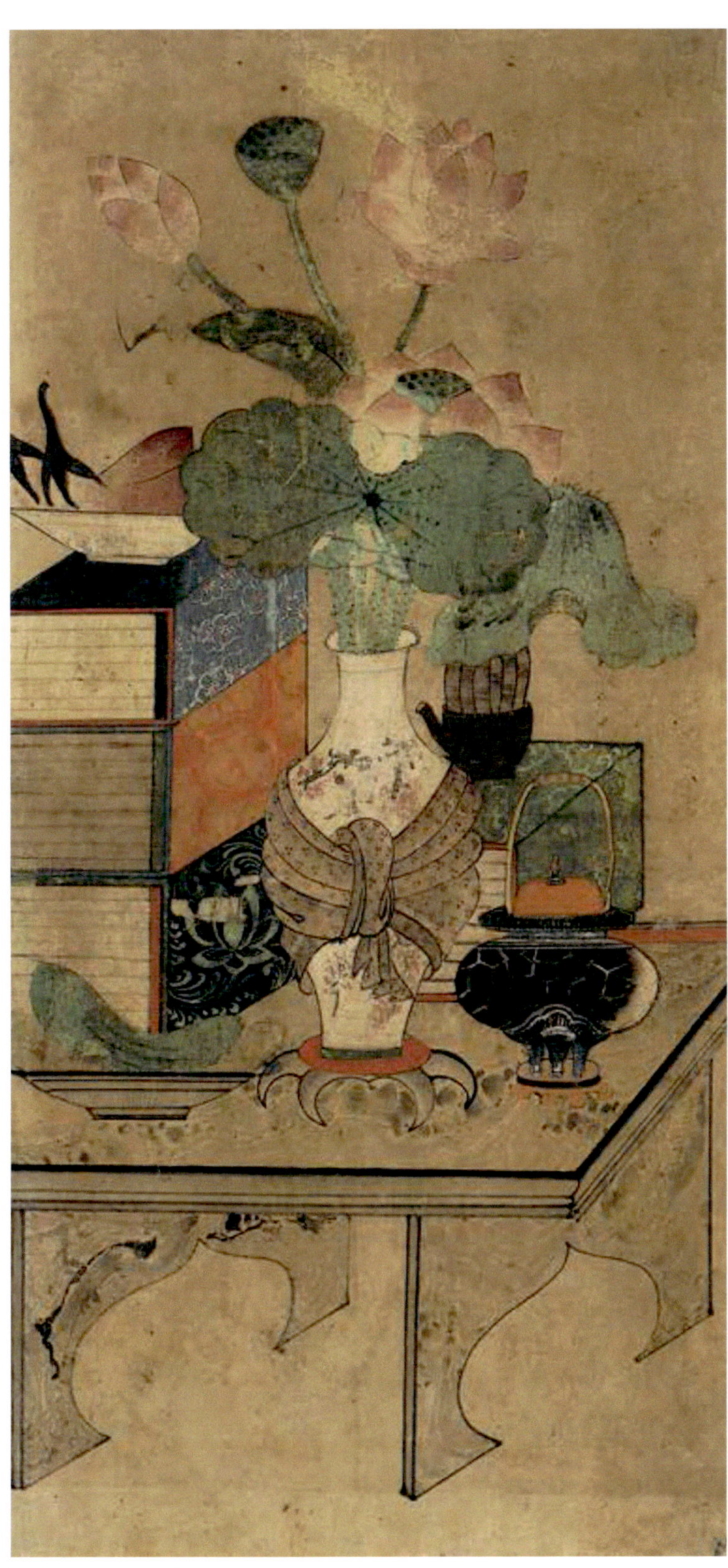

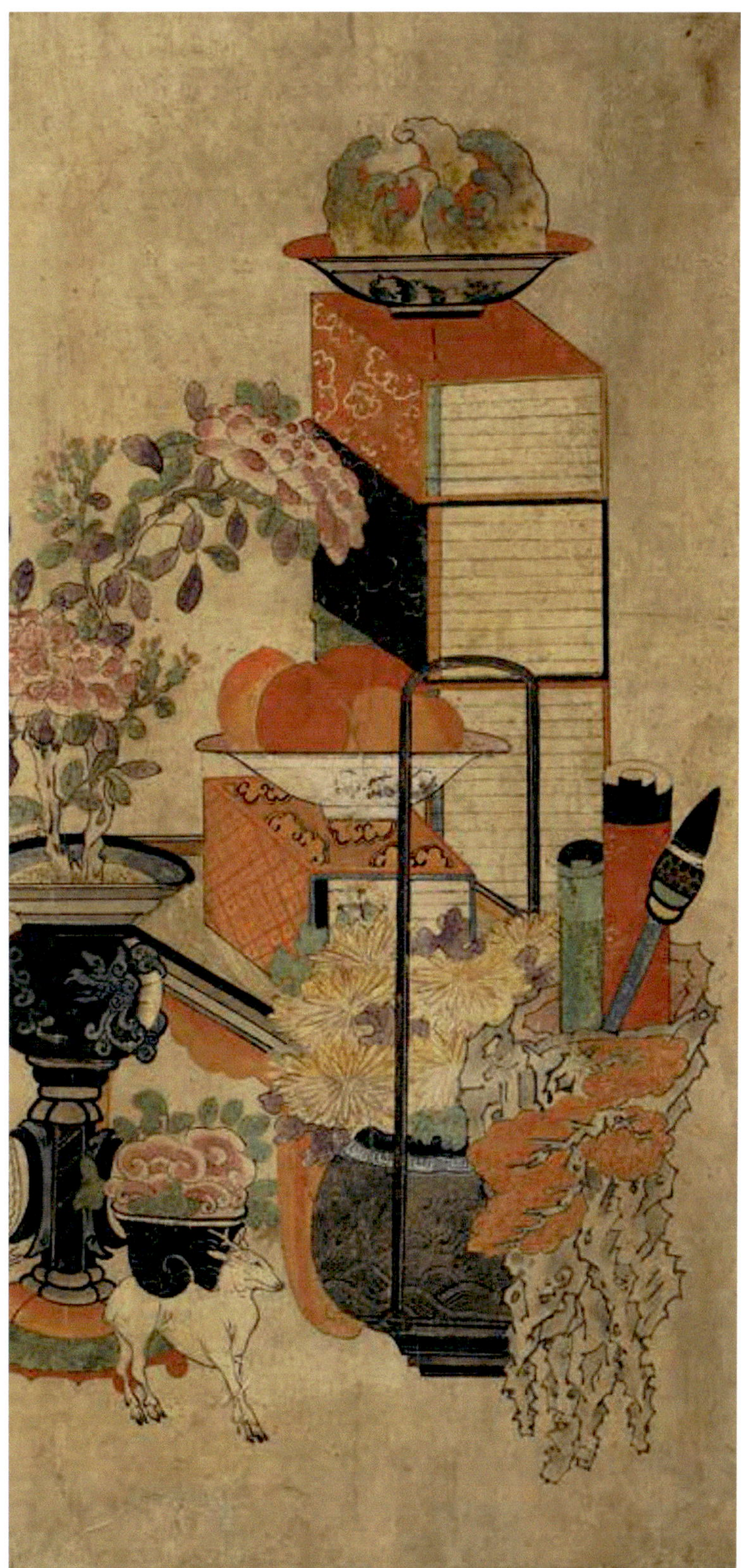

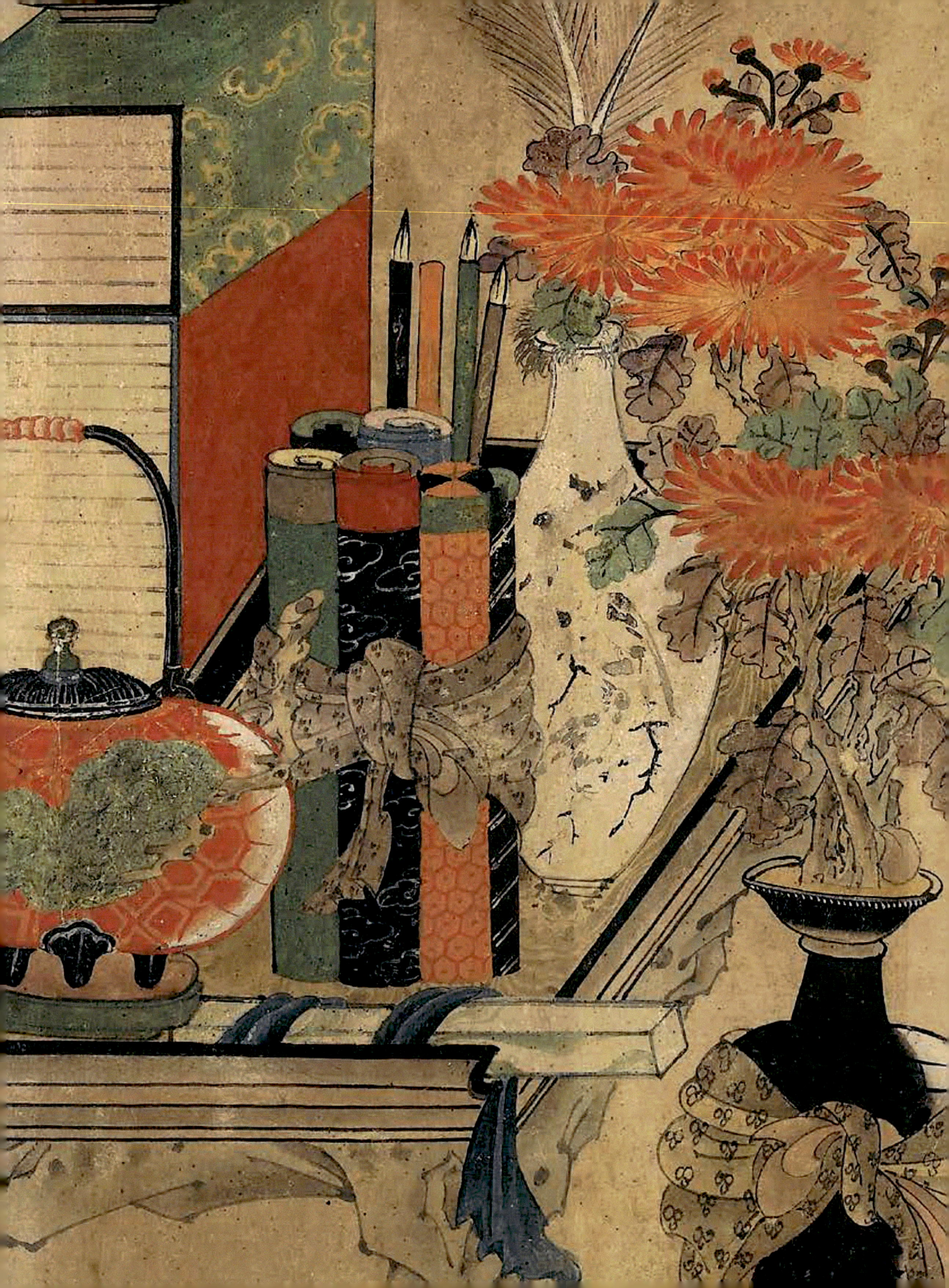

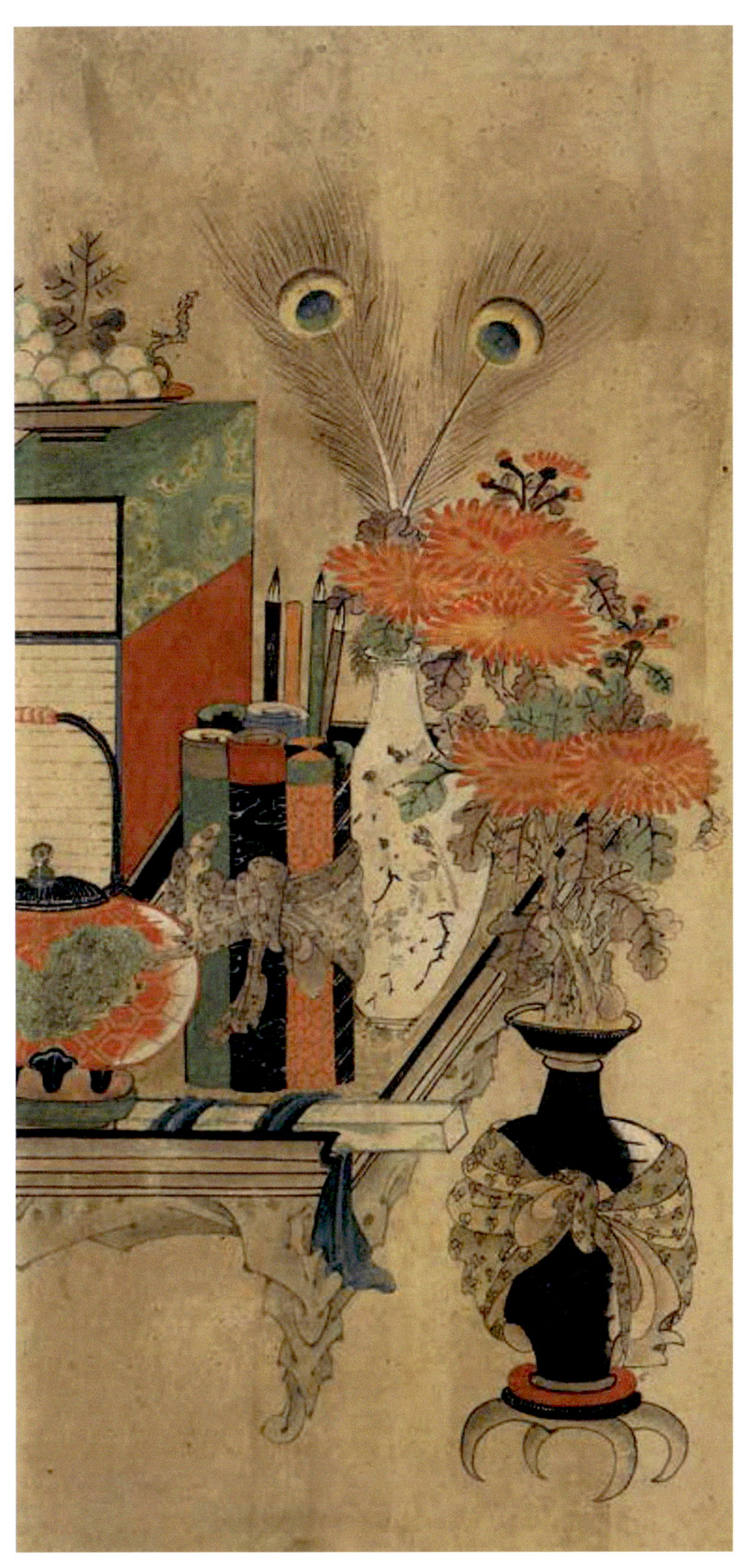

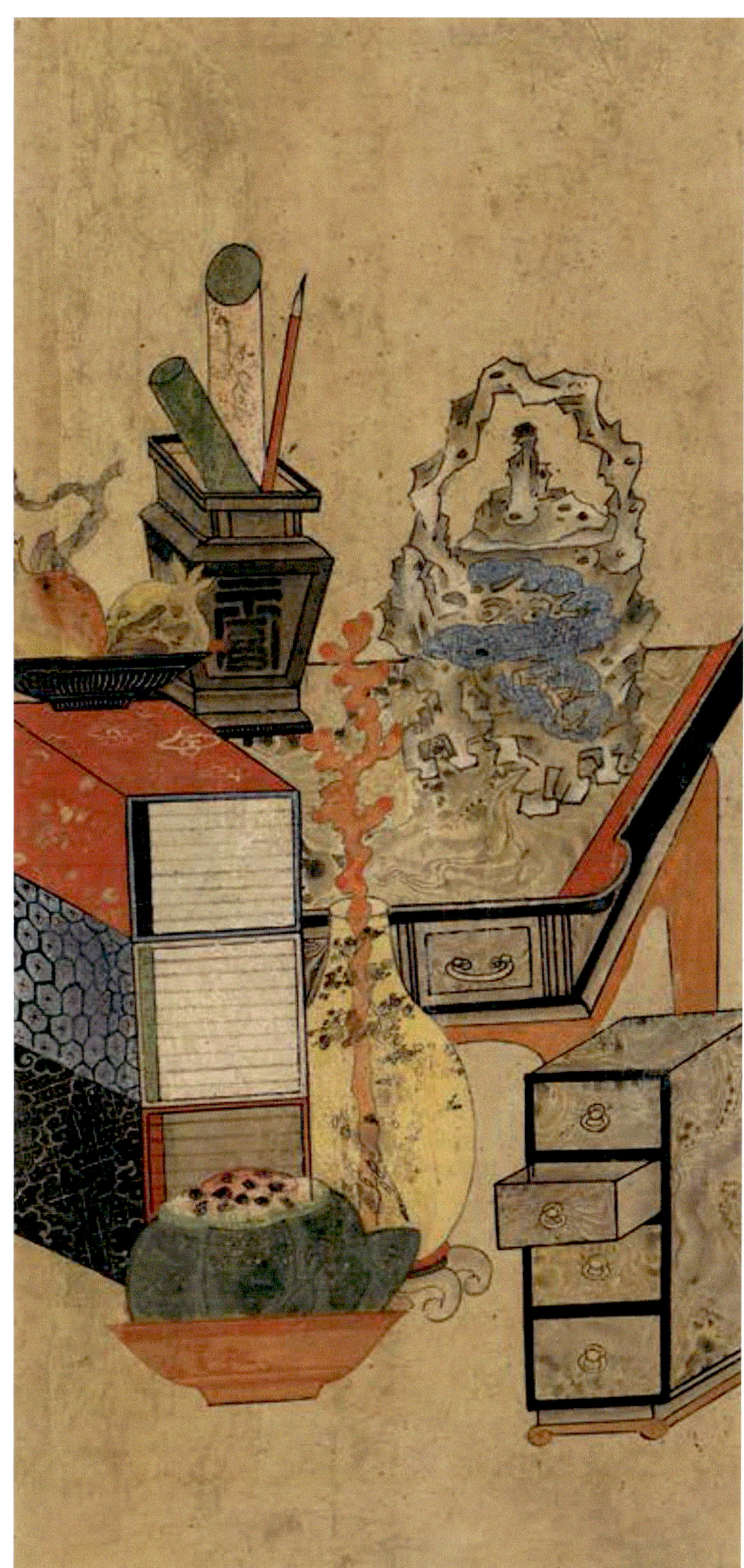

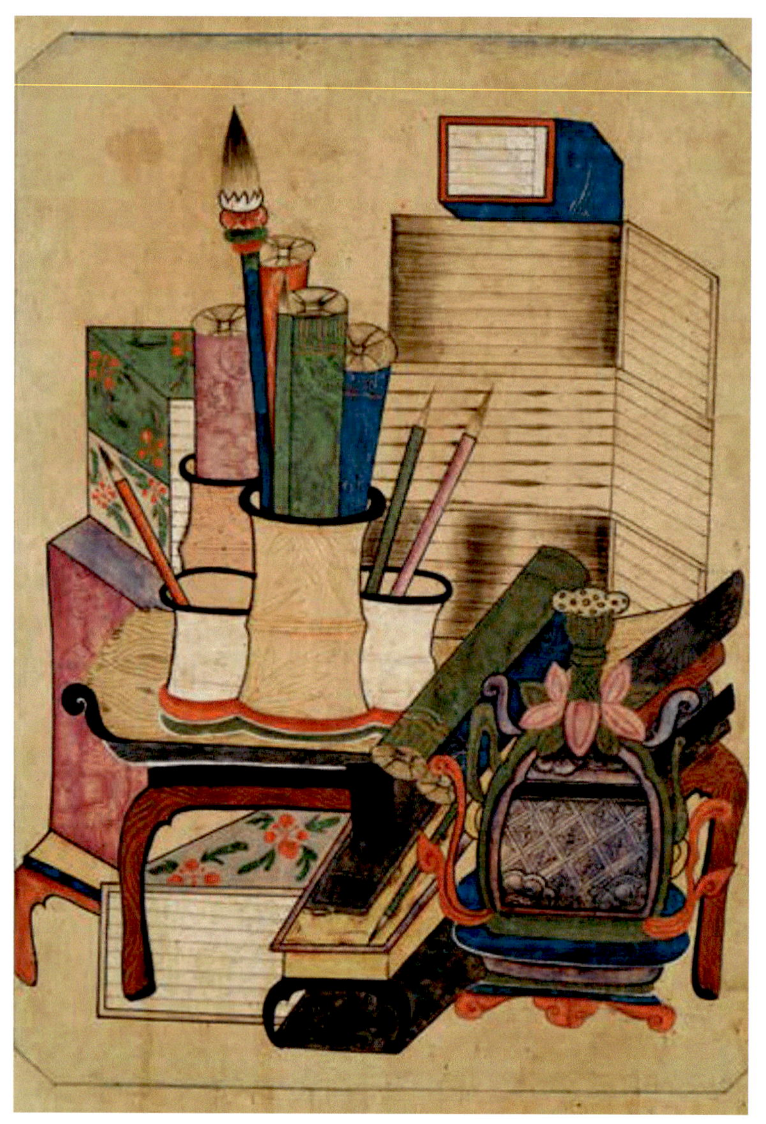
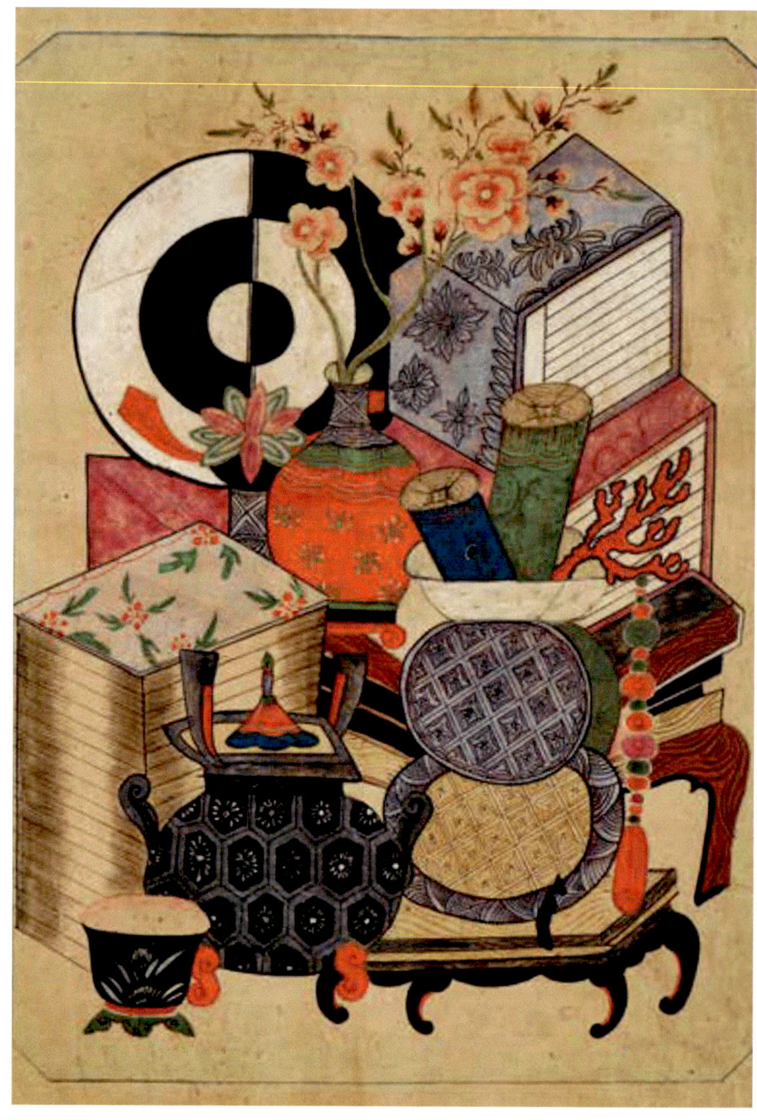

21 *Chaekgeori*

Anonymous, late 19th century
Eight-panel screen
Ink and color on paper, 45.3 x 32.5 cm (each panel)
Private collection

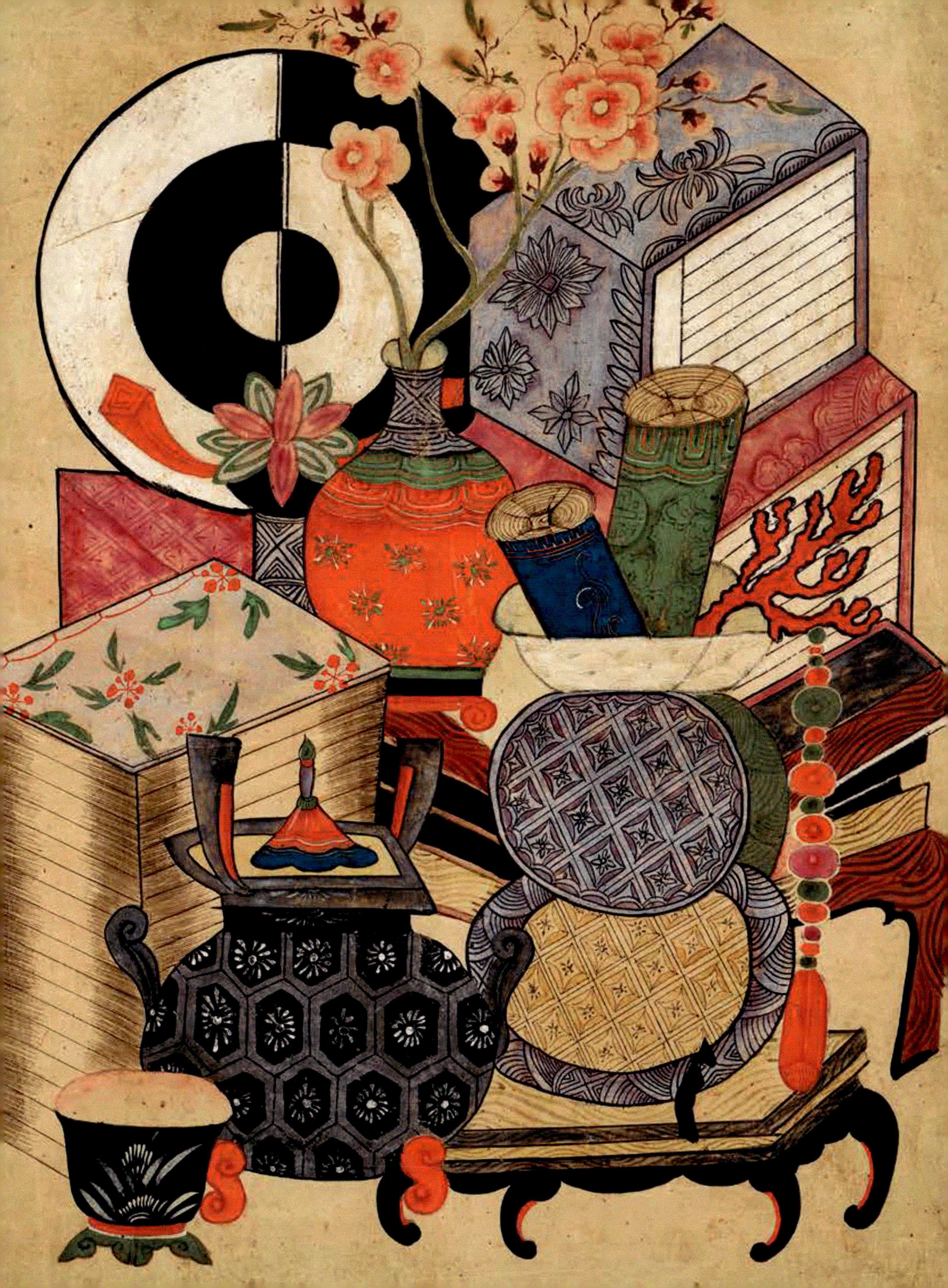

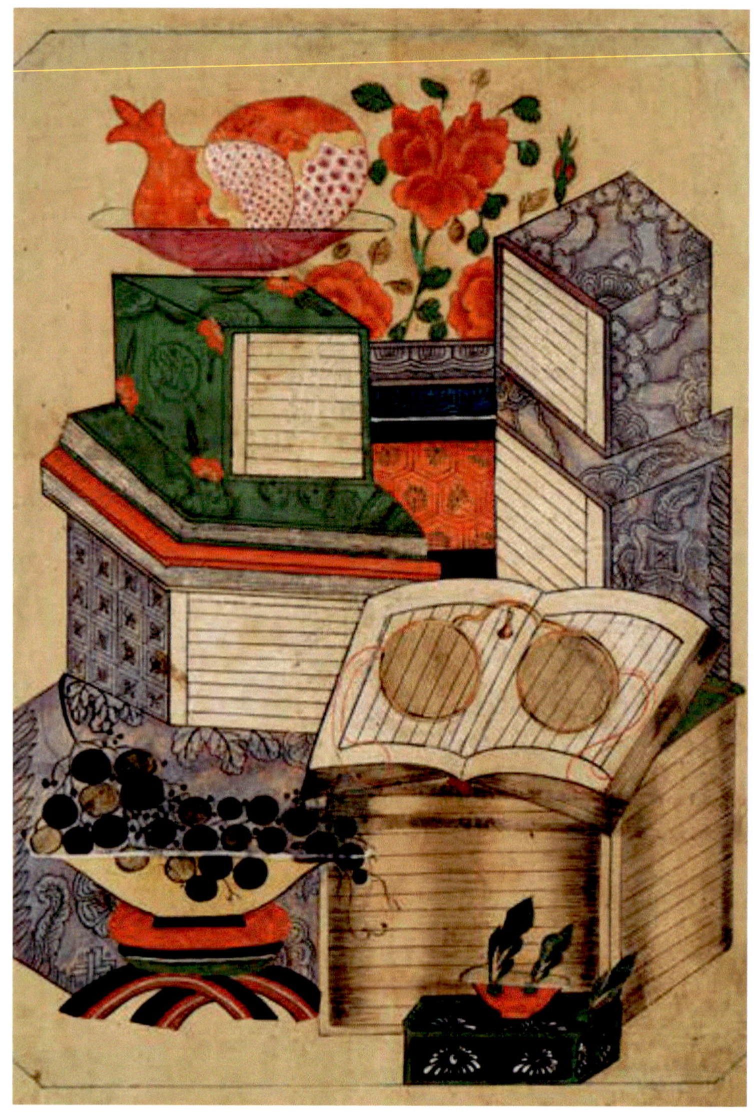

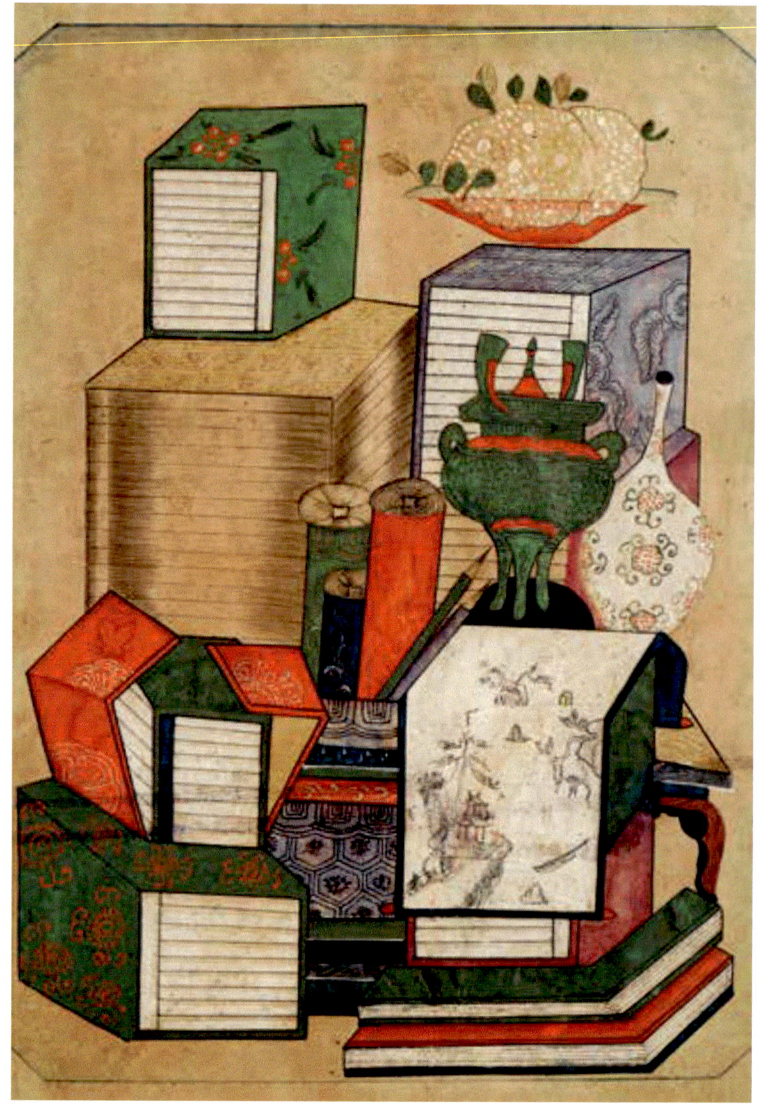

This screen shows an abundance of books, scholar's accouterments, vases, fruits, and a various kinds of colorful flowers, all mixed together. In the late nineteenth century flowers and plants on vases and pots began to appear in folk-style chaekgeori. In this screen, many objects are depicted with several different perspectives and in multiple panels. Also, an artist attempts to add volume to the books by shading them. At the same time, he decorates the bookcases and the surfaces of jars and pots with delicate patterns and enhanced decorative features. By using books as pedestals for other objects, this work illustrates the transformation of chaekgeori from court style to folk style, the latter of which placed more emphasis on auspicious symbols representing wealth, longevity, many sons, peace, and other desirable objectives. BC, JJ

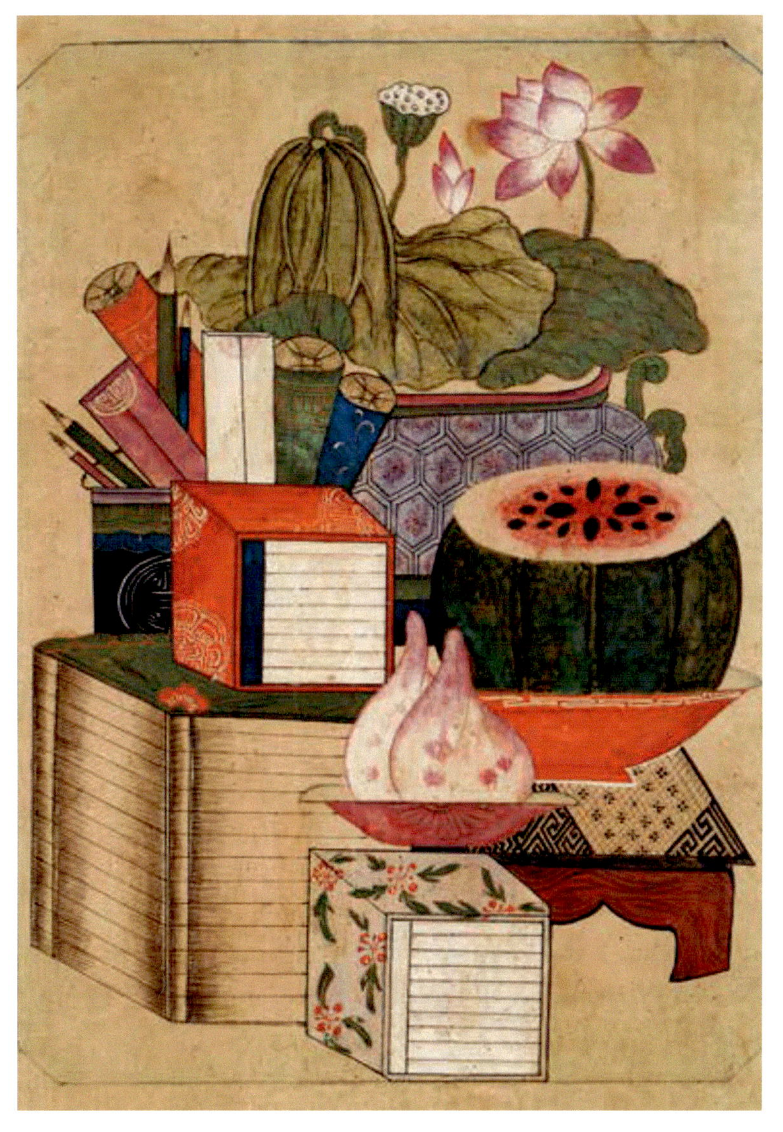

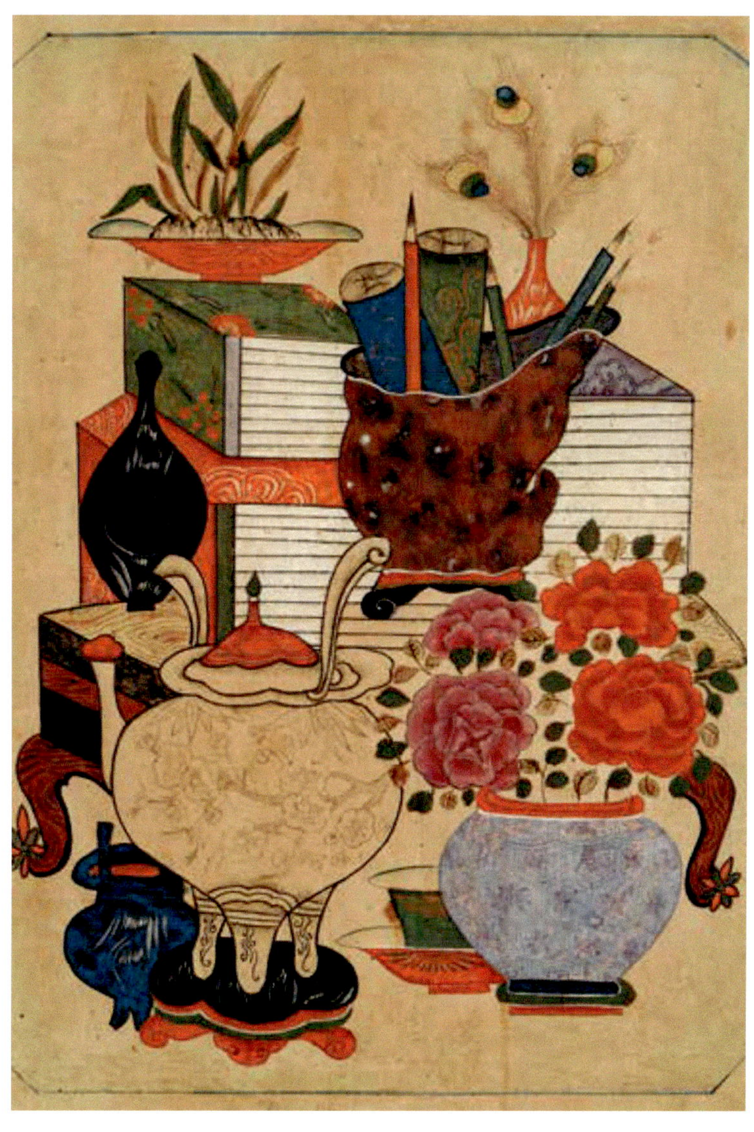

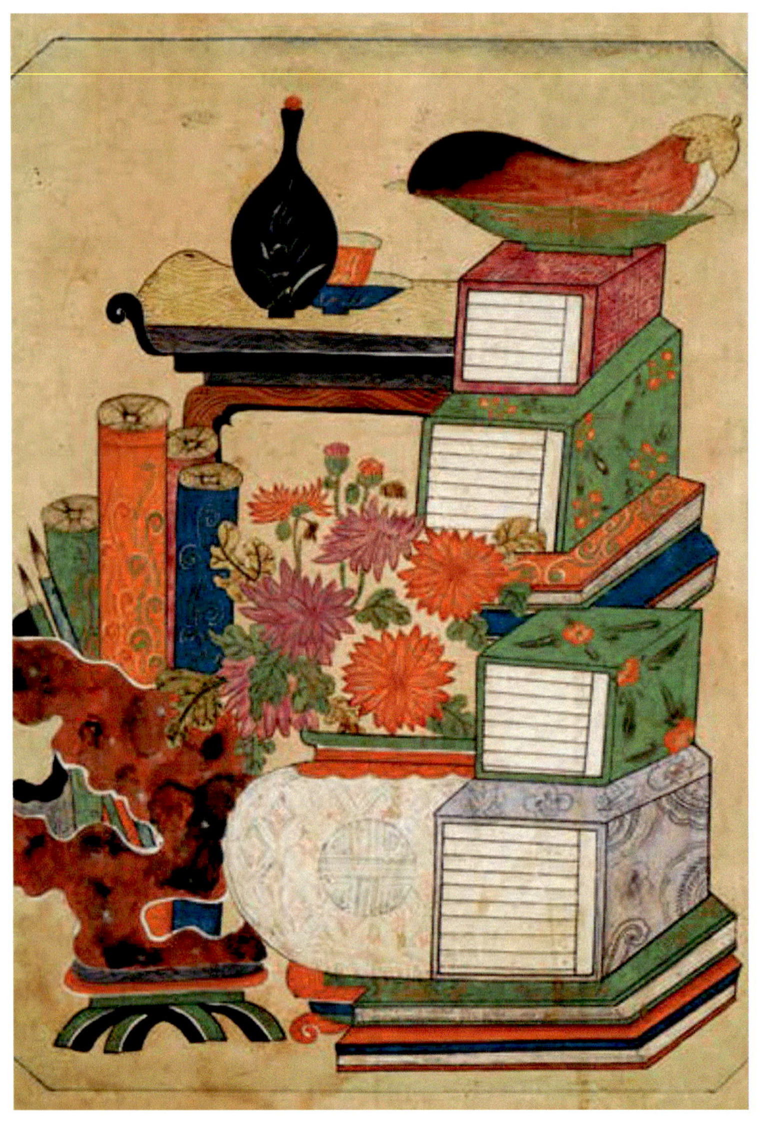

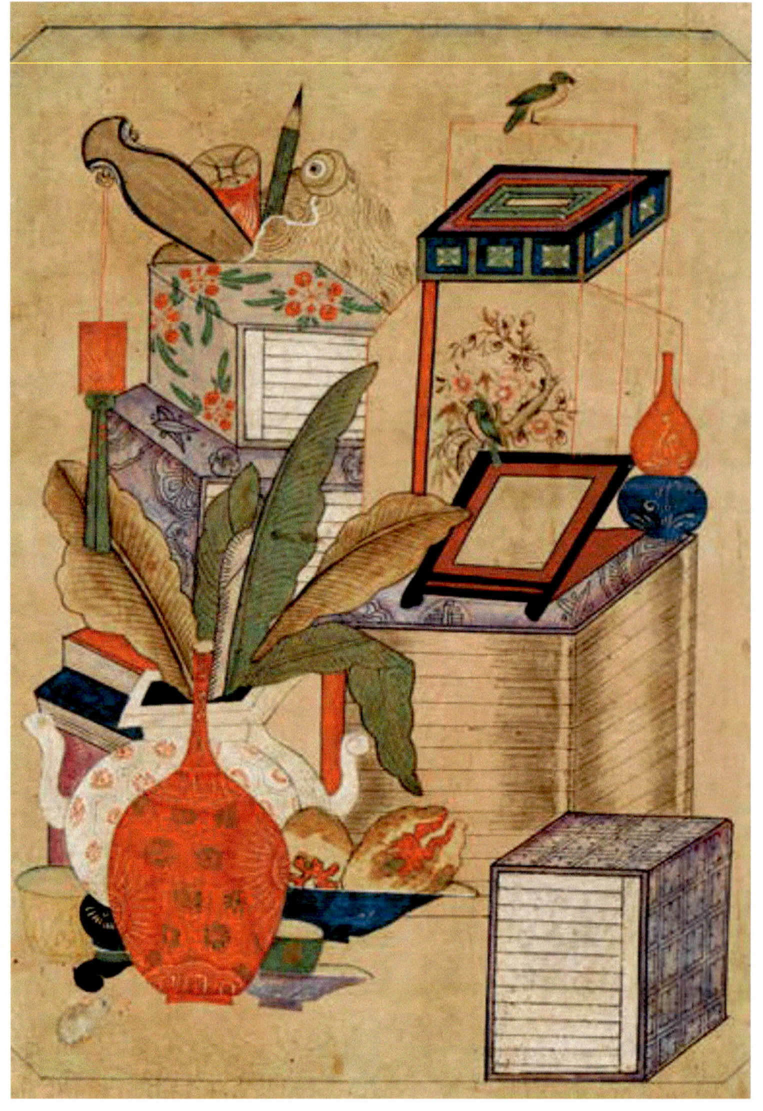

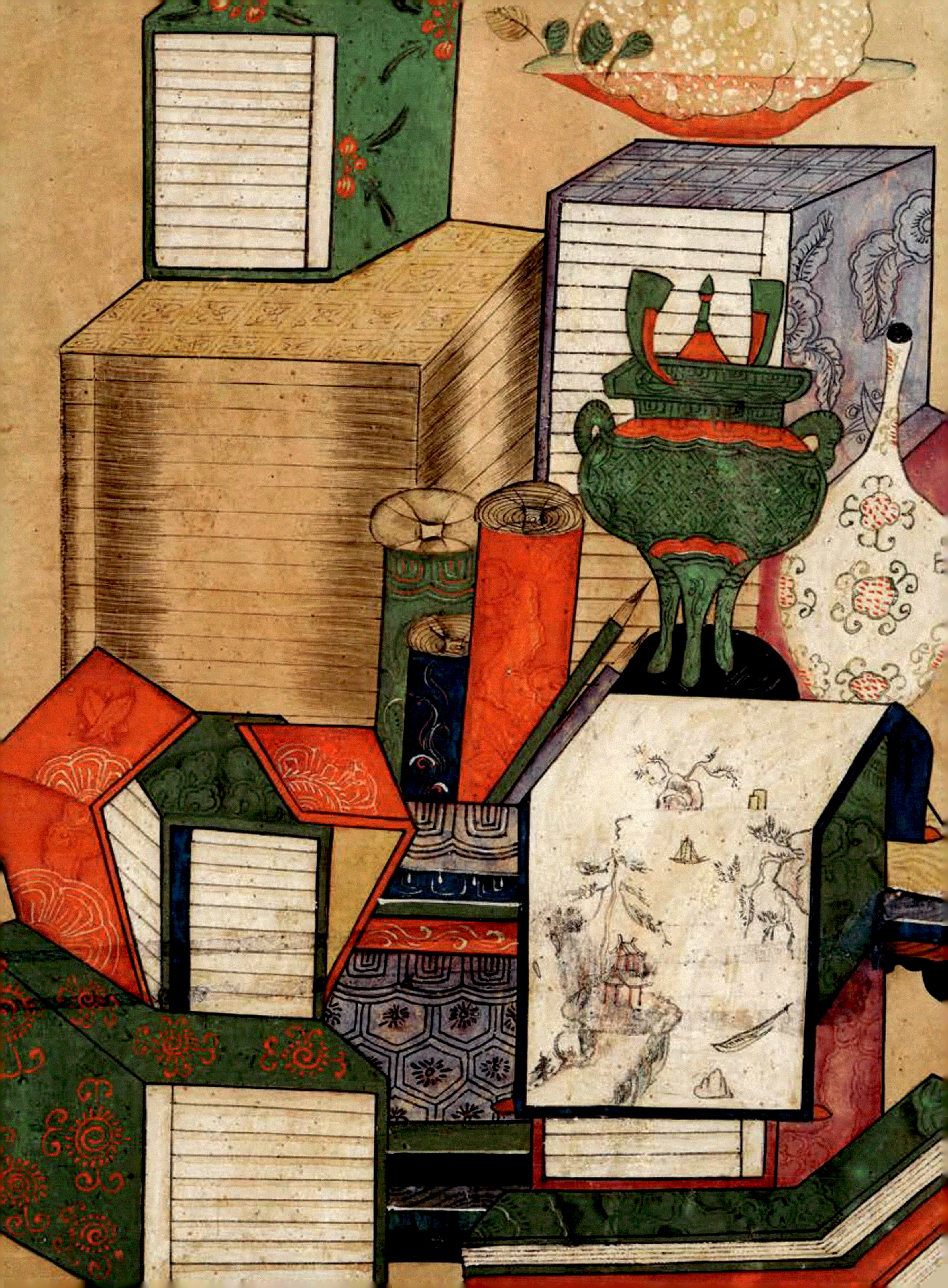

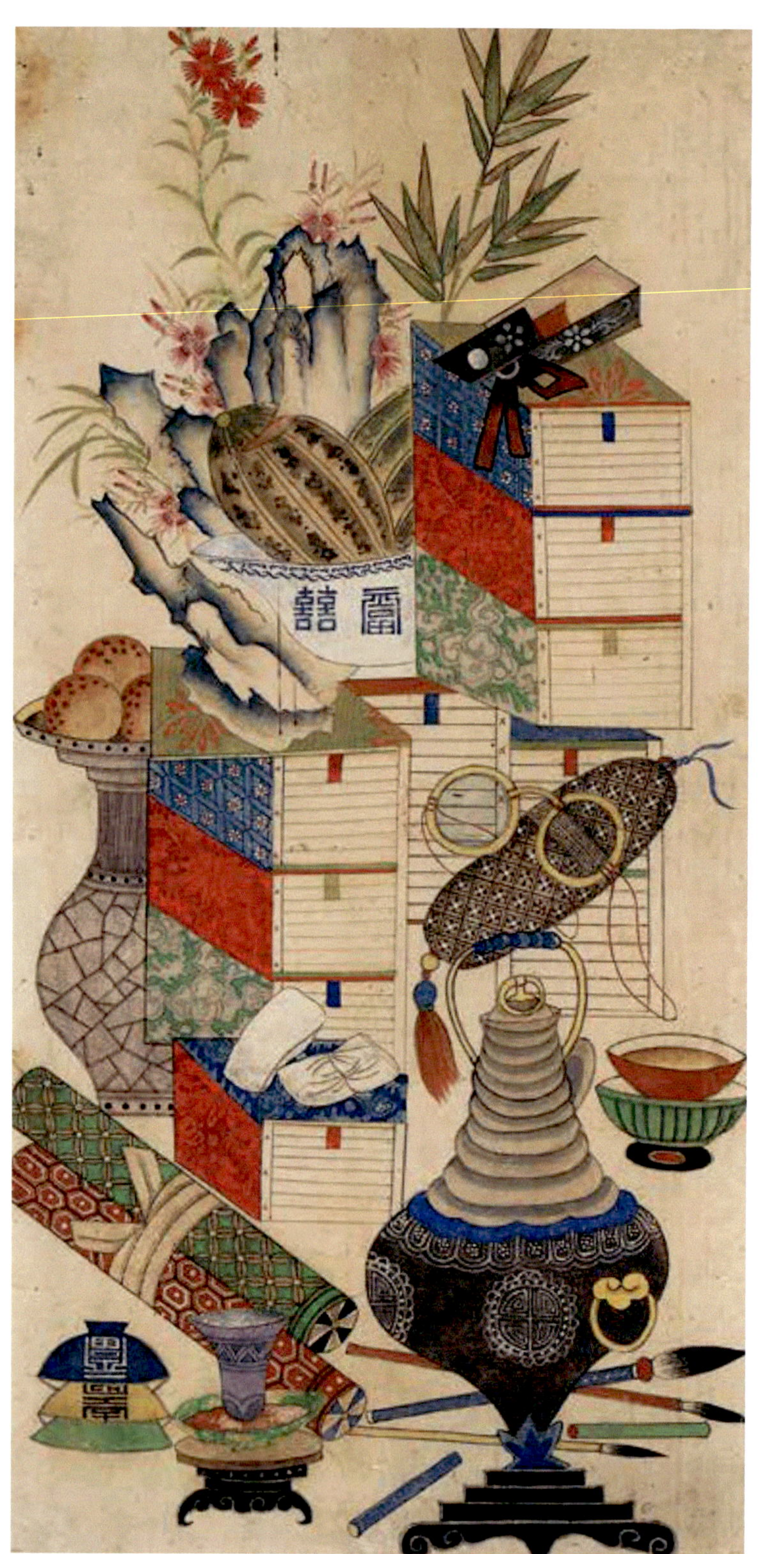

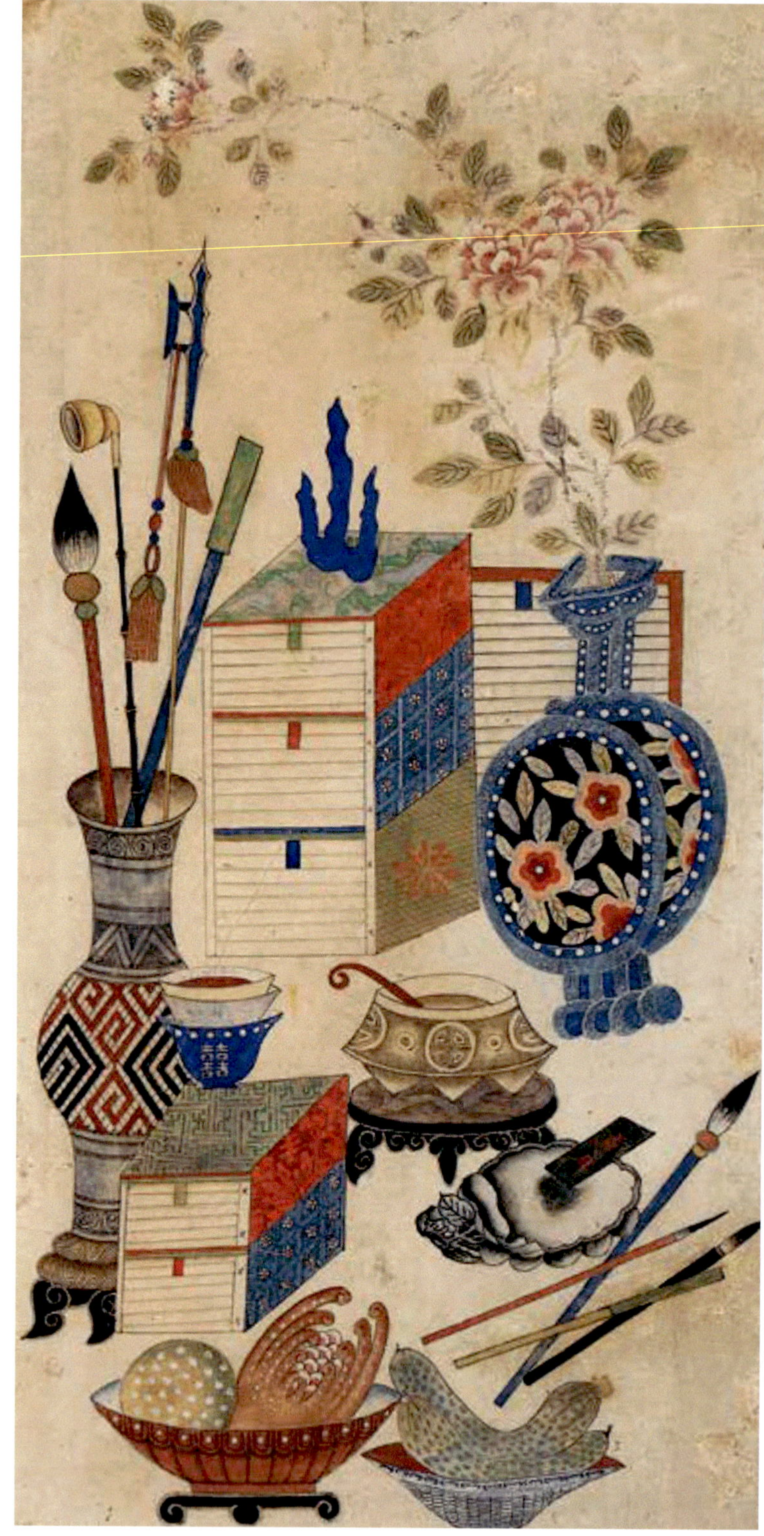

22 *Chaekgeori*

Anonymous, late 19th century
Six-panel screen
Ink and color on paper, 67 x 33 cm (each panel)
Private collection

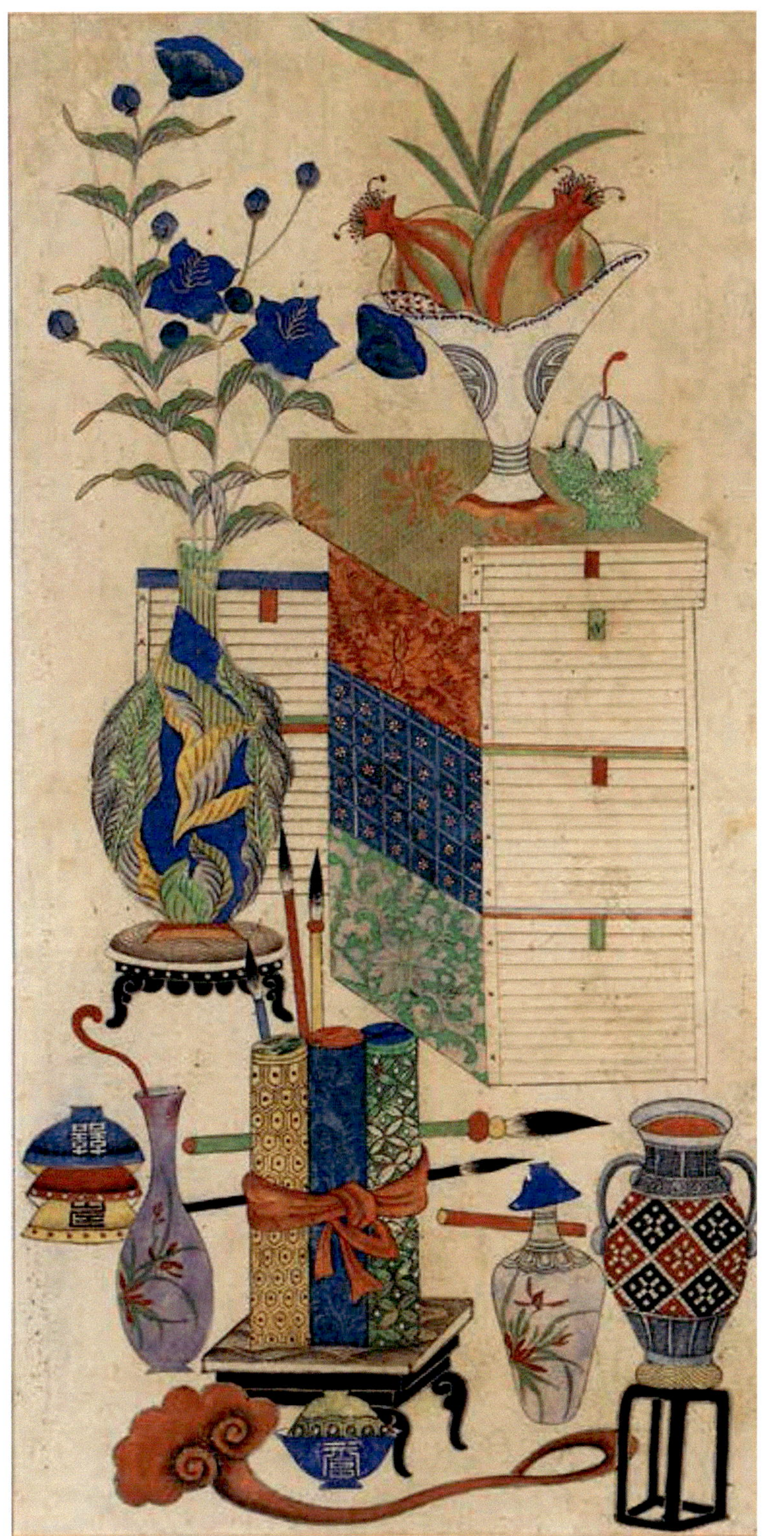

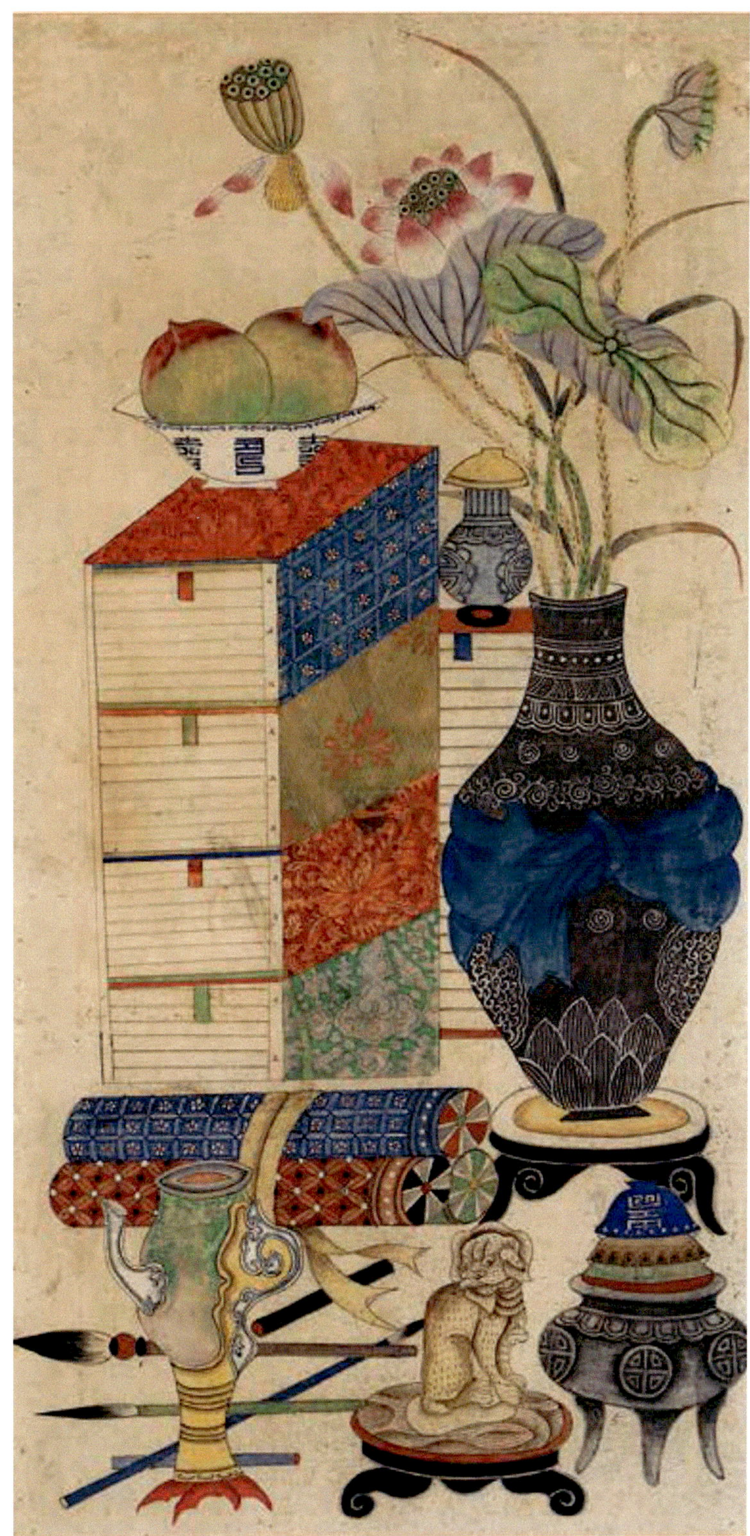

Chaekgeori remained popular for more than two centuries. No other genre or medium in the entire tradition of Korean art, in both literati and folk paintings, has so engaged and documented the image of books and collectible commodities and their place in society. When the genre transitioned into folk-style painting, new and unexpected visual elements emerged. The books and accoutrements started to escape their restrictive, rigid bookshelves. Folk-style chaekgeori often show an exquisite fusion of Korean and Western composition, so much so that screens from the eighteenth and nineteenth centuries feel modern and contemporary to the twenty-first-century viewer's eye. Not only books but also many other symbolic commodities are depicted, representing the commoner's desire for higher social status, wealth, and knowledge. BC, JJ

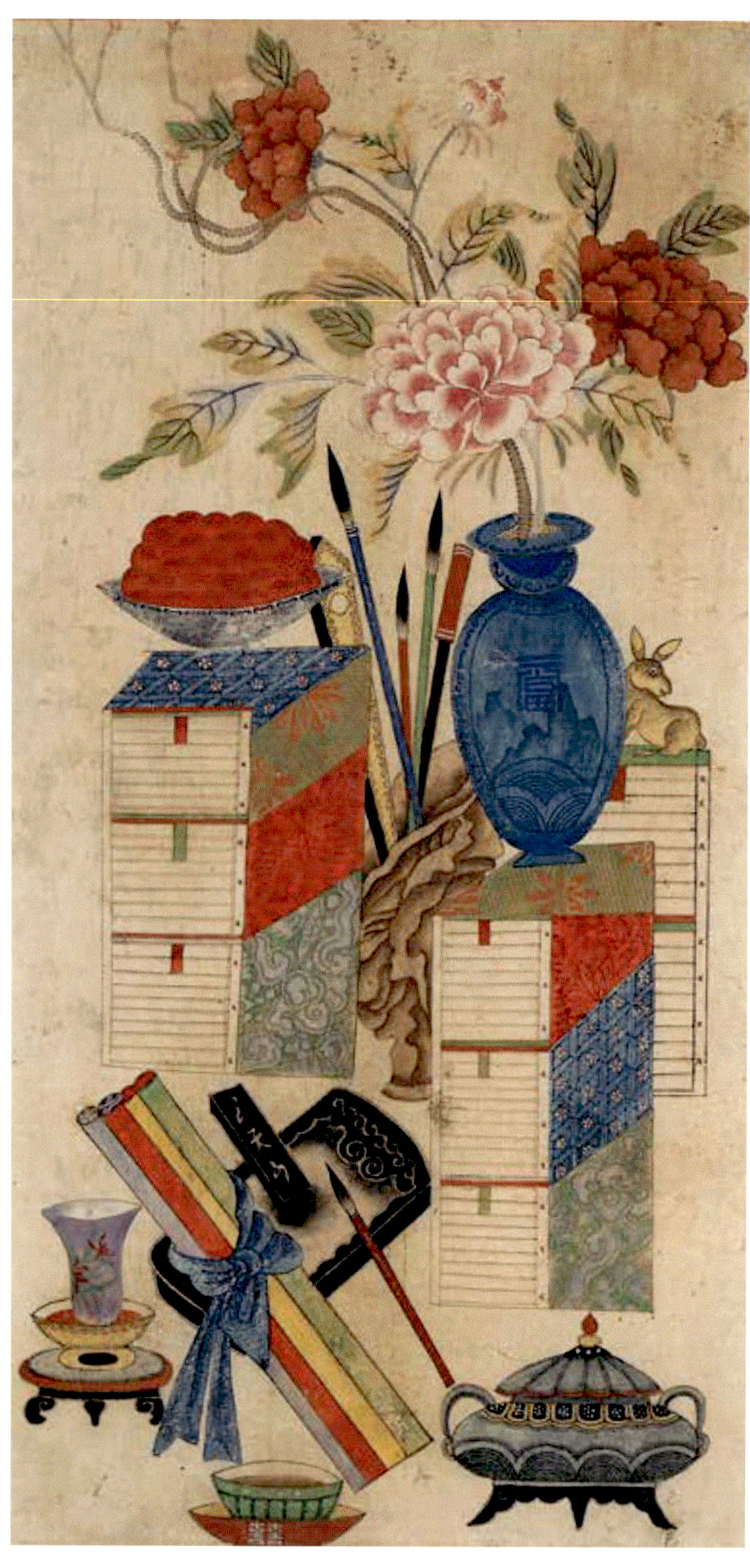

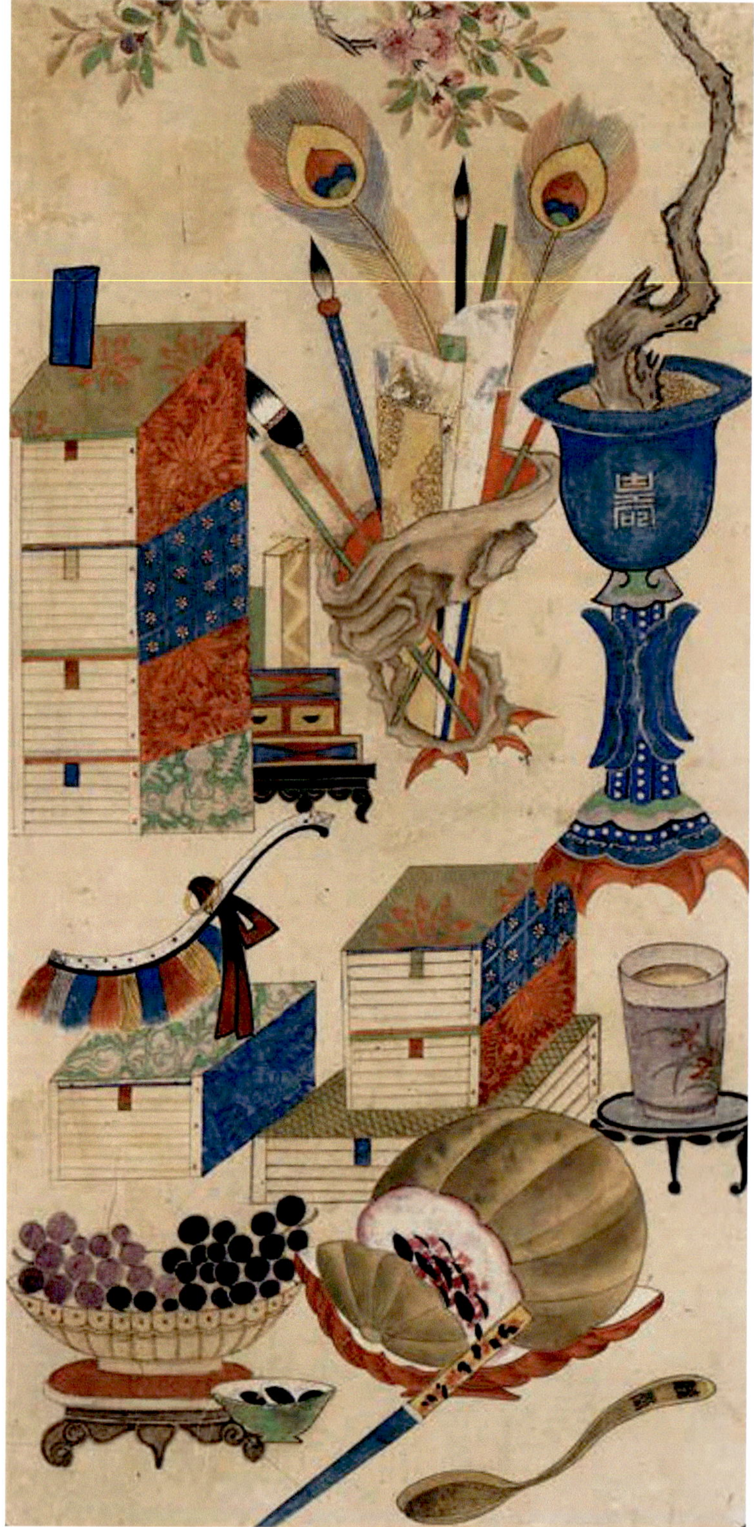

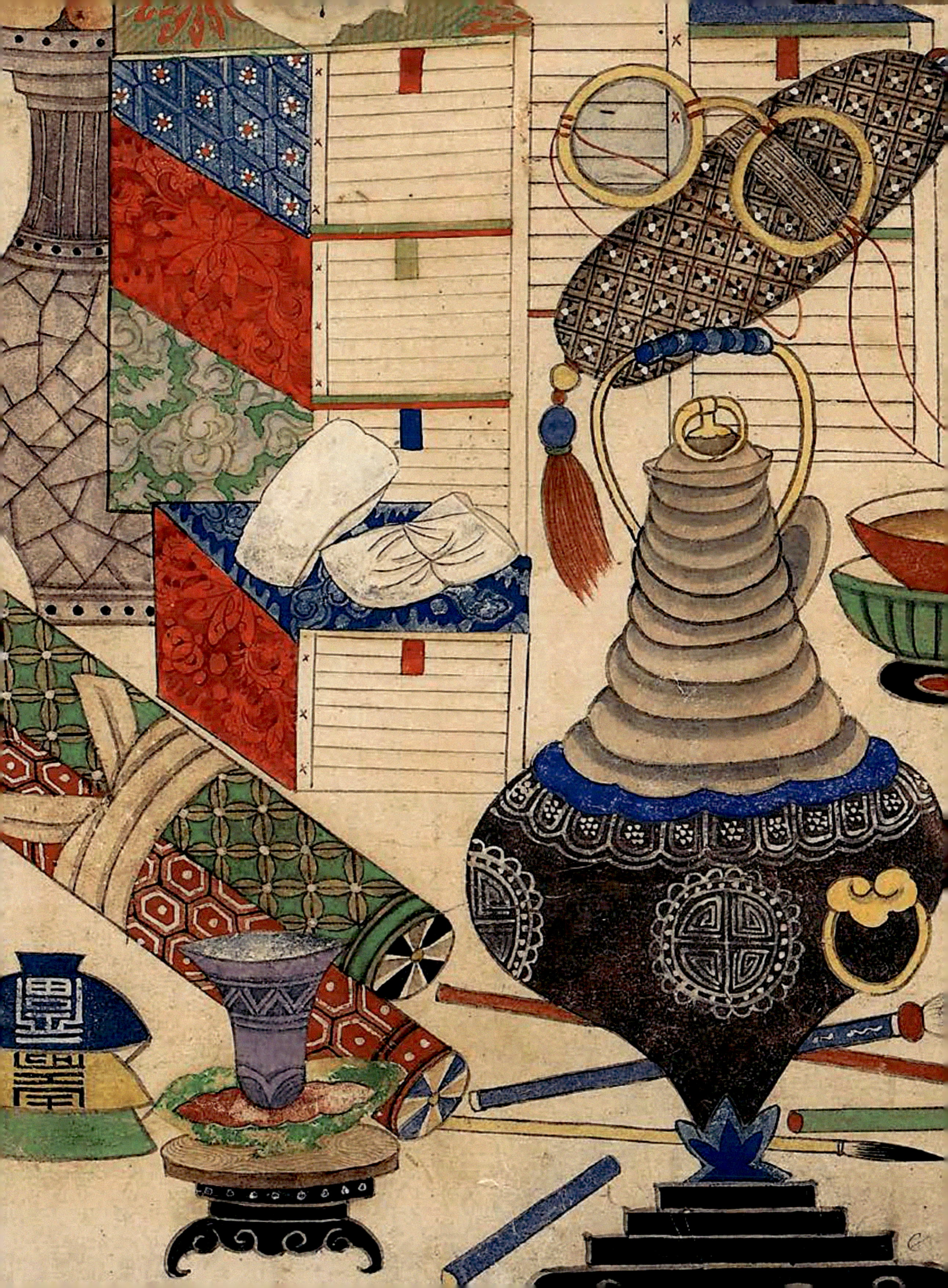

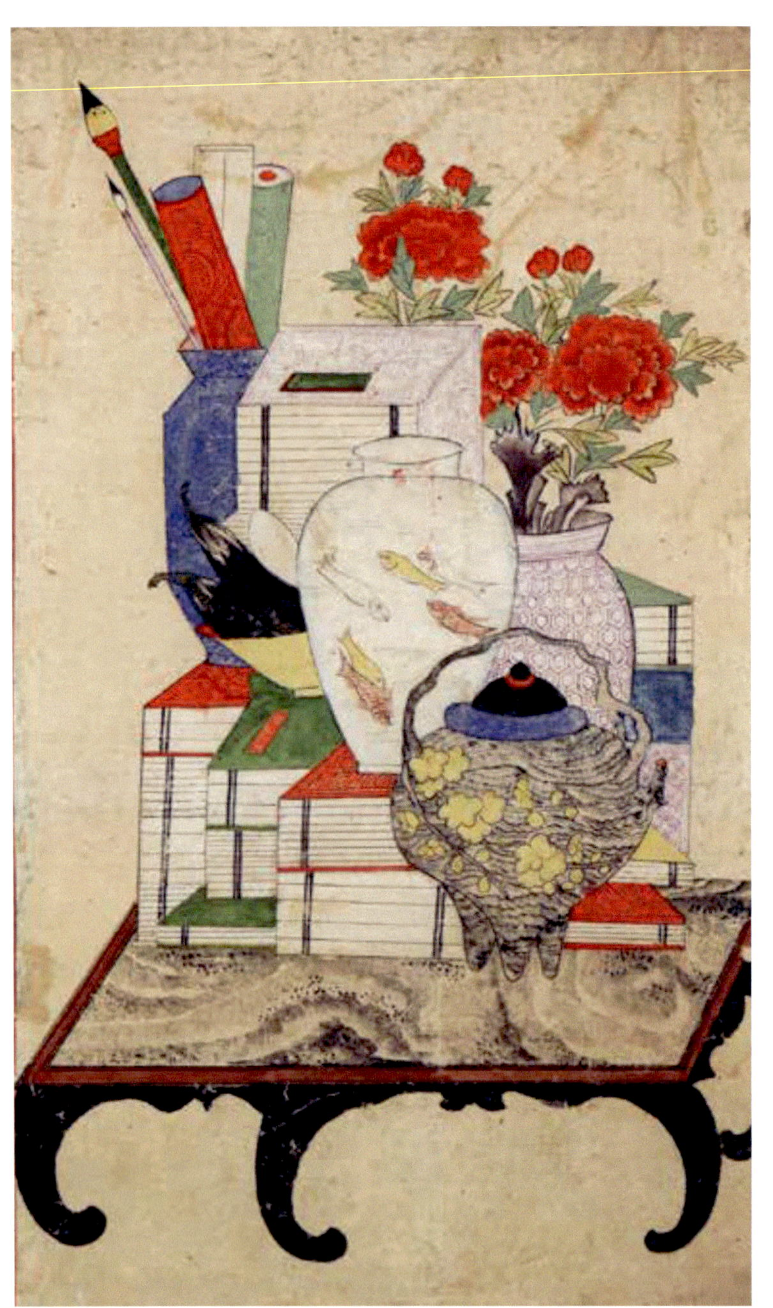

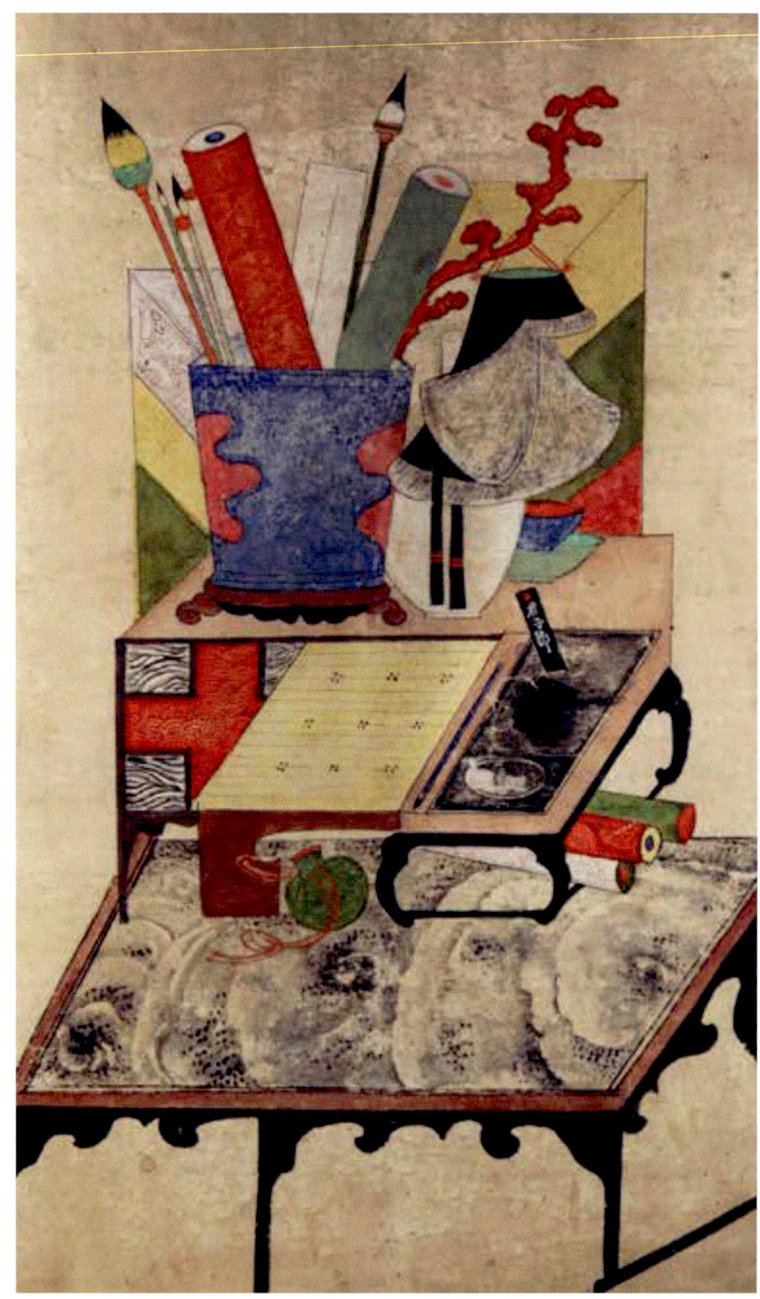

23 *Chaekgeori*

Anonymous, late 19th century
Eight-panel screen
Ink and color on paper, 63 x 39 cm (each panel)
Private collection

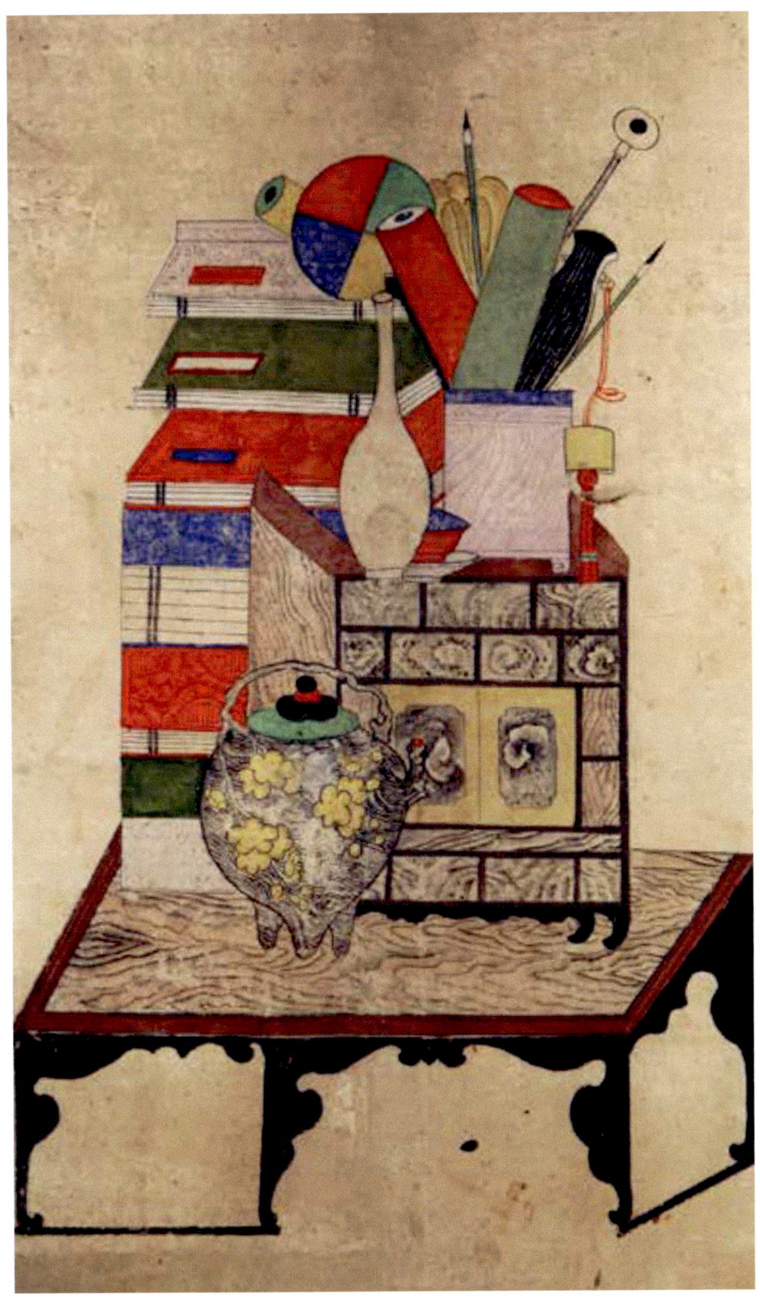

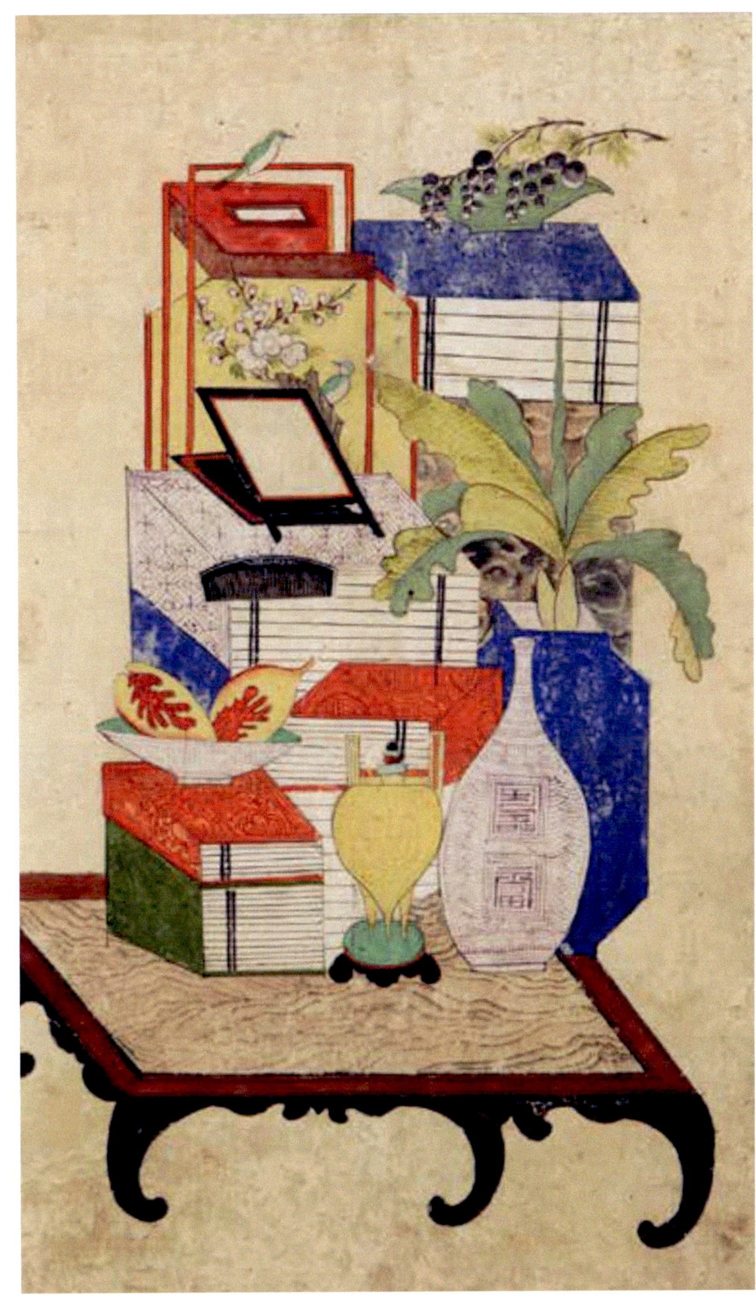

In this chaekgeori, objects such as the case for books, furniture, and vases are placed on desks. This painting seems to represent the interior of a scholar's reception room. The composition may appear simplistic at first glance, but the painter of this folk-style chaekgeori screen uses the desks as highlights—the desktops and the footrests between the legs of the desks stick out in odd directions. For variety, the painter also depicts desks that do not have footrests. This screen may not have been so fascinating a folk-style work if the artist had rendered the desks faithfully. In its unbounded freedom, this work shines as a piece of folk-style chaekgeori. BC, JL

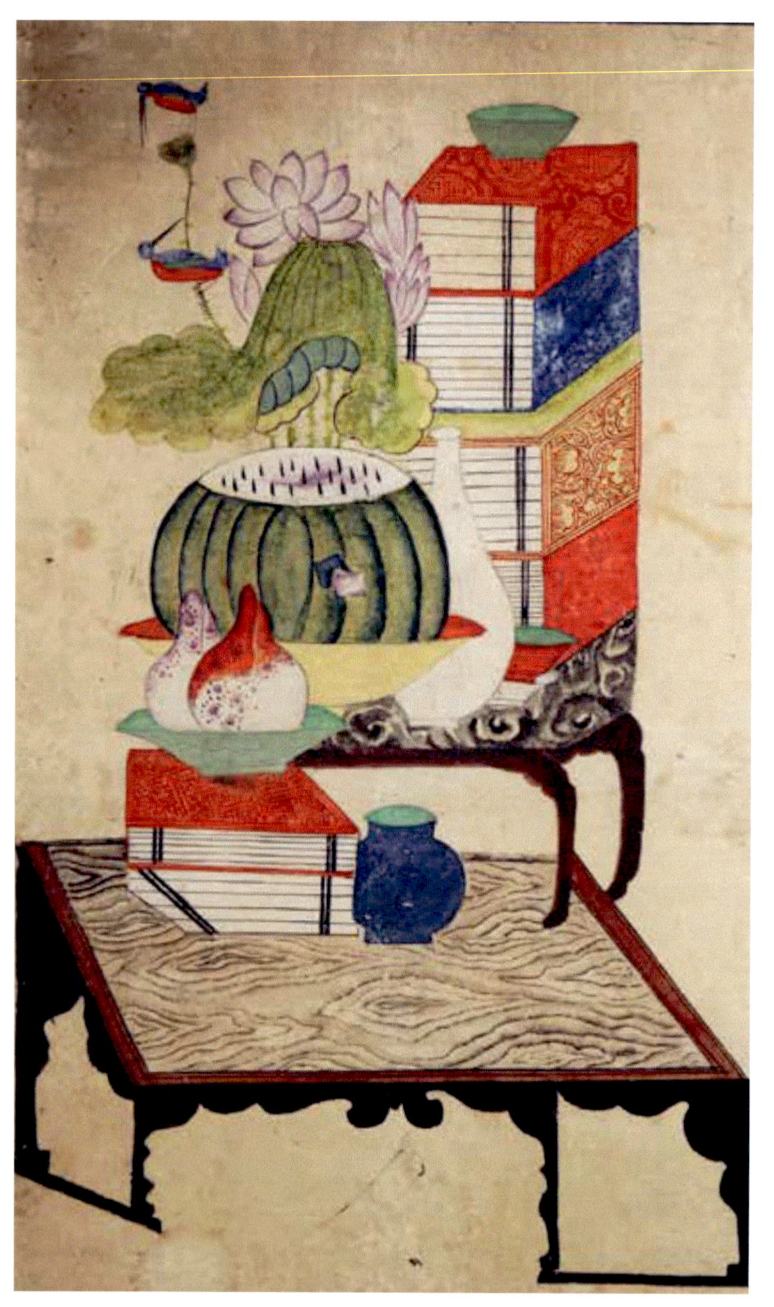

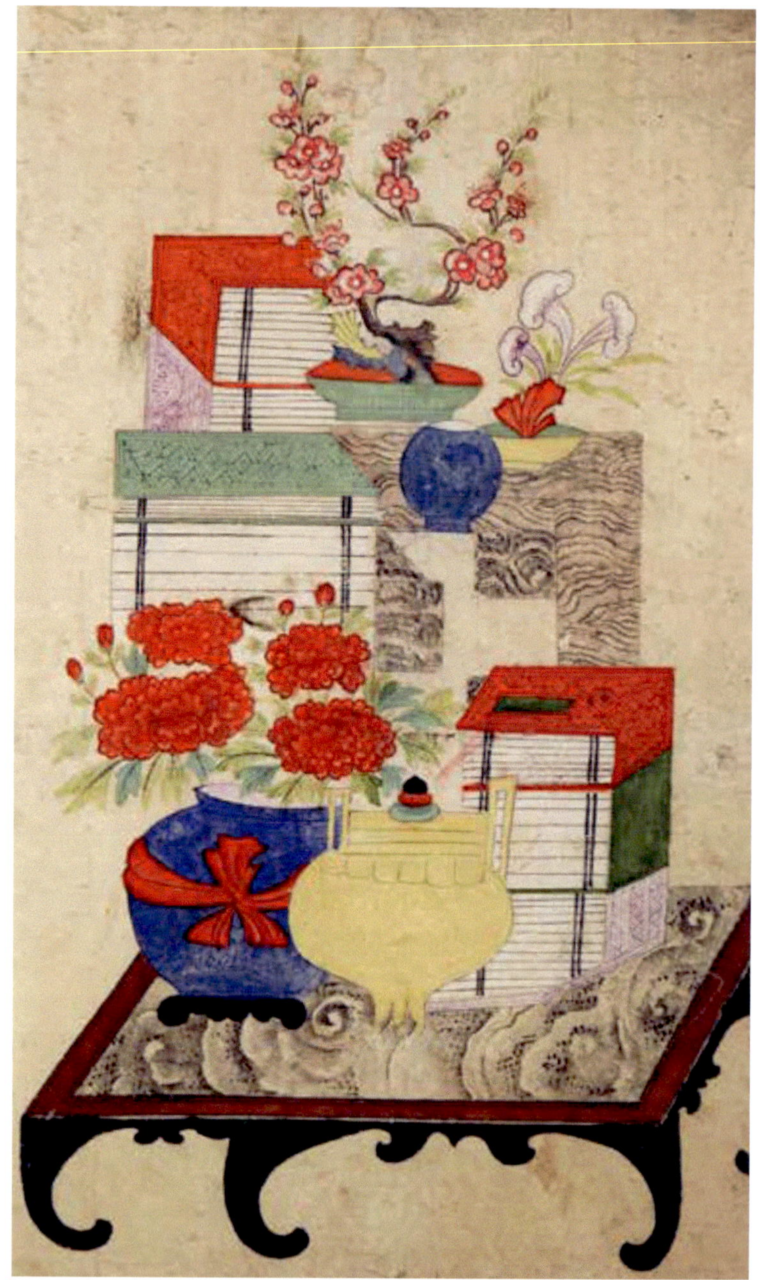

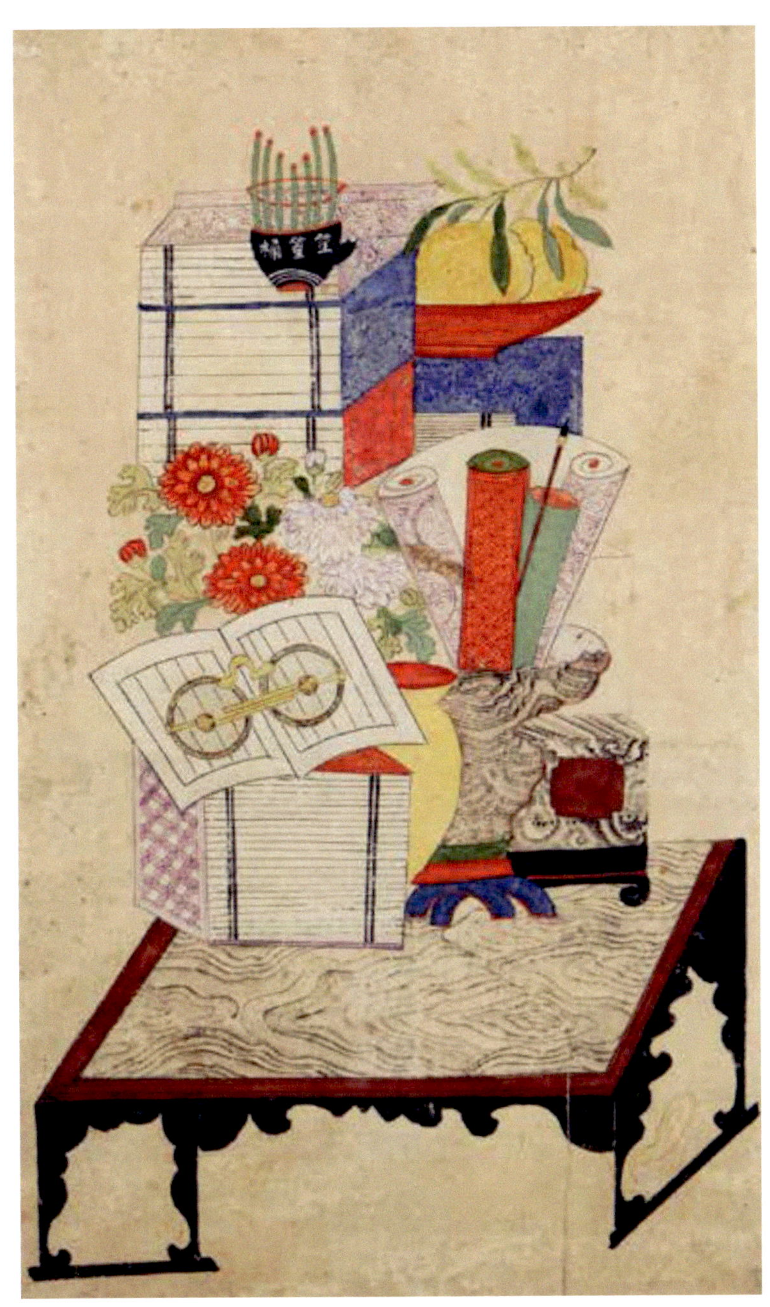

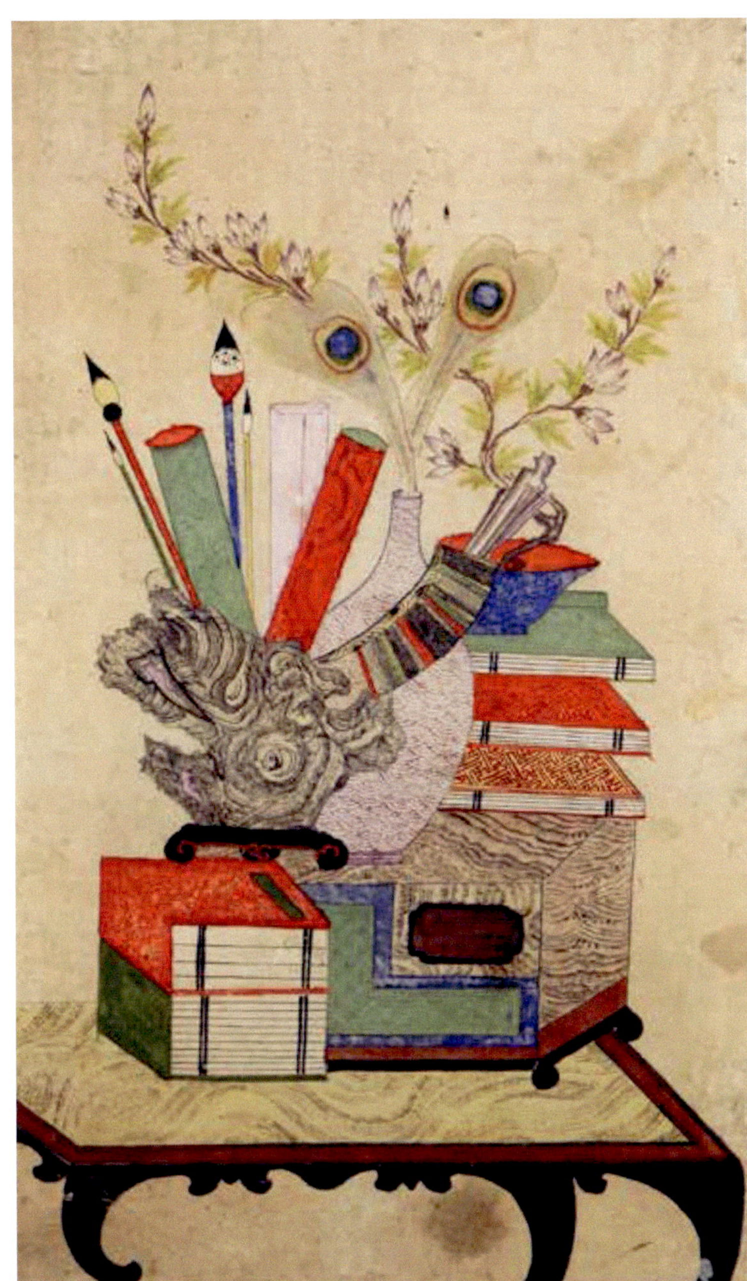

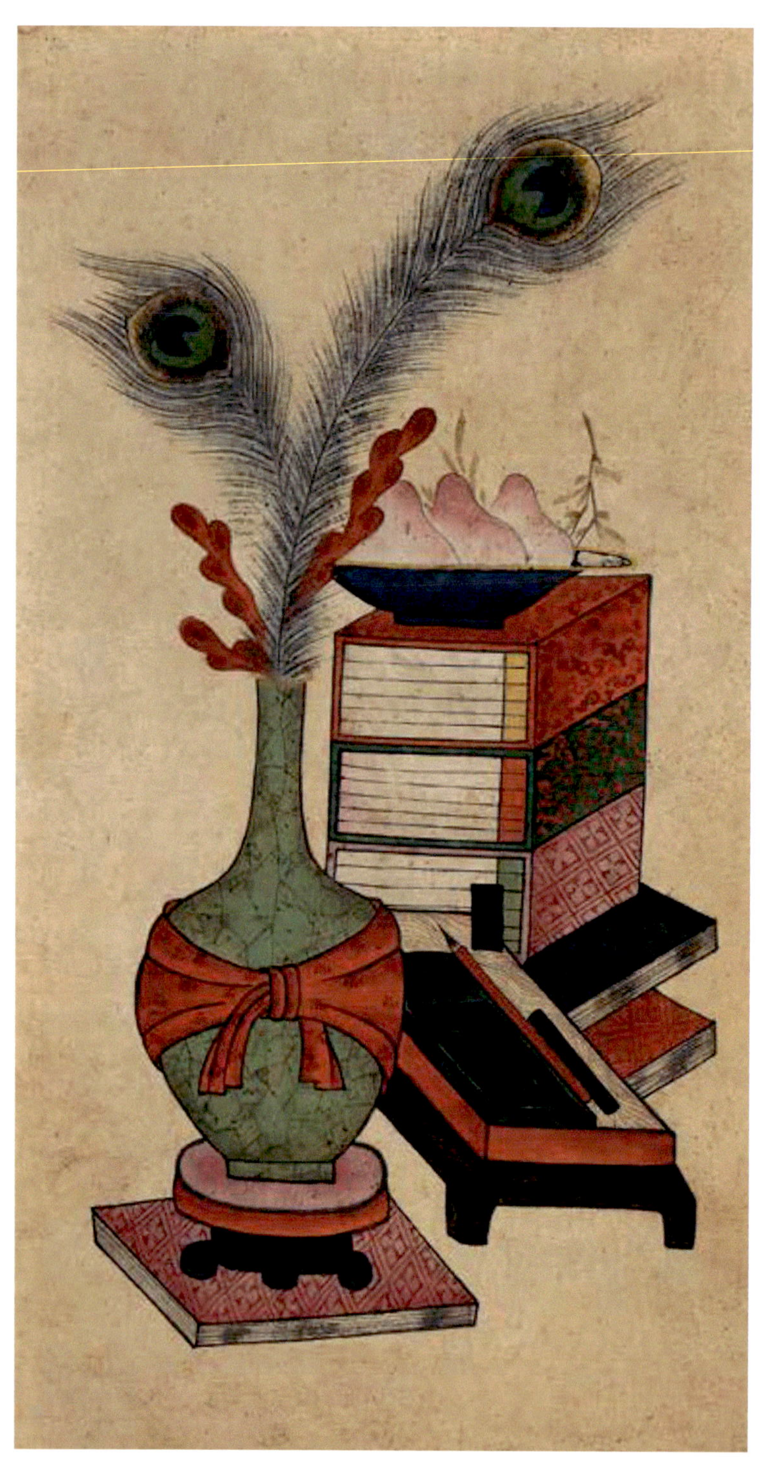

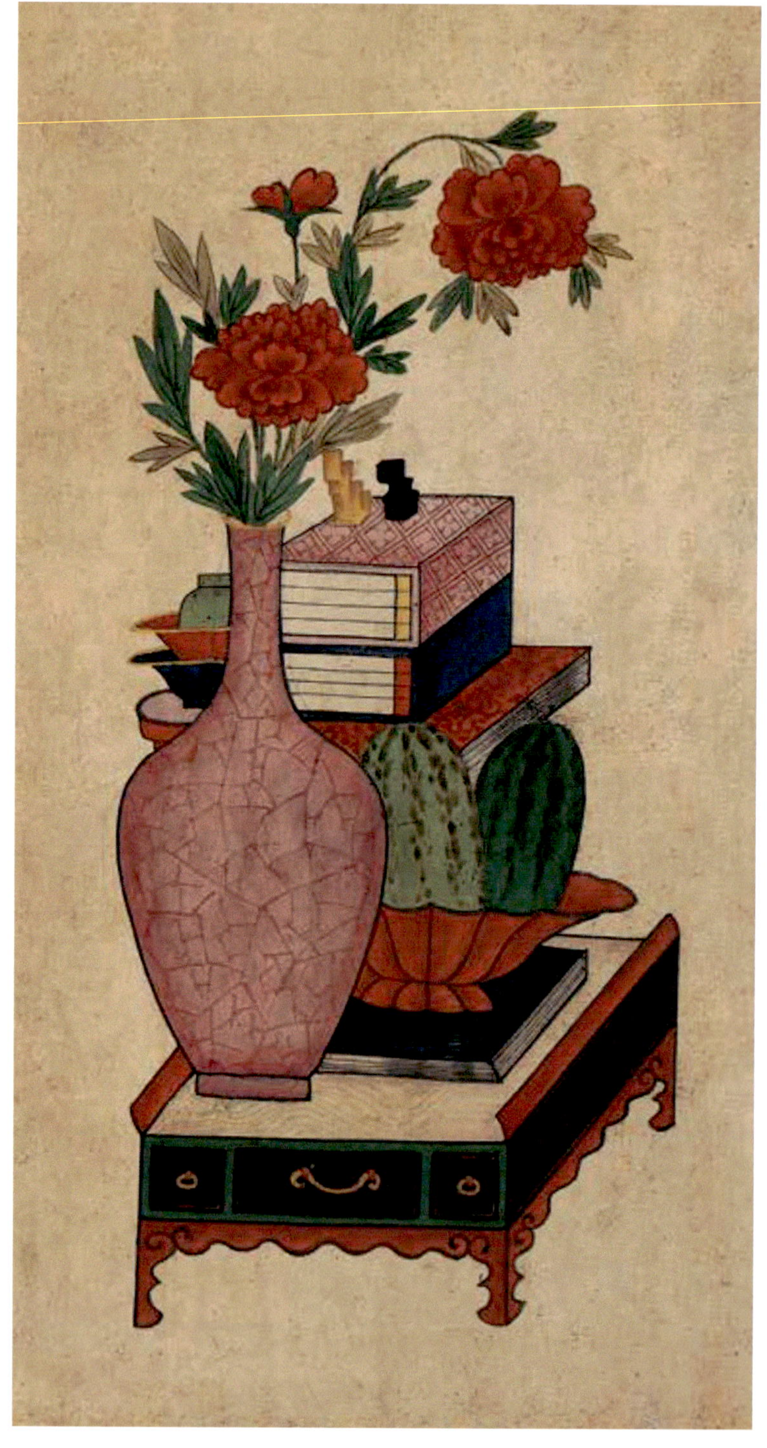

24 *Chaekgeori*

Anonymous, late 19th century
Eight-panel screen
Ink and color on paper, 49 x 28 cm (each panel)
Private collection

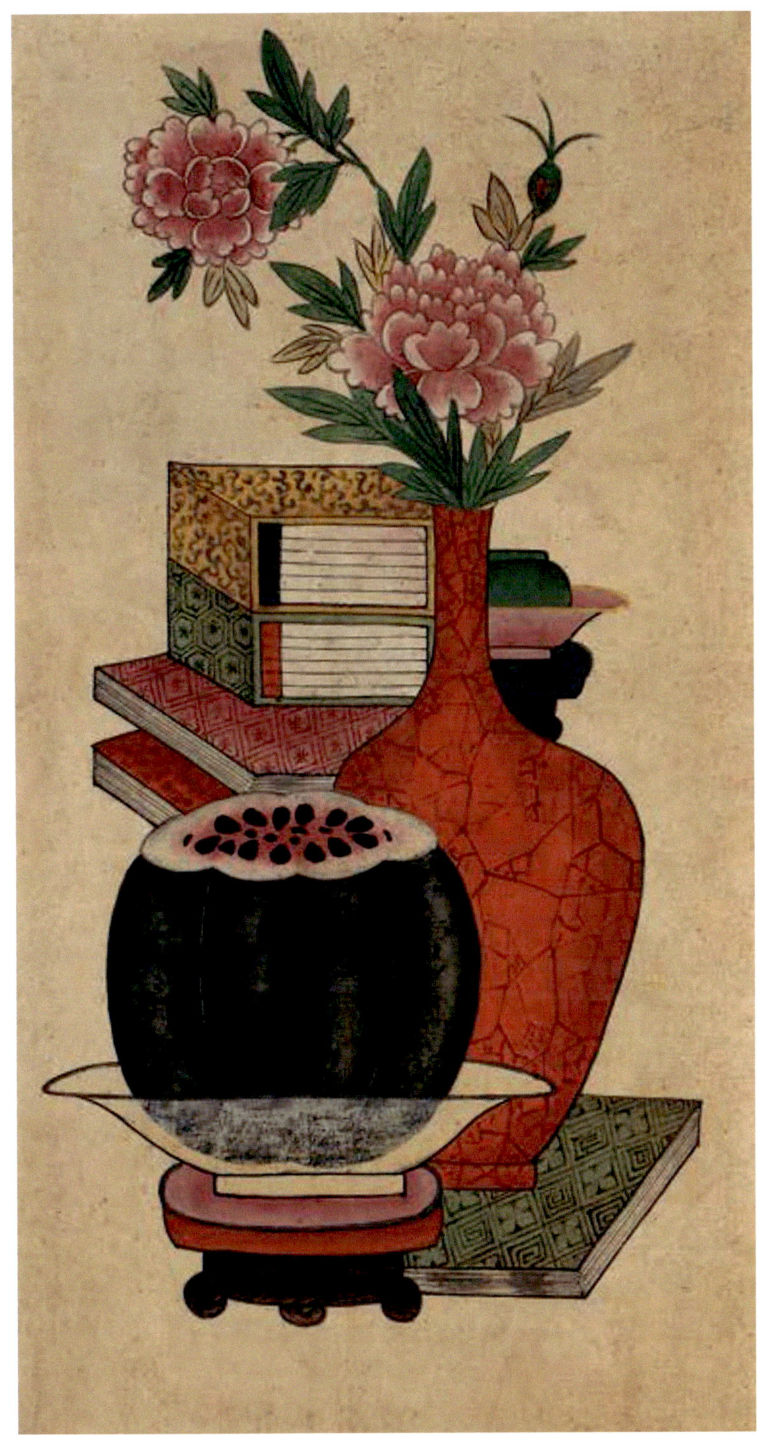

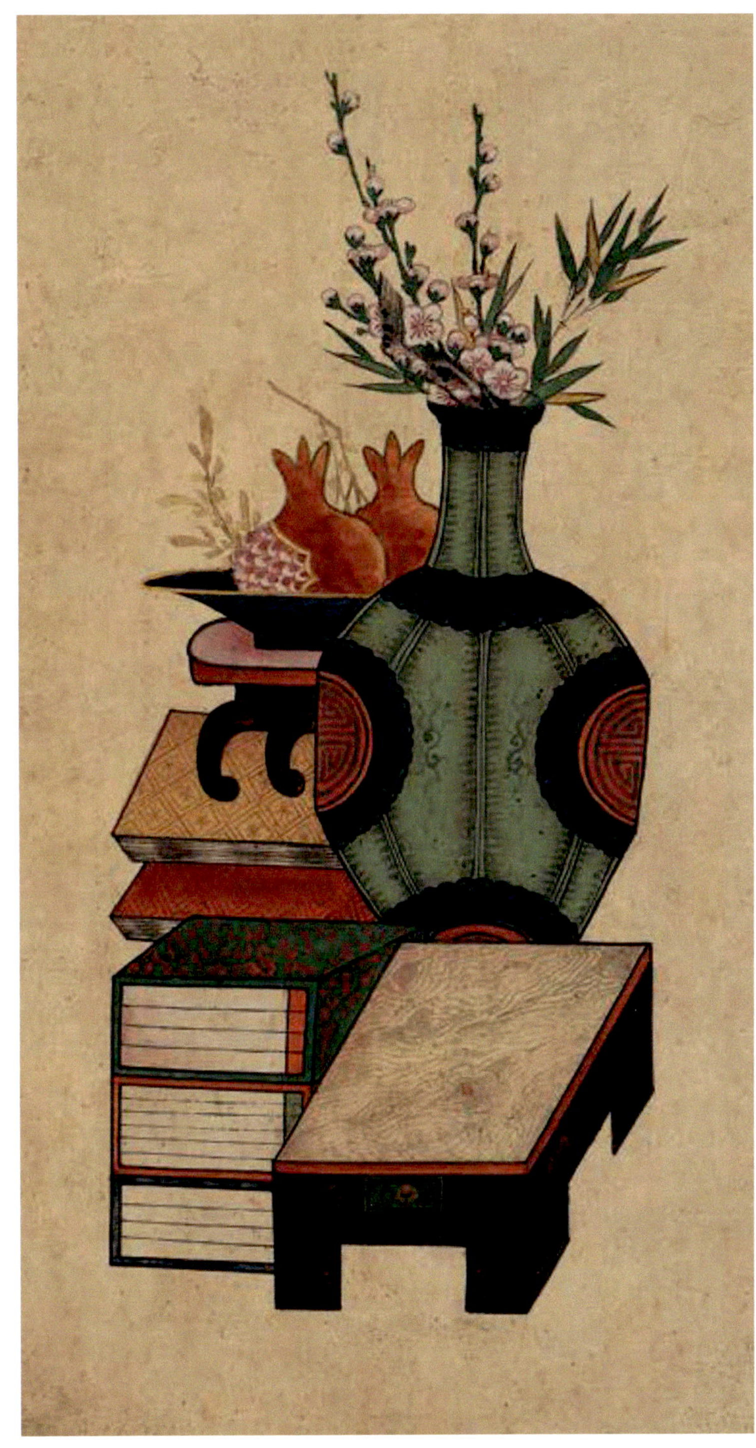

The diverse combination of flower vases, fruits on plates, and books make a very simple yet graceful formation. Each vase holds seasonal and/or symbolic flowers, such as plum blossom (winter and strength), chrysanthemum (autumn and longevity), peony (wealth), and lotus (purity). Although not flowers, the peacock feathers and corals also are symbolic (high rank). Likewise, each plate contains symbolic fruits including peaches (longevity), melons, watermelons, pomegranates, strawberries, and eggplants (fertility). Using as little subject material as possible, this chaekgeori strikes the perfect balance of space in its elegant composition. The screen highlights the harmonious arrangement between objects, such as the calabash, books and their covers, strawberries on a plate, and the colorful porcelain vase. Using five colors - yellow, blue, white, red, and black - accords vitality to this lovely work. BC, JL

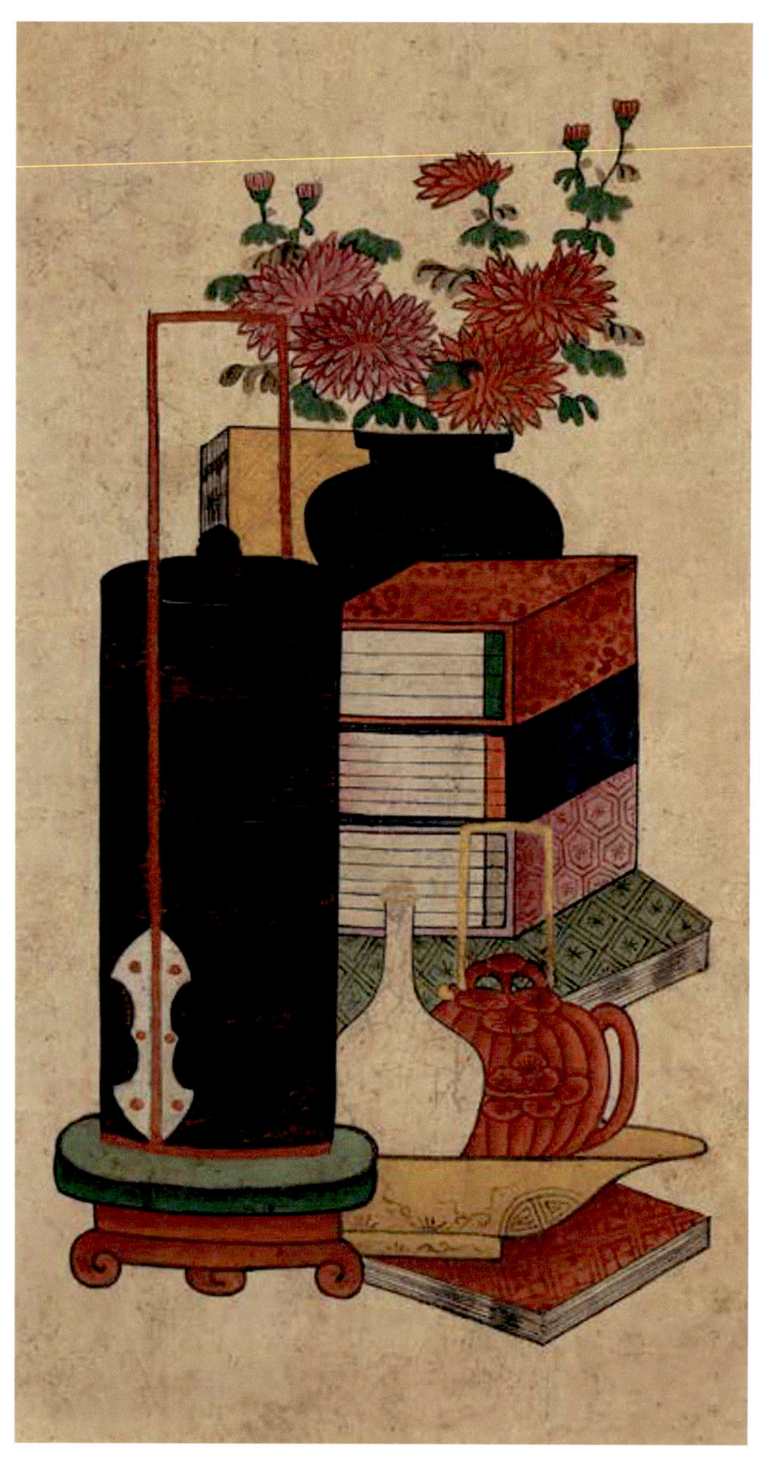

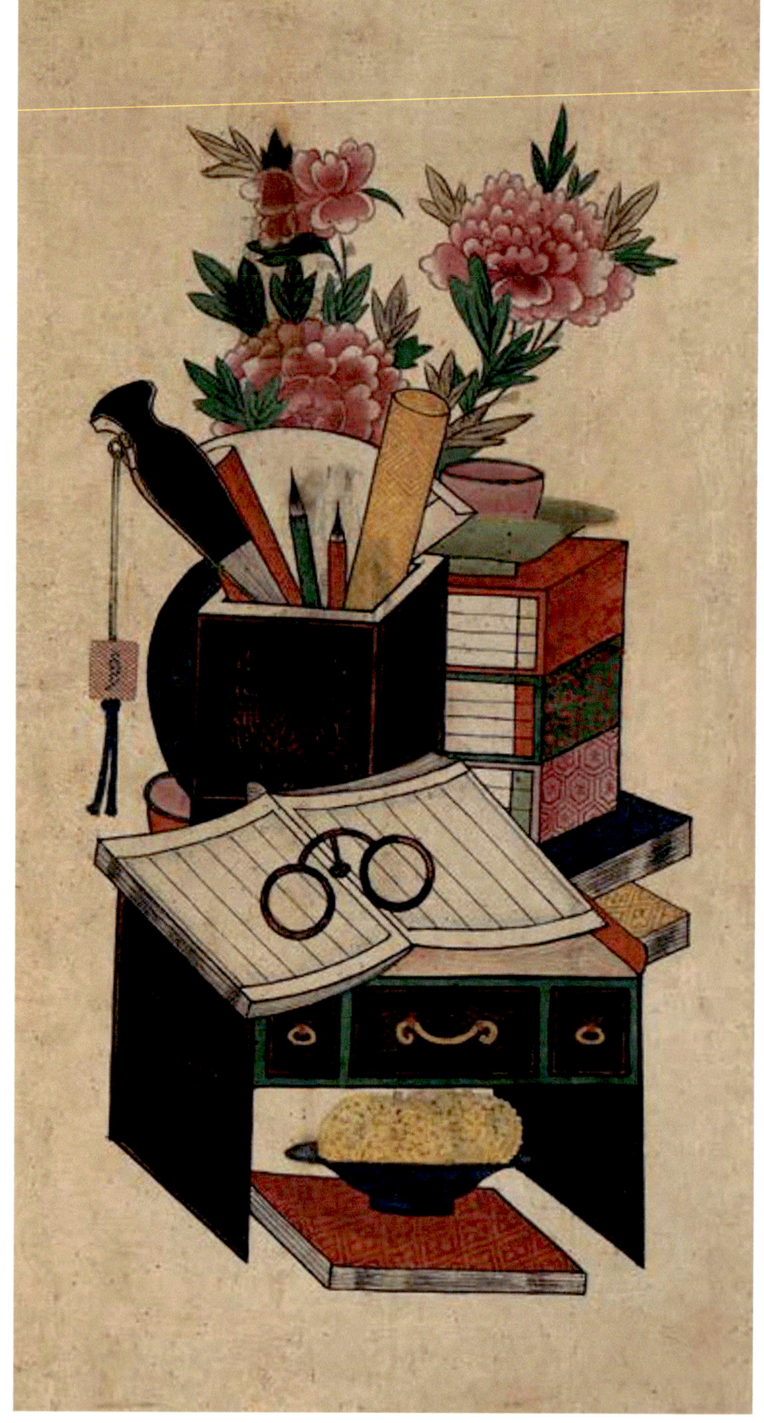

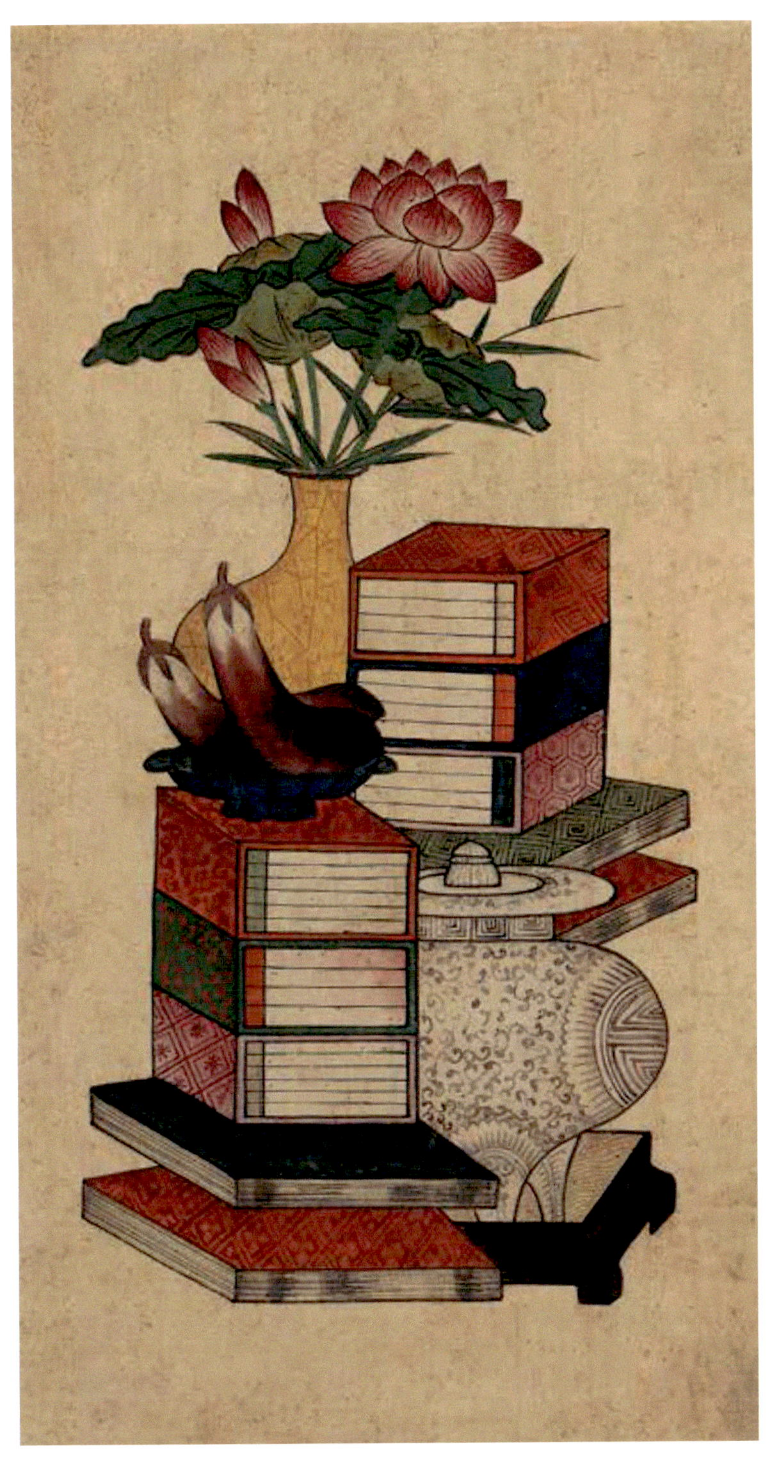

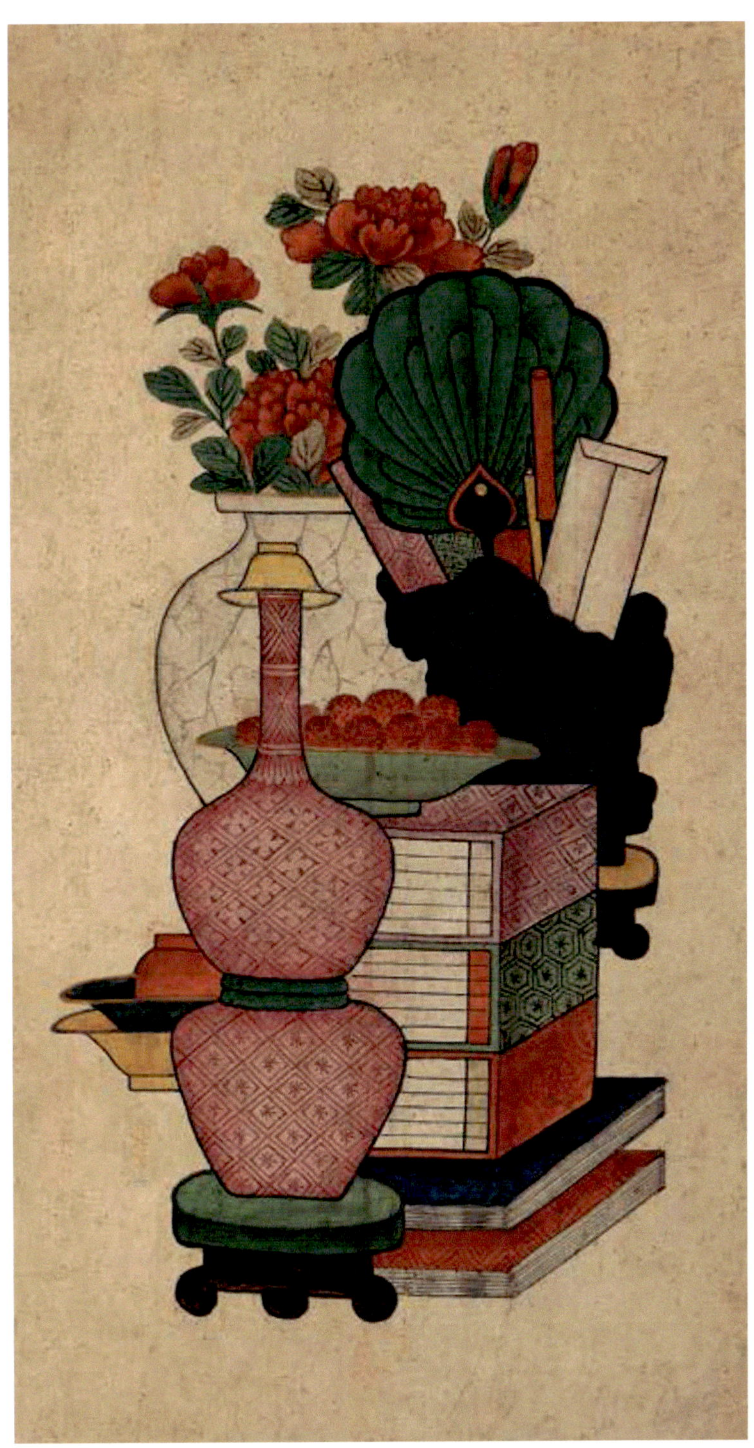

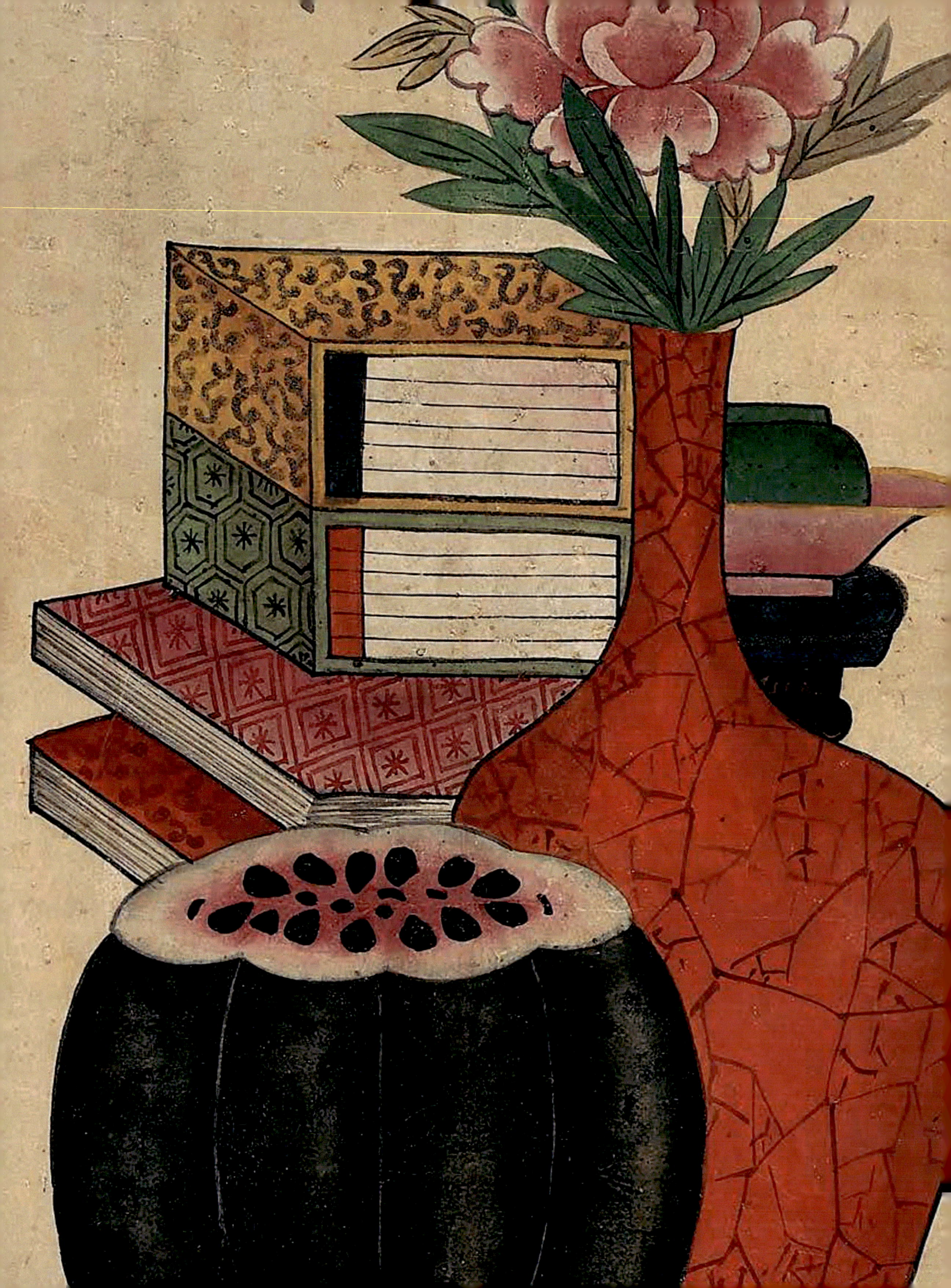

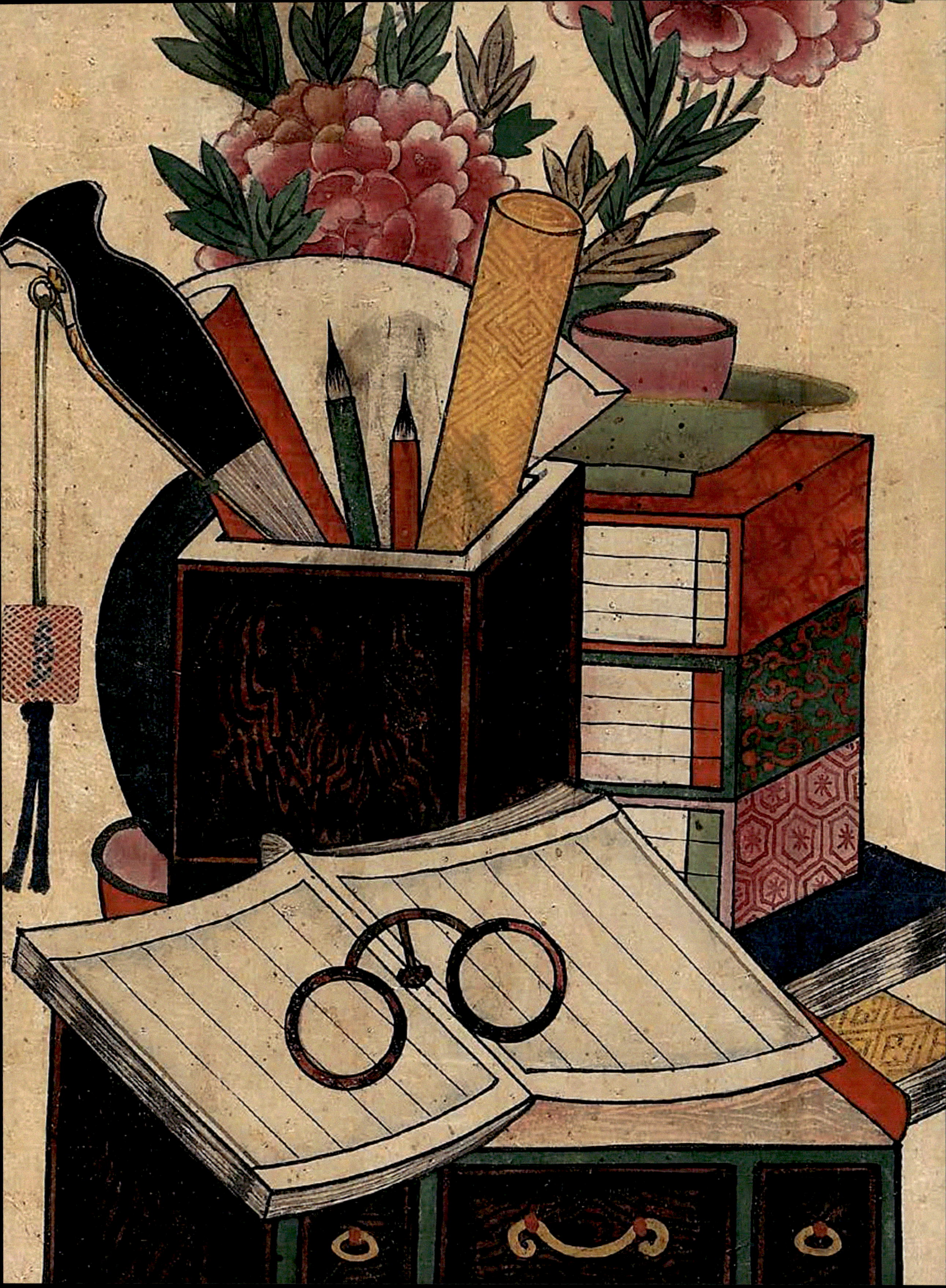

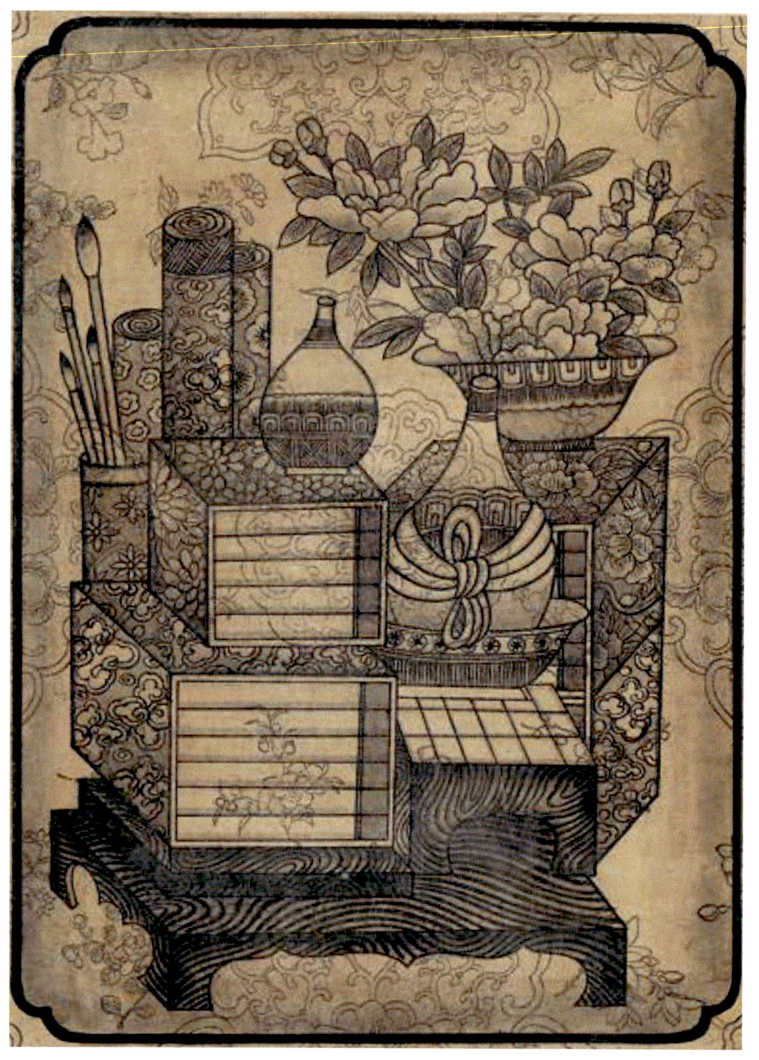
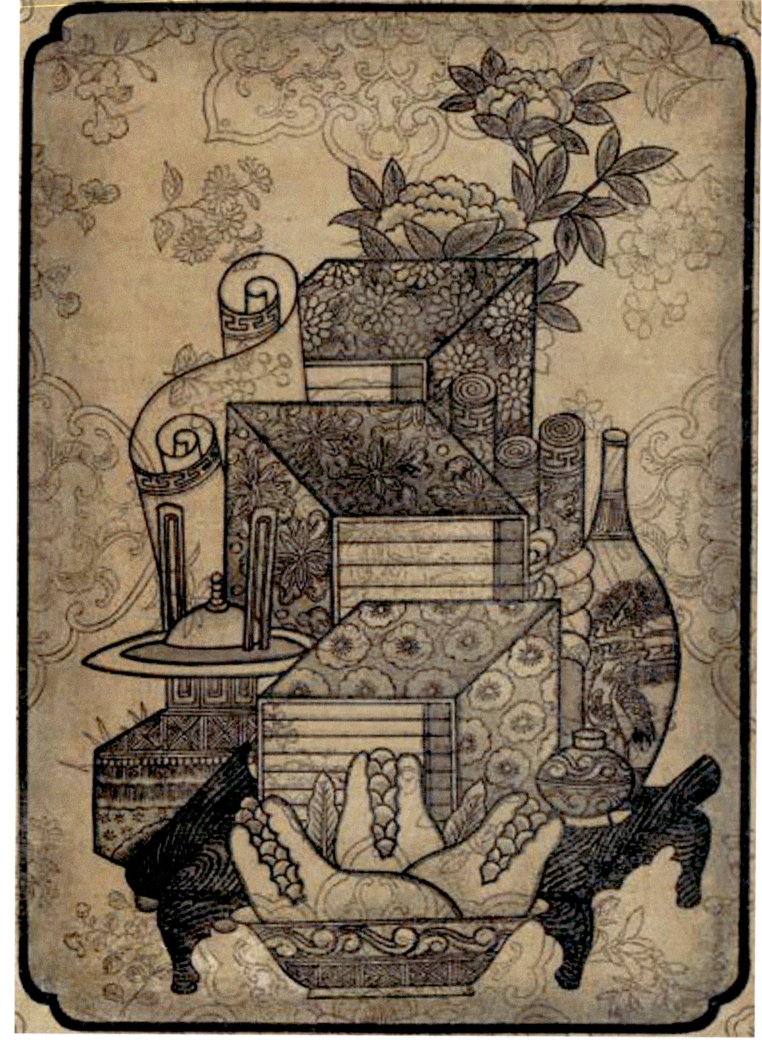

25 *Chaekgeori*

Anonymous, late 19th century
Eight-panel screen
Ink on paper, 49 x 35 cm (each panel)
Private collection

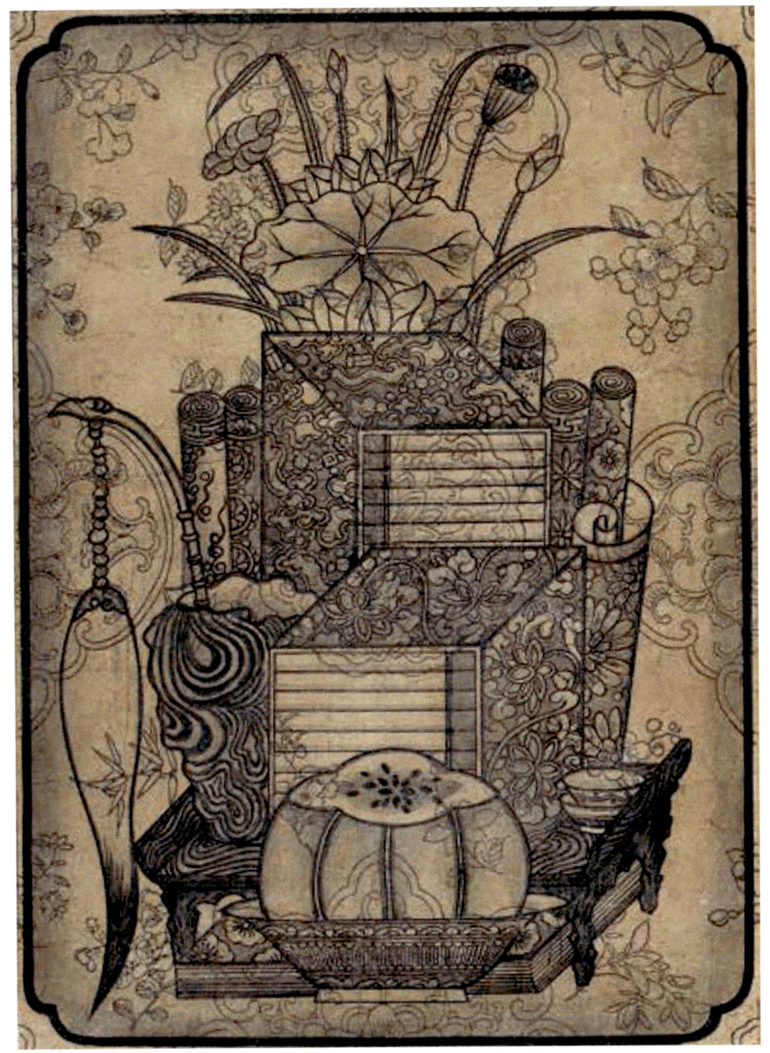

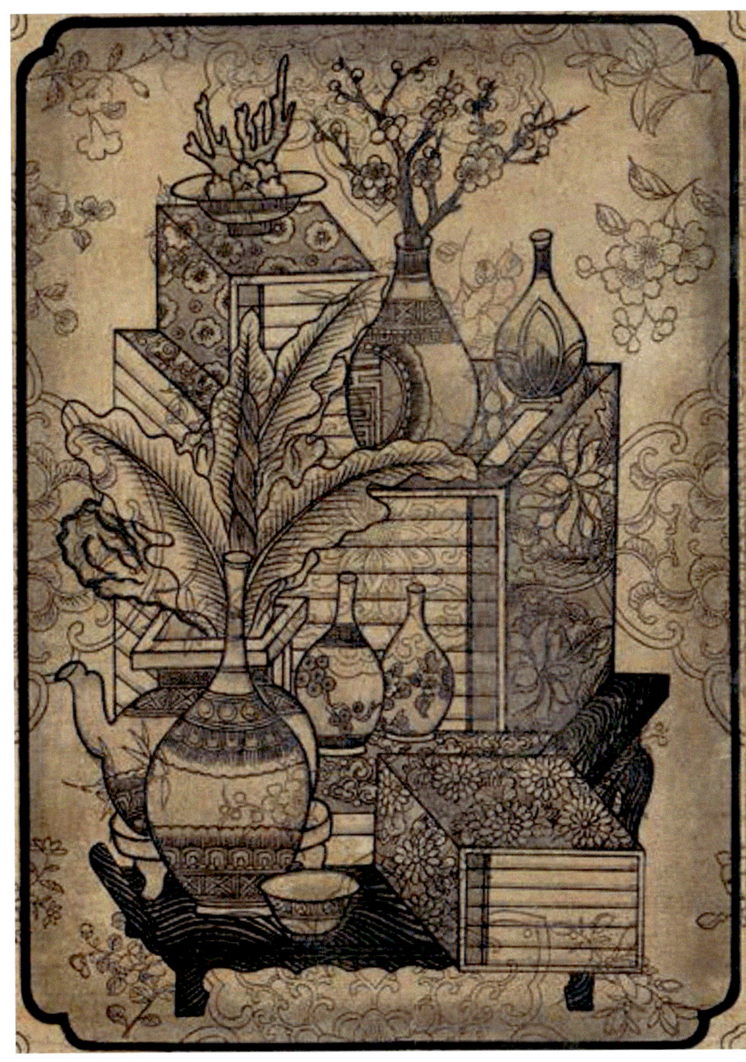

Unusual among chaekgeori, this work is in monochrome and thus stands out from its peers. Not only is this work rare in that it is painted in black ink, but its background is also covered with talismanic Buddhist patterns. The furniture, piles of books, and paper holders are clustered together in one large mass within each panel—as in other folk-style chaekgeori—but here the clustered pattern is not limited to the items. Even the talismanic patterns are placed together in close proximity. By combining numerous and varied auspicious subjects, this painting indicates the desire for both scholarly achievement and prosperity. Without brilliant colors, this screen reflects the aesthetic oscillation between the modest taste of the Confucian gentleman and the human desire for protection and prosperity. BC, JJL

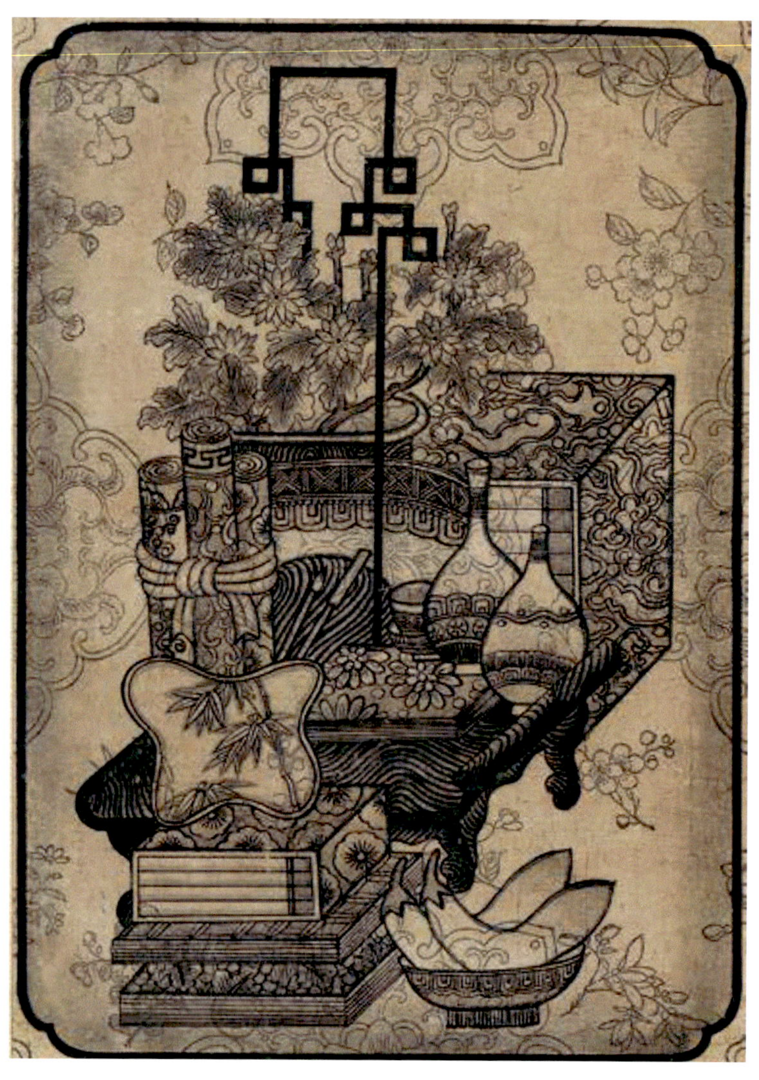

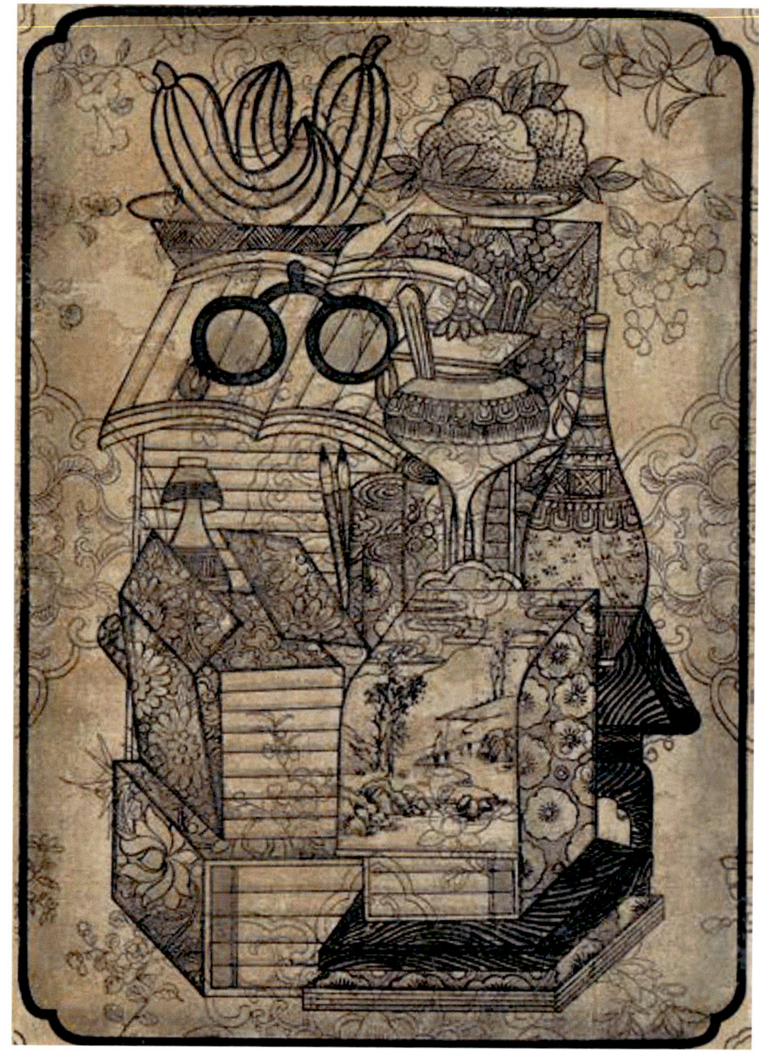

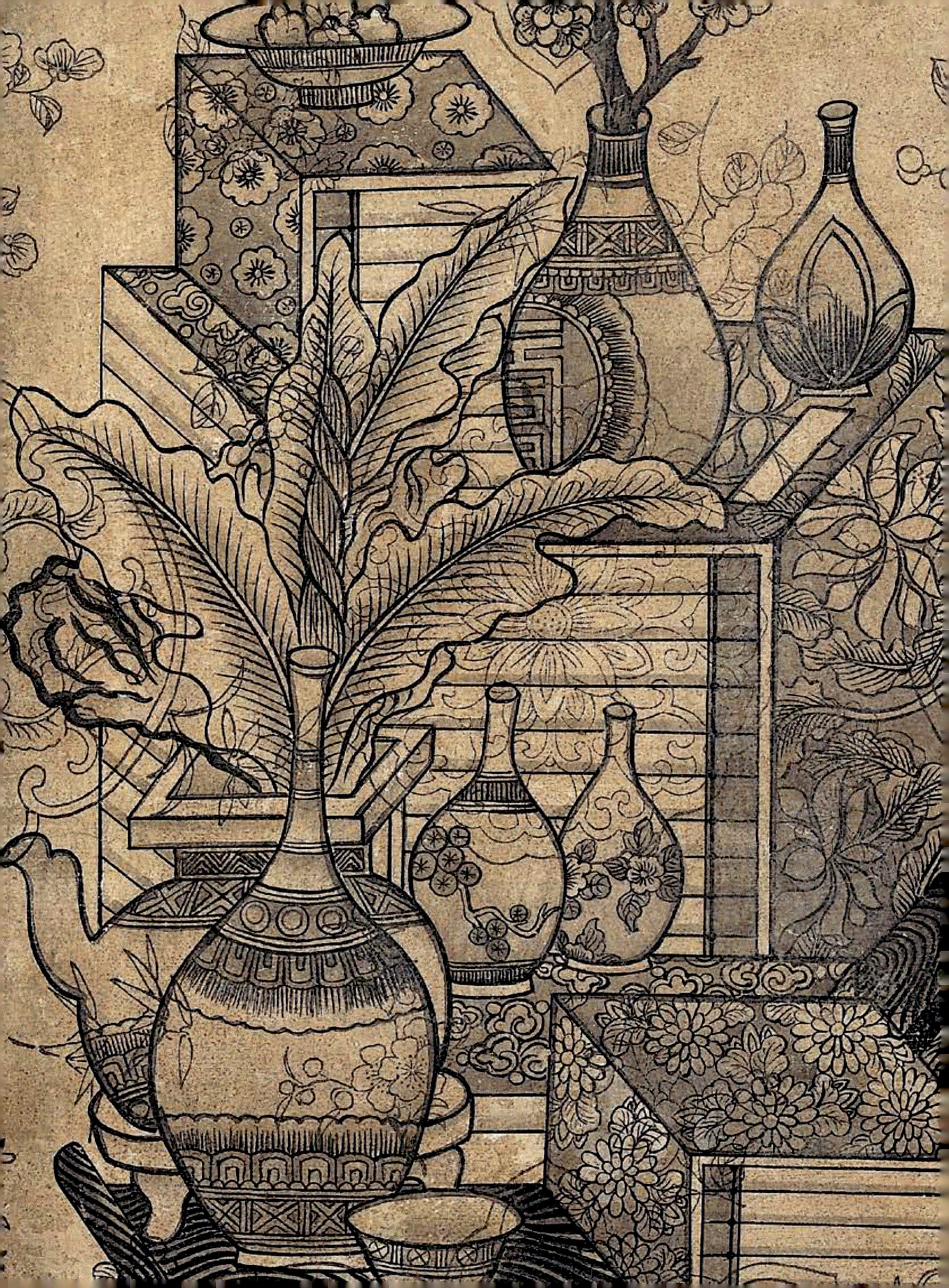

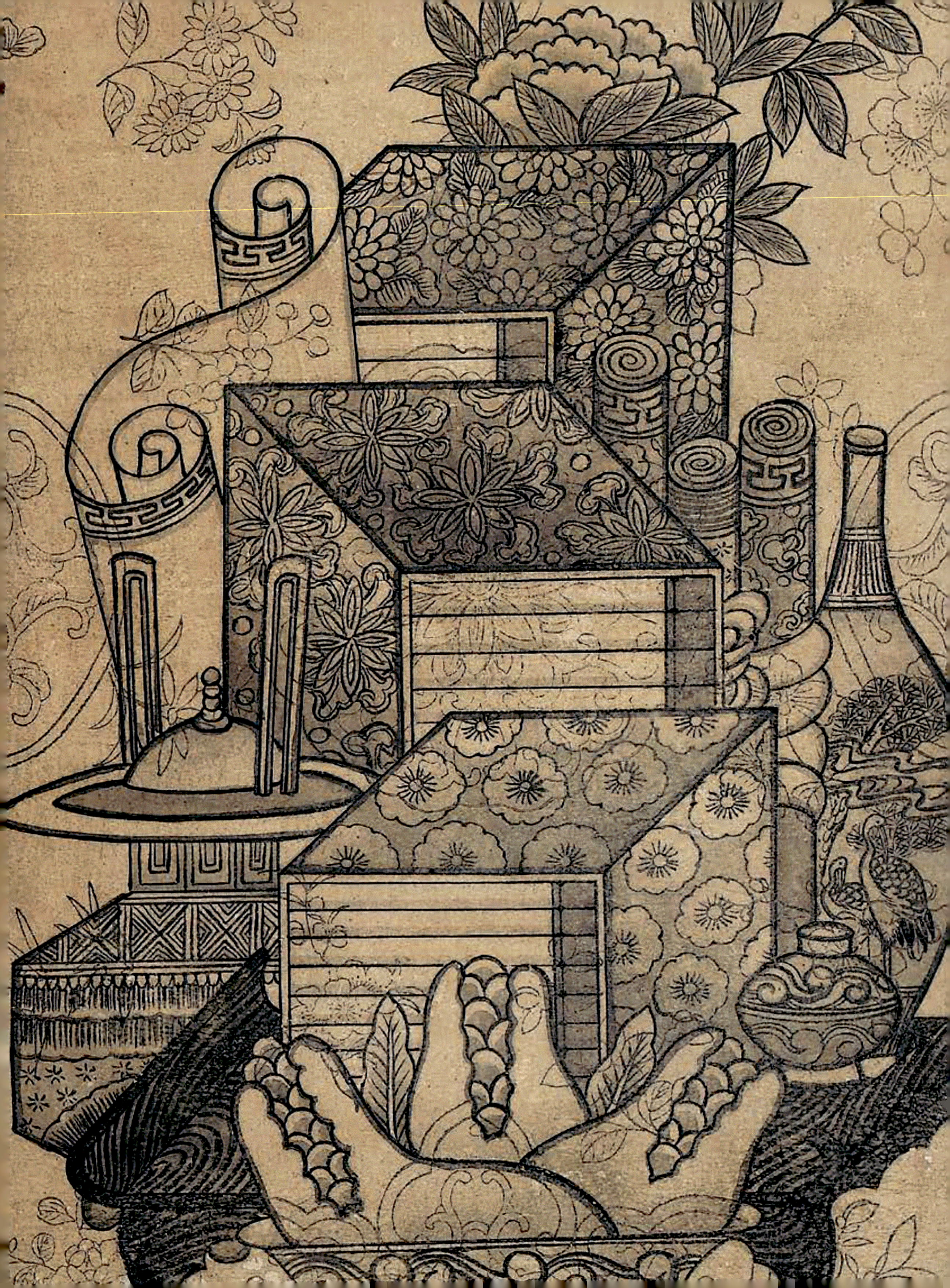

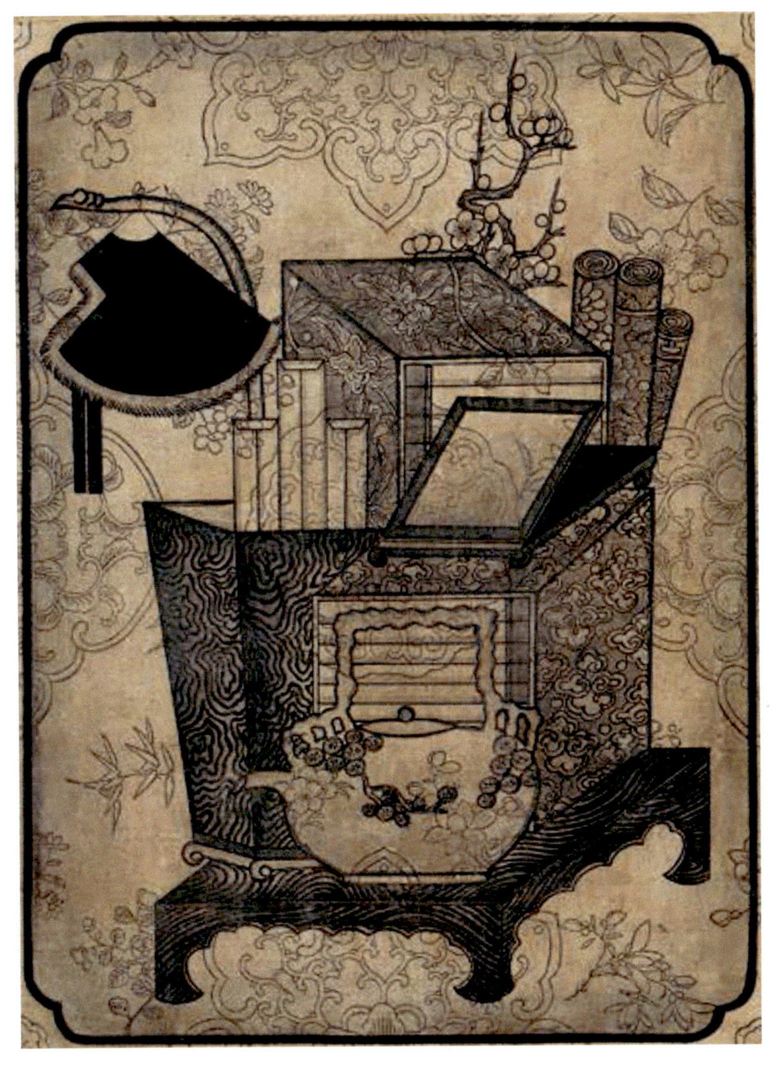

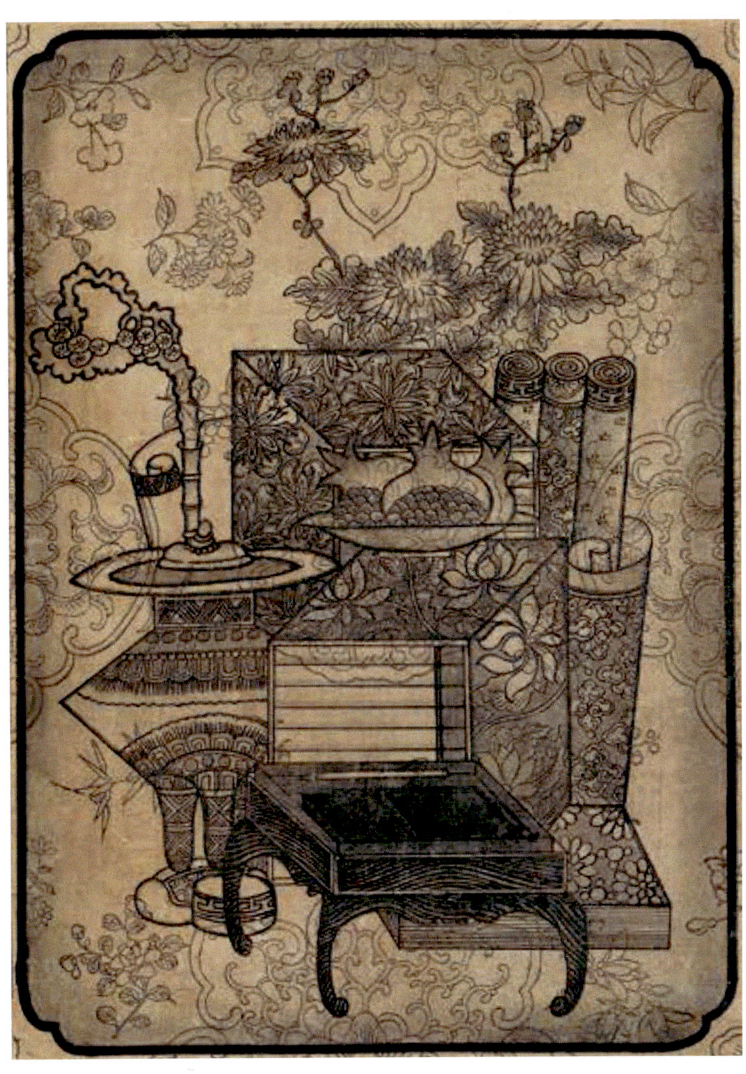

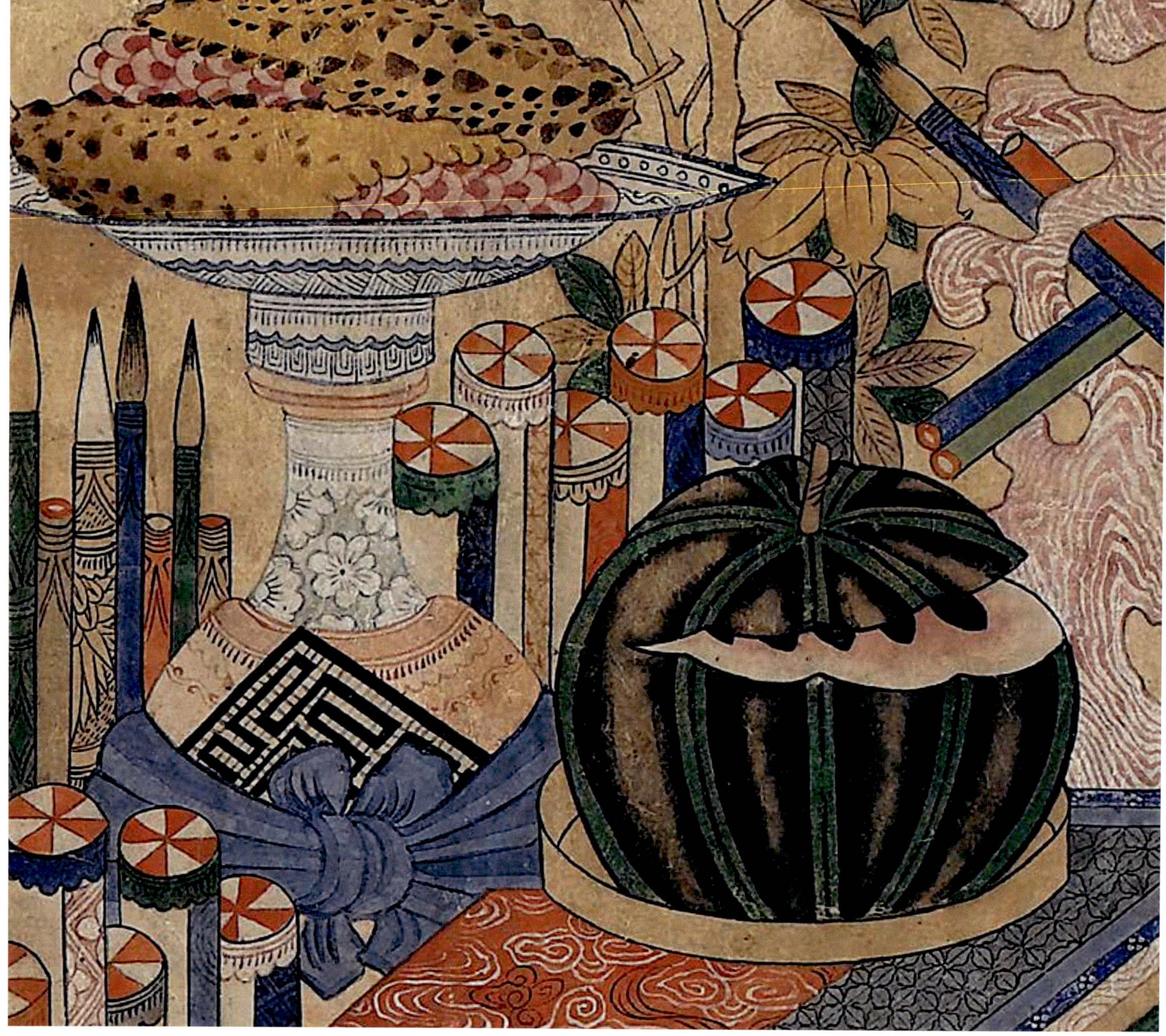

26 *Chaekgeori*

Anonymous, late 19th century
Four-panel screen
Ink and color on paper, 55 x 35 cm (each panel)
Private collection

Although this four-panel screen is relatively in scale, the excellent composition and vibrant colors make this piece highly decorative and unique. The accoutrements and plants in the painting are arranged close together in clusters around books. The patterned corners of the screens create a frame much like a door, adding yet another layer of decorative charm.

The most noteworthy feature, however, is the small child reading among the books. Like a Lilliputian straight out of *Gulliver's Travels*, the child sits before a table piled high with Buddhist texts amid books much larger than he is. Here, subjects of greater importance are drawn larger than subjects of lesser importance, indicating an emphasis on learning.

The child is reading the *Sohak*, a popular ethics book for Korean children during the Joseon dynasty. The open closet (which shows the clothing inside), the palanquin-shaped compass case, the haphazardly stacked books, the messily cut Korean melon slices, and the discarded melon rinds are unusual as subjects in chaekgeori. The painting also shows extraordinary detail when it comes to texture, as seen in the wood grain, book-cover patterns, and accoutrement surfaces. BC, SK

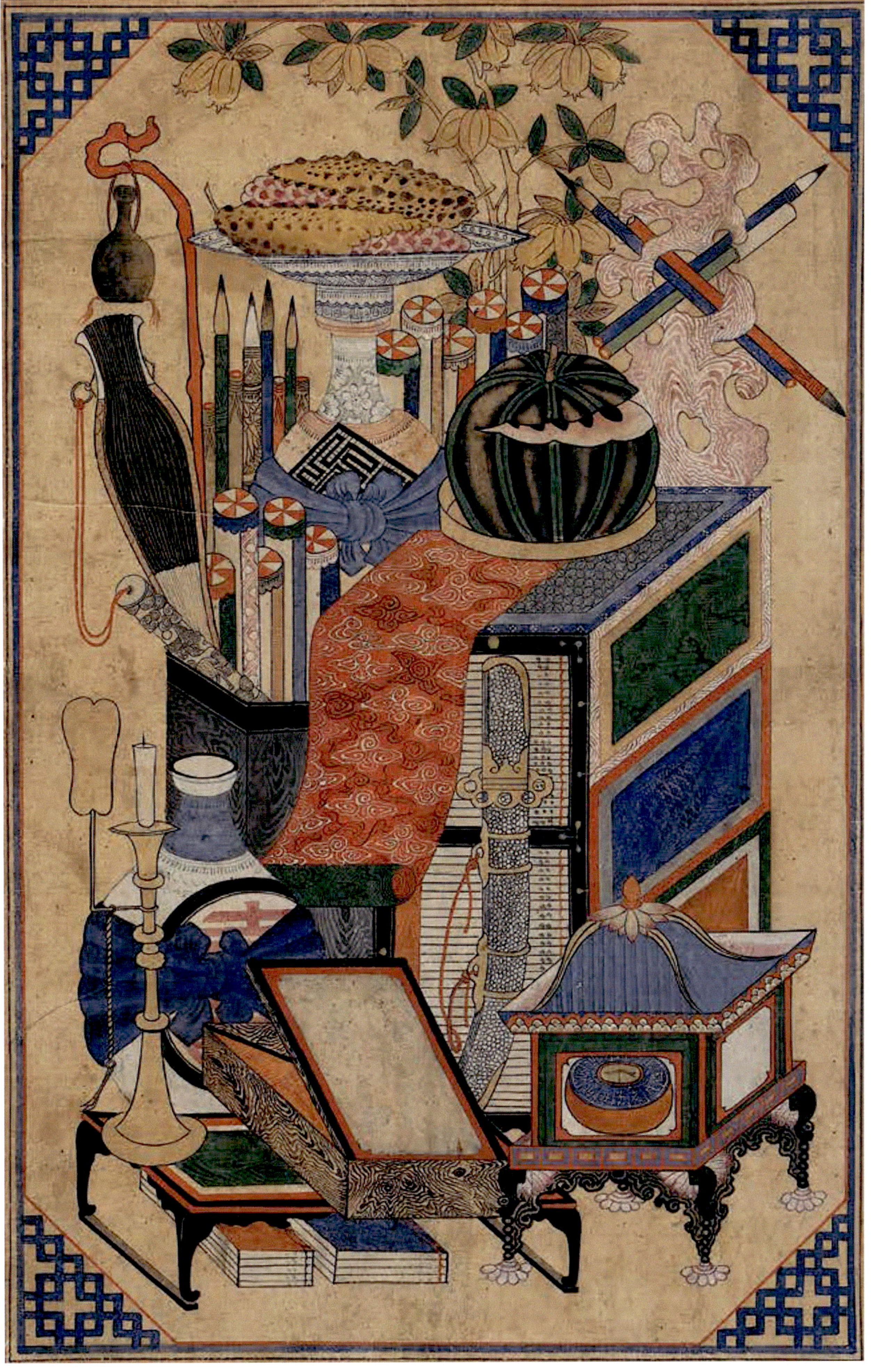

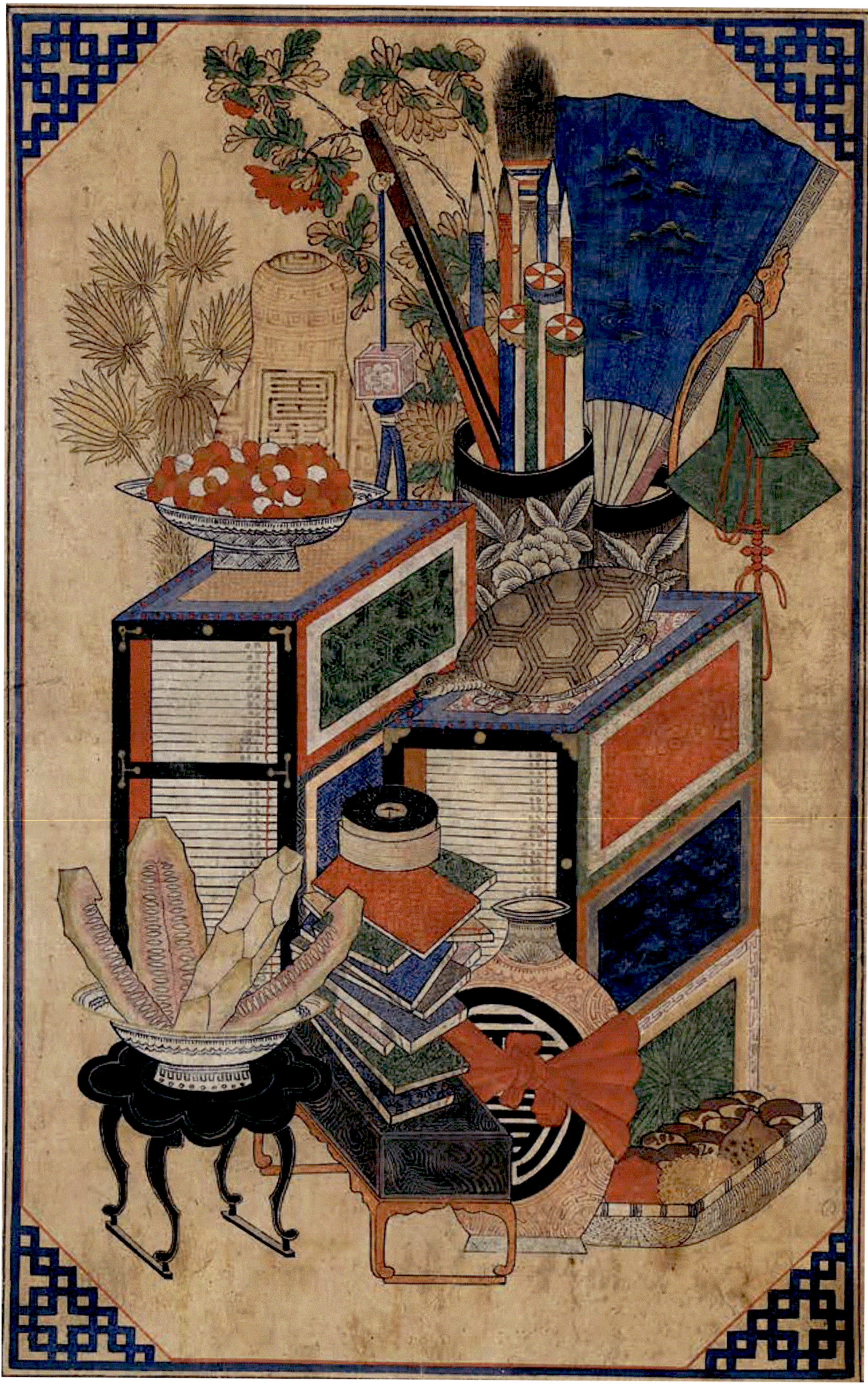

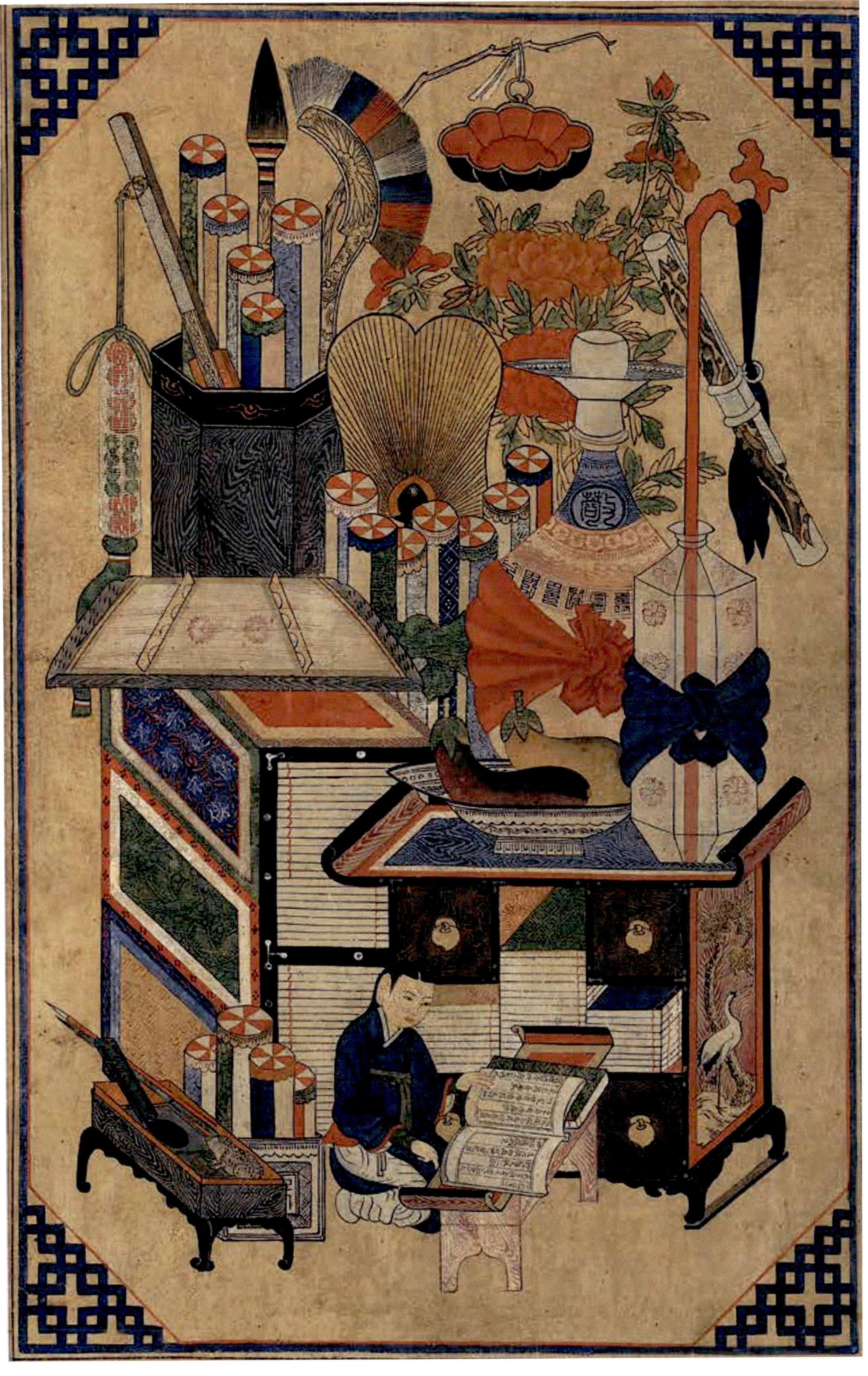

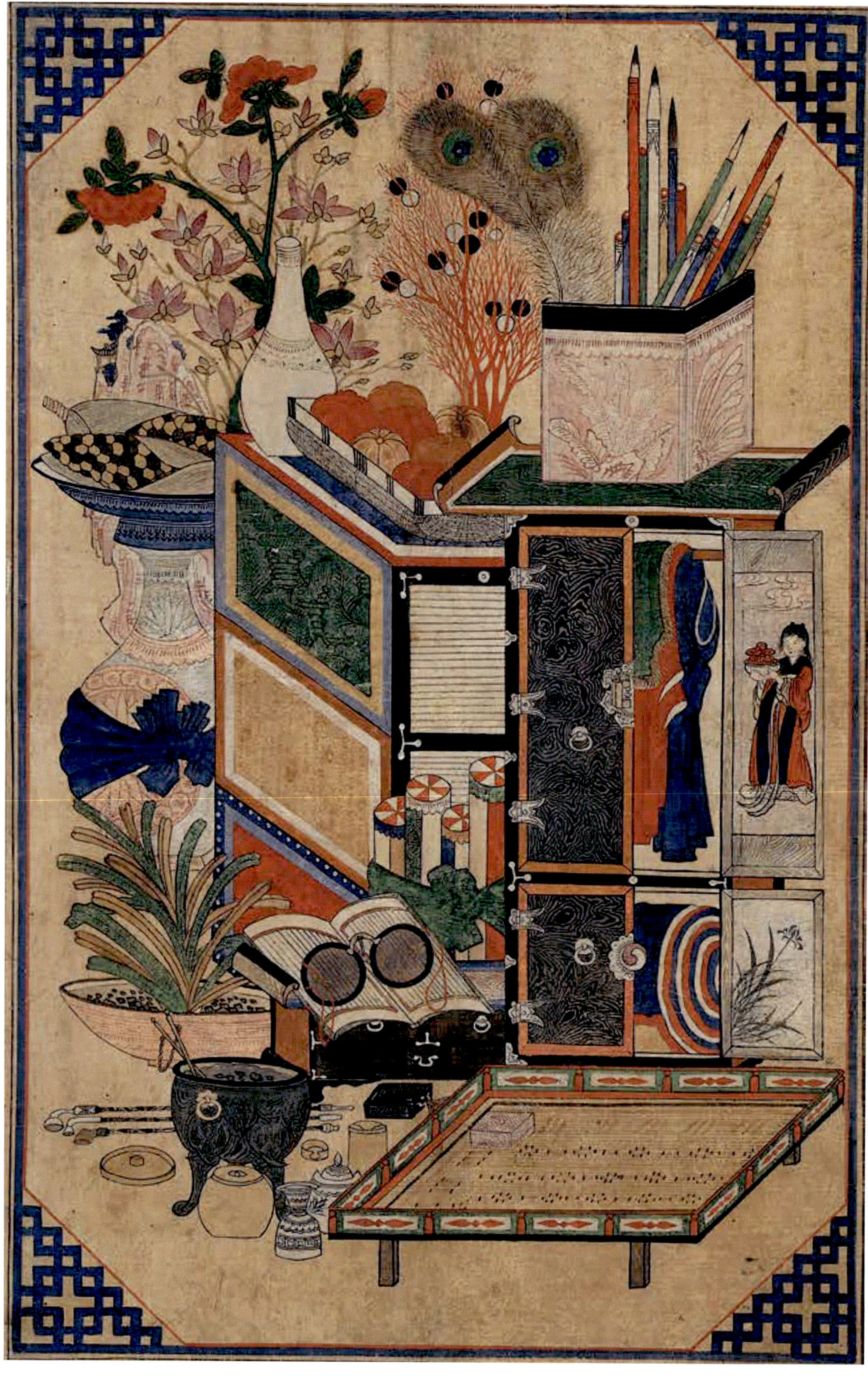

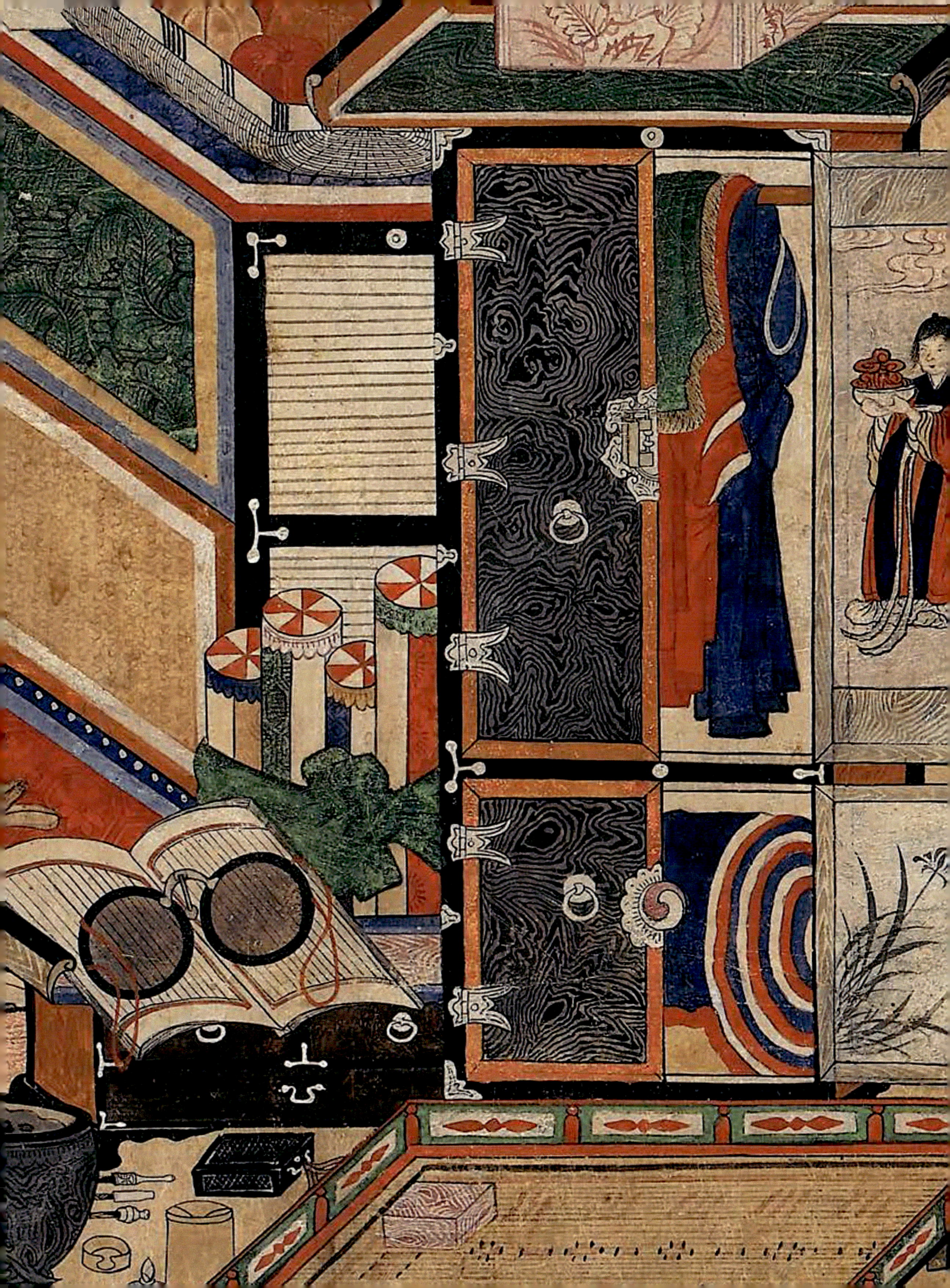

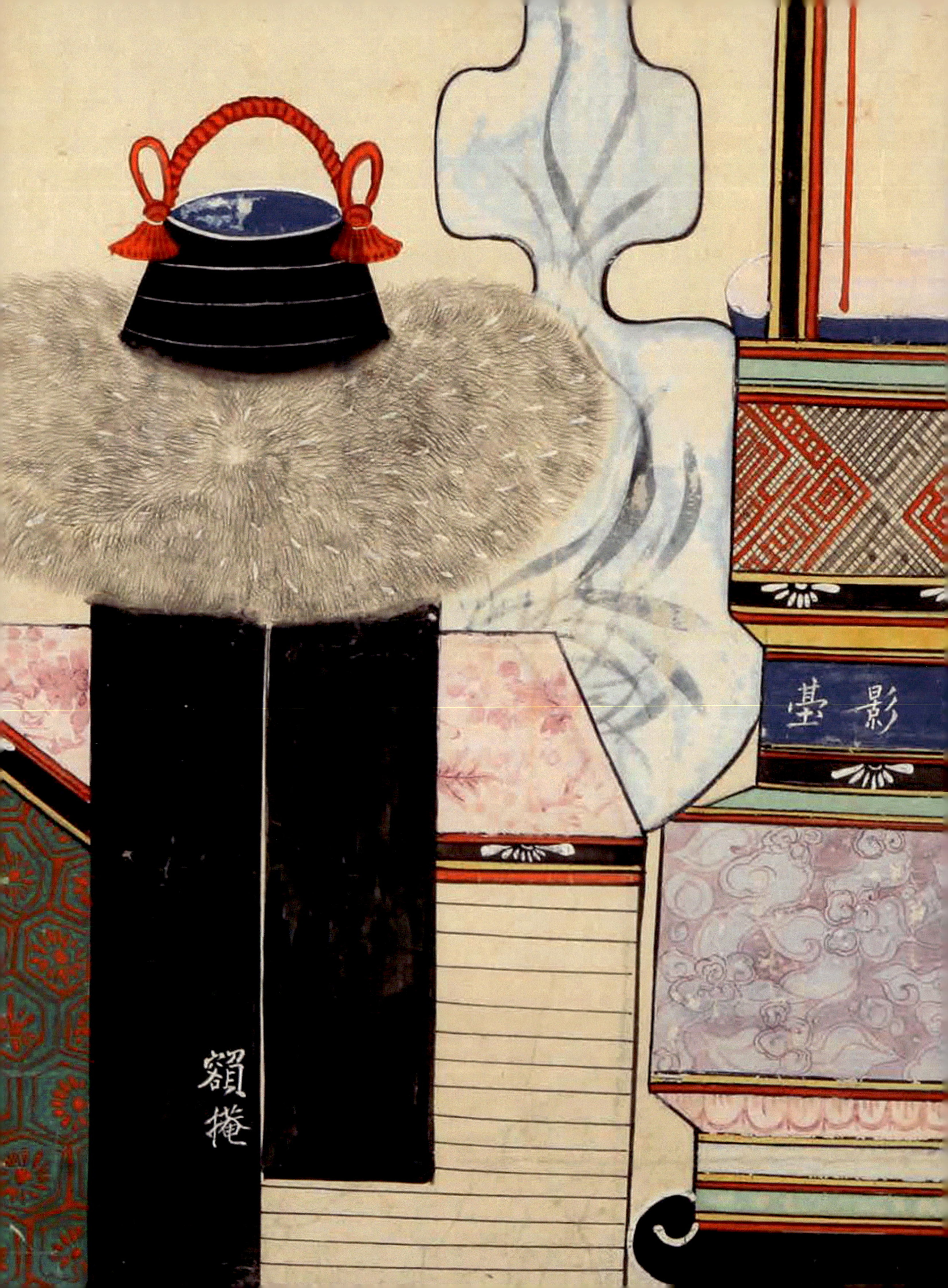
額掩

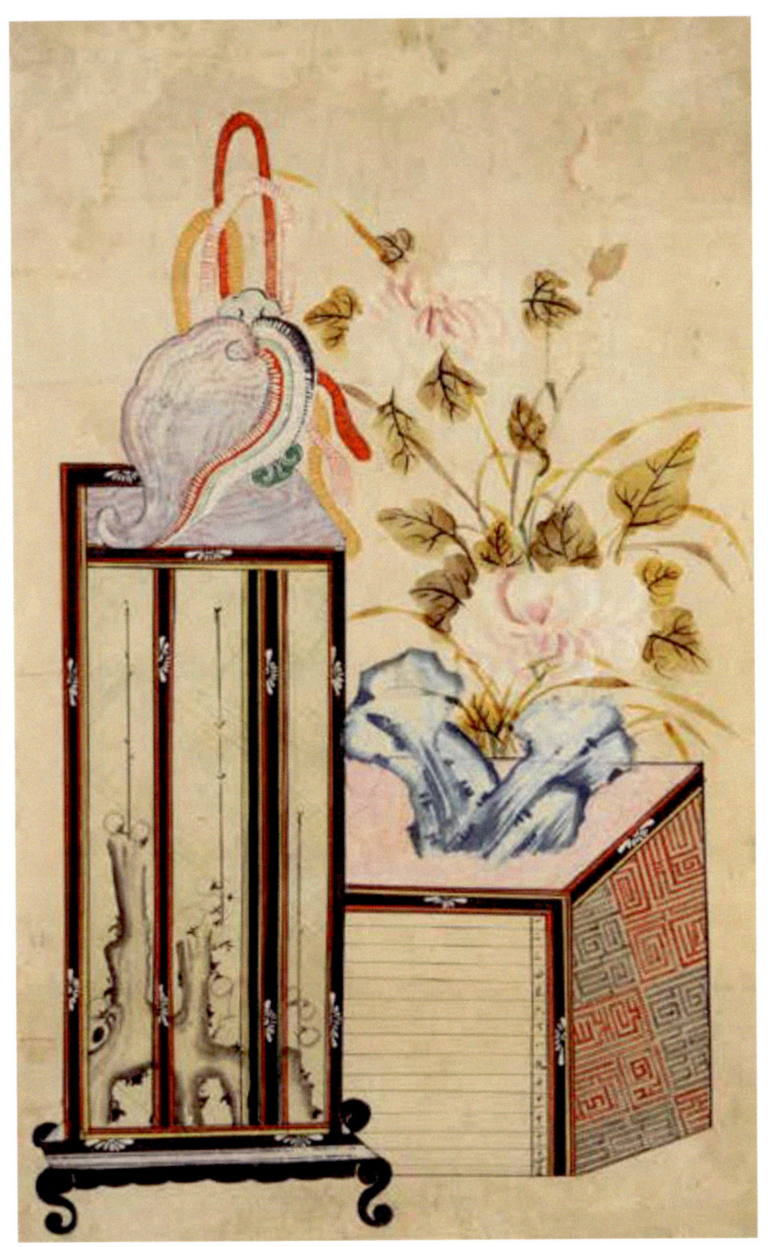

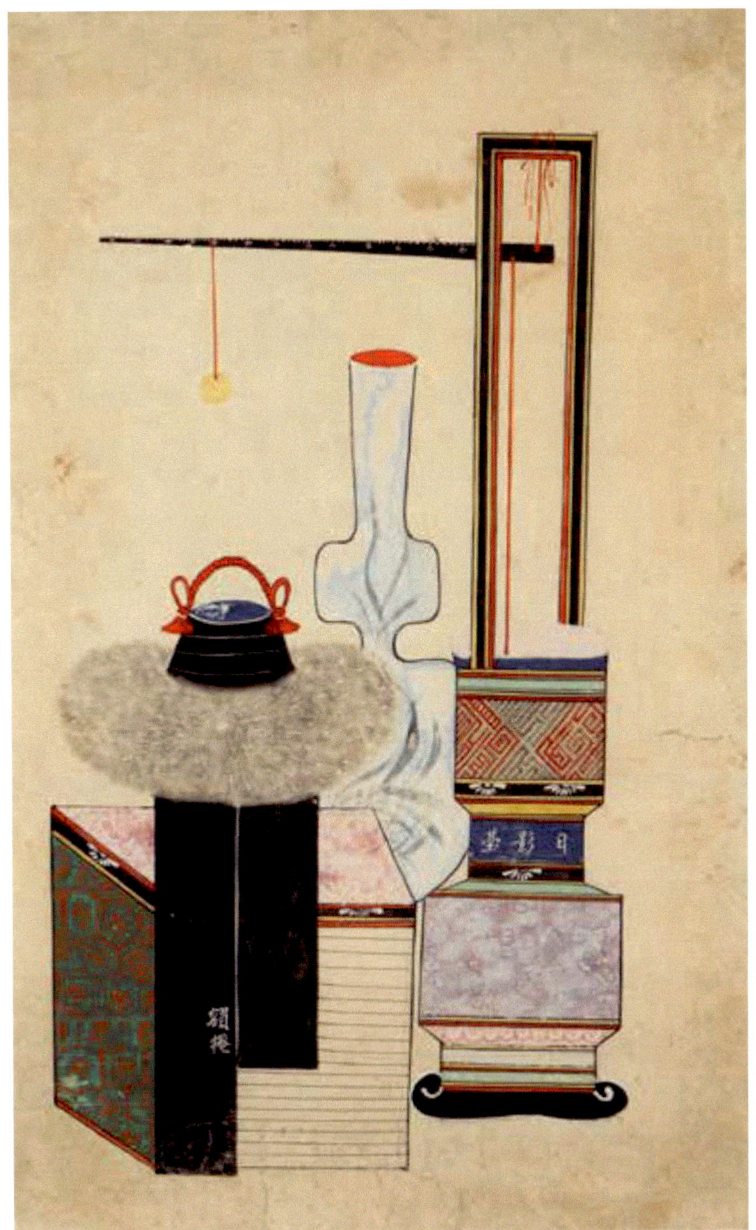

27 *Chaekgeori*

Anonymous, late 19th century
Eight-panel screen
Ink and color on paper, 61 x 37 cm (each panel)
Private collection

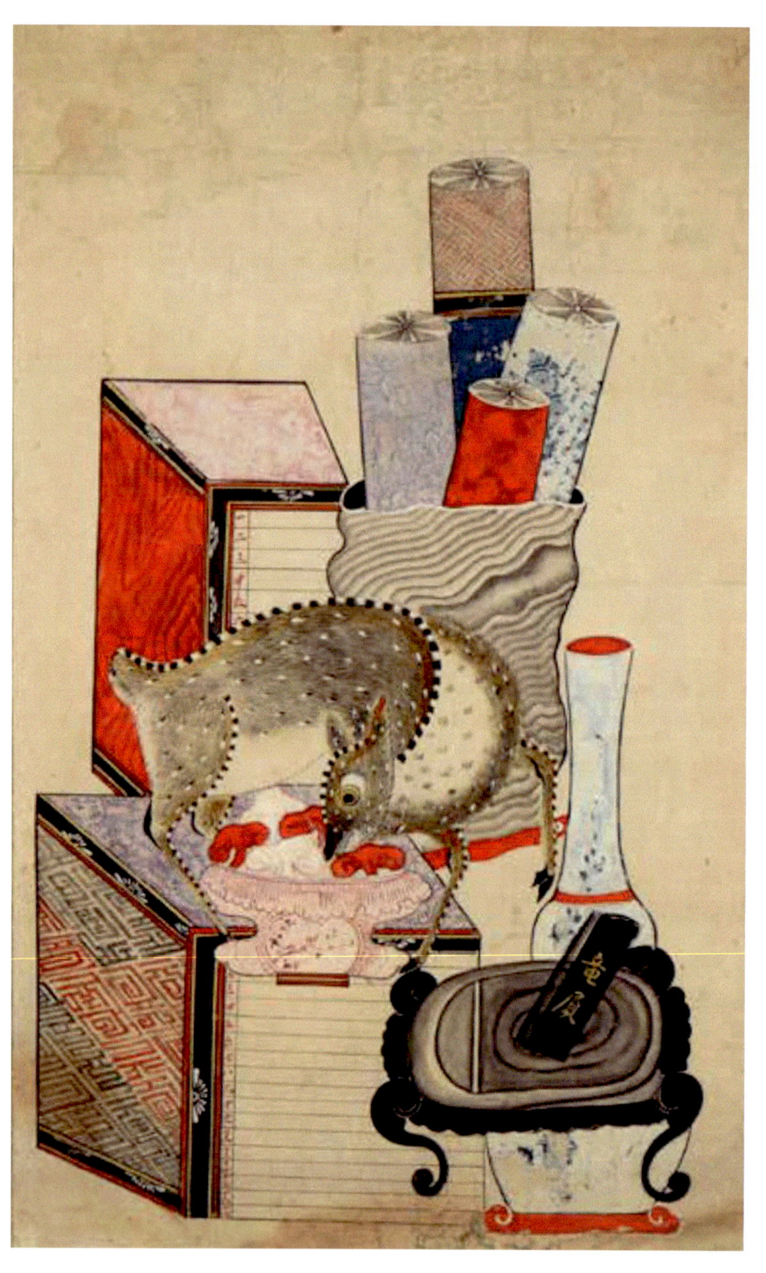

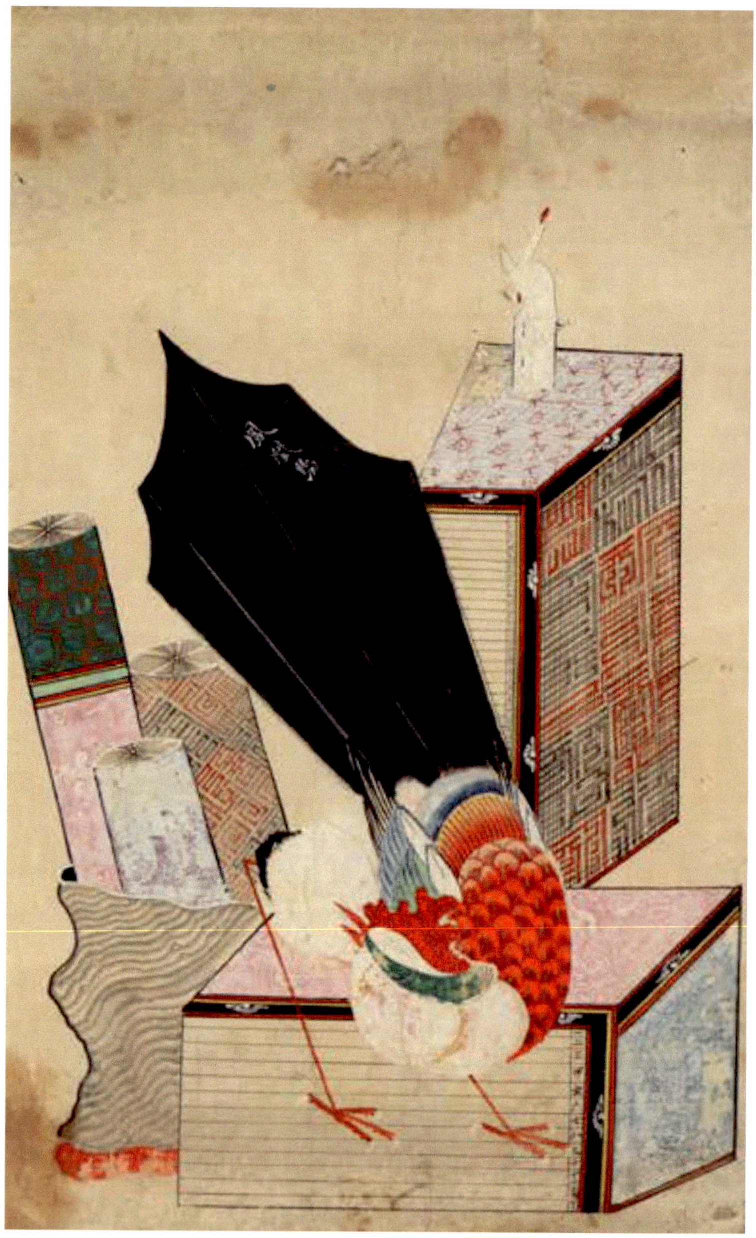

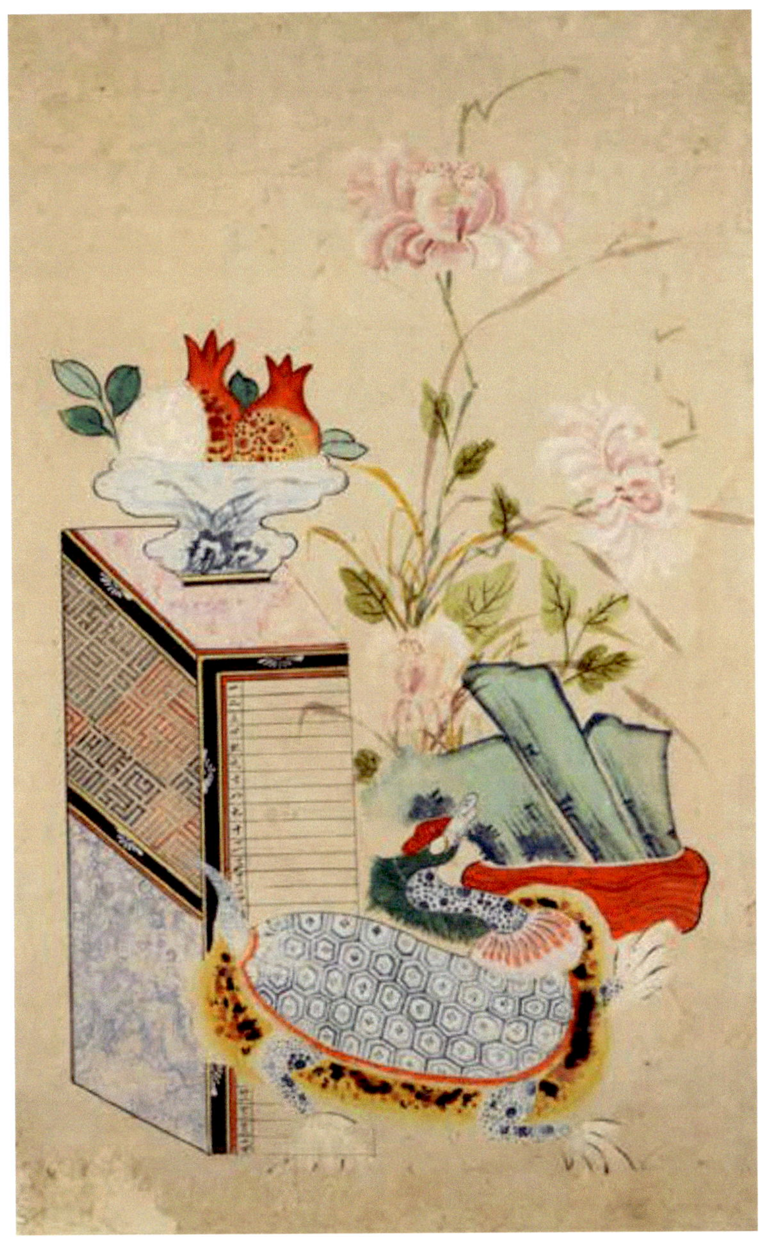

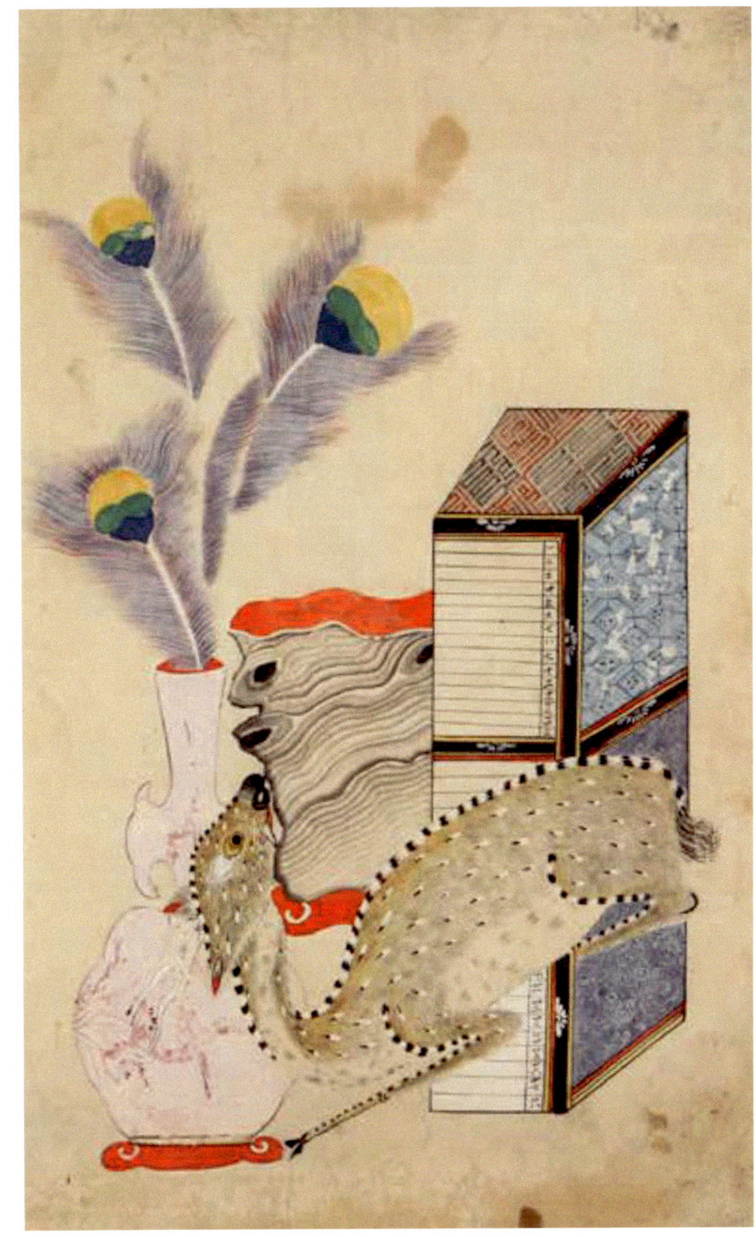

In this work, auspicious animals and accoutrements are placed front and center, with stacks of books behind them. The animals also appear to be floating in the air. Viewing the panels individually from left to right, a roe deer sits atop of a stack of books, a white chicken appears between books, another deer feeds on aspicious lingzhi mushrooms, an Eastern phoenix perches atop a pile of books, and a turtle stands in front of yet another stack of books. The presence of these animals in a chaekgeori screen seems bizarre. Folk-style chaekgeori, however, commonly expresses their subjects and the world in such fantastic ways. Unlike many other chaekgeori, this work is particularly expressive in its style. BC, SK

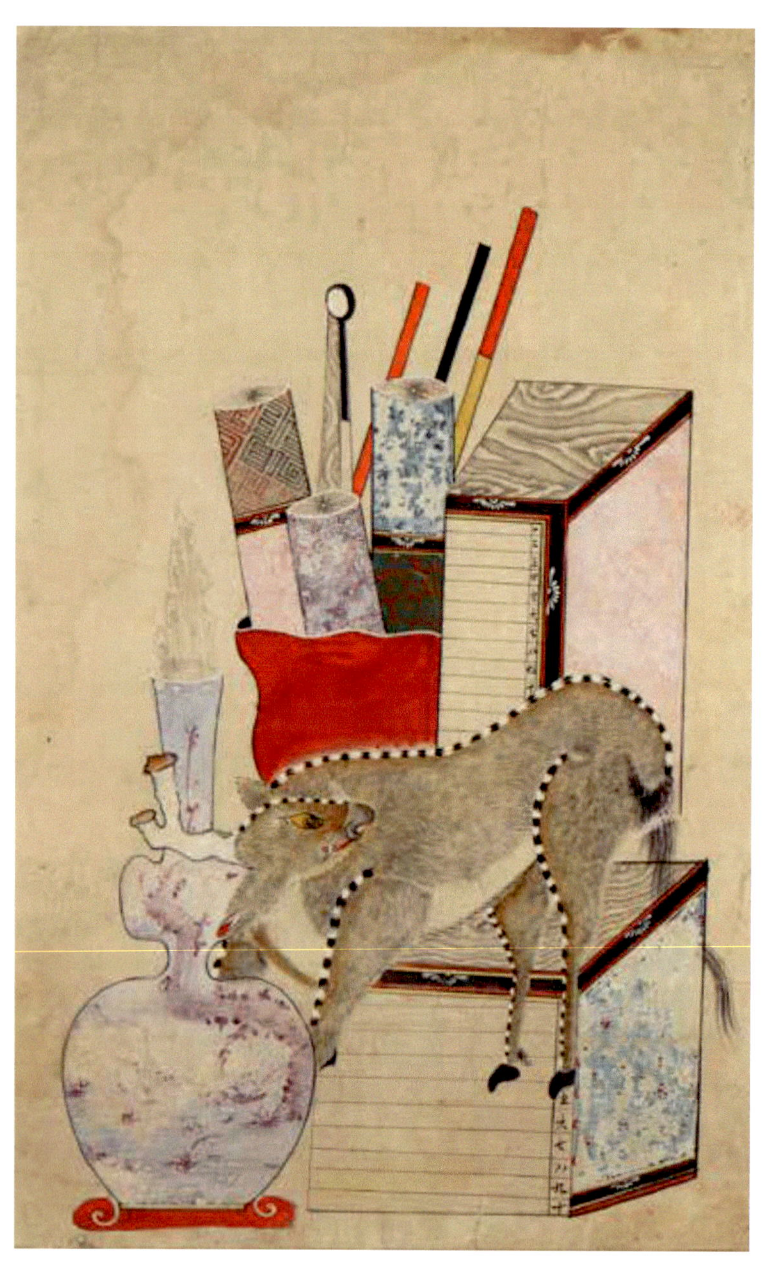

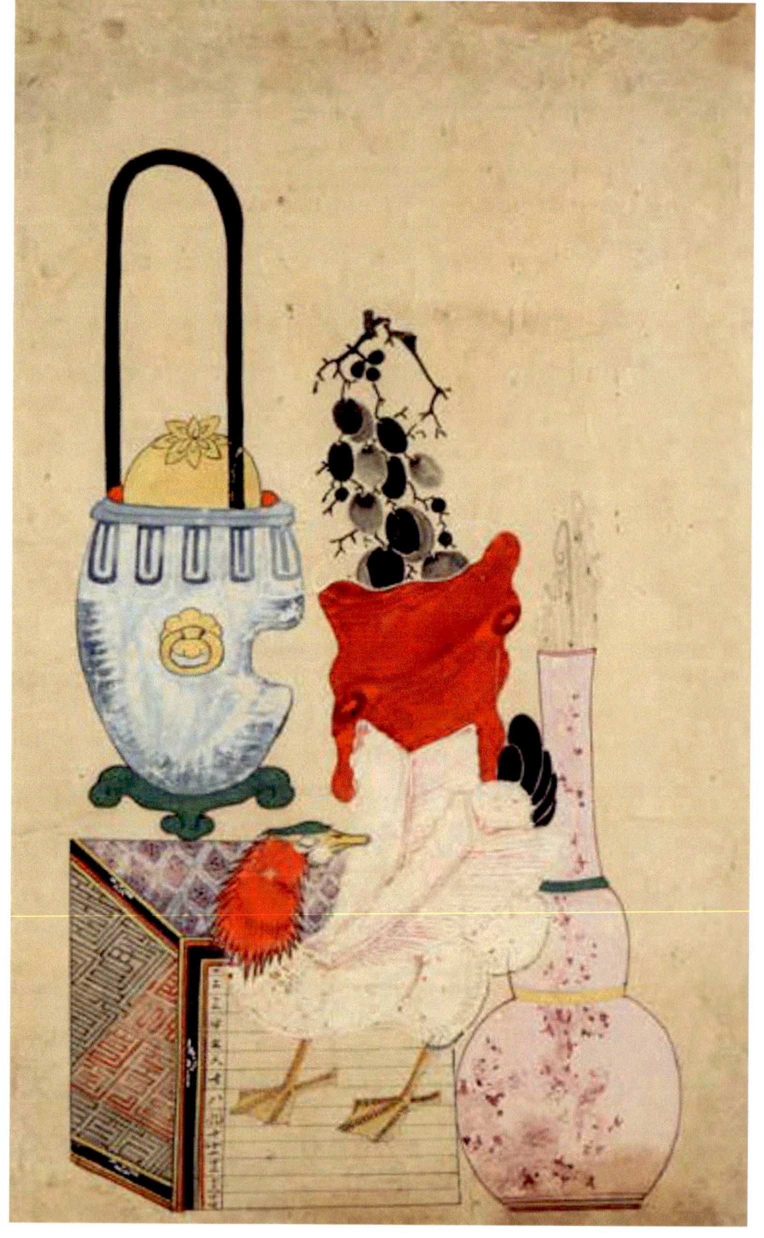

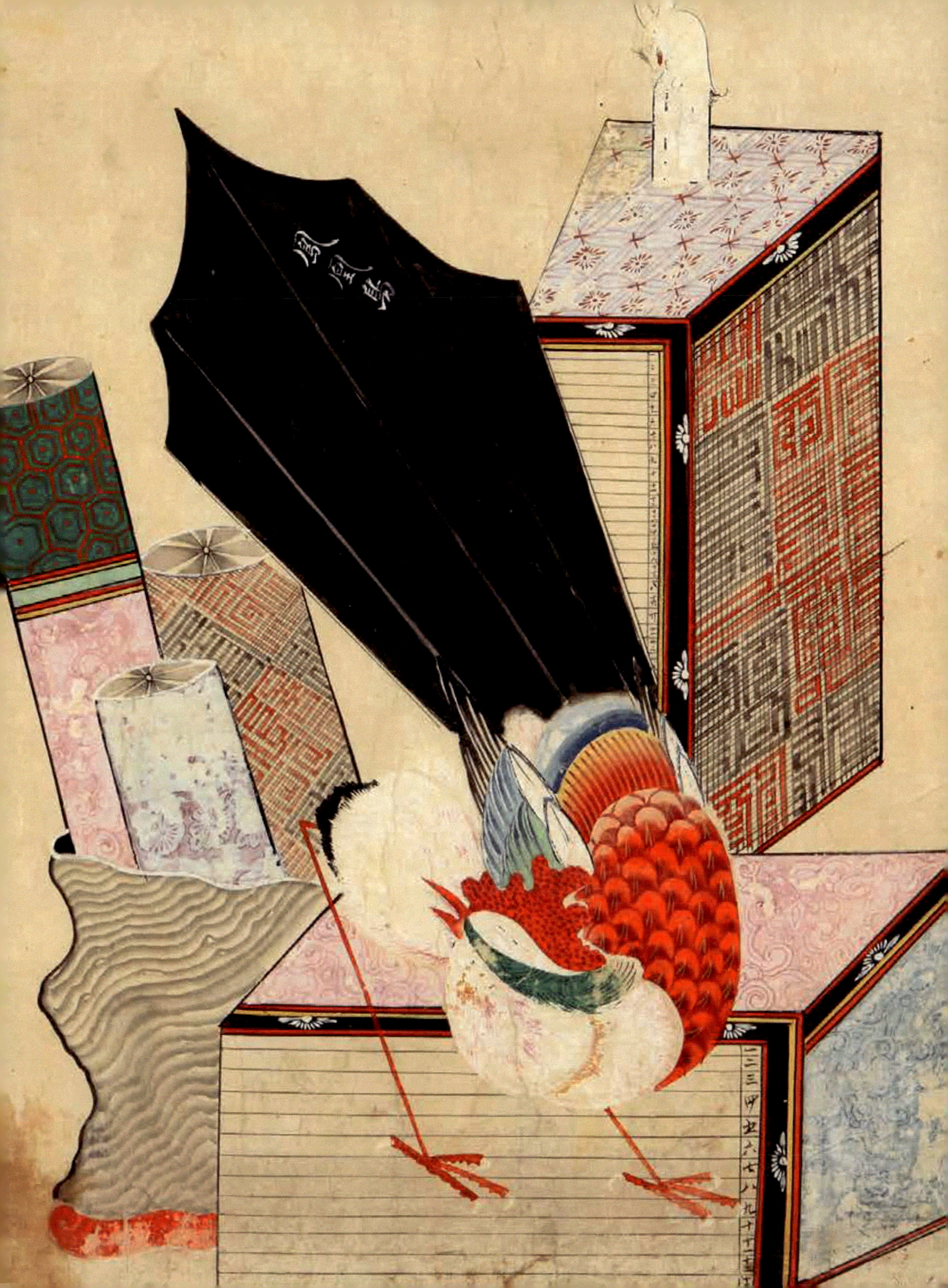

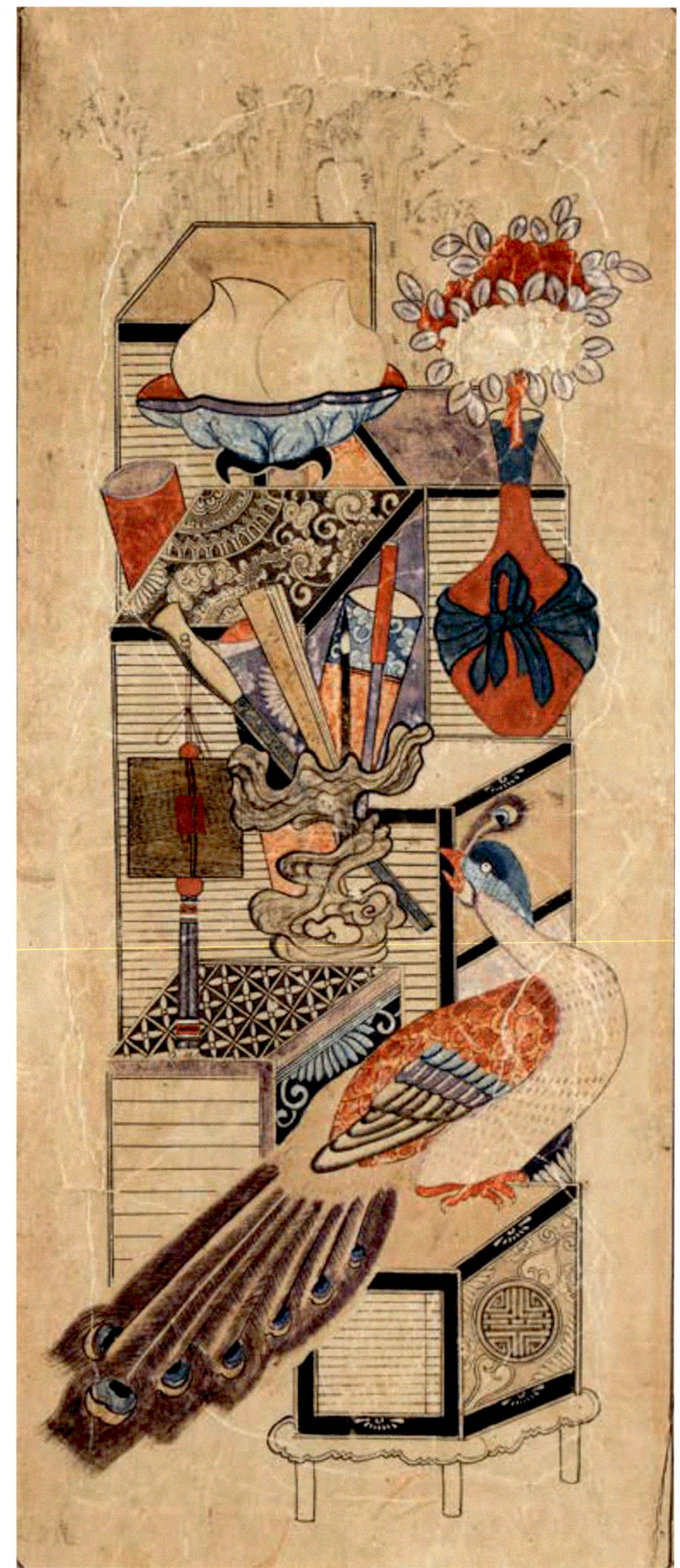

28 *Chaekgeori*

Anonymous, late 19th century
Seven-panel screen
Ink and color on paper, 80 x 31 cm (each panel)
The Chosun Minhwa Museum, Yeongwol

An unusual feature of this screen is its depiction of clouds and a dragon. One can imagine reading books under a transcendent and mystical sky, dragons and phoenixes flying overhead.

Though folk-style chaekgeori expanded the range of subjects to express surreal dreams, the wishes of the commoner were more down to earth in this screen than you might initially deduce. Dragons traditionally symbolize the birth of sons, indicating that this painting is filled with the desire for many prosperous sons, the desire to educate them, and the desire to have them improve their social status through education. The fantastic depictions of such secular, earthly desires is a testament to the incredible imagination of folk-style chaekgeori artists. This work is assumed to have originally been composed of eight panels, but one has been lost. BC, JJ

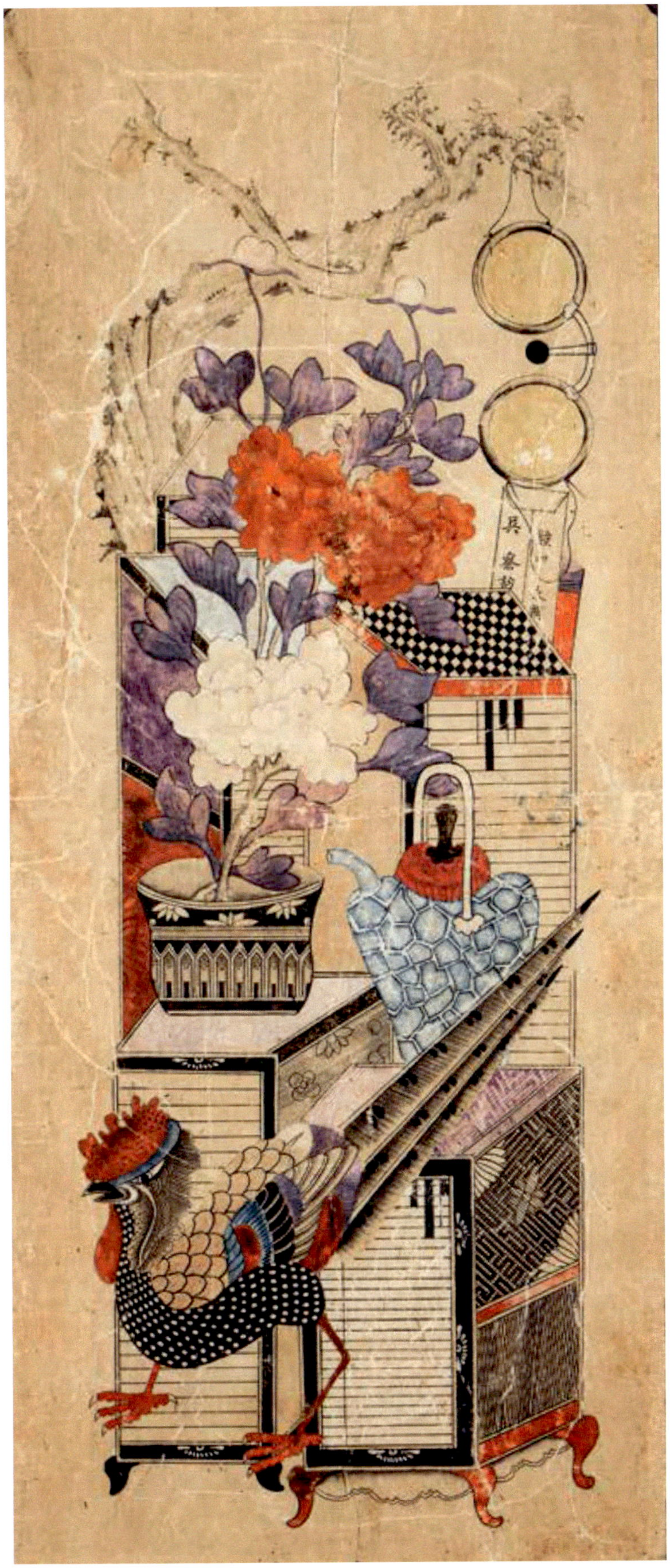

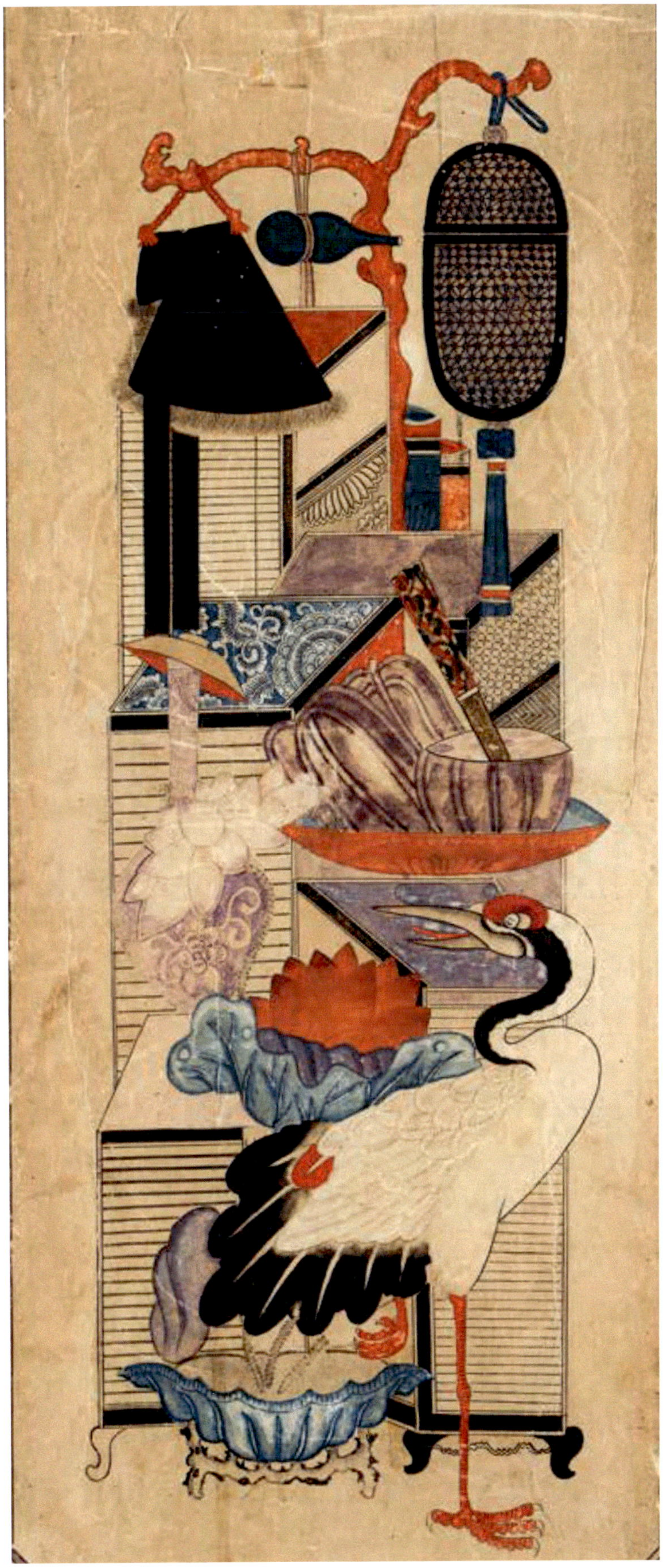

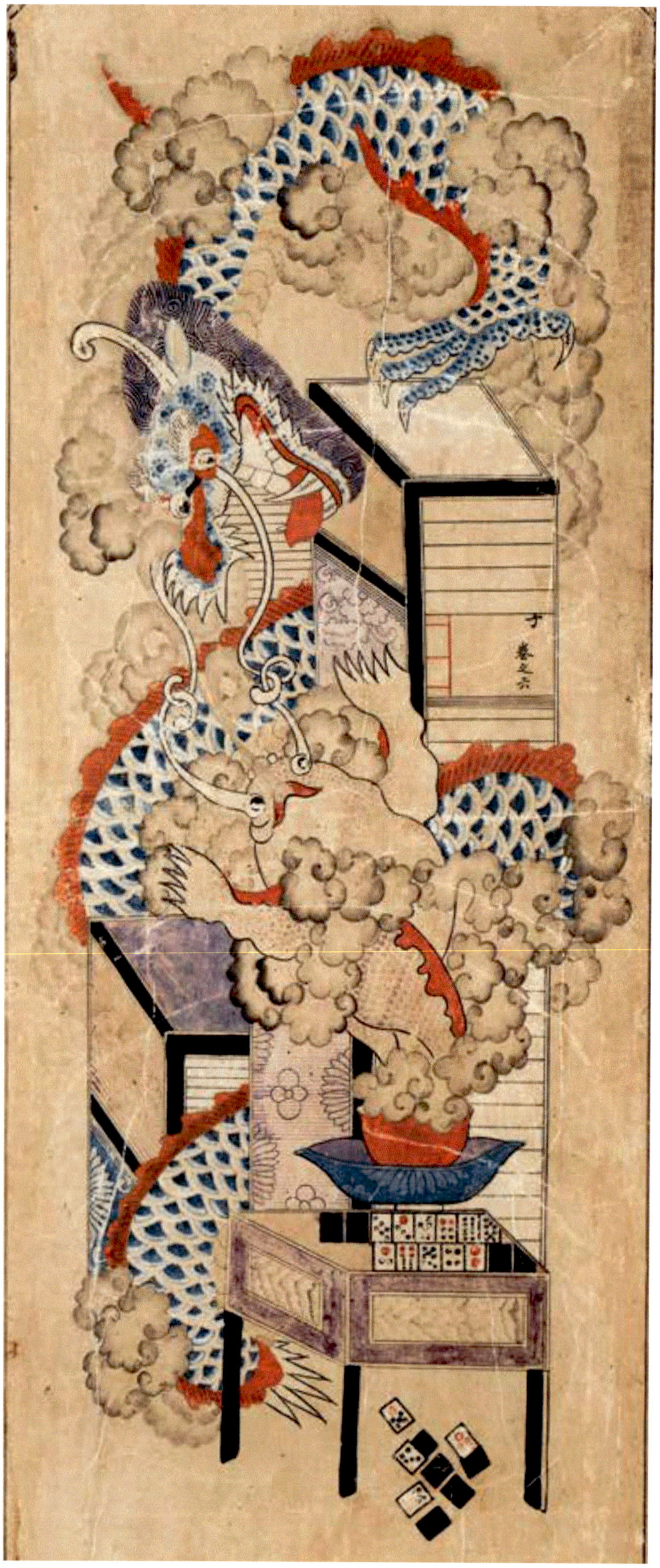

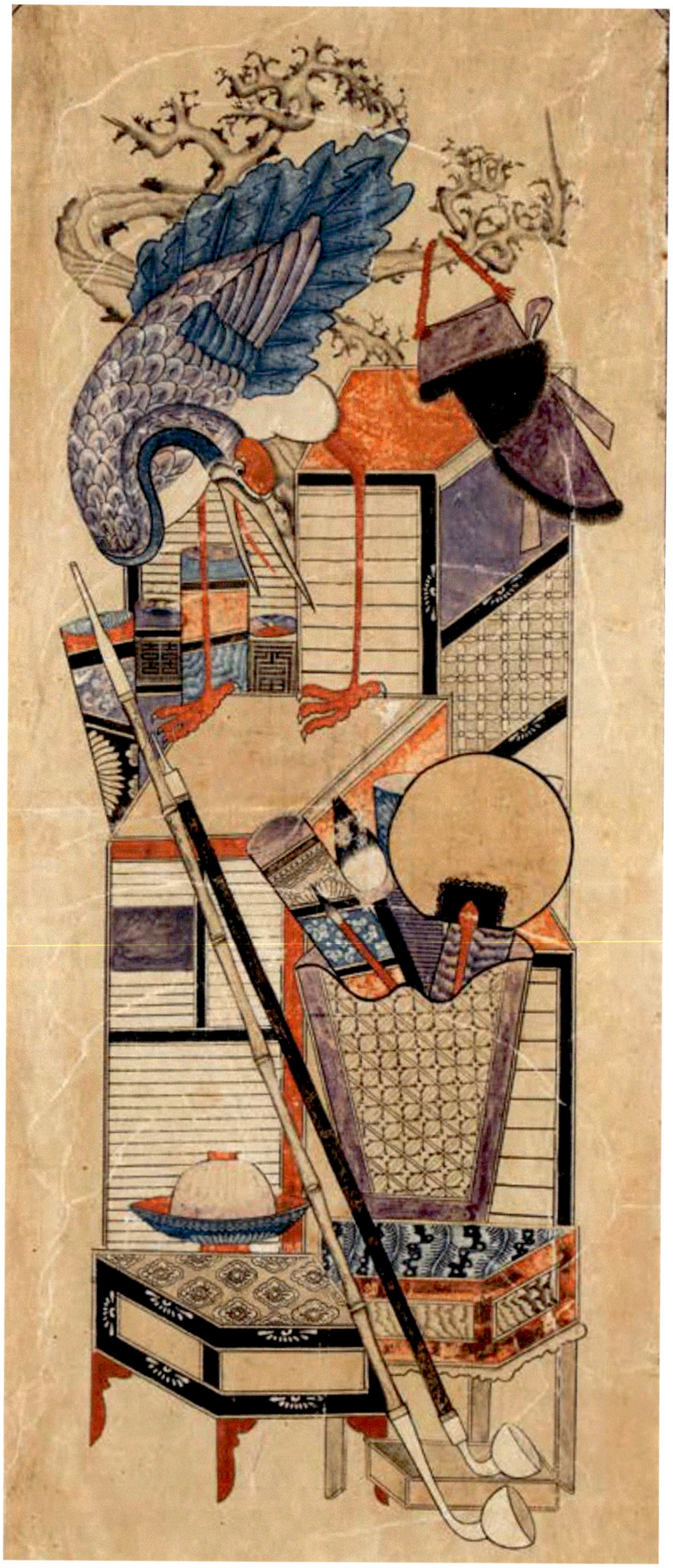

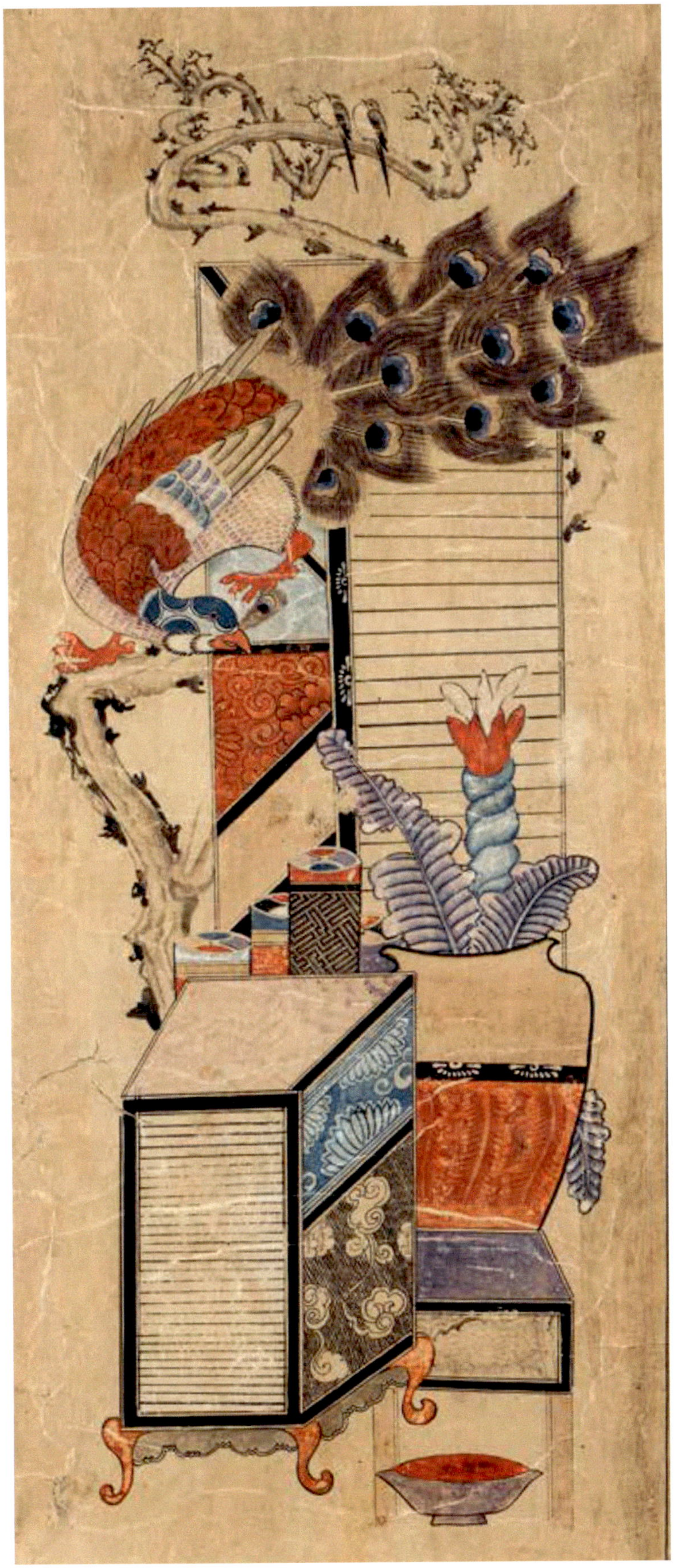

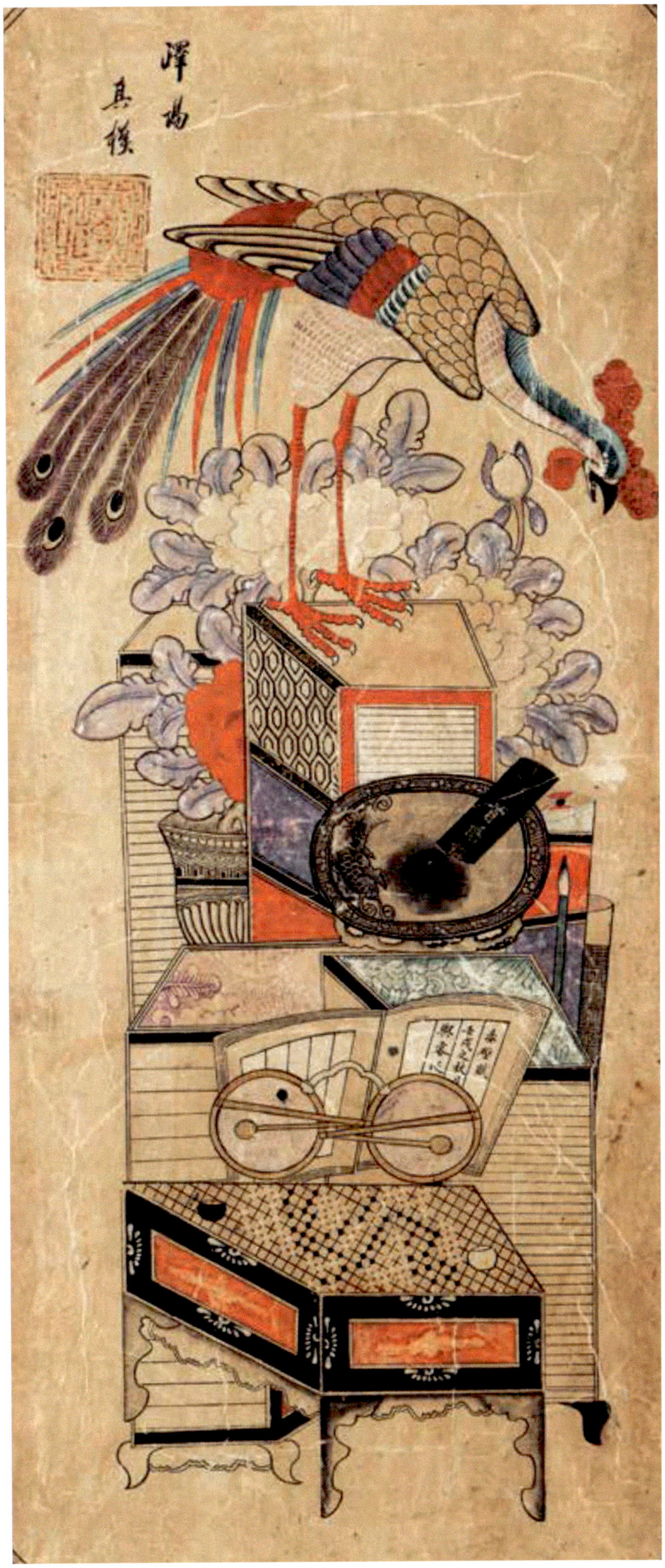

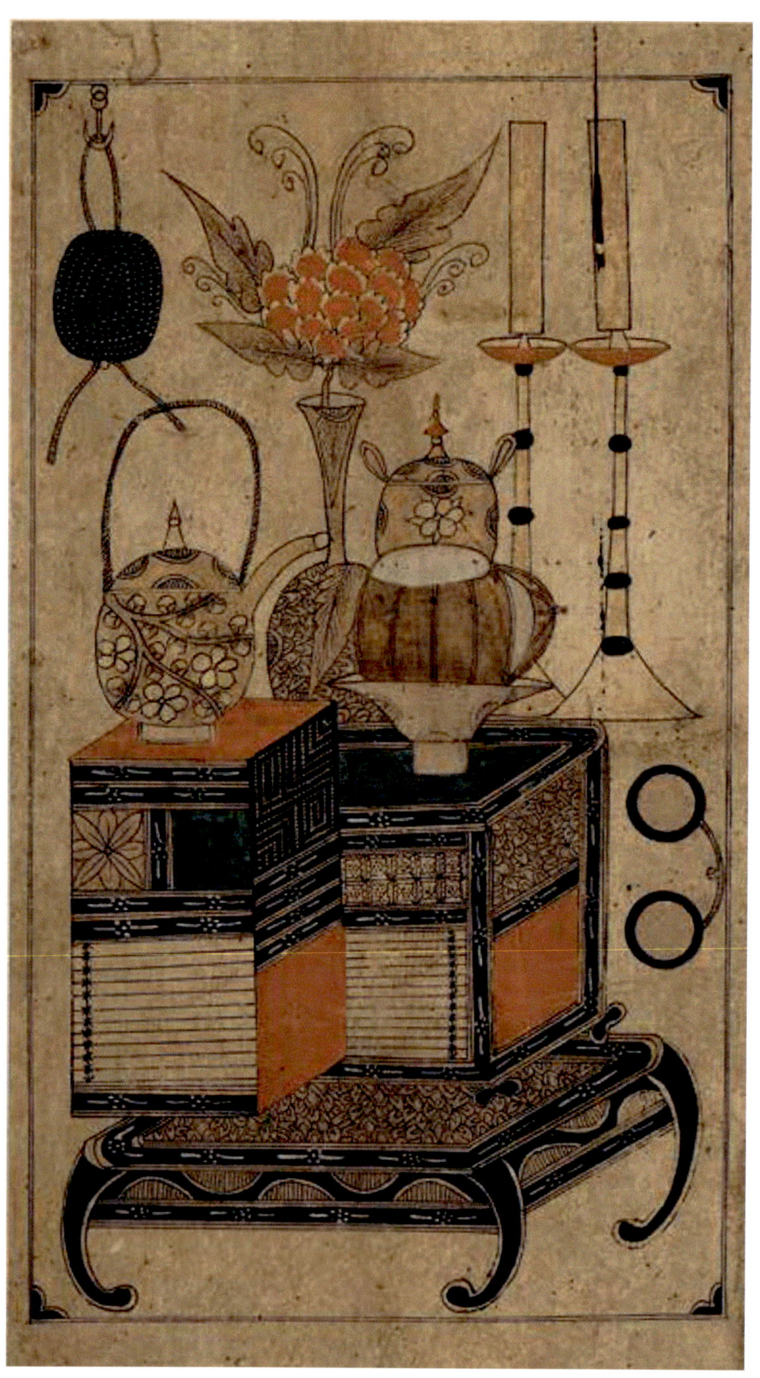

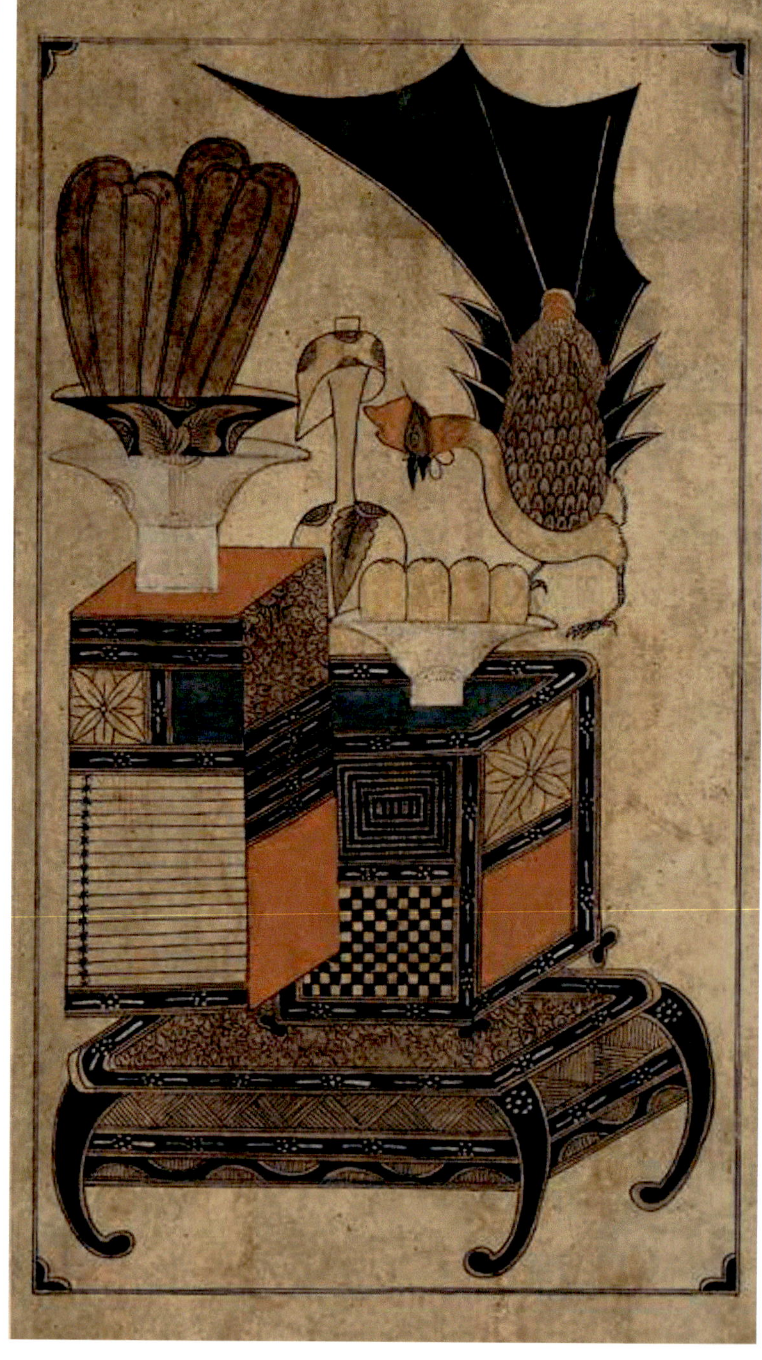

29 *Chaekgeori*

Anonymous, late 19th century
Eight-panel screen
Ink and color on paper, 69 x 38 cm (each panel)
Private collection

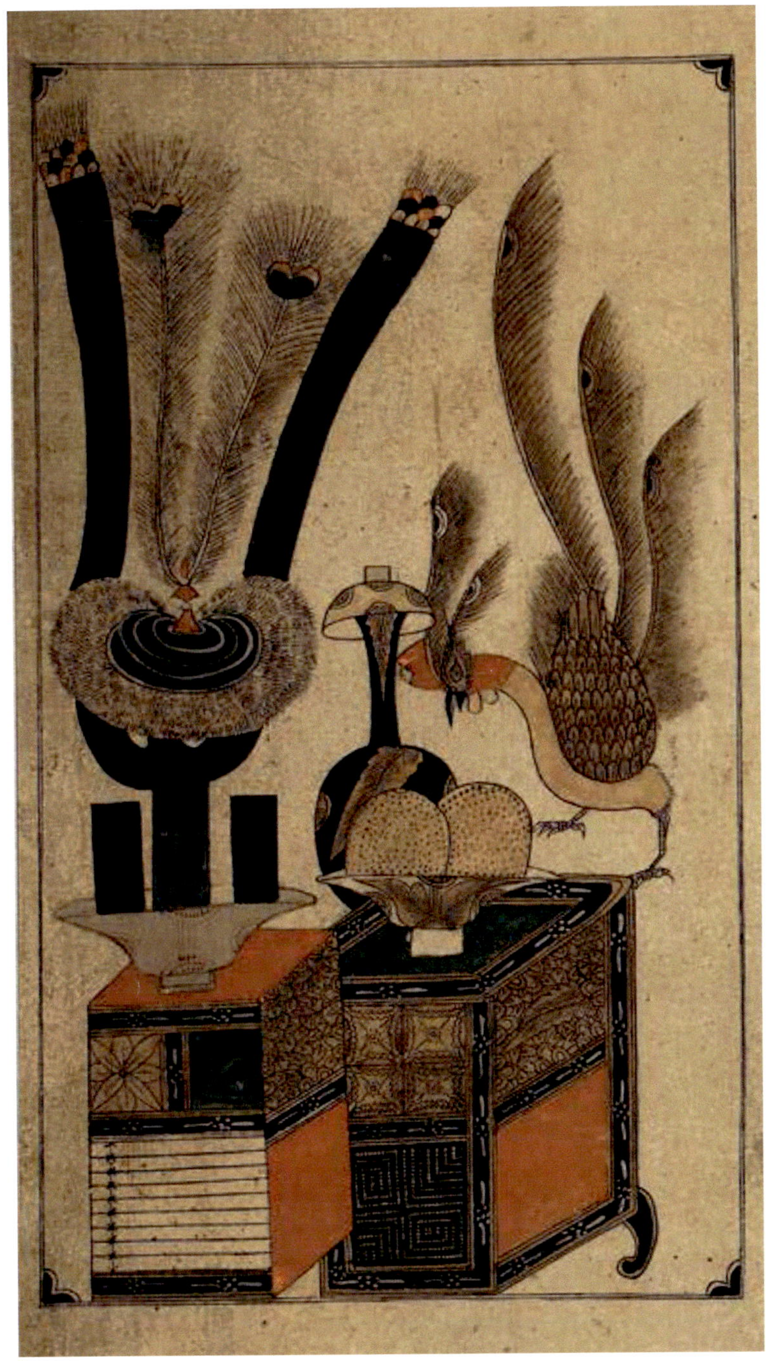

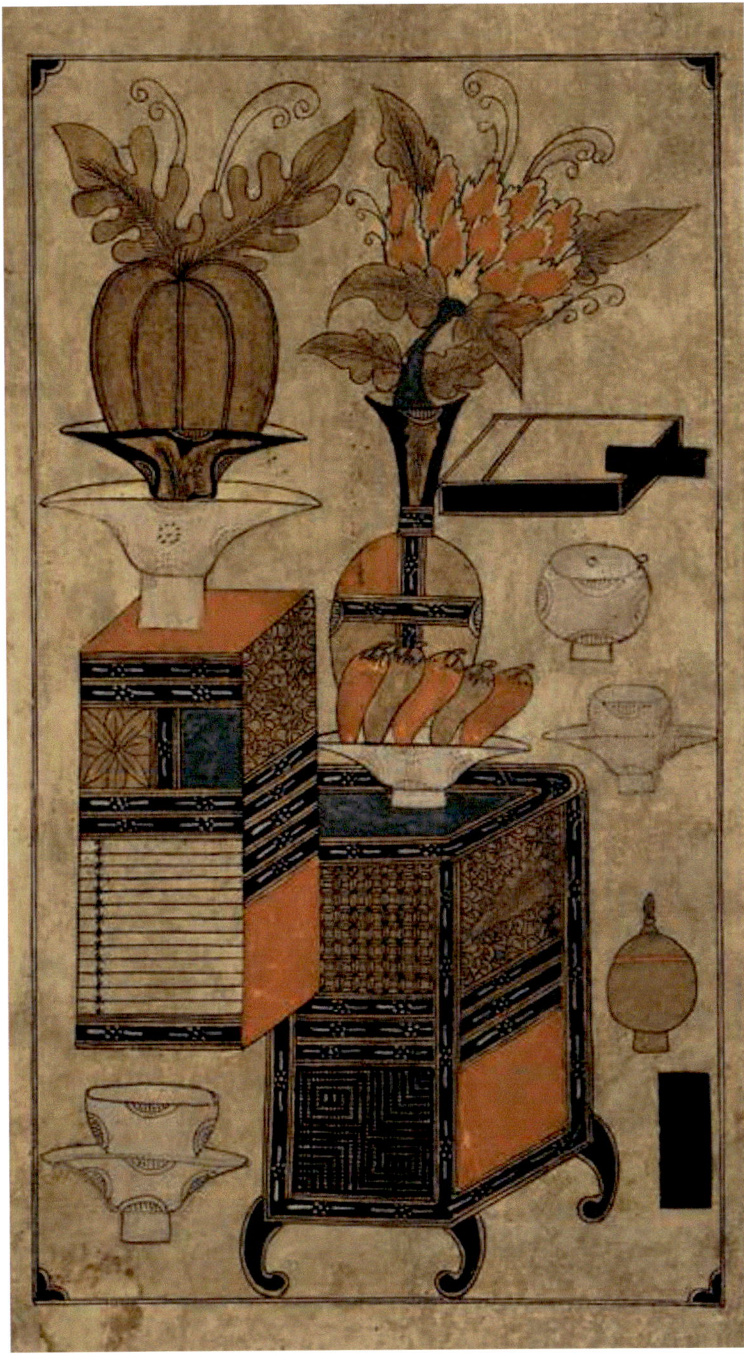

This work is a combination of a chaekgeori and a seosudo, a painting of auspicious beasts. Many of the books and animals seem to be floating in this deliberate expression of blurring the line between reality and the ideal. The understated coloring is another notable feature here. The books have been colored in limited hues, only two main colors, with the orange making the black of the accouterments stand out all the more. The artist enhances verticality and vitality, not only by erecting bird feathers and raising hat straps but also by standing melons, grapes, pomegranates, and even peppers on a plate. The use of limited colors with prominent dark, thick black accents and emphasis on verticality reinforce the feeling of literati exuberance. The measured composition, coloring, and impact of this work come together into one harmonious work of art. BC, SK

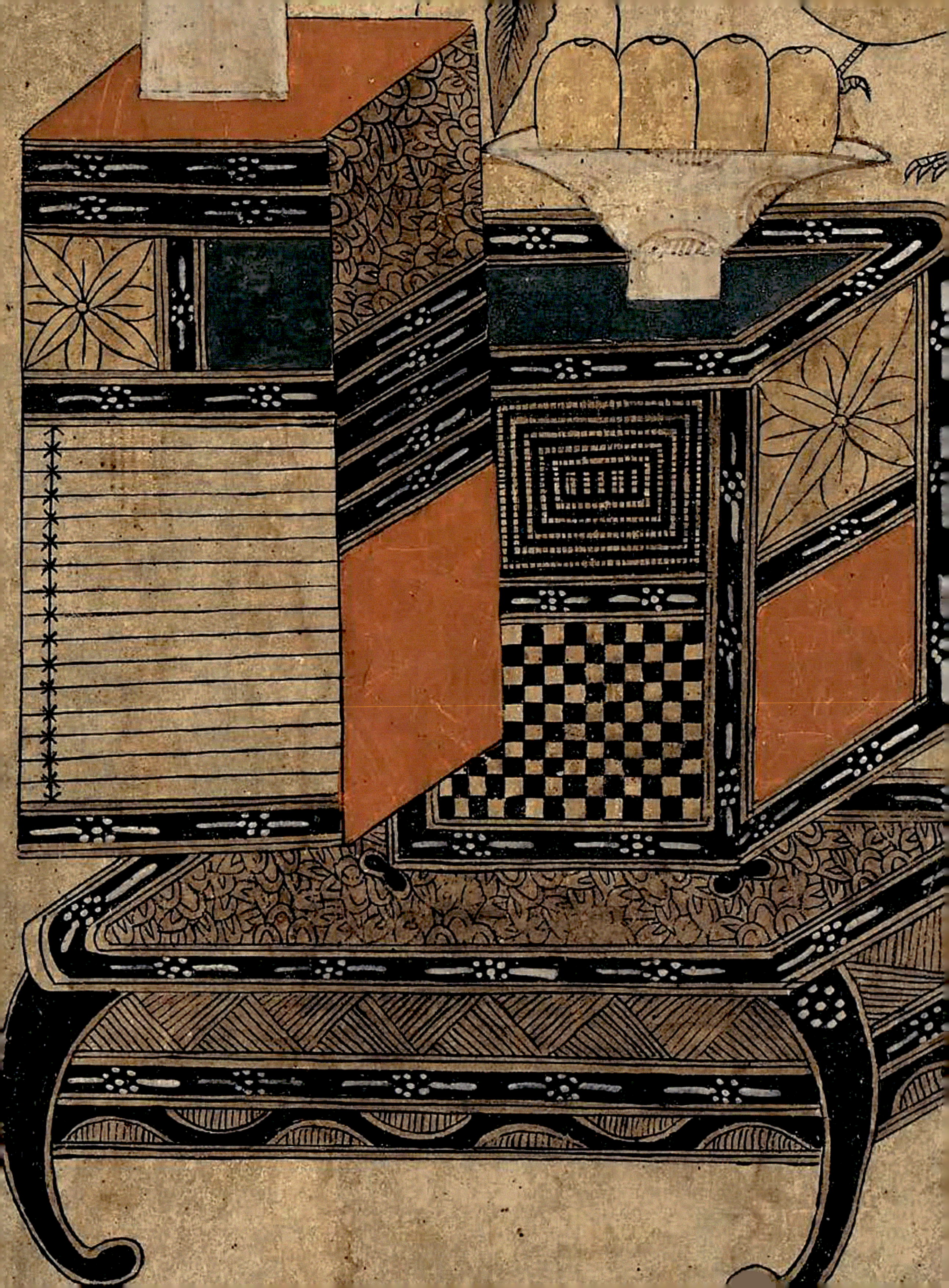

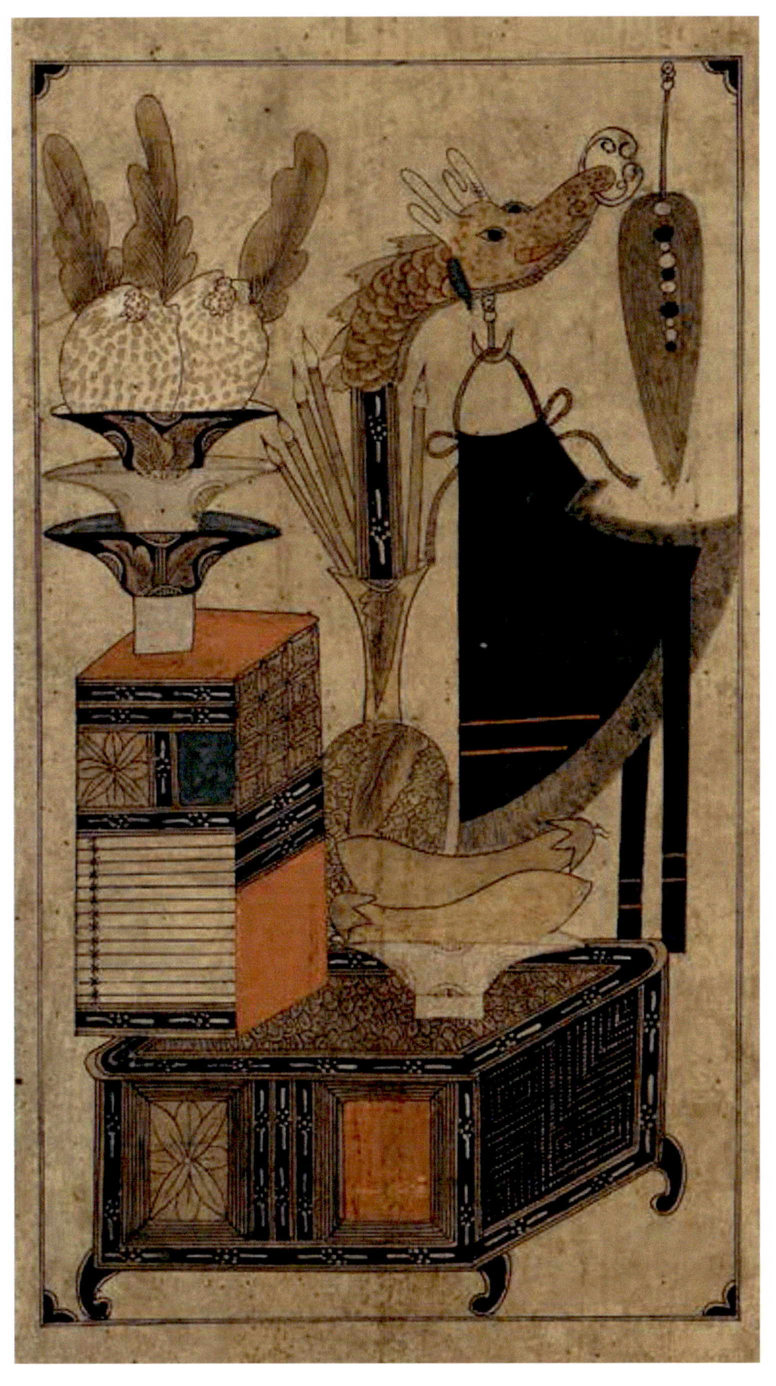

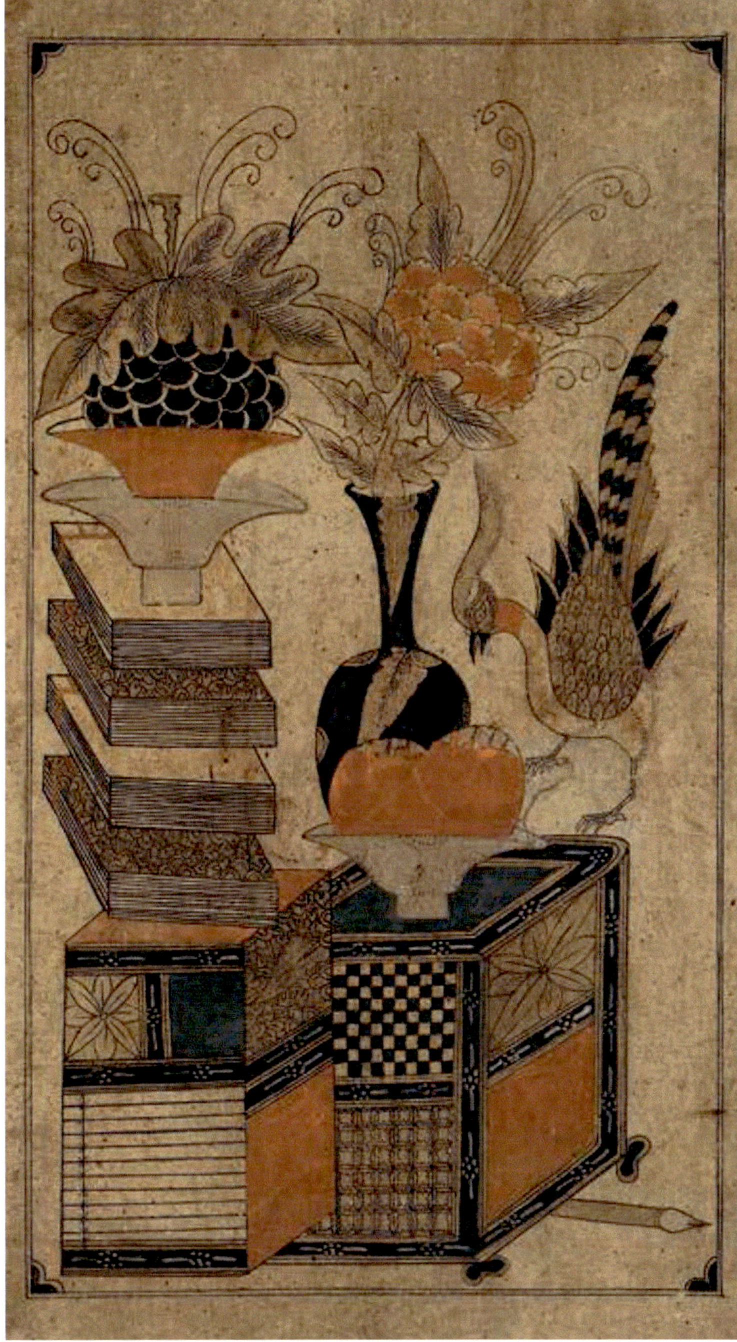

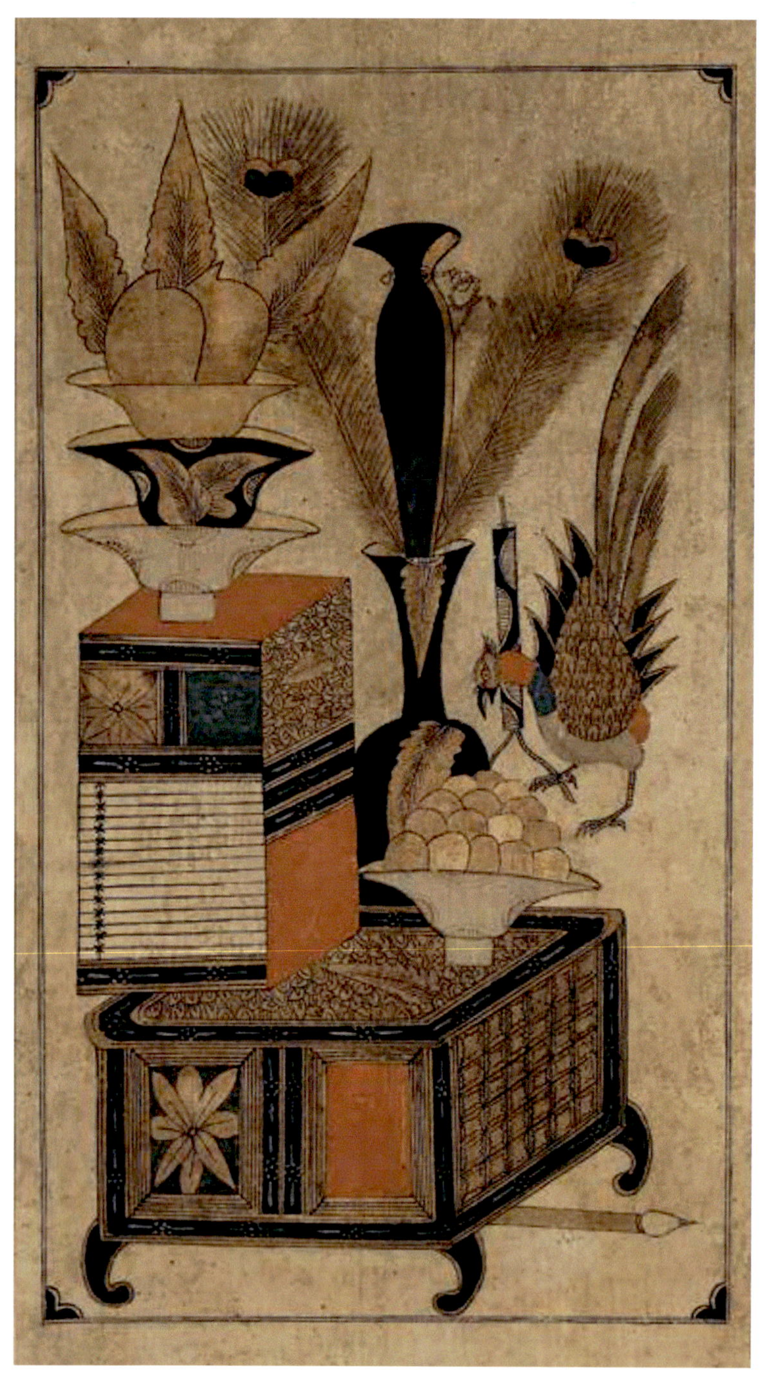

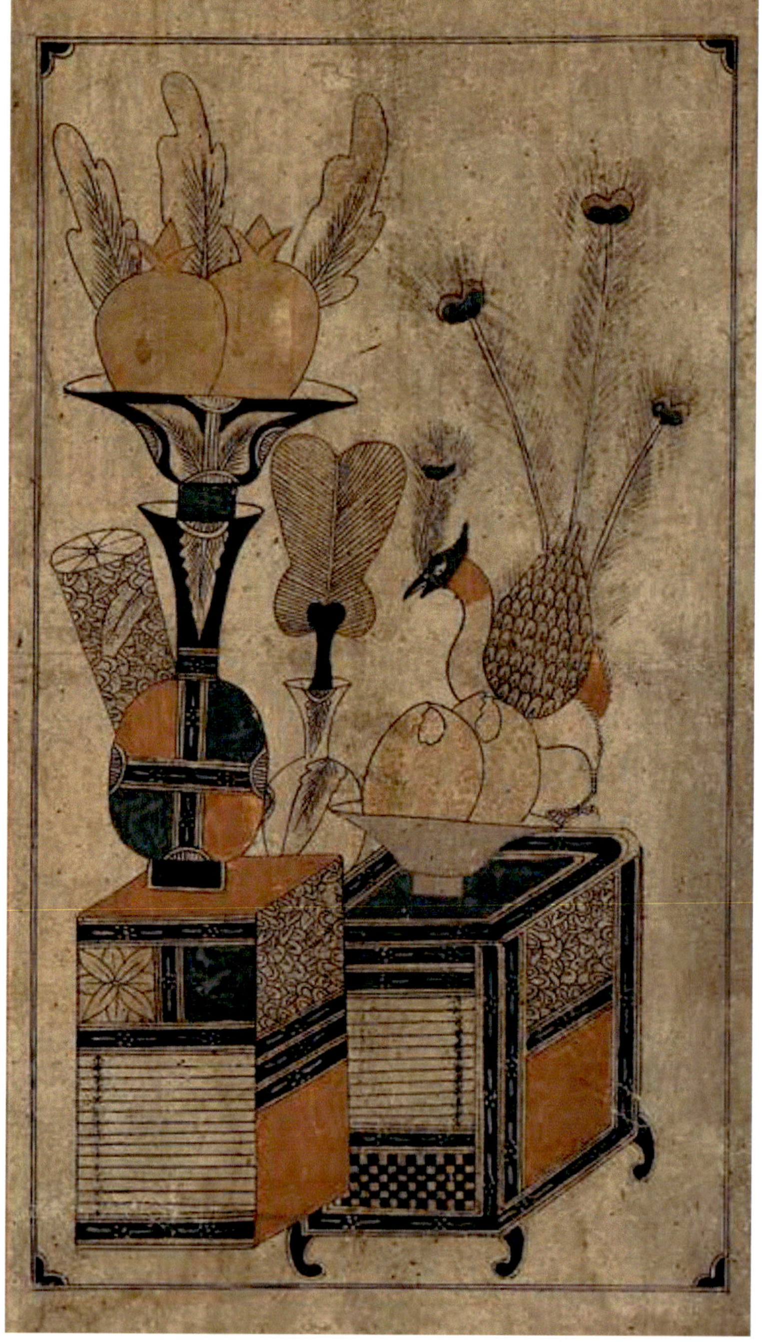

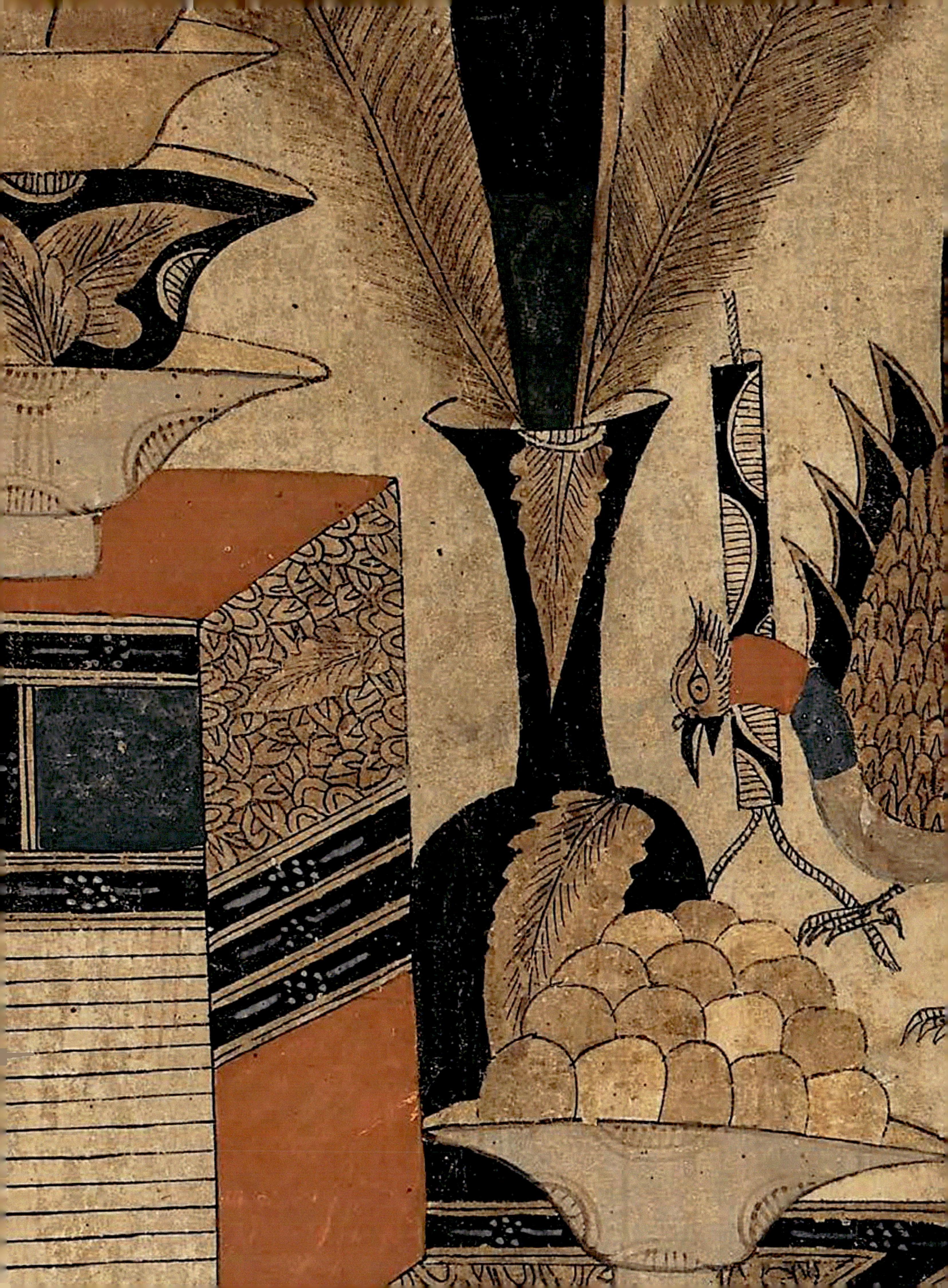

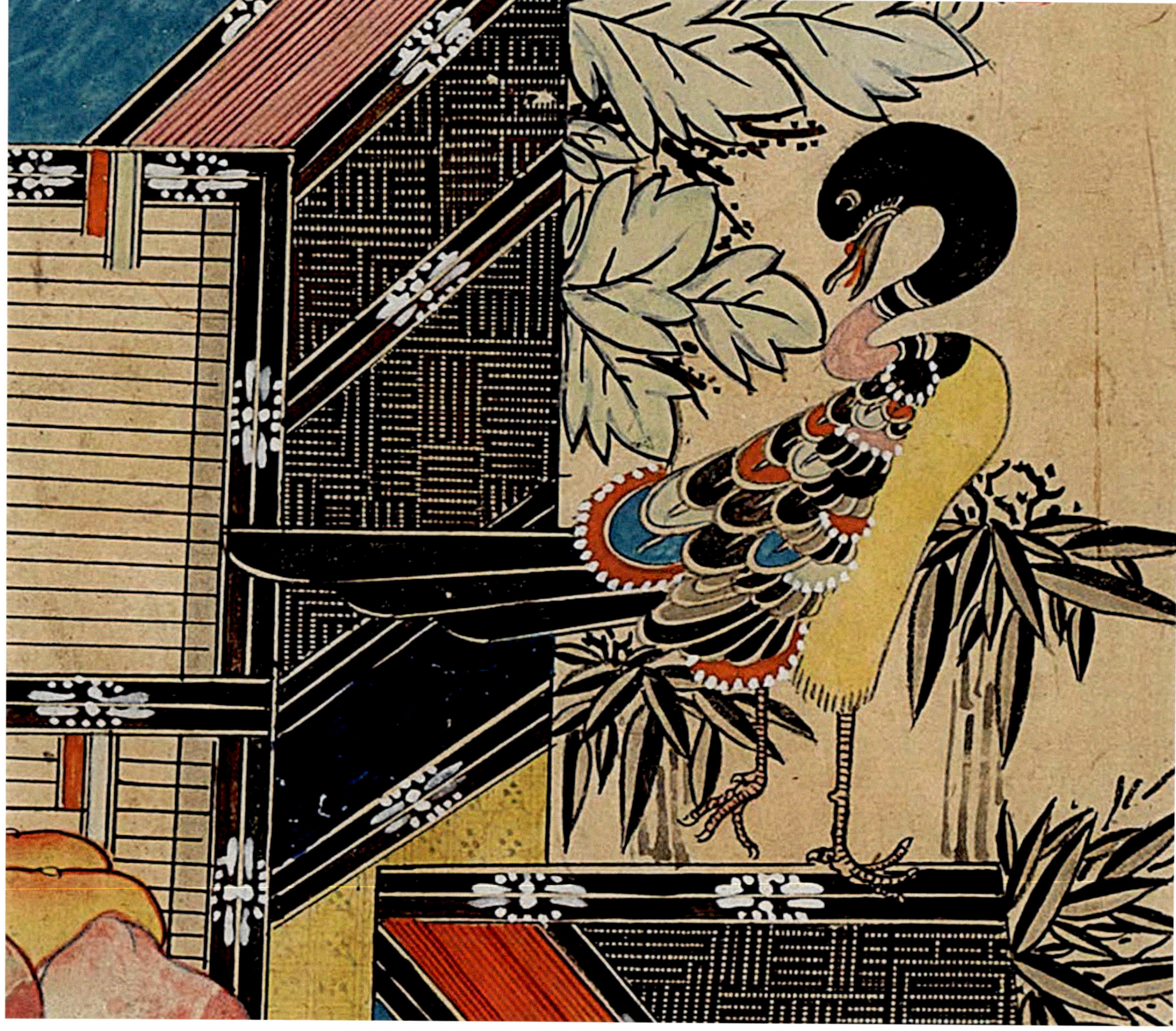

30 *Chaekgeori*

Anonymous, 19th century
Two-panel screen
Ink and color on paper, 105 x 32.5 cm (each panel)
Gahoe Museum, Seoul

This two-panel screen features quotations that show the ideals of the world of folk-style chaekgeori: the turtles emanate auspicious energy, the vase rouses an aromatic spring breeze, and a pair of hundred-year birds relate all this to the people. This particular world of chaekgeori is filled with auspicious energy and the scent of flowers. Although the theme is a realistic one, folk-style artists expressed it through a fantastic and expressive world. This kind of imagination and thought process defines the world of folk-style chaekgeori.

The pair of turtles emanate auspicious energy, and behind the covered books is a vase. Its scent stirs and gives life to a spring breeze, coaxing a song out of the pair of hundred-year birds.
有一雙龜瑞氣濃 書匣而匣後置花盎香動春風其內養 一雙百年鳥向人能言語.

Several peacock feathers stick out of the reddish-brown urn, with stationery-like brushes and an ink stone at their side, making for a perfect sight. [By] Jecho.
齊楚.案上立一古銅壺 挿孔雀尾數莖 其傍設筆硯之類 皆極 齊楚. BC, JJL

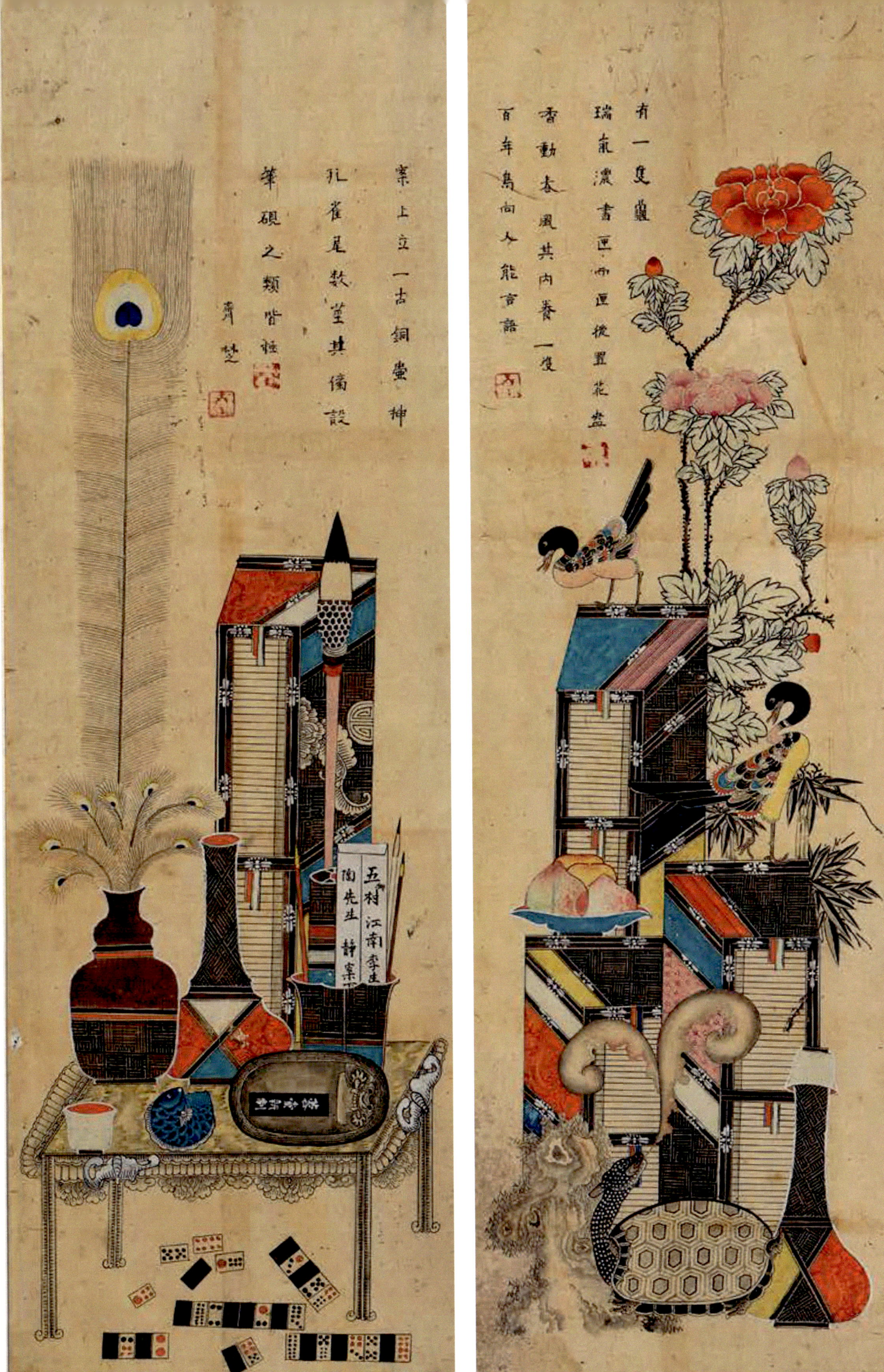
案上立一古銅壺神
孔雀尾數莖其備設
筆硯之類皆極
青楚
五村江南李生
陶先生靜案
有一隻鸞
瑞氣濃書匣而匣後置花盆
香動春風其內養一隻
百年鳥向人能言語

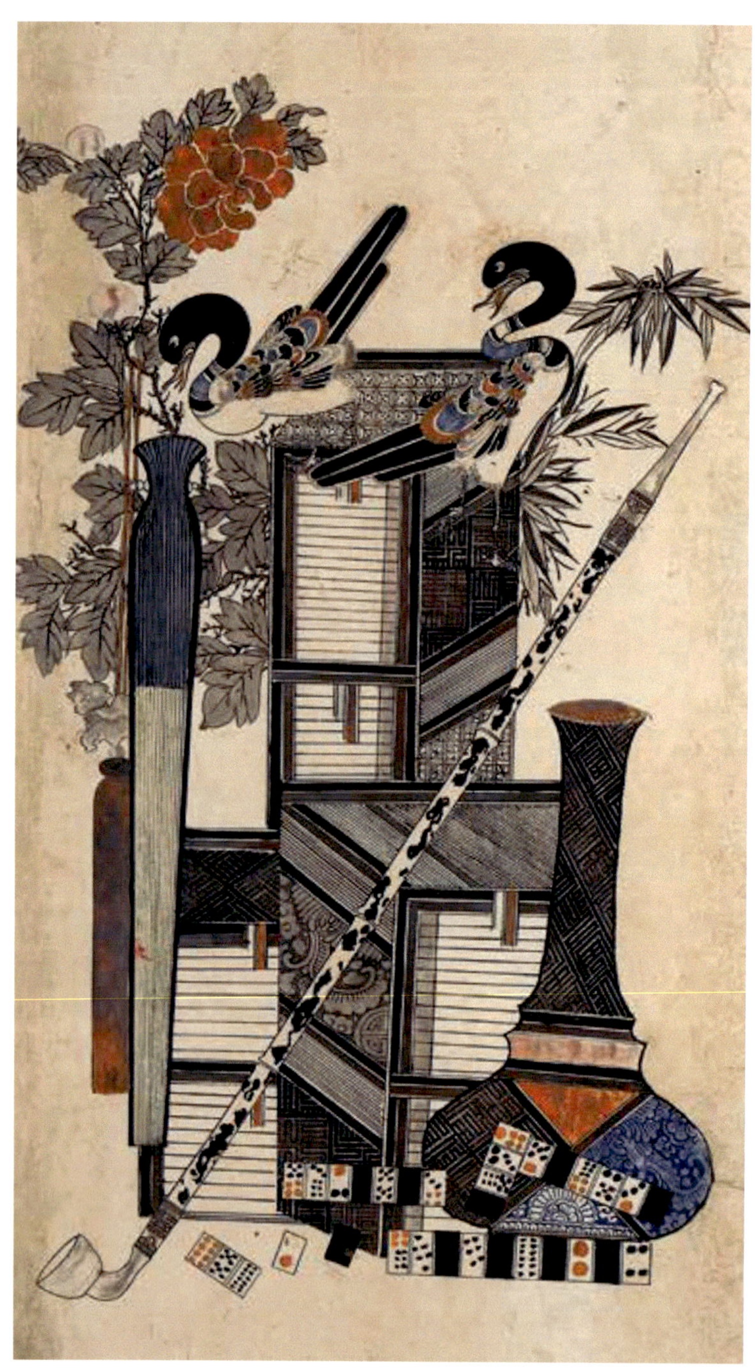

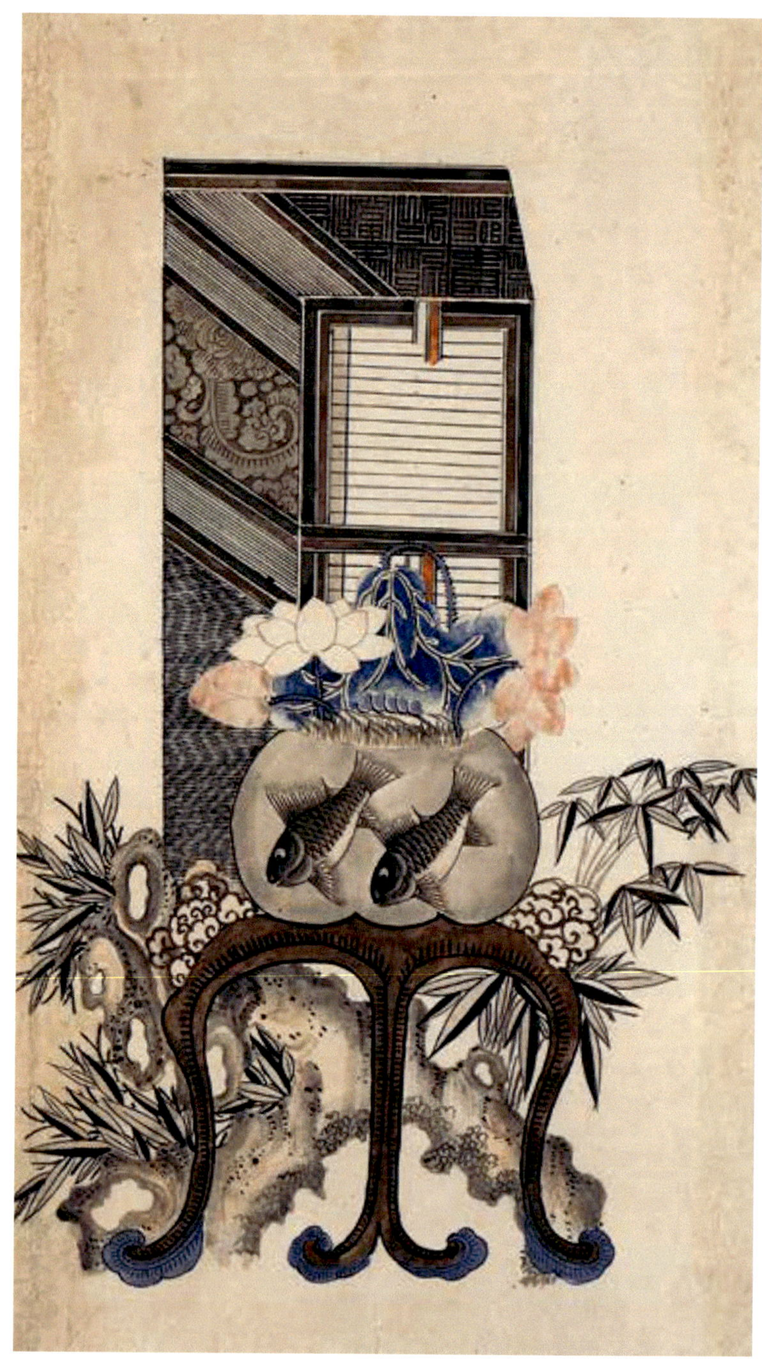

31 *Chaekgeori*

Anonymous, late 19th century
Eight-panel screen
Ink and color on paper, 52 x 29 cm (each panel)
Private collection

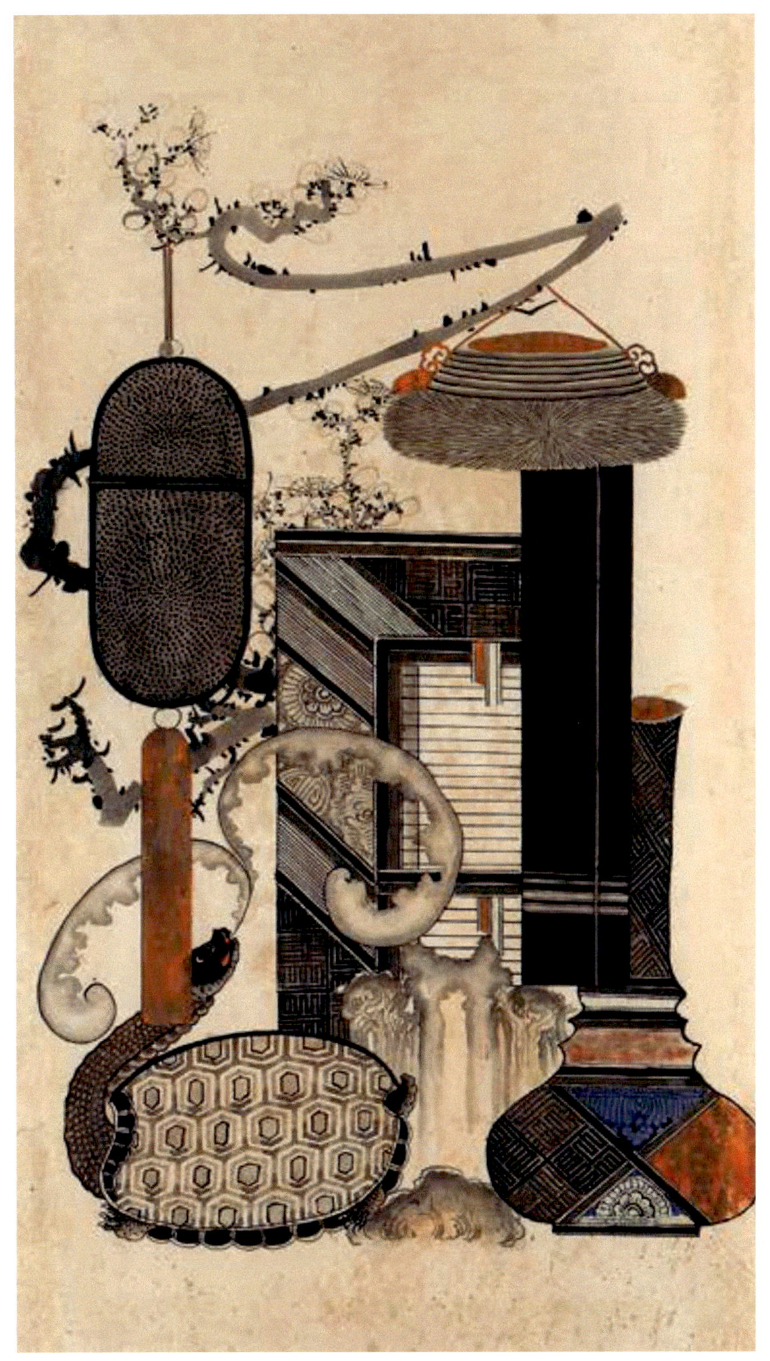

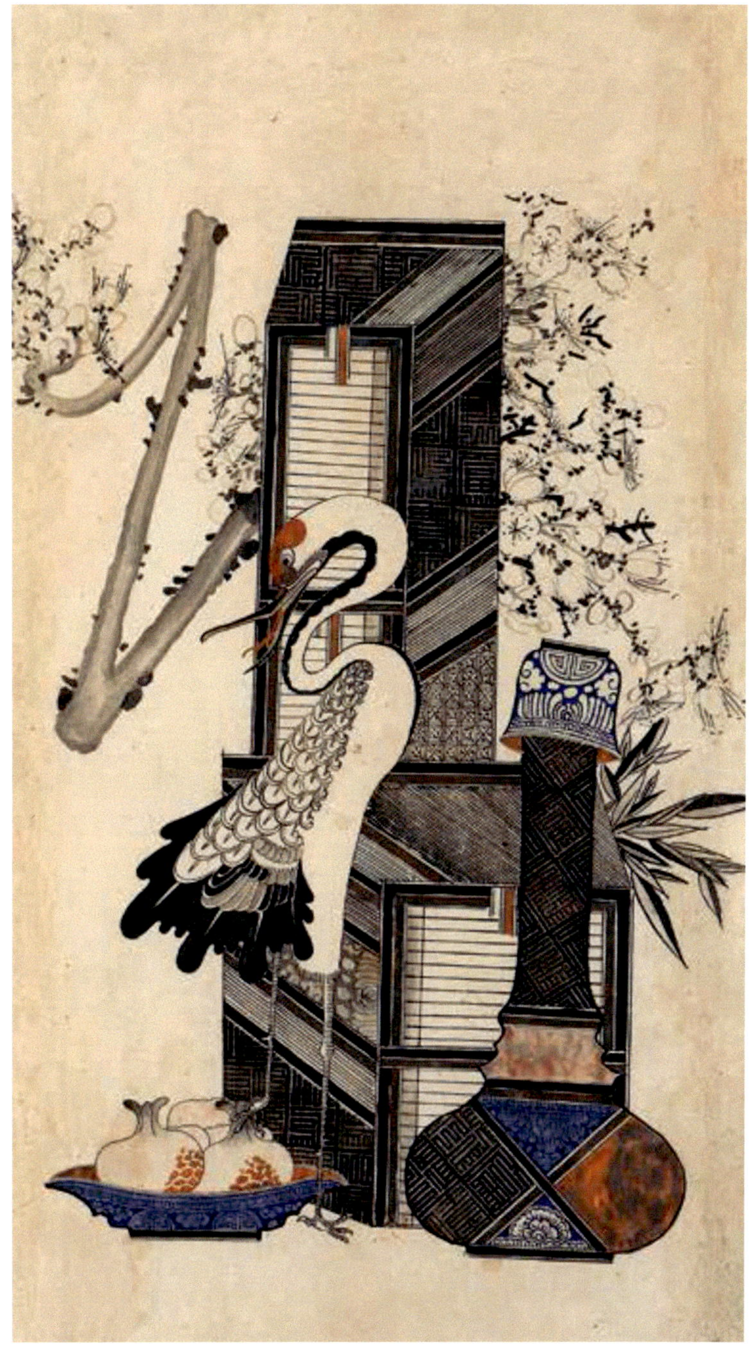

This chaekgeori screen blurs the boundary between reality and fantasy with its sensual composition. Accouterments, auspicious animals, and stationery take center stage, while books are relegated to the background. Trees and decorative stones have been placed between the stacks of books and other objects to soften the rigidity of the arrangement. Although the painter of this screen uses limited colors, there appear to be striking similarities in subject matter with the two-panel screen in figure 30, including a pot with an upright peacock feather and smaller crooked feathers, a brush stand with a large erect brush and short and smaller ones, and an envelope with characters. It appears that either both artists shared the same under drawing, from which they picked and chose, or these works are from the same art studio, if not by the same artist. The artist adds very organic flowering plum branches on the back, smoke-like mushrooms in the middle, and a long smoking pipe diagonally with some standing golpae game tiles; the screen thus becomes interesting and intriguing, whereas it otherwise could have been static and rigid. BC, JL

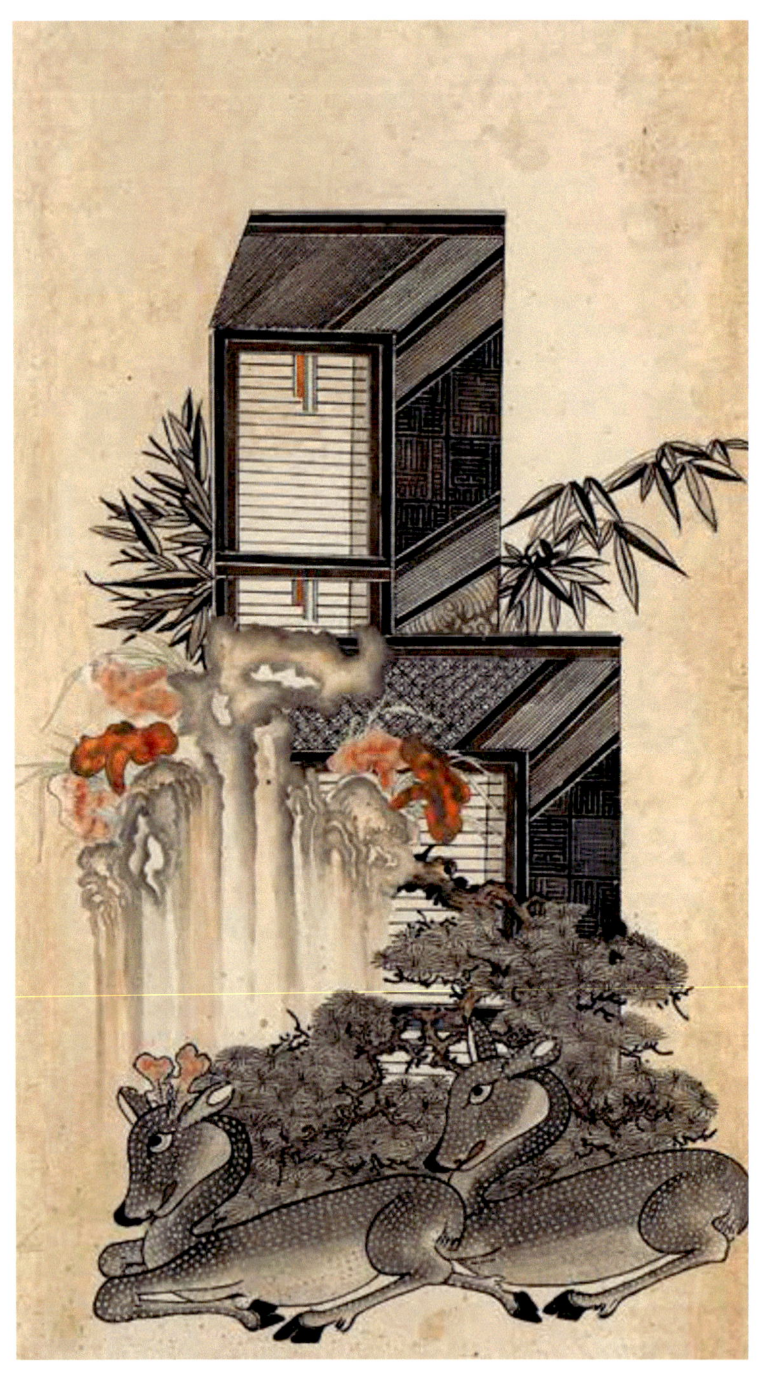

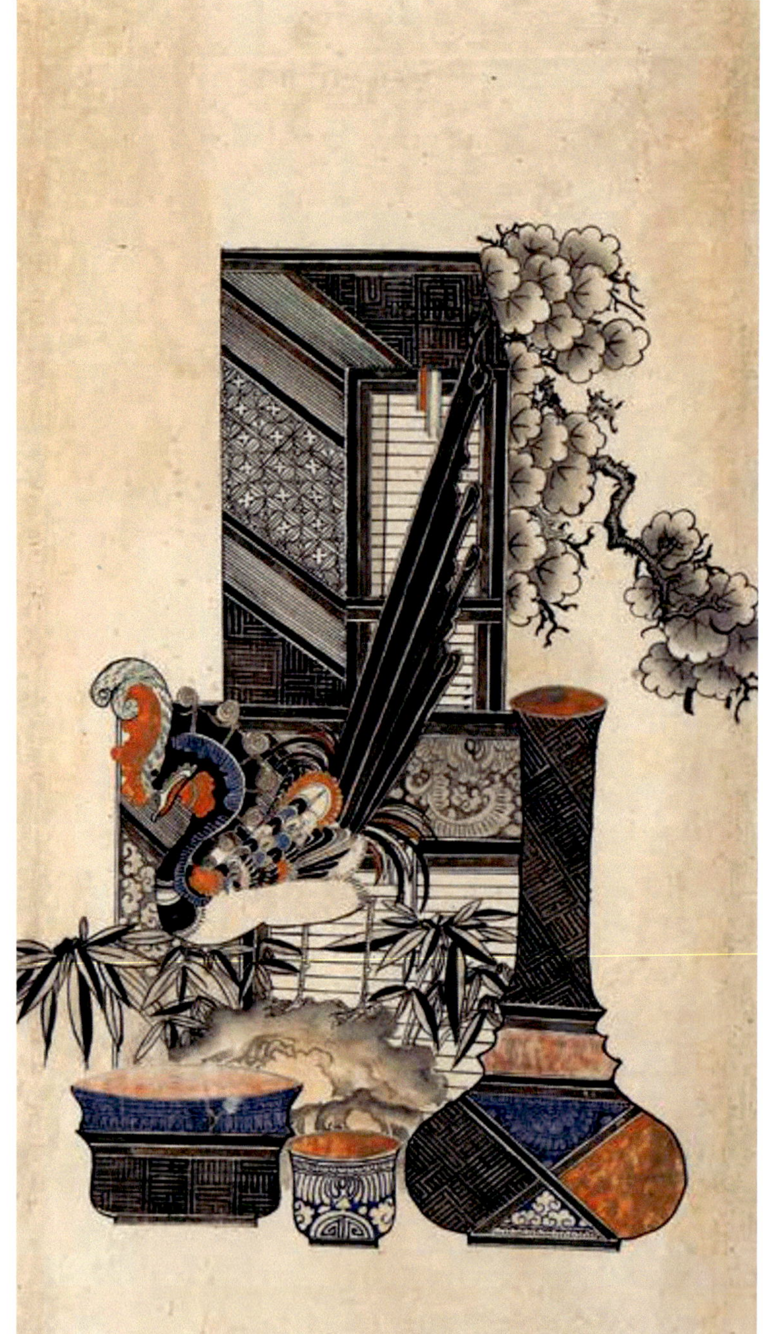

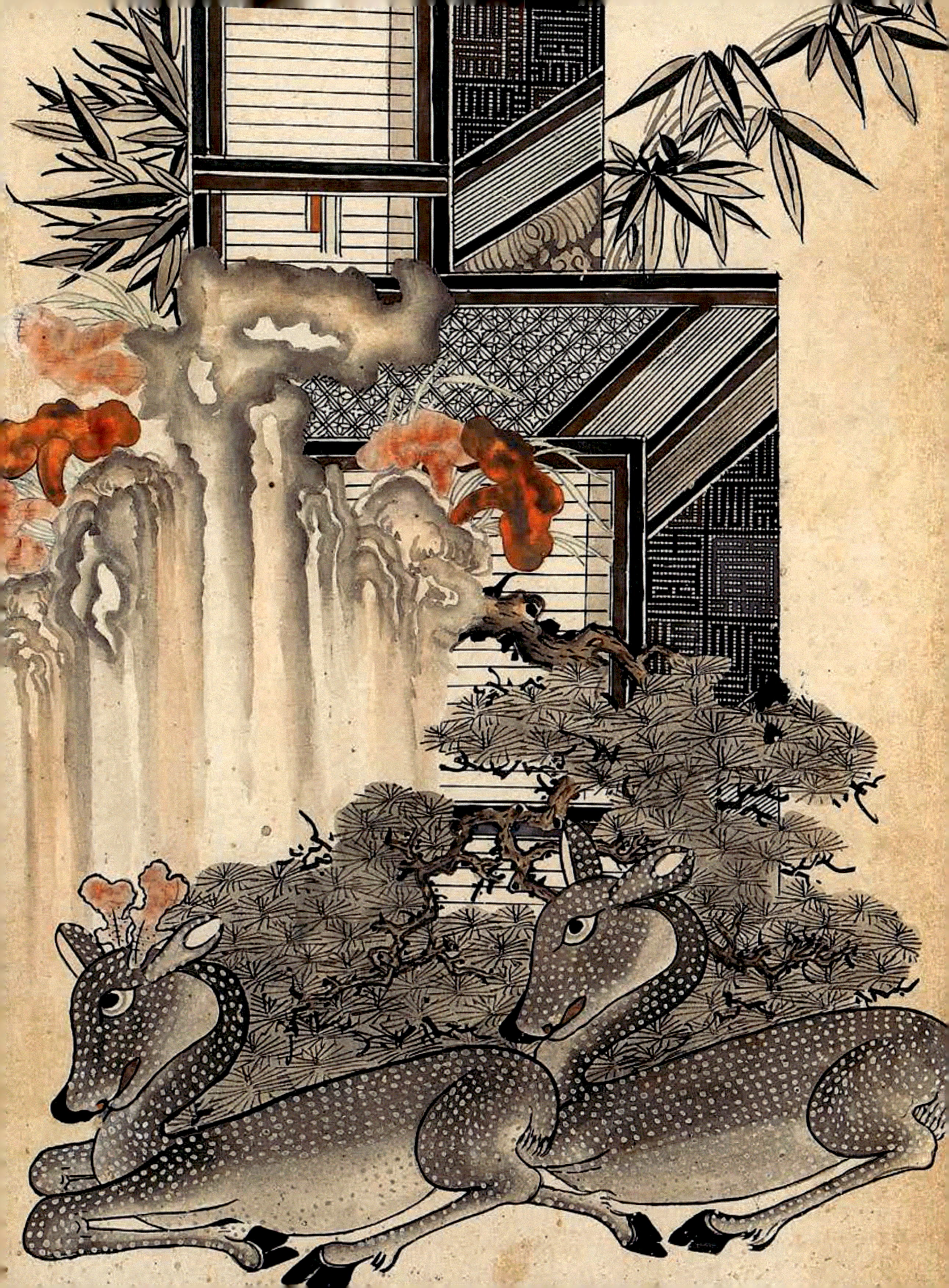

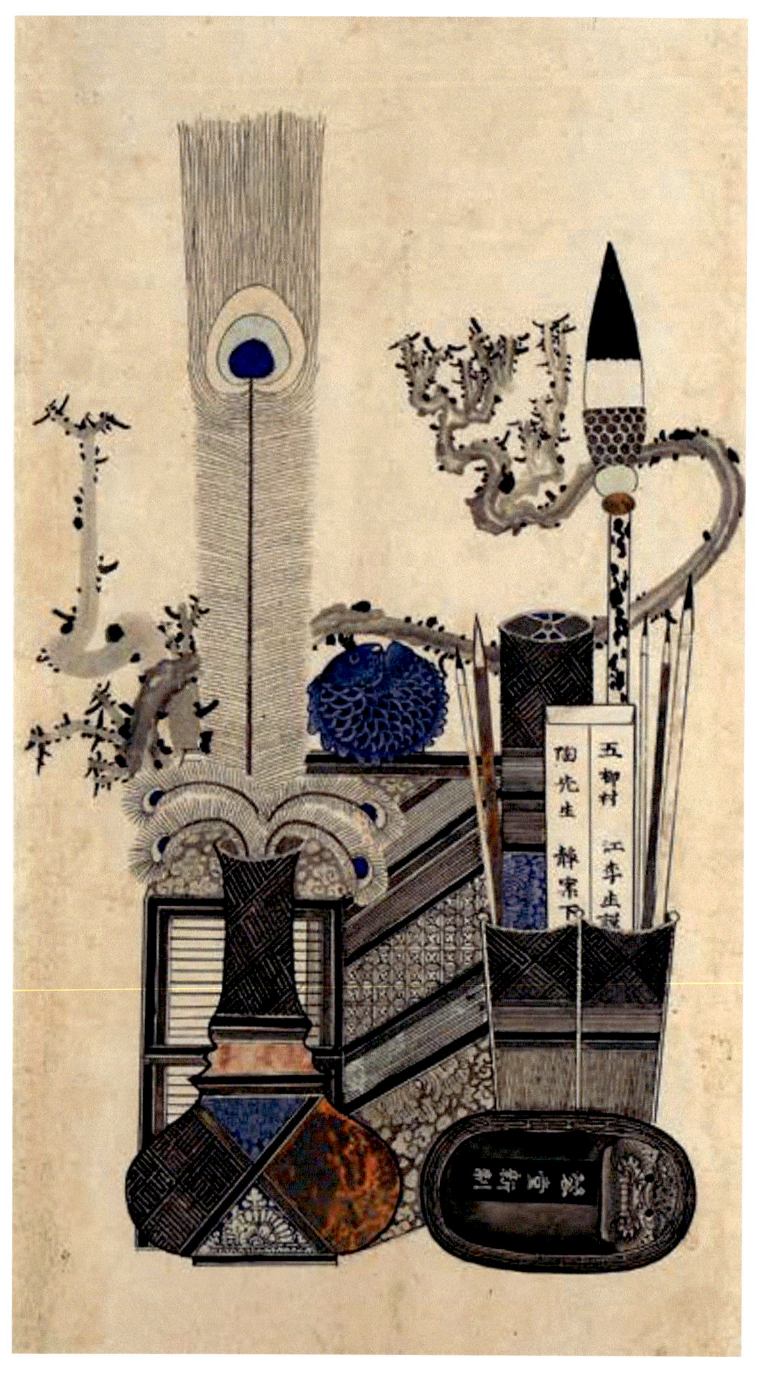
五柳村
陶先生 靜案下

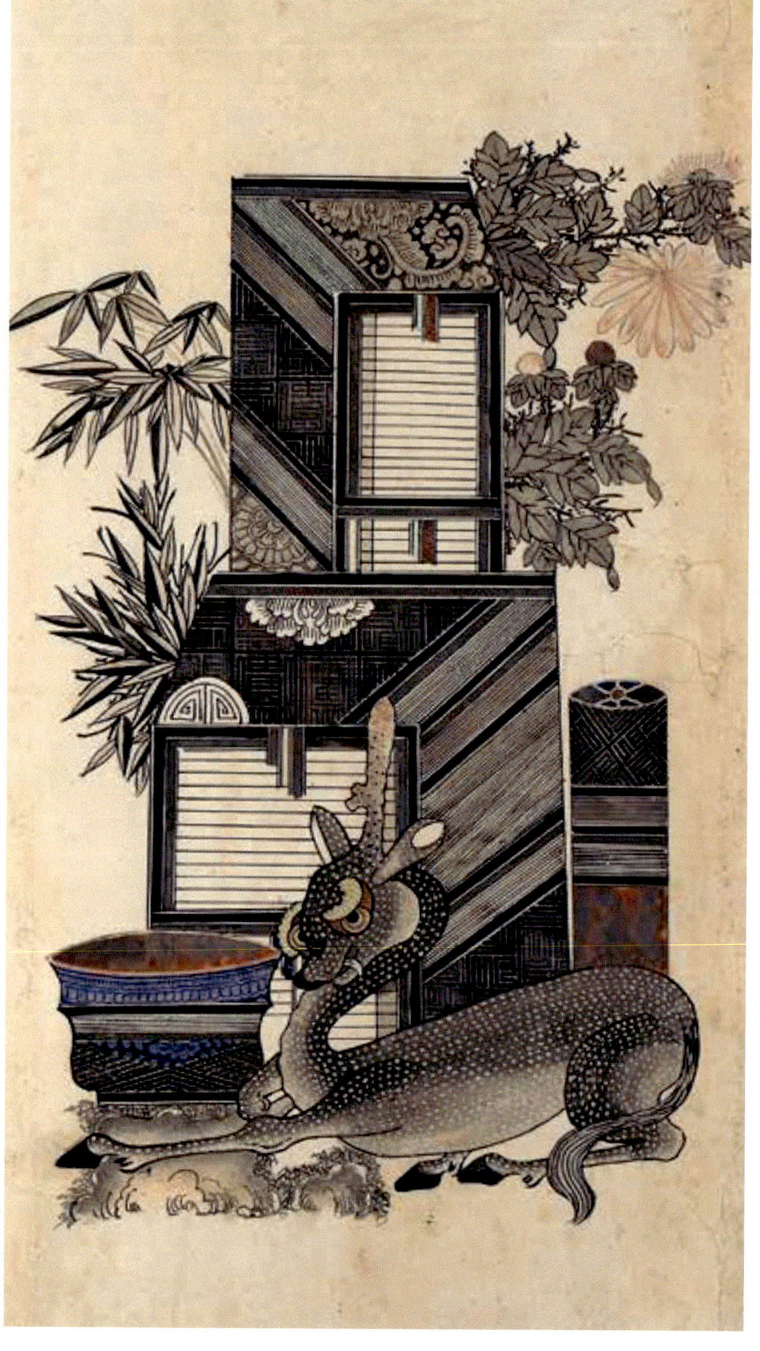

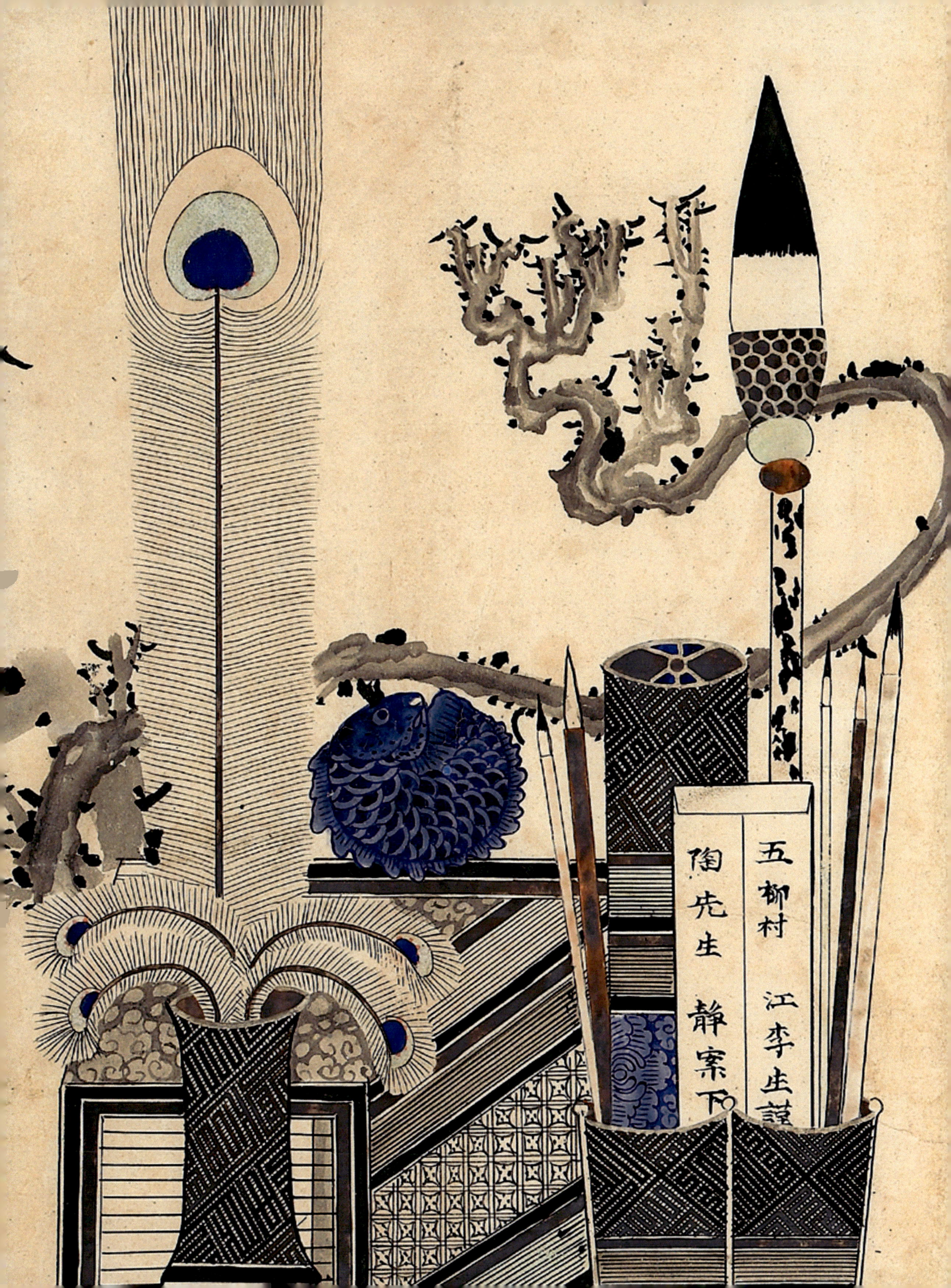
五柳村 江李生謹
陶先生 靜案下

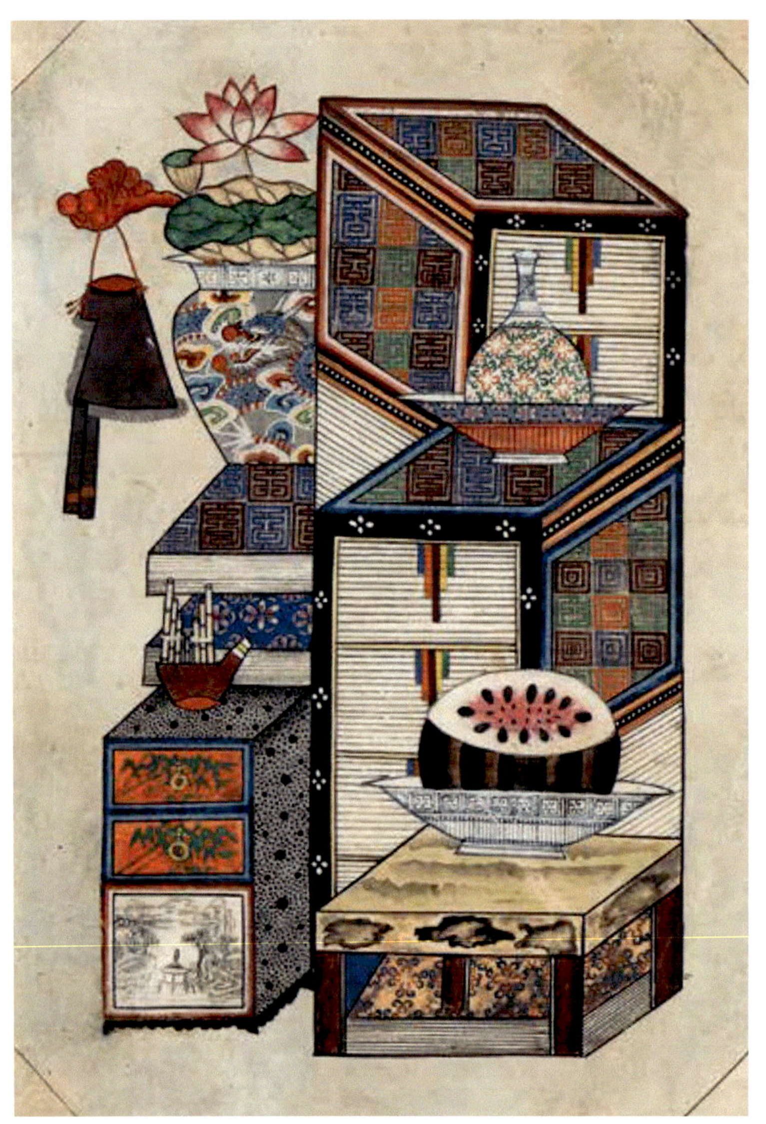

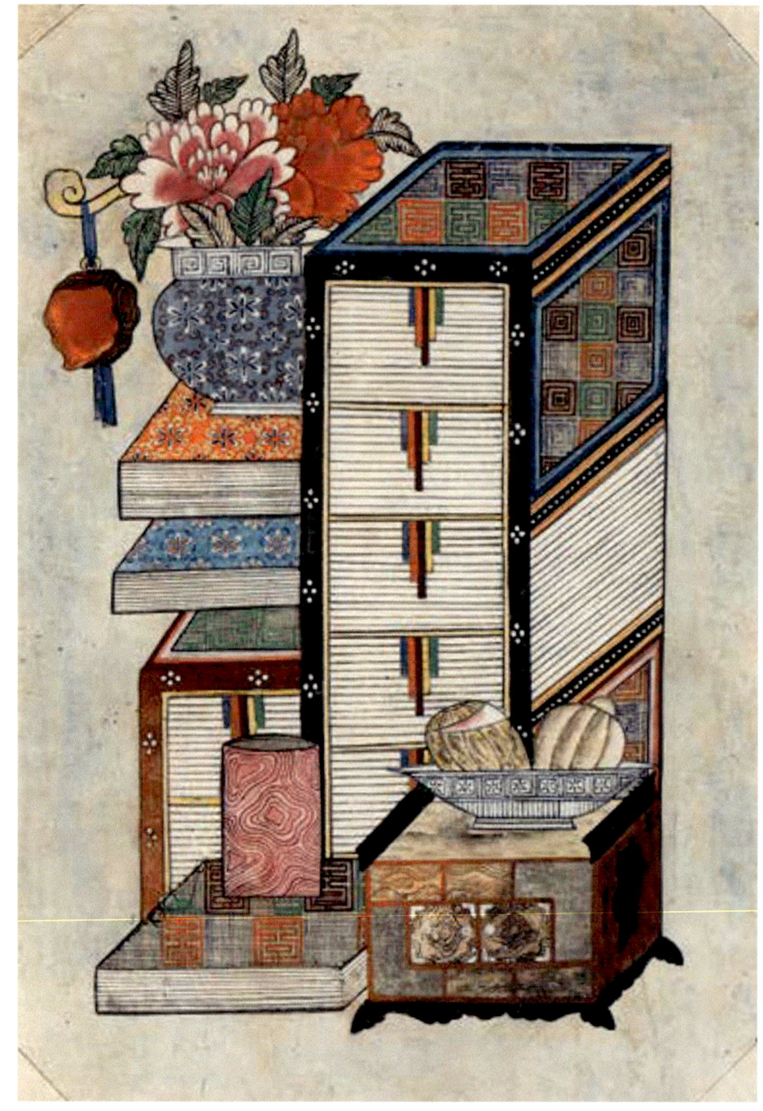

32 *Chaekgeori*

Anonymous, 19th century
Eight-panel screen
Ink and color on paper, 50 x 32 cm (each panel)
Private collection

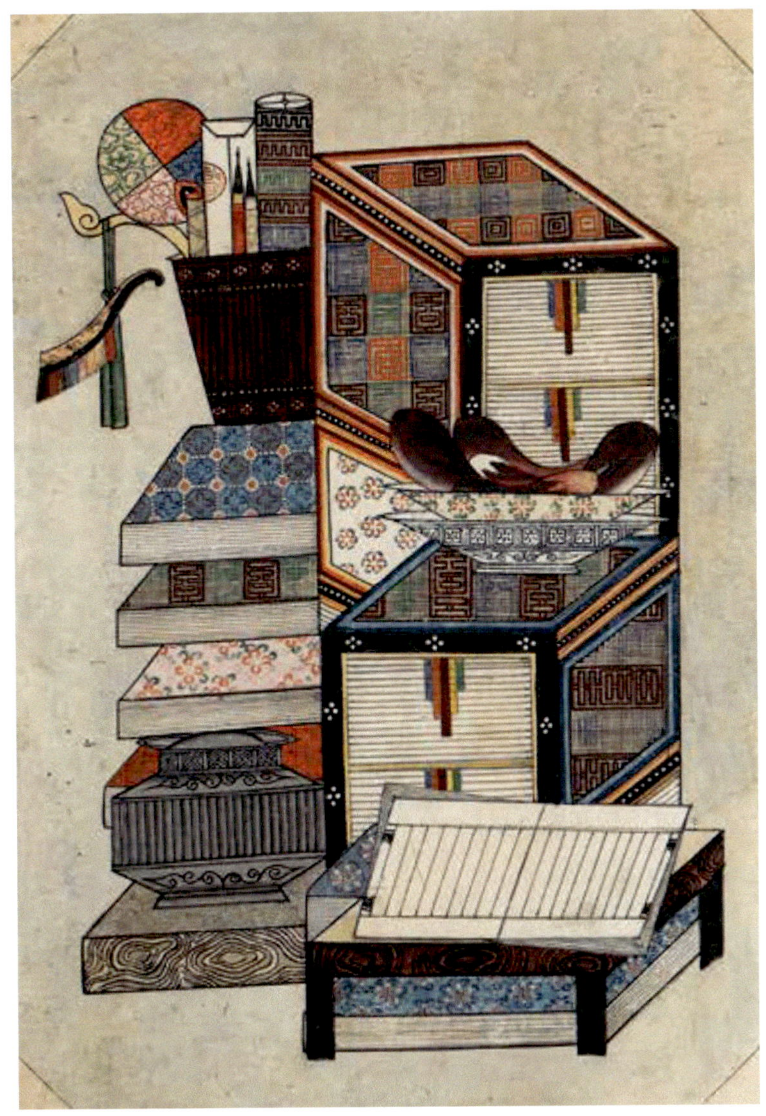

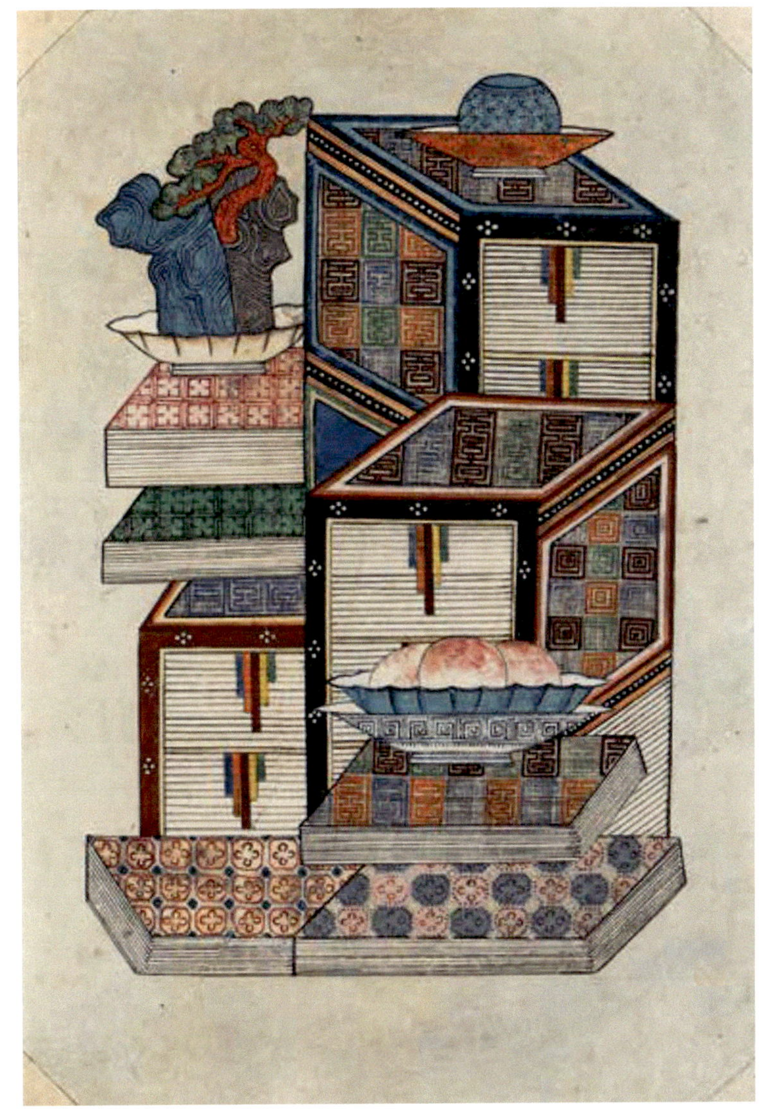

This folk-style chaekgeori makes full use of decorative book-cover patterns. The furniture is depicted as smaller than the books, and accoutrements are arranged freely alongside the covered books. Placed atop the books are bowls of peaches, eggplants, Korean melons, a watermelon, Buddha's hand fruits (fingered citrons), pomegranates, and yuzu. In addition, a pine tree, lotus flowers, tree peonies, peacock tail feathers, herbaceous peonies, and chrysanthemums are placed in porcelain wares or brush holders. The eggplants, Korean melons, watermelon, and pomegranate symbolize the birth of many sons, the peaches longevity, the peacock feathers social advancement, the peony fortune, and the lotus flower happiness—all auspicious symbols. The accoutrements and flora and fauna featured in this work show hope for academic achievement, social advancement, longevity, the birth of many sons, and happiness, in that order. Even the patterns on the book covers use auspicious characters such as 回 (*hoe*) or 壽 (*su*), both alluding to longevity. BC, SK

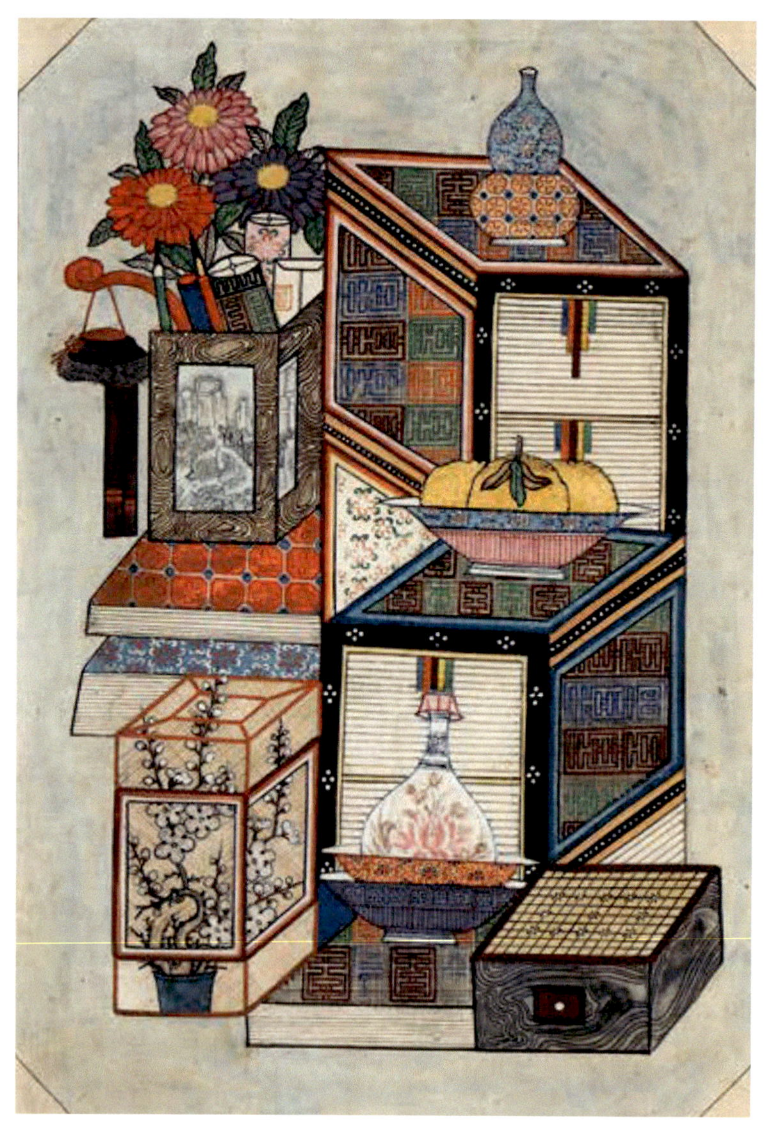
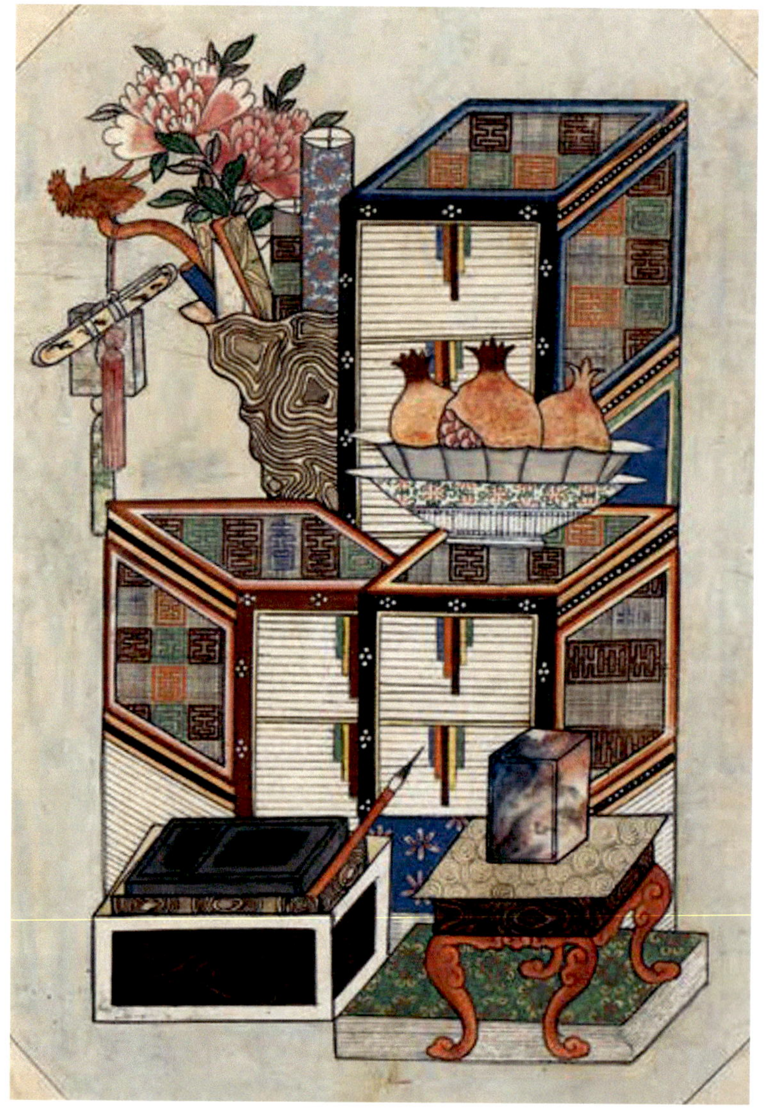

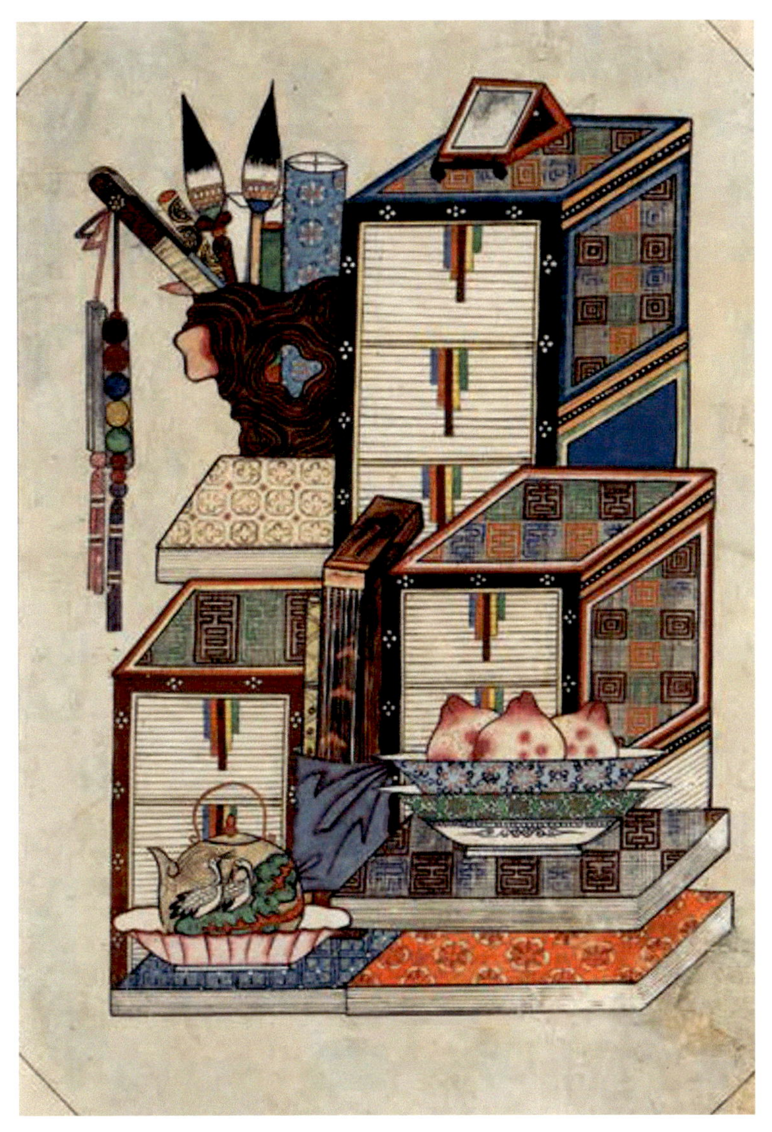
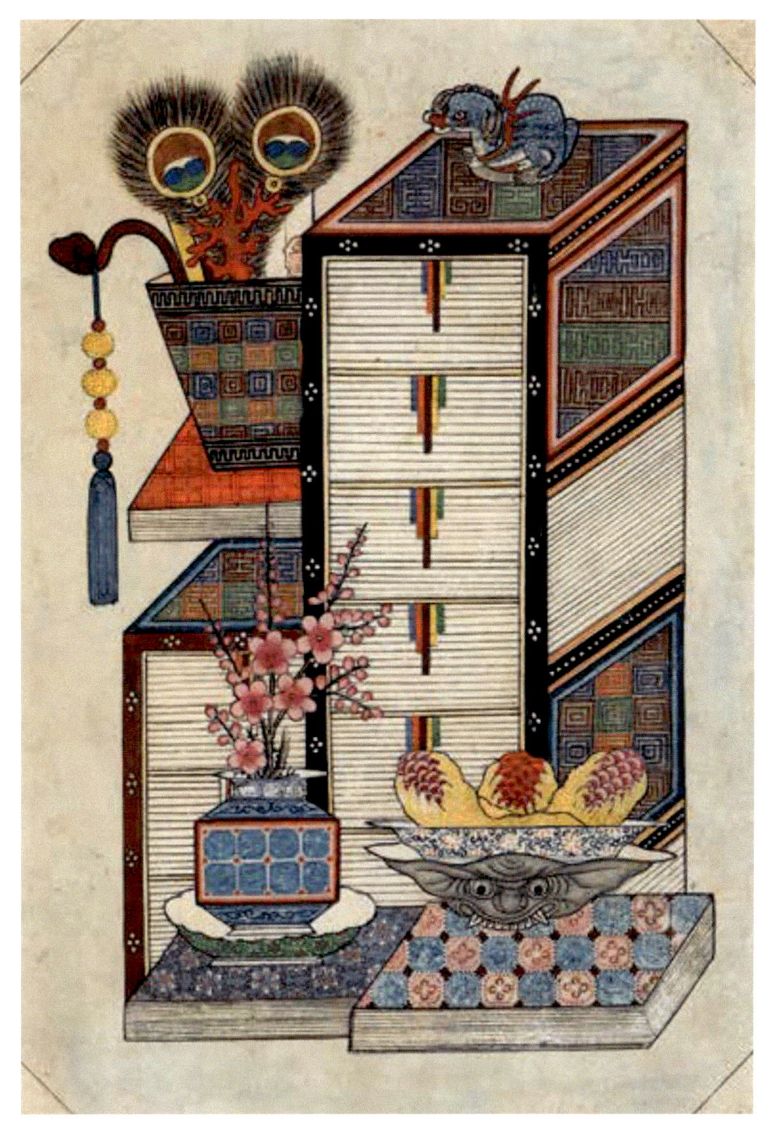

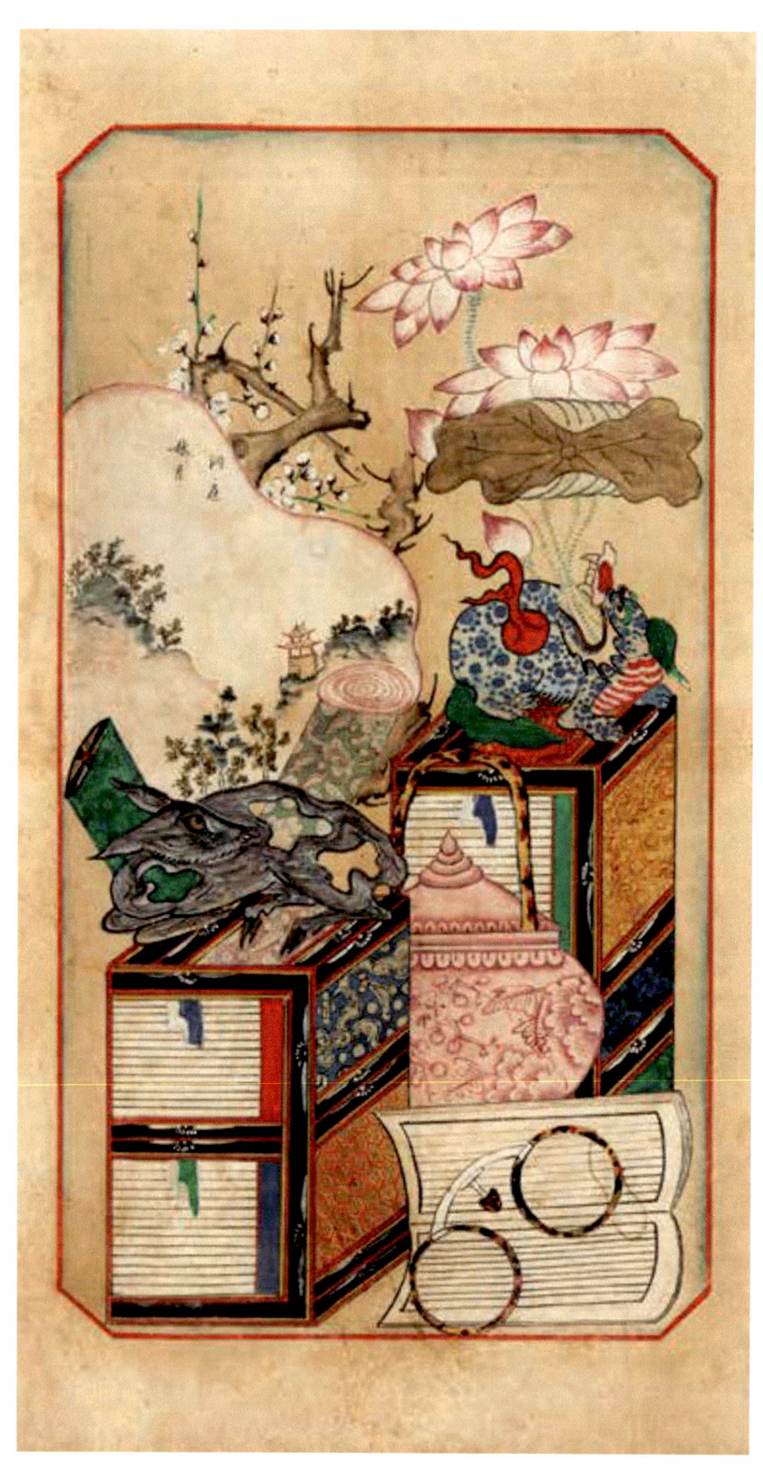

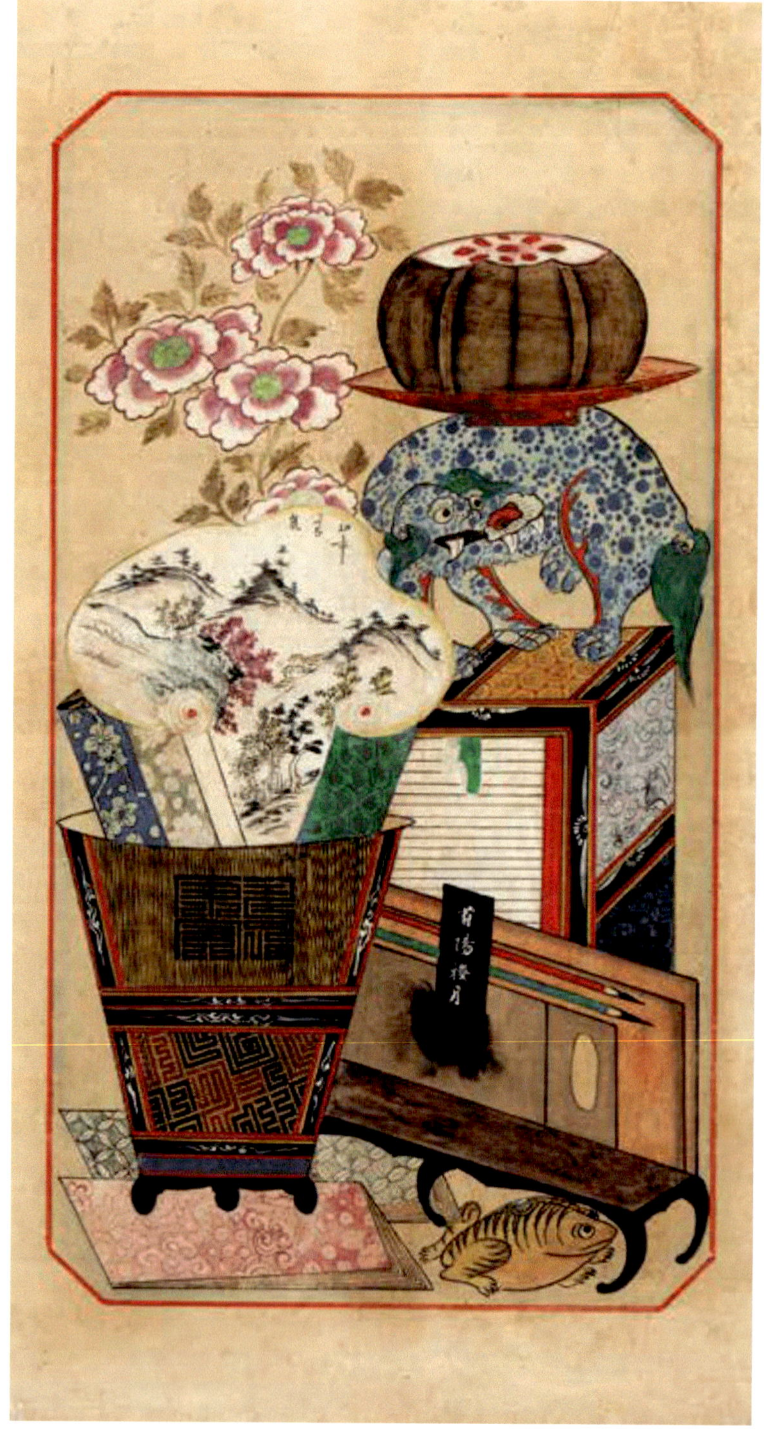

33 *Chaekgeori*

Anonymous, late 19th century
Eight-panel screen
Ink and color on paper, 55.7 x 31.7 cm (each panel)
Sungok Memorial Hall, Mokpo

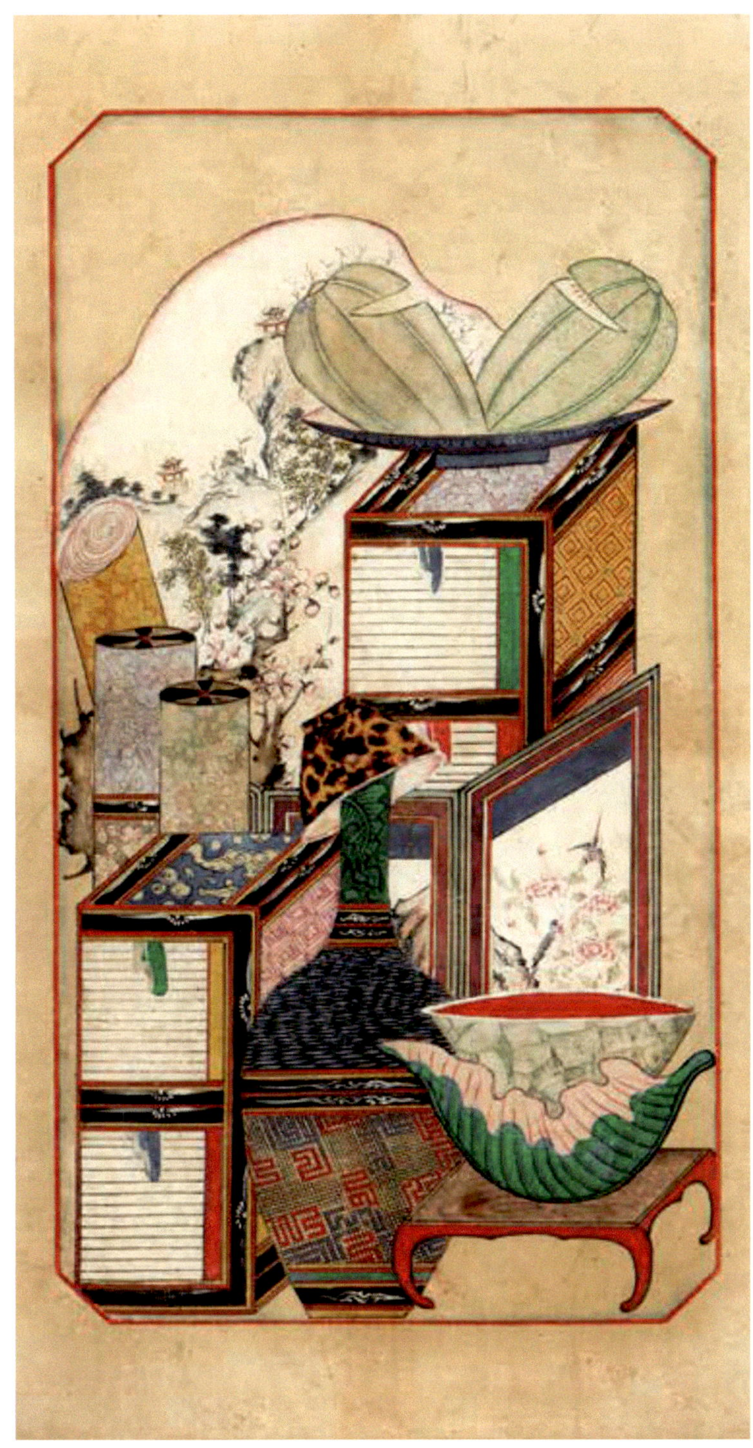

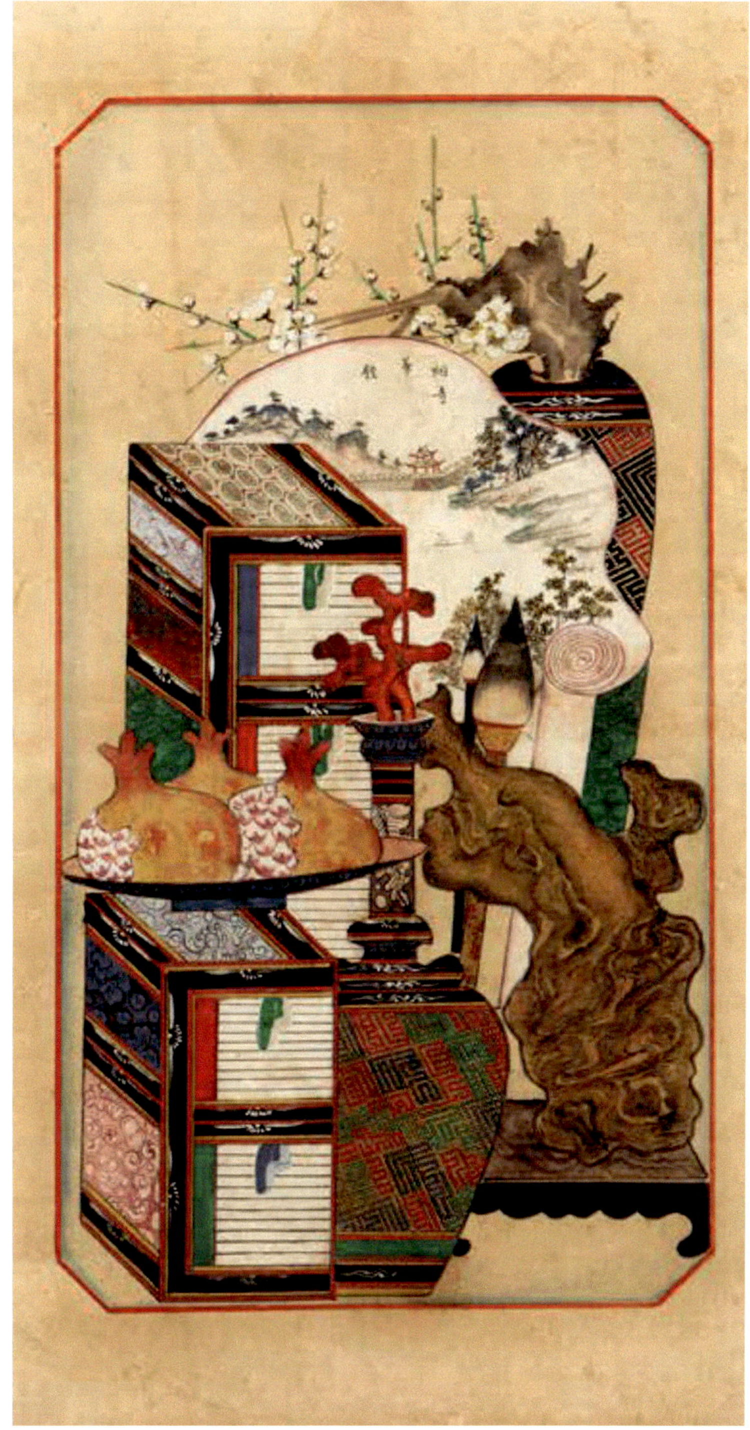

This work is a combination of chaekgeori and Korean landscape painting. Books, accoutrements, and scrolls are arranged harmoniously alongside flowers and trees. The landscapes painted on the scrolls unfurl like scenes out of a fantasy. Not random scenes, these landscapes present nineteenth-century versions of *Eight Scenic Views of Xiaoxiang Rivers*, a Chinese landscape masterpiece that Koreans had held up as an ideal since the Goryeo dynasty. It depicts eight wondrous sights near the Xiang River and Dongting Lake in Hunan Province, China. The geometric forms of the books and furniture, coupled with the sinuous curves of the scrolls, create an exquisite and beautiful composition. The vivid colors also add to the work's many charms. BC, SK

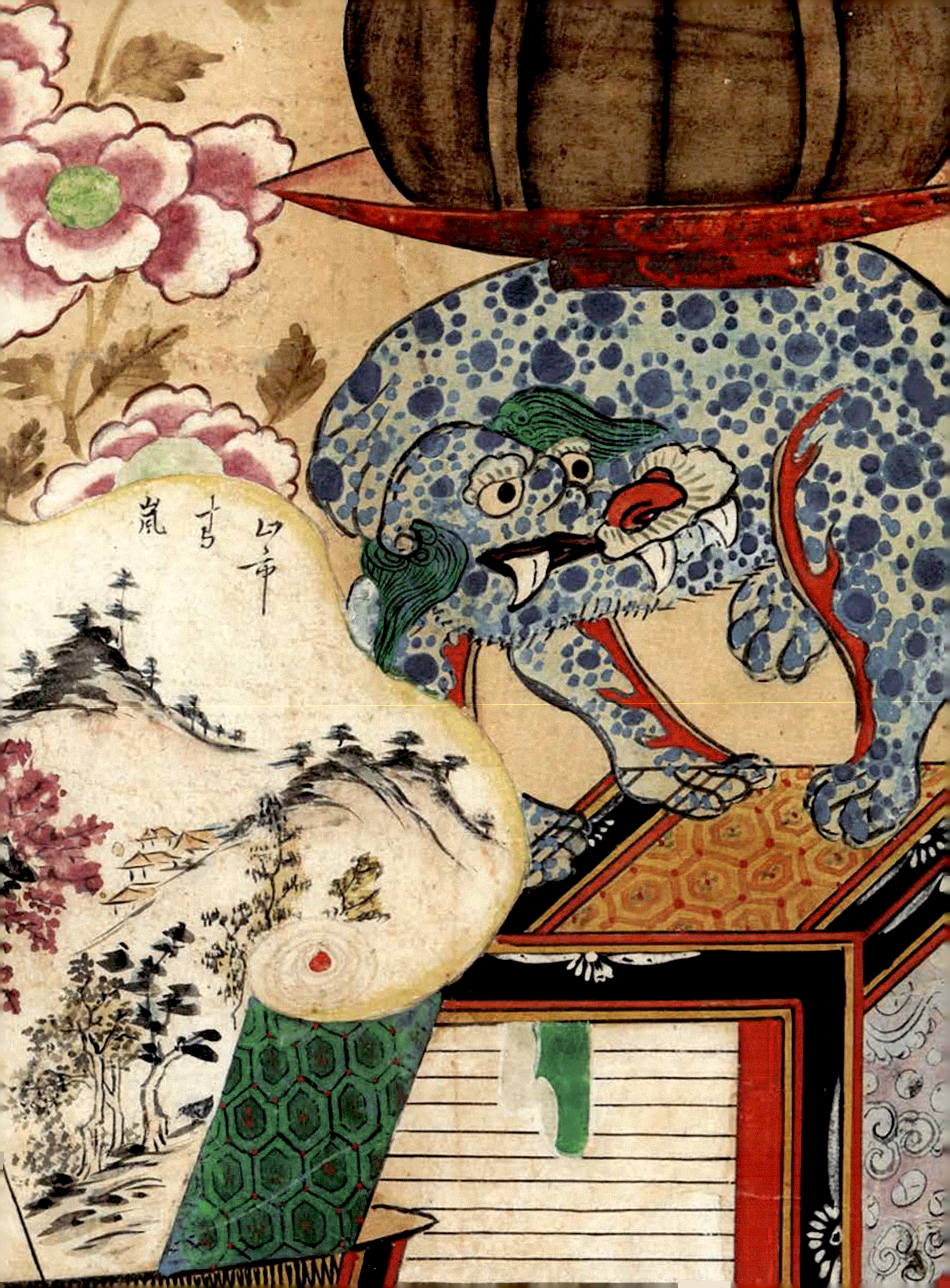
山市
嵐

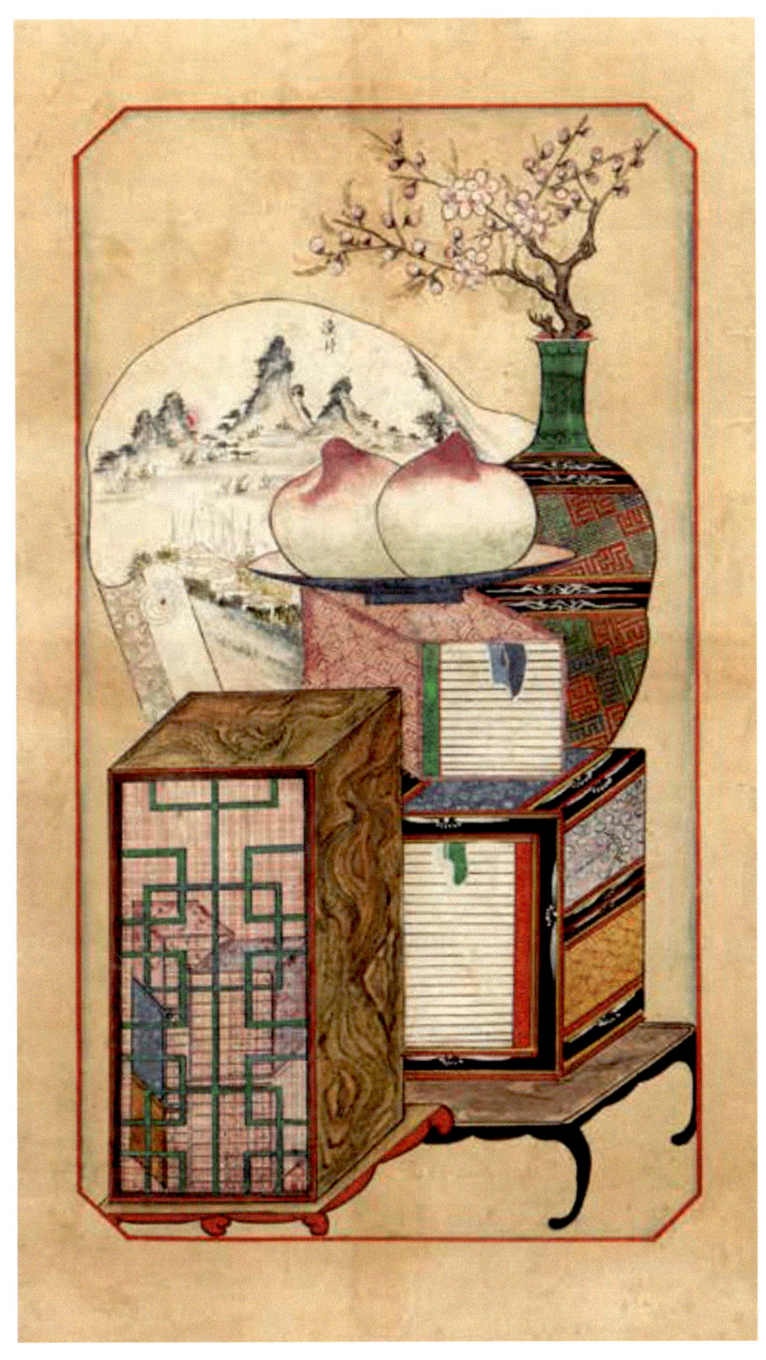

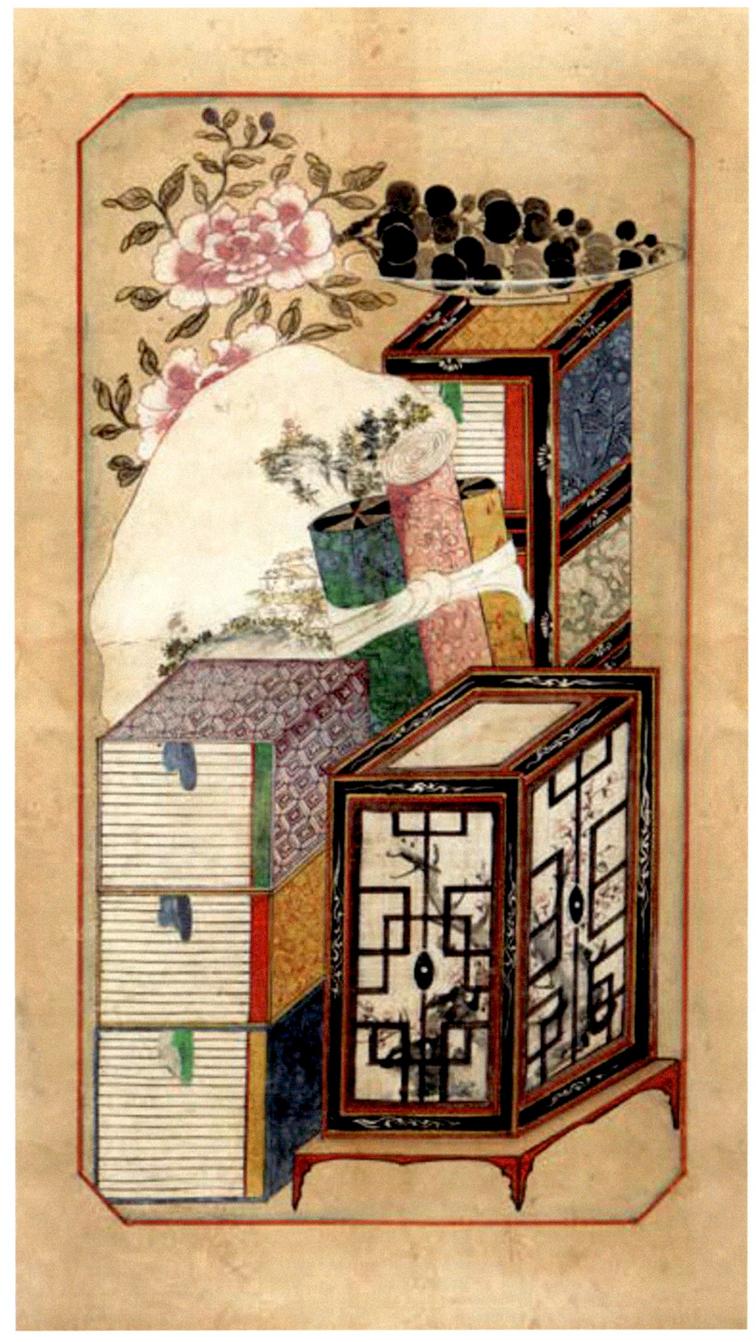

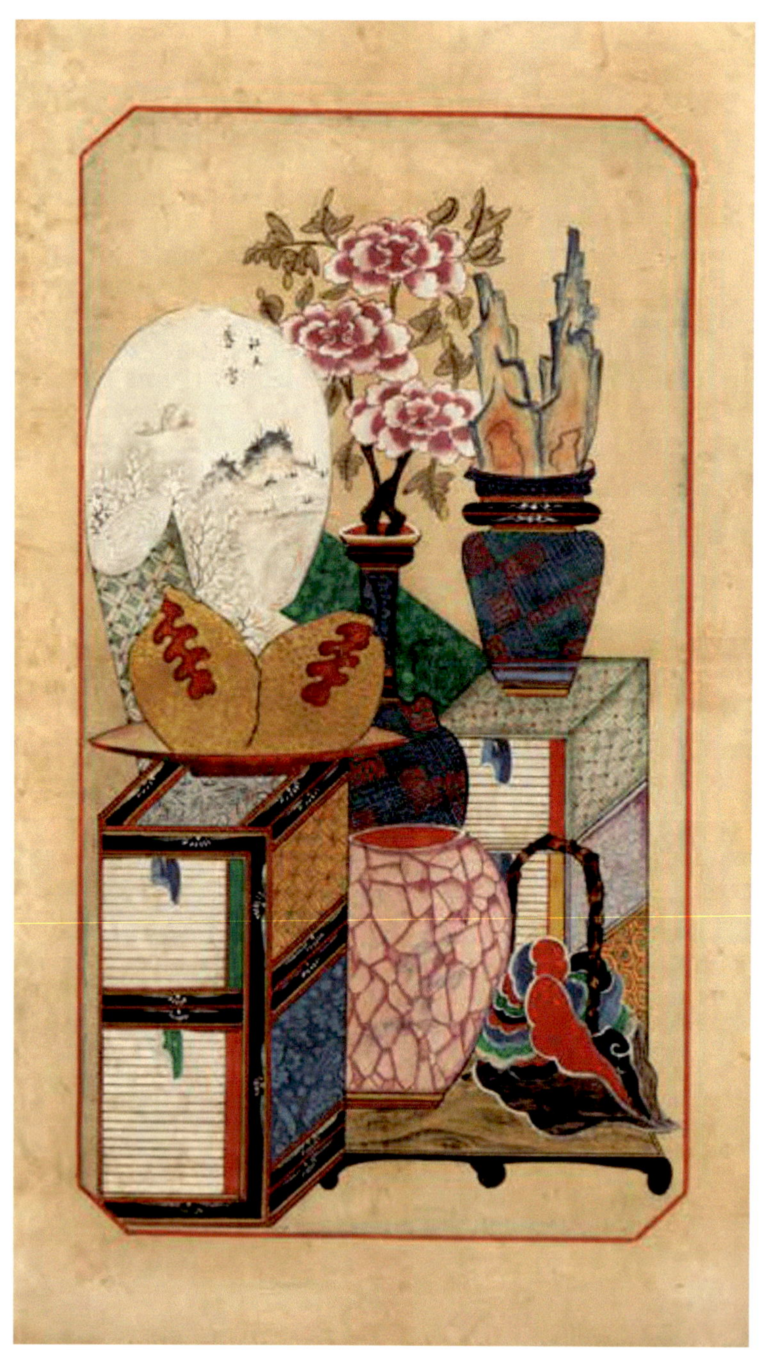
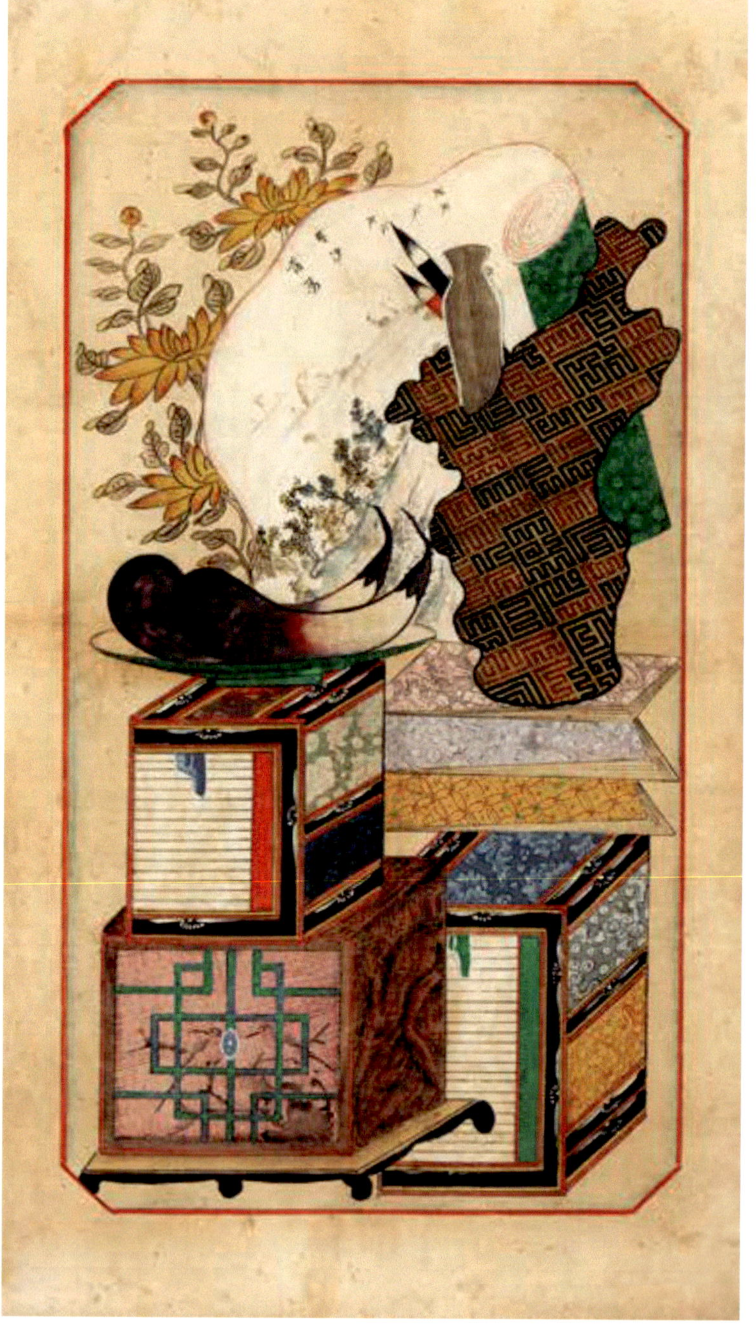

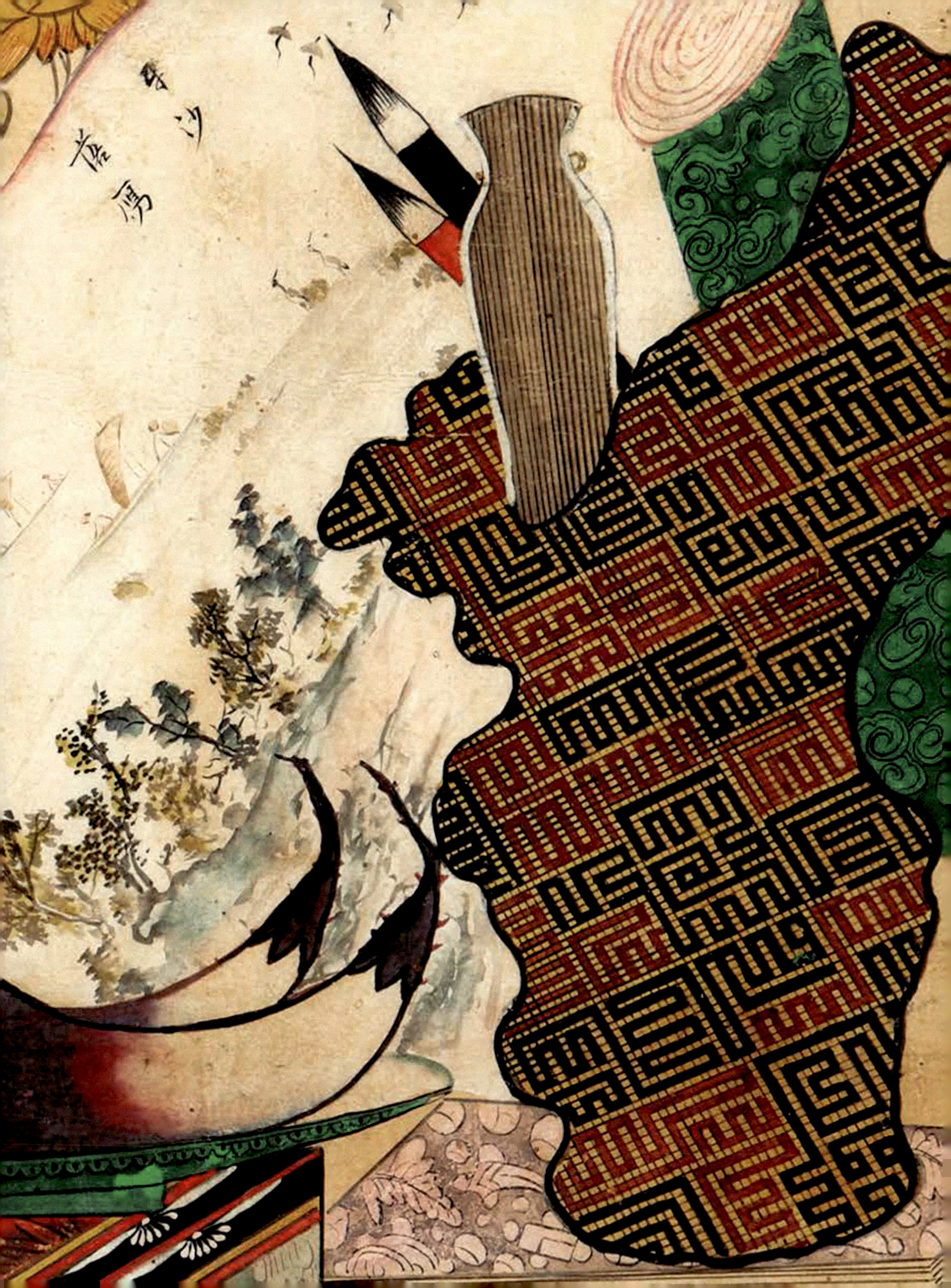

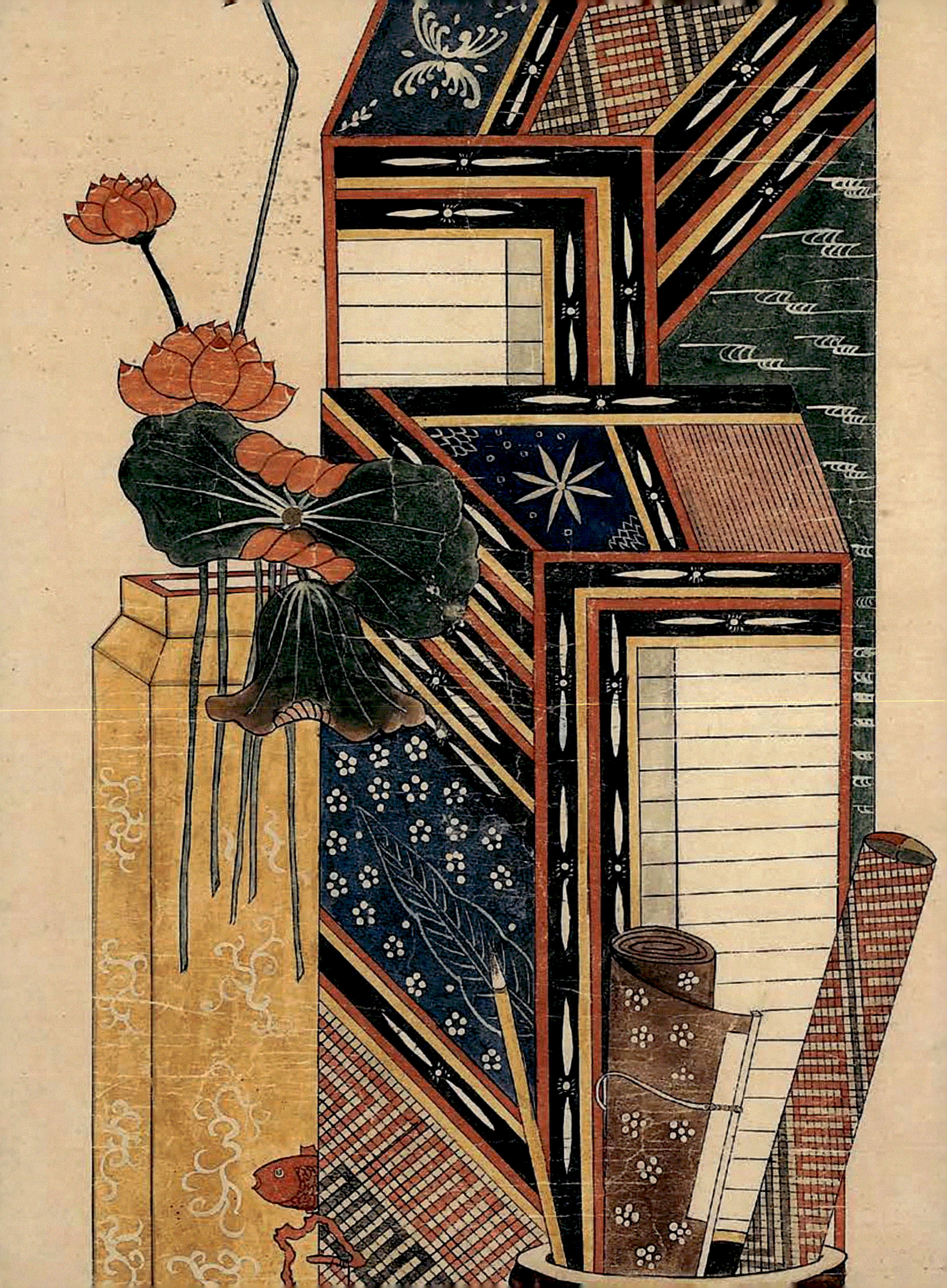

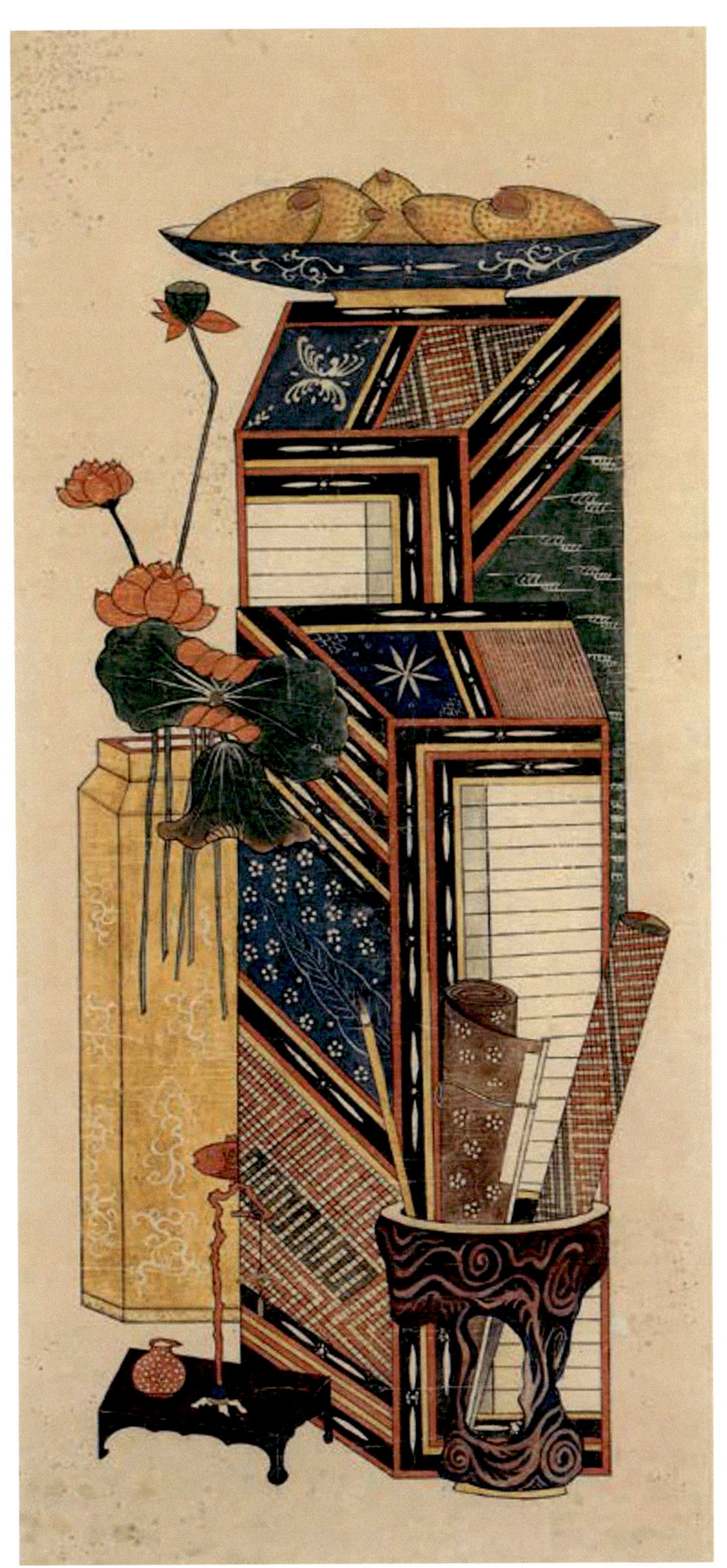

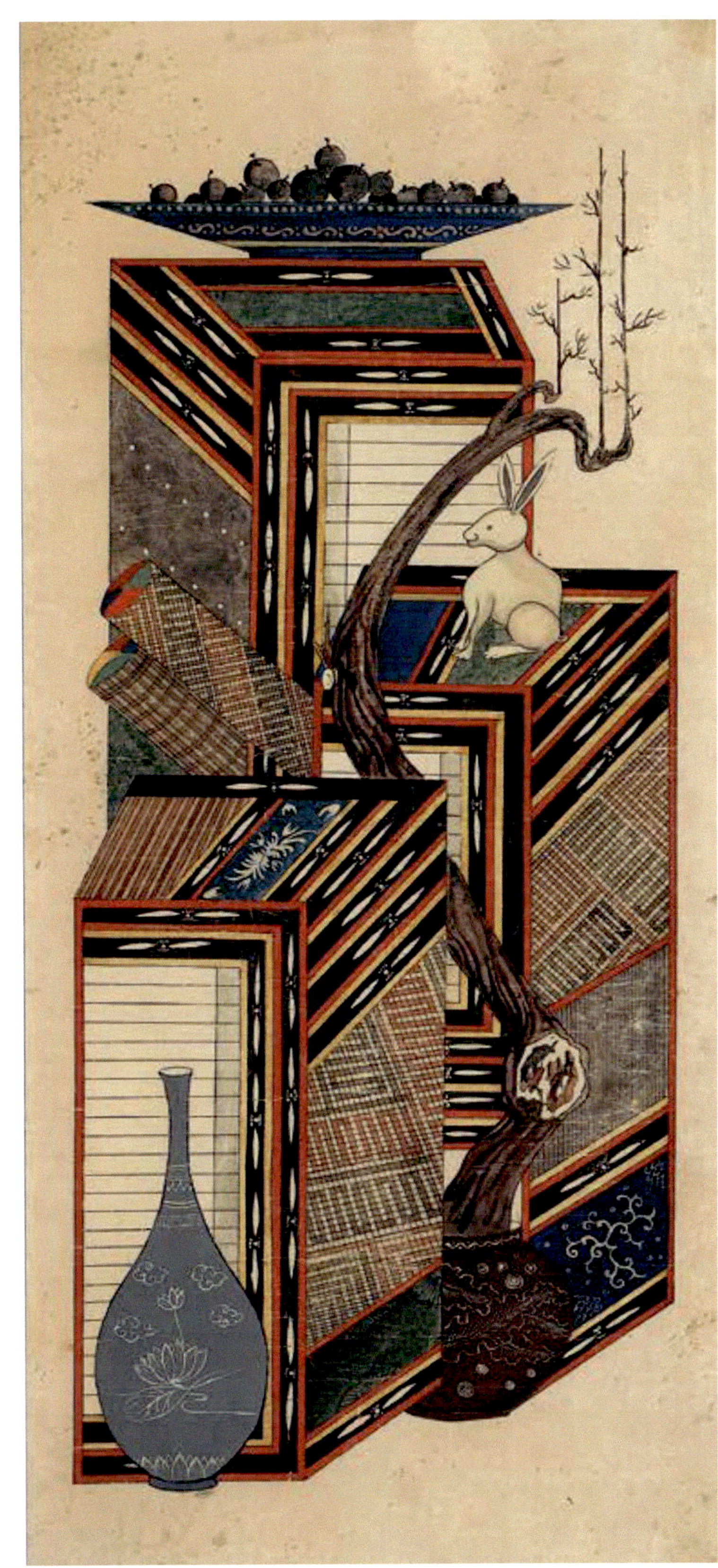

34 *Chaekgeori*

Anonymous, early 20th century
Eight-panel screen
Ink and color on paper, 105 x 46.5 cm (each panel)
Private collection

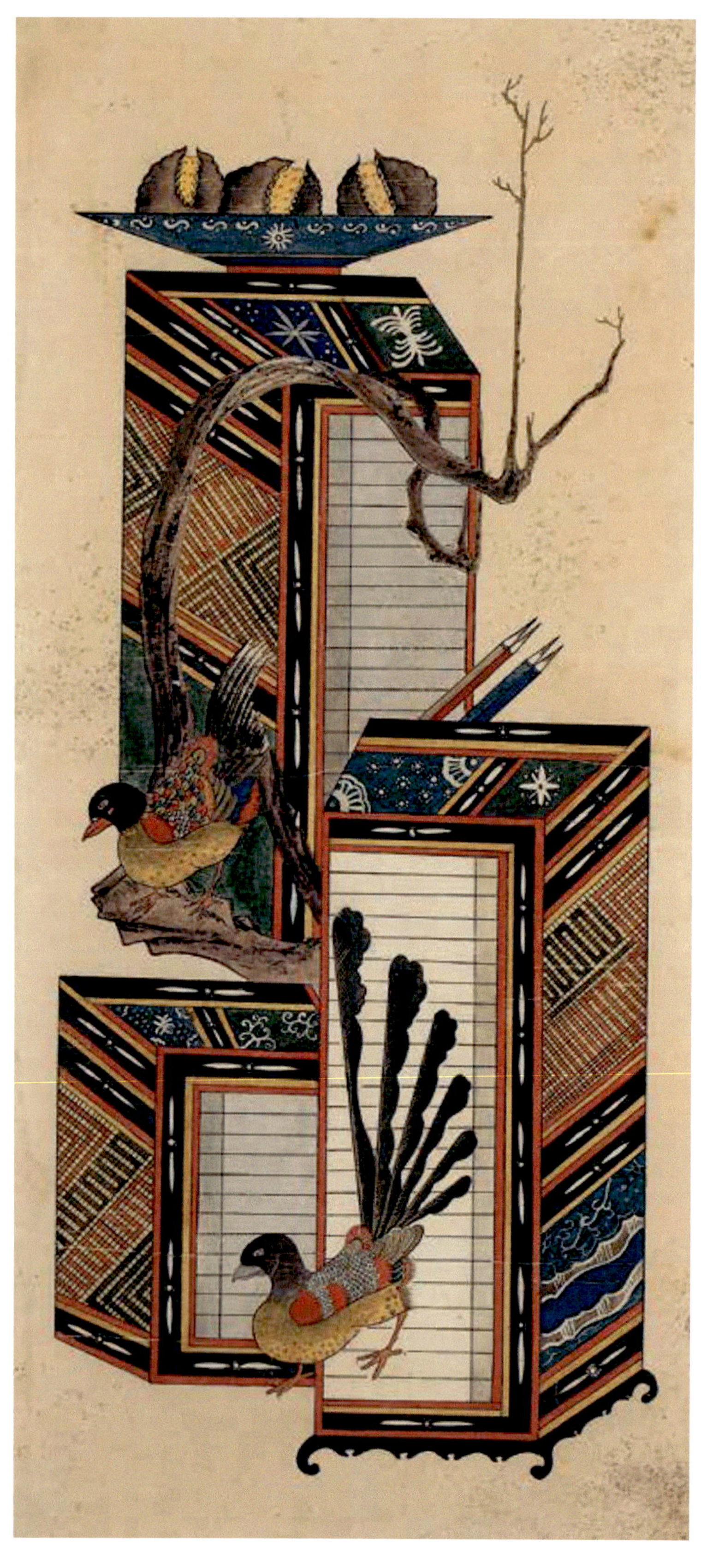

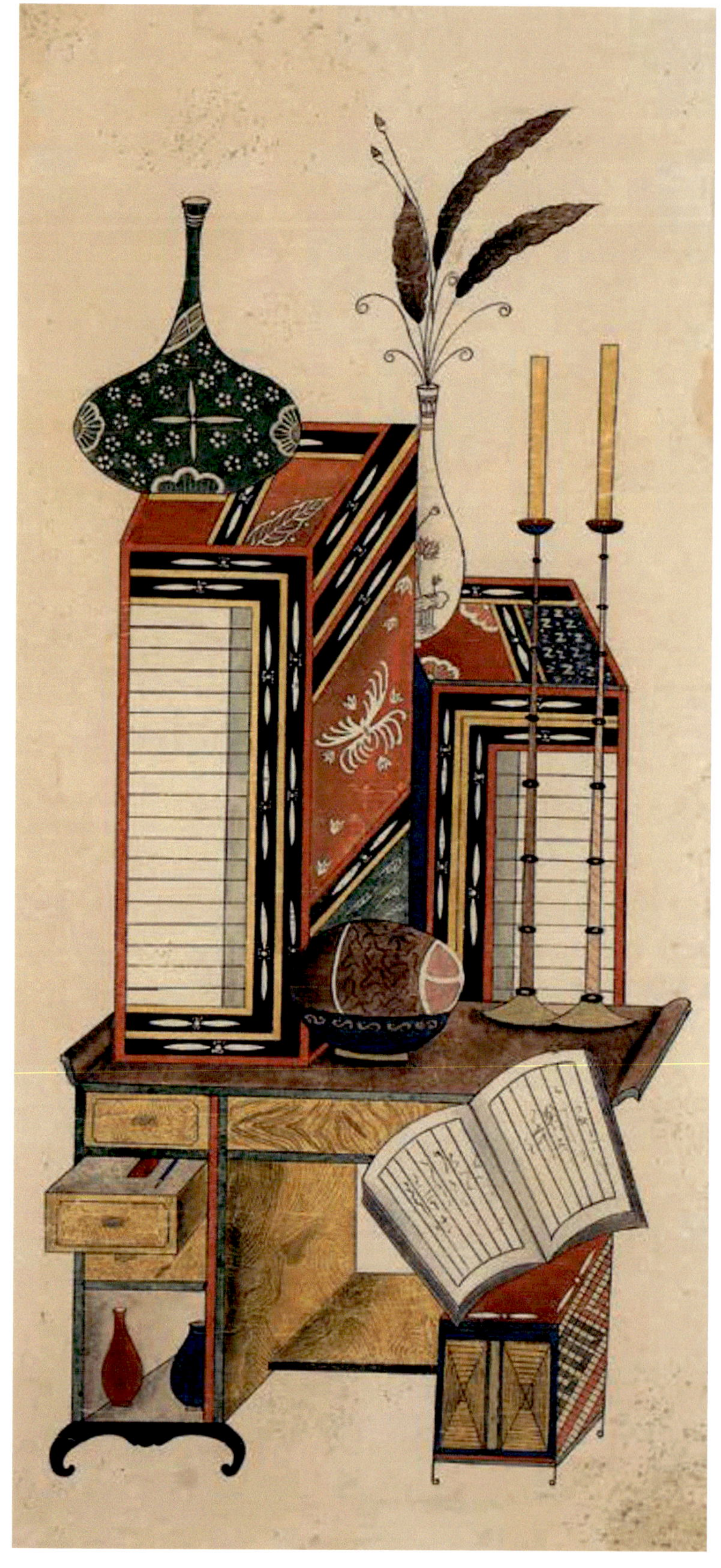

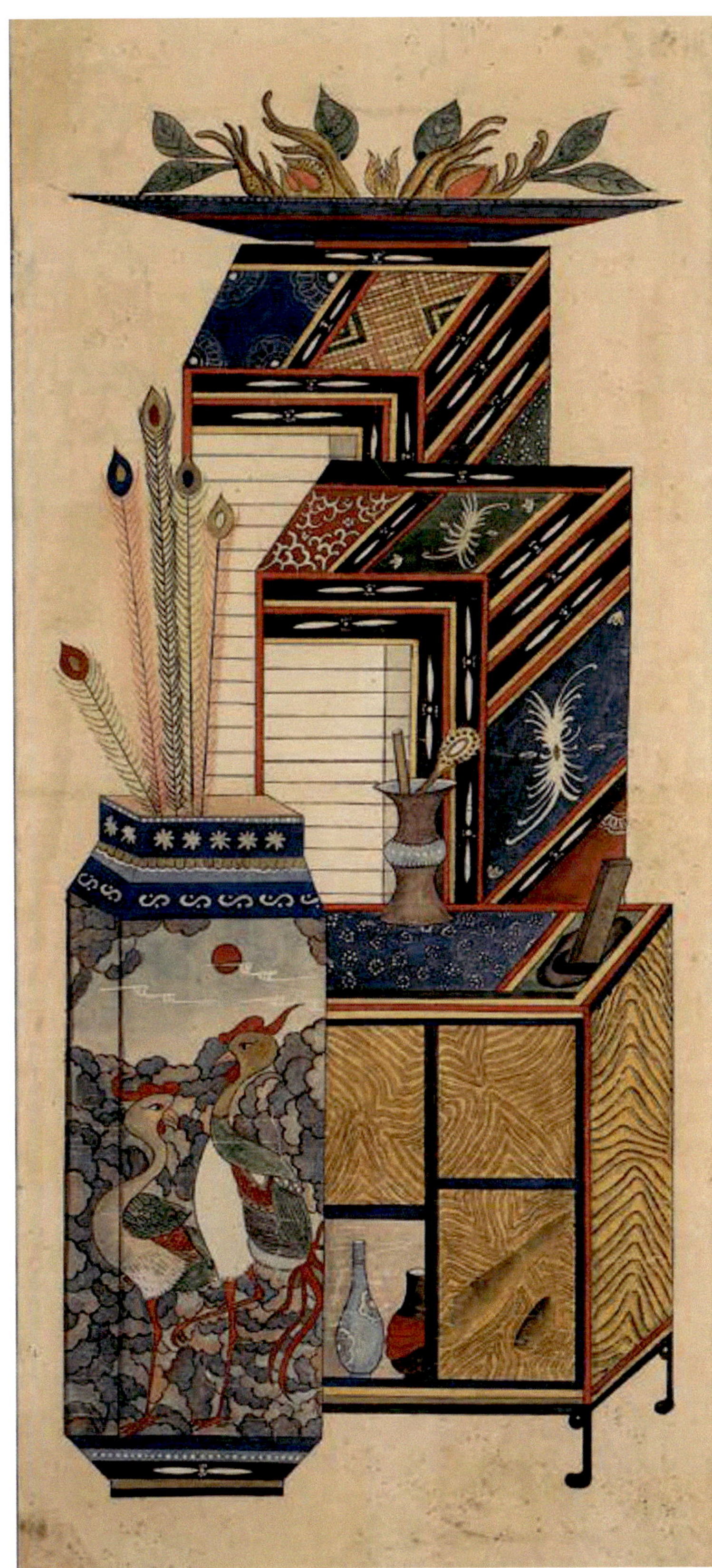

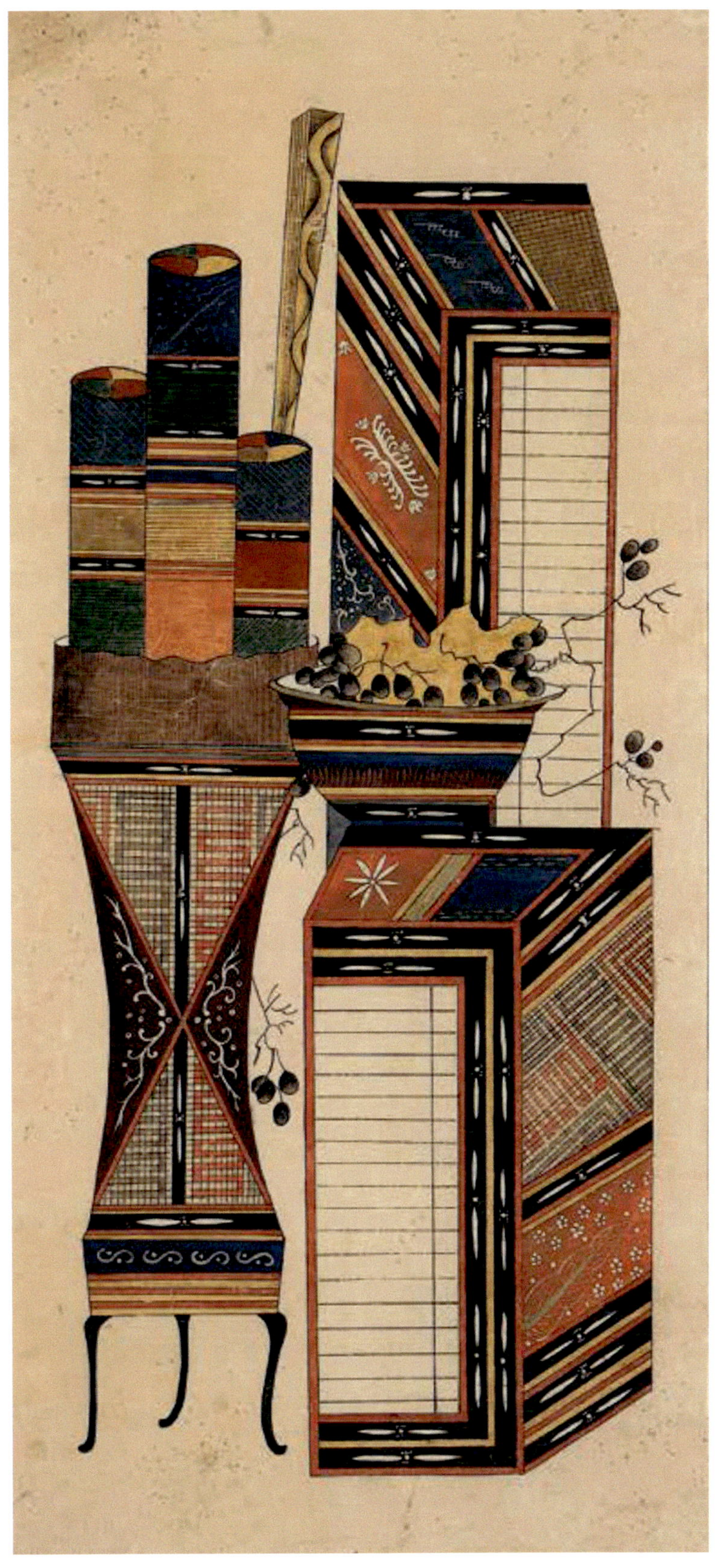

This colorful and strikingly modern-looking folding screen showcases how much this artistic genre had evolved over the course of a century, from a formal royal emblem to a scholar's elegant decorative item, and finally to a grandiose spectacle of popular luxuries. If most chaekgeori were composed of neatly arranged books and other artful utilitarian objects, the painter of this screen was more interested in depicting a sense of abundance and ostentation. In addition to scholarly utensils—books, brushes, an inkstone—a variety of edible delicacies, such as multi-seeded fruits, fingered citrons, grapes, a watermelon, eggplants, and pomegranate, were added to the picture to express the patron's aspiration for many children, the core value of the clan's success. The random apparition of animals—a pair of phoenixes, a white heron, a carp, a pheasant—further emphasizes how much the painter endeavored to convey auspicious messages to his audience. BC, SM

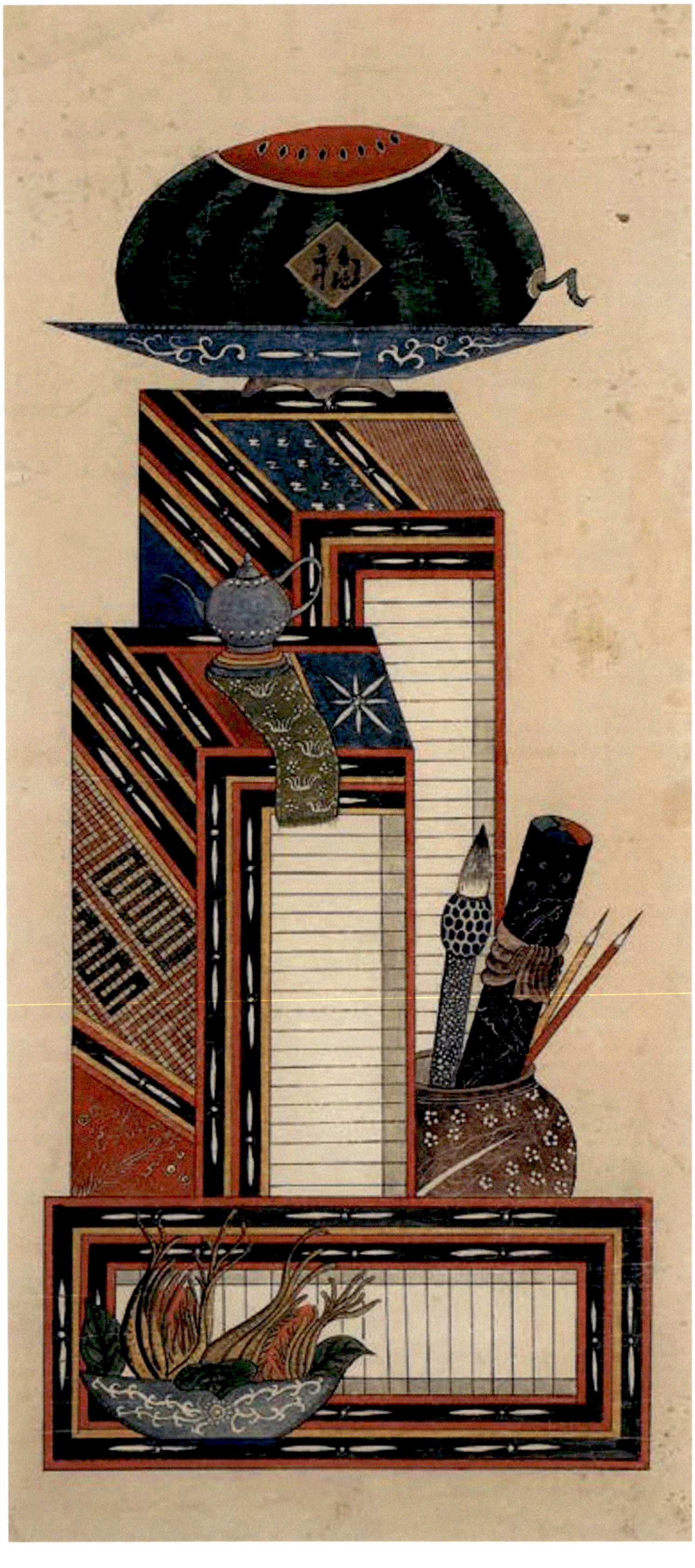

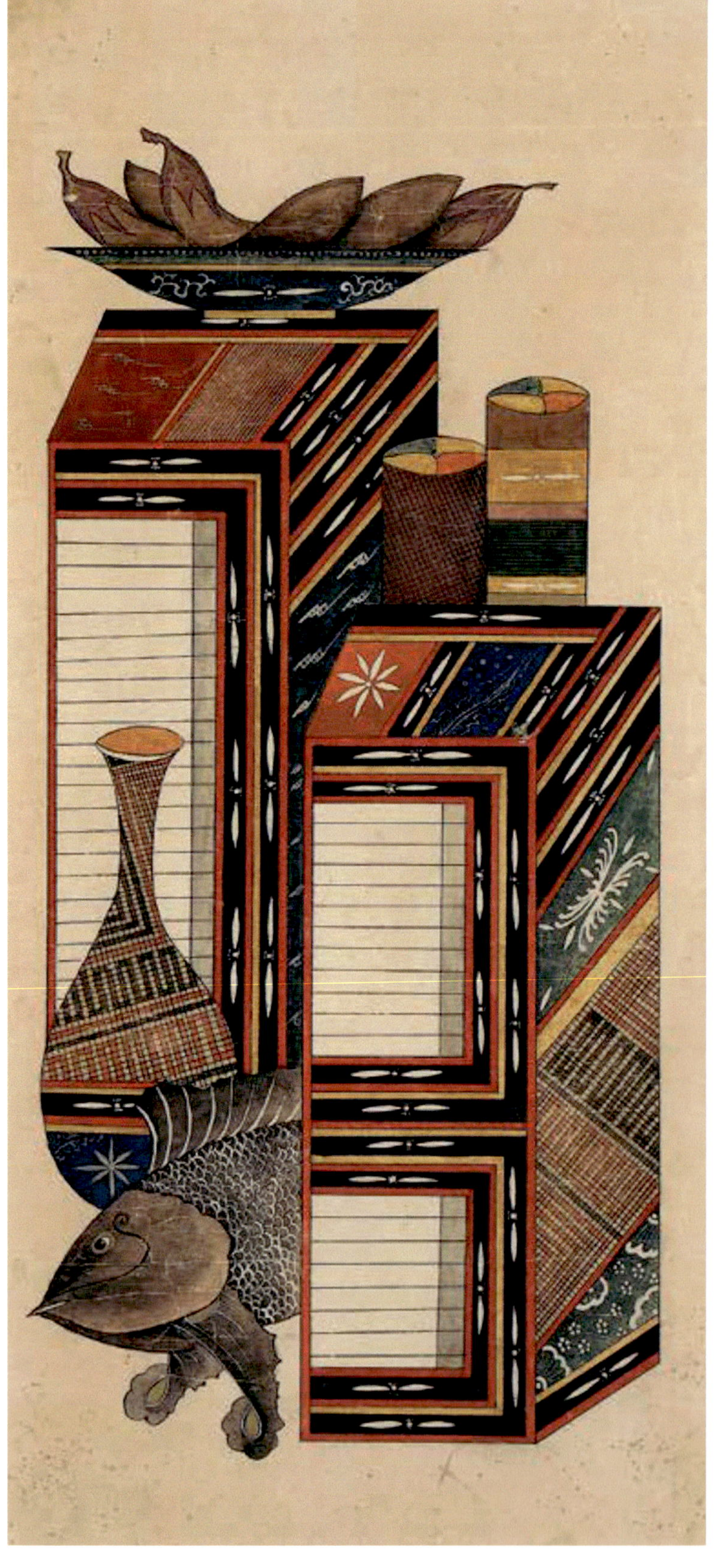

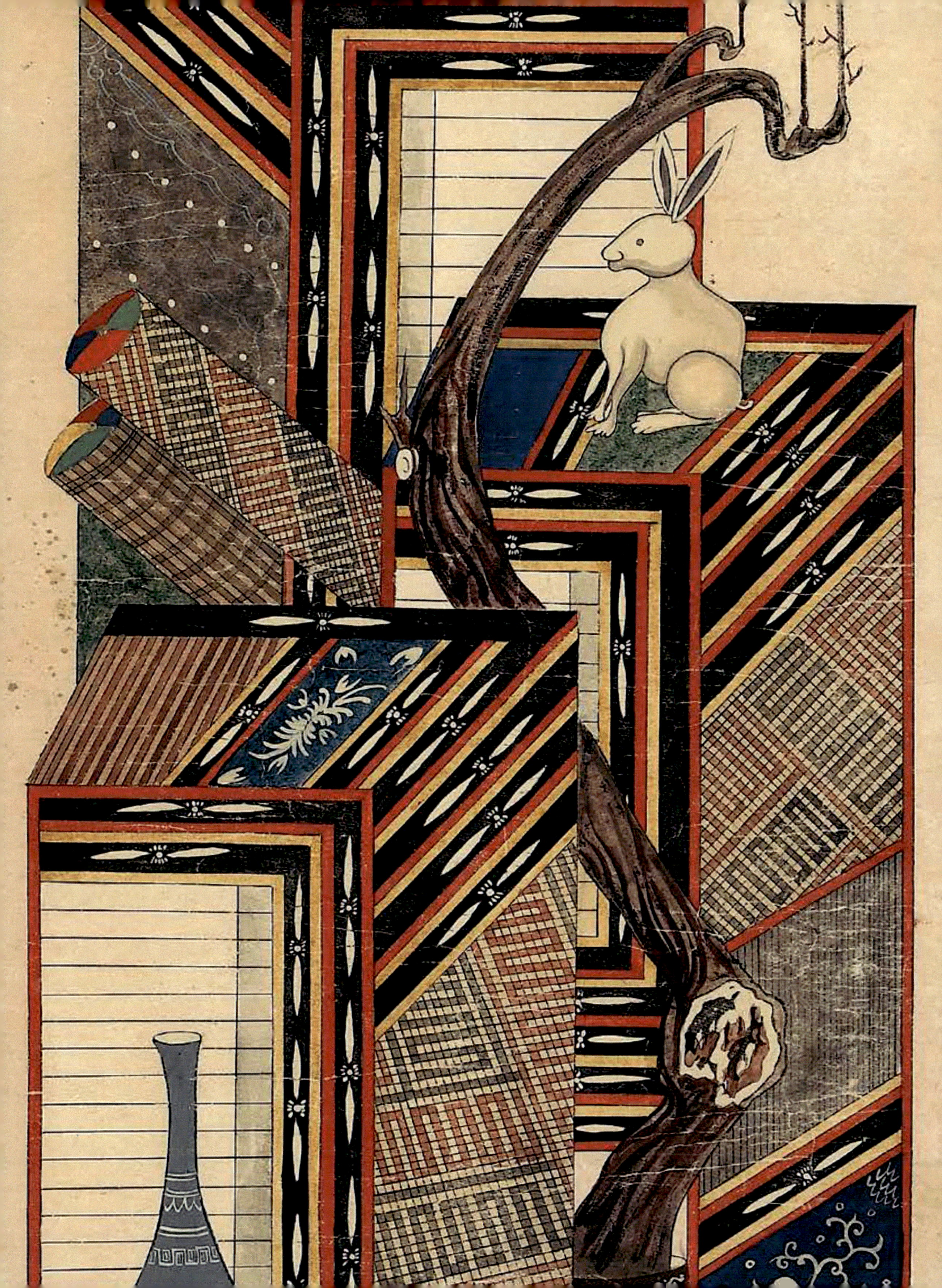

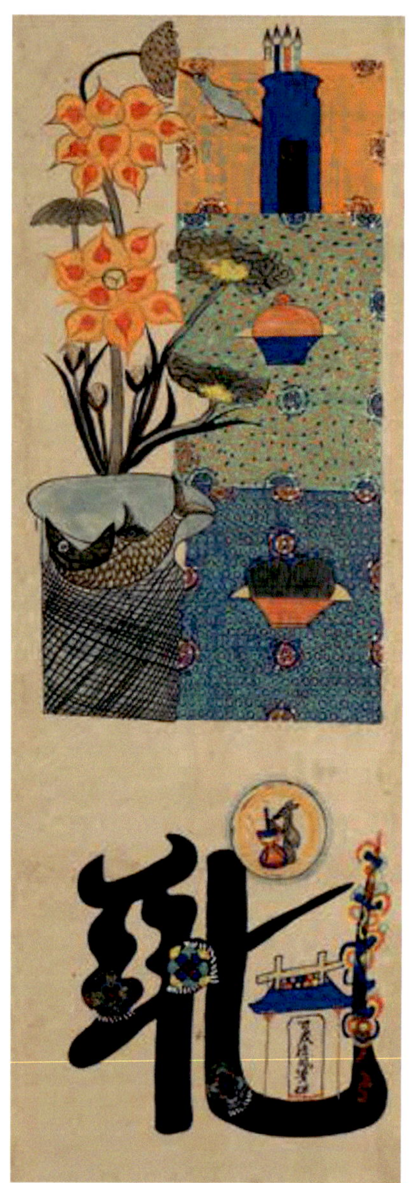
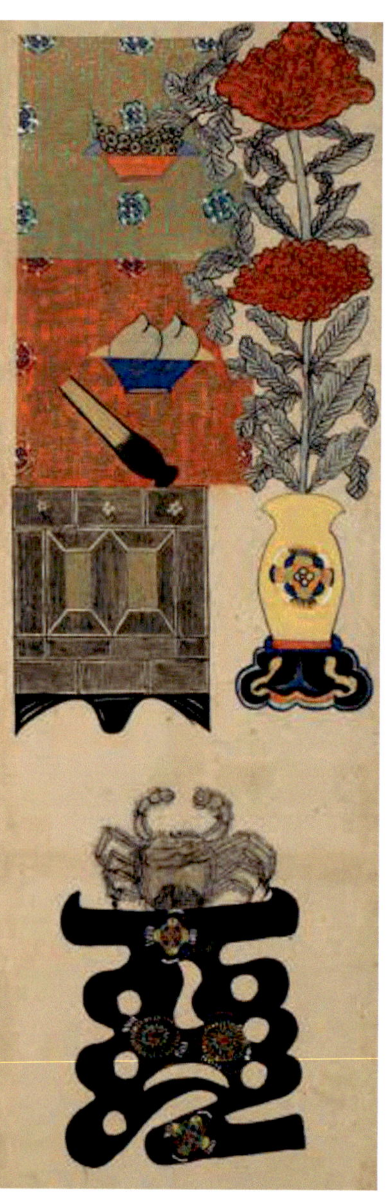
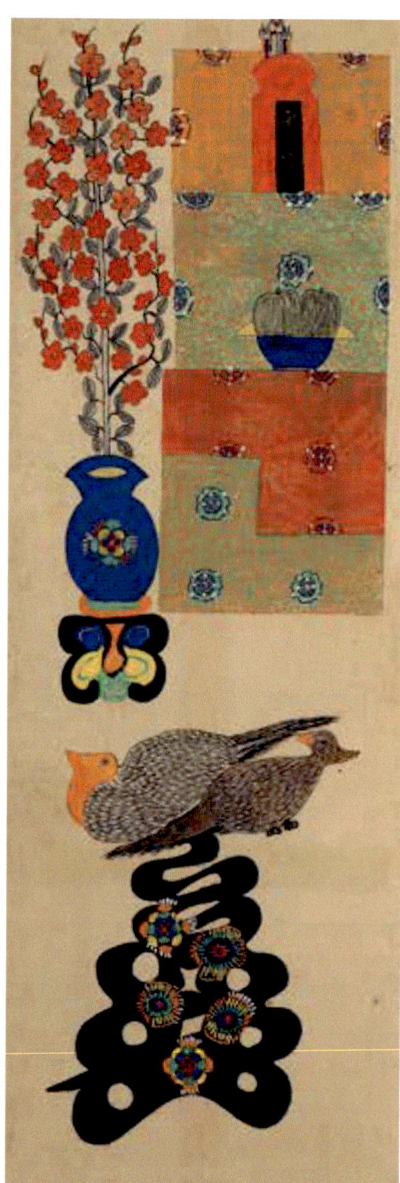
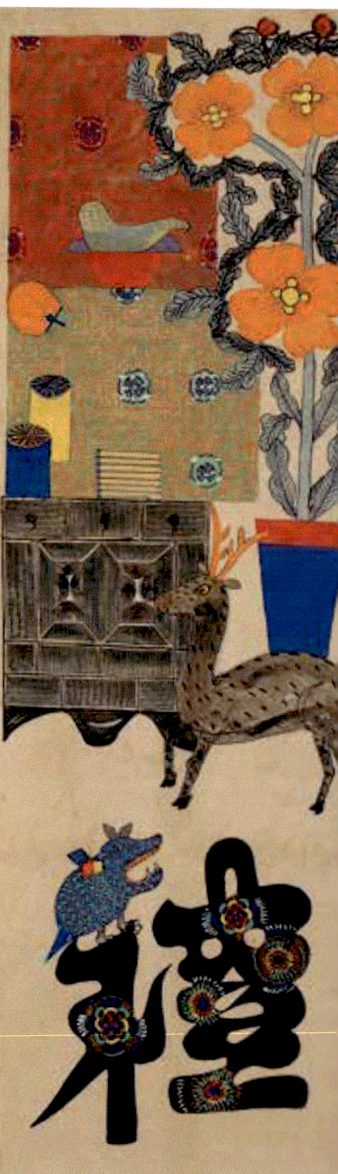

35 *Chaekgeori* and Munjado

Probably Hwang Seunggyu (1886–1962), early 20th century
Eight-panel screen
Ink and color on paper, 95 x 32 cm (each panel)
Private collection

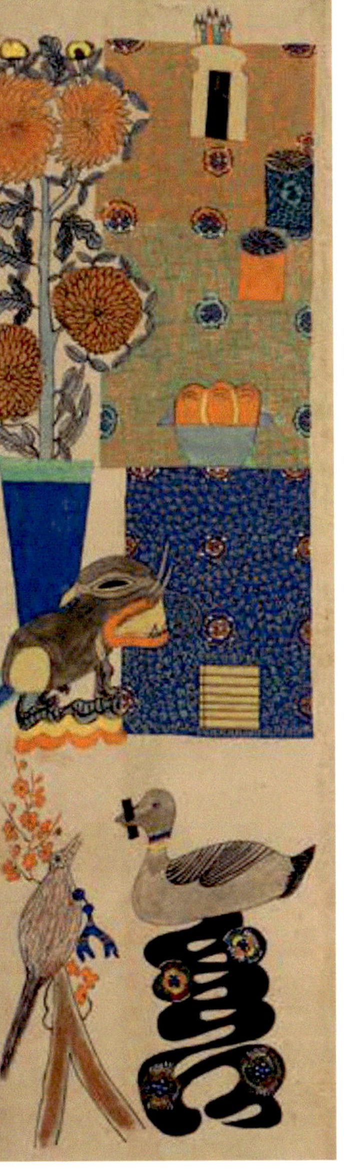
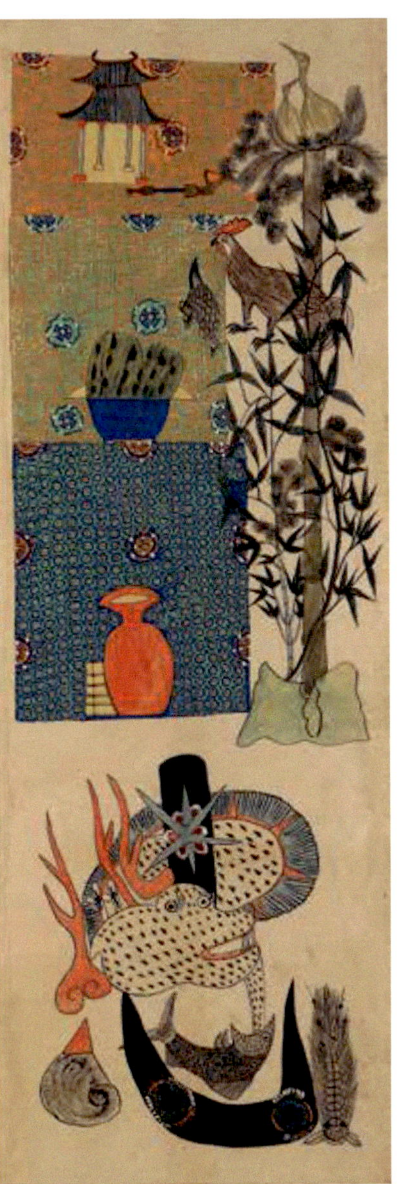
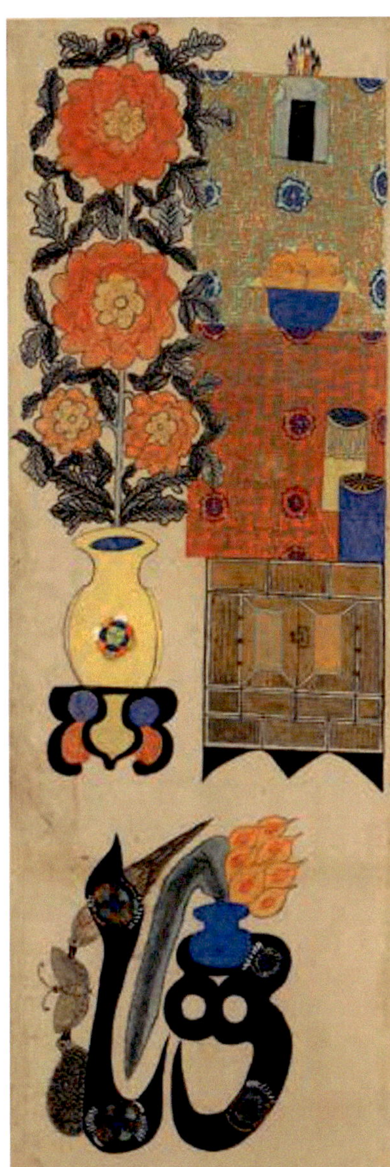
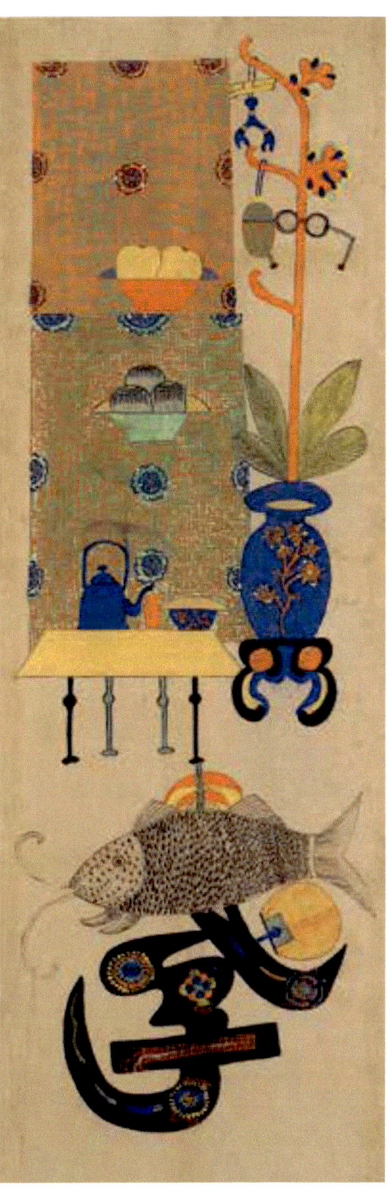

This work is a combination of chaekgeori and *munjado* (picture of eight Confucian characters). In the screen painting, books and furniture have been flattened into abstract, wallpaper-like patterns, while flowers and birds freely weave in and out of the lines and boundaries set by the books. Underneath, bold Korean characters are painted in striking black. This type of folk-style painting was popular in the rural area of Gangwon Province, South Korea. Judging by the style, the artist is assumed to be Hwang Seung-gyu, who worked in Gangwon Province during the Japanese occupation of Korea (1910–45). BC, JJL

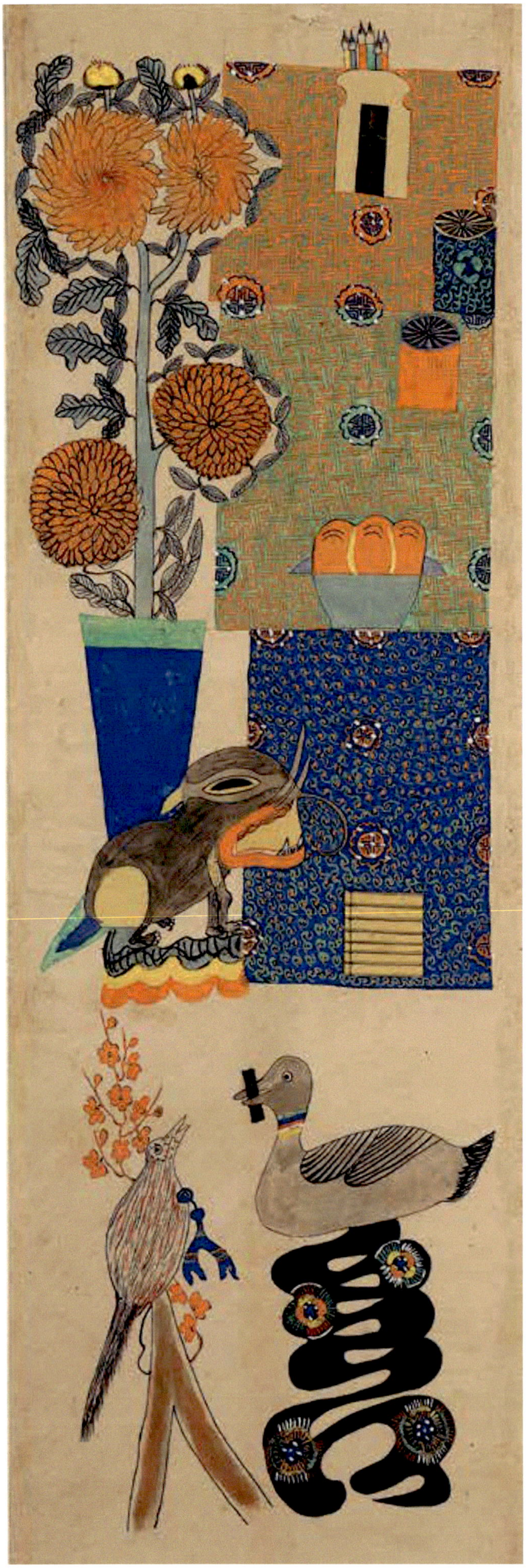

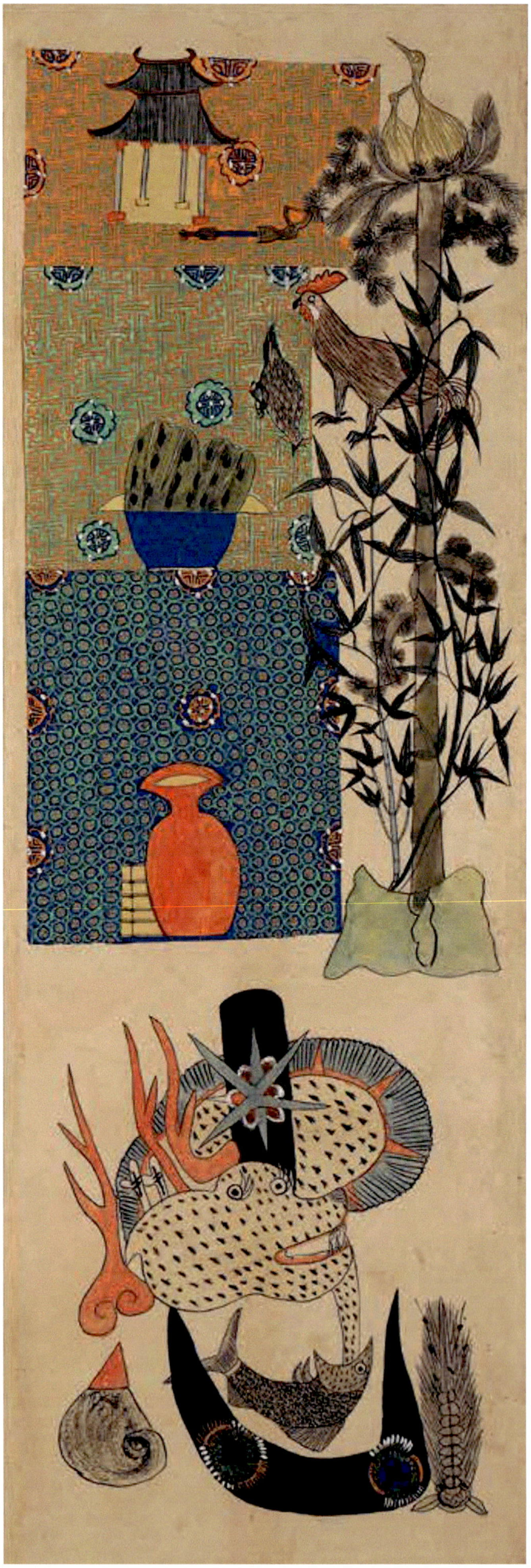

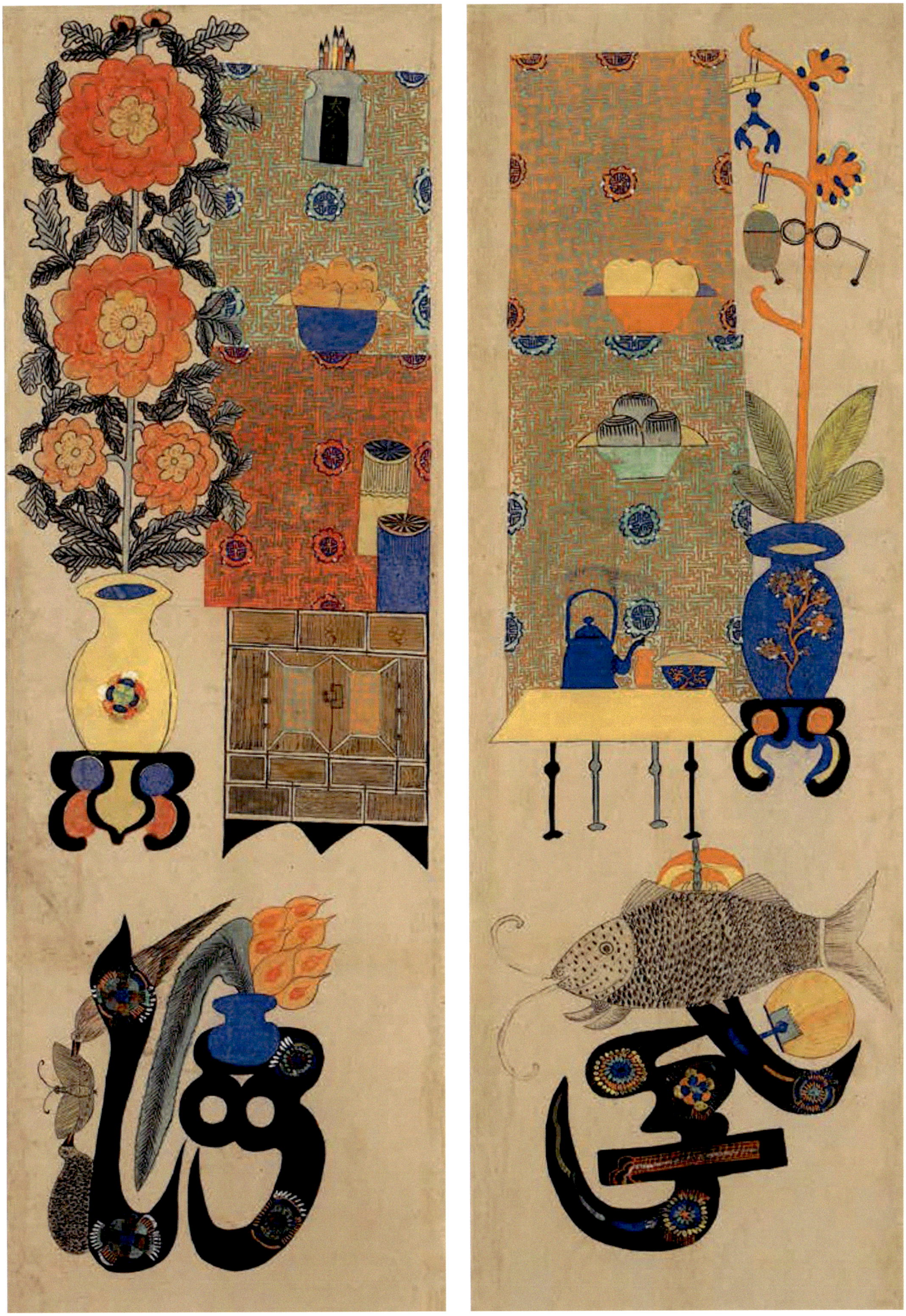

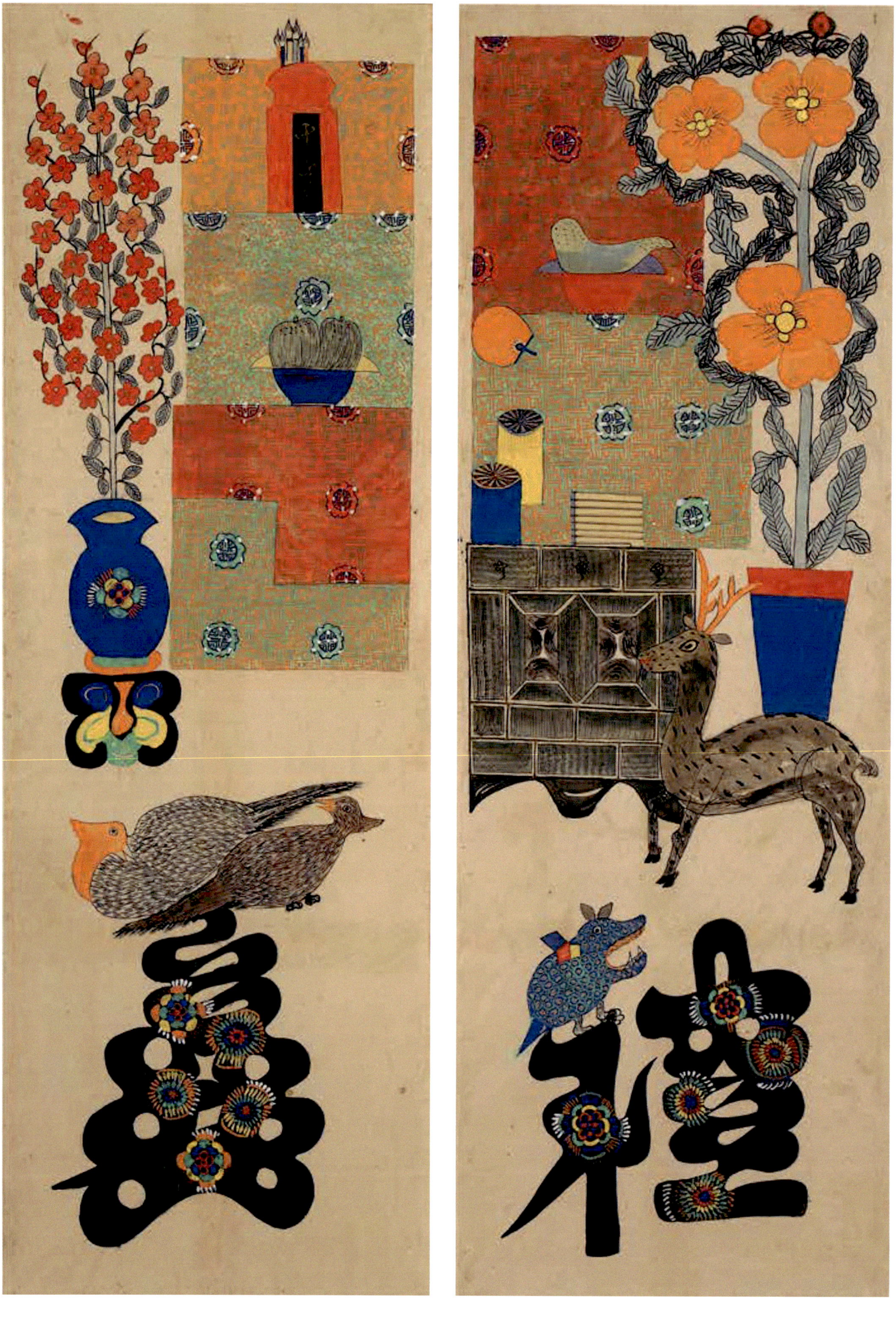

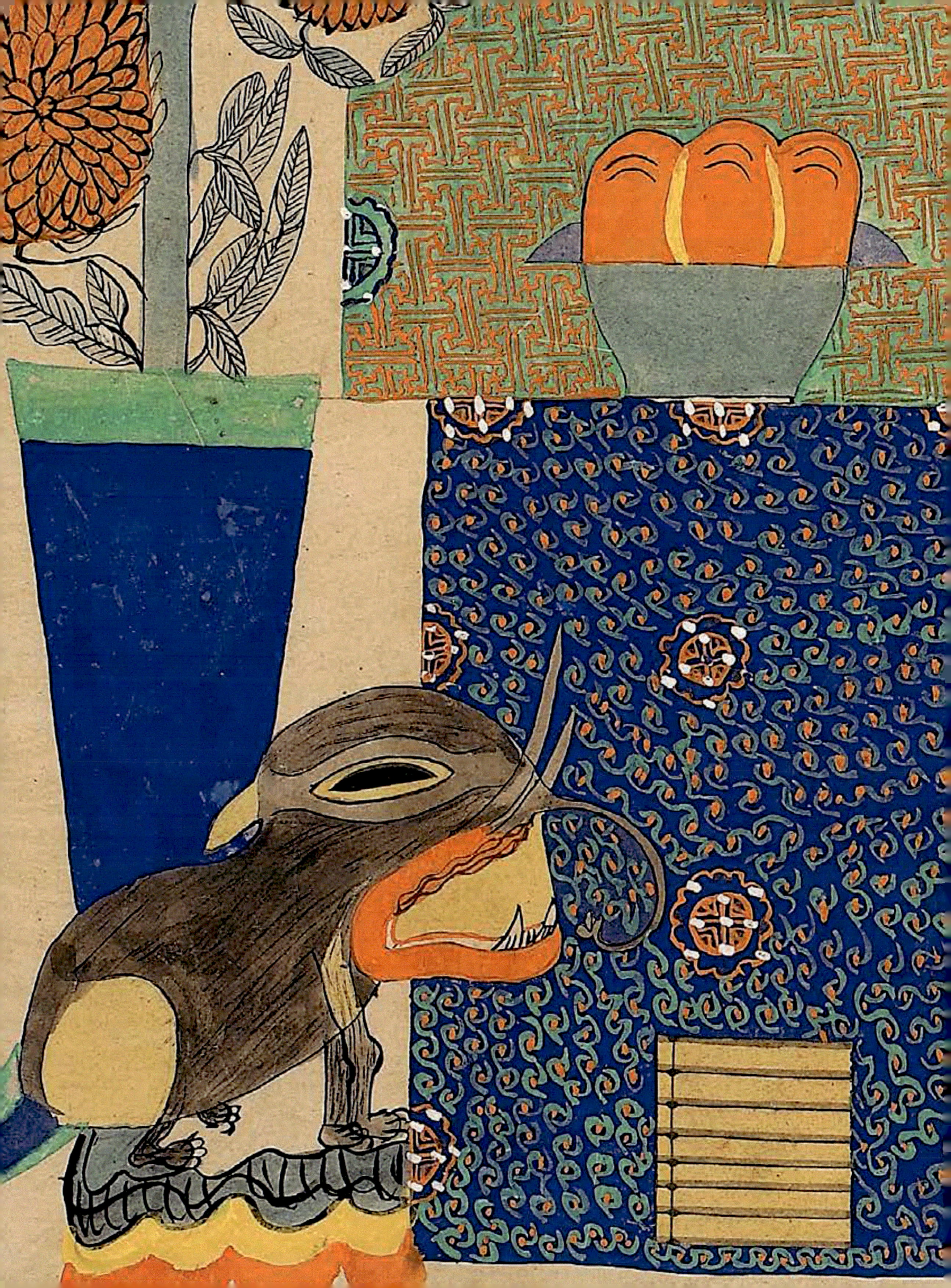

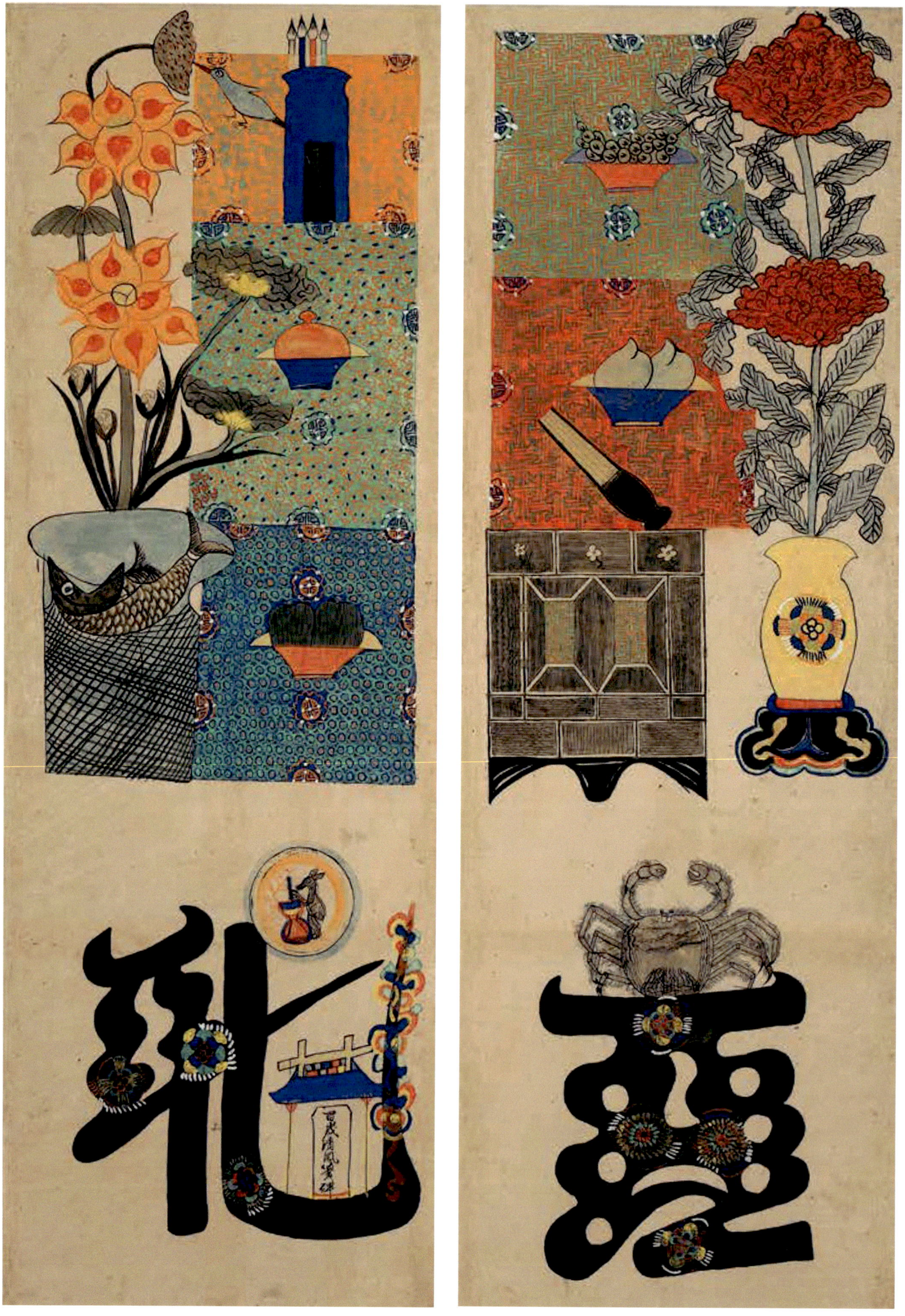

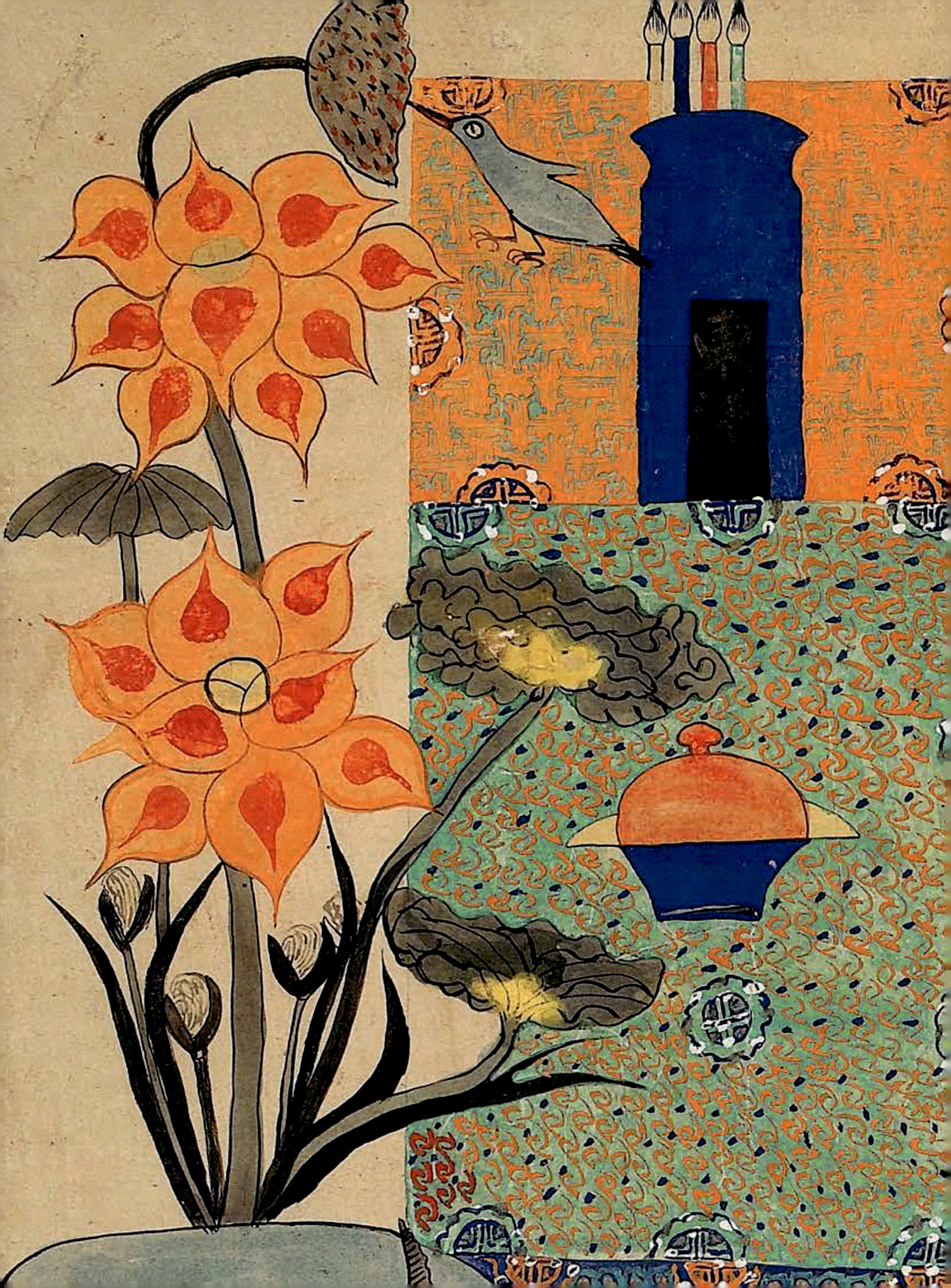

REFERENCE

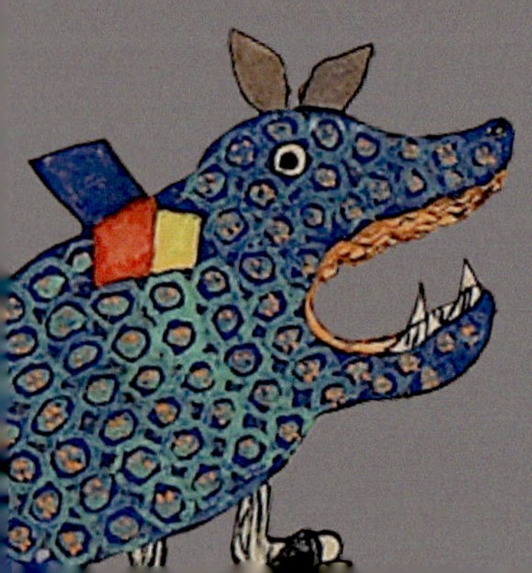

Reference

Accordi 1981
Accordi, Bruno. "Ferrante Imperato (Napoli 1550–1625) e il suo contribuito alla stori della geologia." *Geologico Romana* 20 (1981).

An 2012
An, Daehoe. "Joseon hugi chwimi saenghwal gwa munhwa hyeonsang 조선후기 취미 생활과 문화 현상 [Late Joseon period leisurely activities and cultural trends]." *Hanguk Munhwa* 60 (2012): 65–96.

Bagley et al. 1990
Bagley, Robert W., Jessica Rawson, and Jenny So. *Ancient Chinese Bronzes from the Arthur M. Sackler Collections.* Washington, DC: Arthur M. Sackler Foundation, 1990.

Bailey 1999
Bailey, Gauvin. *Art on the Jesuit Missions in Asia and Latin America, 1542–1773.* Toronto/Buffalo: University of Toronto Press, 1999.

Bak, C. 2010
Bak Cheolsang. "Joseon hugi munindeul ui injang e daehan insik ui ilmyeon 조선후기 문인들의 인장에 대한 인식의 일면 [Late Joseon-period observations on seals]." *Hanguk hanmun gyoyuk hakhoe* 35 (2010): 215–43.

Bak, J. 1968
Bak, Jiwon. *Yeolha ilgi* 열하일기 [Diary of a Journey to Jehol], Gojeon gukyeok chongseo vol. 18 [Series of Korean classics with text and modern Korean translation] Seoul: Minjok munhwa chujinhoe, 1968.

Bak, J. 2007
———. *Yeonam jip* 연암집 [Compiled writings of Yeonam]. Paju: Dol begae, 2007.

Bak, J. 2016
———. *Godong rok* 고동록 [Record of antiquities]. In *Yeolhailgi*[JourneyintoRehe].DatabaseofKoreanClassics. Accessed July 2016. http://db.itkc.or.kr/itkcdb/text/nodeViewIframe.jsp?bizName=MK&seojiId=kc_mk_h008&gunchaId=av002&muncheId=01&finId=006.

Bak, S. 2002
Bak, Simeun. "Joseon sidae chaekgado ui giwon yeongu 조선시대 책가도의 기원 연구 [The origin of *chaekgado* in the Joseon period]." Master's thesis, Academy of Korean Studies, Seongnam, 2002.

Balsiger 1970
Balsiger, Barbara Jeanne. "The *Kunst- und Wunderkammern*: A Catalogue Raisonné of collecting in Germany, France and England, 1565–1750." PhD diss., University of Pittsburgh, 1970.

Bang 2007
Bang, Byeongseon. "Yi Hyeongnok ui chaekka munbangdo palgokbyeong e natanan Jungguk doja 이형록의 책가 문방도 팔곡병에 나타난 중국 도자 [Chinese ceramics in Yi Hyeongnok eight-panel folding screens of scholars' books and accoutrements]." *Gangjwa misulsa* 28 (2007): 209–38.

Barocchi and Ragionieri 1983
Barocchi, Paola, and Giovanna Ragionieri, eds. *Gli Uffizi: Quattro secoli di una galleria.* Florence: Leo S. Olschki, 1983.

Bartholomew 2006
Bartholomew, Terese Tse. *Hidden Meanings in Chinese Art.* San Francisco: Asian Art Museum of San Francisco, 2006.

Beaurdeley and Beaurdeley 1971
Beaurdeley, Cecile, and Michel Beaurdeley. *Giuseppe Castiglione: A Jesuit Painter at the Court of the Chinese Emperor.* Rutland, VT: Charles E. Tuttle, 1971.

Black and Wagner 1993
Black, Kay E., and Edward W. Wagner. "Chaekgeori Paintings: A Korean Jigsaw Puzzle." *Archives of Asian Art*, no. 46 (1993): 63–75.

Black and Wagner 1998
———. "Court Style *Ch'aekgŏri*." In *Hopes and Aspirations: Decorative Painting of Korea*, 23–35. San Francisco: Asian Art Museum of San Francisco, 1998.

Black et al. 2015
Black, Kay E., Edward W. Wagner, and Min Gil-hong, "Gungnip Bangmulgwan sojang Yi Hyeongnok pil chaekgado 국립박물관 소장 이형록필 책가도 [Yi Hyeongnok's chaekgado in the collection of the national museum of Korea]." *Dongwon haksul nonmun jip* 16 (2015): 71–88.

Bourdieu 1996
Bourdieu, Pierre. *Distinction: A Social Critique of the Judgement of Taste*. Translated by Richard Nice. 8th ed. Cambridge. MA: Harvard University Press, 1996.

Brown 2001
Brown, Bill. "Thing Theory." *Critical Inquiry* 28, no. 1 (2001): 1–22.

Burkus-Chasson 2002
Burkus-Chasson, Anne. "Between Representation: The Historical and Visionary in Chen Hongshou's 'Yaji.' " *Art Bulletin* 84, no. 2 (2002).

Byun 2014
Byun, Young-sup [Byeon, Yeongseob]. "Munhwa ui sida e ingneun chaekgado 문화의 시대에 읽는 책가도 [Reading *chaekgado* in an age of culture]." *Minhwa yeongu* 3 (2014): 23.

Cambon 2015
Cambon, Pierre, "Minhwa, hangukjeokin pantaji, geundaejeok hwadu 민화, 한국적인 판타지, 근대적 화두 [Minhwa, a Korean fantasy and modern topic]." In *Hanguk ui Chaesaekhwa* 한국의 채색화 [*Chaesaekhwa*—Polychrome paintings of Korea] 3:53–65. Seoul: Dahal Media, 2015.

Campbell 2003
Campbell, Duncan. "Yuan Hongdao's *History of the Vase*." *New Zealand Journal of Asian Studies* 5 (2003): 77–93.

Chaekgeori 2012
Chaekgeori Screen Painting: History of Studies from the Joseon Dynasty to Modern Times Yongin: Gyeonggi Provincial Museum, 2012.

Chang 2004
Chang, Chin-Sung. "Joseon hugi godongseohwa sujip yeolgi ui seonggyeok: Kim Hongdo ui 'Po'uipungnyudo' wa 'Sa'inchosang' e daehan geomto 조선후기 고동서화 수집열기의 성격: 김홍도의 <포의풍류도>와 <사인초상>에 대한 검토 [Between non-attachment and obsession: the collecting culture of late Joseon period]." *Misulsa wa sigak munhwa* 3 (2004): 154–203.

Chang 2009
———. "Joseon hugi misul gwa 'Imwon gyeongje ji' 조선 후기 미술과 임원경제지 [Administration of our daily life in woods and fields and the art world of late Joseon Korea]." *Jindan hakbo* 108 (2009): 107–30.

Chang 2011
"Joseon hugi hoehwa wa munhwajeok hogisim 조선 후기 회화와 문화적 호기심 [Late Joseon Painting and the Culture of Curiosity]." *Misulsa nondan* 32 (2011): 163–89.

Chang 2013
———. "Ambivalence and Indulgence: The Moral Geography of Collectors in Late Joseon Korea." In Elizabeth Lillehoj, ed. *Archaism and Antiquarianism in Korean and Japanese Art*, 118–42. Chicago: Center for the Art of East Asia, Department of Art History, University of Chicago, 2013.

Chaoxian 2016
Chaoxian ren hao shu. Accessed 22 May 2016. https://babel.hathitrust.org/cgi/pt?id=mdp.39015046647965;view=1up;seq=20Cho 1974.

Choi 2007
Choi, Sang-Hun [Choe, Sanghun]. *Interior Space and Furniture of Joseon Upper-Class Houses*. Translated by Cho Yoon-jung and Min Eun-young. Seoul: Ewha Woman's University Press, 2007.

Chung 2011
Chung, Byungmo. *Mumyeong hwagadeul ui ballan, minhwa* 무명화가들의 반란, 민화 [Minhwa: The rebellion of anonymous Korean folk painters]. Seoul: Dahal Media, 2011.

Chung 2012
———. “Chaekgeori ui yeoksa, eoje wa oneul 책거리의 역사, 어제와 오늘 [The history of *chaekgeori*: past and present],” in *Joseon seonbi* 2012.

Chung 2013
———. “Minhwa e natanan kollaboreisheon hyeonsang 민화에 나타난 콜레보레이션 현상 [Collaboration in ‘minhwa’].” In *2013 Yeongwol poreom* [Yeongwol forum]. Yeongwol: Publisher, 2013.

Chung 2015
———. *Hanguk ui Chaesaekhwa* 한국의 채색화 [Polychrome Painting of Korea]. Seoul: Dahal Media, 2015.

Clunas 1991
Clunas, Craig. *Superfluous Things: Material Culture and Social Status in Early Modern China*. Urbana, IL: University of Illinois Press, 1991.

Clunas 1996
Clunas, *Fruitful Sites: Garden Culture in Ming Dynasty China*. London: Reaktion Books, 1996.

Dam-Mikkelsen and Lundack 1980
Dam-Mikkelsen, Bente, and Torben Lundack. *Ethnographic Objects in the Royal Danish Kunstkammer: 1650–1800*. Copenhagen: Nationalmuseet, 1980.

Feng 2002
Feng, Mingzhu. *Qianlong huangdi de wenhua daye* 乾隆皇帝的文化大業 [Emperor Qianlong’s grand cultural enterprise]. Taibei: Guoli gugong bowuyuan, 2002.

Filarete 1890
Filarete, A. A. *Antonio Averlino Filaretes Tractat über die Baukunst Trattato dell’architettura*. Edited by W. von Oettingen. Vienna: C. Graser, 1890.

Filarete 1965
———. *Treatise on Architecture; Being the Treatise by Antonio Piero da Averlino, Known as Filarete*. Translated by John R. Spencer and edited by W. von Oettingen. New Haven: Yale University Press, 1965.

Filipczak 1987
Filipczak, Zirka Zaremba. *Picturing Art in Antwerp, 1550–1700*. Princeton: Princeton University Press, 1987.

Findlen 1989
Findlen, Paula. “The Museum: Its Classical Etymology and Renaissance Genealogy.” *Journal of the History of Collections* 1, no. 1 (1989): 59–78.

Findlen 1994
———. *Possessing Nature: Museums, Collecting, and Scientific Culture in Early Modern Italy*. Berkeley/Los Angeles: University of California Press, 1994.

Finlay 2001
Finlay, Alec, ed. *The Libraries of Thought & Imagination: An Anthology of Bookshelves*. Edinburgh: Polygon, 2001.

Fontana 2011
Fontana, Michela. *Matteo Ricci: A Jesuit in the Ming Court*. Lanham, MD: Rowman & Littlefield, 2011.

Fučíkova 1997
Fu íkova, Elsa. *Rudlof II and Prague: The Court and the City*. Prague: Prague Castle Administration; London/New York: Thames and Hudson, 1997.

Goffman 1959
Goffman, Erving. *The Presentation of Self in Everyday Life*. New York, 1959.

Gundestrup 1991
Gundestrup, Bente. *Det Kongelige danske Kunstkammer 1737* [The Royal Danish Kunstkammer 1737]. Copenhagen, Nationalmuseet: A. Busck, 1991.

Han 1970
Han, Woo-Keun. [Han Ugeun] *The History of Korea*. Seoul: Eul-yoo, 1970.

Hay 2010
Hay, Jonathan. *Sensuous Surfaces: The Decorative Object in Early Modern China*. Honolulu: University of Hawai’i Press, 2010.

Heidegger 1971
Heidegger, Martin. “The Thing.” In *Poetry Language Thought*. Translated by Albert Hofstadter. New York: Harper Collins, 1971.

Heikamp 1964
Heikamp, Detlef. “La Tribuna degli Uffizi come era nel cinquecento.” *Antichità Viva* 3 (May 1964).

Ho 2004
Ho, Chuimei. *Splendors of China’s Forbidden City: The Glorious Reign of Emperor Qianlong*. London/New York: Merrell; Chicago: Field Museum, 2004.

Hong, D. 2016
Hong, Daeyong. *Yeongi* 연기 [Record of Beijing]. In *Damheon seo* 담헌서 [Book of Damheon]. Database of Korean Studies. Accessed October 2016. http://db.itkc.or.kr/itkcdb/text/nodeViewIframe.jsp?bizName=MM&seojiId=kc_mm_a560&gunchaId=bv007&muncheId=01&finId=012.

Hong, S. 1999
Hong, Sunpyo [Hong Seonpyo]. "Joseon hugi hoehwa ui aeho pungjo wa gampyeong hwaldong 조선후기 회화의 애호풍조와 감평활동 [Late Joseon period trend of appreciating paintings and aesthetic critiques]." In *Joseon sidae hoehwasa ron* 조선시대 회화사론 [Discourse on the history of Joseon period Korean painting]. Seoul: Munye Chulpansa, 1999.

Hooper-Greenhill 1992
Hooper-Greenhill, Eilean. *Museums and the Shaping of Knowledge*. London: Routledge, 1992.

Hsia 2010
Hsia, R. Po-chia. *A Jesuit in the Forbidden City: Matteo Ricci, 1552–1610*. Oxford/New York: Oxford University Press, 2010.

Hu 2011
Hu, Kemin. *The Romance of Scholars' Stones: Adventures in Appreciation*. Warren, CT: Floating World Editions, 2011.

Hu et al. 2008
Hu, Philip K., Robert D. Mowry, Steven D. Owyoung, and Laura Gorman. *Later Chinese Bronzes: The Saint Louis Art Museum and Robert E. Kresko Collections*. Saint Louis: Saint Louis Art Museum, 2008.

Huang and Yu 2004
Huang, Meizi, and Yu Shanglie. "Chaoxian Yanxingshi yu Zhongguo Liulichang 朝鲜燕行使与中国琉璃厂 [Joseon envoys to Yanjing and Liulichang]." *Dongjiang Xuekan* 21, no. 2 (2004).

Hwang 2010
Hwang, Jungyon [Hwang Jeongyeon]. "Joseon hugi seohwa sujangron yeongu 조선후기 서화수장론 연구 [Study of the late Joseon period practice of collecting paintings]." *Gyujanggak* 24 (2010): 193–228.

Hwang 2012
———. "Discourses on Art Collecting in the Late Joseon Dynasty: Perceptions and Practices." *Journal of Korean Art & Archaeology* (2012): 102–13.

Impey and MacGregor 1985
Impey, Oliver, and Arthur MacGregor, eds. *The Origins of Museums: The Cabinet of Curiosities in Sixteenth- and Seventeenth-Century Europe*. Oxford: Clarendon Press, 1985.

Inmul ro 1999
Inmul ro boneun Hanguk misul. Seoul: Samsung munhwa jaedan, 1999.

Jang 2016
Jang, Scarlett. "The Culture of Art Collecting in Imperial China." In *A Companion to Chinese Art*, 47–72. Edited by Martin J Powers and Katherine R. Tsiang. Oxford: Wiley Blackwell, 2016.

Jeong, H. 2012
Jeong, Hohun, "Gyujangchongmokgwa sippalsegi huban Joseon ui woeraejisik jipseong 규장총목과 18세기 후반 조선의 외래지식 집성 [Gyujang chongmok, an eighteenth-century compilation of foreign knowledge]." *Han'guk Munhwa* 57 (2012): 91–125.

Jeong, J. 2011
Jeong, Jongsu, ed. *National Palace Museum of Korea General Catalogue*. Seoul: National Palace Museum of Korea, 2011.

Jeong, JH. 2010
Jeong, Jae-Hoon [Jeong Jaehun]. "Meeting the World through Eighteenth-century Yonhaeng." *Seoul Journal of Korean Studies* 23, no. 1 (2010): 51–69.

Jeong, JH. 2011
———. "Sipgusegi Joseon ui chulpan munhwa 19세기 조선의 출판문화 [Nineteenth-century Joseon publication culture]." *Han'guk Munhwa* 54 (2011): 131–52.

Jeong, M. 2007
Jeong, Min. *18 segi Joseon jisikin ui balgyeon* 18세기 조선 지식인의 발견 [Discovery of eighteenth-century Joseon intellectuals]. Seoul: Hyumeonist, 2007.

Jeong, O. 2001
Jeong, Okja. *Jeongjo ui munyesasang gwa gyujanggak* 정조의 문예사상과 규장각 [The literary ideology of King Jeongjo and the Gyujanggak]. Seoul: Hyohyung, 2001.

Jeong, O. 2013
———. "Jeongjo wa Jeongjodae jeban jeongchaek정조와 정조대 제반 정책 [King Jeongjo and the policies of his reign]." *Seoulhak yeongu* 51 (2013): 1–24.

Jeong, Y. 2016
Jeong, Yagyong. "Dap Bok'am 답복암 [Reply to Bok'am]." In *Dasan simunjip* 다산시문집 [Compilation of Dasan's poems and essays]. Vol. 18. Database of Korean Classics. Accessed July 2016. http://db.itkc.or.kr/itkcdb/text/nodeViewIframe.jsp?bizName=MK&seojiId=kc_mk_c001&gunchaId=av018&muncheId=03&finId=041.

Jeongjo 2016
Jeongjo. *Taehoseok gi* 태호석기 [Record of taihu rock]. In *Hongjae jeonseo* 홍재전서 [Complete works of Hongjae]. Vol. 4. Database of Korean Classics. Accessed October 2016. http://db.itkc.or.kr/itkcdb/text/nodeViewIframe.jsp?bizName=MM&seojiId=kc_mm_a584&gunchaId=av004&muncheId=02&finId=007.

Jiang 1921
Jiang, Shaoshu. *Yunshi zhai bitan, er juan* 韻石齋筆談 [Brush talk of the rhyming stone studio]. Vol. 2. Shanghai: Gushu liu tongchu, 1921.

Jin 2010
Jin, Hao [Kim Ho]. " 'Gujin Tuhua Jicheng' zai Chaoxian de chuanbo yu yingxian 古今圖書集成 在朝鮮的傳播與影響 [Dissemination and influence of the *Gujin Tushu Jicheng* in Joseon]." *Donghai Hanxue* 11 (July 2010).

Joseon seonbi 2012
Joseon seonbi ui seojae eseo hyeondaein ui seojae ro 조선 선비의 서재에서 현대인의 서재로 ['Chaekgeori minhwa' paintings from the Joseon dynasty to modern times]. Yongin: Gyeonggi Provincial Museum, 2012.

Jungmann 2013
Jungmann, Burglind. "Korean Contacts with Europeans in Beijing and European Inspiration in Early Modern Korean Art." In *Looking East: Rubens's Encounter with Asia*, 67–87. Los Angeles: J. Paul Getty Museum, 2013.

Jungmann 2014
———. *Pathways to Korean Culture: Paintings of the Joseon Dynasty, 1392–1910*. London: Reaktion Books, 2014.

Kang, K. 2001A
Kang, Kwanshik [Gang Gwansik]. "Joseon hugi gungjung 'chaekgado'—Joseon hugi 'minhwa' gaenyeom ui saeroun yihaereul wihan sogo 조선 후기 궁중 <책가도>-조선후기 <민화>와 개념의 새로운 이해를 위한 소고 [Painting of bookshelves as late Joseon period court painting: An essay toward new conceptual understanding of late Joseon period 'folk painting']." *Misul jaryo* 66 (2001): 79–95.

Kang, K. 2001B
———. *Joseon hugi gungjung hwawon yeongu—Gyujanggak jabidaeryeong hwawon eul jungsimeuro* 조선후기 궁중화원 연구—규장각 자비대령화원을 중심으로 [Study on late Joseon dynasty official court painters—on the official court painters of the Gyujanggak]. Seoul: Dolbegae, 2001.

Kang, M. 1999A
Kang, Myeong-gwan. "Joseon hugi gyeonghwa sajok gwa godong seohwa chwimi 조선후기 경화사족과 고동서화 취미 [Collecting antiquities as late Joseon-period metropolitan elites' hobby]." In Kang, M. 1999B. 277-316

Kang, M. 1999B
———. *Joseon sidae munhak yesul ui saengseong gonggan* 조선시대 문학과 예술의 생성공간 [Incubator for literature and art in the Joseon period]. Seoul: Somyeong Chulpan, 1999

Kang, M. 2001
———. "Insoe, chulpan ui gukka dokjeom 인쇄, 출판의 국가 독점 [National monopoly of printing and publication]." *Chulpan Journal* (December 2001).

Kang, M. 2015
———. *Joseon e on seoyang mulgeondeul* 조선에 온 서양물건들 [Foreign goods that came to Joseon]. Seoul: Humanist, 2015.

Kang, W. 2015
Kang, Woobang. "Widaehan myeonghwa, sarang ui chaekgeori 위대한 명화, 사랑의 책거리 [Chaekgeori—a masterpiece, a labor of love]." *Wolgan Minhwa* (October 2015): 68–75.

Kaufmann 1978
Kaufmann, Thomas Da Costa. "Remarks on the Collections of Rudolf II: The *Kunstkammer* as a Form of *Representatio*." *Art Journal* 38 (1978): 22–28.

Kenseth 1991
Kenseth, Joy, ed. *The Age of the Marvelous*. Hanover, NH: Hood Museum of Art, 1991.

Kim, E. 2012
Kim, Eun Kyoung [Kim, Eungyeong]. "Chaekgeori e deungjang haneun Jungguk doja ui hamui 책거리에 등장하는 중국도자의 함의 [The meaning of Chinese porcelain wares in *chaekgeori* paintings]." In Joseon seonbi,"; Yongin: Gyeonggi Provincial Museum, 2012.

Kim, J. 2016
Kim, Jeonghui. *Wandang jeonjip* 완당전집 [Complete compilation of Wandang]. Vol. 10. Database of Korean Classics. Accessed July 2016. http://db.itkc.or.kr/itkcdb/text/nodeViewIframe.jsp?bizName=MK&seojiId=kc_mk_h011&gunchaId=av010&muncheId=01&finId=130

Kim, M. 2000
Kim, Munsik. "Gunsa Jeongjo gyoyuk jeongchaek yeongu 군사 정조 교육 정책연구 [A study on scholar-king Jeongjo's educational policies]." *Minjok Munhwa* 23 (2000): 59–114.

Kim, S. 2009
Kim, Sunglim. "From Middlemen to Center Stage: The Chungin Contribution to 19th-Century Korean Painting." PhD diss., University of California, Berkeley, 2009.

Kim, S. 2014
———. "Chaekgeori: Multi-Dimensional Messages in Late Joseon Korea." *Archives of Asian Art* 64 (2014): 3–32.

Kim, T. 2012
Kim, Taehee. "Jeongjo ui munche jeongchaek ui yangmyeonseong— hagmunjeok seonggyeok gwa jeongchijeok seonggyeok 정조의 문체정책의 양면성—학문적 성격과 정치적 성격 [The dualism of King Jeongjo's literary style policies, academic and political]." *Hanguk dongyang jeongchi sasangsa yeongu* 11 (2012): 77–98.

Kim, Y. 2006
Kim, Yeongjin. "Joseon hugi Jungguk sahaeng gwa seochaek munhwa 조선후기 중국 사행과 서책문화 [Late Joseon period ambassadorial trips and book culture]." In *Sipgu segi Joseon jisigin ui munhwa jihyeongdo* 19 세기 조선 지식인의 문화 지형도 [Cultural geography of nineteenth-century Joseon period intellectuals]. Seoul: Hanyang University Publishing, 2006.

Kleutghen 2015
Kleutghen, Kristina. *Imperial Illusions: Crossing Pictorial Boundaries in the Qing Palaces.* Seattle/London: University of Washington Press, 2015.

***Korean Art Collection Brooklyn* 2006**
Korean Art Collection in the Brooklyn Museum, New York, USA. Daejeon: National Research Institute of Cultural Heritage, 2006.

***Korean Art Collection Grassi* 2013**
Korean Art Collection: Grasse Museum für Völkerkunde zu Leipzig Germany. Daejon: Gungnip munhwajae yeongu so, 2013.

Lassels 1670
Lassels, Richard. *The Voyage to Italy, or a Compleat Journey through Italy*. Paris: Vincent du Moutier, 1670.

Laven 2011
Laven, Mary. *Mission to China: Matteo Ricci and the Jesuit Encounter with the East.* London: Faber and Faber, 2011.

Ledyard 1974
Ledyard, Gari. "Korean Travelers in China over Four Hundred Years, 1488–1887." *Occasional Papers on Korea*, no. 2 (March 1974).

Ledyard 1982
———. "Hong Taeyong and His 'Peking Memoir.' " *Korean Studies* 6 (1982).

Lee, S. 2010
Lee, Sumi. "Gyeonggijeon Taejo eojin ui wonbonjeok seonggyeok jaegeomto 경기전 태조어진의 원본적 성격 재검토 [Re-examining the fidelity of the portrait of King Taejo in Gyeonggijeon]." In *Joseon wangsi lgwa jeonju* 조선왕실과 전주 [Jeonju and the royal family of Joseon], 234–42. Jeonju: Jeonju National Museum, 2010.

Lee, U. 1977
Lee, Ufan. *Yijo ui minhwa—gujoroseo ui hoehwa* 이조의 민화—구조로서의 회화 [*Minhwa* of the royal Lee family—painting as structure], 34–43. Seoul: Yeolhwadang, 1977.

Lee, W. 1992
Lee, Wonbok. "Chaekgeori sogo 책거리소고 [Thoughts on chaekgeori]." In *Geundae Hanguk misul nonchong* 근대한국 미술논총 [Compilation of papers on modern Korean art]. Seoul: Hakgojae, 1992.

Leidy et al. 1997
Leidy, Denis P., Anita Siu Wai-fong, and James C. Y. Watt. "Chinese Decorative Art." *Metropolitan Museum of Art Bulletin* 55, no 1 (1997): 11–12.

Li, C. and Watt 1987
Li, Chu-tsing, and James C. Y. Watt, eds. *The Chinese Scholar's Studio: Artistic Life in the Late Ming Period.* New York: Thames and Hudson, 1987.

Li, S. 2003
Li, Shizhen. *Compendium of Materia Medica*. Vol. 30. Beijing: Foreign Language Press, 2003.

Lillehoj 2013
Lillehoj, Elizabeth, ed. *Archaism and Antiquarianism in Korean and Japanese Art*. Chicago: Center for the Art of East Asia, Department of Art History, University of Chicago, 2013.

Lugli 1983
Lugli, Adalgisa. *Naturalia et mirabilia*. Milan: Gabriele Mazzotta, 1983.

Marx 1990
Marx, Karl. *Capital: A Critique of Political Economy*. Vol. 1, translated by Ben Fowkes. New York: Penguin, 1990.

McCune 1983
McCune, Evelyn B. *The Inner Art: Korean Screens* (Berkeley: Asian Humanities Press, 1983.

Min 2015
Min, Gil-hong. "Gungnip Bangmulgwan sojang Yi Hyeongnok pil chaekgado 국립박물관소장 이형록필 책가도 [Yi Hyeongnok's chaekgado in the collection of the National Museum of Korea]." *Dongwon haksul nonmun jip* 16 (2015): 71–88.

Mirandola 1956
Mirandola, Gioavanni Pico della. *Oration on the Dignity of Man*. Translated by A. Robert Caponigri. South Bend, IN: Regnery/Gateway, 1956.

Mun 1996
Mun, Deokhui. "Nam Gongcheol ui seohwagwan 남공철의 서화관 [Nam Gongcheol's aesthetic perspective toward painting]." *Dongbanghak* 1 (1996): 187–214.

Mun 1997
———. "Nam Gongcheol ui *Geumneungjip* e boi neun Jungguk seohwa e daehan insik 남공철의 금릉집에 보이는 중국 서화에 대한 인식 [Nam Gongcheol's understanding of Chinese painting shown in *Geumneung jip*]." *Misulsahak yeongu* 213 (1997): 85–116.

Musillo 2016
Musillo, Marco. *The Shining Inheritance: Italian Painters at the Qing Court, 1699–1812*. Los Angeles: Getty Research Institute, 2016.

Nam 2001
Nam, Gongcheol. *Geumneung jip*. 금릉집 [Collected works of Geumneung] Seoul: Minjok munhwa chujinhoe, 2001.

Neviani 1936
Neviani, A. "Ferrante Imperato speziale e naturalista napoletano con documenti inediti." *Atti e Memorie Accademia di Storia dell'arte sanitaria*. 2nd ser., 2 (1936).

Pak 2013
Pak, Youngsook. "Ch'aekkado—A Joseon Conundrum." *Art in Translation* 5, no. 2 (2013): 183–218.

Paludan 1998
Paludan, Ann. *Chronicle of the Chinese Emperors: The Reign-by-Reign Record of the Rulers of Imperial China*. London: Thames & Hudson, 1998.

Peng 2006
Peng, Iris Ying-chen. "Famous Antiquities Painted in *Shenliu dushutang meiren tu*." *Gugong wenwu yuekan* 278 (2006).

Pomian 1987
Pomian, Krzysztof. *Collectionneurs, amateurs et curieux. Paris, Venise: XVIe–XVIIIe siècle*. Mayennes: Bibliothèque des Histoires/Editions Gallimard, 1987.

Preziosi and Farago 2004
Preziosi, Donald, and Claire Farago, eds. *Grasping the World: The Idea of the Museum*. Aldershot, UK/ Burlington VT: Ashgate Publishing, 2004.

Saravia 2012
Saravia, Luis, ed. *Europe and China: Science and the Arts in the 17th and 18th Centuries*. Singapore/London: World Scientific, 2012.

Scherer 1931
Scherer, C. *Die Braunschweiger Elfenbeinsammlung*. Leipzig, 1931.

Schlosser 1908
Schlosser, Julius von. *Die Kunst- und Wunderkammern der Spätrenaissance: Ein Beitrag zur Geschichte des Sammelwesens*. Leipzig, 1908.

Schulz 1990
Schulz, Eva. "Notes on the History of Collecting and of Museums." *Journal of the History of Collections* 2, no. 2 (1990).

Seong 2005
Seong, Yigeun. "Bosodang injon ui naeyong gwa ibon ui jejak sigi 보소당인존의 내용과 이본의 제작 시기 [Content of *Bosodang injon* and its later copy's creation date]." *Gyujanggak* 14 (2005): 213–34.

Silbergeld 2014
Silbergeld, Jerome. "From Studiolo to *Chaekgeori*, A Transcultural Journey: An Introduction to Sunglim Kim's '*Chaekgeori*: Multi-Dimensional Messages in Late Joseon Korea.' " *Archives of Asian Art* 64, no. 1 (2014): 1–2.

Sin, I. 2009
Sin, Ikcheol. "Yeonhaengnok eul tonghaebon sippal segi jeonban hanjung seojeokyutong ui yangsang 연행록을 통해본 18세기 전반 한중서적유통의 양상 [Book circulation in the first half of the eighteenth century between Korea and China examined through diplomats' diaries]." *Taedong gojeon yeongu* 25 (2009): 227–64.

Sin, I. 2013
———. *Yeonhaengsa wa Bukgyeong Cheonjudang* 연행사와 북경천주당 [Korean envoys to China and Catholic churches in Beijing]. Seoul: Bokosa, 2013.

Sin, M. 2010
Sin, Miran. "Joseon hugi chaekgeori geurim gwa gimul yeongu 조선후기 책거리 그림과 기물연구 [Late Joseon period chaekgeori painting and its painted objects]." *Misulsahak yeongu* 268 (2010): 169–94.

Sin, S. 2011
Sin, Sangcheol. "Misul sijang gwa saeroun chwihyang ui hyeongseong gwangye: 18 segi rokoko misule natanan sinuajeuri yangsik 미술시장과 새로운 취향의 형성관계 [The formative relationship between the art market and new artistic preferences: the style of chinoiserie in 18th-century Rococo art]." In *Art Education*, 155–79. Seoul: Korean Association of Art History Education, 2011.

Sin, Y. 2011
Sin, Yeongju. "Geumneung Nam Gongcheol ui seohwa e daehan gwansim gwa *Seohwa balmi* 금릉 남공철의 서화에 대한 관심과 서화발미 [Geumneung Nam Gongcheol's interest in paintings and "Seohwabalmi"]" *Dongbang hanmunhak* 47 (2011): 93–121.

Stuart 2011
Stuart, Jan. "Practice of Display: The Significance of Stands for Chinese Art Objects." In Jerome Silbergeld et al., eds. *Bridges to Heaven: Essays on East Asian Art in Honor of Professor Wen C. Fong*, 693–712. Princeton: Princeton University Press, 2011.

Thoma and Brunner 1970
Thoma, Hans, and Herbert Brunner. *Schatzkammer der Residenz Munchen. Katalog.* 3rd ed. Munich: Bayerische Verwaltung der staatlichen Schosser, Garten und Seen, 1970.

Wagner 2007
Wagner, Edward W. "A Re-examination of *Chaekgeori* Artists' Renaming and the Dating of Art Pieces." In *Joseon wangjo sahoe ui seongchwi wa gwisok* 조선왕조 사회의 성취와 귀속 [Achievement and ascription in Joseon dynasty], 71–88. Translated by Lee Hunsang and Son Sukgyeong, Seoul: Iljogak, 2007.

Wang, J. 1992
Wang, Jing. *The Story of Stone: Intertextuality, Ancient Chinese Stone Lore, and the Stone Symbolism in Dream of the Red Chamber, Water Margin, and the Journey to the West*. Durham/London: Duke University Press, 1992.

Wang, K. 2011
Wang, Keping. "*Huanghuaji* de wenxue jiazhi 黄华集 的文学价值 [Literary value of the Huanghuaji]." *Liaodong Xueyuan Xuebao (Shehui kexue ban*) 13, no. 2 (April 2011).

Wang, Y. 1963
Wang, Yeqiu. *Liulichang shi hua* 琉璃廠史話 [History of Liulichang]. Beijing: Sanlian shudian, 1963.

Wen 2011
Wen, Zhenheng. *Zhangwuzhi* [Treatise on superfluous things]. Hangzhou: Zhejiang ren min mei shu chu ban she, 2011.

Whitfield 1993
Whitfield, Roderick. *The Problem of Meaning in Early Chinese Ritual Bronzes*. London: Percival David Foundation of Chinese Art, School of Oriental and African Studies, University of London, 1993.

***Xiqing gujian* 1983**
Xiqing gujian 西清古鉴 [Catalogue of Xiqing antiquities]. Taibei: Taiwan shang wu yin shu guan, 1983.

Xu and Li 2016
Xu, Jay, and Li, He., eds. *Emperors' Treasures: Chinese Art from the National Palace Museum, Taipei; Masterworks of the Song, Yuan, Ming, and Qing Dynasties*. San Francisco: Asian Art Museum of San Francisco, 2016.

Yanagi 1981
Yanagi, Muneyoshi. *Yanagi Muneyoshi jeonjip* 야나기 무네요시 전집 [Collected works of Yanagi Muneyoshi]. Vol. 6. Chikuma Shobo , 1981.

Yeonhaeng 2012
Yeonhaeng munhwasa 연행문화사 [Cultural history of missions to China]. Namyangju: Gyeonggi Cultural Foundation/Silhak Museum, 2012.

Yi, D. 2016
Yi, Deokmu. "Kkochkkoji 꽃꽂이 [Flower arrangement]." In *Cheongjang gwan jeonseo* 천장관 전서 [Complete collection of Cheongjang Gwan]. Vol. 62. Database of Korean Classics. Accessed June 2016. http://db.itkc.or.kr/itkcdb/text/nodeViewIframe.jsp?bizName=MK&seojiId=kc_mk_j002&gunchaId=av062&muncheId=02&finId=029.

Yi, D. 1986
———. *Kukyok Cheongjang gwan jeonseo* 국역 천장관 전서 [Compilation of writings of Cheongjanggwan translated into Korean]. Seoul: Minjok munhwa chujinhoe, 1986.

Yi, G. Late 18th c.
Yi, Gyusang. *Ilmonggo* [Manuscript of one dream].Vol. 30. May 2016 http://db.mkstudy.com/mksdb/e/korean-anthology/book/653.

Yi, S. 2014
Yi, Sŏng-Mi [Yi Seongmi]. *Searching for Modernity: Western Influence and True-View Landscape in Korean Painting of the Late Chosŏn Period*. Lawrence, KS: Spencer Museum of Art; Seattle: University of Washington Press, 2014.

Yi, U. 1982
Yi Useong, *Hanguk ui yeoksasang* 한국의 역사상 [Portrait of Korean history]. Seoul: Changjak gwa bipyeongsa, 1982.

Yi, U. 2016
Yi Uiyeon. "Japji 잡지 [Miscellaneous record]." In *Gyeongja yeonhaeng japji* 경자연행잡지 [Miscellaneous record of journey to Beijing in the year of Gyeongja]. Database of Korean Classics, July 2016. http://itkcdb.vacusoft.co.kr/itkcdb/text/nodeViewIframe.jsp?bizName=MK&seojiId=kc_mk_a029&gunchaId=av001&muncheId=01&finId=001.

Yi, Y. 2016A
Yi, Yuwon. *Byeokryeo sinji* 벽려신지 [New record of *Ficus pumila*]. In *Imha pilgi* 임하필기 [Writing of Imha].Vol. 35. Database of Korean Classics, July 2016. http://db.itkc.or.kr/itkcdb/text/nodeViewIframe.jsp?bizName=MK&seojiId=kc_mk_h018&gunchaId=av035&muncheId=01&finId=002.

Yi, Y. 2016B
———. *Hwadong oksam pyeon* 황동옥삼편 [Section of East Asia's delicacy called Ok'sam]. In *Imha pilgi* 임하필기 [Writing of Imha]. Vol. 34. Database of Korean Classics. Accessed October 2016. http://db.itkc.or.kr/itkcdb/text/nodeViewIframe.jsp?bizName=MK&seojiId=kc_mk_h018&gunchaId=av034&muncheId=01&finId=083.

Yoo, H. 1990
Yoo, Hongjun. [Yu Hongjun] *Danwon Kim Hongdo* 단원 김홍도 [Danwon Kim Hongdo]. Seoul: National Museum of Korea, 1990.

Yoo, H. 1992
———. "Lee Gyusang 'Ilmonggo' ui hwaronsajeok uiui 이규상 '일몽고의' 화론사적 의의 [The significance of Yi Gyusang's *Ilmongo* in the history of Korean painting]." *Misul sahak* 4 (1992): 31-76

Yu, JG. 1857
Yu, Jaegeon, "Lee Hyeongnok." In *Ihyang gyeonmunnok* 이향견문록 [A record of illustrious persons]. After 1857.

Yu, JS. 2008
Yu, Jinsang. "The West Psyche by Kibong Rhee: Art of Humidifying Surfaces." In *Kibong Rhee: The Wet Psyche*. Seoul: Kukje Gallery, 2008.

Zeitlin 1991
Zeitlin, Judith. "The Petrified Heart: Obsession in Chinese Literature, Art, and Medicine." *Late Imperial China* 12 (June 1991): 1–26.

Zhang, H. 2003
Zhang, Hongxing. *The Qianlong Emperor: Treasures from the Forbidden City.* Eidenburg: National Museum of Scottland, 2003.

Zhang, Y. 1968
Zhang, Yingwen. *Qing bi cang*. Taibei: Yi wen yin shu guan, 1968.

Zo 1974
Zo, Zayong. *Hanho ui misul* 한호의 미술 [Korean tiger art], 188. Seoul: Emile Art Gallery, 1974.

GLOSSARY

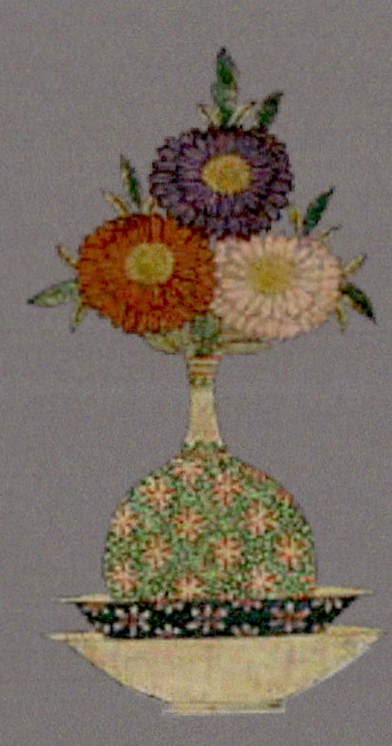

Glossary

Jungsil Jenny Lee

A. B

ajip / yaji 아집 / 雅集 elegant gatherings
anātman non-self
Attiret, Father Denis (1702–1768)
baduk 바둑 a strategic board game (go in Japanese)
Bak [Park] Jega 박제가 / 朴齊家 (1750–1815)
Bak [Park] Jiwon 박지원 / 朴趾源 (1737–1805)
Bak [Park] Seonsu 박선수 / 朴瑄壽 (1821–1899)
bakgodo 博古圖 painting of ancient bronze, porcelains, and jade vessels
banggeon 방건 / 方巾 a square-shaped men's hat worn during the Joseon dynasty
Bencao gangmu 本草綱目 Compendium of materia medica, a major pharmacological work published during the Ming dynasty
Bogutu 博古圖 Illustrated catalogue of antiques
Bologna, Giovanni da (1529–1608)
Bukhak 북학 / 北學 Northern Learning, a branch of Practical Learning (Silhak)
Bukhakui 북학의 / 北學議 Discussion of Northern Learning

C. D

Castiglione, Father Giuseppe (Lang Shining) (1688–1766)
chaekgado 책가도 / 冊架圖 literally, "picture of bookshelves"
chaekga munbangdo 책가문방도 / 冊架文房圖 literally, "picture of a book study [with] bookshelves"
chaekgeori 책거리 / 冊巨里 literally, "books and things"
Changdeokgung 창덕궁 / 昌德宮 Palace of prospering virtue, one of the five royal palaces built during the Joseon dynasty
Chenghua 成化 (r. 1465–87)
Cheongjanggwan jeonseo 청장관전서 / 青莊館全書 Collected writings of Cheongjanggwan
cheongsang 淸賞 pure appreciation
Damheon yeongi 담헌연기 / 湛軒燕記 Record of Damheon's trip to Beijing
Daodejing 道德經 Book of the way
ding 鼎 tripod bronze vessel
doenjang 된장 fermented bean paste
dokhwa 독화 讀畵 reading a painting
Du Wan 杜綰 (act. in the 12th century)
dui 敦 tureens
duobaoge 多寶格 literally, "a cabinet of myriad treasures," a furniture developed in China during the late Ming period.

F. G

fangding 方鼎 rectangular bronze cauldron
Gao Lian 高濂 (1572–1620)
ge yao 哥窯 stoneware with crackled glaze
Geumneung jip 금릉집 / 金陵集 Collected works of Geumneung
Gheradini, Father Giovanni (b. 1654)
gimyeong jeoljido 기명절지도 / 器皿折枝圖 literally, "painting of vessels and cut-flowers"
Godong gak 고동각 / 古董閣 pavilion to store calligraphy, books, antiques and paintings, which Nam Gongcheol owned
Gojong 고종 高宗 (r. 1897–1907)
golpae 골패 / 骨牌 a traditional Korean domino game
Goryeo dynasty 고려 / 高麗 (918–1392)
guwantu 古玩圖 picture of ancient playthings
Gujin tushu jicheng 古今圖書集成 Comprehensive collection of books and pictures of the past and present (first edition; 1726)
guan yao 官窯 state wares
Gunok sogi 군옥소기 / 群玉所記 Record of a group of jades
Guwen zhenbao 古文眞寶 True treasures of ancient literature
Gyujanggak 규장각 / 奎章閣 Royal library during the Joseon dynasty

H. I

Han Eungsuk 한응숙 / 韓應淑 (act. late 19th century)

Hanyang 한양 / 漢陽 modern day Seoul
Heo Gyun 허균 / 許筠 (1569–1618)
Heo Yong 허용 / 許容 (1753–?)
Heonjong 헌종 / 憲宗 (r. 1834–49)
Heungbuga 흥부가 / 興夫歌 Song of Heungbu, one of the popular repertoire of Korean musical story telling
Hong Daeyong 홍대용 / 洪大容 (1731–1783)
Hong KyoungTack 홍경택 (b. 1968)
Hongjae jeonseo 홍재전서 Completed works of Hongjae
hsiu-ts'ai [xiucai] 秀才수재 genius
Hu Wenming 胡文明 (act. late 16th–early 17th century)
Huang Tingjian 黃庭堅 (1045–1105)
Huanghua ji 皇華集 poetry diplomacy
hwahwehwa 화훼도 / 花卉圖 flowering plant pictures
hwajohwa 화조도 / 花鳥圖 flower-and-bird paintings
Hwang Seung-gyu 황승규 / 黃昇奎 (1886–1962)
Ilmonggo 일몽고 / 一夢稿 Manuscript of one dream
irworobongdo 일월오봉도 / 日月五峯圖 Sun, Moon, and Five Peaks screen

J. K

Jang Hanjong 장한종 / 張漢宗 (1768–1815)
Jeong Seon 정선 / 鄭敾 (1676–1759)
Jeongjo 정조 / 正祖 (r. 1776–1800)
Jeong Yagyong 정약용 / 丁若鏞 (1762–1836)
Jiao Bingzhen 焦秉貞 (act. 1689–1726)
Jiang Shaoshu 姜紹書 (d. ca. 1680)
Joseon dynasty 조선 / 朝鮮 (1391–1910)
jungin 중인 / 中人 literally, middle-people; technocrat class during the Joseon dynasty
Kang, Airan 강애란 (b. 1960)
Kang Dalsu 강달수 / 姜達秀 (act. second half of 19th century)
Kangxi 康熙 (r. 1661–1722)
Kim Hongdo 김홍도 / 金弘道 (1745–1806/14)
Kim Jaegong 김재공 / 金在恭 (act. in the second half of the 18th century)
Kim Jeonghui 김정희 / 金正喜 (1786–1856)
Kim Sangheon 김상헌 / 金尙憲 (1570– 1653)
Kim Yunsik 김윤식 / 金允植 (1835–1922)

L. M

Lee, Stephanie S. 김소연 (b. 1977)
li 鬲 cauldrons with three hollow legs
Li Shizhen 李時珍 (1518–1593)
Lin Youlin 林有麟 (act. mid-17th century)
lingbishi 灵璧石 a type of scholars' stones are found in the Lingbi county of Anhui province, China.
Liulichang 琉璃廠 a street at Beijing famous for book and antique stores
Matisse, Henri (1869–1954)
Mi Fu 米芾 (1051–1107)
minhwa 민화 / 民畵 literally, "art for common folks"
Ming dynasty 明 (1368–1644)
Miyosawa Motozu 三代澤本壽 (1909–2002)
munjado 문자도 / 文字圖 ideographs, Calligraphy of character pictures
mungbando 문방도 文房圖 literally, "painting of scholar'saccoutrements"
munbang sau / wenfang sibao 문방사우 / 文房四寶 Four Friends of the Scholar's Study (brush, ink, paper, ink stone)

N. O. P. Q

Nam Gongcheol 남공철 / 南公轍 (1760–1840)
Nam Yongik 남용익 / 南龍翼 (1628–1692)
Nam Yuyong 남유용 / 南有容 (1698–1773)
Nokchwijae 녹취재 / 祿取才 special examination given to court-painters-in-waiting
Northern Song dynasty 北宋 (960–1126)
Okamura Kichiemon 岡村吉右衛門 (1916–2002)
pansori 판소리 musical storytelling performance
pildam 필담 / 筆譚 brush talk; written communication
Ping shi 瓶史 History of flower vase
Pozzo, Andrea (1642–1709)
Qianlong 乾隆 (r. 1736–95)
Qing dynasty 清 (1644–1911)
Qing bi cang 清閟藏 Collecting the pur and rare

R. S. T

Rhee, Kibong [Yi Gibong] 이기봉 (b. 1957)
Ricci, Father Matteo (1552–1616)
Ripa, Father Matteo (1682–1754)
sabang takja 사방탁자 / 四方卓子 four-direction shelf
sarangchae 사랑채 / 舍廊 men's quarter, multifunctional room for dinning, sleeping, reading, and receiving guests
Schall vol Bell, Father Adam (1591–1666)
Schreck, John (1576–1630)
Seo Hosu 서호수 / 徐浩修 (1736–1799)
seogado 서가도 / 書架圖 literally, "painting of book shelves"
seosudo 서수도 / 瑞獸圖 painting of auspicious beasts
Serizawa Keisuke 芹沢 銈介 (1895–1984)
Shang dynasty 商 (about 1600 BCE–about 1046 BCE)
Shen Defu 沈德符 (1578–1642)
Silhak 실학 / 實學 School of Practical Learning
Sin Hanpyeong 신한평 / 申漢枰 (b. 1726)
Sin Jaehyo 신재효 / 申在孝 (1812–1884)
Sohak 소학 / 小學 ethics book for Korean children
Crown Prince Sohyeon 소현세자 / 昭顯世子 (1612–1645)

Song dynasty 宋 (960–1279)
studiolo (pl. studioli) private study/room
Su Shi 蘇軾 (1037–1101)
Suyuan shipu 素園石譜 Suyuan stone catalogue
Suzhou 苏州
taihushi 太湖石 a type of scholars' rock, limestone produced at the foot of Dongting Mountain in Suzhou, which is close to Taihu lake
Tangpyeongchaek 탕평책 / 蕩平策 policy of impartiality
taotie 饕餮 a motif of zoomorphic mask from Shang and Zhou dynasties
Three Kingdoms period, China (220–265 CE)
Tu Long 屠隆 (1543–1605)

V. W. X

Verbiest, Father Ferdinand (1623–1688)
Wang Yemei 王冶梅 (1832–after 1892)
Wanli 萬曆 (r. 1572–1620)
wanmul sangji 완물상지 / 玩物喪志 dallying too much with objects kills one's will
Wen Zhenheng 文震亨 (1585–1645)
Wen Zhenming 文徵明 (1470–1559)
Xie Huan 謝環 (1377–1452)
xingyuan yaji tu 杏園雅集圖 Painting of elegant gathering in the apricot garden
Xiqing gujian 西清古鉴 Catalogue of Xiqing antiquities (1749)
Xuande 宣德 (r. 1425–35)
Xuandelu 宣德爐 type of censer made during the Xuande period
Xuanhe 宣和 (r.1119–1125) Era of Emperor Huizong of the Song dynasty
Xunzi 荀子 (298–238 BCE) an ancient Chinese philosopher of Confucianism

Y. Z

yabok 야복 / 野服 a white plain robe
Yanagi Muneyoshi [Yanagi Soetsu] 柳宗悦 (1869–1961)
Yanjing 燕京 old name of Beijing
Yang Rong 楊榮 (1371–1440)
yangban 양반 / 兩班 educated scholar-officials
Yeolha ilgi 열하일기 / 熱河日記 Jehol diary
Yeondaejaeyurok 연대재유록 / 燕臺再遊錄 Record to the second visit to Beijing
Yeonhaengnok 연행록 / 燕行錄 Record of the journey to Beijing
yi 彝 a wine bronze vessel
Yi Deokmu 이덕무 / 李德懋 (1741–1793)
Yi Eungnok 이응록 / 李應祿 (1808–after 1871)
Yi Giji 이기지 / 李器之 (1690–1722)
Yi Gyusang 이규상 / 李奎象 (1727–1799)
Yi Haeung 이하응 / 昰應 (1820–1898)
Yi Hancheol 이한철 / 李漢喆 (1812–after 1890)
Yi Hwang 이황 / 李滉 (1501–1570)
Yi Hyeongnok 이형록 / 李亨祿 (1808–after 1871)
Yi Imyeong 이이명 / 李頤命 (1658–1722)
Yi Jonghyeon 이종현 / 李宗賢 (1718–1777)
Yi Taekgyun 이택균 / 李宅均 (1808–after 1871)
Yi Uihyeon 이의현 / 李宜顯 (1669–1745)
Yi Yunmin 이유민 / 李潤民 (1774–1841)
Yeongjo 영조 / 英祖 (r. 1724–76)
yingshi 英石 limestone from Yingde, Guangdong province
Yixing 宜興 the city of Yixing in Jiangsu Province known for purple clay
Yongzheng 雍正 (r. 1723–35)
Yu Deukgong 유득공 / 柳得恭 (1748–1807)
Yu Jaegeon 유재건 / 劉在建 (1793–1880)
Yuan Hongdao 袁宏道 (1568–1610)
Yun Dongseom 윤동섬 / 尹東暹 (1710–1795)
Zhang Yingwen 張應文 (1530–1594)
Zhangwuzhi 長物志 Treatise on superfluous things
Zhou dynasty 周 (ca. 1046–221 BCE)
Zhou Lu Ding Er 周魯鼎二 rectangular cauldron of the Zhou dynasty
Zhou Wen Wang 周文王 (1152–1056 BCE) King Wen of the Zhou dynasty
Zhou Wen Wang Ding 周文王鼎 a tripod bronze vessel dedicated for King Wen of Zhou
Zhu Xi 朱熹 (1130–1200)

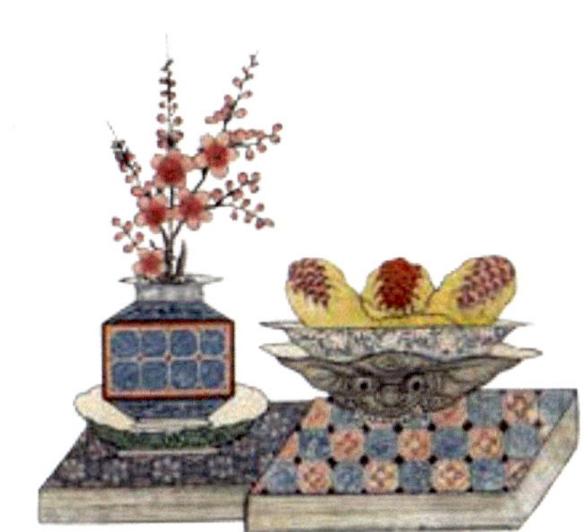

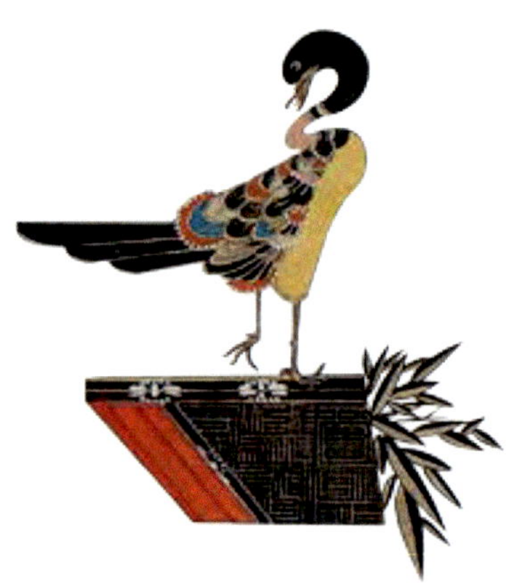